They Dared to Dream

UNIVERSITY PRESS OF FLORIDA

Florida A&M University, Tallahassee
Florida Atlantic University, Boca Raton
Florida Gulf Coast University, Ft. Myers
Florida International University, Miami
Florida State University, Tallahassee
New College of Florida, Sarasota
University of Central Florida, Orlando
University of Florida, Gainesville
University of North Florida, Jacksonville
University of South Florida, Tampa
University of West Florida, Pensacola

THEY DARED TO DREAM

Florida Women Who Shaped History

DORIS WEATHERFORD

WITH THE FLORIDA COMMISSION ON
THE STATUS OF WOMEN FOUNDATION, INC.

University Press of Florida
Gainesville · Tallahassee · Tampa · Boca Raton
Pensacola · Orlando · Miami · Jacksonville · Ft. Myers · Sarasota

VIVA FLORIDA 500
1513-2013

A Florida Quincentennial Book

Printed in the United States of America on acid-free paper

This book may be available in an electronic edition.

20 19 18 17 16 15 6 5 4 3 2 1

Library of Congress Control Number: 2014951466
ISBN 978-0-8130-6060-6

University Press of Florida
15 Northwest 15th Street
Gainesville, FL 32611-2079
http://www.upf.com

Contents

1 A Time Before

Florida is going, not coming. Our fragile peninsula used to be almost twice as big, extending more than a hundred miles farther west into the Gulf of Mexico. As the last Ice Age ended and northern glaciers melted, the sea level rose in the Atlantic and the Gulf, covering the land. The change, of course, was slow and not perceptible to our prehistoric ancestors. Yet it occurred recently enough in time for divers to have found evidence of prehistoric humans on undersea ledges on the continental shelf of Florida's west coast. As the science of oceanography grows, we should learn more about this era when our peninsula was larger.

The first Floridians probably arrived about twelve thousand years ago, following the southerly route that their ancestors began from Mongolia, when our human predecessors crossed the land/ice bridge that then connected Alaska to Siberia. The Florida that these prehistoric families found was not only larger but also drier and colder, and many creatures lived here that now are extinct. Archaeologists have found bones from huge animals that were akin to bison, camels, mastodon, mammoth, and the giant tortoise. Some bones have butchering marks, indicating that humans killed them.

Florida's archaeologists also have been exceptionally fortunate to find, in muck bottoms of shallow ponds, actual corpses of people who lived as long ago as 6000 BC. These aboriginals apparently buried their dead under the water, weighting or tying down the bodies—and when conditions were exactly right, even tissue did not decay.

Excavation at Little Salt Springs also indicates that these long ago Floridians understood some aspects of astronomy. Artifacts include a deer antler with twenty-eight marks on it; because there are twenty-eight days in a lunar month, experts believe this was an early calendar. University of South Florida archaeologist Brent Weisman concluded that the salinity of Little Salt Springs, which greatly reduces the chance of decomposition and therefore allows bone and animal tissue to remain intact, makes the spring "globally significant." Longtime diver John A. Gifford estimates that less than 5 percent of the area has been explored. More is known about Windover Pond in Brevard County. Airless peat there preserved "an array of normally perishable artifacts and human tissues, including brains."[1]

Because the peninsula was also drier, the earliest peoples lived near watering holes, and their lives revolved around catching animals that came to drink. Despite an abundance of potential game, many animals were larger than humans, who had not yet developed effective methods of trapping or spearing. The Windover Pond bodies show malnutrition, especially in children—an indication that their mothers lacked enough calcium for strong bones at birth and during lactation. The backbones of both men and women were bent, probably from carrying heavy loads, and teeth were badly eroded.

With women in other places and times, anthropologists consider ground-down teeth as evidence that women used their teeth incessantly. They not only chewed tough meat before giving it to children and the toothless elderly, but also—even especially—women used their teeth to soften materials that they intended to sew for both clothing and shelter. Another reason for poor teeth is that female bodies use their own calcium to build bones for developing infants, and among peoples not keeping domesticated animals for milk, women lacked replacement calcium.

Paleoindians expanded their living area as watering holes became lakes and rivers. They also developed better wooden spears and stone arrowheads, which allowed them to be better nourished. As early as 5000 BC they had learned to weave cords, mats, and clothing fabric from natural fibers, especially palms and palmettoes. Textiles found at Windover Pond "are some of the oldest hand-woven fabrics in North America."[2] By 800 AD some groups were growing corn—which means making the big anthropological leap from a hunter-gatherer economy to settled agriculture.

Social scientists seldom speculate on women's part in that transition, but the probability is that they were key. Everything we know about early peoples indicates that weaving and sewing were likely "women's work," and the probability is that women made the fabric in 5000 BC. It is likely, too, that it was women who did the cooking and carrying, which motivated them to grow gourds for containers. By 2000 BC early Floridians—again, most likely women—made pottery from clay. And because women bear the next generation of children and endure the hardships of pregnancy, delivery, and lactation, it was apt to be women, more than men, who saw growing food as preferable to gathering it. These are huge—if often unacknowledged—factors in human history.

Indeed, it is possible that prehistoric people had a greater appreciation for women than is the case in today's world. Florida had little rock for pictographs or other carved-in-stone records, but in places where prehistoric history was memorialized, the theme of female fertility is important. Although cartoon Neanderthal males are stereotyped as dragging women by the hair, that degrading depiction does not show up in cave drawings. Instead, women are honored for their vital role in giving birth to the future, often receiving more attention than that given by later artists and historians.

Women's health is vital to population growth, and by the time that Europeans arrived in Florida during the 1500s, experts estimate that almost a half-million people made their homes here. They ranged all the way from the Panhandle to the Keys, usually living in bands of fewer than fifty people, which was the best group size to sustain their society on the resources they were using.

Like other North American natives, they lived in a communal economy in which all members of the group could expect that their basic needs would be met. A group might experience famine during drought or other natural disasters, but no one starved while others grew fat. Archaeological evidence has been found showing that even permanently disabled people who were an economic liability were nonetheless kept with the group and cared for as well as possible.

A key characteristic, as among all North American natives, was that the idea of private ownership of land or other natural resources was an unknown concept. Although clans or tribes might fight over which group had the right to hunt or fish in a particular area, no individual of any clan claimed to own land permanently—that could not apply, any more than one person could own the sky.

Because their view of property ownership differed so radically from that of Europeans, natives would find themselves endlessly betrayed. When they accepted gifts from the strange white people who arrived, and in turn presented gifts to the newcomers, they had no idea that this exchange would cause the whites to believe the natives had sold their homeland. That was simply an impossible idea. Nor did the natives take more of nature's resources than they needed. Ecological chains were respected, as early humans were not ambitious to accumulate wood or game or fish in greater quantities than could be immediately used.

Moreover, whatever personal property a family did have—in terms of pottery, clothing, and so forth—belonged to the women. This was not only because women were most likely to have manufactured the items but also because, unlike in the European patriarchal structure, most North American natives lived in matrilineal societies. Unlike among whites, who traced descent through the father, native children took their mother's name and belonged to the mother's clan.

This system had several important implications that arguably gave Native American women a higher status than that of European women. Not only were women seen as owners of any property that a family might have, but also, and more important, because children took their mother's name and clan identity, a child never was seen as "illegitimate." Neither mother nor child suffered socially when a baby was born "too soon," and the idea of bastardy was as unfathomable as the concept of owning land. Because fatherhood therefore was much less significant, women axiomatically had more freedom, especially prior to marriage. Teenage girls and boys swam naked together, for instance, and the property-oriented courtship customs of Europeans—in which a girl's sexual innocence was essential—again was an unknown concept.

Women also felt free to control their reproductive lives. Some who wanted to become pregnant, according to a 1596 report, drank sassafras tea "to make them with child."[3] Sassafras was also grown as a cure for venereal disease. An expert on the natives of northeast Florida reinforces the point of personal control by saying that "abortion was standard practice for unmarried women who became pregnant. Some used herbs to provoke the miscarriage. Others used physical means to injure or strangle the fetus and thereby induce a miscarriage."[4] The use of abortion, however, was not based in shame as in European society but was an individual decision. The matrilineal structure of most North American tribes meant that pregnancies—and even the resulting children—were matters best left to women, who would deliver, nurse, and rear the next generation.

Some women in northern Florida may have used what anthropologists call "menstrual huts," places where women went during their monthly periods and for childbirth. Academics almost invariably deem this to be based in a taboo on women at these times, with the implication that a menstruating woman should be hidden—but it seems just as likely that the women created these places as a welcome retreat from field work and household duties. Instead of being a house of shame, women might well have thought of these isolated structures as akin to going to a modern spa for relaxation and recovery.

Europeans, of course, misinterpreted many aspects of matrilineal societies, but they were accustomed to class structure—which existed in native America more than is generally acknowledged. Within the class structure, though, it was uncles who mattered more than fathers—and specifically the uncles who were the brothers of the mother, not the brothers of the father. Because there is never any doubt as to who is a baby's mother, families of every class were structured on female lineage.

A child's inherited status thus depended on that of the mother—as well as on the maternal grandmother and her sons, the uncles. This was especially important in determining leaders: "Solid evidence," says a Florida scholar, "indicates that succession to chieftainships and some other leadership positions followed the matrilineal pattern under which a deceased chief was succeeded by a nephew or niece, children of his eldest sister, rather than by his own son or daughter."[5] Men were favored for leadership roles—but if the ruling family had no males, then powerful positions went to females.

Some pre-Columbian societies were very democratic with little class structure, but others—especially in South America—were highly ranked by status at birth. In general, the poorer the people, the less class structure there was, and when there was great wealth, as among Mexico's Aztecs and Peru's Incas, class lines were as strict as any in Europe. Even there, though, it was the maternal family that mattered: when a chief died, it was probable that his replacement would not be his son, but instead his nephew, the son of his sister.

Another important result of matrilineal family structure was that when couples married, they lived with the bride's clan. This was fundamentally different from circumstances in Europe and Asia, where girls barely into their teens often had to leave their families and move into the household of a husband. Especially in Europe, upper-class families sent their daughters to fulfill property-related marriage contracts far away from home, and teenage brides perhaps never saw their mothers or sisters again. In Asia it was customary to mistreat a new daughter-in-law, especially if her family had not paid a large dowry or if she did not bear sons.

Native North Americans, in contrast, brought the new groom to join his wife's family—and if a couple broke up, it was the man who went home to his mother. Indeed, as late as the nineteenth century, Seminole tribal law required a man to live with his wife's family. Divorce was easy, with either party simply deciding against living together; no courts or councils interfered with these individual decisions. Children stayed with their mother, not so much because that was "natural" but because of the matrilineal social structure of Seminoles and their ancient ancestors.

The prehistoric peoples who occupied Florida lived in small groups and were sufficiently isolated to develop differing languages and identities, with little interaction between cultures. Indeed, many of the hundreds of tribes in North America considered themselves to be singular and were confused when asked for a tribal name. Most eventually gave themselves names that reflected the geography where they lived, although many names also mean variants of "the people" or "the original ones."

* * *

As the population grew and peoples interacted increasingly, an important effect was that trading systems began to arise in Florida at about the same time that the first inter-continental commerce began between Europe and Asia. Obtaining things not available in one's own land is a major step forward in human progress, and about 1200 AD, Floridians began to acquire innovations from elsewhere.

We know this because archaeologists have found many items hundreds of miles away from their places of origin. The presence in Florida of rock that originated in the mountains of Tennessee or tar from North Carolina shows that trading systems developed about two millennia before the first whites arrived. A Tennessee clan, for instance, might barter their hard stone, which was useful for tools, with a Georgia group who had flint, useful for lighting fires. Eventually such chains of exchange reached their way to Florida, which had other resources never seen by the natives to the north.

Palmetto fibers, for example, may have been a miracle to women farther north, who were accustomed to sewing with the sinews of animals. For

Florida women, the most important result of trading would probably have been items made from rock and metal. Although the women had become skilled at weaving baskets from tall grasses, stone containers were vastly superior for cooking and for holding water. Instead of carrying water in gourds or fragile clay pottery and roasting meat on a spit, women could make more digestible stews with cooked vegetables in containers indifferent to fire.

Both men and women, however, seemed to have prized the new imports at least as much for decoration. Pre-Columbian metal utensils, for instance, are almost nonexistent, but jewelry made of both copper and gold has been found in numerous burial mounds that date to about 1200 AD. Especially at Lake Jackson, near Tallahassee, materials that came from farther north indicate not only a trading system but also a fondness for the artistic.

Indeed, much evidence points to men being more likely than women to spend time and wealth on adornment. The more powerful the man, the more he decorated his body with tattoos and dyes as well as necklaces and earrings of feathers and shells. Early drawings of natives in northeast Florida also indicate that men cared more about their hair. While women's hair was naturally free flowing, men bound theirs up in a tight bun at the top of the head. The absence of loose hair in these portrayals may indicate that men used grease or some other smoothing method.

People buried with gold jewelry doubtless were at the top of their society—literally so at Lake Jackson. The people in this Tallahassee-area culture seem to have preserved their history by burying their important individuals with one generation literally on top of the preceding one. Archaeologists theorize that when a tribal leader died, "the Indians would burn the house in which the person had lived, offering his possessions to the fire and closing or sealing his memory." Another house would be built over the ashes, to be occupied by the next generation's leader. Lake Jackson experts estimate that this process was repeated "at least twelve times over a 250-year period."[6] A similar burial in the Lake City area may have been created for a powerful woman:

> Ceramics recovered . . . suggest the house was home to a village leader, a person of great importance. That person, a woman or very gracile male . . . was buried in a very shallow grave dug into the floor of the house. He or she was interred on the back with arms bent at the elbows and palms up. Red ochre colored the hair, which was decorated with . . . an anhinga. . . . Cause of death could have been . . . a stone

> arrow point . . . embedded in the bone. [There was] evidence of a severe infection which had lasted . . . several months.[7]

Burial mounds may have been built high to ease concerns that floods or animals might disturb the bones of loved ones. Gravesites have a clear intent, but experts debate the purposes of other mounds left by aboriginals. Mound-building societies lived throughout the Southeast, as far west as Arkansas and north to Illinois, with some earthen structures hundreds of feet high. Some mounds are merely garbage piles (or middens, the archaeologists' term), the discarded remains of ordinary life. These are most common in coastal societies that accumulated huge quantities of shells, especially oyster shells, from centuries of a seafood-based diet.

In addition to burial sites and refuse dumps, archaeologists believe that some mounds were intended as high places for sacred ceremonies. No skeletons or castaway items seem to be buried in them; instead, they may have served as earthen temples. Religions worldwide share a general belief that the netherworld of hell is down below, while heavenly reward comes in rising upward. Creating mounds that reached toward the sky in flat Florida could have been akin to Europe's building of high cathedrals in the same era.

Archaeologists seem more willing to speculate that mounds were built for religious reasons than to think of them as hurricane shelters, but that also may be possible. Mound building continued after whites arrived, and one early diary spoke of this usage. When Jonathan and Mary Dickinson were shipwrecked off the coast of St. Lucie in 1696, he recorded their experience with a four-day hurricane—during which they found relative safety on "oyster hills":

> The house we were in was afloat, and . . . the wind and rain still violent. I then saw a house on another oyster hill that the water was not got over; I . . . asked by signs if I might be there. The Indians seemed willing: so thither I got my wife. . . . The flood continued. We imagined that the sea was broke in upon the land and that we should be drowned. . . . The Indians seemed much concerned. . . . [On day four] the storm of wind and rain . . . began to abate. . . . The water fell many feet . . . I went out to see our people whom I left. . . . The flood had risen within two or three inches of the top of the cabin, and they said they expected to die there.[8]

Whatever their exact purpose, shell mounds existed on all Florida coasts. Tampa Bay, for instance, was ringed with mounds that reached from northern Pinellas County down through southern Hillsborough and Manatee counties. Most were destroyed by whites who did not recognize them as anything other than a natural hill—or who deliberately took them down in the twentieth century, when crushed oyster shell became a valuable material for road construction.

Other mound sites that still exist run from the Panhandle's Fort Walton down through the west coast's Crystal River, Weeden Island in Tampa Bay, and on south through Key Marco in Collier County. The artifacts in these mounds include valuable items that people gave up to be entombed with the dead, signaling not only sentiment for the lost loved one but also a probable belief in an afterlife. The dead, presumably, would want these things in the next world.

One striking artifact was discovered at Myakka in Sarasota County: beautifully crafted from clay, this water bottle featured a round base with a narrow top and was "found in 1934 over a skeleton near the center of the mound."[9] North of Jacksonville, "layers of sand and shell were deposited to form 'steps' up the side of the low mound. A human fetus or newly born child, dressed in clothing decorated with a shell bead 'apron,' was placed in a grave dug into the steps."[10]

Archaeologists also have found elaborately carved wooden masks, often featuring an animal, especially at Fort Walton. Hundreds of miles farther south, a Key Marco mask presumably was worn by a fierce Calusa; with spaces for the eyes and nose, it conveys a severe look. A third in Volusia County was made from human bone. Presumably the wearers intended to disguise themselves as frightening creatures in the hope of warding off enemies or supernatural evil.

Nor was sculpture the only form of art. The records of early whites tell us that drumming and dancing were important, with women and men having specific roles. Some clans seemed to hold dances as a daily ritual, beginning about ten o'clock and lasting well past midnight. Singing, too, was frequent, although its atonal quality was nerve wrecking to most whites. Some early Floridians also had woodwind music, as Spanish newcomers wrote of being welcomed by marching flutists.

Both men and women participated in sports and gambled. As is the case today, men spent more time on these activities, and intra-tribal ball games were taken very seriously. Men also were privileged to use the "Black Drink" that women prepared, which had intoxicating and religious significance. Because tobacco does not flourish in Florida, neither men nor women smoked—but men were quick to take up the habit when white men introduced it.[11]

* * *

With arrival of Europeans in the 1500s, Florida tribes began to enter the historical record as named entities, from the Ais to the Timucua, each composed of several named clans. None had a written language, and European spellings varied wildly. Ais, for example, is pronounced "eyes" and also has been spelled Aix, Aiz, Alis, and even Jece, the name of an aboriginal town near Hobe Sound. To confuse things further, some Spanish writers referred to this tribe as the Costas, meaning "coastal." Both they and the Timucua lived on the East Coast, with the Ais to the south.

By far the biggest group in the region, the Timucua had developed a sophisticated civilization by the 1500s. They lived in villages that ranged from modern Amelia Island inland through Lake City and Live Oak. Because this area is colder than elsewhere in Florida, they built permanent wooden homes. Some villages had more than a hundred buildings, and the entire

Trail of the Lost Tribes

The Florida Humanities Council brochure *Trail of the Lost Tribes* maps some two dozen mound-related places in western Florida. The farthest inland is Blueberry Mound in Highlands County.

One of the four sites in Manatee County, the Madira Bickel State Archeological Site, is named for the woman who donated the land in 1949, when it became the state's first such preserve.

The Portavent Temple Mound, also in Manatee County, has had a succession of white women associated with it since Civil War days. Mabel Morrow bought it in 1924; she died in the Manatee River while vainly trying to save her drowning husband.

Mound Key in Estero Bay has mounds that are more than thirty feet high; they probably were the Calusa's religious and military headquarters when Ponce de León unsuccessfully attempted settlement there in 1521.

Most of these sites charge no admission and are open until sunset. They are wonderful places to reflect on real Florida.

Timucuan population probably was about 200,000 when the Spanish established St. Augustine in 1565.

An early Frenchman reported that syphilis was common among Timucuan men because of "their too great love for women and the maidens whom they call daughters of the Sun."[12] Fondness for women, body adornment, and a time-consuming hair style did not make Timucuan men weak, however, as the tribe had more modern weaponry than other Floridians, including the bow and arrow.

Timucuan villages ranged north of the modern Georgia border, and they adopted the agricultural system of the Cherokees to their north, with women as the primary farmers. Men did the initial groundbreaking, but it was women who were responsible for planting and cultivating corn, beans, and members of the squash family—the sustenance of life for most North American natives.

It is difficult to grow these food staples farther south on the East Coast, where the Ais lived. Their territory ranged from modern Brevard County down to Palm Beach County; Indian River is thus named because the largest Ais settlement was there. They remained a hunter-gatherer society, without the crop growing of settled agriculture. It would have been the Ais who witnessed the first white expedition, led by Ponce de León, in 1513. They remained hostile almost two centuries later, when they captured the shipwrecked Dickinsons.

To their south, in the modern Broward/Dade area, lived the Tequesta, who probably arrived there about 500 BC. The southern peninsula climate was so mild that clothing was virtually unnecessary; both men and women covered only their pubic areas, and children generally went naked. Women, however, wove strong baby-carriers, much like the slings that modern mothers use. The Tequesta depended on a water-based diet and developed elaborate systems of wooden dams and weirs to trap fish. Women likely spent much of their time digging for clams and collecting oysters and turtles.

In 1998 archaeologists working near the mouth of the Miami River discovered a prehistoric landmark that is interestingly different from others. The "Tequesta Circle" or "Miami Circle" is not a mound but a careful alignment of holes in the ground that form a large circle. It is possible that the pattern had some religious or astrological significance, but it also is possible that the holes merely held posts or beams for a large circular building. It may have been used as a temple, a council meetinghouse, a storehouse, or even a storm shelter.

The inhabitants of the Keys were a small tribe that whites named the Matecumbe. According to a Spanish teenage boy who was shipwrecked there in 1545, these people were exceptionally large, and "the men used palm leaves to cover their lower body, and the women wore skirts of Spanish moss."[13] The implication is that the women went topless, which was usual for native women in warm climates.

By the time of this shipwreck, the Matecumbe were under the firm control of the militaristic Calusa, whose main settlement was near modern Fort Myers. The Matecumbe paid regular tribute—or taxes, in our terms—to their Calusa conquerors. Later Spanish writers confirmed the warlike nature of the Calusa, and the Tequesta, on the eastern side of the Everglades, also feared them. The Tequesta developed a strategy to pacify them through intermarriage: they sent their sons to wed Calusa women, thereby hoping to lessen hostilities.

Calusa warriors made themselves more fearsome by wearing frightening masks, and they used tattoos, dyes, and jewelry that probably were considered magical protection against harm. They had a hunter-gatherer economy, so women's work of gardening was eliminated. Their major highway to the Gulf was the river named for them, the Caloosahatchee, and their diet was primarily seafood, especially conchs.

Discarded shells again made high mounds, and Mound Key in Estero Bay is the most famous of these. The excavated site also held some post-Columbian artifacts, "including fragments of sixteenth-century olive jars" and other ceramics introduced by the Spanish—making it clear that mound building continued into the 1600s.[14] Again it is possible that some Calusa may have built their homes atop these mounds as protection against flooding.

The cabbage palm was a staple of their diet—and that of other Floridians where it was warm enough for the tree to grow. The heart of that palm is edible, and natives cut down mature trees to reach the core. Newcomers may have dubbed it "cabbage" because of its mild taste and because, like the European ground plant, cabbage palm can be eaten raw or cooked.

North of the Calusa lived the Tocobago. Their villages ranged roughly from modern Sarasota to Tarpon Springs, with the land around huge Tampa Bay as the chief settlement. Within that, northern Pinellas County's Safety Harbor was the "capital city," and this sacred site, which the Spanish called Bahia de Espiritu Santo (Bay of the Holy Spirit), is now Philippe Park.

Like other tribes, the Tocobago depended on fish, especially mullet, and on seafood, leaving immense piles of shells. They considered the Calusa to be enemies but did not try to pacify them as the Matecumbe and Tequesta did—perhaps because the Tocobago developed an unusual weapon, a saber made from the sharp spine of the stingray.

Around the Big Bend of the Gulf of Mexico and to its north were the Apalachee, the tribe most familiar to the English-speaking settlers who followed the Spanish into Florida much later. Tallahassee, then as now, was the capital city. The Apalachee were akin to the tribes north of them in Georgia and Alabama, including the people whom the English called Creeks (Miccosuke or Muskogee) as well as the Choctaw and Cherokee. Some of those peoples would migrate into Florida by the 1700s, fleeing the whites who took over Georgia, the Carolinas, and Alabama. Place names reflect this later presence: in the Muskogee language, for instance, Homosassa means "place where pepper grows"; Panasoffkee means "deep valley"; and farther north,

Approximate Timeline of Florida's Prehistory

10,000 BC	The first Floridians arrive from the north, their ancestors having come from Mongolia via Alaska
6000 BC	Aboriginals apparently bury their dead underwater, as indicated by corpses found in the twentieth century
5000 BC	People—probably women—weave household goods and clothing from natural fibers
2000 BC	Crude clay pottery is produced, again probably made by women for carrying and cooking needs
500 BC	The southernmost part of the peninsula is settled by the Tequesta
300 AD	Mound building begins; pottery is more sophisticated and demonstrates artistic intent
600 AD	Carved wooden bowls have decorative detail
800 AD	Corn is grown in north Florida; women have the primary responsibility for its cultivation
1200 AD	Trading systems begin, exchanging goods with tribes in modern Alabama, Georgia, and the Carolinas
1513 AD	Two women are part of the de León expedition that brings the first whites to Florida

Chattahoochee indicated "marked rock." Pensacola is Choctaw for "long-haired people," as native men and women there did not cut their hair.

Like the Choctaw and other tribes to their north, the Apalachee practiced settled agriculture and had permanent villages. Women were responsible for growing two corn crops per year. They roasted and stewed large animals that did not thrive in lower Florida, especially deer and bear. Their wood-based homes were round and snug, with only a hole at the top for emitting smoke from the fires needed in winter.

Another female responsibility was to gather—and later, to grow—herbs that were useful as medicine. In an era when European physicians used leeches to bleed out "bad" blood and plastered their patients in mercury-based poultices, Native Americans administered less dangerous medications. In North Florida, among the common wild herbs used as medicine were the may apple, wild yam, and witchhazel.

The world in which these peoples lived had its tribulations, but it was far more serene and ecologically sound than would be the case a half-millennium later. "The American presence in Florida accounts for only 2 percent of Florida's human history," says author Barbara Purdy, "but Americans are responsible for nearly 100 percent of the modifications of the landscape."[15] That negative change—and the destruction of all Florida's indigenous tribes—began with the Spanish, who arrived in La Florida about three centuries prior to the first Americans.

2 Newcomers

The First European Women, 1513–1819

Christopher Columbus, that visionary sailor of 1492, used maps that he obtained from his mother-in-law. His historic journey, in fact, owed a great deal to women.

Born in Genoa, Italy, to weavers Susanna and Domenico Columbo in 1451, he married Doña Felipa Perestrello e Moniz in 1479. She was a member of "one of the first families of Portugal"; they had been in the sailing business for a long time and thus understood and supported his innovative ideas.[1] Moreover, Felipa herself was an experienced sailor. She had not only explored dangerous waters with her father but had also made geographic drawings that her husband would use in shaping his vision of the globe. The couple lived with her mother, Doña Isabel Moniz, in Lisbon, where Doña Isabel gave her new son-in-law maps, logs, and other useful items that had belonged to her late husband.

With their son Diego, Felipa and Christopher (or, more properly, Cristoforo) moved about 1482 to the Madeira Islands—then on the edge of the known world. They returned to Lisbon prior to Felipa's premature death in 1485, but even after that, her family continued to be key. When he could not get financing in either Italy or Portugal, he turned to Spain. With five-year-old Diego, Columbus went to the port town of Huelva on Spain's southern shore—where "he knew no one" other than Felipa's sister.[2]

That he was finally able to make the historic voyage was also largely due to a woman. No man with sufficient funds was willing to champion this first perilous venture—but Queen Isabella of Castile was an equal monarch with

King Ferdinand of Aragon in the creation of the new nation of Spain, and it is no myth that she put up her personal jewelry as collateral for the risk-filled investment. Moreover, when she died in 1504, their daughter, Juana, replaced Isabella as monarch. Ferdinand shared the throne with first his wife and then his daughter as joint rulers.

Columbus, having lost his wife, appeared to be serious enough about a woman that before heading out into the Atlantic, he directed his three-ship fleet to Gomera in the Canary Islands, where Doña Ines Peraza de García was *gobernadora* (governor). Queen Isabella had sent the young Doña Ines, a beautiful and intelligent widow, to develop this new Spanish possession. Columbus visited her again on his second voyage, even though it was somewhat risky with the seventeen vessels he had in 1493—and Gomera's harbor was "tiny." According to an Italian man who wrote in 1495, "Columbus was in love with Doña Ines."[3]

Juan Ponce de León was a teenage sailor on the 1493 trip. Nine years later he was fortunate enough to marry one of the few prominent Spanish women available in the Caribbean. Leonor Bint Pedro was a native of Sevilla, in Castile, and their 1502 wedding took place on the island of Santo Domingo. Her family was sufficiently wealthy and venturesome to have built an inn there; de León had substantially improved his status via the marriage. His bride was constantly pregnant or nursing during the couple's first six years: between 1502 and 1508 she bore Juana, Isabella, María, and Luis.

The young family moved to Puerto Rico (rich port) in 1508. The "forty-two persons and eight sailors" had a disastrous trip, taking four months to cover the short distance between Santo Domingo and Puerto Rico.[4] Repeated tropical storms—new to Europeans—caused them to run aground and lose their supplies. As governor of Puerto Rico, Juan continued to travel; Leonor and other women often were without their husbands in the tenuous new home. It probably was she who supervised the building of their residence—actually a fortress designed for protection in expected rebellions of natives. He described it as a "house with [a] terrace and tall battlements . . . metal within and without."

The year that Juan and Leonor wed, 1502, also was the year that a rough outline of the southern coast of Florida first appeared on a map. The Spanish had heard of this place from the people Columbus called "Indians." The great admiral died in 1508 still believing these lands were in or near India. Queen Isabella also used that terminology when she commanded Columbus in 1503 "that the said Indians be converted to our Holy Catholic Faith. . . . See to it that the said Indians are well treated, those who become Christians better than the others." She further specified: "the Indians shall perform [work] as free people, which they are, and not as slaves."[5]

After her death the following year, however, enslavement of natives became routine. The Mediterranean area had a long history of slavery dating back to biblical days, and in the context of the times, it was not surprising that slavery quickly spread to the New World. The first African slaves arrived in Santo Domingo in 1501, less than a decade after Columbus's first voyage, and Native Americans also were routinely enslaved when their territories were conquered. Because of the intervention of Catholic priests, slavery in South America would develop in slightly less repressive ways than in of English-speaking North America.

Spanish officials placed legal limitations on hours and conditions of work, which allowed slaves to earn money and buy their freedom. Most important, marriage between the races was not banned, and the shortage of potential brides meant that white men married outside their race. Children were born slave or free according to the mother's legal status—as in the matrilineal systems of Native Americans and Africans and unlike in Europe's patriarchy. The ultimate result was that Spanish (and French) colonies in the New World escaped the worst of the profound racial strife that would plague the United States.

* * *

Whether slave or free, however, natives in the Spanish Empire certainly were sufficiently mistreated that they consistently encouraged newcomers to leave by telling them of greater riches in another place. In Arizona, for example, the fable was "seven cities of gold"; in Florida, it was the "fountain of youth." The Taino people living in Puerto Rico saw Juan Ponce de León go off in search of this fountain—and in response to the omnipresent predictions of gold—on March 3, 1513.

He believed he was sailing toward the rumored island of Bimini when he departed with three ships; onboard were two women, perhaps sisters or sisters-in-law, Beatriz and Juana Jiménez.[6] They reached what probably was the Melbourne area on April 2, and according to a 1601 history:

> They called it *La Florida*, because it was very pretty to behold with many and refreshing trees, and it was flat, and even: and also because

> they discovered it in the time of Flowery Easter [*Pascua Florida*], Juan Ponce wanted to agree in the name.[7]

The name La Florida would apply to the whole of North America for many decades thereafter. The Ais tribe who lived on the East Coast did not appear during the de León party's six-day stay, but after turning south and rounding the Keys, the Spanish reached the land of the fierce Calusa on Florida's West Coast. The Calusa rowed out in eighty canoes to confront the Spanish near Sanibel, and de León retreated. Further explorations in the Ten Thousand Islands area meant the group did not return to their Puerto Rican home until October 1513—eight months after setting out. Juan headed to Spain the next year; the New World pattern for Leonor de León meant an independent life, her husband away much of the time.

Although there is no evidence that she went with him during other Caribbean ventures, some unnamed women did. According to the detailed chronology of Spanish historian Andres de Barcia:

> Juan Ponce sailed in May [1515] to pacify the Caribs and continue the conquest of Florida. After a good voyage he reached the island of Guancane (which is also called Guadalupe), where he put a party ashore to get water and firewood. With soldiers as guards, some women also landed to wash clothes. The Carib . . . boldly rushed upon the men who had landed, massacring the majority and capturing all the women.[8]

Rape probably was part of such capture, and almost certainly these European women were forced to live and work as slaves. Barcia said nothing to indicate that de León made any attempt to ransom or retrieve these women from what probably was a very harsh fate.

Women also were part of de León's next voyage to Florida, which proved fatal. Early in 1521, some two hundred "male and female settlers" sailed to southwest Florida, intending to colonize near the Caloosahatchee River.[9] Again, despite superior European technology, the Calusa managed to thwart their plans. After an arrow landed in the conquistador's leg and infection set in, the group abandoned their aim and departed for Cuba.

Juan Ponce de León died there in July, soon after arranging the marriage of his second daughter, Isabella, to Antonio de Gama—which enabled de Gama to become Puerto Rico's next governor. Once more a son-in-law gained a prestigious and profitable position via his wife. Historian Barcia concluded his brief commentary on de Gama by noting that he "remained a resident there [San Juan], husbanding the considerable dowry he had received."[10]

Other Europeans briefly visited Florida, but no conquistador attempted a major invasion until 1528, when Pánfilo de Narváez led three ships there from Cuba. Ten women sailed with him. They disembarked at Tampa Bay, where Narváez decided to march north with some three hundred soldiers, while ordering a hundred men and the "ten married women" back onboard.[11] He told the ship's captain to sail along the coast and meet the army farther north. It was a thoughtless plan: no one knew what lay ahead or even if Florida was an island or a peninsula, and the two groups never found each other.

One of the women had the temerity to warn Narváez that he and his soldiers were headed to their doom. Although unnamed, she apparently had a reputation for wisdom, as "Narvaez had consulted with the soothsaying woman at other times during the expedition." This time, however, he heedlessly reassured her that even if "many would die, those who remained would . . . end up very rich."[12] But she was right, and he was wrong. In a saga of disaster on all sides, eventually Narváez and all but four of his men perished. The four spent eight years aimlessly going west.

Back at Tampa Bay, when the groups separated in May 1528, the clairvoyant told the other women to assume that they would be widows. According to Cabeza de Vaca, one of the saga's four survivors, she said "to see whom they might marry, because she planned to do it."[13] Along with the male mariners, the women sailed for almost a year, vainly searching the Florida coastline before returning to Cuba.

Narváez's wife, María de Valenzuela, sent out search parties. She already had expended a great deal of money and effort on her husband's behalf: Narváez spent the first three years of the 1520s adventuring in Mexico, where his rival, Hernán Cortés, imprisoned him. A widow when she wed Narváez, Valenzuela brought a significant amount of property to the marriage and was a good business manager. According to Gonzalo Fernández de Oviedo y Valdés (called Oviedo), Narváez returned from Mexico to find "his estate increased in value. . . . She also had for him 13,000 or 14,000 gold pesos, which the woman had mined with their slaves and Indians."[14] María would never again see her Pánfilo, however, and like the women who sailed with his expedition, spent years wondering if she was a widow.

Florida women, meanwhile, had the unfortunate experience of meeting the cruel Narváez. Like other conquistadors and modern fascists, he followed a policy of inducing terror by demonstrating extreme insensitivity

Our Own Pocahontas

When Pánfilo de Narváez failed to return from his 1528 voyage, his wife, María de Valenzuela, hired men to hunt for him. As they sailed into Tampa Bay, natives made it clear that they would resist invasion. No more than three or four Spanish men dared to disembark. All were killed by arrows except Juan Ortiz, who was sentenced to be slowly roasted alive.

Fortunately for Ortiz, women sometimes played a strong role in deciding the fate of prisoners of war. Ulele, a daughter of the local chief, pleaded for Ortiz. His screams from the fire moved her; she asked that he be released; and he was. One source says her mother and sisters joined in this pleading—which would demonstrate a remarkable willingness to forgive, given that presumably it was Ulele's grandmother, the mother of chief Hirrihigua, who had been killed by Spanish dogs.

Ulele treated Ortiz's wounds and nursed him back to health, and he lived with her people for the next seven years. She saved his life a second time and helped him escape when others in the clan were convinced that he intended to betray them. He repaid Ulele's kindness by doing just that.

When the de Soto expedition arrived in 1539, Ortiz eagerly joined it, and because of the language and survival skills that Ulele had taught him, he was of great value to the Spanish. He died in Mississippi in 1543, but not before his knowledge of native ways had enabled the conquistadors to inflict fatal pain on Ulele's people.

Thus almost a century prior to the famous Pocahontas, Florida's Ulele set the model for native women who saved the lives of European men, a pattern that would recur as America's first peoples won the occasional victory during the genocide against them.

from the beginning. He greeted the Tocabago chief, Hirrihigua, by cutting off his nose, and when the chief's mother objected, Spanish dogs were set on her to eat her alive.

The pattern of cruelty was repeated with the third major invasion of Florida, that of Hernando de Soto in 1539. Like Narváez, he would die in the attempt; after three years of horrendous conflict, his soldiers dropped de

Soto's body into the Mississippi River. During their rampage from Tampa Bay to Louisiana, de Soto's men killed, captured, enslaved, and disfigured thousands of Indians. Some of the first archaeological evidence of this moving disaster was found in Citrus County, where the Tatham Mound, probably built by a Timucuan clan known as the Ocale (Ocala), appears to have had more than two hundred burials at the same time. The casualties "probably all had been inflicted by Spanish soldiers, quite likely members of the de Soto expedition."[15]

But we need not depend on archaeological evidence of the atrocity that was the de Soto conquest: we know of it from their own mouths, as the expedition's four male chroniclers did not hesitate to detail the horrors inflicted on natives. Men, predictably, were more likely to be killed outright, while women, especially young women, were kept alive as sex slaves. Chronicler Oviedo wrote that men captured the women for "foul uses and lewdness, and then they had them baptized for carnal intercourse."[16] The presumption seemed to be that forcing baptism on the victim excused the rape.

A second chronicler of the de Soto expedition demonstrated the influence of the New World's matrilineal culture. Called "the Inca," he bore the Spanish name Garcilaso de la Vega; he was the child of a Spanish man and a high-ranking woman of Peru's sophisticated Inca culture. His mother's native name was Chimpu Ocllo; she changed it at baptism to Isabel Suarez. She had a strong effect on her son; indeed, one writer said the boy "absorbed from his mother's milk" an understanding of history and language.[17] The Inca offers an important entry into the question of Spanish women on the de Soto expedition.

Until recently, historians ignored any hint of female presence, but it now appears that at least a dozen Spanish women joined de Soto. The best known are Francisca Hinestrosa, whose death was recorded by the Inca, and the valiant Ana Méndez, one of relatively few survivors. Historian René León details:

> The Inca separates the narrative of the expedition into what he calls "books." In the third one, in Chapter 38, "The Battle of Chicaca Continues until the End of It," he explains [that] . . . Francisca Hinestrosa was married . . . with Hernando Bautista. She would die when Indians set fire. . . . At the time she died she was pregnant. This happened about the end of March 1541 in the northwest part of the [modern] state of Mississippi.[18]

Francisca Hinestrosa was part of a distinguished Havana family; she is believed to have disguised herself as a man to accompany her soldier husband. Ana Méndez, on the other hand, was an illiterate woman who was a servant (or slave) to de Soto's wife, Isabella Bobadilla, and presumably Méndez went because she was ordered to do so. She lived to testify in 1560 to a Spanish commission about her experience, when she petitioned the Spanish government for "the benefits they usually gave . . . to the survivors of that type of adventure."[19] The testimony included a reference to Méndez having been sent to attend de Soto as a servant and for "his other necessities"—which, of course, implies sex. Historian León candidly added, "Vasco Parcallo de Figueroa might have taken some of his concubines on the trip."[20]

Beyond Hinestrosa and Méndez, it is probable that a dozen women were on the de Soto expedition. That number had traveled with Isabella Bobadilla and Hernando de Soto when they left Spain for Santiago, Cuba, in 1538—and less than a year later, "most of these passengers made the trip to Florida."[21] At least two were African slaves. Several writers reported that one of these women took the first opportunity to escape, fleeing soon after landing at Tampa Bay and joining the local Tocobaga.[22]

Isabella Bobadilla did not go on with her husband from Santiago to La Florida, but it is entirely possible that this was not—as stereotype might have it—because she was too frail to endure the wilds of North America. Instead, it is likely that she stayed behind as a stabilizing presence in Cuba, where she served as governor.[23] She was qualified by family heritage for this position, as her father was governor of both Panama and Nicaragua. Bobadilla was sufficiently known throughout the Spanish Empire that the Inca mentioned her "at least ten times in his *La Florida*." He pronounced her a "prudent and wise woman," capable of acting with "discretion."[24] This thoughtful chronicler also reported that the female chief of Florida's Cafachiqui clan gave de Soto a string of pearls intended for Bobadilla. Moreover, his report on "the Lady of Cafachiqui" was entirely positive: he called her an "able ruler" and "intelligent diplomat."[25]

* * *

Although this is seldom spelled out in history textbooks, women thus participated in all six of the initial Spanish attempts to colonize to Florida. There were women on de León's first and second voyages, as well as on the epic

Timeline: European Women in Early Florida

Future researchers may be able to find more detail on these adventurous women involved in the first expeditions to Florida:

1513 Beatriz and Juana Jiménez accompany Juan Ponce de León from Puerto Rico to the Melbourne area; in addition to the East Coast, they explore the Keys and other southwestern islands

1521 De León leads some two hundred men and women to the Sanibel area, where the Calusa repel them

1528 "Ten married women" go with Pánfilo de Narváez; after almost a year sailing Florida's West Coast, they return to Cuba

1539 Ana Méndez, Francisa Hinestrosa, and probably others travel with Hernando de Soto; Méndez survives and reports to a Spanish court

1549 Magdalena guides Father Luis Cancer from Vera Cruz, Mexico, to Tampa Bay

1559 Spanish women are part of attempted settlement at Pensacola

1564 French women are part of attempted settlement at Fort Caroline on the St. Johns River

1565 Permanent settlement finally succeeds at St. Augustine; of course women are present—because without women, there is no future

ventures of Narváez and de Soto. A woman actually served as the navigational guide on the fifth major effort at settlement of Florida.

That was in 1549, a decade after de Soto's 1539 misadventure—and more than the earlier expeditions, it was an attempt to carry out Queen Isabella's original mandate to Christianize natives. Father Luis Cancer led an expedition from Vera Cruz, Mexico, to—again—Tampa Bay. That was exactly the locale that the Spanish should have avoided because of the enmity created there by Narváez and de Soto. Whether Father Luis felt compelled to convert these particular natives or his guide betrayed him remains a subject of debate.

The guide was Magdalena, a native Floridian who had gone to Cuba, converted to Catholicism, taken a Christian name, and somehow ended up in Mexico. Because she was familiar with Florida, Father Cancer went from Cuba to Vera Cruz for the explicit purpose of recruiting her.[26] She may have followed his intent to go to Tampa Bay, or she may have led the sailors guilelessly to the deep harbor she knew best—or she may slyly have taken this opportunity to return home, while repaying the Spanish for the harm they had caused her people. Spanish historian Barcia wrote:

> Padre Fray Luis . . . went forth from Mexico. . . . With him he took an Indian woman named Magdalena, a Christian and native of the country of their destination. He reached Florida on the eve of the Ascension [June 1549], and a few days later . . . arrived at the Bay of the Holy Spirit [Tampa Bay]. Fray Diego de Penalosa disembarked here with Fuentes, and upon going into the interior, they were killed by Indians. A Castilian by the name of Juan Munoz came to the ship. This man had been . . . with Hernando de Soto . . . and was so disfigured that if he had not spoken Spanish they would have taken him for an Indian. . . . Fray Luis wanted to go ashore . . . [and] nothing would dampen his ardor. Throwing himself into the water, he came up on shore, where he was cruelly murdered by the Indians in plain view.[27]

The ship "thereupon set sail for Havana . . . , having left Magdalena among the barbarians."[28] She seemed happy to stay. Even before Cancer's death, she "appeared suddenly on the shore among a crowd of natives" and seemingly taunted those with whom she had recently repeated Catholic litany, for "she had shorn herself of her Christian clothing and had taken on the old habits of her Indian upbringing."[29]

Magdalena's intentions probably will remain a mystery, but in any case, she appears to have been a remarkably competent navigator and linguist.

How she ended up in the Caribbean also remains unknown, but during the half century after Columbus, there were many cases of piracy and capture that displaced natives and Europeans all over the Gulf of Mexico. Indeed, in the same year as Father Cancer's demise, historian Barcia recorded that "three vessels en route from New Spain were cast away on the Florida coast. Most of the people survived, but only to undergo greater hardships."[30] Four years later, in 1553, "a furious wind" swept ships bound for Spain onto a Florida shore:

> Of the thousand people aboard the wrecked vessels, more than three hundred came ashore clinging to ships' planks or boxes of merchandise. . . . They had hardly begun to march when the hundreds of Indians loosed a shower of arrows. . . . Many Spaniards were killed, and with each day's march the number of Indians increased. . . . They seized two Spaniards and stripped them naked, but . . . then sent them on. . . . The rest thereupon abandoned their garments, believing the savages were after the clothing . . .
>
> They arrived naked at the Rio de Palmas. Here the last of the women and children died. . . . They went on, and met a naked negress, who . . . helped a great deal, for she found herbs that they could eat. . . . The Indians deprived them of this alleviation, however, for they murdered the negress.[31]

Such horrors occurred fairly regularly, as shipwrecks were frequent in the treacherous Bermuda Triangle. Indeed, the Calusa told Pedro Menéndez in 1567 that during the previous decades as many as two hundred bodies had landed on their beaches, presumably the victims of shipwrecks. Nor were all wrecks accidental: many of the region's ships were sailed by pirates whose occupation was robbery—along with murder, rape, and other terrorism.

Yet knowing the perils, even more Spanish women participated in the fifth major attempt to colonize La Florida. This one did not go to Tampa Bay, and it came closer to success than any before. Don Tristán de Luna y Arellano, a nobleman from Aragon, led as many as a thousand people from Vera Cruz, Mexico, to what now is the Pensacola area—although he named it Santa Maria. They landed at its fine harbor on August 14, 1559—and on August 20 a hurricane struck.

Europe has no storms comparable to those in the Americas, and newcomers were unprepared for the destruction that hurricanes cause. This one smashed the fleet to pieces, so there was no way to return to Mexico even if they had wished to go. Once the fleet's salvaged provisions were eaten, the newcomers began moving inland. It probably would have been smarter to stay by the sea, where at least they might find seafood, but Aragon is a mountainous, arid region of Spain that provided de Luna with little knowledge applicable to the Gulf of Mexico. Nor was he an innovator or a good leader, and matters worsened as winter approached:

> Acorns became the soldiers' principal sustenance. The acorns were so bitter that . . . the women and children could not eat them at all, and

were compelled to . . . forage for leaves and twigs of trees. . . . They began to eat their leather trappings and rawhide. . . . Others were poisoned by the unknown herbs they ate.[32]

The writer's assumption that women and children could digest "leaves and twigs" but not acorns is perplexing—but serves to show the lack of chivalry. As would be the case with the later English Pilgrims in Massachusetts, it was natives who saved these Spanish invaders: "Indians began coming over; they brought maize, vegetables, and fruits." By the following summer, however, "the Indians of Olibahali had already tired of having guests."[33]

Spanish men further wore out their welcome by taking sides in a conflict between local clans, while infighting between de Luna and some of his officers added to the mismanagement. The friars also failed as missionaries. They lamented that only one Indian had agreed to be baptized—and that was a woman on her deathbed who accepted all shots at salvation.

Finally, at the end of 1560, two ships arrived. The colonizers hung on for another year, but Tristán de Luna and his men—including some of the clerics—seemed more interested in competition with each other than in truly building a settlement. Finally, in the spring of 1561, "they all embarked and went back to Havana, with the exception of Don Tristán, who remained with a few of his followers." When the survivors told their story in Cuba, the viceroy "ordered Don Tristán to return to New Spain," and he "complied, although with great dejection."[34]

* * *

No nuns were among the Spanish women who went to the New World, nor would there be any among the French people who briefly settled Florida in the 1560s. The first nuns in what would become the United States did not arrive until 1727, in French New Orleans.

To put early Florida in its global context, it is important to know that at nearly the same time as the first explorations, Germany's Martin Luther had begun the great Protestant revolution against Catholicism. By the mid-1500s, wars between religious zealots raged throughout Europe. Indeed, getting away from religious persecution would be a major motivation for settlers to the north of Florida. The Spanish Empire, however, was a theocracy: Catholicism was the official religion, and non-Catholics were not permitted to live in any part of it. In the 1560s Florida was not yet fully claimed by Spain, and so French Protestants, called Huguenots, sought to make it a haven for dissenters from state-imposed Catholicism.

"The heretics," said Catholic historian Barcia, "asked Elizabeth of England for help."[35] She responded with funding for a 1562 exploratory journey led by Frenchman Jean Ribault. Catherine de Medici functioned as the French monarch for her young son, Charles IX, and she was akin to Elizabeth in astute use of power. Although Catherine later would be violently pro-Catholic, at this point she seemed to believe that ridding France of dissenters would be good policy, and she "offered royal support to a colony expressly for Protestants."[36] Thus, supported by two powerful women with opposing interests, "300 men and four women" left France for Florida on April 22, 1564.[37]

They settled at the mouth of the St. Johns River where modern Jacksonville stands, calling the site Fort Caroline (or Charles Fort or Charlesfort). Things did not go well with such a preponderance of males, and among other incidents, some "restless members of the group staged a mutiny, stole two small sailing vessels, and set out to sea in search of quick wealth."[38] Specifics on the four women were not spelled out, but the settlers were on the verge of abandoning their efforts when about five hundred men and seventy women arrived from France in the summer of 1565.

Meanwhile, Spanish spies were keeping an eye on the colonists—who were not only French but, much worse, Protestant (Spanish writers called them all "Lutheran"). Just weeks after the additional Huguenot women arrived, they would find themselves under attack by Spaniards led by Pedro Menéndez de Avilés. When his forces surprised the French at daybreak on September 20, 1565, "fifty women and children and six noncombatant[s] . . . were taken prisoner."[39] Women also were among about sixty people who fled and hid in the woods until they could manage to slip away on two ships. Although some noblemen were kept alive as prisoners of war, most of the men were chained together and brutally hacked to death with axes and swords. The site still is remembered as Matanzas, "place of slaughter."

Spanish troops did not have far to go that September morning when they attacked Fort Caroline. Just days prior to the massacre, they had established a base at what is known today as the oldest continuously occupied European-style city in the United States, St. Augustine, only about forty miles to the south of Fort Caroline. Unlike other expeditions, this one came directly from Spain, with the direct intent of destroying the French settlement. Pedro Menéndez de Avilés led "two thousand, six hundred, and forty-six people, among them twenty-six married citizens and their families."[40] This was by far the largest of the expeditions to Florida, which probably was key to its success; it also may have had better supplies, given that it came directly from Spain instead of the Caribbean.

Menéndez had intended to take "five hundred slaves . . . a third of them female," but free volunteers appeared in such numbers that there was no need.[41] This expedition was unlike earlier ones in its diversity: in addition to mariners, soldiers, and clerics, it included skilled male workers such as carpenters, men who expected women and children to join them in building a lasting colony.

Also onboard the flagship was Menéndez's wife, Doña Ana María de Solís. Called María, she had been "affianced from childhood."[42] The de Solís family may have regretted that decision as the years passed: Pedro was one of twenty children born to Juan Alfonso Sanchez de Avilés and María Alonso de Arango, and soon after Pedro's engagement at age eight, his father died.[43] Although his mother soon remarried, "the family was not wealthy," and Pedro went to live with a guardian, with whom he frequently quarreled.[44]

The marriage contract was nonetheless fulfilled, and by the time of the expedition to Florida, Doña María was forty-eight years old—past the time of life when most people are willing to move to a new land. She came from an adventurous family, though, and it is likely that they helped finance the expedition. Her brother, Gabriel de Solís, was a leading officer, and another brother, Gonzalo Solís de Merás, probably was the designated historian; his first report appeared in Spain in 1567, just two years after the expedition.[45] Moreover, the couple had lost their only son to a shipwreck, and a daughter had taken vows as a nun in Avilés. Thus Doña Catalina Menéndez de Avilés became her father's "heir and universal successor."[46]

As storms once again interfered, and several vessels ended up in Puerto Rico, it was with "few ships" that the expedition arrived at Cape Canaveral on August 28, 1565.[47] Upon sight of land, chronicler Gonzalo Solís de Merás wrote that everyone kneeled and repeated the "Te Deum Laudamus." They continued up the coast, disembarking at the harbor they named St. Augustine. On September 8, "a solemn Mass was offered in honor of the Nativity of the Blessed Virgin Mary," constituting what many Floridians argue was America's first Thanksgiving.[48] As with Massachusetts natives at the later Plymouth colony, Timucuans shared food with the newcomers. After giving thanks, these Spanish men went about the business of killing French "heretics" just twelve days later.

Most of the early chroniclers were priests, and few bothered to mention women. We do not know how many Spanish women were with Menéndez, let alone exactly who they were—or whether they cooked the Thanksgiving meal. The same is true of the French women at Fort Caroline: we do not know who among them was the mother of "the first Protestant white child born in America."[49] Although most of these women had lived in Florida for only a matter of days before the massacre, there seems to be evidence that some were pregnant or had recently delivered when the Spanish attacked. Records include a deposition from a man who said "he saw eight Frenchwomen and four of their babies" in Puerto Rico soon after the raid on Fort Caroline. Word also reached Madrid "that thirty women and eighteen children" had survived and were in Santiago, Cuba.

Fearful of Catherine de Medici's wrath about this attack on her colony, Spain's King Phillip issued an order in March 1566 that "all the women be brought back [to Europe] and freed, and also the children." No documentation has been found that the order was fulfilled, however, and no female names are recorded on survivor lists—unless women were included under "other poor people who are in different places in the Indies."[50]

Not only did these French women suffer, but many more women back in France found themselves widows dependent on charity: an organized effort began in 1566 "to raise funds for the support of the widows and orphans of Huguenots murdered by Menéndez."[51] Other French women may have stayed in captivity at St. Augustine. Some French men did, as a Catholic apologist for Pedro Menéndez de Avilés explained that the "Black Legend" of his cruelty resulted in part from an "inability to feed the French captives from his meager stores."[52]

If some "heretics" managed to escape to the Timucuans, it is likely that they were sheltered, for natives did not respond to Catholicism in the way that Menéndez expected. During the next few years Jesuits established missions from western Georgia's Chattahoochee River to Parris Island off the coast of South Carolina, but few Indians accepted the new faith; instead, they killed several missionaries.

The internal conflict between Spanish preaching and practicing of their faith can also be seen in that the specialty of South Carolina's Santa Elena colony was sassafras—which was grown as a cure for syphilis. By 1572, just seven years after their arrival, the Jesuits abandoned Florida for Mexico.

* * *

That we know so little about St. Augustine's pioneer Spanish women also is affected by the fact that even socially prominent women often were only semi-literate. In rural Spain it was not unusual for the priest to be the only person in a village who could read and write—and the church especially distanced itself from female education. Hispanic women were discouraged from showing any interest in books or learning; instead they were expected to focus all their attention on their families. Thus even the adventurous women who became the first Europeans in Florida were likely to lack the skills to record their activity.

But they were there, and without them the colony would have disappeared within a generation. Mothers of St. Augustine also included black women, both slave and free, who lived in the town from its beginning. Other women with roots in the Old World lived elsewhere in Florida, the fallout of earlier expeditions or shipwrecks or piracy. While exploring the southwestern peninsula in 1566, for example, Menéndez found "four women and three Christian men." He "had his tailors make them clothes, and "the Christians wept for joy" at their rescue, "although two or three women regretted leaving their children in that country."[53]

The Spanish did not understand that under the natives' matrilineal system, these women probably could have taken their children with them if they had asserted themselves. The Calusa men who were the probable fathers might well have seen the children as naturally belonging with their mother and her "clan." In Spain, contrastingly, both wives and children were viewed as property viewed as belonging to the man—and these "Christian" women appeared to have absorbed those values so thoroughly that they did not envision themselves as having a right to the babies they bore.

More serious for both cultures, Menéndez failed to understand the political role of women in a matrilineal society. When the Calusa chief known as Carlos told Menéndez that "he wanted to adopt him as his elder brother," a natural part of the deal—in Carlos's mind—was that Menéndez should take Carlos's "elder sister whom he loved dearly" as a wife. Carlos further asked that Menéndez "take her to a land of Christians, and then bring her back, whereupon he and all his vassals would become Christians."[54]

Shocked Spaniards assumed that the woman was being forced into this marriage, but that was not at all the case. Instead, Carlos clearly respected and trusted his sister: he was appointing her as an ambassador between the two cultures and believed her capable of learning the new ways and teaching them to the Calusa. Far from throwing his sister into sexual slavery, he intended to indicate her high status as the mother of his successor. But rather than recognizing this, Spanish writers did not even give her the dignity of a name—the name that literally would be of highest importance in this matrilineal society.

Like an appreciable number of Native American chiefs, Carlos had several wives, but Menéndez did not explain that Christianity required monogamy and that he already was married. Instead, he refused the marriage because she was not Christian and created non-existent Christian rules. She nonetheless went to the harbor, along with "some Indian men and women to accompany her," and made it clear that exclusion would be a great insult to her people. Yet, although she "asked about religious matters with considerable penetration," no priest encouraged her conversion. Instead, "Christian women"—also unnamed—dressed her in Spanish clothes, and "that night they baptized her and gave her the name of Doña Antonia."[55]

Doña Antonia and seven other Calusa, four women and three men, did in fact sail to Havana. Although Menéndez's legal wife, Doña Maria, also lived there, Menéndez deposited Doña Antonia with a family named Rojas and continued his wanderings. Initially she seemed happy, and Menéndez's friend Juan Hinestrosa testified to her intelligence:

> He thought highly of the Indian woman because she was very discreet, and her dignity, and her prudence even more, caused her to be admired by the entire city, for in a few days, together with a maidservant of hers, she had learned her prayers and Christian Doctrine.[56]

But being treated as something of a pet and not either the wife or the emissary that she considered herself to be, she grew depressed. This worsened when all but two of her Calusa companions died, presumably from European diseases. When Menéndez returned several months later, his highest priority became returning Doña Antonia to the Calusa, lest she also die and he be blamed. Again, she did not want to go, but she, "her Indian maidservant, and two of the captive Christian women" soon found themselves back in Florida.[57] Presumably the "Christian women" opted for life among the Calusa instead of in Cuba. Menéndez did not even escort the women to their village.

Carlos took his behavior for the insult that it was. He did not convert, and relationships between the Spanish and the Calusa would never again come so close to harmony. Nor did Doña Antonia quietly retreat: whether or not Menéndez wanted her as a wife, she continued her political role. When

Menéndez later supported the Tampa Bay Tocobaga against their traditional enemy, the Calusa, Doña Antonia said "he had two hearts, one for himself, and one for Tocobaga, but none at all for her and her brother." Continually assertive, "she said other things to vex him."[58]

The East Coast Timucua, who were monogamous and practiced settled agriculture, suited Spanish values better—although even there, clerics complained that Timucuans asked annoying questions, including "does God have a wife?" Despite theological skepticism, northeast Florida was the most hospitable place for the capital, and in 1569 another two hundred Spaniards arrived at St. Augustine. The Spanish population, however, remained so overwhelmingly male, especially west of St. Augustine, that men routinely forced themselves onto native women.

Even priests seemed to think that the shortage of Spanish women meant soldiers had a right to rape. Friars at Apalachee, for example, justified rape in a 1567 letter to the Spanish governor: "Sir, these Indians are very jealous and they are excited beyond measure when someone approaches their wives, daughters, or sisters. And the lieutenant and the soldiers who are there are men and by that fact are weak."[59]

"Weak" men nonetheless assumed political power, and when Pedro Menéndez de Avilés died in Spain in 1574, King Phillip II did not appoint his heir, Doña Catalina Menendez, as governor, but instead named her husband, Hernando de Miranda, "to carry out all that his father-in-law had contracted for concerning the government of Florida."[60]

Franciscans, a gentler order than the Jesuits, began arriving in 1584 but suffered an immediate setback when England's Sir Francis Drake raided St. Augustine in 1586. Rebuilt by monies from Spain, the village grew slowly, with captive natives supplying much of the labor. Even Franciscans routinely exploited those they attempted to Christianize, and a major rebellion occurred in 1597, when Guale Indians, who lived along the coast and on the islands north of modern Jacksonville, killed five friars.

The probable cause of this event, sometimes called Juanillo's Revolt, was that the friars had chastised the chief Juanillo for his polygamy. He gathered his warriors and murdered all but one of the area's clergymen. Ultimately, though, native revolts were not successful anywhere in Spanish Florida. Church and state were the same, and both clergy and civilians continued to run their settlements with enslaved labor. The very next year, for example, in 1598, "fifty-four men, women, and children" from the area now called Cape

Canaveral were "brought to St. Augustine where they were distributed to families and to the military."[61]

Christians did not engage in polygamy, but they routinely forced children into marriage. In 1598, when María Menéndez y Posada turned twelve, she married Juan Menéndez Márquez. She was the niece of St. Augustine founder Pedro Menéndez de Avilés, and her dowry brought Juan the title of royal treasurer. The family dynasty that María began before she reached her teens would hold power for five generations.

* * *

Arranged marriage was not routine in native societies—nor did women necessarily object to polygamy, which many saw as a kind of sisterhood that allowed them to share household work. Spanish chroniclers also wrote of several Timucuan women who held direct power. As the 1600s began, at least three towns had female chiefs with Christian names.

St. Augustine's original mission, Nombre de Dios (Name of God) was "under Cacica [female chief] Doña Maria." She married a Spanish soldier, Clemente Vernal, and they had three children—but she nonetheless was recognized as the source of authority for her nephew, the male chief [cacique] at San Mateo, the Spanish name for the old French Fort Caroline. Cacica Doña Ines headed the village of San Juan del Puerto, and the most powerful of all was Cacica Doña Ana. "A number of soldiers spoke explicitly of dona Ana as cacica of San Pedro," which was in modern south Georgia, while a Spanish friar said that Doña Ana was "head chief and head of all the . . . maritime villages down to St. Augustine."[62]

With such powerful women as converts to Christianity, by the 1630s sixteen missions had been established in what now is north-central Florida. They ranged south to the Santa Fe (Holy Spirit) mission near modern Gainesville and north into Georgia; from the mother church in St. Augustine on the East Coast, missions extended west to Tallahassee. As there was no separation of church and state in Spanish Florida, these missions fulfilled both religious and military functions. They were built as walled fortresses, surrounded by small villages of natives who had converted.

In Florida's humidity, the wooden structures of these missions have long since disappeared, but in the drier climate of California a similar-sized chain of missions from the 1700s remains well preserved; they run from San Diego to Sacramento. Such sites also are extant in Arizona, New Mexico, and other parts of the Southwest. They were run from Mexico City, while those in the Southeast were administered from Havana.

All used the model of the church as fronting on a central plaza, with housing for both soldiers and civilians, and a bell that called natives outside the compound for worship and other activities. The mission bell was the Timucua's first experience with keeping time as measured by anything other than the sun, moon, and stars and was particularly symbolic of cultural change. Missions included schoolrooms, but the emphasis was on doctrine with little secular education, and boys were much prioritized over girls. Priests taught Latin to promising boys, but most natives learned Spanish by osmosis, not through formal instruction.

Within the mission walls there also were stables, forges, leather-making space, and other workplaces traditionally for men, while women probably dominated the kitchens, laundries, and rooms for weaving and candle making. Extant sites in the Southwest are surrounded by orchards, gardens, and vineyards, and women prepared and preserved this produce. In Florida, says a modern historian:

> Women . . . did most of the work in or near the town. With the help of larger children, they collected firewood, shelled and ground the maize, and gathered and processed the cassina [herbal medicine], nuts, and oysters. They cleaned the church and its grounds. They planted and hoed the . . . fields and gardens, guarding them against birds and other garden raiders. No doubt they raised pigs and chickens as part of their gardening routine.[63]

The plan was to have missions no farther apart than could be walked in one day, and eventually dozens were built in northern Florida. Those for the Timucua stretched from Amelia Island nearly to Tallahassee, while later ones for the Apalachee went west from Tallahassee. Florida's missions never grew to be as large and permanent as those in the Southwest, but by 1620, Father Francisco Pareja wrote that his Timucuan congregants "did not remember the old ways and that the new generation made fun of people who occasionally still practiced them."[64] He noted that women as well as men participated in Catholic routines, writing in 1614 that "there are Indian women who catechize other Indian women," and that "many persons are found, men and women, who confess and who receive [Holy Communion] with tears."[65]

It was nonetheless true that all over the Americas, Catholicism and native life blended in ways that church authorities chose to ignore—sometimes shockingly so. In 1630, for example, a decade after Father Pareja said the old ways were forgotten, another Florida Franciscan referred to child sacrifice without any condemnation:

> They are a most pious people toward their deceased. . . . They cry with great tenderness for the time of 30 days. . . . When the principal cacique [chief] died, they buried some children from the common . . . people along with his body. For this benefit, their mother and father are . . . esteemed as leading people from then on.[66]

Other friars, too, opted to overlook long-held beliefs and customs that officially were condemned as "sorcery." The likelihood is that the clerics were even less aware of women's customs than of men's, and they probably neither knew nor cared if women continued to practice herbal medicine and other forms of their ancient beliefs. At childbirth, for example, a midwife acted as physician, while a female shaman performed rituals to invoke supernatural aid. These women served as consultants on romantic and other problems, predicted the future, and otherwise continued practices that did not fit with Christianity. The same was true of African women, who continued to worship their own gods in the quiet of their quarters. Rarely did any priest challenge such double-thinking of dogma.

While the missions developed, so did the fortress town of St. Augustine, and the pattern of positions and property for Spanish men via their wives also continued. When naval captain Juan Rodríguez, for example, petitioned the Crown for promotion in 1612, he cited his wife's family as a reason:

> I am married . . . to a daughter of one of the first conquerors . . . who served Your Majesty for thirty years until the Indians killed him . . . and my aforesaid wife is a granddaughter of the captain Juan de Junco who died there and was present on many occasions . . . with the Adelantado Pedro Menéndez.[67]

Rodríguez gave no name for his wife, but she was Francisca Ramírez—and in 1627, after she was a widow, she petitioned the Crown in her own right. On behalf of their seven children, she argued that compensation was due because Rodríguez had served in the military "when the enemy Hollanders and [those] from other nations came to infest these [Florida] coasts, as with the Indians native to the land." She added that she "had already lost her father, cut to pieces by Indians, and a brother, drowned."[68]

Not only were the emotional costs high for Spanish women in the Florida frontier, but so were the economic costs—and how could the Crown expect a widow with seven children to support her household without financial help? Indeed, it is probable that she and other St. Augustine civilians did not live as well as the male clerics and soldiers at outlying missions and forts, who had natives to grow their food and do their work for them.

* * *

Missionaries made sporadic efforts to convert the Apalachee of northwestern Florida from 1608 onward, but both a shortage of priests and Apalachee uncertainty about the new religion meant that a formal program did not begin until 1633. When Spanish soldiers and governmental authorities followed, "the inevitable liaisons that soldiers formed with Apalachee women were undoubtedly a source of friction."[69] Apalachee men also resented the imposed labor that was expected, and in February of 1647, they

> killed three friars, as well as the deputy governor . . . his wife, and a married pregnant daughter along with her husband and child. The unborn child was cut from the mother's womb. The deputy governor also had a teen-aged daughter. . . . She appears to have been particularly bold and was preaching the word of God to the Indians as the others were being tortured. In reprisal, the Apalachee cut off her breasts and her tongue.[70]

Nonetheless, the most important of Apalachee missions, San Luis near modern Tallahassee, began in 1656. Permanence on anything was far from predictable, though, and just three years later, in 1659, a terrible epidemic of measles killed at least ten thousand Florida natives. Measles was just one of the European diseases to which Native Americans had no resistance, and the tragedy would be repeated over and over again as whites settled the continent. Two centuries later, for example, measles would spread through the Pacific Northwest's Cayuse tribe, motivating them to kill Narcissa Whitman, the first white woman there. Her Anglo name appears in history texts, while the Spanish women who suffered more horrific fates go unnamed.

Florida violence again erupted in 1675, when a priest attempted to force an elderly Apalachee leader to separate from three of his four wives. In the same year, thirteen-year-old Juana Cathalina de Florencia married Jacinto Roque Pérez in St. Augustine; they moved to San Luis [Tallahassee] about 1678. The teenage mother went on to bear at least ten children, and these descendants were known by her name, de Florencia. Her dowry doubtless was a factor in making the de Florencia family "the province's most important ranchers, with property in Apalachee worth an estimated 10,000 pesos in 1704."[71] Following the male tradition of drafting native labor, Juana Cathalina became known as exploitive; she is especially remembered for slapping "a hapless chief who failed once to bring her the fish she expected every Friday."[72]

It was not so much the threat of natives, but instead rival whites, that motivated the 1675 beginning of construction of St. Augustine's Castillo de San Marcos, a huge fort that still stands. Spanish officials understood that they would need it to deal with the growing English colonies to the north, which had begun in Virginia in 1607. Englishmen also lusted after the free labor available by capturing and enslaving natives, and they began exploiting old resentments between tribes to create warfare that would result in captives. Especially after South Carolina's Charleston (then Charles Town) began in 1670, Englishmen joined with local Yamasee warriors to raid Timucuan villages in Spanish Florida.

One of the worst raids was in 1684, when warriors from Carolina conquered Amelia Island and moved down the coast to St. Augustine. Again the town was burned, and Spanish women lived in the new fortress for most of two months before the Carolinians retreated—taking some five hundred captives, including many women.

An unexpected result of forcing these Floridians into slavery in the Carolinas and Georgia was that, after adjustments for differing languages, the newcomers could tell the enslaved of those colonies that life was freer in Florida, with Spain's legal limitations on the severity of slavery. The precedent for fleeing to Florida was set in 1687, when three black women, eight men, and a breast-fed infant managed to sail from Georgia to St. Augustine. When their owner discovered where they were and demanded their return, Governor Diego de Quiroga y Losada refused, saying that they had converted to Catholicism and were assets to St. Augustine.

The following year, Governor Quiroga traveled to western Florida in an attempt to address Apalachee complaints against Spanish governance. He was largely successful—except for an Apalachee woman named Qua. She allied herself "with the English of Charles Town" and advocated a confederacy of natives in modern Alabama and Georgia against the Spanish.[73] The majority of Apalachee leaders, however, took up the governor's offer and sent a letter to Spain's King Charles II assuring him of their loyalty.

They did so in 1688, and five years later, the king issued a proclamation intended to harass the English by encouraging more escapes of their African slaves. In surprisingly liberal language, he promised freedom to those who had the courage to leave their masters and come to Florida: the 1693 proclamation "granted liberty . . . to all . . . the men as well as the women."[74]

During the following decades many African, Native American, and mixed-race slaves would leave Georgia, the Carolinas, and even Virginia for the relative freedom of Spanish Florida. Some would succeed in the difficult trek; others would die in the attempt; and still others would be captured and returned to a harsh future. In Florida the result would be many free people of color. Indeed, as the eighteenth century dawned, Florida slaves were more likely to be Native Americans than African Americans.

One of the women who took advantage of the freedom that Spanish Florida offered blacks was an enterprising baker. According to historians Kathleen Deagan and Darcie MacMahon:

> Isabel de los Rios was a free black woman who lived in St. Augustine and sold fresh baked "rosquetes" (spiral rolls), sugar syrup, and possibly other provisions from her home. We know of Isavel and of Captain Crispin de Tapia, a free black man who ran a grocery store, through court records. Both . . . testified in a 1695 court case against several Apalachee Indians that the Indians had given them counterfeit money for the purchase of rolls and other goods.[75]

Some people of color, both free and slave, toiled far inland from St. Augustine, as huge haciendas began effectively displacing missions. Florida missions had begun their decline with the 1656 rebellion; there were twenty-three sites then, but by 1689 just thirteen remained in operation. Instead of the completely male-dominated missions, Spanish women played key roles on the new cattle-growing ranches.

For example, Antonia Basalia de León married Francisco Tomás in 1689; she was the daughter of a widow who owned large amounts of land near modern Jacksonville, and Tomás was a member of the founding Menéndez family. Together they controlled tens of thousands of acres, and just one ranch, La Chua near modern Gainesville, had some seven thousand cattle. Although Spanish women rarely did any physical labor in association with such ranches, it was often their dowries that made these ventures possible. Widows in particular actively managed their property and workers, kept the accounts, and made the decisions to buy and sell, hire and fire.

The hacienda lifestyle also encouraged departures from rigid European behaviors, especially in dress. Spanish women adopted looser clothing than Anglo women to the north, and they made further accommodation to Florida's heat by sometimes sleeping outside in hammocks or ramadas. Boston's Puritans of the 1600s would have been shocked by St. Augustine's women of the same era: not only did Spanish women keep their maiden names—they also routinely danced, gambled, drank alcohol, and even smoked cigars. Although they were less likely to be literate, Florida's women arguably had more fun.

* * *

As the 1700s began, Florida's founding Menéndez family again had women in top positions, at least on paper. In the fifth generation after Pedro Menéndez de Avilés and María de Solís married, there again was no male heir, and Doña María Catalina Menéndez de Avilés was "lady of the Adelantadoship of Florida."[76] The same proved true in the seventh generation, when again males died in infancy, and Doña Ana Antonia Menéndez de Avilés held a string of titles. These women lived in castles in Spain, though, not in frontier Florida—where natives continued the sad decline that had begun two centuries earlier.

Mission bells regularly tolled as cases of illness became epidemics and epidemics became plagues. Already in 1689 a census of Timucuans had indicated that the tribe had been reduced by 98 percent from the estimated population in 1492. One historian summarized: "ten generations after Ponce de León's first voyage to Florida, one Timucua Indian remained for every fifty who had lived then."[77] Entire clans had disappeared, and tribes that had formerly had populations in the tens of thousands now numbered in the mere hundreds. Indeed, huge stretches of Florida were without population. Tampa Bay, where the Tocobaga had lived so successfully, would be completely without permanent residents from the early 1700s until well into the 1800s. Only the occasional fishing boat passed by; otherwise, decades of waves and wind went unseen by a human population.

In north Florida raids by English speakers and their Indian allies continued. The town of St. Augustine was taken over by a British invasion in 1702, but women joined men in surviving a months-long siege of Castillo de San Marcos. San Luis, however, the important mission to the Apalachee at Tallahassee, never recovered from a 1704 attack by Carolinians and their Creek allies. They had made their first attempt in 1702, but a Christian woman of the Chacato people who lived near the Apalachee rushed to warn them that enemies were on their way. In 1704, however, repeated raids from January to August meant that "Apalachee lost its entire native population and its Spanish community."[78] Some thirteen hundred people surrendered and agreed to go north in return for their lives, while others escaped west to Pensacola, a new Spanish colony established six years earlier, in 1698.

The natives went west by land, driving their cattle, but eight Spanish families fled from San Luis to Pensacola by sea. One refugee was Cathalina de Florencia, by then a widow. Her presumably Spanish fellow passengers showed no chivalry, as she "was robbed of all her valuables during the voyage."[79] She went on from Pensacola to Vera Cruz, Mexico, and in 1709 the Spanish Crown compensated her for her Florida losses.

Another founding mother of San Luis (or Tallahassee), María Magdalena de Florencia, ended up in Cuba. Born in St. Augustine in 1675, she was just twenty-nine when the British took her husband, Diego Jiménez, to Charleston, South Carolina, as a prisoner of war after the 1704 collapse of San Luis. She somehow had to support their five children even after he was released, as his health never recovered.

Yellow fever in Pensacola killed many of the Apalachees who had managed to get there, and most survivors went on to Mobile, which was French territory governed by New Orleans. There they found that the French treated them much better than the Spanish—something that was true all over North America. While Spanish men often sexually exploited native women, French men were much more likely to marry them and assimilate into their culture. That probably happened to the Apalachee as they intermarried with the tribes of Alabama, Mississippi, and Louisiana as well as with the French and other Catholics who came to the western Gulf Coast in the eighteenth century.

English men were both less likely to exploit native women and less likely to marry them: they had less need, because English colonizers typically included women in their expeditions from Europe. Most Britons, however, were perfectly willing to enslave anyone they could, and by 1708 St. Augustine officials reported that some ten thousand natives had been sold into slavery in the British-controlled Carolinas. In the same year a British agent for the Carolinas candidly reported that his men "drove the Floridians to the Islands of the Cape, have bought and sold many Hundred of them, and Dayly now continue that trade so that in some few years they'el Reduce these

Barbarians to a farr less number." The next year, a map in London's Colonial Office tersely summarized the situation of Tampa Bay: "Tocobaga Indians, Destroyed 1709."[80]

While native numbers plummeted, the African population rose. In 1738, six years after the British established the colony of Georgia, Florida set an important record with the first legally sanctioned community of free blacks outside Africa. On an island just off the coast of St. Augustine, it was officially Gracia Real de Santa Teresa de Mosé, but more commonly called Fort Mose (pronounced "Mo-say"). News of this shelter for slaves spread quickly, and as early as 1739 South Carolina lawmakers offered rewards for the capture and return of slaves. Despite their reproductive capabilities, women were worth less than men: the bounty for male slaves was £40; for women it was £25. The next year the South Carolina House passed a resolution that read:

> Part of our Calamities [are] . . . from the frequent attempts of our Slaves, [which] arises from the Designs and Intrigues of our Enemies the Spaniards in St. Augustine. . . . Many [slaves] have already deserted, and others encouraged daily to do the same; and even those who have committed the most inhuman Murders, are there harboured, entertained and caressed.[81]

The charge that escaping slaves were murderers had little foundation: indeed, the 1739 bounties encouraged murder in the opposite direction. In addition to rewards for returning live slaves, the law also provided:

> an encouragement . . . for bringing in the scalps of such men and women Negro slaves that . . . cannot be taken and brought home alive, to wit, for each scalp with the two ears £20 to be paid out of the Publick Treasury. Such Negroes as shall be executed . . . their owners shall be reimbursed by the Publick.[82]

With such laws that encouraged their deaths, Fort Mose residents had to be constantly on the alert. Moreover, the Spanish officials who authorized the community were not truly intent on creating an outpost for freedom; instead, they wanted Fort Mose to serve as the first defender of St. Augustine against the English. With free blacks two miles out of town, the whites of St. Augustine could feel more secure. Despite the dangers, though, thirty-eight households were immediately established at Fort Mose, and the colony lasted as long as Spanish governance did.

English newcomers in the Carolinas and Georgia, of course, also harassed the Creeks, Choctaws, Cherokees, and others who remained there. Often of mixed race, these people fled to Spanish Florida, and by 1750 they were settling in the vacant middle of north Florida, on land left unoccupied by the vanishing Apalachee and Timucua. The name Seminole, in fact, means "runaway" in the Creek language, or "people who choose to live alone." The term appears to have originated only shortly before the 1763 British occupation of Florida.

Few Spanish soldiers bothered these runaways, as Spain itself was on the decline. The empire had reached its zenith in 1588: after England's navy under Elizabeth I defeated the Spanish armada that year, Spain never truly recovered. It lost more power during Europe's long religious warfare of the 1600s, and by the mid-1700s, Britain, France, and even Holland had replaced Spain as world powers. Already in 1719, for instance, the flag over Pensacola "changed four times, from Spain to France and vice versa."[83]

Raids by Englishmen from Georgia continued through the 1730s and 1740s, and a 1750 yellow fever epidemic hit St. Augustine hard. Even as the city's Castillo de San Marco finally was declared finished in 1756, the Spanish government clearly was faltering. By 1759 only two Franciscan missions remained: Tolomato, just north of St. Augustine, and the city's original mission, Nombre de Dios (sometimes called Nuestra Señora de la Leche, or Our Lady of the Milk).

Then in 1763 France lost its North American colonies to Britain at the end of what Americans call the French and Indian War. Because Spain had backed the losing French against the English, part of the complex European negotiations meant that Florida was transferred from Spain to Britain. This would last for only twenty years—but no one could foretell that future, and news of British government was terrifying to longtime Spanish Floridians.

Those at Fort Mose had the most immediate reason to be fearful, and America's first community of free blacks came to an end in 1763, twenty-five years after it had begun. Along with "86 Indians who lived in St. Augustine," they escaped to the relatively greater freedom of Cuba.[84] The buildings they left behind would be used by the British but fell into disrepair under the Americans and were finally destroyed in 1812. Not until 2000 was Fort Mose declared a national historic landmark and restored to the attention merited by the African Americans who undertook personal peril to create this haven.

Spanish people also left Florida for other parts of Latin America or for Spain. The result was that the British did not gain much with their new acquisition: almost two centuries after its first permanent European settlement,

East Florida (basically St. Augustine) and West Florida (basically Pensacola) remained separated by four hundred miles, and "neither colony had more than a few thousand, mostly illiterate, inhabitants."[85]

* * *

As English speakers replaced Spanish speakers in Florida, "the English Board of Trade advertised in London that it would make grants of up to twenty thousand acres of land to persons undertaking to settle them with a specified number of families."[86] By far the best known land grant recipient was Scottish physician Andrew Turnbull. He had migrated to the Mediterranean, where he married Maria Gracia Dura Bin, a Greek woman whose wealthy family lived in Smyrna, a town in modern Turkey that is directly across the Aegean Sea from Athens.

Florida's New Smyrna, about seventy miles south of St. Augustine, thus was named for Dura Bin's hometown. The Turnbulls recruited some fourteen hundred Mediterranean people to the colony, including peasants from Greece and southern Italy as well as from the islands of Corsica and Minorca. Floridians generally lumped them together under the name Minorcan.

Dr. Turnbull may have been influenced by one of the first Florida land promotion pamphlets written in English, a 1763 piece by Scotsman Archibald Menzies, which encouraged the working of British estates in Florida by free labor from the Mediterranean. Menzies appears to have been a humanitarian who wanted not only to cut down on slave importation from Africa but also to liberate Mediterranean peasants from "their severe masters" and give them "the protection of a free government." He understood the importance of including women in planned colonization and expected that the "remarkably handsome" Mediterranean women would attract British men, which would "naturally prompt inter-marriages." Centuries ahead of his time, he hoped that such unions would "soon put an end to all distinctions."[87]

Similar globalism lay behind Turnbull's intention to specialize in indigo, a plant that produces blue dye; it would be used in the new textile factories that were beginning the industrialization of England. Indigo had been perfected by America's first important agriculturist, Eliza Lucas Pinckney of South Carolina, who experimented with it and other plant hybridizations from 1739 onward. She actively managed seven plantations and was so well respected that President George Washington served as a pallbearer at her funeral.

New Smyrna's Andrew Turnbull, however, did not prove to be the successful manager that Eliza Pinckney was, and the colony ended up a "miserable failure."[88] Although his workers were indentured servants, not slaves, their treatment was as bad as that of most slaves, or worse, including frequent whippings and "other harsh punishments." One overseer, for example, "allegedly beat a married Minorcan because she would not sleep with him, and in another instance, beat a husband when he objected because his wife did."[89] Not surprisingly, colonists revolted in 1768 and again in 1777.

Turnbull's colony also suffered from bad timing, as he began it when talk of revolution against Britain was growing in the American colonies to the north. The new United States, however, would not find many allies south of Georgia, and almost all Floridians remained loyal to the established government. African Americans certainly did not want to live under the United States government. Most had escaped to the relative freedom of Florida, and they rightly feared American law. The same was true of Native Americans, who understood that Americans were a greater threat to their way of life than the British.

Experts estimate that only about eight thousand people lived in vast Florida in 1775—many fewer than had been the case centuries earlier. Whites were a definite minority, as both African Americans and Seminoles (including many individuals who identified with both groups) were much more numerous. There also was appreciable diversity among the whites: in addition to longtime Spanish Floridians, there were newly arrived Britons, especially Scots; the Mediterranean peoples of the New Smyrna colony; and French-speaking, New Orleans-based families who lived around Pensacola Bay. Almost none had any good reason to support the American rebels, and many had very sound reasons to oppose the new United States.

On the other hand, few actively fought for the British, either, and Florida's history during the American Revolution was almost entirely one of victimization. That pertained especially in the west, where "from one month to the next, British commanders in Jamaica and New York never knew who occupied Pensacola."[90] While the harbor was repeatedly claimed and counterclaimed by either the British or their French and Spanish enemies, Pensacola residents spent endless days under siege in their blockhouse.

In St. Augustine a particularly egregious case occurred at a tavern run by a Greek couple, Lorenzo and Mary Magdalena Capo. British soldiers, armed and drunk,

> marched the Capos at gunpoint to the fort and threw Mary in the guard room, where Ensign Manning raped her. Several hours later, soldiers prodded the Capos with bayonets to force them to return to the tavern and serve punch and rum for the rest of the evening. When Manning was eventually formally charged with rape, he blew out his brains. Angry soldiers, blaming the Capos for the death . . . , pulled down the tavern timber by timber.[91]

This was not isolated behavior, and women in the American colonies also were terrorized by gang rapes committed by soldiers on both sides. Most went unpunished, as few women had Mary Magdalena Capo's courage in making public her frightening experience. Other Florida women may have been raped, and we know for a fact that they suffered in other ways because after the war ended, many British loyalists filed financial claims for wartime losses.

Among them was West Florida's Mrs. Ann Shakespeare, who filed her "memorial" for reimbursement of property damage on May 8, 1783. In East Florida, Mary Peavett "had lived throughout the Revolution in the substantial Oldest House . . . near the St. Francis barracks."[92] After her husband died in 1785, the fifty-year-old Peavett married a young Irish soldier who spent her money so quickly that she soon had to sell her house.

When the 1783 Treaty of Paris worked out the settlement details of this intercontinental war, British loyalists who stayed in Florida were shocked to learn that they were again under Spanish governance: Britain exchanged the insignificant Florida peninsula for the Bahamas, which Spain had captured during the war. Hundreds of English speakers left for those islands or other British territory, especially from West Florida, where "almost without exception, British subjects . . . evacuated Pensacola."[93]

The most enduring indication of the twenty-year British reign over Florida may have been in place names. Among the most notable are Charlotte Harbor, which was named for the current English queen, and the Hillsborough River in what is now Hillsborough County was named for Lord Wills Hills, who never saw it. British headquarters remained at St. Augustine (East Florida) and Pensacola (West Florida), and neither city's name changed.

A second influence in the last year of British control was Florida's first newspaper. For more than two centuries, from the 1565 settlement of St.

Augustine, no Spanish person had begun a newspaper, but the English *East-Florida Gazette* was founded in 1783.

In another hopeful omen the next year, Spanish emissaries to Native Americans wrote a treaty that was one of the most respectful ever. A council on June 22, 1784, at Mobile Bay replicated an earlier one at Pensacola. According to historian Caroline Mays Brevard:

> The [Indian] warriors brought with them their wives and children, all of whom were generously entertained. As at Pensacola, gifts were lavished . . . and a treaty of commerce was concluded. [In] one clause of the treaty of Pensacola . . . , the Indians renounced the custom of taking scalps and of enslaving white prisoners. . . . The Indian nations were confirmed in the possession of lands owned within Spanish dominions; and should they be deprived of these by the enemies of Spain, they were to be granted elsewhere in Spanish territory the same extent of equally good lands.[94]

Spain soon proved powerless to enforce this or any other treaty, however, as rebellions in South America increasingly doomed the Spanish Empire. For the next four decades Florida would stagnate as a backwater that was neither truly Spanish nor American.

* * *

When the U.S. Constitution was written in 1787, one of its clauses prohibited the importation of slaves after 1808. The buying and selling of slaves within the United States continued—even in such northern states as New York—but no more were legally allowed in from Africa. Illicit importation did not cease, however, and Florida's long and undeveloped coastline became an ideal spot for smugglers to deposit their illegal human cargo. Fernandina on Amelia Island became an unofficial headquarters of this covert activity. Slave traders and pirates controlled the area, as local government was unwilling to enforce either U.S. or Spanish law, both of which now banned new slaves.

The Keys and the Ten Thousand Islands area of southwestern Florida also were infested with pirates. Although the Spanish had known of Key West's strategic site for centuries, no lighthouse had been built there. Nor did the locals truly want one, as "the little island town prospered on the unique business of wrecking." Although not as inhumane as high-seas pirates, Key West residents nonetheless profited by going "to the aid of wrecked vessels. Their payment . . . was a percentage of the value of the property they saved."[95]

The state of anarchy that supported pirates was indicative of how different Florida was from the new United States—and cultural differences were even more striking than political ones. The life of Francisco Xavier Sánchez provides an excellent example. Owner of a huge north Florida ranch, he lived with "Maria Beatriz Stone (Pierda), a free mulatto born in Charleston," for two decades. They "had three sons and five daughters":

> All these children were recognized by their father and baptized in the Catholic church. By 1790, Sanchez had moved the children into town, and they lived in St. Augustine attended by slaves of their own. . . . Sanchez's mulatto sons attended the public school in St. Augustine. His daughters also received an education. . . . Three of Sanchez's mulatto daughters married white . . . Spaniards.[96]

But he apparently had a midlife crisis. At age fifty-one Sánchez married Maria del Carmen Hill, the seventeen-year-old daughter of a wealthy South Carolina family. His common-law wife, living in "poverty" and doubtless depressed, soon died. With his new wife, this patriarch had another ten children, "the last of whom was born days before her father's death in 1807." Francisco Sánchez thus fathered eighteen children, and despite his abandonment of the mother of the first eight, they all seemed to live in amity: "Maria del Carmen and her children apparently enjoyed a close relationship with the children of Sanchez's first union and served as godparents for his quadroon grandchildren."[97]

In addition to the end of legal importation of slaves, the year 1808 marked the first land grant in the area that became Miami. The Spanish government gave John Egan title to one hundred acres at the mouth of the Miami River; this and additional acreage later passed to Egan's sister, Harriet English. Her son William farmed there, but when he died young, the land reverted to Harriet English.[98] Although she never lived there, it was her property that decades later was bought by Julia Tuttle, "the mother of Miami."

South Florida was largely vacant of human life in the early 1800s, though; St. Augustine and Pensacola continued to be the only substantial towns. Both were Spanish, but Pensacola was greatly influenced by French speakers from New Orleans. That area, too, saw governance change in 1803, when the United States purchased Louisiana from Napoleon's cash-starved France—but again, such changes on maps meant little to local residents.

"Balls in Every Direction": Spanish Life Near Its End

In two travelogues, *A View of West Florida* and *Voyage to the Spanish Main*, John Lee Williams described colonial Spanish life in the early 1800s. Of Pensacola residents, he said:

> They were a temperate, quiet, and rather an indolent people. Affectionate and kindly to each other, and kind to their slaves, the even tenor of their way was not frequently interrupted by business. . . . Dances [and] card-parties were frequently indulged in, but never to excess. . . .
>
> Sherrivarees are parties . . . [when they] dress themselves in masquerade, whenever a widow or widower is married. They often parade about, and play buffoon tricks, for two or three days; haunting the residence of the married pair, and disturbing the whole city . . . until they can be bought off with money or liquor.

Of St. Augustine, he wrote:

> Masks, dominoes, Harlequins, Punchinellos, and a great variety of grotesque disguises, on horseback . . . and on foot, paraded the streets with guitars, violins, and other instruments; and in the evening, the houses were open to receive masks, and balls were given in every direction.

Note: John Lee Williams originally published *View of West Florida* in Philadelphia in 1827, and the University Presses of Florida reissued it in 1976.

Pensacola's Moreno family of this era was similar to St. Augustine's Sánchez family. "The eldest of 26 children," Angela Moreno learned leadership in that role.[99] She married Stephen Mallory, and the Spanish-English family that they established became influential for two centuries. Angela and Stephen moved to Key West and later, when he was elected to the U.S. Senate, to Washington. When Florida seceded from the Union, she would go with him to Richmond, where he was the Confederate secretary of the navy, before ending their days back in Pensacola. Many Floridians were akin to the Mallory-Moreno families in drifting easily between governments. Speaking both Spanish and English and sometimes French, their cultural tradition was hugely different from that of their neighbors in the new United States.

Florida was Spanish territory in 1812, when the United States again went to war with its old motherland, Great Britain. The causes of the War of 1812 repeated many of the same issues of the American Revolution, especially with British-allied Indians in the Upper Midwest and Britain's maritime attacks on the fledgling U.S. Navy. The war's effect in Florida, however, was quite different: it gave Georgians an excuse to make raids against former slaves who had fled to Florida. At least ninety, including women, were forcibly returned to Georgia.

The war ended early in 1815, but African Americans continued to escape from American slavery to Spanish freedom, and some occupied an abandoned fort on the Apalachicola River. Called "Fort Negro," this settlement included Seminoles and mixed-race families—and drew immediate attention from General Edmund Gaines. From a headquarters about sixty miles north on Georgia's portion of the river, Gaines notified the U.S. War Department in May 1815 that "certain negroes and outlaws have taken possession of a fort . . . in the Territory of Florida."[100]

The stirring words of an abolitionist writer during the Civil War still seem best to tell this story. The author refers to the runaway slaves and Seminoles as "Exiles," meaning that they had exiled themselves from Georgia, Alabama, or other parts of the United States to the Apalachicola River of Spanish Florida:

> For more than a year . . . General Gaines made the Exiles a subject of frequent correspondence to the War Department. . . . Of these communications the Exiles were ignorant. . . . In the autumn of 1815, they gathered their crops . . . ; they lived in peace and enjoyed the fruits of their labor. The following spring and summer found them in this enviable condition. . . .
>
> Power is never more dangerous than when wielded by military men. They usually feel ambitious to display their prowess. . . . On the sixteenth of May [1816], General [Andrew] Jackson wrote General Gaines, saying, "I have little doubt . . . that this fort has been established . . . for the purpose of rapine and plunder, and that it ought to be blown up, regardless of the [Spanish] ground on which it stands. . . . Destroy it and return the *stolen negroes* and property to their rightful owners."[101]

Gaines was happy to obey. He attacked at dawn, when everyone was in the fort and asleep. "Mothers and children shrieked with terror as the roar of cannon" awakened them.[102] Soon "a hot-shot from one of the boats . . . caused a terrible explosion. The scene was horrible," as people were literally blown apart, while others burned to death. "Of the three hundred and thirty-four human beings in the fort, two hundred and seventy were instantly killed, and most of the remainder died from their injuries."[103] Just three were unwounded—and two of them were leaders, who then were executed by Indians allied with Gaines. The relatively few who survived their wounds were re-enslaved; the livestock and property that they had begun to accumulate was confiscated.

American victory in the War of 1812 meant that unemployed soldiers encouraged other raids against Seminoles and their black allies. They understandably retaliated, and there were atrocities on both sides. In 1817 natives ambushed a boat on the Apalachicola that included seven white women and four children. They fired on the boat, and four unchivalrous white men who swam away were the only survivors. "All on board were horribly massacred . . . , with the exception of . . . a woman, whom the Indians carried away with them."[104]

Later called the First Seminole War, this conflict continued into 1818, as Andrew Jackson and his men pursued native civilians deep into Spanish territory. With an army of approximately fifteen hundred white men and eighteen hundred Indians, most of them Creeks, they chased the runaway Seminoles. They found the Seminole village of Miccosukee deserted, as residents had had enough warning to flee. Jackson felt his cause justified, however, when he discovered "a warpole planted before the council house, and suspended from it were fifty recently-taken scalps—men's, women's and children's."[105]

Jackson's forces also attacked the "Old Town of Suwanee," where they "entered the town and set fire to the buildings. . . . He captured some three hundred Indian women and children," a big enough victory that he declared the war over in May. By then, "nearly the entire population residing on the Apalachicola River had been massacred. Their villages at Mickasukie and Suwanee had been burned; and it is probable that nearly one half of the [Seminole] population had been sacrificed."[106]

What sealed Florida's fate, however, happened the next year, when Jackson hanged two British men at St. Marks, southwest of modern Tallahassee, for alleged conspiracy with Seminoles. Although massacres of women and children caused little concern, the execution of these British citizens created an international crisis. U.S. Secretary of State John Quincy Adams was angry about Jackson's unauthorized activities, and the two became lifelong enemies.

Florida's Jewish First Family

In 1817, two years before Spain ceded Florida to the United States, Moses Elias Levy bought some 60,000 acres of land in west-central Florida that he had not yet seen. He made the transaction in Cuba with Fernando de la Maza Arredondo. A Sephardic Jew, Levy also had lived in Spain, Morocco, and the Virgin Islands, and he hoped to create a utopian colony for Jews.

He arrived in 1818—presumably with a wife whose name goes unrecorded; biographers focus on their son, David Yulee Levy. David had been born on the Caribbean island of St. Thomas 1810 and was eight when they arrived in Florida. He soon went on to boarding school in Virginia, but Mrs. Levy apparently had other children.

When other Jews did not follow them to Florida, Moses Levy bought slaves and developed a sugar plantation of some 36,000 acres near Micanopy. After David completed his education, he married a woman whose father was governor of Kentucky, and he named their plantation "Margarita" for her. The plantation featured what probably was the area's most modern sugar mill.

David Levy was a member of Florida's first constitutional convention in 1838. With statehood in 1845, he became not only Florida's first U.S. senator but also the nation's first Jewish senator. When Florida left the union just fifteen years later, he dropped out of politics to provide sugar for the South. Ammunition was stockpiled in the Levy mansion, and a Union naval force therefore burned everything to the ground in 1864.

The Citrus County Federation of Women's Clubs preserved a six-acre site around the sugar mill in 1923 and donated it to the state in 1953. Exhibits at the mill ruins are uncommon in that they demonstrate industrial work done by slave women. These women not only toiled in the cane fields but also refined sugar.

At the same time, however, Adams used his diplomatic skill to make the point that Spain obviously could not control this territory and that the only way to end the anarchy in Florida was for Spain to cede it to the United States. He met with Spanish ambassador Luis de Onis, and they signed the Adams-Onis Treaty on February 22, 1819. In exchange for $5 million in claims, Spain's centuries-long governance of Florida came to an end.

If a vote had been taken, most of the people living in Florida at the time probably would have voted against joining the United States. Certainly this was true of the Seminoles and their African American allies, who absolutely dreaded the thought of being in U.S. territory. It also was true of most of the Spanish-speaking people in the old cities of St. Augustine, Pensacola, and even Key West. Within a few years, however, they would have been outvoted by the Americans who founded Jacksonville, Tampa, and Tallahassee during the 1820s.

Florida's Spanish-Seminole-African-Minorcan majority would begin to disappear in the 1820s, soon outnumbered by Anglo-American newcomers. The change would be huge—and most modern Floridians have no idea that not until 2055 will the American flag have flown over Florida for as long as the Spanish flag did.

3 From Spanish Colony to Statehood and Secession, 1820–1859

"The Era of Good Feelings" is a phrase historians use to denote the unique political unanimity of 1820, when President James Monroe was reelected without opposition; no presidential election since has gone uncontested. The previous year, on February 22, 1819, Spain had peacefully ceded Florida to the United States. The 1820s were indeed notable for "good feelings," for peace and harmony.

All was not entirely calm for the Seminoles in that decade; as whites and their black slaves moved into north Florida, Seminoles moved farther south. Some of Florida's Spanish residents, especially upper-class people and government officials, moved to Cuba, Mexico, or other Spanish colonies after the United States took over Florida—but many stayed and adjusted to life under American governance. Although the transition was emotional and sad for the Spanish, there were no riots or rebellions when their flag came down and the Stars and Stripes went up—at Pensacola on July 7 and at St. Augustine on July 10, 1821.

Rachel Donelson Jackson watched the Pensacola ceremony from a balcony on Main Street, facing the harbor. Her husband, General Andrew Jackson, was the first governor of the Florida Territory, but she wrote empathetically of the Spanish. The ships, she said,

> hove in view under the American flag and a full band of music. . . . They marched by to the Government House, where the two Generals met in the manner prescribed, then his Catholic majesty's flag was lowered,

and the American hoisted high in the air, not less than one hundred feet.

O how they burst into tears to see the last ray of hope departed of their devoted city and country—delivering up the keys of the archives. . . . Next morning they set sail.[1]

The four months of 1821 that Rachel Jackson spent in Pensacola were the only time in her married life that she left her Tennessee home, aptly named the Hermitage. Although her husband's political opponents hurled horrible insults about her morality, she was a pious (albeit pipe-smoking) Presbyterian. That was clear when she lived in Pensacola, where behavioral standards differed from those of Puritanical Americans. She did not hesitate to take matters into her own hands:

The Sabbath was profanely kept; a great deal of noise and swearing in the streets; shops kept open; trade going on, I think, more than on any other day. They were so boisterous on that day I sent Major Stanton to say to them that the approaching Sunday would be differently kept. . . . Yesterday I had the happiness of witnessing the truth of what I had said. Great order was observed; the doors kept shut; the gambling houses demolished; fiddling and dancing not heard any more on the Lord's day.[2]

Rules changed, too, in St. Augustine, as the new government imposed a tax structure to discourage luxury. New levies included "a tax of one dollar a year on each slave over seven years of age, two dollars a year upon each dog, twenty-four dollars a year upon every dram shop [liquor store], fifty dollars a year upon billiard tables, [and] ten dollars for every 'riding carriage.'"[3]

Because Andrew Jackson was no natural puritan, these changes seem to reflect Rachel's influence. He preferred a military and political life to that of a territorial executive, however, and soon was ready to leave. Although Rachel "pronounce[d] Pensacola that most healthful place she had ever seen," the Jacksons returned to Tennessee.[4]

* * *

President Monroe took a surprisingly personal interest in appointing Florida's first officials, even explaining his choices by referring to the needs of some of the nation's leading families. "The Era of Good Feelings" had the ironic effect of impoverishing military officers: the Revolution and the War of 1812 had swelled the ranks, but now military cutbacks negatively affected the families of founders. Monroe's words also show the significance of women: at least two appointees seem to have gotten their jobs because the president respected—and was concerned for—their wives. He detailed his choices to the new governor:

> Steuben Smith . . . married the daughter of Mr. [John] Adams, former president. He is the nephew of the present Secr'y of State, & his wife is the sister of Mrs. [John Quincy] Adams. . . . Mr. Hackley's . . . wife is the sister of Govr Randolph of Virginia. . . . As these persons are I believe literally poor . . . , I wish you to place them, if possible, in some of the public buildings.[5]

Cases abound. Francis Wayles Eppes, for example, was three times the mayor of Tallahassee, but his name alone reveals little about his connections. His mother was the daughter of President Thomas Jefferson, and his wife, Elizabeth Randolph Eppes, was the prime mover behind the Florida relocation of many of Virginia's famed Randolph family members. Jefferson's mother's was a Randolph, and after the cousins Francis and Elizabeth married, the next generation saw a similar trend, when Thomas Eaton Randolph became U.S. marshal in Tallahassee. These links between the seats of power in Florida and in Washington were very real, and many were based on the personal connections of women.

The Walton family, for whom Walton County is named, is another example. Acting governor George Walton Jr. probably would not have gotten that appointment but for his family background. Prominent but relatively poor, they arrived in Pensacola on July 12, 1821—and Sarah Walker Walton soon found herself in charge of hosting state events out of her family budget:

> The expense of living is even greater here than at New Orleans; and besides, the example of General Jackson, who was remarkable for hospitality, rendered it almost impossible for me to pursue a course entirely different, without . . . lessening respect for . . . the Government. Instead of renting an Office distinct from the House in which I live, I have made one of the rooms in it serve the purpose, not a little to the inconvenience of my family.[6]

President Monroe appointed William Duval as governor in 1822—but Duval spent so much of his early tenure in Kentucky, where his wife lived,

"Such a Woman Occurs But Once": Octavia Walton

Octavia Walton had a strong role model in her grandmother, Dorothy Walton, who was a prisoner of war during the American Revolution. Her husband signed of the Declaration of Independence, and when the British captured their Savannah home, they imprisoned both Dorothy and George Walton in British-owned territory in the Caribbean.

Their granddaughter, Octavia, was ten in 1821, when their son George Walton Jr. was appointed acting governor of West Florida. According to a Florida historian, "tradition has it that young Octavia . . . was influential in giving the new capital village its old Indian name." She also performed unpaid government work for her father: "a linguist in her early teens," she "helped him with translation of Spanish documents."

Like other prominent men in this era, it appears that Governor Walton obtained his position partly because of the women in his life. His wife, Sarah Walton, "inherited a small fortune from her father," and they owned seventeen slaves when he began building their Tallahassee residence in 1825. The Walton women, however, chose not to join him there but continued their matriarchal life in Pensacola. Revolutionary War veteran Dorothy Walton lived with her daughter-in-law and granddaughter, making it a three-generation woman-centered family. A Tallahassee historian said that after fourteen years of Florida politics:

> Sarah Walton appears to have despaired of her husband attaining the station to which she aspired. . . . His mother, too, cut him off in her will, leaving what little she had to his children, Octavia and Robert. A year after Dorothy Walton died and was buried at Pensacola, [Sarah] took her own patrimony and the children for a long-cherished social tour of the North. . . . Octavia was socially triumphant in the nation's capital . . . , [where] she could talk politics with [men], as well as dance with them.

They went on to Europe, and Queen Victoria broke precedent by inviting this new cultural star to a ball before Octavia had been formally presented at court. Upon their return the women moved from Pensacola to Mobile, where Octavia married into a prominent French family. By then both she and her mother were completely estranged from her Florida father.

Her Mobile home became "a popular attraction for the wise and witty," and among her guests were Swedish author Fredrika Bremer and England's Lady Emmeline Stuart-Wortley. Both published travelogues in Europe about their visits to America, and Octavia Walton Le Vert reversed this in 1853 and 1855, when she published her European experiences, *Souvenirs of Travel*. She demonstrated her organizing talent by raising a thousand dollars in one day for the Mount Vernon Ladies Association, which preserved the home of George and Martha Washington. In 1855 Alabama's governor appointed her as the state's representative to the World Exposition in Paris.

Octavia Walton Le Vert moved to New York City in 1865, at the end of the Civil War and after her husband's death. She was sufficiently feminist and cosmopolitan to be welcomed as a founder of Sorosis, which historians recognize as the nation's first female professional organization. Elizabeth Lummis Ellett, the first historian of American women, featured her in *The Queens of American Society* (1867), and Jane Cunningham Croly included her as a founding feminist in *History of the Woman's Club Movement* (1898).

Octavia died in 1877 at the Walton family home in Georgia. Famed author Washington Irving said of her, "such a woman occurs but once in the course of an empire."

Note: These and other quotes are from Malcolm B. Johnson, *Red, White and Bluebloods in Frontier Florida*, published by the Rotary Clubs of Florida and copyrighted by Johnson in 1976, when he was editor of the *Tallahassee Democrat*.

that Congress later passed a law requiring territorial governors to live in the territory they presumably governed.[7] When Duval finally arrived in Pensacola and the first Territorial Council was due to meet, five of the thirteen delegates were weeks late because of storms. Then yellow fever broke out, and Governor Duval wrote to President Monroe:

> It is with deep sorrow that I announce to you the death of . . . Doct. Bronaugh. . . . I lived with [him] in Col. Walton's family. It is almost a wonder that I escaped—for every member of his family has been or is now down with the fever except himself and his venerable mother . . .
>
> The Spanish inhabitants stand it much better . . . not that they are exempt, for many of them have been . . . sick—but few have yet died. . . .
>
> The distress occasioned in Pensacola by the fever cannot be described, poor little children, without parents or friends are thrown on the charity of strangers [and] we have not a cent to relieve the wretched. The Spanish citizens act nobly, they have done and continue to do all in their power.[8]

Joseph and Mary Ellen Adair White traveled with Governor Duval from Kentucky. Her father had been Kentucky's governor, and her husband's political appointment was due to her influence. When the capital moved to Tallahassee in 1824, the Whites moved again—and the following year Joseph White became the Florida Territory's first elected delegate to the U.S. House. Mary Ellen White's friends there soon nicknamed her "Florida," and she was known by that name the rest of her life.

Their Florida home was Casa Bianca, a Jefferson County plantation, and she not only ran it but also ran her husband's reelection campaigns during the twelve years he served in Congress. She soon had a "reputation as an astute politician and campaigner for her husband."[9] Tallahassee pioneer Ellen Call Long admired Ellen White, even though the men in their lives were political enemies. Long wrote that "White has a pillar of strength in his wife."[10] Later Long described her and her sister, Harriet Pleasant, campaigning at the horse races that then were popular:

> Both [are] brilliant conversationalists, [have] vast tact, and [are] of fine personal appearance; and they are here [at the races] to electioneer . . . in behalf of the incumbent who remains at his post in Washington, while

these two young ladies, accompanied by one or more young men of the territory, have canvassed every county in the interest of the absent candidate, much to his advantage. . . . Mrs. Florida White . . . [is] of high natural intelligence. . . . [Her] adaptiveness to electioneering is said to be wonderful, and most of his [Joseph White's] success is owing to this fact.[11]

At a time when most of the nation held a strong taboo against public speaking by women, Florida White not only spoke to the all-male electorate but also conducted early versions of press conferences—and deftly handled loaded questions. For example, the era was virulently anti-Catholic, but when a hostile journalist asked about her recent trip to Rome, her reply was nothing short of brilliant:

I was told . . . that excepting the daughters of crowned heads, ladies were not received at the vatican . . . I replied that I was an American woman, and thereby the daughter of a sovereign. . . . My spunk so pleased the cardinal that I was admitted to the sanctified presence, whom we found affable and courteous as any other gentleman.[12]

* * *

The Territorial Council met in St. Augustine in 1823 and authorized the land survey that created Tallahassee as the new capital in 1824. Midway between the old West Florida capital of Pensacola and the East Florida one at St. Augustine, the area was already called Tallahassee, meaning "old field" or "abandoned village" in the Mikasuki language.[13] It had once been a prominent site on the chain of Native American towns; Hernando de Soto's expedition had camped there in the winter of 1539–40. By the 1820s, though, it had been depopulated for more than a century, ever since the 1704 destruction of Spain's Fort San Luis.

Like the nation's capital—which was established less than thirty years earlier—Tallahassee was very much a planned city, started from scratch with governmental purposes as the top priority. Newspapers and capital cities go hand in hand, and within three months of its founding, Tallahassee had a newspaper, the *Florida Intelligencer*. Its parent company, the Washington-based *National Intelligencer,* reprinted a lengthy portion of the Florida paper's first issue, which read like a real estate promotion. On April 9, 1825, it said:

"This young capital of Florida is already attracting the attention of capitalists. Many buildings are erecting [sic] . . . even before the sale of the lots. . . . It is situated on a beautiful and commanding eminence."[14]

More than a nice view or good soil, however, a key to making a capital compare favorably with its counterparts elsewhere is the city's social life. From the beginning, Florida women contributed to creating a capital worthy of respect, including through attention to the arts. The undisputed head of local society was Catherine Willis Gray Murat.

Her maternal great-grandmother was George Washington's sister, while her paternal great-grandmother had been his godmother. The oldest of the eight children of Byrd and Mary Willis, she was called Kate and grew up wealthy near Fredericksburg, Virginia. She married young, but her husband, Atchison Gray, died within a year and she returned to her parents' lively home. Her father later acknowledged that he wasted the family fortune: "I was an idle fellow, fond of fox hunting, racing, and convivial parties, paid no attention to plantation business. . . . In 1825, finding that things were getting worse and worse, I sold off, paid off, and came off, to . . . Florida."[15]

The family settled in a log house on Monroe Street—and the next year, in the wilds of pioneer Tallahassee, Catherine married the presumed heir to the French throne. He was Prince Achille Murat, the nephew of Napoleon Bonaparte and son of the king of Naples (then a separate Italian kingdom). Exiled from Europe after Napoleon's fall, the prince had gone to St. Augustine in 1824; unimpressed with it, he moved on to Tallahassee, where he met the young widow from Virginia; they wed on July 12, 1826.

Despite their prestigious lineages, however, the Murats were relatively poor. When he tried to persuade his mother, Queen Caroline of Naples, to send him money, the prince apparently thought it necessary to explain that he had not married a wealthy woman: "my wife did not bring me a cent as a dowry," he wrote. He then went on to complain that although "she has some property of her own, which in accordance with the law of this country, is now mine," that "property" was largely in the value of ten slaves, "seven of whom are children who have to be fed and do not bring in any income."[16]

With the labor of these slaves, they carved a plantation in Jefferson County. Trees had to be cut and trails created to reach such unsettled places, and families—including those with a legitimate claim to the French throne—lived in huts for years while land was cleared and crops were planted until finally a fitting home could be erected. But they carried in their minds another sort of world, as the prince pointed out:

> Beneath the roof of this wild habitation, you will find a family almost as well brought up and educated as many in Boston and New York. . . . The women, above all, support these privations with a patience truly angelic, softening by their presence the natural wilderness.[17]

The Murats prospered and moved to New Orleans, where they lived too extravagantly. Bankrupt, they returned Florida and managed to buy a small plantation, Econchattie. Prince Achille died in 1847, while Catherine lived on another twenty years. She was buried next to her prince in Tallahassee's Episcopal cemetery.

Tallahassee was not the era's only new town. Quincy, named for President John Quincy Adams, began in 1825. Monticello, the name of Thomas Jefferson's Virginia home, was established in 1828, while the Gulf Coast towns of St. Joseph and Apalachicola followed in 1829. The last had been a capital city for earlier natives; in the Seminole language it meant "place of the ruling people."

At the other end of the long peninsula, Key West—which remains the southernmost city in the United States—was officially established in 1821. Ellen Mallory was an early influence there. An Irishwoman, she immigrated first to Trinidad in the British West Indies, where she married John Mallory from Connecticut and bore a son, Stephen Russell Mallory. The family arrived Key West in 1823 and built a large house. When her husband died soon afterward, she turned it into a boardinghouse. She thus supported her son, while boarders created an international network. After marrying Angela Moreno, Stephen Mallory would become one of the most important politicos in the South.

A lighthouse had been needed on this fragile ocean point during the centuries of Spanish governance. The U.S. government finally built it in 1825—and a woman, Barbara Mabrity, would be the lighthouse keeper for most of its existence. Although Key West had a much more Caribbean flavor than any other American town, it also soon became home to wealthy New England families in the shipping business. In addition, its working class would differ from that in other towns—including more employed women than most nineteenth-century cities. Key West's first cigar factory began with Cuban workers in 1831—both in Europe and in the Americas, women were cigar makers.

Jacksonville, too, was a blue-collar town. Renamed in 1822 to honor Andrew Jackson, it was then a six-year-old settlement formerly called Cowford

A Lady Lit the Lamp: Key West Lighthouse Keeper Barbara Mabrity

Born in 1782, Barbara Mabrity was already middle-aged when she and her sailor husband moved to Key West with their six children in 1826. President John Quincy Adams appointed Michael Mabrity as keeper of the new lighthouse there—but he would die of yellow fever six years later. From 1832 to 1864, the indomitably strong Barbara Mabrity operated the Key West Lighthouse.

She was not alone in this occupation—Maine's Ida Lewis became famous for rescues during the same era—but Mabrity held the position longer than others. She endured wild tempests during hurricanes in 1835, 1841, and 1842, and a record storm on October 10, 1846, was truly devastating.

Key West residents—including her children, their spouses, and her grandchildren—took refuge in the seemingly strong lighthouse. The wind and rain were too powerful, however, and the building collapsed. Mabrity and one of her children managed to run away before it fell, but everyone else was killed.

Despite this trauma, she again climbed the lighthouse stairs when it was rebuilt. She stayed at her duty another eighteen years, finally resigning in 1864 at age eighty-two. The year is significant: 1864 was the last full year of the Civil War, and the U.S. Navy controlled the waters off Florida. Florida was part of the Confederacy, however, and U.S. Navy officials might have invited criticism if they had allowed a Floridian to run the vital lighthouse.

Barbara Mabrity died three years later. Her family—including granddaughter Mary Carroll and granddaughter-in-law Mary Elizabeth Bethel—ran the lighthouse until it was automated in 1915. The Coast Guard recently named a buoy tender *Barbara Mabrity*, and she is honored at the Lighthouse and Keepers Quarters Museum in Key West.

or Cowfordia.[18] It began as a trading post during the First Seminole War—and that too had a female connection: trader L. G. Hogan built his store on land that belonged to "his Spanish wife, Dona Maria Suarez."[19] Her family had lived in the area for generations, and she had received this land grant in 1816 from Spanish Governor José Coppinger as compensation for the death of her first husband, Turnel Taylor, in the War of 1812. Suarez not only kept her maiden name during two marriages to Anglo men; she also brought her legal case to the attention of the governor, who granted her two hundred acres of land on the St. Johns River.[20]

Another Jacksonville founder was engaged in a business in which women have dominated since time immemorial: "In 1821, Mrs. Sarah Waterman with four daughters and two sons came up from Saint Johns Town at the bluff to manage the first inn."[21] Other female founders of Jacksonville include Nancy Hart, mother of future governor Ossian Hart, and Sarah Tucker, who signed Duval County's first marriage license when she wed Robert Robertson in October 1823.

Like Tallahassee, Tampa began in 1824 as a result of federal expansion in Florida: while Tallahassee was the civic capital, Tampa's Fort Brooke would long be its military headquarters. Only two families, named Gonzalez and Caldez, lived on Tampa Bay when the fort was established—but American women came along with their men. The first civilian was Nancy Dixon Collar, a Massachusetts native who had five children when she and her husband, Levi, arrived; she would bear six more while they built their farm at Six Mile Creek. The creek was six miles from Fort Brooke, where more American women lived.

Finding the details of their lives, however, can be difficult. Few traditional historians included much about women, and in military circumstances, it is even harder to discover the women. Because of their babies, however, we know that there were at least four pregnant women at Fort Brooke soon after its 1824 establishment.

The fort was named for its commander, Colonel George Mercer Brooke; his wife, Lucy Thomas Brooke, bore a son on December 18, 1826. Six months earlier, on June 14, 1826, Joseph Fry was born; his mother remains anonymous. The previous year, on October 12, 1825, Adele Senac Sands delivered a boy; her husband was Captain Richard Sands. The first baby of all, however, appears to have been a girl, Marianna, born to Martha Coffin Pelham in August 1825.

Pelham soon moved from Tampa. As Martha Coffin Wright, she would become a popular pioneer feminist. Although part of an old Quaker family, she was not a picture of piety and may have been pregnant when, at age eighteen, she married an army captain, Peter Pelham, over her family's objections. She went with him to Fort Brooke, but he died just two years later, and the young widow had no choice but to go back north—where her neighbors considered her an "infidel."[22]

After marrying lawyer David Wright in 1829, Martha Wright bore six more children. In 1848 she joined her sister, Lucretia Coffin Mott, in calling for the world's first meeting on women's rights. That was in Seneca Falls, New York, where Mott's friend Elizabeth Cady Stanton lived. Martha Wright—once a friendless single mother in Tampa—went on to be elected the 1874 president of the National Woman Suffrage Association.[23]

* * *

Tampa remained an outpost, however; growth centered around Tallahassee—where women joined men in pioneering today's still ongoing industry of promoting Florida land development. Just three years after the capital was proclaimed, for instance, young Elizabeth Randolph Eppes led her family in moving from Virginia—and noted that the females were more willing than the males to take this risk.[24] Although part of a very distinguished family and recently married to Thomas Jefferson's grandson, Francis Eppes, she clearly viewed herself as a businesswoman. Her younger sisters, moreover, were prepared to earn money by beginning a school. She was still in Virginia when she argued for the move in an 1827 letter:

> Emigration has been the sole topic of conversation, the one engrossing subject. . . . Mama is quite willing to remove, I believe, and the girls wish it exceedingly, and even Papa, who opposed it at first . . . seems now to be coming round. . . .
>
> Florida, Tallahassee and its neighborhood, will be our location . . . , the girls to keep a school . . . Francis and myself will settle in a log house in the woods, he to begin life anew as a sugar planter and I as—what? for I know not what my particular avocations will be there, or how I shall employ myself beyond the customary occupation of our unlucky sin in "making children."[25]

Elizabeth Randolph Eppes's strong will prevailed, and although she may have been pregnant, she made the rough wagon journey with help from about twenty slaves. At least two sisters, Harriet and Mary Randolph, also moved—and Harriet summarized the experience by saying "Bonaparte's Russian campaign could not have been harder." They settled on a site about twelve miles from Tallahassee and called their plantation L'Eau Noir, or the Black Water. Harriet used typical masculine language in referring to the new property as belonging to the one man of the group—but her letter to their mother also shows that the women of this genteel Virginia family accepted the frontier hardships cheerfully:

> This is a very comfortable house of Francis's, roomy and airy and quite good looking for a log pen. The floor of our loft (Mary's and mine) is not nailed down, and the seams gape rather more widely than is pleasant, but we have remedied the evil by spreading down your parlor carpet. . . .
>
> The yard is fenced in, and nicely cleared up with only a few trees left standing; at the back of it is a fine crop of cotton . . . and the most splendid growth of forest trees I ever beheld—superb oaks covered in the long moss of this country. . . . I never even imagined anything so beautiful.[26]

They were expecting still another sister, Lucy, and Harriet asked her to bring supplies for their new school: the list included "ink powder, quills . . . , good drawing paper, crayons, and paints."

The "unlucky sin" of childbearing, however, caused Elizabeth Randolph Eppes to die after the birth of her sixth baby. Her husband sold L'Eau Noir, built a house in Tallahassee, and married Susan Ware, the daughter of a Georgia governor. The Randolph sisters, however, built a plantation, Ethelmere, and carried on with their plans for a school. This was clearly intended as a business, not a charity, as Harriet reported to her father in 1829:

> We set the price of Board (including washing) at $100 for boys. . . . Tuition in the English branches will be at three prices. . . . French and Spanish [courses] . . . I had once set lower, but on further consideration thought it better to be above. . . . I shall not give myself the least uneasiness as to our success. The plantation is our . . . anchor.[27]

But Harriet too died young, in 1832, soon after her marriage to Dr. Lewis Willis. Lucy married planter John Parkhill, and the carefully laid school plans came to naught; it was indeed plantation agriculture that would be the territory's anchor. Schools would be a low priority for a long time to come—and, in fact, the 1830 census did not even recognize any towns on this new frontier.

That census showed 34,730 people in the vast Florida Territory, an area so big that the distance from Key West to Pensacola is farther than that from New York to Chicago. Of these inhabitants, 19,220 were free, while 15,501 were slaves. The free people included 844 "colored," more than half of whom were women: 461 black females had managed to acquire their freedom, while 383 men had done so.

White men outnumbered white women by 10,236 to 8,149, or 20 percent. This four-women-to-every-five men ratio was not nearly as imbalanced as on many frontiers. At an analogous point in their histories, territories in the Far West often had a male:female ratio of ten to one, and in mining, lumber, and railroad settlements it was not unusual to find a hundred men for every woman. Florida was more akin to the rest of the Southeast: despite images of soldiers and cracker cowboys, family settlement was the rule, not the exception.

Nor were all the incoming families from the United States. As early as 1820 a large group of families named with names such as McLendon, McKinnon, McCaskell, and McLeod moved to the Euchee Valley of modern Walton County. Many came directly from Scotland and were Presbyterians. "A hardy, honest, industrious people . . . , they lived always at peace with their Indian neighbors. . . . They built schoolhouses, though in the wilderness, had good teachers, every man paying for the teaching of his own children. They built a church . . . even when they could have no regular minister."[28]

The plantation economy that grew in the 1830s had a negative effect on such middle-class farmers—but in both types of agriculture, women played a major role. The reality was not an absence of women but a lack of recognition of them. While their men engaged in the public activity that got their names into the history books, the women assumed the daily management of the farms and plantations that anchored the economy, while also bearing and rearing the next generation.

* * *

The ghost of Rachel Jackson returned in 1834. Her husband Andrew was president, and he appointed Secretary of War John Eaton as Florida's third territorial governor. In doing so, Jackson made a point to Washington society. Like Rachel Jackson, Peggy Eaton had had an unhappy first marriage. Her husband was an alcoholic and a sailor, often away at sea. He did not return from one of his voyages, and word finally reached her that he had died in the Mediterranean, leaving her with three children. When she married John Eaton shortly afterward, rumors flew: Washingtonians said the Eatons had had a prior relationship and that John Eaton was responsible for the assignment that caused the death. Mostly, though, they argued that Peggy Eaton's Irish origins were too lowly for a Cabinet wife. The Jacksons had suffered from the same sort of shunning, and the president took revenge on Washington's societal leaders with his appointment. He even dropped Vice President John Calhoun from his reelection ticket because Floride Calhoun—a South Carolina belle—led the Cabinet wives in excluding Peggy Eaton from society.

Unaware of this Washington gossip, Tallahassee residents welcomed the Eatons with a cannonade. At least parts of the cannon dated to the 1704 destruction of Fort San Luis, and it took "all night" to fire them—but Peggy Eaton was delighted to be greeted with such distinction. Decades later, she summarized:

> We resided in Florida two years. They were beautiful years to me. My neighbors were pleasant. I had no ugly passages in my history, and I was away from my husband's political persecutors. . . .
>
> In Florida, our residence of course was at Tallahassee, the capital, to which [John] took us from Pensacola as soon as he could make the necessary arrangements. We had two happy years in Florida. To me it was the land of flowers as Washington had been the land of briars.[29]

Peggy Eaton left Florida when John Eaton was named ambassador to Spain, and the fourth territorial governor was Richard Keith Call. He was the first to consider himself a Floridian. A decade earlier he had fathered the first white child born in Tallahassee. Call assumed the governorship at a terrible time both publicly and personally: the Second Seminole War erupted in late December 1835, and his wife, Ellen Kirkman Call, died two months later. At thirty-three, she had given birth to six babies in ten years; only two of them survived more than a few days.

The December events that began the war brought immense hardship to Seminole women, as they would see their community subjected to what amounted to nationally authorized genocide. At the urging of President Jackson, Congress had passed the Indian Removal Act (1830), under which all eastern tribes were to relocate to the Indian Territory of Oklahoma/Kansas. The date for completion of this forced exile was January 1, 1836. Florida's Seminoles—whose very name meant "runaway"—did not accept the mandate, and as the deadline approached, conflict increased.

Several incidents in the autumn of 1835 portended serious trouble, and "a large number of [Miccosukee] women and children sought protection at Tampa Bay."[30] There they may have seen white women at Fort Brooke, who "labored through the night of December 22 knitting flannel sacks to hold cannon charges."[31] Christmas would be forgotten as 110 men, under Major Francis Dade, marched to Fort King, at Ocala, to reinforce that smaller fort after an attack there by a rising young warrior, Osceola.

Born in Georgia, his mother was a Red-Sticks Creek woman, and his father was Englishman William Powell. The family split up about 1808, when Osceola was aged about ten. The two daughters stayed with their father, while the son moved south with his mother; they eventually settled in the Ocala area. Osceola, who was called Powell in most of the era's records, grew up near Fort King.

The matrilineal structure of native life, which encouraged Osceola to stay with his mother, disappeared during the early nineteenth century as native men emulated white men in excluding women from political and military decision making. Cherokee women in Georgia, for example, had spoken out on moving west "in separate National Council meetings in 1817 and 1818," but by the 1830s, women's views were ignored.[32] If Osceola's mother had an opinion on removal to Indian Territory, it is not known; the same is true for his Creek wife, Chechoter (Morning Dew), with whom he had four children. He was said to have been a good husband and father, and even an early white historian credited Osceola with trying to exclude white women and children from violence. "It is not upon them that we make war and draw the scalping knife," he reputedly said. "It is upon men. Let us act like men."[33]

He presumably thought he was "acting like a man" when he stalked his former friend, Fort King agent Wiley Thompson, who was in charge of Indian removal. Osceola and other young warriors caught Thompson outside the fort's store on a pleasant Sunday afternoon; after shooting him and a lieutenant, they invaded the store and "fired upon the party within, and after scalping them and cutting in pieces their bodies, set fire to the building."[34] They left without attacking the fort itself, which allowed its commander to send a runner to Tampa's Fort Brooke to reinforce his forty-six troops.

When Fort Brooke women said goodbye to their men on Christmas Eve, it would be forever. Because of rain near Bushnell on December 28, Commander Dade allowed his men to button their (too colorful) coats over their ammunition. Dade died with the first bullet, and after hours of horrific violence, all but two of the professional soldiers were dead. It was the most complete failure in the history of the American army, and Seminoles and their African American allies rejoiced.

* * *

The first of the two badly wounded survivors of the "Dade Massacre" reached Fort Brooke on New Year's Day, while the mutilated bodies of the others lay unburied well into the next year. Their wives at Fort Brooke went uncomforted, largely forgotten as violence gripped Florida from coast to coast:

> In the neighborhood of New Smyrna . . . during the month of January, 1836, sixteen plantations . . . were entirely destroyed. . . . The country was desolated in every direction, and many of the settlers, men, women, and children, were ruthlessly massacred. . . . About the last of August, the post at Micanopy [near Gainesville] was broken up, and the whole country between Newnansville and Tampa abandoned to the Indians. . . . The Johns family [near] Jacksonville was attacked; Mr. Johns was killed, Mrs. Johns shot and scalped, and the house burned.[35]

Osceola's advice about not attacking women and children was ignored, and terrorism continued all over the state during the next years. In 1839 "murders were committed by Indians within a few miles of Tallahassee and St. Augustine." An officer's wife at Micanopy, a Mrs. Montgomery, "was shot through the breast" a few days after Christmas, 1840.[36] Almost a year later, a few days prior to Christmas of 1841, the Mandarin settlement near Jacksonville was attacked. Two men, two women, and a child were killed, and most of the houses were burned. Because this was an area where the population was denser than in most of Florida, fear again paralyzed whites. A letter writer near Mandarin said, "I had just gotten settled. . . . This is the third time I have been obliged to abandon my place and sacrifice time, money, and everything but my life."[37]

Perhaps the most noted attack on civilians occurred all the way south in what is now called Indian Key, where "the family of Dr. Perrine, a botanist" was attacked. Mrs. Perrine and her children were saved "by concealing themselves under a wharf." They had big plans for plant experimentation in the balmy keys, and "the Perrines brought 36 families from the Bahamas. . . . A major part of them were driven away by the Indians." Mrs. Perrine and her children courageously stayed in Florida, but she ultimately "was unable to carry out . . . the contract . . . made by her late husband."[38]

Lines of enmity were not blind, however, as cases also occurred of friendly Seminoles who warned whites of an expected attack. Tampa's Nancy Dixon Collar was one whose kindness toward Florida's original residents was repaid when danger threatened early in the war. And, of course, Seminole women suffered infinitely more. Professional soldiers hunted them as though they were animals—to the extent that Congress received many petitions from non-Floridians objecting to the army's use of bloodhounds in tracking the natives.[39]

Seminoles found it impossible to buy ammunition or weapons to protect themselves—all they could do was go into even wilder country and hide. The swampland that made the best hiding places was not their accustomed terrain, and they often went hungry. Soldiers found fields of corn, which meant that women had used precious seed to plant but had been forced to abandon their crop.

Some gave up. Through the long years of being hunted, occasional bands surrendered and volunteered to be transported to Oklahoma. In one case, a chief even used a woman to recruit others to leave: Coacoochee sent "his younger brother and an Indian woman" to the Peace River interior, where she "was to carry a talk to [chiefs] Arpeika and Billy Bowlegs."[40]

Those least likely to heed such messages—those who had the most to lose by surrendering—were black Seminoles, who justifiably feared that they would not be sent west but would instead be sold into slavery. They fought so fiercely that General Thomas Jesup averred "it was not an Indian war, but a Negro war."[41] The war's first historian used the era's more openly biased language in crediting blacks for its ferocity: "The negroes exercised . . . a wonderful control [of the Seminoles], and they undoubtedly added very much to the barbarity and savage manner with which the war was prosecuted."[42]

A Sister Spirit

Coacoochee's name meant "Wildcat," but he showed a tender demeanor. Like men in most American tribes, he derived his status through his mother: she was a sister of powerful chief Micanopy.

Caroline Mays Brevard admired Coacoochee, calling him "by far the greatest chieftain of the Seminoles after the death of Osceola." The niece of historian Ellen Call Long, Brevard became an even more serious writer. Her two-volume *History of Florida* was not published until after her death—perhaps because it was more thoughtful than most histories of that era, including respect for the Seminoles. She wrote of Coacoochee that "he had a twin sister who died in her youth," As he told it:

> She died suddenly. I was out on a bear-hunt, and when seated by my camp-fire alone, I heard a strange noise—it was something like a voice, which told me to go to her. . . . The night was dark and gloomy; the wolves howled . . . I thought she was speaking to me. At daylight I reached her camp—she was dead. When hunting some time after . . . , I heard strange sounds. . . . I felt myself moving, and thought I went far above to a new country, where all was bright and happy. . . .
>
> I then saw a small white cloud . . . and out of it, came my twin-sister. . . . Her long black hair, which I had often braided, hung down. . . . She sang the peace song of the Seminoles . . . , stepped into the cloud, and was gone. . . . I may be buried in the earth, or sunk in the water, but I shall go to her, and live with her. Game is abundant there; and there the white man is never seen.

Panic-stricken whites who abandoned their plantations also offered slaves an opportunity to escape, and some historians claim that as many as a thousand may have done so. Records in other places and times show that women were almost as likely to flee for freedom as men, even though often burdened by children. It is entirely possible that several hundred black women took advantage of the Second Seminole War to leave their white owners.

On the other side of the social scale, future First Lady Margaret Mackall Taylor lived at Fort Brooke: General Zachary Taylor was the commanding officer during much of the conflict, and not only his wife but also his daughter joined him there. The daughter, Ann Taylor Wood, was married to the fort's surgeon, Dr. Robert Wood, and both women assisted in nursing. They lived in Tampa for almost three years, from the fall of 1837 to the spring of 1840, and biographies of President Taylor credit the two women with saving lives during a severe attack of malaria.

They were a tiny minority, as just a handful of women were among the approximately forty thousand men who passed through Tampa during the Second Seminole War. The 1840 census showed only ninety-six civilians (eighty-one whites and fifteen "colored") in all of Hillsborough County, a huge area that ran from modern Dade City to Charlotte Harbor. Not surprisingly, soldiers complained about the lack of women—and some complained about those they did find. West Point graduate Lt. Henry Prince, a Maine native, wrote contemptuously upon leaving the Santa Fe River area: "Farewell, ye Crackers. . . . Farewell the dirty foot, . . . the unwashed face, ropy hair, the swearing, lazy, idle slut. . . . Ye drinking . . . sluggards, fare ye well!"[43]

When he, Taylor, and others left to promote their careers in the West, the power of a professional army slowly showed results. A captured Osceola had died in 1838 while imprisoned on an island off Charleston, South Carolina. He may have been poisoned or died of maltreatment, and the effect was disheartening for Seminoles. As they saw the odds against them, other bands surrendered or were captured. Some were marched in chains, with the first deportees leaving Tampa Bay just months after the war began. On April 11, 1836, more than four hundred natives said farewell to their homeland—and twenty-five of them would die before reaching their new, unchosen land. Their dogs were not allowed to board, and even hardened soldiers were touched by cries from abandoned pets.

Yet, despite the army's hugely superior ability, this was guerilla warfare of the sort that is almost impossible to win. When the war was declared over on August 14, 1842, it was less a genuine peace than a truce made necessary by the diversion of military attention to potential war with Mexico because of Texas and with Canada because of the Oregon Country. The cost to the United States of the Second Seminole War was huge: some $40 million dollars and the deaths of 1,466 professional soldiers. As was their habit, military record keepers did not enumerate either Seminole or civilian deaths, including those of women.

* * *

Except for new forts and some improvement of water transportation, the long state of terrorism understandably prevented investment. Beyond that, northeast Florida suffered a severe freeze in 1835; the temperature dropped to eight degrees and killed its nascent citrus industry. The nation suffered its first major economic depression in 1837, and the effects were felt in Florida. "Things got so bad," said one historian, that "the Legislative Council suspended taxes on land and slaves for fiscal 1839–41."[44] Duval County, unable to fund construction of its courthouse, resorted to selling lottery tickets. On the other hand, Leon County officials closed down their racetrack, declaring it a public nuisance in 1842.

It had not always been so. A genteel woman who visited Tallahassee a decade earlier said "nothing is talked of here except the races." Race week was "a gala time, when homes were filled with guests. . . . All the folk went to the races. Stakes were high, and interest was keen; but . . . [with] good humor. . . . The ladies entered into the spirit of all—their wagers, however, being gloves or, perhaps, books. A ball would close the activities."[45]

The end of the Second Seminole War also created a national precedent, as in 1842 Congress passed a law for the Florida Territory called the Armed Occupation Act. It was intended to settle the land that had been wrestled from natives by filling it with farm families who would substitute for the departed professional soldiers. To persuade people to accept this potentially dangerous situation, Congress gave them free Florida land.

Families in northern Florida were especially likely to take advantage of the act, as the Gambles, Bradens, and others moved to the new frontier of the Manatee River. Joe and Julia Atzroth also settled at the mouth of the Manatee about 1841, and "Madam Joe Atzroth" was long influential there. The life of the Armed Occupation Act, however, was brief. Most wealthy planters who settled the Deep South in the 1830s and 1840s did not want competition from middle-class farmers, and they controlled the congressmen who blocked homesteading. When the national Homestead Act finally passed in 1862, it was because the South had seceded.

Like the later national act, the 1842 Armed Occupation Act granted 160 acres of free land to any "head of family" who settled south of Gainesville, built a home, cleared five acres, and lived there four years. During its nine-month life—before congressional aristocrats killed it—about thirteen hundred claims were filed, with approximately one in every six filed by female household heads.

Some who moved south initially stayed at the Gates House, which opened in 1841 in the wilderness of what became Manatee County. Although historians credit "Josiah Gates and his wife" with running this hotel, doubtless most of the work was done by their eight slaves—and most of the daily management probably fell to Mrs. Gates. Operating inns historically has been a female occupation, and Tampa's biggest hotel at the time was owned by Margaret F. (May) Palmer.

She purchased it in 1845 in her own name, even though her husband was alive and apparently healthy; later she bought a huge parcel of land at the tip of Tampa's inner peninsula, signing the deed "M. F. Palmer." When a devastating hurricane struck in 1848, the Palmer House proved the town's best refuge. The Hillsborough River rose to the point that only the tops of tall trees could be seen and tables floated in May Palmer's dining room, but the two-story hotel kept everyone alive.

By the time of the 1848 hurricane, Florida had been a state for three years. The old Spanish settlements of St. Augustine and Pensacola resisted statehood, but in Middle Florida, from Tallahassee to Tampa, almost all new residents came from the United States and expected to live in a state, not a territory. Men accustomed to voting in Massachusetts or Kentucky found it intolerable that the president appointed the officials who governed them in Florida. Women, of course, lived with a lack of democracy all of their lives—and women such as May Palmer were not exempted from taxation because they had no representation. Most accepted gender inequity as immutable, however, and unlike in some western territories, Florida women made no attempt to be included in the governance of the new state.

The first moves toward statehood had been made in 1837 at a constitutional convention in the boomtown of St. Joseph's, on the Gulf south of

Tallahassee. Since the 1820 Missouri Compromise, however, the U.S. Senate had been equally divided between (all-male) senators from states with and without slavery. Florida, as a slave territory, had to wait until the Iowa Territory, which had no slavery, grew large enough to be admitted to the Union. Neither had quite enough population when Congress went ahead and admitted Florida—and that was another effect of conflict with Mexico during the 1840s. Having spent so much money to acquire Florida from Spain and then to drive out its Seminoles, Congress wanted to ensure loyalty along the Gulf of Mexico, and on March 3, 1845, Florida became the nation's twenty-seventh state. Iowa followed the next year.

Women in other places found that territorial governments were friendlier to women's rights than the state governments that replaced them, and that also was true in Florida. One of the last bills that the Territorial Council passed was a Married Women's Property Rights Act in 1845. This was remarkable in the context of the times, as feminists in much more liberal parts of the nation were only beginning to organize on the issue. Elizabeth Cady Stanton and other well-known women's rights leaders concentrated on property law in the 1840s, but nowhere in the thousands of pages of records that these women left is there any indication that they were aware of Florida Territory's enlightened act.

The explanation probably lies in the transition from territorial to state law, and even more in the reality of court decisions—which often depended less on the law than on the status of the plaintiffs and defendants. An affluent woman with a good civic reputation who was backed by a supportive family could sometimes work her way around archaic property laws, especially if her husband was known to be abusive. In any case, the innovative law was not publicized, and certainly no flock of feminists moved to Florida because of it.

* * *

The census conducted for statehood in 1845 showed five counties in which the black population was larger than the white, all along the Georgia-Florida border. They were Leon, with a 69 percent black majority; Jefferson, with 64 percent; Gadsden and Jackson, which both averaged 53 percent; and Nassau County on the East Coast, where 50 percent of residents were slaves. Their work on the Atlantic Coast differed from than in the Middle Florida plantations: rice and high-quality sea cotton grew in the marshlands north of Jacksonville, while in the Tallahassee area, most slaves toiled in fields that produced lower-quality, cheaper cotton.

Slave women often performed the same farm tasks as men, including at the clearing stage of plantations. They removed trees, dug ditches, and plowed fields; they drove oxen and horses, planted seeds, and then—in what was called "chopping cotton"—endlessly hoed weeds. In the long days of summer they worked from daylight to dark, sometimes sixteen hours a day. Their food was meager compared with their physical labor, and pregnant women were particularly likely to be malnourished.

After the initial stage of primitive frontier living, however, most plantations established a routine that included some time off. No fieldwork was done on Sundays, and Madison County's Nancy DeLaughter was not unusual in ending the workweek at noon on Saturdays. Susan Eppes understood that slave women needed more "time off" than men, as she wrote "Saturday afternoon was a holiday for every mother of a family."[46]

Less farm work was necessary in winter, of course, and Christmas often was celebrated with a week of extra food, dancing, and visiting. Most slaves expected and got gifts from their masters, and the holiday often was the occasion of distributing new clothes and shoes for the following year—most of them made, of course, by slave women. Occasionally there even were bonuses for exceptional workers: a woman called Marenda on the DeLaughter plantation, for example, got $9 in 1858; only one man was given more.

Although most slave women labored like men in the barns and fields, women were more likely than men to be trained as household servants. A plantation home usually would have only one male butler and valet, but several women worked as cooks, servers, cleaning maids, laundresses, and child nurses. The most talented became ladies' maids, who worked as seamstresses and hairdressers; they sometimes traveled with their mistresses to other plantations or even northern cities.

Genuine emotional bonds often arose between families and household slaves, and feelings of respect could last a lifetime. A Jacksonville pioneer was not unusual when he recorded in his daily journal: "Dick and George [are] making Peggy's coffin. . . . Buried the old and faithful servant in the evening."[47] That he called her "servant" instead of "slave" also is typical; white people rarely referred to the household workers by that harsh term. Women such as Peggy clearly were valued by their owners—and sometimes

A Voice from the Grave

William Ashley, for whom one of downtown Tampa's main streets is named, defied all that was sacred in southern society to proclaim his love for a woman who legally was his slave. He acknowledged their intimate relationship by instructing the executor of his will—John Jackson, another Tampa founder—to have this message carved on the tombstone that he shared with his beloved Nancy. Under the shadows of office towers, in Oaklawn Cemetery, you can read this eternal wisdom:

> HERE LIES
> WM. ASHLEY AND NANCY ASHLEY
> MASTER AND SERVANT
> FAITHFUL TO EACH OTHER IN THAT RELATION
> IN LIFE, IN DEATH THEY ARE NOT SEPARATED.
> STRANGER, CONSIDER AND BE WISER,
> IN THE GRAVE ALL HUMAN DISTINCTION
> OF RACE OR CASTE, MINGLE TOGETHER
> IN ONE COMMON DUST.
> TO COMMEMORATE THEIR FIDELITY TO EACH OTHER
> THIS STONE WAS ERECTED BY THEIR EXECUTOR
> JOHN JACKSON
> 1873

became so well respected within the white community that owners had to offer preferential treatment to keep them. This applied especially for women who were talented at cooking or sewing. Many cases exist of black women who bought their freedom by earning money in their "off-hours," usually by sewing or ironing.

There were numerous variants on how slaves became free. Almost a thousand free blacks or mixed-race "Creoles" lived in Florida during the decade prior to the Civil War. Most were in Pensacola or St. Augustine: old Spanish cultures there meant that these two towns, four hundred miles apart, offered free African Americans perhaps the fullest civil rights in the United States at the time. There "they owned property . . . , could carry firearms without a license . . . and served on juries with whites."[48] What the historian failed to note, of course, was that these rights did not apply to women of any race.

Sexual harassment was an infinitely greater problem for black women than for white, as owners, overseers, and other white men were not culturally condemned for abusing black women. No laws protected a black woman from rape—and if her husband or anyone else tried to interfere, that person likely would be whipped or otherwise punished. Many white men managed to avoid outright rape merely by using the threat of violence, and some offered bribes—particularly a new dress—for "consensual" sex. Occasionally genuine feelings arose in these illegal liaisons, but like all human relationships, they differed with different circumstances and individuals.

Evelyn Beasley, for example, was always aware that her siblings were fathered by their master—and that she was the daughter of a different white man. Her mother "was forced into companionship" with her father, and "although he appeared to have developed a real affection for her . . . , she always hated him." Her mother's relationship with her master, in fact, was better than that with the "lover" who had fathered Beasley. Although the master was married to a white woman and had legitimate white children, he also acknowledged that he had "several half-Negro children." Beasley said that "to these he was always as considerate as to his other children, and when two of the latter grew older and objected, he drove them from the plantation."[49]

The Parker family who lived near Fort Meade in Polk County was similar. William Parker fathered three children by his slave Rachel Davis, and after his death in 1858 his brother John—who had been Hillsborough County's sheriff—became the apparent father of her three additional children. Both men were married to white women, and the "black" and white families spent time together. Rachel Davis's sons used their mother's name and eventually became quite successful in the citrus and cattle industries. Near Plant City, Matthew Albritton also had both legitimate and illegitimate mixed-race children, and again the two families reportedly had close relationships.

A Duval County case is more complex: "owner Jacob Bryan fathered eight mulatto children by his slave mistress, Sarah," but one of those children, Celia, stabbed him to death and "denounced her mother" as the ultimate cause of the crime. Celia apparently got a reasonably fair trial but nevertheless was hanged nine months after the patricide. The white male jurors were doubtless influenced by the testimony of estate's executor, who said Sarah and her children were the victim's "only family."[50]

Such open acceptance, however, was unusual. More commonly, a white mistress would make life very hard for a slave woman whose children resembled their owner. Often the mother or the child would be sold, ridding the white woman of the painful daily evidence of her husband's infidelity. On the other hand, if a man chose not to sell the woman whose cabin he visited at night, there was little that his wife could do; usually her only recourse was to pretend that she did not see what everyone else saw. An 1857 visitor to the Fort Meade area empathized, writing: "Oh, what must be the degraded, hopelessly sickened, desolate heart of the wife, who, perhaps childless herself, sees around in the slave children . . . the features of her husband."[51]

Only very rarely did the reverse situation occur; Florida documentation of relationships between white women and slave men is virtually nonexistent. If a pregnancy resulted, the probability is that the white woman would have committed suicide or died in an unsafe attempt at abortion. Black women were in the opposite position: because the children of slave women were born into slavery, they were assets. An occasional woman so intensely hated her life that she attempted to prevent children from being born into it, and a few cases exist of black mothers who killed their children rather than see them live as slaves, but that was rare. The common situation was that everyone welcomed a black woman's pregnancy, and no one asked who the father was.

Some owners rewarded women for bearing children and applied the principles of eugenics. A Madison County slave, Charlotte Martin, for instance, said that her master selected the "strongest and best male and female slaves and mated them exclusively for breeding," adding that "the huskiest babies were given the best of attention in order that they might grow into sturdy youths, for it was those who brought the highest prices at slave markets."[52] The mothers of such "husky babies" were given less work, with their prime responsibility limited to pregnancy, nursing, and caring for their children. Always, however, they lived with the emotional pain that these children likely would be sold as teenagers.

Despite such profound racism, Charlotte Martin's master nevertheless trusted her father enough to send him on unsupervised wagon trips between Florida and Virginia—even bringing back whiskey. Respect for such dutiful slaves often was great enough that owners also respected their marriages and, in occasional cases, even provided proper weddings with a cake, formal clothing, and so forth. Although slaves were not issued marriage licenses by legal authorities, ministers presided over such ceremonies. Such clergymen were sometimes white, sometimes black—but always men. Most were Protestant, but in St. Johns County, Catherine Solana engaged a white Catholic priest to perform an 1839 wedding for her house servant John Solana, who married Harriet Alvarez, a slave belonging to Geronimo Alvarez.

That ceremony also reflects the greater social liberalism of Spanish culture. Slaves in those areas often were free to move about after their work day ended, and city officials did not really try to enforce the 9:00 p.m. curfew. It was another cultural difference between those areas and the fast-growing American culture in Middle Florida—and a reason why Pensacola and St. Augustine citizens had been reluctant about statehood.

The same was true in Key West, which never had the plantation system that entrenched slavery farther north. One result was a slow-paced economy—something that bothered Catherine Hart, a mainland Floridian who lived in Key West in the 1840s. She complained not only of boredom and the monotony of island life but especially about the seeming unwillingness of anyone to engage in the sort of agriculture that required work. "Such a thing as vegetables cannot be bought here," she said. "We have no variety in our market; beef, turtle, and fish is all that is ever for sale." Her underlying complaint, though, was that the color line was not drawn as sharply as she expected. Some Key West slaves even had their own homes and did not live with their masters, so that she and her husband "found it difficult to tell which blacks were free and which enslaved."[53]

That was not the case in north Florida, especially in Tallahassee. Men from Virginia, Georgia, and the Carolinas increasingly dominated the state government, displacing Spanish influences and making Florida more akin to the United States and less akin to the Caribbean. Now free to write their own laws without interference from the federal government, Florida legislators quickly made the new state more conservative than it had been as a territory.

New laws aimed to exclude free persons of color from the new state, and owners were not allowed to emancipate slaves unless they also provided the money for the freed person to move out of Florida. Curfews were passed, and restrictions on travel were especially likely to be enforced in coastal towns. Black sailors, for example, were confined to their ships while in port—something that was a real regression in places such as Key West and Fernandina. Worst of all, from 1848 onward, even African Americans whose families had been free for generations were forced by law to choose a white legal guardian.

At least thirty-five Pensacola victims of this new law opted to move to Tampico, Mexico, while others in the St. Augustine area went either to Cuba or to the new colony for former slaves, Haiti. Florida's new "black codes" had no identifiable basis beyond bald racism, as Florida's free blacks did not encourage slave rebellions. Indeed, according to one historian, some of these newly restricted free blacks had themselves been slave owners.[54]

Not only did conditions for free blacks worsen during the 1850s, but slavery itself became harsher. The possibility of escape plummeted after 1850, when Congress passed the federal Fugitive Slave Law. Applicable nationwide, the act made it a crime for anyone, black or white, to assist a fleeing slave. Owners, who had always advertised for the return of missing slaves, felt even more empowered. An ad in the Jacksonville-area *Florida News* read:

> Twenty-five Dollars Reward
> RUNAWAY in November last my negro woman HANNAH. She is about 5 ft., 7 or 8 inches high, black, no front teeth and about 40 years of age. Hannah has a mother in Newnansville or Tallahassee known by the name of Mary Ann Sanchez, formerly the property of Roman Sanchez of Newsnansville. The above reward will be given upon her being lodged in any jail where I can get her or upon being delivered to me.
> Louis M. Coxetter
> Jacksonville, June 5, 1852
> The Tallahassee papers will please copy and send their bills to this office.[55]

Opposition to slavery was growing in the North, and abolitionists used such advertisements to make their case. Even non-abolitionists often had a negative image of Florida, and many continued to write scornfully about whites. An army officer, for example, spoke disparagingly in 1854: "Each one owns perhaps, two or three negroes, and two or three hundred acres of pine which . . . most . . . do not take the trouble to clear, but merely fence in. They raise cotton, sweet potatoes, and turpentine."[56] An 1849 traveler between Palatka and Ocala was contemptuous of "the log-cabin habitations of 'crackers,' each with its swarm of tow-head, dirty urchins and their slatternly mother." He continued:

> Every Saturday all of the families from far and near came into the town ostensibly to do what little shopping their circumstances demanded. . . . It was a gala occasion. . . . The mother, always at the head

> [was] followed by daughters in order of age. The garb of these females, always the scantiest patterns, was picturesque with ingenious patching. . . .
>
> The jug was filled with the weekly supply of whiskey. . . . Tobacco and snuff were the next items of consideration; for the men all chewed, the women all dipped, and both men and women smoked pipes. . . . Whatever was left over from the [sales] of the hides or skins or whatever else they chanced to have, was judiciously expended in a few groceries and some calico or other stuff for the women-folk. The latter would then retire, squatting themselves down in shady nooks to enjoy their pipes or snuff-dipping in peace and contentment.[57]

Similar depictions came even from women less likely to be prejudiced. Catherine Hart, who would be the state's first lady after the Civil War, was a Floridian, but her travel diary attests to an unpleasant 1852 journey from Hillsborough to Levy County. The best of the available lodging was in Pasco, yet it was merely "a small room put up in the yard separate from the main house." At the Hernando stop, "We found very poor people, a man and his wife and five children":

> Their residence consisted of a log house all in one room with a fireplace and three beds in it. . . . [The female innkeeper] made her sick husband get up out of his bed and take another and put us in the one he had left, and when I laid down it was hot from the fever the man had; and the fleas were so thick we could not rest a minute.[58]

Schooling was not a priority for such families—nor was it for the aristocrats who made the laws. In his 1843 call for statehood, Governor Richard Keith Call spoke of Florida's nonexistent public schooling: he reminded legislators that ever since 1787, Congress had provided land that could be sold to fund education. Northerners took advantage of this, selling surplus land and spending the money on education, but southern states did not.

Wealthy families hired tutors and governesses for their children; they sent sons to colleges up North and daughters to finishing schools in Savannah or Charleston. Leaving the majority illiterate helped maintain upper-class control; as one Tallahassee observer noted, "swarms of children are running about the streets, improving rapidly in dissipation and vice."[59] An army officer said of Tampa in 1856:

> It has about eight hundred inhabitants, and contains a court house, a ten pin alley, two churches, two hotels, and any quantity of oyster houses and groggeries. There is neither agriculture or manufacturers to support the place and all the inhabitants derive their living either directly or indirectly from government appropriations."[60]

Those government appropriations were seldom spent on schools, another thing that affected women negatively, as teaching was one of few employment opportunities. Some attempted to run their own private schools, usually called "academies," or, if they were limited to girls, "female seminaries." Those who began such schools were almost always widows or spinsters; often they had a house large enough to board girls who came in from rural areas, sometimes for a school "year" that was as short as three months. No matter what form it took, "keeping a school" was financially precarious, and none in Florida became prestigious.

The 1851 legislature finally accepted the federal offer to fund education with land sales, and some ninety thousand acres were sold for this purpose—but even then, the institutions were not true colleges. East Florida Seminary opened in Ocala in 1853; today's University of Florida claims descent from it. Three years later, West Florida Seminary began in Tallahassee; it eventually became Florida State University. Both actually were in Middle Florida, not the true east and west of St. Augustine and Pensacola—something that again echoed an American bias against the old Spanish towns.

On the positive side, however, although these institutions were slow to begin, they admitted both men and women, which was still quite uncommon in the 1850s. Their primary purpose was to train teachers, and "after twenty weeks of study students could be certified to teach if they passed an examination."[61]

If the schoolhouse was neglected, so was the church. The era was not nearly as pious as many want to believe today, and church building typically waited until a town had several saloons. Private Bartholomew Lynch, who was stationed at Fort Brooke after the Second Seminole War, doubtless was telling the truth when he almost grinned aloud: "Tampa is a perfect arcadia. . . . Whiskey at 50 cents a gill, plenty [of] women in the market, absolutely at the disposal of the highest bidder. Nor church or meeting-house parson or any thoughts of Religion to mar the liberty so universally enjoyed here."[62]

He was right. Even though it was settled in 1824, Tampa had no church until 1853, when the Methodists began one. Until that time they met at the home of Nancy Walker Givens, who cleared her parlor of furniture when an itinerant preacher passed through. A Baptist church soon followed, funded by Scottish immigrant Sarah Cail—perhaps Florida's first philanthropist and the maternal ancestor of the McKay family still prominent today. Yet, although the 1850 census showed 441 residents in Tampa, the Baptist congregation that she endowed numbered just twenty-four souls—some of whom may not have joined of their own free will. One-third of the congregants were black; the membership included seven slaves and a free black.

The same was true of Jacksonville's St. John's Episcopal Church in 1856, where 90 of the 140-member congregation were African Americans. A statewide report by Methodists in 1860, the year before the Civil War, showed that of its 8,110 members, 42 percent were slaves. Blacks sat in segregated space, often in balconies where they could not be seen by the whites below. Their attendance sometimes was coerced, and virtually all of their preachers emphasized the Bible's admonition, "slaves, obey your masters."[63] When the Civil War loomed, clergymen—including the cleric at the powerful Episcopalian church in Tallahassee—preached for secession and slavery.

Some whites allowed some African American preachers for their slaves. They almost always were male, but Duval County saw at least one exception: "A slave woman known as 'Mother Sam' preached there, accompanied by her owner or some other white person." She attained appreciable popularity and conducted baptisms "in the St. Johns River at the foot of Jacksonville's Hogan Street."[64]

She likely did not mention that Jacksonville did not necessarily appear to be in God's grace. The town suffered a serious fire in the spring of 1854, with seventy buildings entirely destroyed. A few months later yellow fever threatened so seriously that residents actually fired a cannon at a steamship from Savannah to prevent it from landing and potentially reintroducing the dread disease. In 1859 the (all-male) city council adopted several puritanical legal codes. "Selling or Giving Liquors to Slaves" became a serious offense, punishable by a $50 fine or fifteen days in jail. In comparison, however, "An Ordinance Relating to Houses of Ill-Fame" imposed a fine "not exceeding twenty dollars, or imprisonment not over five days."[65]

The decade's social changes also included divorce. Hillsborough County's first divorce decree was granted to Ann M. Robarts in 1855, and all the rest of the county's pre–Civil War divorces also were suits filed by women. The statistic unintentionally reveals how much more women suffered from a bad marriage than did men. With no prohibitions on physical violence and no real protections in terms of property or economic support, some women finally got up the courage to break social taboos and terminate the marriage contract. Limited though their employment opportunities were, many clearly preferred a meager economic life to one of abuse from the man who had promised to love and cherish.

* * *

As the 1850s drew to a close, violence again appeared with the last of the wars against the Seminoles. As middle Florida farmland became scarcer, whites who had scorned south Florida began to reconsider. Newspapers and politicians not only called for Seminoles to leave this last reservation land but even advocated their outright extermination if they refused to go to Oklahoma.

Just as Andrew Jackson had encouraged the Second Seminole War, the Third Seminole War was caused in part by the policies of Secretary of War Jefferson Davis, soon to become president of the Confederate States of America. His War Department goaded Seminoles into violence by closing their trading posts, which made it impossible for them to earn a living by selling alligator hides or other products. Nor could Seminoles buy items that they had grown accustomed to, such as metal utensils—and ammunition.

Like the war in the 1830s, this one also began near Christmas, with the first deaths on December 18, 1855. During the next year Seminoles terrorized whites with random raids that killed twenty-eight civilians. Many moved into stockades: Manatee River women, for example, spent most of 1856 living in a quickly built fort, where three children were born in ten months. Army headquarters moved from Tampa's Fort Brooke to Fort Myers, while the wilds of future Miami became known as Fort Dallas.

Still, to call it a war is to dignify the impossible odds. The army had fourteen trained soldiers for every Seminole warrior—but even then, it was largely volunteer militiamen, not the professional army, who won the war. The volunteers were attracted, sadly, by the bounties placed on humans by the federal government. On August 2, 1857, for example, a man marched fifteen Seminole women and children into Fort Myers at gunpoint and got fifteen hundred dollars for his "heroism." But even that was not enough: the conflict finally ended when Chief Billy Bowlegs decided to take the money offered to him.

At a conference in Fort Myers, he and the white men with whom he negotiated made traditional assessments of human value: in return for moving to Oklahoma, he accepted "$6,500 for himself; $1,000 for each of four subchiefs, $500 for all other warriors, and $100 for women and children."[66] Other clans joined them, and the federal government paid out $44,600. Between two and three hundred Seminoles, however, refused the terms. Including women, these defiant people hid deeper in the Everglades, where they would remain legal fugitives until 1917.

On May 1, 1858, 124 natives left Tampa on a steamboat appropriately named *Grey Cloud*. They stopped at Egmont Key and picked up another forty-one deportees who had been held on this island between Hillsborough and Pinellas. The ship stopped again at St. Marks, a Panhandle port where they refueled. According to Seminole oral history, a woman named Polly Parker slipped away unnoticed and somehow managed to walk more than five hundred miles back to the Everglades.

That was the last of the wars against Florida's natives, but there would be little respite from organized violence. Just as Florida's Second Seminole War was a prelude to the national Mexican War, so the Third Seminole War was almost immediately followed by the Civil War, the most terrible that the nation has ever known. And as earlier, most Florida women supported their men in this decision, little realizing how much they all would suffer.

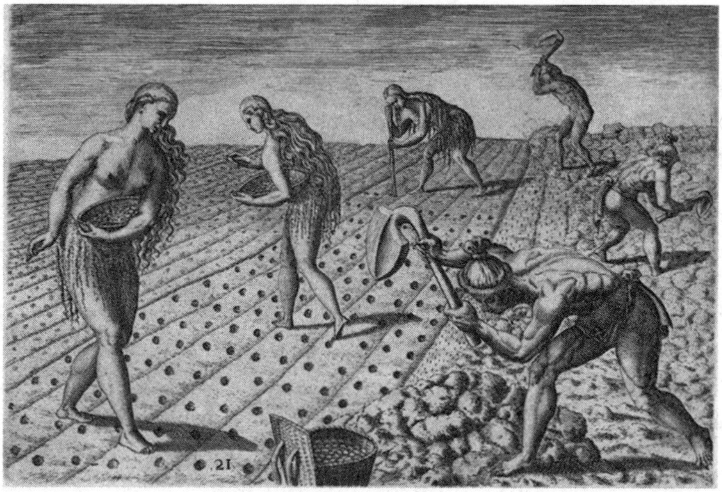

Jacques le Moyne, a member of the French colony of Fort Caroline that existed briefly in the 1560s, painted many scenes on native life in northeast Florida. This one shows that both men and women of the Timucuan tribe worked at settled agriculture. Engraving published by Theodor de Bry in *Grand Voyages* (1591), State Archives of Florida, *Florida Memory*, http://floridamemory.com/items/show/254220.

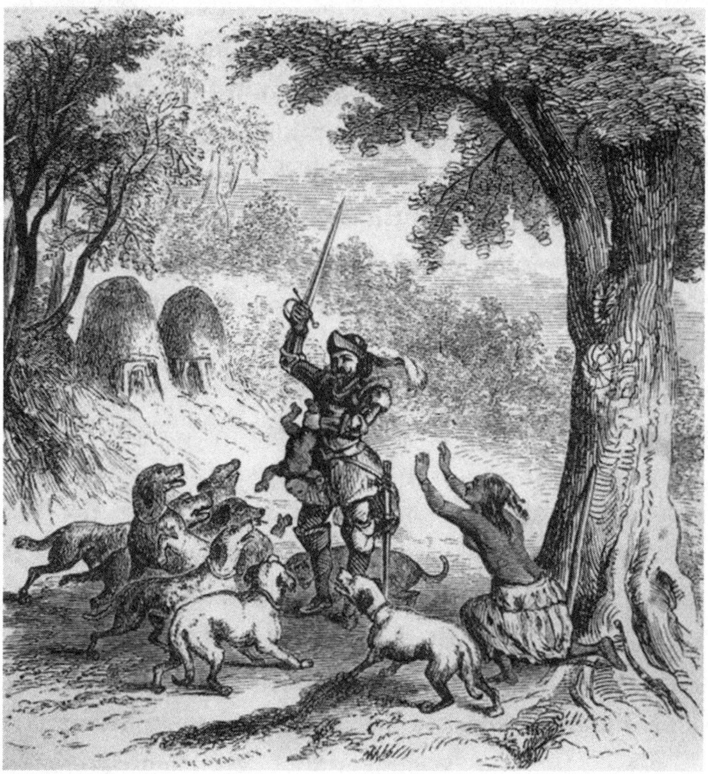

The State Archives dates this drawing to the 1520s, which likely would make it a scene from the Spanish invasion of Tampa Bay led by Pánfilo de Narváez. Conquistadors indeed were cruel and did not hesitate to depict the terrorism they inflicted, including upon women and children. State Archives of Florida, *Florida Memory*, http://floridamemory.com/items/show/4332.

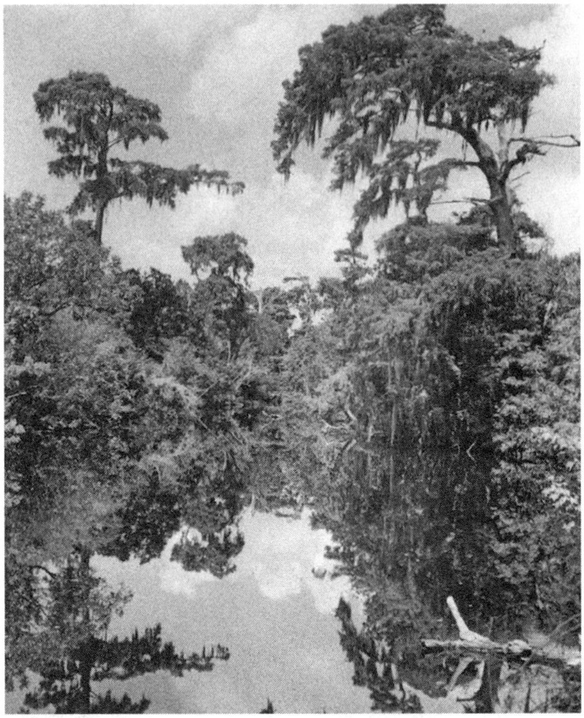

Jonathan Dickinson State Park in Hobe Sound is named solely for him, but his wife and infant child—along with several other people—also survived a 1696 shipwreck there. Mary and Jonathan Dickinson were Quaker missionaries who were returning from the Caribbean to Charleston, South Carolina, where an appreciable number of Quakers lived.

Natives of the Ais tribe captured them and stole most of their apparel. Barefoot in cold weather, they nearly starved while being marched to St. Augustine, where other Europeans ransomed them. At least six died, including a white boy, a black boy, a young black woman, and two black men. Hagar, a black woman, managed to carry her baby's body to St. Augustine for a Christian burial. State Archives of Florida, *Florida Memory*, http://floridamemory.com/items/show/41425.

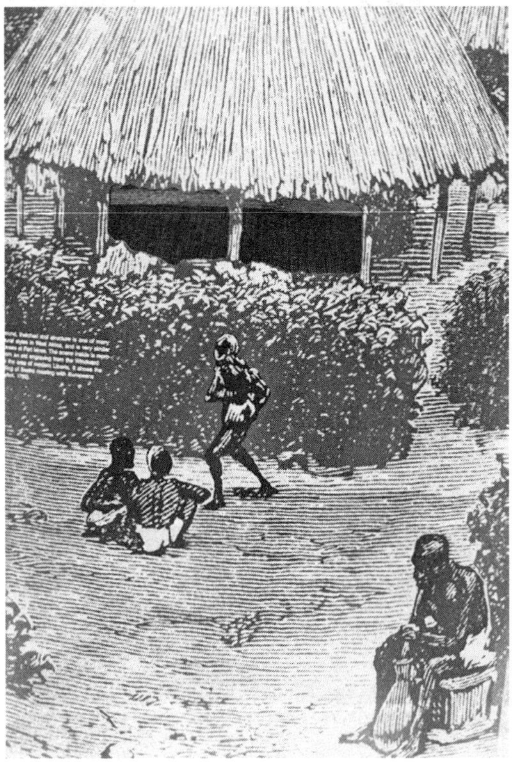

This drawing of a West African village probably is the style that escaped slaves would have built when they created Fort Mose, off the coast of St. Augustine, in 1738. It was the first legally sanctioned free black community outside of Africa, as the Spanish governors of Florida intended to encourage slaves to leave their British masters further north. State Archives of Florida, *Florida Memory*, http://floridamemory.com/items/show/142766.

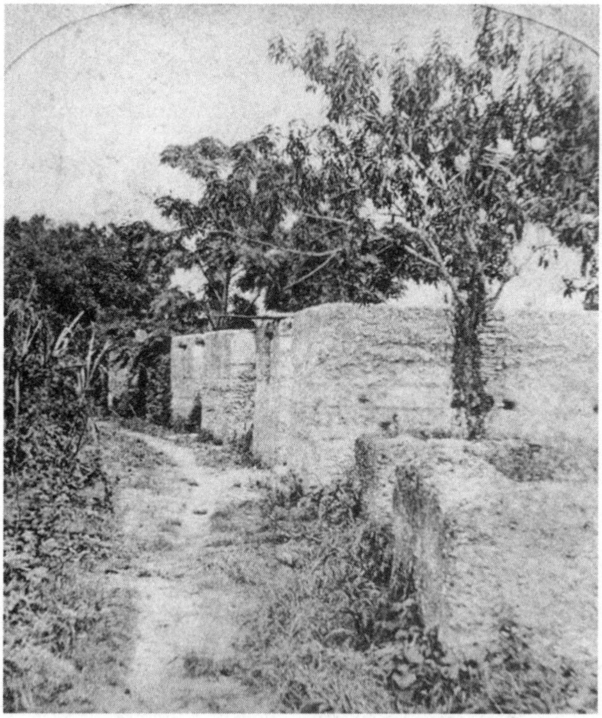

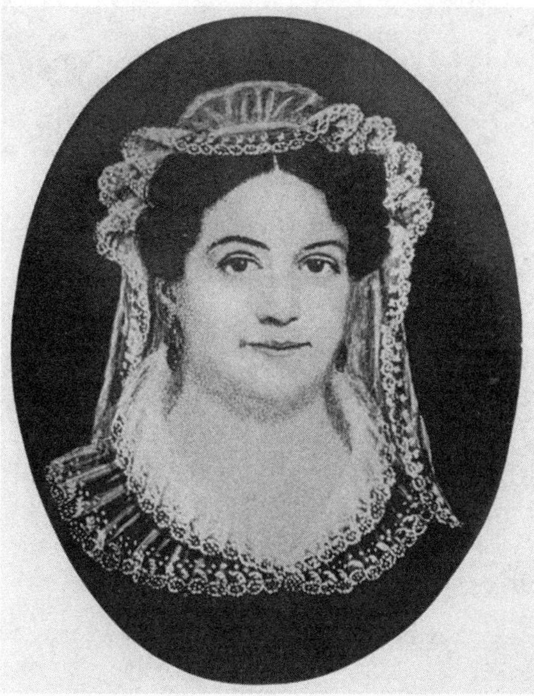

These are remains of slave cabins at Kingsley Plantation on Fort George Island near Jacksonville, which was run by Anna Madgigine Jai Kingsley. Taken as a slave in Senegal when she was about ten, she was sold to Zephaniah Kingsley in Cuba in 1806. He brought her to his Florida plantation, where he also fathered children with other "wives." He frequently traveled on business, and she proved an astute manager, eventually owning slaves and other property in her own name. She lost legal rights when Spain ceded Florida to the United States in 1819 and moved to Haiti, but later returned. Her mixed-race daughters married wealthy white men and were accepted in Jacksonville society. (Please see Daniel L. Schafer, *Anna Madgigine Jai Kingsley: African Princess, Florida Slave, Plantation Slaveowner*, as well as a fictionalized account, M. C. Finotti, *The Treasure of Amelia Island.*) State Archives of Florida, *Florida Memory*, http://floridamemory.com/items/show/9015.

Rachel Donelson Jackson joined her husband, future president Andrew Jackson, at Pensacola, the first capital of the Florida Territory, in 1821. This was the only time that she left their Nashville plantation, The Hermitage, where she hid to avoid painful gossip about her first marriage to an abusive man at a time when women could not file for divorce. Painting by Anna Claypoole Peale, 1815, State Archives of Florida, *Florida Memory*, http://floridamemory.com/items/show/129075.

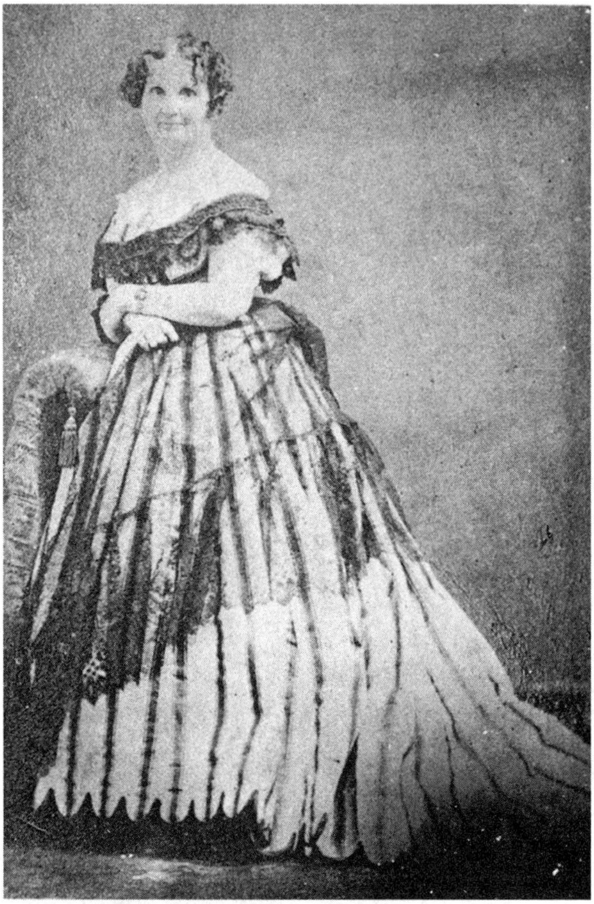

Catherine Willis Gray Murat was the queen of Tallahassee society when the capital was new. The great-grandniece of George Washington, she married Prince Achille Murat, the son of the king of Naples and an exiled nephew of Napoleon Bonaparte. Both had experienced serious economic loss, but after their 1826 wedding in Tallahassee—and with the help of slaves—they carved out a plantation in the wilderness of Jefferson County. State Archives of Florida, *Florida Memory*, http://floridamemory.com/items/show/75747.

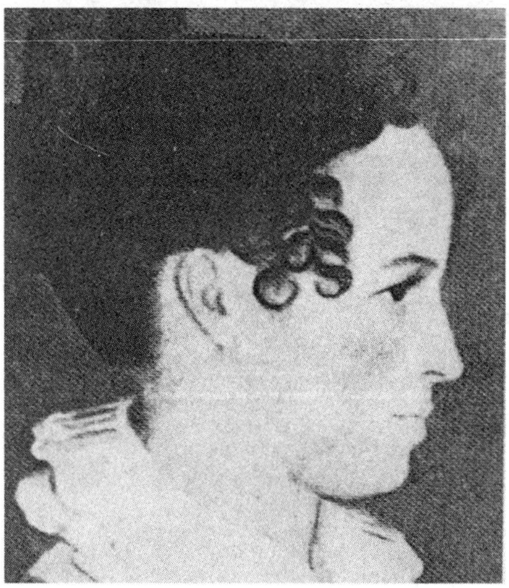

When Seminoles killed botanist Henry Perrine in an 1840 attack on Indian Key, his wife (whose first name remains unknown) led her three children to safety by hiding under a burning wharf until she could get them into a boat and row away. She tried to continue their botanical experiments on her own, but ultimately was "unable to carry out his contract." State Archives of Florida, *Florida Memory*, http://floridamemory.com/items/show/153446.

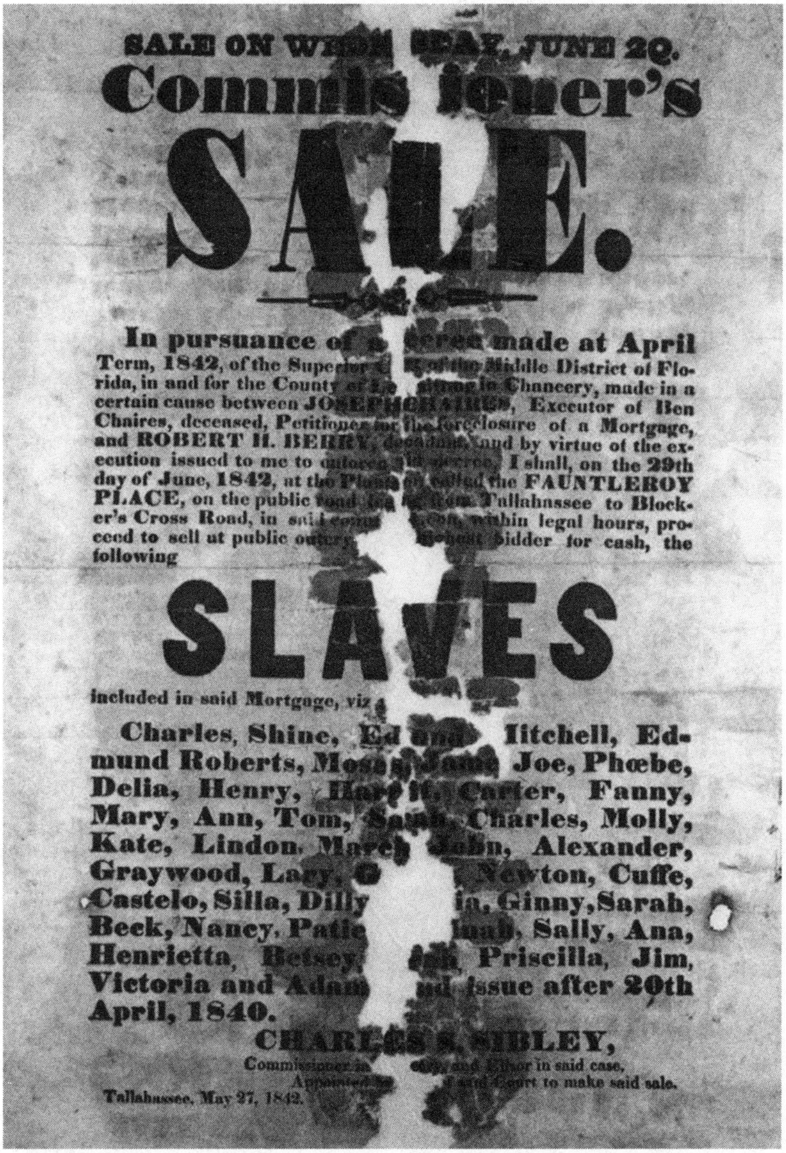

This 1842 advertisement is for the auction sale of slaves owned by a Leon County man who died in debt. Note the last line, which creates legal inclusion of any unborn children of pregnant women. State Archives of Florida, *Florida Memory*, http://floridamemory.com/items/show/34910.

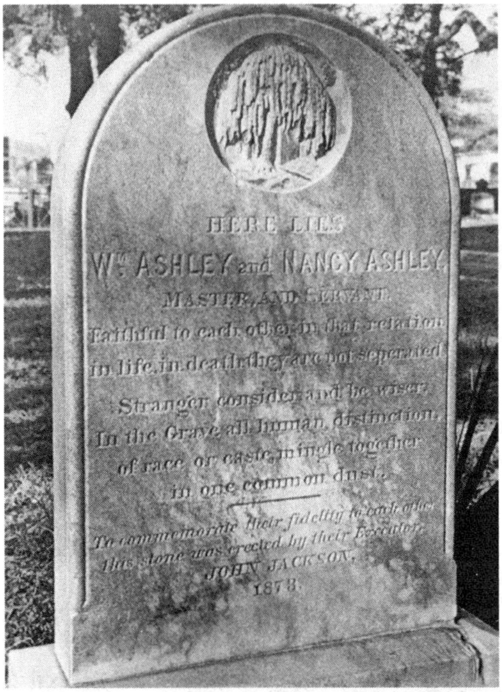

More men impregnated their slaves than generally is realized today, but very few were as openly affectionate as William Ashley was for his slave, Nancy. They could not have legally married even after slavery ended, as Florida law would prohibit miscegenation for another century, but Ashley mandated that his executor place a tombstone in Tampa's Oaklawn Cemetery to bear witness to the strength of his love and the immorality of such law. State Archives of Florida, *Florida Memory*, http://floridamemory.com/items/show/10841.

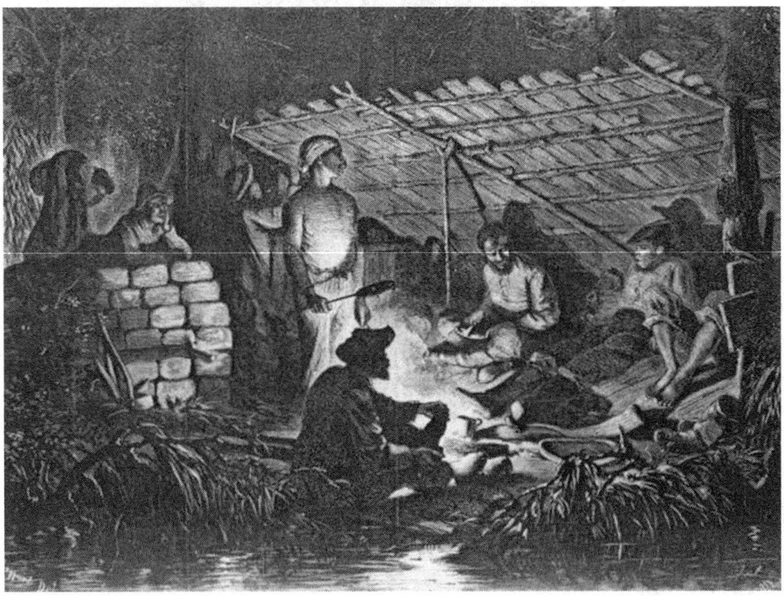

This 1873 engraving depicts black people hiding in a swamp after an attack by vigilantes. The era after the Civil War brought lynching, lawlessness, and anarchy—but even fifty years later, in 1923, racists destroyed the African American town of Rosewood, massacring its residents. State Archives of Florida, *Florida Memory*, http://floridamemory.com/items/show/35632.

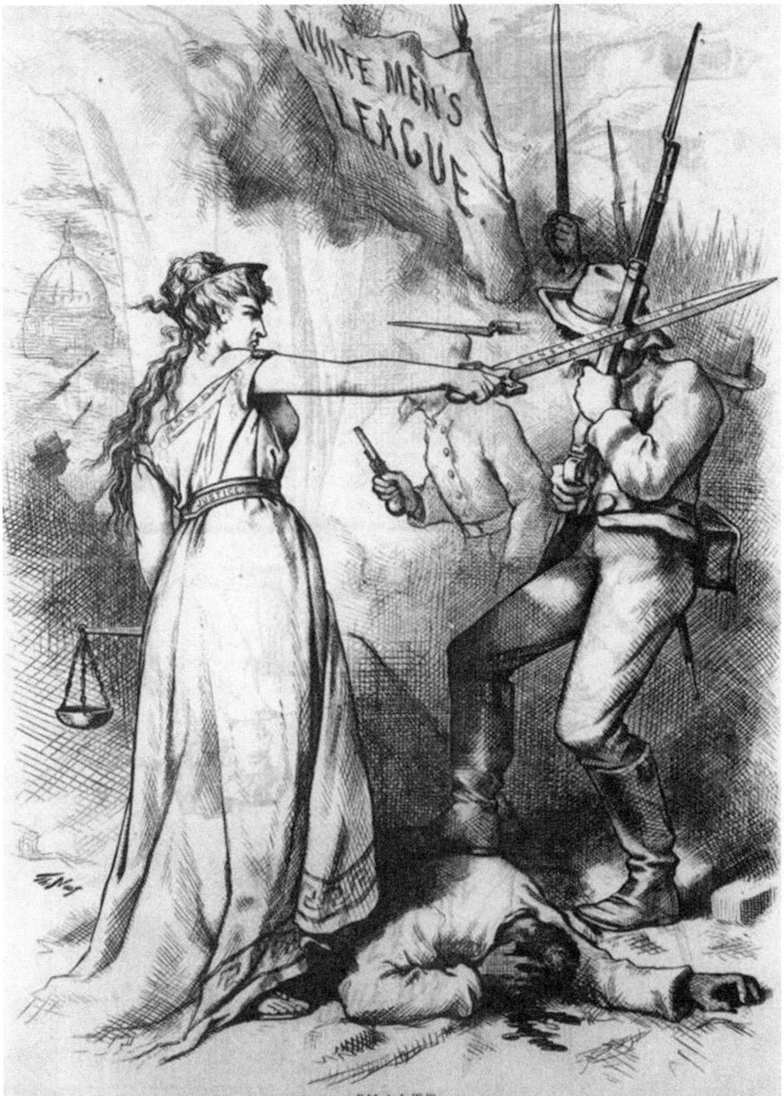

"HALT!"

"This is not the way 'to repress corruption and to initiate the Negroes into the ways of honest and orderly government.'"

This 1874 sketch shows the kind of terrorism that forced many blacks into the semi-slave status they had in Southern states after the federal government withdrew its Civil War troops. The artist recognizes that more than men, women resisted such vigilante behavior. Cartoon by Thomas Nast, *Harper's Weekly*, 1874, State Archives of Florida, *Florida Memory*, http://floridamemory.com/items/show/35630.

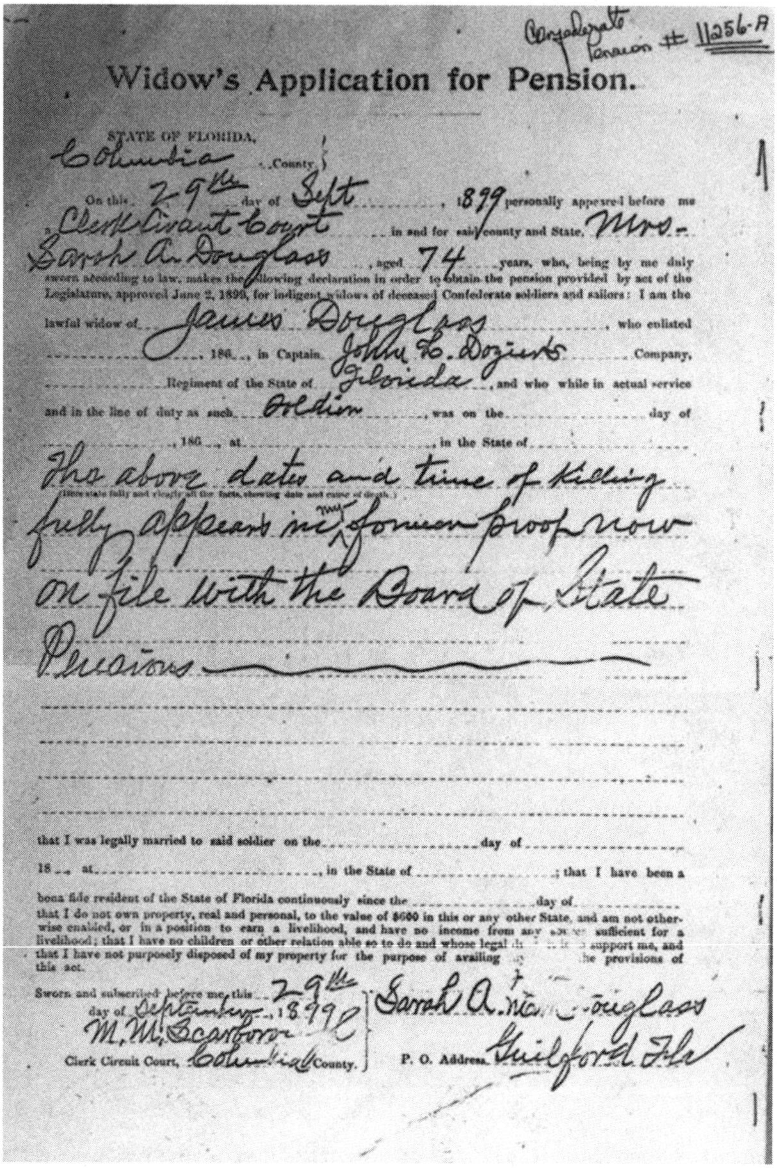

Confederate Pension # 11256-A

Widow's Application for Pension.

STATE OF FLORIDA,
Columbia County,

On this 29th day of Sept 1899 personally appeared before me Clerk Circuit Court in and for said county and State, Mrs. Sarah A. Douglass, aged 74 years, who, being by me duly sworn according to law, makes the following declaration in order to obtain the pension provided by act of the Legislature, approved June 2, 1899, for indigent widows of deceased Confederate soldiers and sailors: I am the lawful widow of James Douglass, who enlisted ..., 186.., in Captain John C. Dozier's Company, ... Regiment of the State of Florida, and who while in actual service and in the line of duty as such soldier, was on the ... day of ..., 186.., at ..., in the State of ...

(Here state fully and clearly all the facts, showing date and cause of death.)

The above dates and time of killing fully appears in my former proof now on file with the Board of State Pensions

that I was legally married to said soldier on the ... day of ... 18.., at ..., in the State of ...; that I have been a bona fide resident of the State of Florida continuously since the ... day of ... that I do not own property, real and personal, to the value of $600 in this or any other State, and am not otherwise enabled, or in a position to earn a livelihood, and have no income from any source sufficient for a livelihood; that I have no children or other relation able so to do and whose legal duty it is to support me, and that I have not purposely disposed of my property for the purpose of availing myself of the provisions of this act.

Sworn and subscribed before me, this 29th day of September, 1899.
M. M. Scarborough
Clerk Circuit Court, Columbia County.

Sarah A. Douglass
P. O. Address Guilford Fla

A Columbia County widow, Sarah Douglass, applied for a state pension in 1899, but it was based on her husband's service in the Civil War thirty years earlier. During and immediately after the war, many women were forced to support themselves and their families with little or no resources. State Archives of Florida, *Florida Memory*, http://floridamemory.com/items/show/1969.

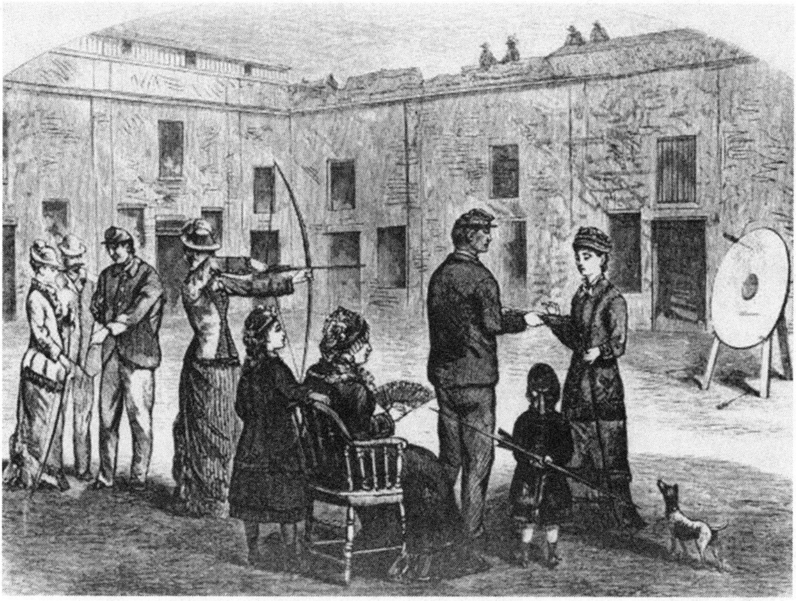

This unusual 1878 drawing is titled "Indians Instructing Their Teachers in Archery." It depicts Native Americans who were taken from the Midwest and Southwest and imprisoned in St. Augustine at the ancient fort of San Marcos, which was called Fort Marion in this era. Harriet Beecher Stowe and other white women taught them the fundamentals of reading and writing, and in return, they taught the women to shoot arrows. State Archives of Florida, *Florida Memory*, http://floridamemory.com/items/show/4254.

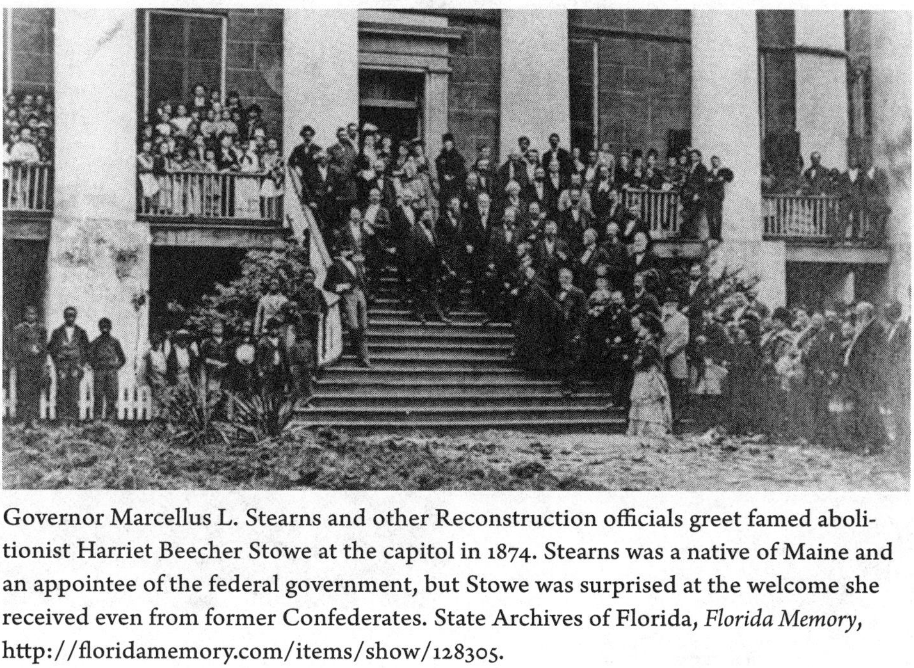

Governor Marcellus L. Stearns and other Reconstruction officials greet famed abolitionist Harriet Beecher Stowe at the capitol in 1874. Stearns was a native of Maine and an appointee of the federal government, but Stowe was surprised at the welcome she received even from former Confederates. State Archives of Florida, *Florida Memory*, http://floridamemory.com/items/show/128305.

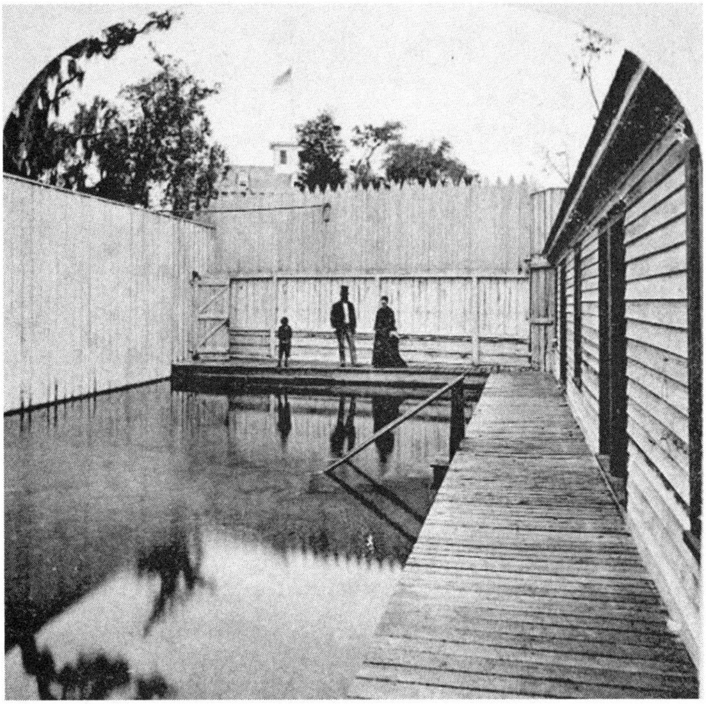

This photograph from the 1870s is of an "enclosed ladies swimming pool" at Green Cove Springs. Complete with a pier that could serve as a diving board, it allowed privacy to Victorian women. Green Cove Springs is near Jacksonville, an area that began attracting winter residents after the Civil War. The first Florida affiliate of the General Federation of Women's Clubs was at Green Cove Springs. State Archives of Florida, *Florida Memory*, http://floridamemory.com/items/show/8842.

Historians do not yet know if Sarah Ann Blocker was born slave or free. She was born in Delaware in 1857, but Delaware was the very last state to abolish slavery, six months after the war ended in 1865. By the 1870 census, her family had moved to Albany, Georgia, and in 1883, she earned a degree from the institution that became Atlanta University. A co-founder of the school that eventually was named Florida Memorial College, she gave the rest of her life to educating black Floridians, dying in St. Augustine at age 87. Courtesy of Florida Women's Hall of Fame (hereafter "FWHOF").

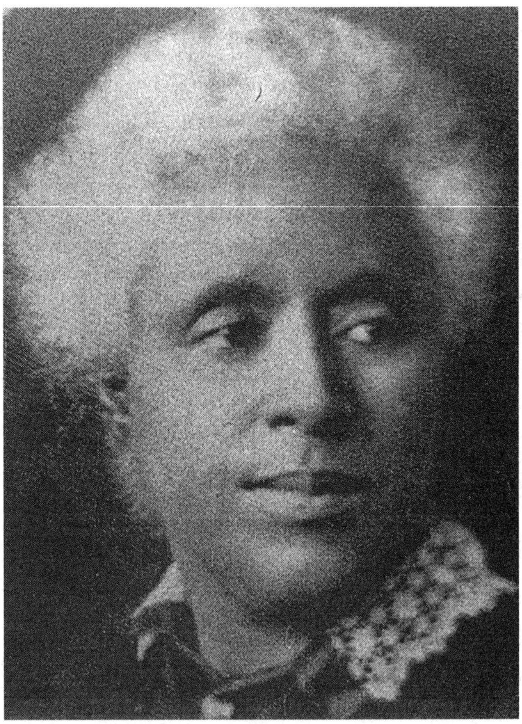

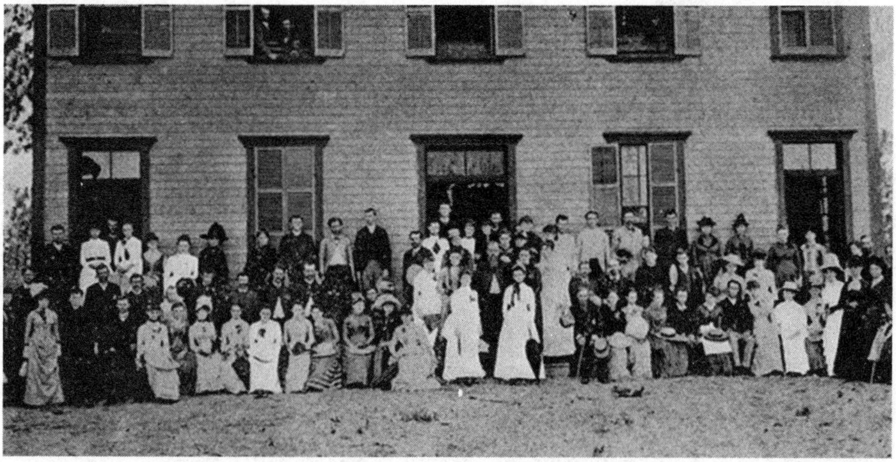

This photo depicts charter members of the Florida Education Association, which began in 1886 at DeFuniak Springs. Although the majority of teachers were women, no woman would be president until the late twentieth century. State Archives of Florida, *Florida Memory*, http://floridamemory.com/items/show/140262.

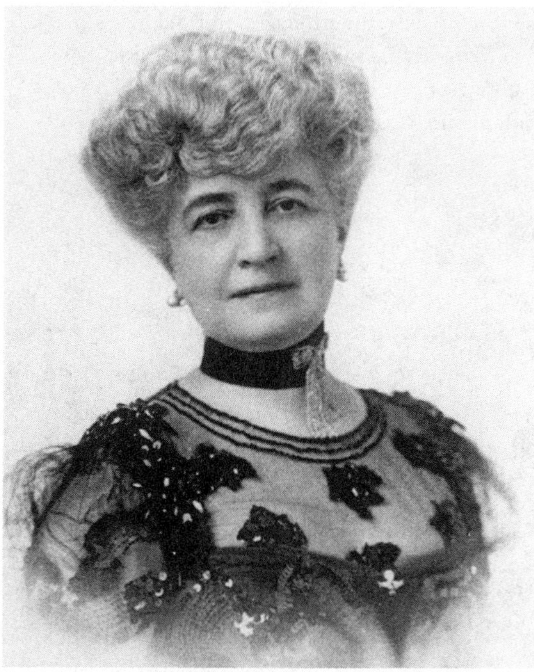

Congress appointed Bertha Honore Palmer to head women's activities at the Chicago World's Fair, a year-long event in 1892–1893 that honored the 400th anniversary of Columbus's voyage. She and her committee built a Woman's Building that was designed by a female architect, decorated with art and sculpture by women, and women composed the music performed. Millions of people from all around the world viewed its exhibitions and participated in hundreds of seminars that were held. Palmer was a winter resident of Osprey, near Sarasota, where she built an innovative home. She also owned huge amounts of land in southwest Florida and conducted experiments in cattle breeding. State Archives of Florida, *Florida Memory*, http://floridamemory.com/items/show/28043.

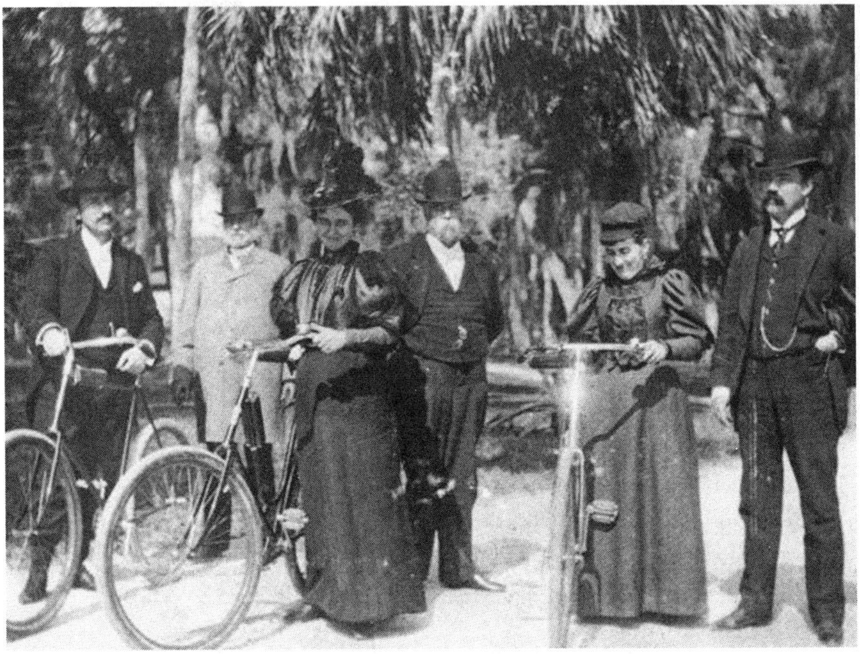

Blanche Peck and Grace Taylor pose in 1896 with their bicycles in Rockledge. Bicycles were liberating for women with no access to horses, and even middle-aged women such as these took advantage of that new freedom. State Archives of Florida, *Florida Memory*, http://floridamemory.com/items/show/29358.

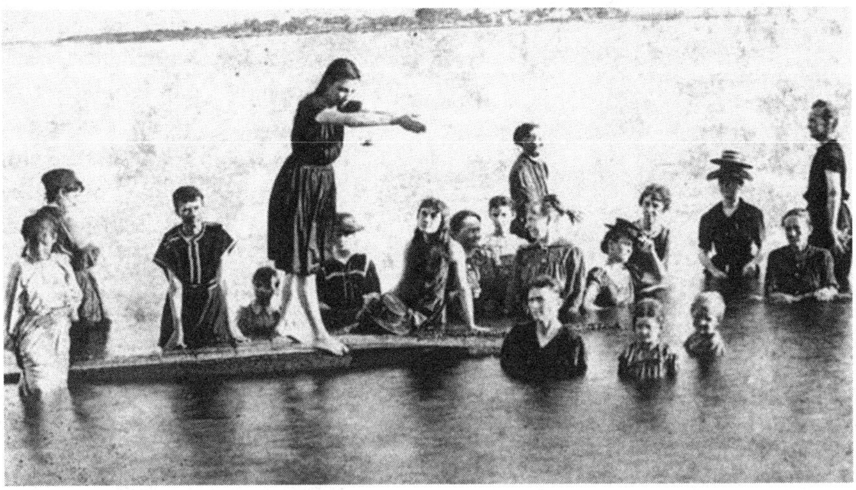

In another indication of changed standards near the end of the Victorian era, this 1896 photo shows women and girls in the water at Cedar Key—along with men. None have the new "bathing costume" worn by the diver and the man behind her, but note that one woman jokingly has a man's hat on top of her own. State Archives of Florida, *Florida Memory*, http://floridamemory.com/items/show/32000.

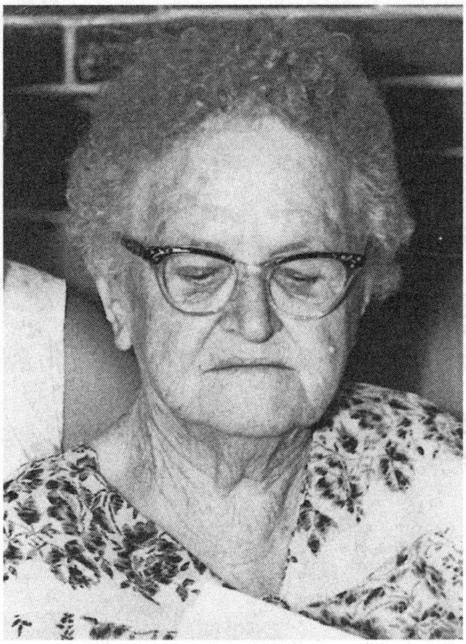

Born in 1876, Lillian Pierce Voss was the first white child in southeast Florida. Both she and her mother joined her father in piloting boats for cargo and passengers on the Atlantic and on inland waterways. A fifty-year resident of Hypoluxo, she helped make Palm Beach County what it is today. Courtesy of FWHOF.

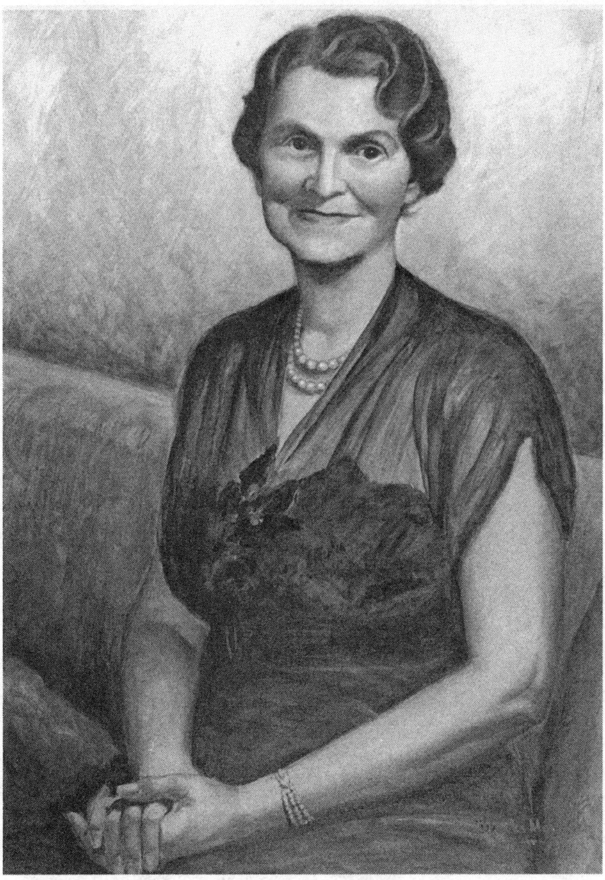

Called "Aunt Frances" by her Fort Walton Beach friends, Sarah Brooks Pryor was born in an Okaloosa County log cabin in 1877 and rowed a boat to school. She became a teacher, operated a historic hotel, and in 1917, was appointed postmaster by President Woodrow Wilson. Other women ran post offices, too, including Victoria Brandon, who founded the Hillsborough County town of Brandon. Courtesy of FWHOF.

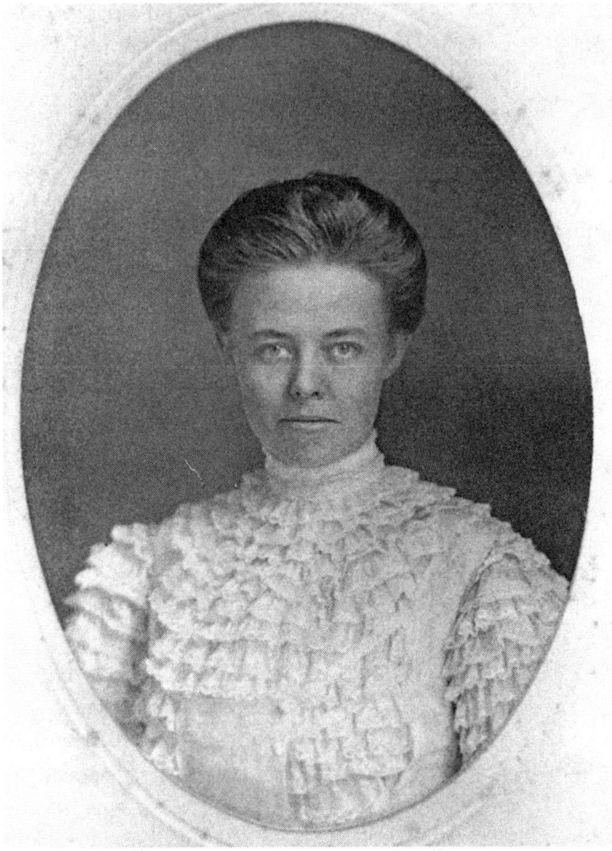

Ivy Cromartie Stranahan pioneered in Broward County with her husband, Frank, when Fort Lauderdale was merely a small trading post. Long known as the best friend of Seminoles, she was key to their acceptance of reservation status in 1924. Stranahan also served as president of the Florida Woman Suffrage Association and lobbied in Tallahassee for women's right to vote. Courtesy of FWHOF.

Known as "The Mother of Miami," Julia Tuttle was a real estate developer from Ohio. After her husband's death in 1891, she bought a square mile of land at the mouth of the Miami River and astutely gave much of it away to induce others to move there. She died at age fifty in 1898, just two years after successfully advocating for a railroad to Miami. Courtesy of FWHOF.

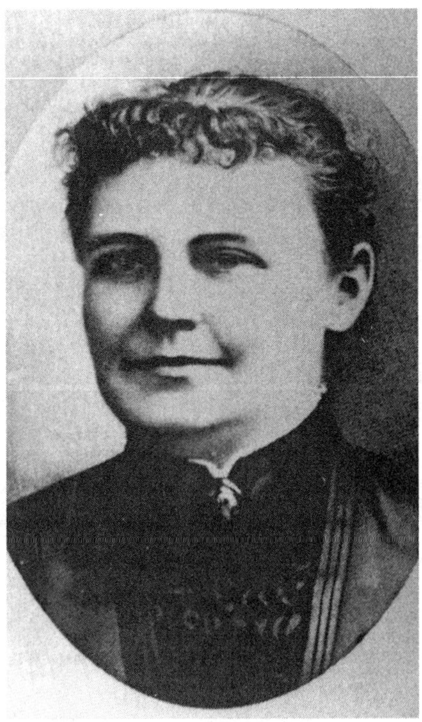

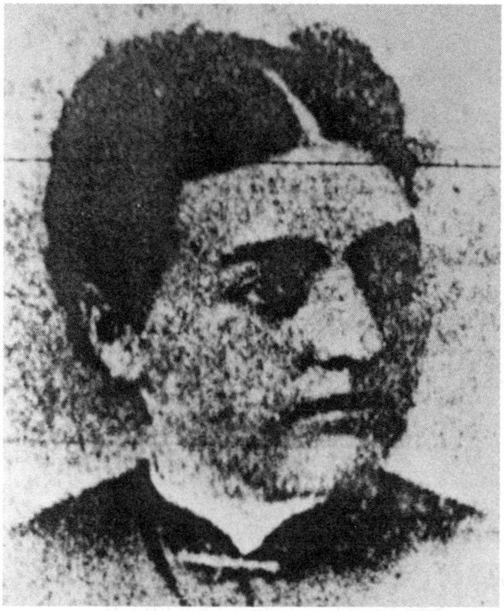

Northern women had edited newspapers since colonial days, but that tradition did not develop in Florida—which had no newspaper during the centuries of Spanish government. After Reconstruction, however, women began to establish themselves in the newspaper business, and this 1897 photo is of Neva C. Child, who published the *De Soto County Champion*. Other women were editors and publishers elsewhere even earlier, including Bartow and Tampa in the 1870s. State Archives of Florida, *Florida Memory*, http://floridamemory.com/items/show/137575

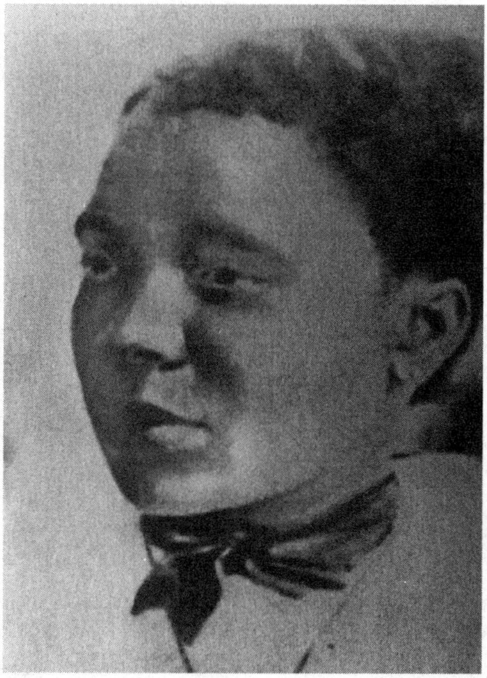

Born in Cuba in 1845, Paulina Pedroso was a cigar maker in Key West and Tampa. When Cuba sought its independence from Spain in 1895, she organized La Sociedad Libres on behalf of Cuban freedom. The great José Martí headquartered his activities in her home in the Ybor City section of Tampa, and they worked closely together—although he was white and she was black. Courtesy of FWHOF.

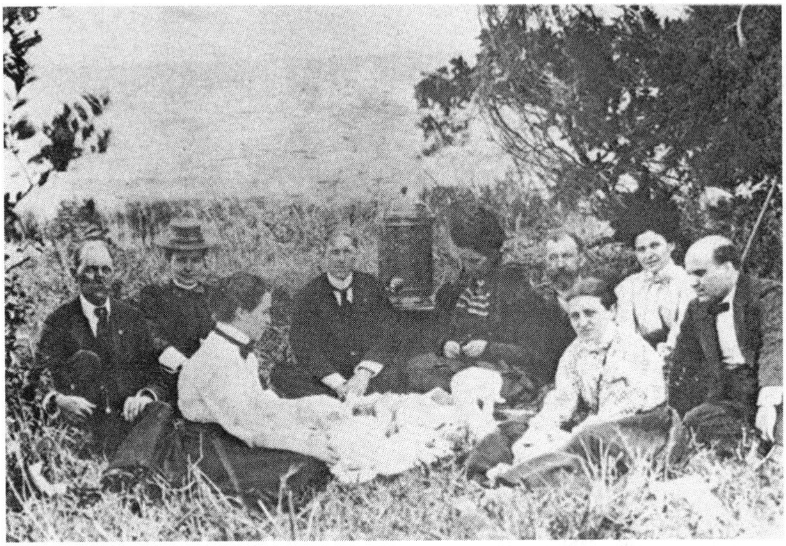

Clara Barton, founder of the American Red Cross, picnics with colleagues in Tampa while awaiting permission to take relief supplies to Cuba in the 1898 Spanish-American War. Although modern Tampa has many reminders of the presence of Teddy Roosevelt's Rough Riders during that time, Barton's contribution is neglected. State Archives of Florida, *Florida Memory*, http://floridamemory.com/items/show/35991.

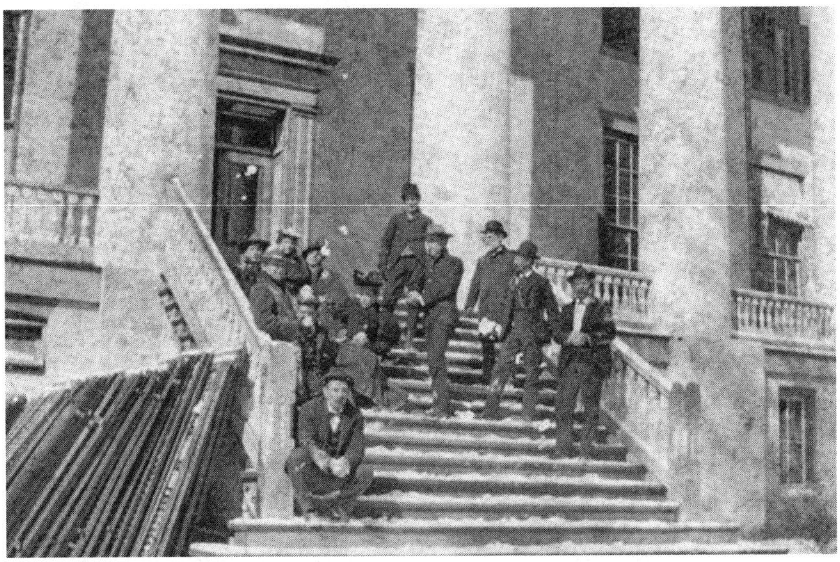

This 1899 photo depicts women and men on the snow-covered steps of the state capitol. Winters in the late 1890s were uncommonly cold, and freezes bankrupted many farm families. Especially the citrus industry moved further south, an important factor in the growth of Dade, Broward, and Palm Beach counties—and in the forced relocation of Seminoles to the Everglades. State Archives of Florida, *Florida Memory*, http://floridamemory.com/items/show/24747.

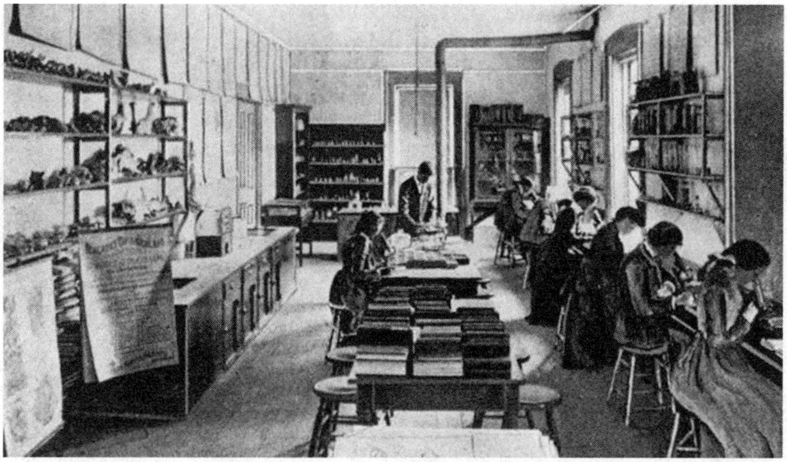

Women use microscopes in the biology lab of West Florida Seminary in Tallahassee in 1900. It would become Florida State College for Women in 1905 and open only to white women, while white men attended the University of Florida in Gainesville. State Archives of Florida, *Florida Memory*, http://floridamemory.com/items/show/25066.

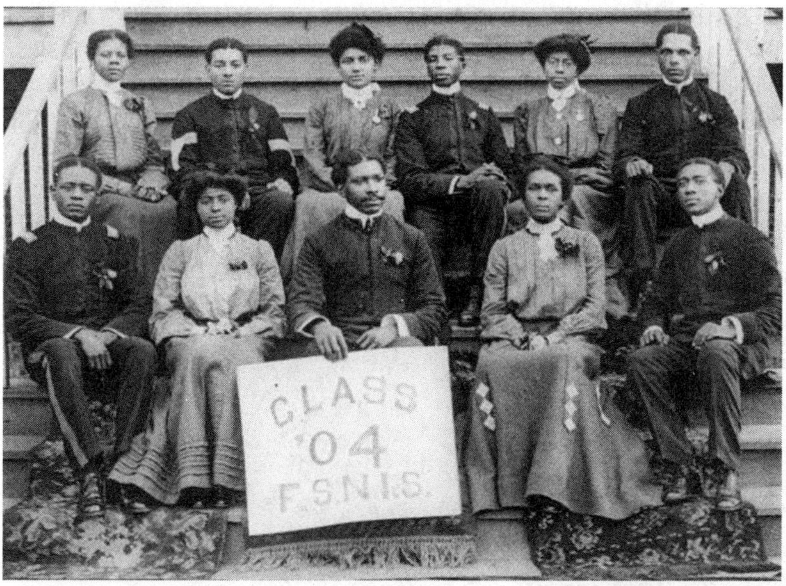

This is the graduating class of 1904 at Florida State Normal & Industrial School in Tallahassee. "Normal" at that time meant a teacher-training school, and blacks of both genders attended. A legislative act the next year would change the name to Florida Agricultural & Mechanical College; much later, it would gain university status and the institution now is commonly known as FAMU. All public higher education was in north Florida until 1956, when the University of South Florida began in Tampa. State Archives of Florida, *Florida Memory*, http://floridamemory.com/items/show/26289.

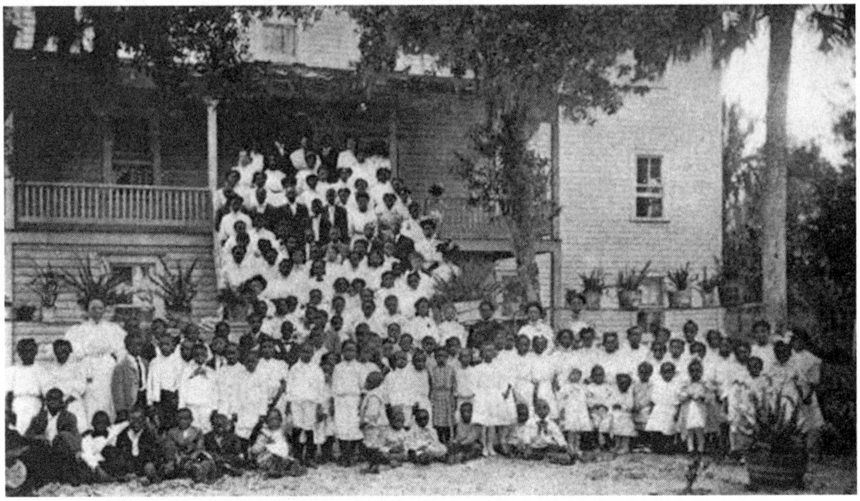

Mary McLeod Bethune stands with students and staff at what then was called Daytona Normal and Industrial School in 1919. She began a Daytona Beach boarding school in 1904 with less than $5 and five female students. Although initially there were times when they had nothing to eat, they cleared a junkyard, learned to sing to entertain winter visitors, and soon built a thriving institution that eventually became Bethune-Cookman University. Bethune went on to international fame and was the only woman of color at the founding of the United Nations. State Archives of Florida, *Florida Memory*, http://floridamemory.com/items/show/764.

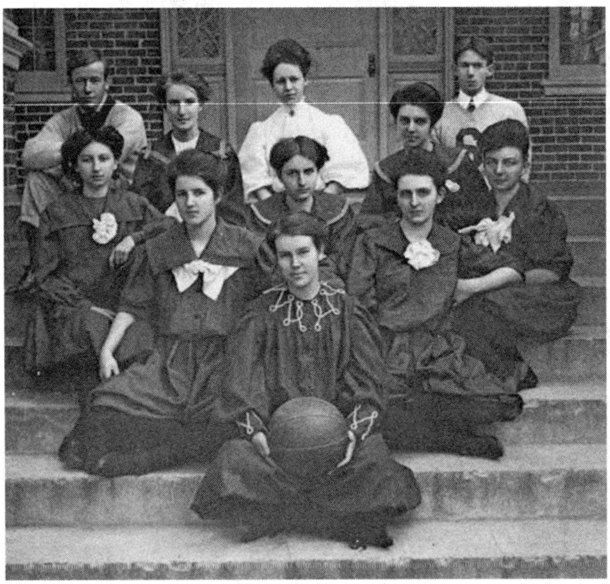

For many decades, Florida offered no tax-supported public law school that was open to women, and Stetson University, a private college in DeLand, educated most of the state's early female attorneys. This is Stetson's women's basketball ball team in 1907. State Archives of Florida, *Florida Memory*, http://floridamemory.com/items/show/11457.

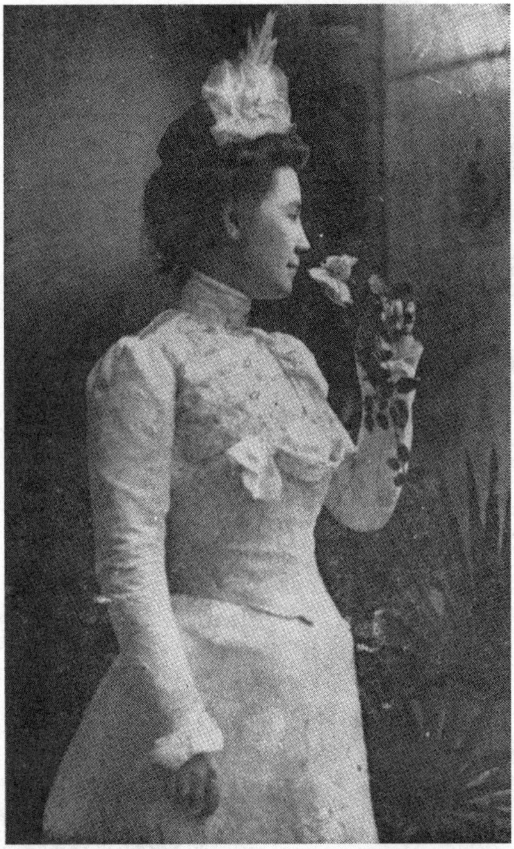

May Mann Jennings is dressed in 1901 for the gubernatorial inauguration of her husband, William Sherman Jennings. In the next decade, she would lead the movement for women's right to vote along with her kinswoman, Mary Baird Bryan, the wife of former Democratic presidential nominee William Jennings Bryan. Both women were astute politicians, although Florida did not grant women voting rights for any elections other than those in a few municipalities. State Archives of Florida, *Florida Memory*, http://floridamemory.com/items/show/128316.

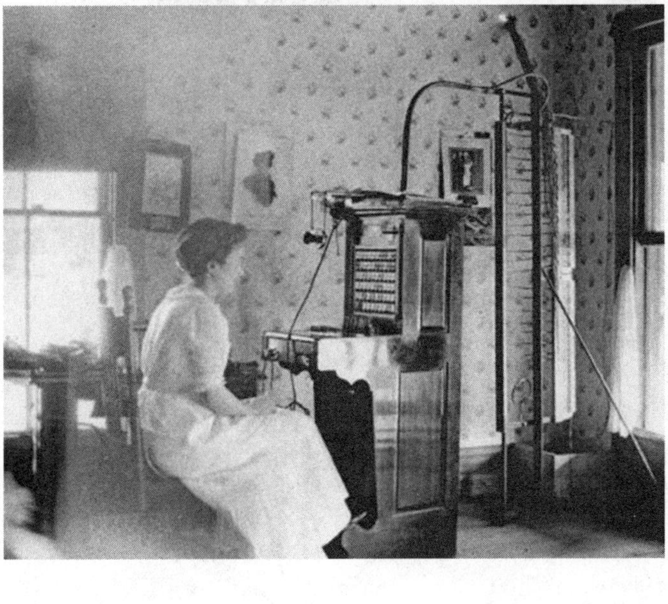

An anonymous woman operates a telephone switchboard from her home in Coleman, near Gainesville, in 1906. Employers initially tried young men as phone operators, but found women to be more patient and dependable. This was a wholly new employment opportunity for women—and for the phone company, women who worked from home were advantageous because the operator was available day and night. State Archives of Florida, *Florida Memory*, http://floridamemory.com/items/show/154754.

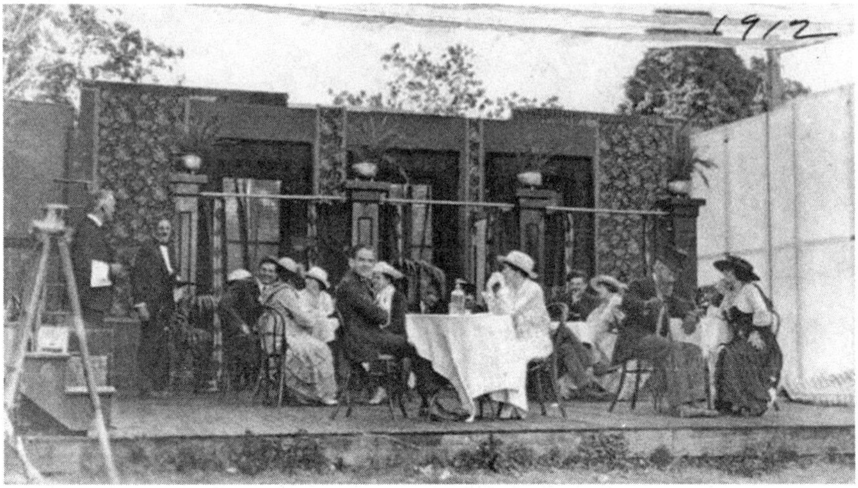

The motion picture industry briefly took hold in Florida, and this photo of a movie set is in Jacksonville in 1912. This was still another new employment opportunity for women, not only as actors, but also and especially as costumers. Florida's weather is more temperamental than that in California, however, and most of the industry moved there in the next decade. State Archives of Florida, *Florida Memory*, http://floridamemory.com/items/show/5921.

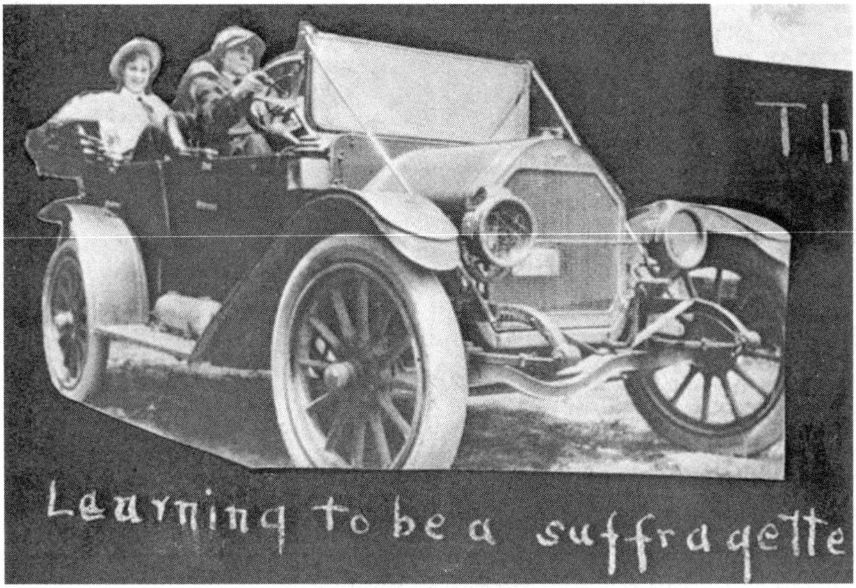

This 1914 depiction of women smoking, dressed as men, and driving a car was ahead of its time. In Florida, such change would not occur until the next decade, and the state's women who lobbied for the vote between 1913 and 1920 dressed and behaved conventionally. State Archives of Florida, *Florida Memory*, http://floridamemory.com/items/show/34564.

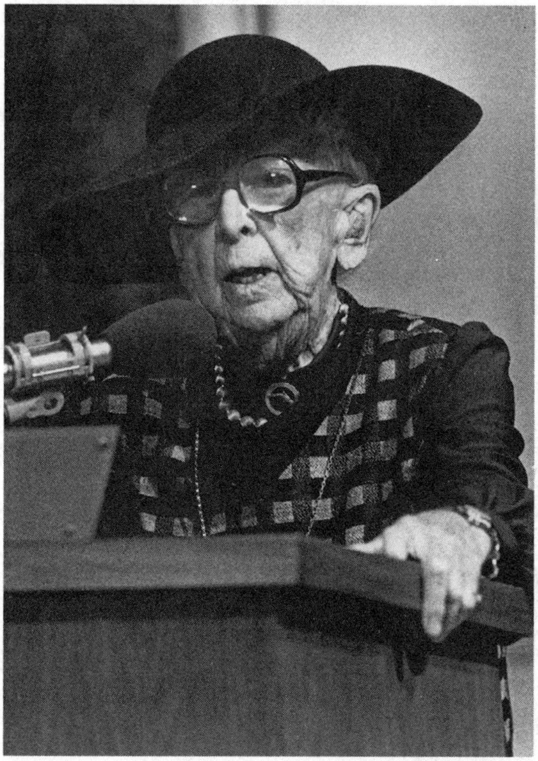

Marjory Stoneman Douglas lived to 107 and is shown here in her old age, but she was a young divorcée when she went to Tallahassee to work for the vote. Born in Massachusetts, she graduated from Wellesley College in 1912 and moved to Florida in 1915 with her father, who published the *Miami Herald*. One of the first women sworn into the military in World War I, she became famous for her writings about Florida, especially *River of Grass* (1947). She was key to preservation of the Everglades and was awarded the Presidential Medal of Honor in 1993. Courtesy of FWHOF.

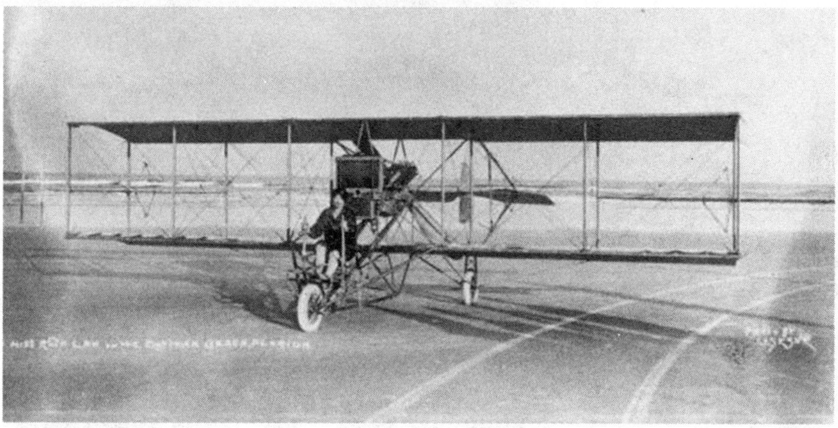

The title of this 1915 photo says only "Ruth Law Lands Her Plane—Daytona Beach." That was early, as the first American pilot licenses were issued in 1911. A Massachusetts native, Ruth Bancroft Law kept her maiden name when she married Charles Oliver, and he watched as she performed unprecedented air acrobatics before a large Florida crowd. The next year, she set a speed record racing from Chicago to New York, and President Woodrow Wilson attended a banquet in her honor. From then on, Florida developed a rich history of female aviators—called "aviatrixes" in their time. State Archives of Florida, *Florida Memory*, http://floridamemory.com/items/show/31269.

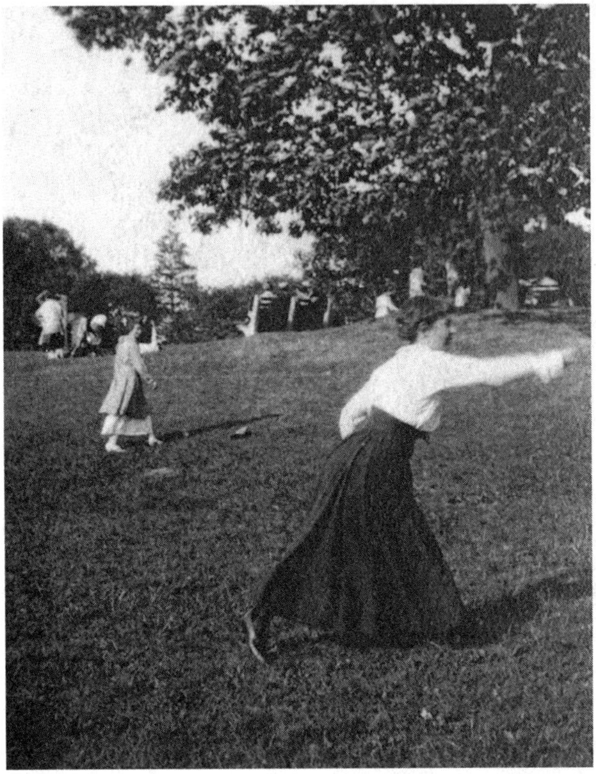

Koreshan women play baseball in 1916. This utopian community began in 1894 with settlers from Chicago, and they soon owned some 6,000 acres of land on the Estero River near Fort Myers. Koreshan Unity members believed that God was both male and female, and because Jesus had appeared in male form, there soon would be an appearance of a female form of God. Its major female leader was Annie G. Ordway, and she led missions as far away as Nicaragua. Both men and women belonged, but they were celibate, a factor that led the community to eventually fade. The site that commemorates these unusual Floridians is off of I-75 at Exit 123. State Archives of Florida, *Florida Memory*, http://floridamemory.com/items/show/256505.

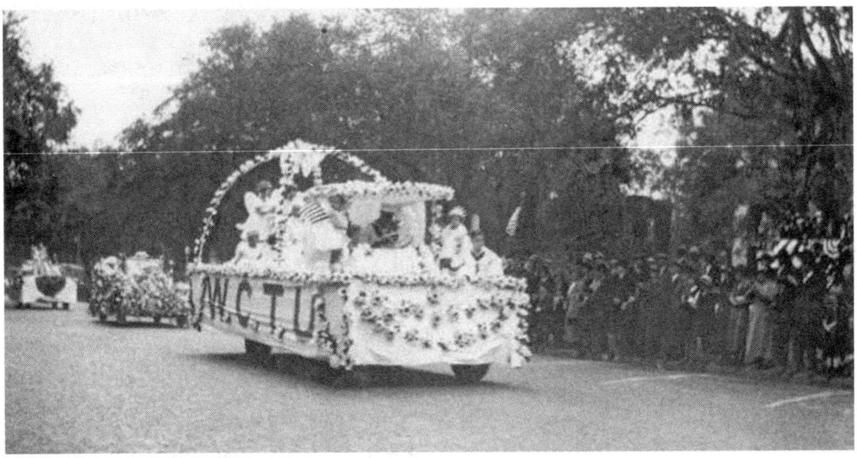

The WCTU (Women's Christian Temperance Union) celebrates Tallahassee's centennial in a parade on November 11, 1924. Although they had achieved their goal of banning alcohol, the WCTU remained politically visible. Note also that although this is the midst of the Roaring Twenties, most women still are wearing long dresses. State Archives of Florida, *Florida Memory*, http://floridamemory.com/items/show/24266.

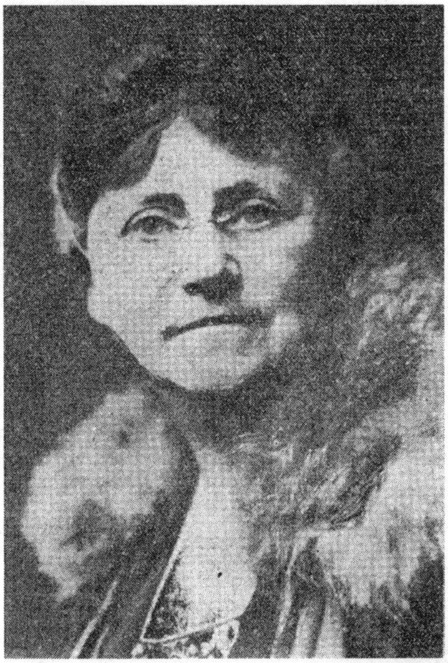

Orlando's Edna Giles Fuller was the first woman elected to the Florida legislature in 1928. Called "Mrs. John T. Fuller" in the press, she organized the state's food conservation program during World War I and was the last president of the Florida Woman Suffrage Association prior to winning the vote. She chaired a House subcommittee on education already in her first term. State Archives of Florida, *Florida Memory*, http://floridamemory.com/items/show/31077.

Women did well in the 1928 election, and Ruth Bryan Owen of Miami became the first U.S. congresswoman from the South. A widow with four children, she drove her own car to campaign in the district, which ran from the Georgia border to Key West. From Congress, she went on to play other important roles as the first female ambassador (to Denmark) and as a founder of the United Nations. Courtesy of FWHOF.

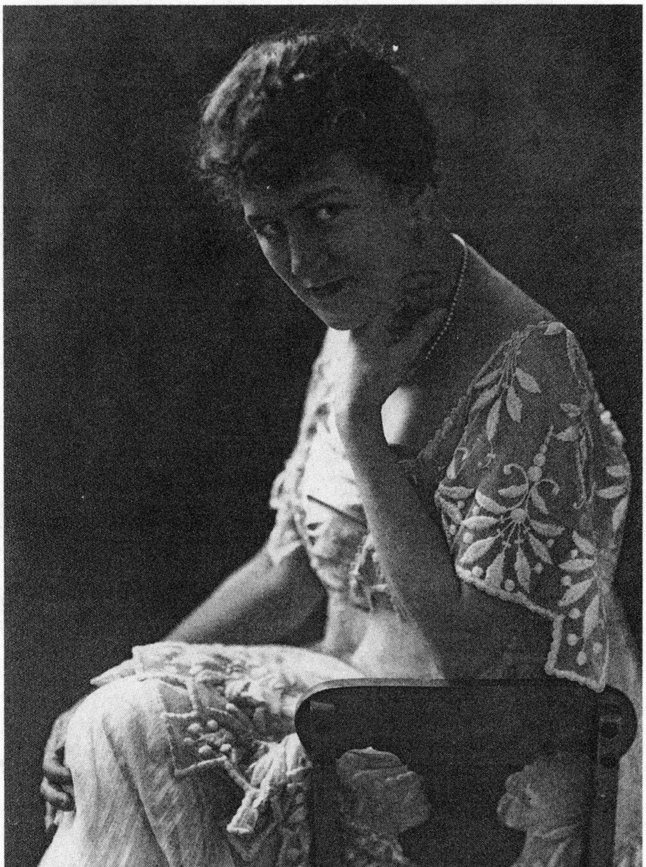

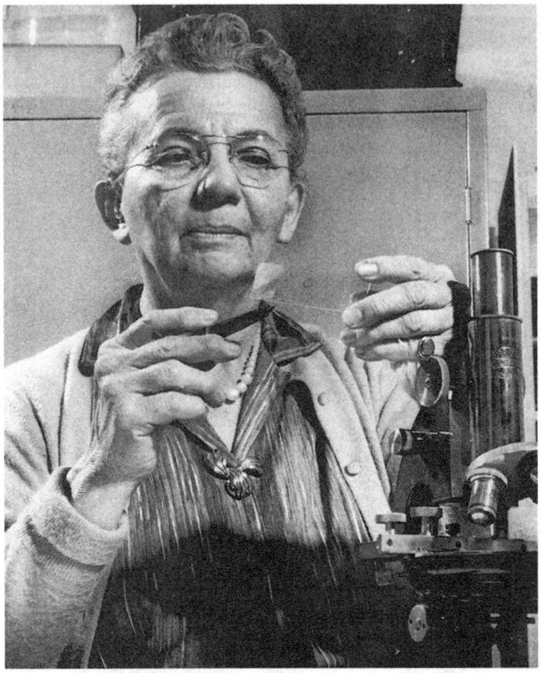

Although older in this photograph, Florence Seibert earned a doctorate from Yale University in 1924 despite being crippled by polio. She made major contributions in intravenous therapy and is considered the creator of the skin test that identifies tuberculosis. During three decades of "retirement" in St. Petersburg, she researched cancer and was inducted into the National Women's Hall of Fame. Courtesy of FWHOF.

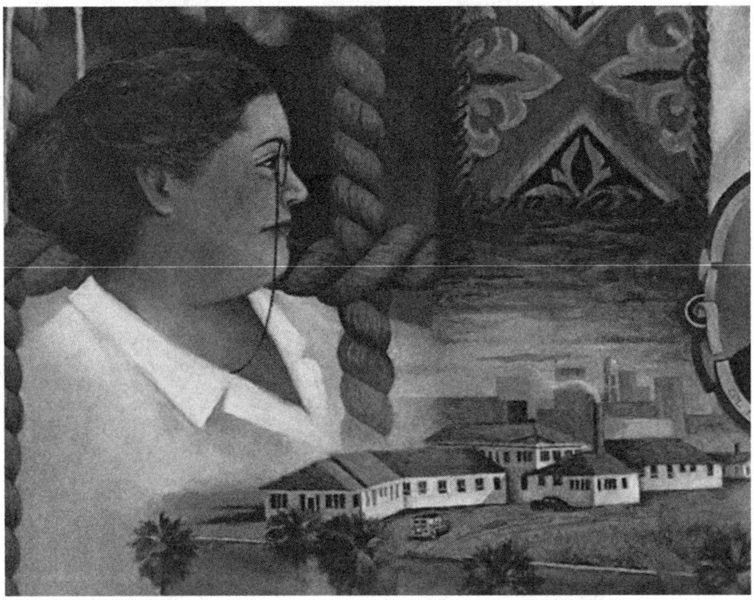

Although so light-skinned that she could have passed for white, Clara Frye identified as black and founded Tampa's first hospital for African Americans in 1908 in her home; the first surgery was on her dining room table. With expansion in the 1920s, the hospital was the only one available to blacks on Florida's West Coast. Courtesy of FWHOF.

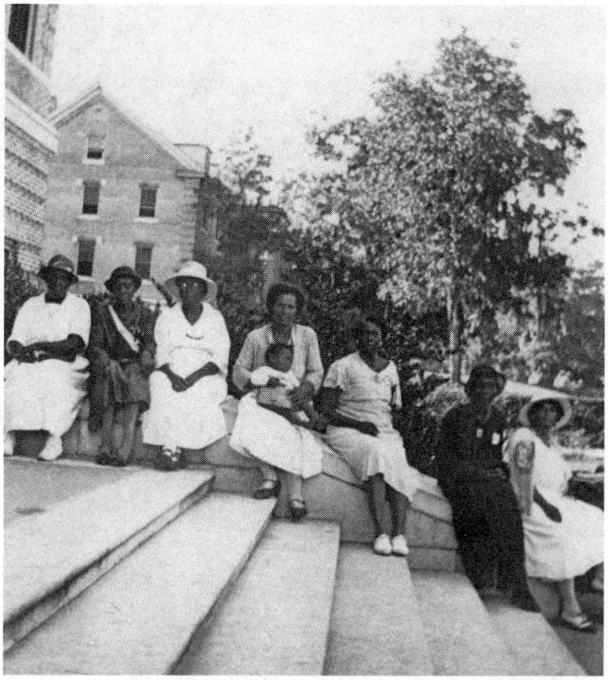

These are some of the women enrolled at the West Florida Midwives Institute at Florida A&M in Tallahassee in 1933. The State Board of Health created training programs for midwives in 1931 to deal with Florida's huge rate of infant mortality and maternal death. Although these and other trained midwives safely delivered thousands of babies, they later had to fight for their right to practice. State Archives of Florida, *Florida Memory*, http://floridamemory.com/items/show/44582.

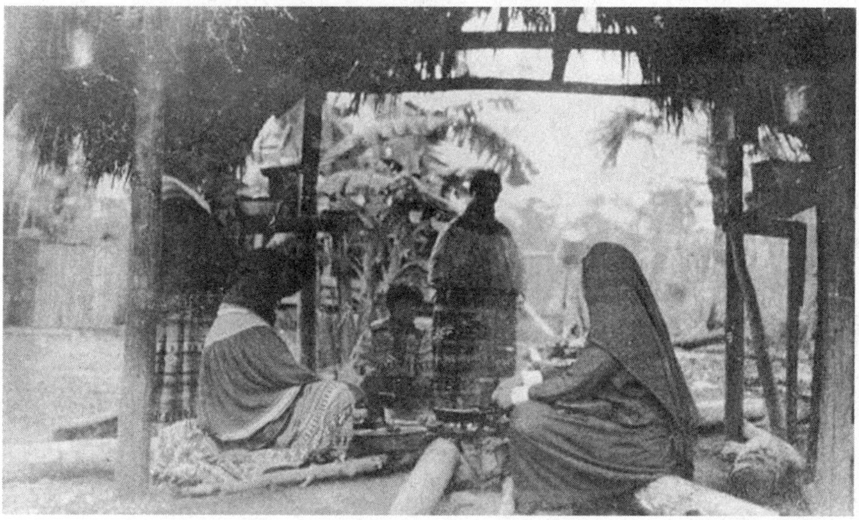

According to state archivists, this photo could be as early as 1933 or as late as 1960, as that was the period during which Deaconess Harriet Bedell was a missionary to Florida Natives. Here she is shown at a cooking chickee, a style of architecture that Seminole women used as late as the 1970s. Bedell lived from 1867 to 1969; in her early career, she drove a Model A to visit Seminoles and Mikasuki in homes throughout the Everglades. State Archives of Florida, *Florida Memory*, http://floridamemory.com/items/show/63762.

Economic conditions were so bad in the late 1920s and early 1930s that many previously middle-class families from other states were reduced to migrant labor in Florida. Whether or not a man headed this family in Belle Glade is not clear, but the woman certainly saw endless days of toil and despair. Yet the iron on the stove indicates that she tried to keep up standards—and that she had no electricity. Getting fuel for the stove would be still another worry. Photo by Marion Post Wolcott, 1939, State Archives of Florida, *Florida Memory*, http://floridamemory.com/items/show/26421.

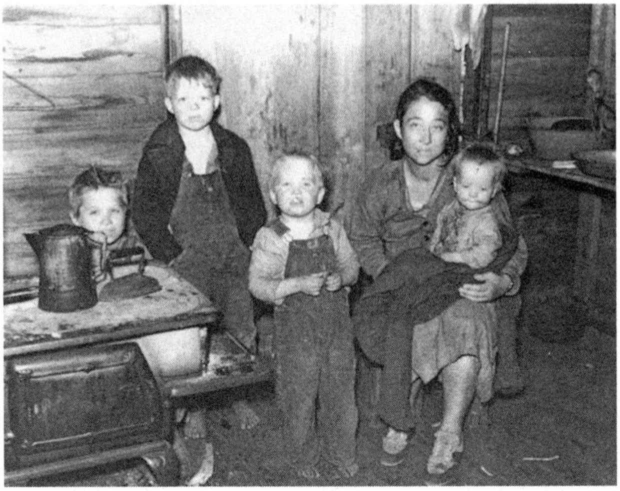

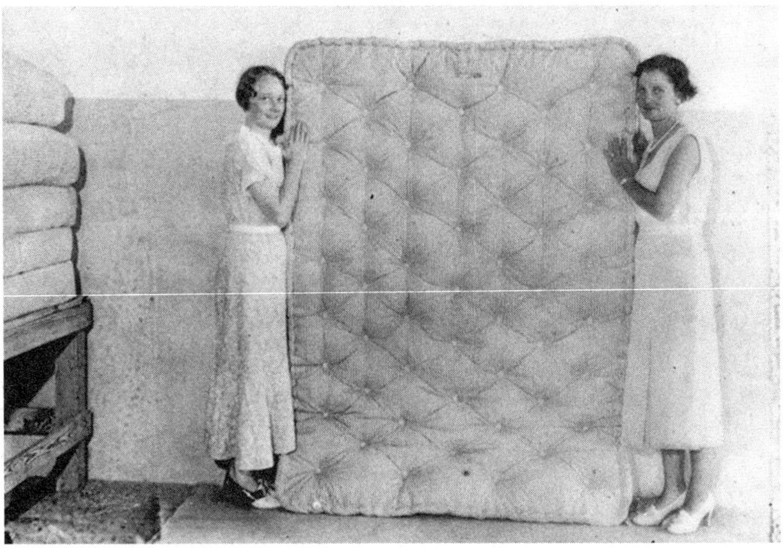

After the Great Depression deepened, the federal government created a number of programs to provide jobs, including jobs for women. Working under the Federal Emergency Relief Administration (FERA), these Jacksonville women doubtless dressed up to pose for a 1935 photo that shows the end product of their mattress making. The State Archives has a series of photos of this work, which women did at every stage from carding the cotton onward. FERA women in Orlando, Pensacola, and elsewhere did similarly heavy labor in what were genteelly called "sewing rooms." State Archives of Florida, *Florida Memory*, http://floridamemory.com/items/show/144056.

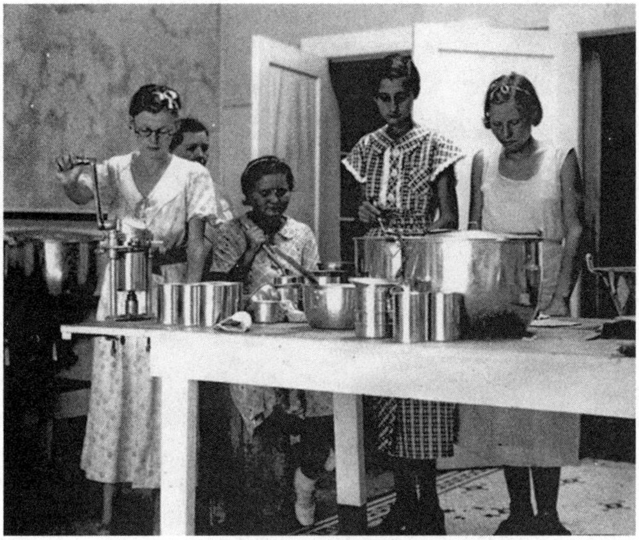

This 1935 photo is of women in Hastings, near St. Augustine, using a cannery funded by the Federal Emergency Relief Administration (FERA). They are learning to safely can (in glass jars) seasonal produce from their gardens. The FERA's communal canneries provided necessary equipment, including running water and electricity. In addition to home canning, Florida women long worked in commercial canneries and in packinghouses for both fruits and vegetables. They also worked in the seafood industry, including digging oysters, cleaning shrimp, and picking crabmeat. Florida traditionally had more female agricultural workers than any other state. State Archives of Florida, *Florida Memory*, http://floridamemory.com/items/show/141014.

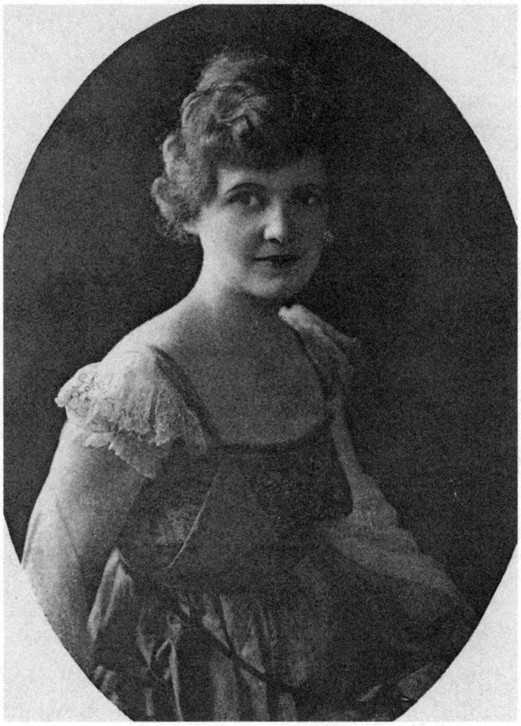

White-collar workers also were unemployed during the Great Depression, and Congress created the Federal Writers Project (FWP) to assist that portion of the population. Carita Doggett Corse of Jacksonville was one of very few women who headed the FWP, and she did an extraordinary job of hiring writers to preserve Florida history and folklore, as well as to create tourist guides. Unlike many administrators, Corse hired blacks as interviewers for the Slave Narrative project, which recorded the memories of elderly people born in slavery. Courtesy of FWHOF.

4 "We Live On Cornbread and Hope"

The Civil War and Its Aftermath, 1860–1880

Abraham Lincoln's name was not on the Florida ballot for the 1860 presidential election: the men who governed the state refused to allow that voting option. Male voters in other states, however, cast more votes for him than for any of the other three candidates, and although that was less than a majority, he won the presidency. Florida lawmakers almost immediately resolved to secede from the Union that they had been eager to join in 1845, a mere fifteen years earlier.

Although Florida women seldom expressed themselves politically, some participated in the decision to go to war. On November 6, 1860, as soon as election results were known in Jacksonville, "the ladies" of the Duval County area known as Broward's Neck drafted a petition to the "Politicians of Florida." Asking not to be left "to the tender mercies of the Yankees," the women challenged men to "avail themselves of the means given them by God and nature and defend themselves."[1]

At a November 24 rally on the Alafia River, near modern Hillsborough and Manatee counties, twenty-six women joined several dozen men in signing a petition for secession. From leading families, they were married and unmarried, as the *Florida Peninsular* indicated in "The South Should Govern the South." The paper quoted the petition: "Whereas, it is now certain that Abraham Lincoln has been elected president of the United States, and whereas [because] of that election . . . the powers of Government have passed into the hands of a section implacably hostile to our interests and institutions . . ."[2]

The "interests and institutions" they had in mind, of course, were an economy and lifestyle based on slavery. The 1860 census showed Florida's population as 140,424, of whom 61,745 were slaves. They belonged to 5,153 owners, or 15 percent of the white population. Many in that 15 percent owned only one or two slaves, and some whites worked on farms and in homes alongside them. Yet, although 85 percent of Floridians owned no slaves at all, virtually all the men who controlled the government held large amounts of human property. Despite rhetoric about constitutional rights, they understood that the coming war for Southern independence was based in their desire to maintain slavery.

When a convention gathered in Tallahassee to amend the state's constitution for secession, a mere seven voted to stay with the United States: the tally to leave the Union was 62–7. The vote was taken on January 10, 1861—and Florida seceded ahead of Georgia, Louisiana, and other states usually considered more rebellious. The news spread quickly, with many Floridians joining in celebration:

> The parades and gun salutes, speeches and toasts, and pure jubilation that greeted the news of secession was evident in every hamlet in Florida. Crowds filled the hotels in Pensacola, Tallahassee, and Jacksonville and danced in the streets amidst torchlight parades and fireworks. Bonfires and the sounds of church bells and cannon-firings were common. Militia units paraded jubilantly. Unionists became cautious and soft-spoken.[3]

Three months before the Fort Sumter engagement regarded as the beginning of the war, shots were fired in January 1861 at Pensacola's Fort Pickens, where Confederates pulled down the U.S. flag. Several contemporary writers, including Elizabeth Cady Stanton, credited women with resisting the rebels, and the Union ultimately prevailed. No first names were recorded for these women, but two were newlyweds married to young lieutenants, Slemmer and Gilmore. They were not, of course, native Floridians, and most Floridians enthusiastically supported the rebellion.

Caroline Mays Brevard later recalled that her Madison County friends—or at least the men among them—were firm in the common Southern belief that they could easily defeat the established government in Washington. "Prominent men predicted that the war would not last sixty days," she said, "and some men offered to drink all the blood that was spilt. The young men were eager to enlist and go forward at once, for fear that the fighting would be over before they arrived."[4]

Elizabeth Randolph Eppes, the Tallahassee granddaughter of Thomas Jefferson, arguably followed his reasoning on the right to declare independence from an incumbent government. An artist, she embellished "The Declaration of Independence of the Sovereign State of Florida" and wrote that she was pleased to present it "on behalf of the ladies . . . of Florida who go heart and hand into the cause."[5] Other women sewed flags for the new government, including at least one in Jacksonville: a few months later, the "Jacksonville Light Artillery" formally thanked "Mrs. Lena Coker for the handsome flag."[6]

Even ethnic minorities who had lived in a semi-slave status during the Spanish era joined the cause of slaveholders. A historian of St. Augustine's Minorcans said that they "were almost all Southern sympathizers" and pointed out that on a still extant "Confederate monument in the plaza of St. Augustine . . . a majority of the names are Minorcan." While these men used rifles, he added, "the women used beauty as their weapon, acting as spies among the Union troops."[7]

Representatives of Florida went in early February to join the Confederate States of America in Montgomery, Alabama; the capital was there until Virginia seceded and Richmond became the Confederate capital. Strategic parts of Florida, however, remained under Union control throughout the war. The U.S. Navy was so superior to that of the new Confederacy that Southern rebels never attempted to occupy key outposts such as Fort Taylor on Key West and Fort Jefferson in the Dry Tortugas. Nor would there be any military action on the nearby mainland of south Florida. Few whites lived south of Bradenton, and Miami, Palm Beach, and other cities of today did not yet exist.

In northeast Florida, in the coastal areas around Jacksonville, many lacked a strong allegiance and were willing to switch sides depending on which army was in control. Spying was most common there, and Union officials fretted about women they suspected "were able to keep in contact with the mainland by use of an intricate system of signals." On further investigation, however, they decided that "the signals were primarily between wives and husbands or sweethearts, and no arrests were made."[8]

Still, most observers agreed that women were more passionate in their political allegiance than men. After Union troops occupied St. Augustine, for instance, a federal official there said: "There is much violent and pestilent

On a Desert in the Ocean

The Dry Tortugas are a group of ten islands sixty miles west of Key West and are the most southern portion of the United States. Because winds keep rain away, the islands are a desert surrounded by salt water. The Army Corps of Engineers built Fort Jefferson there and used it as a prison.

Emily A. Holder moved there just before the Civil War began. She came from Massachusetts in 1859 with her husband, a physician and zoologist employed by the federal government, and their eight-year-old son. She wrote of her first glimpse:

"The exterior of the fort was bare and repulsive, the interior offering a decided contrast. Here were trees of deep green belonging to tropical vegetation, so restful to the eye in the glaring sun. . . . I lost the feeling of being so far away."

She and a handful of other women were surrounded by the fort's male workers—and, as the Civil War wore on, its prisoners. Fort Jefferson was a Union fort and was so impregnable that the Confederacy never threatened it. Most of its prisoners during the war, ironically, were other Northerners—deserters or criminals in the Union Army.

Ironic, too, is the fact that even after the Emancipation Proclamation, slavery remained legal in Union territory. One of the women at the fort was a Mrs. Fogarty, "an immigrant from Ireland who ran the mess hall," and she owned a slave called "Aunt Eliza." Emily Holder had no qualms about hiring this elderly black woman to do her domestic work—with the pay going not to the worker but to her owner, Mrs. Fogarty. Indeed, Holder's writing indicates that she thought Eliza should be grateful to have a room above the kitchen and was shocked that Eliza smoked a pipe, saying she would "smoke until she was dizzy."

Dr. Holder was reassigned in December 1865, the same month that the Thirteenth Amendment abolished slavery. Nothing was said about Aunt Eliza's fate.

Note: Quotations are from Thomas Reid, *America's Fortress: A History of Fort Jefferson, Dry Tortugas, Florida* (Gainesville: University Press of Florida, 2006).

feeling among the women. They seem to mistake treason for courage, and have a theatrical desire to figure as heroines."[9] Several writers attested to the activism of St. Augustine's Confederate women:

> The women . . . had a meeting . . . and cut down the [Union] staff. . . . Mrs. Mitchell [said] the men behaved like cowards, but there were stout hearts in other bosoms, striking her own.

A second observer added:

> The night before the men . . . landed, this pole was cut down by a group of women to prevent the Union flag from ever flying from it. Rumor had it that the first chip was cut by Mrs. Judge Smith. . . . Later the halyards holding up the Union flag were secretly cut, so it came down.

And a third said in a letter:

> I sent old Sam to . . . the flag staff [that] a parcel of the girls had cut down in the square (Anna H. giving it the first blow). . . . The Marshal stopped him, but . . . I paid 50 cts. to help put it up.[10]

Union strategy was to eliminate the St. Johns River as a transportation vehicle for the Confederacy. Such naval blockades inherently mean attacking civilian vessels, and women often were on these ships. Early in 1862, for example, a Union gunboat, the USS *Ottawa,* chased the civilian *Darlington* up the St. Johns, "firing eleven-inch shells. . . . The boat was crowded with men, women, and children," but the captain refused to surrender—despite "appeals by the women on their bended knees, for God's sake, to surrender." Doubtless more concerned with losing his cargo than with loss of life, he surrendered only after he accidentally ran aground.[11]

The situation had been reversed the previous year, when Confederates succeeded in capturing a Union vessel off the coast of Fernandina. In that case "the Yankee captain, his wife, and a negro were aboard, who refused to come ashore, and who raised the American flag." A mob of several hundred gathered and forced them off the boat; they put the woman ashore by tying "a rope around her waist and lowering her down."[12] Senator David Yulee managed to calm the crowd and invited the frightened woman to his home.

Transplanted Yankees indeed could expect trouble, but some nonetheless made their views known. According to historian Tracy Revels, Clarissa Anderson was "a wealthy Boston-born widow and bastion of St. Augustine society"—but she "canceled her newspaper subscription in 1861, unwilling to pay for the *St. Augustine Examiner* because it advocated that "all Unionists leave the Oldest City or 'be hung.'"[13]

Secessionist feeling was strongest in the Panhandle, an area that still reflects the culture of nearby Georgia and Alabama. In Tallahassee, Ellen Call Long lived surrounded by Confederates, although she deplored leaving the Union, as did her father, former governor Richard Keith Call. He died of natural causes during the war, and she kept her opposition quiet after secession became a fact. She had been around politics long enough to become cynical, as she said in a letter soon after the war begun:

> Men seem to join the Southern forces, throw up batteries, contribute money and material, then . . . spend a few weeks, gather together their families and effects, and either go abroad or back to their homes. . . . Persons claiming to be Union . . . live within the seceded States [and] help along the disunion cause. Others . . . avow secession, yet carry the stars and stripes. . . . A very civil war, indeed![14]

The Union initially hoped that Pensacola would stay loyal like Key West and did not move to reinforce its forts. Southerners quietly occupied them, but the situation remained so calm that Virginia Clayton of Eufaula, Alabama, took a pleasure trip to visit her husband's regiment. She found other Confederate women doing the same, "occupying houses in the Navy Yard . . . filled with lovely flowers, roses, geraniums, and bright little annuals."[15]

That changed as diplomacy failed to work; the war got serious; and the United States tried to retake its forts. In the words of a modern historian, Pensacola became "the scene of invasion, occupation, skirmishing and foraging, bombardment, a scorched-earth strategy, massive deployment of troops, a Union naval blockade, and refugees."[16] Virtually all of the population fled inland after naval bombardment destroyed the town—some five thousand shells were fired in two days in 1861. That December, "during the shelling of the Pensacola navy yard, . . . the wife of a Marine Corps sergeant was killed."[17]

Newly married Mary Caro Gromley was one of the few civilians who stayed in Pensacola, and when she and her family finally left in mid-1863, she worried about repercussions from Confederate friends who would condemn them for living under Union occupation. After leaving their once beautiful mansion for the coastal town of Warrington, the family found refuge in a structure that had been built for an Odd Fellows hall, there being one large room on the first floor and another in the second story with a small room off one end. . . . I was almost afraid to go to sleep as there was no shutters or glass to the windows and also no doors. But I was so tired I went to sleep. . . . [My] heart ached to think that my parents had to live in such a place.[18]

* * *

In coastal cities throughout the South, residents fled inland. Countless women had to welcome kin who lived in dangerous places—sometimes for months and years. Not only were these refugees needy, but so was the Confederate military itself. It never had the resources for such a serious war, and this soon became apparent to legislators. In the same 1861 session that took Florida out of the Union, lawmakers appropriated ten thousand dollars for the Ladies Military Aid Society. Based in the Tallahassee area, society members used the money for cloth that they sewed into uniforms. As the Union blockade of Florida's ports proved successful, however, importing cloth would become all but impossible.

Although the South grew cotton, it had not developed textile mills, and some women therefore relearned their grandmothers' skills of spinning and weaving. Susan Bradford Eppes attributed most of this skill and teaching to female slaves. "In nearly every [slave] quarters," she said, "some old woman could be found and employed with the spinning of either cotton or wool into knitting yarn." By 1862, she wrote, "the whirl of the wheel and the noise of [its] baton could be heard in almost every house."[19]

Spinning wheels produced yarn that then could be knitted into respectable-looking socks and sweaters, but loom-woven fabric remained scarce. Even upper-class women simply patched old clothes until the cloth was literally threadbare. Lake City's Mrs. M. M. Scarborough wrote that when supplies did reach the area, "a great crowd of us hurried . . . , hoping we might be able to purchase at least a calico dress, but after . . . our long ride, we had to be content with our homespun dresses."[20]

Getting shoes was likewise problematic. All factories were in the North, and especially late in the war, many Floridians went barefoot. Even Eppes, the teenage daughter of one of Florida's most prominent families, wrote in April 1864: "Today I have no shoes to put on. . . . The very touch of my bare foot to the ground made me shiver." She dealt with the crisis by creating shoes made of soft cornhusks and scraps of velvet, which she said, "made everybody laugh," but she felt "quite proud."[21] Women wore bonnets woven of palmetto fiber, another skill had that to be relearned. "Dixie Bonnets" became popular, selling in Tallahassee for a costly ten dollars.

Most Florida soldiers served outside the state, which meant that they endured unaccustomed winters. Again the military was not prepared, and soldiers sent home letters asking for warm underwear. Women collected shoes and blankets for them too and, like women in the North, held fundraisers to buy supplies that the government did not provide. Catherine Hopley, an English governess for the children of Governor John Milton, was cynical about the peer pressure that women put on each other to sacrifice for the new government. She wrote in 1862:

> At this time there was a perfect *furore* throughout the Confederacy for Ladies gunboat funds: Having supplied their soldiers with winter clothing . . . , their attention has turned to the gunboats. . . .
>
> Ladies were forming societies for this object. One saw columns of names and subscriptions [donations] in the papers. Those who had money gave it, those who had not gave [silver] plate and Jewelry.[22]

When the *Florida Sentinel* announced the fund drive, it named women who had "already donated" and listed "$5 and 2 silver forks; $2 and one pair of sugar tongs; 1 fork, 1 spoon, and 1 napkin ring."[23] The silver would be melted down and used to support the Confederate dollar, which decreased in value as time went on. Whatever the money was worth, however, fundraisers continued—including a Tallahassee concert in the House of Representatives that raised eight hundred dollars on April 9, 1865—two days after the South surrendered.

Women in Jefferson and Madison counties raised money with suppers and plays; in the north Florida town of Quincy, two concerts raised more than twenty-three hundred dollars. In addition to money, women made and sent things: they fashioned fans of palmetto leaves to cool hospitalized soldiers in summer; in fall and early winter they sent as much ripe citrus as wagons could carry before frost arrived. They did such work enthusiastically, and Ellen Call Long wrote:

> I don't know how the women would do if they had to go to be shot at, but as it is, they are tremendous in the desire to fight, and certainly those in [Military Aid Society] offices . . . are indefatigable. . . . Night

> and day is spent cutting out and making clothing. . . . The most delicate and refined women [are] devoting themselves to nursing the sick, tending the hospital and taking soldiers into their own homes. . . . All delicacies are reserved for the hospitals; jellies, preserves, pickles, wines and condiments made at home are not used as formerly in hospitality, but sacredly kept for the soldiers far and near.[24]

Some soldiers indeed were "near," as women took individual men into their own homes—men who were traveling on furloughs and/or after they had been discharged because of wounds or illness. There were few trains in the South, and most soldiers did not own horses; they walked literally hundreds of miles, and injured men especially needed breaks to recuperate before moving on. The most prominent of these "soldiers' homes" was the Monticello mansion of the aptly named Mrs. Guardian. It became so popular that the legislature appropriated money to assist H. Louisa Guardian.[25] Florida also had six official Confederate hospitals. Each had fewer than one hundred beds, however, and the six were relatively close together: two at Madison and one each at Lake City, Tallahassee, Quincy, and Mariana.

Most women who wanted to nurse went where they were most needed—Virginia. The first major battle was on July 21, 1861, at Manassas, Virginia, between the U.S. capital of Washington and the Confederate capital of Richmond. The area would be regularly visited by cruel war for the next four years, as both sides won and lost huge battles that involved tens of thousands of men. Tallahassee's Ruth McLean was in Richmond and exchanged letters with Ellen Call Long. As the combat went on, McLean summarized:

> Our women are most active and generous in lending their aid wherever needed. Many articles indispensable to the soldier are impossible to be purchased within Southern limits. Women, inventive and ever ready to help in an emergency, have given carpets [to cover the ground in tents], piano-covers [to do the same], blankets; all and everything that can be useful. . . . No moment is idle—in the [railroad] cars traveling, visiting, in the dark and in the light—the knitting needle is going perpetually.[26]

The most prominent among Florida women who served in Richmond was Mary Martha Reid, the widow of former governor Robert Raymond Reid. She worked hard at the difficult business of running Florida's hospital in Richmond and was especially affected by the war when her own son was killed in 1864. After that tragedy, Floridian Ruth McLean, who also was in Richmond, wrote that Reid was "filling the waste places of her heart in painful labor. . . . In the hospital and on the field, she mingles [her tears] with motherly tenderness for the despairing, stricken, home-sick soldier."[27]

Not all soldiers and sailors were nursed because they were injured: equal numbers were sick with the diseases that war brings to men who live without proper nutrition and sanitation. Pensacola Bay, for instance, was already full of sick men before the end of 1861, and Confederate General Braxton Bragg asked Catholic officials to send nursing nuns. When Sisters of Charity came there from Mobile, they found deplorable conditions. A measles epidemic had spread to at least eight hundred soldiers, some of whom had no choice but "to lie on the floor with their knapsacks under their poor heads and one blanket . . . fairly alive with vermin and fleas."[28] Sister Mary Agnes wrote:

> A few days after our arrival, I asked the daily physician if he knew that nearly all the fever cases had very serious bed sores and some were fetid with gangrene and two others' clothing had grown into their backs. . . . We could not induce the . . . [male medics] to assist in cleaning or purifying their sores. . . . [It] required a strong stomach and cologne was in great demand.[29]

For most men, being in any hospital at all was a new experience, and most also were prejudiced against the Catholic women who tried to nurse them. Sister Agnes said some Pensacola patients took several days to accept the sisters' services: "they covered their heads with blankets," she wrote, "and nothing would induce them to uncover them." Within a short time, however, the Sisters were running the Pensacola Naval Hospital—still occupied by Confederate troops—with such efficiency that a soldier described it as "large, well lighted and well ventilated; the walls, furniture, and bedding scrupulously clean." He added that "dressed in black and wearing white sun-bonnets," the Sisters of Charity "were often seen fluttering through the wards."[30]

* * *

Tampa's Sophia Crane is an example of the hard choices women faced when the men in their lives developed differing political views. Although a Florida native, she went with her husband to his New Jersey home, while her son joined the Confederacy and lived the rest of his life in Florida. Tampa, however, suffered less than other towns. It was true that gunboats invaded in June 1862, October 1863, and May 1864, but Union troops did not find Fort Brooke or anything else worthy of their continued presence.

To the north, two Gulf Coast communities had strategic importance: Union troops burned the Levy mansion near Homasassa and destroyed its sugar mill, while Cedar Key was important because of its saltworks. In a time before refrigeration, salt was vital to preserving meat—and marching men on both sides of the war depended on beef jerky and salt pork. Cedar Key also was the terminus of the only railroad that Florida had, which ran there from Fernandina Beach on the Atlantic Ocean.

Fernandina merchants also had strong shipping ties with the North, and the town surrendered soon after the war began. Nearby Jacksonville, however, was different: it was invaded four times, including in 1862, when Union troops "began an orgy of destruction." Among the buildings burned was a hotel run by the Keene family, and "a bullet passed through Mrs. Keene's bonnet."[31]

By 1864 the state was spending more than $290,000 in aid to 13,248 Floridians, but such aid often was distributed according to the whim of the dispensing official.[32] The lack of defined rules left women subject to inequity based on social status or friendships as well as to sexual harassment. Most women simply supported themselves and their children as best they could.

Amanda Comerford, who lived near the Peace River in central Florida, wrote that when her husband enlisted, "he left me on a farm with . . . four small children . . . and these responsibilities were afterwards added to by the birth of twins." Not only did he leave her heavily pregnant; she doubtless had to do the farm work. Probably a cow had to be milked, chickens fed and eggs gathered, water pulled from a well, wood gathered, and so forth. As the oldest child was eleven and she mentioned no slave or hired help, she had much work on her hands: "It is difficult to describe my struggles to provide food and clothing for this large family. . . . But somehow I managed to survive through as did many other women during these trying times."[33]

She had every right to be angry with her husband. Gainesville's Mrs. L. W. Jackson remained angry much later, especially with those who failed to give women any credit for their hard work. "No historian," she wrote, "dipped his pen in ink to tell of the grand and glorious deeds of this or that *woman*. . . . How she spent her days in at hard labour to provide for her fatherless children and then half of the night spinning and weaving cloth . . . and even making shoes for their tiny feet. It is beyond the power of the Historian or his pen to picture her . . . [and] her mental sufferings."[34]

Others said it would have been easier to describe what women did *not* do during the war than to summarize what they did. Three women, one of them unmarried, later recounted:

> Every where women did man's work, as well as women's. They curried leather, did blacksmithing, plowing, cobbling. They made fence, drove ox-carts, went to mill, repaired the furniture, drenched sick horses, butchered hogs, set traps for the thieving larks and crows, pulled the corn and hauled it to the barn. It would be [a] much easier task to tell what they did not do.[35]

But if they resented these newly imposed roles, comparatively few said so. Martha A. Robertson, who lived on the edge of civilization in little-settled Orlando, was cheerful and sensible, without a complaint in her letter. Part of a small network of female farmers who helped one another, she wrote to her soldier husband on March 27, 1864:

> I seat my Self to inform you that we are all well at this time and I hope these fiew lines will find you in good health I have no news to write much the children is all hearty And the baby grose a rite smart and he is a good boy and the Pretyest you ever saw and Alice has quit crying you wanted to no what we got to eat we got Patatoes and a little milk. . . . I have got Some cane planted and this peas and corn hear by the house and it looks verry well And I have got all the rest of the ground . . . ready to plant when I can get a horse to plant it with . . . Two of the sows has got pigs But I . . . couldn't find them . . . I received a letter from you on the 18th of this month that was rote on the 8th of March and I was glad . . . to hear you was well.[36]

* * *

War would not directly affect her little Orlando community, but it became real in the Jacksonville area soon after its beginning at Fort Sumter, South Carolina, just off the coast of Charleston. Union ships soon took over the Sea Islands farther south, including Nassau County's Amelia Island and Little Talbot Island. The United States controlled this area so thoroughly that by

1862 large numbers of slaves, called "contrabands," escaped from the mainland to freedom on these islands. Ellen Long Call quoted a letter from a friend who lived on the St. Johns River near Jacksonville:

> A few nights after the Yankees came up the river, father discovered our servants [slaves] about to bid farewell to the place; so next morning he packed them all off to the interior. Can you imagine how we got along without a single servant? I assure you that we have some funny experience, and cut, burnt, and sore fingers enough. However, now we are more accustomed to house-work and manage quite well. . . . It is impossible to keep Negroes now, so father determined it was better to have a home without servants. . . . So we stay here living on cornbread and hope, our only consolation that we are no worse off than our neighbors.[37]

Many black people understandably fled to Union armies whenever they appeared. Others did not, and some even assisted their owners in the crisis. When St. Augustine was invaded, for example, H. B. Jenckes wrote to an absent friend about a sympathetic report from his "servant," which was the polite term for household slaves. "Your servant Lucy," he said, "came here this morning and wished me to write." Someone had broken into the mansion in Lucy's absence, "and everything was taken out . . . and the books strewn all over the floor. And Lucy [was] robbed of . . . the best of her clothes."[38]

Occasionally, the usual status actually reversed, as fleeing slave owners abandoned slaves who were not valuable enough to be worth transporting. In Pensacola, for example, a Union officer wrote of one such case, a woman who was "trying to read and is learning very fast. . . . Her children are all in slavery, [but] she was too sick to be moved when the rebels fled, and was left to live or die as best she could."[39]

Even healthy contrabands posed a problem for Union officers. On the one hand, officers welcomed escapees because their arrival meant that the Confederacy had lost the value of slave labor—but at the same time military men had no desire to cope with refugees. Most were women and children of no military value, and even the men generally were unskilled and had no assets. A Union officer near Jacksonville described the situation to the *Philadelphia Inquirer* on April 5, 1862:

> A scene of the wildest confusion exists here. Masters are running and leaving their negroes with no one to look after them. . . . The lines of the

railroad are thronged with refugees, and bread is sold to them at $1 per loaf. Some of them have no place to go and are starving in the woods.[40]

But Northern white women soon came to distribute food and clothing—and went on to build schools and orphanages. Among the first in Florida were Chloe Merrick, Cornelia Smith, and Sarah Slocum. When they arrived at Amelia Island in autumn of 1862, they found that most plantation owners had fled, and some of their former slaves, both children and adults, had created a school in an unused Episcopal church. Within a few months, Merrick wrote, "seventy or eighty pupils had learned the alphabet and some were able to read."[41]

Sarah Slocum probably gave her life to the cause: she died in Fernandina in 1864, likely because of subtropical heat, mosquitoes, and poor public sanitation that led to disease. Indeed, as much as teachers, such women were

Confidence amidst Crisis: College in Wartime

Florida in the 1860s had no institution that could be called a college—for either men or women—but its neighbor to the north, Georgia, has a legitimate claim to having the first to call itself a college for women. Georgia Female College began in Macon in 1836, and it survives today as Wesleyan College. Tampa's Emma Miller went there in 1863, but the next year Macon fell to Union troops, and communications with Florida were cut. Emma and her family did not hear from each other for a year and a half.

The college closed for just two weeks of General William T. Sherman's devastating 1864 march through Georgia, but without money from home to pay her tuition, young Miss Miller arranged to teach school at Cuthbert, in western Georgia. When the war ended in 1865, she was able to go home for summer vacation. Instead of traveling through the war-torn land, she went by boat down the Chattahoochee River to the Apalachicola River and the Gulf. She returned to college that fall and graduated in 1866—as valedictorian.

That enabled her to be hired as a mathematics professor at Cuthbert's newer Andrew Female College. Emma Miller probably was Florida's first female college graduate and almost certainly was its first female professor. Marriage later changed her name to Edwards, and she died back in Tampa in the 1887 yellow fever epidemic.

nurses and social workers—professions that had not yet formally developed. Nor could they necessarily expect support from Unionists, and some military men even exploited their young black pupils sexually. Merrick later wrote of a former student impregnated and abandoned by a white soldier: in frustration and anger, Merrick said, "We cry out from the depths of our soul, God, what lessons art thou teaching the nation in this scourge thou art permitting thus to visit this oppressed people?"[42]

Such women also functioned as executives, usually raising the money for the budgets they administrated. In the summer of 1863 Merrick returned to the North to raise money for the Fernandina project. The *Syracuse Journal* reported that at a dinner meeting, her "remarks were of an interesting character, giving an account of her labors among the refugees in Florida," especially the "dire needs of Florida's blacks and orphans."[43]

Several such Sea Island women kept diaries of this unusual place and time, and the one most pertinent to Florida was that of Dr. Esther Hill Hawks of Lynn, Massachusetts. Her husband was also a physician, and in July 1864 they went together from Port Royal, South Carolina, for what she wryly termed "the third annual conquest of Florida"—meaning the third time that Union troops headquartered themselves in the nearly defenseless city of Jacksonville.

The objective was to capture a Confederate supply depot near Lake City, and Dr. Hawks thus was part of Florida's largest Civil War confrontation—the Battle of Olustee, northeast of Lake City. Confederates inflicted a big loss on the Union, which suffered almost two thousand casualties. Survivors quickly retreated to Jacksonville, and Dr. Hawks jotted in her diary:

> The work of repairs went bravely on—and by 1 p.m. the wounds are all dressed. The men fed and supplied with clean shirts and clean straw to lie in. Most of the wounds are comparatively light—but many of them may prove severe from . . . exhaustion from the long march. Many touching instances of friendliness occurred among our patients, who were a mixed company of black and white . . . The black Regts [regiments] had borne the fiercest onslaught of the enemy, and the white soldiers were loud in their praise. . . . When I saw white soldiers sharing their tobacco with the black ones, I concluded that . . . the millennium had begun![44]

Such black regiments were experimental, and many whites on both sides were surprised at how determinedly they fought. Some of these men may have been recruited by the famed Harriet Tubman, who spent most of the era scouting around the Sea Islands and running a hospital for black soldiers in Beaufort, South Carolina. Confederate men reacted to these former slaves in uniform with extreme anger, and when Confederates won, as at Olustee, black soldiers would not be taken as prisoners of war: instead, they were murdered, usually brutally, on the field of battle. They therefore had genuine reason to fight to the death—and the same was true for black women caught in similar circumstances. They could expect not only brutality but also rape.

A teenager called Sarah took the risk of joining the Union soldiers, and she especially impressed Dr. Hawks:

> She is, apparently, about fourteen—quite black, good features—bright and keen. . . . She belonged to a Mrs. Brooks, living sixteen miles beyond Lake City. . . . On hearing that the Yankees were so near . . . , they [came] the whole eighty miles on foot—the women toting the babies. Sarah shows more bitterness in speaking of her old mistress than I have ever seen. She says—"I'll always hate her 'cos she never gave me 'nuff to eat. . . ." The greatest incentive she has to learn is that she may be able to write to her old mistress to tell her that she has "bacon and hominy and rice, too, all I can eat, and if you come here I'd like to see you starve."[45]

* * *

Although the Confederacy won at Olustee, the Union was winning more significant battles farther north, and some Southerners began to realize that they would lose. Especially after the Confederacy started drafting men in April 1862, many poor whites felt betrayed. The conscription of soldiers was class based in both the North and South, with wealthy men able to buy substitutes, and even Confederates who had enlisted enthusiastically began to see this as "a rich man's war and a poor man's fight."

Some historians estimate that as many as one in every ten Confederate soldiers deserted. Truly crass men repeatedly deserted and reenlisted for the money, but as it became evident that the South would not prevail, more Floridians deserted permanently and came home to hide. Some went as far south as the islands around Fort Myers, where wives and children joined them in a lifestyle much like that of the persecuted Seminoles.

Even Ruth McLean, who had strongly supported secession, became ambivalent—especially after Confederate President Jefferson Davis called on

Sarah Pamela Williams and the Battle of Olustee

A young widow with a toddler son when the war began, Sarah Pamela Williams ran a farm at Ocean Pond, which now is part of the Osceola National Forest near Lake City. Because her brother-in-law had gone to fight in Virginia, she explained, "my sister and her two children were living with us." The "us" referred to her fourteen-year-old nephew Norman and her slaves: an unmarried man called Jiggins and a family composed of Henry, Bet, and their children. She wrote of the Battle of Olustee, which occurred on February 20, 1864, as well as the years that followed:

> I shall never forget the day of that battle. From early morning, vehicles of all sorts and descriptions, filled with people, traversed the public road in front of my house, fleeing from the town and seeking safety in the settlements south of us. I was having sugar cane planted back of the kitchen, and Henry, my oldest negro man, advised me to bury some provisions in case the Yankees did come. I told him to go ahead and so he and Jiggins, the other negro man, dug a hole and buried in boxes—meat, salt, sugar and other necessities . . .
>
> We gave tithes of all our crops (except cotton) to the Confederate States Government. . . . Poor Norman and all of our neighbors' boys had to go into the army or navy at sixteen years of age. . . .
>
> We heard the news of General Lee's surrender at Appomattox with anguish—to us it was as though the heavens had fallen. My brother-in-law had been taken prisoner at Gettysburg and my sister didn't hear anything of him. . . . When at last he returned to us, he was quite broken down. . . .
>
> We all saw hard times for several years after the war closed. The negroes were declared free in May 1865 in our part of the country. Jiggins left me immediately, though he attended to the crops on the land I let him use. . . . Henry, Bet, and their children remained for eight months until the crops were gathered in. I gave Henry a fourth of all we made. As I furnished the seed, land, horses and mules, that was a lawful division.

Note: From James M. Denham and Canter Brown Jr., eds., *Cracker Times and Pioneer Lives: The Florida Reminiscences of George Gillett Keen and Sarah Pamela Williams* (Columbia: University of South Carolina Press, 2000), 121–23.

women to report deserters. She quoted the *Richmond Enquirer*, adding from her personal knowledge that Florida was indeed a haven for draft dodgers:

> In desperation President Davis appeals to the women of the Confederacy, that they "will make so intolerable those who linger that they dare not. . . . They know those stragglers, one by one, and where they are to be found. They, the mothers and sisters, may, if they will, be a conscript guard impossible to evade. . . ." Florida is a refuge; so all who linger here are not her sons. . . .
>
> My desponding patriotism may incline me to consider matters not my province . . . , but the appeal of President Davis to women to countenance no home chivalry . . . would not prevent . . . men from staying at home. And we hear of women who fell trees, roll logs, clear fields, and plant and grow crops.[46]

When a woman such as she expressed ambivalence about Confederate policy, it is not surprising that lower-class families gave up on the South. A semi-literate Madison County man wrote to his mother from an unspecified Northern battlefront in December 1863: "Wright to me [if] Brother Ben is gone back to Virginia and Tell Him If He Haint Gone Not Go Take the Woods First."[47]

Many men indeed took to the woods, especially around north Florida's Econfina, Fenholloway, and Aucilla rivers. Hundreds of people, including women and children, stayed with men who hid in the wilderness rather than go north to continue the war. So many deserters and draft evaders were in the area by 1864 that Confederate cavalry units systematically destroyed the property of people they believed were aiding deserters. Families whose homes were wiped out were sent to Camp Smith near Tallahassee, where—in a sad forerunner to modern concentration camps—they were imprisoned until Governor Milton protested this war "on women and children."

Milton's own household, too, was feeling the pain of the war that, just months earlier, he had thought would be so easy. Family governess Catherine Hopley returned to England midway through the war, while Florida's first family was suffering. Hopley said of conditions in Tallahassee:

> Of medicines there were none. . . . Stimulants there were none . . . [We were] without mustard, black pepper, and many other trifles. . . . We often had no rice . . . , no white sugar, very little molasses, no more tea, and no more imported fruits. The cook was limited in her baking for

want of [baking] soda. . . . Mrs. Milton was in perpetual dread of illness on account of the scarcity of medicines. Quinine sold for twenty dollars an ounce; castor oil, twenty dollars a gallon . . . ; common cotton cloths . . . half a dollar a yard; children's shoes, and very inferior ones, from three dollars upwards; full-sized shoes from five to ten dollars a pair; and other things in proportion.[48]

Rum from Cuba, however, was widely available at a fairly low price, as that was what blockade-runners valued. Piracy and profiteering added to the cynicism, and many women began to question their previous beliefs. The Stephens family, for instance, was well established on plantations in Marion, Putnam, and Clay counties, but by 1864 some were refugees—along with their slaves. Their men had gone to war, and Augustina (Tina) Stephens referred to herself as "alone" when she wrote to Octavia ("Tivie") Stephens about her evacuation from her Putnam County home of Welaka. Clearly, however, she had help from slaves—and more interestingly, some of the slaves rode, while some of her children walked. In a long letter without paragraphs, she said on June 19, 1864:

My own dear Tivie

You no doubt will be surprised . . . to hear that we are homeless. . . . Soon after I wrote last to you Welaka was occupied by . . . 17th Connecticut troops. . . . You may imagine my feelings all alone no one to exchange a thought with and in hourly expectation of those Devils riding up and burning the house over my head. . . . I had the oxen [brought] up and had borrowed Mr Bassfords horse cart, expecting the Emergency, so in a short time one Boat was full of our things. . . . [Ten-year-old daughter] Minnie and I rode on old Charley. . . . [Sons] Willey, Louis, and [slave] Sophia walked nearly every step of the way, and [slave] Minja with [son] Charlie and [slave] Mary, rode on the cart. . . . The old place and all of your things were burned to the ground.[49]

Six months later, after deaths in the family, Tina was truly despondent. She wrote cynically to Tivie from a temporary home near Ocala on January 8, 1865:

No one knows the mortification one has to endure to get barely enough to keep soul and body together. I went yesterday and tried to get a little cotton for spinning from Col Martin (enormously wealthy)

> and as a great favour and only to accommodate me [he] let me have a few pounds for two dollars and a half a pound. Aint that patriotism . . .
>
> I see no Earthly hope for our success now, we hear that [Jefferson] Davis has gone to Europe deserted in time to save his neck and that his Coffin was taken out and buried in Richmond to express his fate and the public sentiment, but I do not credit any such a report, it is only raised by some enemy or friends to the Yankees, but I really believe we are whipped.[50]

She was right, although instead of fleeing, President Davis fought on for more deadly months. After Atlanta fell late in 1864, the massive Union army marched south through Georgia and went into South Carolina, where the war had begun at Charleston. Dr. Esther Hawks was in Florida when she wrote in her diary on March 26, 1865, "Glory to God! Charleston has fallen!"[51] Fighting was fierce in Virginia, but Union troops entered the Confederate capital of Richmond on April 3, 1865, and Confederate General Robert E. Lee officially surrendered to Union General U.S. Grant on April 7.

Mary Martha Reid fled Richmond as it fell, along with Confederate officials who hurried south in the hope of finding a ship and exiling themselves in the Caribbean or Europe. Confederate Attorney General George Davis fled to the isolated Columbia County plantation of his cousin, Mrs. Thomas Hill Lane; after months of elusive travel down the Florida peninsula, he was captured at Key West. Secretary of State Judah P. Benjamin hid at the Gamble Mansion in Manatee County and managed to board a ship to England. Confederate Navy Secretary Stephen Mallory made it to LaGrange, Georgia, where Angela Moreno Mallory had fled from Virginia—but Union officials soon traced him, and he was imprisoned for the next two years.[52] Dr. Samuel Mudd, who treated John Wilkes Booth for the leg that Booth broke in Lincoln's assassination, was imprisoned in the Dry Tortugas. Governor John Milton, one of the war's strongest advocates, saw its results and killed himself on April 1.

That was two weeks before Lincoln's assassination on April 14, but Tallahassee did not fall until May 10, when Union troops quietly occupied it. It was the only capital city in the South that had not rated Union attention—which was a mark of how far from important Florida remained. Yet even though their state was not a major battleground, Floridians made great sacrifices: out of a white population of about 70,000, some 14,000 men served in the Confederate Army. Another 2,000 or more Floridians joined Union forces, almost half of them blacks who enlisted during the last two years of the war. Some of them died, as did about a third of the Confederate men. Thousands of women became widows, and many more women lived with men who were mentally or physically disabled for the rest of their lives.

Almost all Floridians suffered economically. Especially in Jacksonville and Pensacola, most homes were damaged. Even if a house remained standing, refugees found when they returned that things had been vandalized or stolen. Soldiers on both sides confiscated horses, mules, and other animals that were essential to farm families. Already midway through the war in Pensacola, for example, "poor whites, who have come in from the surrounding country to avoid starvation and the conscription" helped themselves to the contents of abandoned homes. Some Union officers also abused their rank by taking valuables: one directed his soldiers to move four pianos to the mansion that he occupied, including one that was "carved rosewood, reported to be worth $1,500."[53] Others shipped the confiscated property of Florida women to their wives or sweethearts in the North.

Pensacola's Fannie Bushnell Stevens was one whose home was pillaged by the piano-stealing commander. She thought he "must have been crazy, for while he took much of value, he also took [family mementos], which could have no possible use or value to him."[54] He may have been drunk with power—or simply drunk. It is possible, too, that his motivation was not greed but instead anger against secessionists who started the war. In situations such as this, few took time to determine the political views of the owner whose home was plundered: although a mansion might belong to cruel slave owners, it might also be the property of Union loyalists. But pillagers did not ponder such matters.

* * *

Doubtless because of the leadership of quiet Unionist Ellen Call Long, Florida women led the nation in their willingness to forget and forgive. They met in Tallahassee on June 22, 1865—just a month after federal troops occupied their city—to organize a Memorial Association. Showing themselves to be fine diplomats, the Tallahassee women adopted a statement on the tragic war just ended. They spelled out their thoughts:

> The object of this meeting is to initiate a Memorial Association . . . that shall perpetuate in an honorable manner the memory of the gallant dead, who sacrificed life in our defense.

> Our purpose is . . . to reclaim from oblivion and defamation the memory and graves of those who, right or wrong, stood by their country's cause, firmly believing that when the clouds of prejudice are dissipated, posterity will acknowledge "we did our duty. . . ."
>
> In no invidious spirit do we come; the political storm that shook our country to its foundation, we hope, is passed. . . . We are done with the cause . . . and are willing to do all that women can do to stem the tide of bitterness . . . and angry feelings. . . . We will practice and teach forbearance and patience, that must finally bring peace and justice.[55]

Having lost the war, of course, meant that men who had been traitors to the United States were disenfranchised, and Union soldiers—some of them black—enforced martial law. Legislatures throughout the South were taken over by (male) white liberals and educated black men, and they amended state statutes to provide civil liberties for former slaves. More than in other Confederate states, however, Union officials in Florida were willing to please powerful whites, and Florida's revised 1865 constitution retained many vestiges of the past.

Blacks could testify in court, for example, but only in cases involving other blacks. Punishments also varied by race, so that a black person was flogged for offenses for which a white was merely fined—which almost invariably meant that it was a white man who took a whip to a black woman's body. Strict laws on vagrancy also were aimed at newly freed slaves: they were passed at a time when "vagrancy" was especially likely because many blacks were homeless, having been forced to leave plantations by owners no longer willing to feed them. Worse, if an alleged vagrant could not pay the court's fine, his or her labor could be sold as payment.

Florida's "black codes" made it illegal to sell a gun to a black person, and it was a crime for a black to "enter a public assembly of white persons or any vehicle reserved for whites"; both these "crimes" incurred a penalty of thirty-nine lashes. "The rape of a white woman, or assault with intent to rape" merited the death penalty—but the law said nothing about the rape of black women.[56]

Even if laws were fair, administrators often applied them unfairly. For example, Jackson County officials allowed Mary Jane Baker, a black woman, to swear out a warrant for the arrest of William Parker, "a white man who had beaten her"—and charged her six dollars for the warrant, while he was fined five dollars for his crime. Not even Freedman's Bureau officials could

The Graves of Strangers and the Beginning of Memorial Day

The Tallahassee women who began the 1865 Memorial Association spelled out their premises and proposals:

> To every battle-field Florida gave her . . . youth, whose unmarked graves extend from Yorktown to the Gulf, which to neglect or ignore, would haunt us. . . . It was woman's tender fingers that twined the Palmetto Cockade, that presented the banner; it was her bright smile . . . that sent him forward to duty and too often to death; and it is woman now that shall preserve from reproach and forgetfulness our brave soldier dead.
>
> The object of this meeting is to organize a society that shall not be ephemeral in its character, but a permanent institution . . . , establishing an Anniversary of Memorial Observances, the object of which will be to renew and ornament . . . the graves of soldiers, whether strangers or Florida's own sons. . . .
>
> This society proposes, moreover, to make provision for the education of as many children of deceased soldiers in every county of the State of Florida . . . as may be compatible with the means of said Association. It is hoped that it will be unanimously agreed upon to have the proposed monument placed in the capitol grounds of Tallahassee.
>
> Our stern alarums are not charged to merry meetings, nor are "our brows crowned with victorious wreaths," and worse than all, we are not sure that we have secured the peace that valor extends to valor, or which brother should meet brother. The memories of the past are written in blood, and cannot be effaced. But forward we must, crushed, oppressed, and heartsick. Yet we shall not forget.*

Other organizations, often called Women's Relief Societies or similar names, soon began in both the North and South—but Tallahassee's Memorial Association, which announced its aims just weeks after the war ended, probably was the first in the nation.

Note: * From Ellen Call Long, *Florida Breezes; or, Florida New and Old*, originally published in 1883; reprinted with an introduction by Margaret Louise Chapman (Gainesville: University of Florida Press, 1962).

be trusted to take the side of newly free women, as Baker County's Martha Richardson discovered. Mrs. James DeWitt ordered Richardson to do laundry as in the past, and when Richardson refused the job, DeWitt got a judge to rule that the former slave was a vagrant—and the Freedman's Bureau refused to intervene.[57]

Hernando County's Adeline Frierson behaved like DeWitt, as though she could not accept that she no longer owned human property. In 1867, two years after the war was over, she tried to collect the wages of her former slave. The local court granted her the right to do so, but a military official countermanded it.[58] That was not always the case, though, and in scenes akin to slave auctions in the past, the labor of blacks was sold for allegedly unpaid debts—sometimes in humiliating circumstances, such as on public squares or courthouse steps.

Understandably, there was violence, especially in north Florida, where blacks were the majority, and both black and white women were victims. In March 1867 "a Mrs. Rushing, the wife of a minister, was murdered in Gainesville by a freedman who sought revenge."[59] In Jacksonville the next month, "a Negro living with a white woman was riddled with bullets as he lay in bed with her."[60] In the Ocala area in 1868, "a pregnant white housewife, a Mrs. Dupree, was brutally murdered near Orange Springs by a Negro. The culprit was seized by a mob of Negroes, given 100 lashes, and hanged."[61] The situation worsened after the 1868 election: Unionists won and federal troops withdrew, feeling secure that the law could be enforced. Resentful former Confederates and their new Ku Klux Klan soon retook power through terror.

White men ambushed black people on their way to a picnic in Mariana, and a two-year-old boy was killed. A Jewish merchant there, who had spent the war in the North and was a known Unionist, was kidnapped and killed because he told blacks he would sell them guns; he left a widow and children. A few days later in September 1869, young Maggie McClellan was shot dead as she sat on the veranda of the Mariana Hotel with her father and another Confederate man, the presumed target. The cycle of violence continued as the would-be victim led an attack on Matt Nickels. A mob of white men attacked the Nickels's home and forced him, "his wife, and his young son to march a quarter-mile to a limesink and there slaughtered all three of them. A daughter who had escaped . . . witnessed the killings from a distance."[62]

Anarchy prevailed, as ostensible law enforcement officials failed to enforce the law. In Clay County a black couple, Samuel and Hannah Tutson, "were flagrantly assaulted and brutally beaten by some white men, including a deputy sheriff."[63] On the other side of the state, in Washington County, a reformist government tried to protect black rights—with the result that "the state tax collector and his wife were brutally murdered."[64] In Baker County the Klan targeted R. W. Cone, a white man who had served on a jury that convicted a leading conservative:

> On the night of June 24, 1871, nine men broke into the house where Cone and his family were in bed, struck Cone and his wife, who was about six months pregnant, and dragged both of them from their bed. Cone was taken into the yard and beaten savagely. When his wife sought to come to his aid, she was clubbed and was told that if she moved or cried out, the men would "blow her damn brains out."[65]

The next month, "a band of disguised white men" invaded the Columbia County home of a prominent black family, the Nobles. Again, both husband and wife were severely beaten. Nor were these isolated cases, as in Alachua County alone, "nineteen persons, mostly Negroes, were murdered during the period from 1867 to 1871."[66] Jonathan Gibbs, a respected African American who was secretary of state under Reconstruction governance, said "153 persons were murdered in Jackson County during the period from 1867 to 1871." Given that Alachua County is appreciably south of the Georgia border where slavery was strongest and that Jackson County had a small population, as remains the case today, any extrapolation must reasonably conclude that a thousand black Floridians lost their lives, including many nameless women. People were randomly killed by the Klan and its confederates; every black person lived with daily terrorism.

The same could apply to whites who tried to help blacks by accepting appointments from the Reconstruction government. In 1873 the ousted Columbia County sheriff led a mob that attacked the Lake City homes of three newly appointed officials, Sheriff George C. Keene, Clerk of the Circuit Court Keight Waldron, and Tax Collector W. W. Moore. All were married, and a correspondent for the *New York Sun* interviewed their wives. Mrs. Keene, the sheriff's wife, acted strongly while he hid. She told the reporter:

> We knew there was going to be trouble. Threats had been repeatedly made against us. . . . I drew down the curtains of the sitting room. It was dark, and more dangerous to attempt to leave the house than to remain in it. We went to bed early, and between 12 and 1 o'clock I awoke with the noise of the firing. . . . I saw from the direction of the shots that

> they intended to shoot Mr. Keene while in bed if possible. I lighted the lamp and got him out of bed, and made him lie down on the floor. . . . I then went to the window. . . . There was a man standing at the picket fence only twenty feet away. I went to Mr. Keene and asked him to let me have his repeater [rifle], so that I could kill the scoundrel. I am sure that I could have put a bullet through him. Mr. Keene said that if I did it would only be a random shot, and he had better keep the repeater.[67]

Mrs. Waldron, wife of the clerk of the Circuit Court, also seems to have demonstrated at least as much professional ability as her husband—even though the reporter described her as "a thin, feeble woman" who "had a baby in her arms" and "was apparently much frightened." He added that when the Keenes had told their neighbors to anticipate trouble, Waldron's "husband didn't believe any attack was intended." He left to protect a black family, and Mrs. Waldron thus was alone when the terrorists returned:

> They began to shoot into the house again. I held my baby tight to my breast, and shouted to them. I told them that I was alone, and asked them if they wanted to murder me and my baby. They didn't say anything, but began to shoot into the roof. I told them that if they shot me or my husband, there would be trouble. We had many friends, and they would have revenge. . . . They didn't make any answer, but after a time they went away.[68]

The reporter also interviewed Mrs. Moore, "a delicate woman" whose husband had not known—or at least had not told her—about the anticipated attack. Shocked when a "deadly volley" of fire "poured through the window, Mrs. Moore and another lady barely escaped with their lives. The bullets struck articles that they were carrying in their hands." The reporter counted nearly fifty bullet holes in the house; at the Keene home, there had been sixteen in the sitting room alone.

The mob may have intended only to terrorize—or their poor aim may have been because they were drunk—but they also shot up the vacant home of Judge A. P. Holt, who was out of town. Mrs. Holt and "her twin babies" were staying with her father and thus were spared the violence. She also appeared to have the courage to face down the lawless, as the reporter called her "a spunky little woman with snapping black eyes, and as brave as a lioness." Indeed, he added that she was so firm in her right to fight back that "it is thought that she may hurt some of the assassins before the trouble is over."[69]

* * *

Living in such anarchy may be a factor in explaining why Southern women did not demand the vote as Northern women did during this era. Casting a ballot could cost a Florida man his life, and it is understandable that most women wanted no part of such government. Northern women, however, continued to argue for "no taxation without representation."

Their legal case was bolstered by the Fourteenth and Fifteenth Amendments, which were added to the U.S. Constitution to assure civil rights for former slaves. The Fifteenth Amendment especially gave women a strong argument for the vote: its language is completely gender neutral, and both black and white women in at least a dozen jurisdictions from New Hampshire to California attempted to cast ballots in the 1868, 1870, and 1872 elections. Among them was famed orator Sojourner Truth, who owned a house in Battle Creek, Michigan, and tried to vote there.

The case that finally reached the U.S. Supreme Court, though, was that of a white woman, Virginia Minor of St. Louis, Missouri. In an 1874 decision that quoted the Bible as much as the Constitution, the court ruled that states were free to define their voters—a direct contradiction to the federal troops who enforced the right of black men to vote in former Confederate states. These states had to ratify the amendments to reenter the Union, but the court effectively ruled that if the plaintiff was a woman of any color, the words did not mean what they said.

Few Florida women cared. They lived in lawlessness and had many more immediate concerns. Even Dr. Esther Hill Hawks, who was listed in the records of the National Woman Suffrage Association as vice president for Florida, spent very little time on the right to vote. Instead, it was the temperance movement that attracted reformers. In an era when many states made it almost impossible for a woman to sue for divorce and gave fathers complete custody of children, countless women lived with drunken and abusive husbands. Most towns had more saloons than churches, and some women developed the courage to change that. In Tampa a temperance-oriented "Band of Hope," composed of seven women and six men," began in 1870, but it would be another decade before any significant number of women joined.[70] Instead, Dr. Hawks and similar feminists concentrated on achievable charities, not political justice.

Supported by the federal Freedman's Bureau—an idea originated by Ohio's Josephine Griffing—"freedman" schools run by Northern women welcomed former slaves of all ages and both genders. By 1866 Florida had thirteen freedman's schools with a combined 27 teachers and 16,663 students. Teaching learners of such varied ages was difficult, but as almost all former slaves were illiterate, work began with the alphabet. The same was true for poor whites, a few of whom also ventured to these schools. Often nearly as impoverished as former slaves, they usually were attracted by free food and clothing—the donations of Northern women.

Vermont's Anna M. Kidder began a school in Ocala in 1870. Although she was finally able to write, "I haven't heard any grumbling from the Whites about my school lately," whites were far from welcoming.[71] Chloe Merrick had been working in the Jacksonville area since 1862 but was still a social outcast in 1866, when she wrote that local white women "shrank" from her and her colleagues as though they were "a pestilence." They bore "the reproach . . . of being 'n______ teachers,'" an attitude that "came from Northern as well Southern whites."[72]

These women nonetheless maintained a cheerful approach, especially in letters home. Freedman teachers knew that their families worried about them, as mosquito-borne diseases endangered lives. Kidder and her associates promoted well water instead of polluted surface water—and accepted that segregation would extend even to water. She wrote, "I know of one colored well and two white ones that have been dug since Emancipation."[73]

She probably avoided writing about Ocala's postwar violence lest her family be upset, but Harriet Barnet and Catherine Bent, Northern white women who began a Gainesville school in 1867, revealed shocking incidents to a Freedmen's Bureau official. He reported that these teachers said:

> The bitter hatred of whites for Negroes often manifested itself in cruel treatment of freedmen. They cited incidents in which a drunken white man gouged out the eyes of a Negro who happened to get in his way, and the stabbing of two Negroes at Archer by a group of white men because the Negroes had served in the Union Army. The young teachers reported that their greatest trouble came from the assaults of white boys who often harassed them by throwing missiles into the schoolroom, sometimes hitting the teachers, and who manifested their disrespect in other ways.[74]

The "other ways," in all probability, were of a sexually harassing nature that a Victorian man could not bring himself to record. At a minimum, these women could expect catcalls and wolf whistles. Often, though, they had pleasant surroundings as compensation because freedman schools frequently were located in mansions that owners had abandoned. Usually they were the confiscated property of secessionists who had fled invaded cities, but occasionally they were property donated by Unionists. The school in Palatka, called Sunny Point, was among the latter. It was a relatively new mansion, built by Judge and Mrs. Isaac Bronson in 1854. He died the very next year, but she lived there until the war began, when she returned to New York. At the war's end she supported New Yorker Charlotte Henry in beginning a school there. In 1904 Bronson willed the house to her nurse, Mary Mulholland, who lived at what now is called the Bronson-Mulholland House until the 1930s. It still stands on the St. Johns River in Palatka.

Northern white women did not build all such schools, as some Florida blacks acted on their own initiative. Although postwar Tampa was occupied by federal troops, it had no freedman school, and local blacks—especially women—raised the money to fund their own. Iola Brumick recalled: "The first school building for colored children was erected in 1868. . . . It was 35 × 75, one room with no partitions and few windows—but it was very dear to the hearts of colored people."[75]

* * *

No Northerner in Reconstruction Florida was more famed than Harriet Beecher Stowe, the author of the nineteenth century's best-selling novel *Uncle Tom's Cabin* and many other books. In 1866, the first year after the war ended, she bought Laurel Grove, a vacant plantation near Orange City, to rehabilitate a son who had become an alcoholic during the war; later she moved across the river to Mandarin.[76]

Abbie Brooks, who called herself "Sylvia Sunshine" when she issued *Petals Plucked from Sunny Climes,* wrote amusingly about the Stowes' first visit to a Jacksonville church:

> Mrs. Harriet Beecher Stowe is here to-day from her home in Mandarin. . . . Dr. Stowe, her husband, accompanies her [because] he preaches. When they both entered the Southern Methodist church a slight rustle was heard in the congregation, and a few persons left the house. Mr. and Mrs. Uncle Tom were more than a Sabbath dose for some of the Jacksonville community.
>
> Harriet B. has no resemblance to a perpetrator of discord or scandal.

The three snowy curls on each side of her face give her a matronly look, and her stout-built frame, well covered with flesh, [gives] a substantial appearance. . . .

The service was opened by a very long prayer from Dr. Stowe, after which he preached a purely orthodox sermon. . . . Mrs. Harriet had confidence in the ability of her husband . . . and she went to sleep.[77]

Florida also was home to Constance Fenimore Woolson, who followed her famed great-uncle, James Fenimore Cooper, as an author. She had a solid reputation with literary giants such as Henry James, and her work was popular with ordinary readers too. With her invalid mother, Woolson spent winters in Florida from 1873 to 1879, when her mother died. She set some stories in Reconstruction Florida but was not a crusader in the mold of Harriet Beecher Stowe; Minorcans who had settled in the area a century earlier were her favorite topic. She told friends in Europe that she wanted to return to Florida but never did. Her death in Venice may have been a suicide, and her Winter Park home now belongs to Rollins College.

"A Florida Housekeeper" and Non-Tourist Florida

The most interesting thing about Sidney Lanier's travelogue may be a long quote from an anonymous "Florida housekeeper" in the Jacksonville area. She was disgusted with tourists who traveled without leaving their boat and believed whatever their guide told them. Apparently some of these boat captains saved money by telling passengers that only inferior food was available, and this farmwoman wrote an outraged letter to the *New York Evening Post* in response to that calumny:

> Much is written of "no milk," of "tough beef," of "canned fruit," etc. . . . We have three cows . . . [and] rich milk daily . . . and have as good beef as you can get in the North. . . . We have . . . all year round, Irish potatoes, sweet potatoes, cabbages, lettuce, tomatoes, peas, turnips and beets. . . . We also have figs in the autumn, oranges . . . , lemons and citrons, grapes and blackberries, huckleberries, and musk and water melons, and peaches and bananas. All these were grown and not canned.

Note: Sidney Lanier, *Florida: Its Scenery, Climate, and History*, originally published in 1875 (repr. Gainesville: University of Florida Press, 1973).

Sidney Lanier, a famous poet based in Georgia, traveled through Florida in the winter of 1874–75. He visited Harriet Beecher Stowe, describing her home as a "brown cottage, near the shore, nearly obscured by foliage."[78] She lived there in winter (and occasional summer months) with her husband Calvin, a retired theology professor, some of their unmarried daughters, and constant visitors. Her collection of columns on Florida, published as *Palmetto Leaves* in 1873, was credited for bringing fourteen thousand visitors to Florida the next year. Another member of her family settled near St. Mark's, south of Tallahassee. Somewhat to her surprise, Tallahassee welcomed Harriet Beecher Stowe with a reception in 1874. She posed for a photograph on the capitol steps and spoke about harmony between former Civil War enemies.

Stowe's calm resolve to do right included hard physical work when that was needed, which she demonstrated with a communal plantation project that resettled former slaves from the Carolinas and Virginia. On the opposite side of the St. Johns from Mandarin, it was called the Mackintosh Plantation, and two young men from New England began it after the war's end. She toiled there prior to the arrival of any other white women, and said:

> The Negro women . . . were all . . . born and bred as field-hands. . . . Many were as strong as men. . . . They showed a most affecting eagerness to be taught to read and write. We distributed a stock of spelling books, which they eagerly accepted and treasured. . . . Sundays and evenings after work, certain of them would appear with [book] in hand, and earnestly beg to be taught. . . .
>
> One of the most dreaded characters on the place was the dairy-woman and cook Minnah. She had been a field-hand in North Carolina, and worked at cutting down trees, grubbing land, and mauling rails. She was a tall, lank, powerfully-built woman . . . and a tongue that never hesitated to speak her mind. . . . Minnah's back was all marked and scored with the tyrant's answer to free speech. Her old master . . . stretched her over a log, staking down her hands and feet, and flayed her. . . . For all that, Minnah was neither broken nor humbled.
>
> Minnah . . . abominated housework like a man. . . . A regular domestic routine was simply disgusting in her eyes. So . . . it was agreed that Minnah was to go back to field-work, where she was one of the most valuable hands. . . . We obtained a cook from Jacksonville, trained,

accomplished, neat, who made beautiful bread. . . . But [she] was worth more than we could give, and went from us to enjoy forty dollars per month as a cook in a hotel. Such as been the good fortune of all well-trained house-servants since emancipation. They command their own price.[79]

Forty dollars was indeed a good salary: monthly wages for blacks averaged about ten dollars for men and eight dollars for women. There were other black women on this communal plantation, but they apparently also preferred agricultural work. The only one who took any interest in learning domesticity was a young woman pathetically eager to please her "husband": she wanted to keep him there instead of going back to the "wives" he had in both North Carolina and Virginia.

According to Stowe, the majority of couples at McIntosh never formalized their relationship, but that was not the case in the Tampa Bay area. Slaves there were much less likely to be field workers and more likely to emulate white families, and most black couples rushed to establish legal marriages as soon as they could do so. Some blacks had weddings in slavery, but most were performed by black preachers who themselves may have been slaves, and such marriages were not officially recorded. Even free blacks had not been allowed to wed: although there were many cases of a free man or woman buying the freedom of a spouse, Florida law did not allow them to register as a married couple.

Thus many Reconstruction newlyweds had long relationships. Fort Brooke scout Sampson Forrester, for instance, bought the freedom of Rose Bennett in the early 1840s, but they could not pronounce themselves legally married until 1866. Molly Williams and Andrew Varnes, who had been brought as slaves from South Carolina fifteen years earlier, also married in 1866. Fortune Taylor, a landowner in what now is downtown Tampa, had been with Benjamin Taylor so long that he died of old age just three years after they wed in 1866. Near Lakeland, Bryant Horton and Olive Bell married; they had belonged to Bathsheba Gross Wilder, a widow who moved them from Georgia.[80]

The Hortons settled in Bealsville, an all-black community south of Plant City that began with the war's end. Sarah Howell, a former slave owner, offered land and farming equipment to ten families, and the community was called Howell's Creek until 1923, when it was renamed for a man. In Orange

County, too, the all-black community of Eatonville sprang up soon after slavery ended. In north Florida, where as noted, blacks were the majority, there were numerous all-black communities.

Generous former slave owners such as Sarah Howell were the exception, not the rule. Many others were eager to rid themselves of the human beings they now deemed a liability. Some took their newly free human capital to urban areas and abandoned them. Emma D. Bryant, the daughter of slaves, said in 1936 that "many plantation owners from . . . Sumter County brought [former slaves] as far as Tampa and dumped them there."[81]

Catholic sisters assisted some. Although they never had a presence during Spanish Catholic days, nuns came to what had become an almost wholly Protestant Florida during the Civil War and Reconstruction. They aided not only the minority who were Catholic but anyone who wanted their services. Sisters of the Holy Cross opened an academy in postwar Pensacola, while Sisters of Mercy ran St. Mary's Academy in St. Augustine, and other nuns ran schools at Fernandina and Mandarin. All these institutions opened or reopened between 1866 and 1870, and in 1873 Sisters of Mercy began a Jacksonville home for needy whites. "Most of the support" for this work came from Catholics in France—as did some of the nuns themselves.[82] A historian summarized:

> The French Sisters of St. Joseph arrived in St. Augustine in . . . 1866, where they resided in an old house on St. George Street and took their meals with the Sisters of Mercy. To the French sisters, Florida life represented work in a foreign mission. Since they spoke only French, they first needed to learn English. They soon succeeded in that regard, and in 1867, the sisters opened one school for black children and another for white boys. White girls, Catholic and Protestant, still were taught by the Sisters of Mercy until . . . 1869, [when] the Sisters of St. Joseph opened St. Joseph's Academy for white girls.[83]

The nation had three orders of African American nuns, but none was south of Baltimore, where the Oblate Sisters of Providence had been the first in 1831. Black Protestant women in Florida, however, often used the same nomenclature for their benevolent work. During Reconstruction, Florida saw such African American organizations as Sisters of Protection, Sisters' Beneficent Society, and Sons and Daughters of Bethlehem.

Reconstruction government emphasized education, and the next decade brought appreciable progress. Duval High School was Florida's first:

it opened in 1874, and an 1888 report said it was "scarcely inferior to the colleges of the state." For African Americans, the first advanced education was at Jacksonville's Cookman Institute, which had sixty students and a long waiting list by 1876. A visitor that year questioned students in an algebra class and said they were equal "to pupils in any of our schools in the North."[84]

Freedman schoolteacher Chloe Merrick married Governor Harrison Reed, and despite becoming pregnant for the first time at age forty, continued her interest in education. In response to her suggestion the governor appointed Charles Beecher, brother of Harriet Beecher Stowe, as education commissioner. Under him and other Reconstruction leaders, including African American Jonathan Gibbs, school enrollment rose. In 1860, the year before the war began, Florida had some 6,500 students—most of whom were in private schools that nonetheless received tax dollars. By 1873 enrollment was 191,916 students in 511 schools. Beecher believed that this "represented almost one-third of all Floridians between the ages of six and eighteen."[85]

Under liberal leadership in Washington, at least three women were appointed as postal officials during Reconstruction: Amanda Mann became postmaster at Brooksville in 1867, and Clementine Wilkinson and Sarah Fountain each served as postmaster in Bartow—or postmistress, in the usual term of the time.

Catharine Hart, who was called Kate, had a circuitous route to this role at Kissimmee. She had lived in numerous Florida towns while her husband, Ossian B. Hart, pursued a career as a Republican. He became governor in 1872, but as the state did not have a home for governors, they lived in Jacksonville most of the time. When he died in 1874, she stayed there and supported herself by turning their home into a boarding house. He left many debts, however, and the house burned. She also was sued in a probate case involving Northern relatives, and when Hart's debtors foreclosed on the land, she lost her Jacksonville home.

The former first lady lived with friends in Tallahassee and Bradenton while recovering financially to the point of establishing a new household in Kissimmee. It was a frontier, where "cowmen simply rode up to [an] outside refreshment stand and ordered their poison—whether it be corn whiskey, peach spirits, rot-gut, or cane skimming whiskey."[86]

Kissimmee organized as a municipality in 1883, and Kate Hart organized a chapter of the Women's Christian Temperance Union the same year. She also began writing a regular column on the subject in the *Kissimmee Valley Gazette* and became the town's postmistress the same year. This provided the first financial security she had had since her husband's death. Kissimmee grew quickly, with mailboxes rising from eighteen to a hundred during her first year. But she was one of the few Republicans in Florida, and when Democrat Grover Cleveland became president in 1886, Kate Hart lost her position to a Democratic man. She was near poverty when she died back in her native New Jersey.

In Jacksonville, Martha Reed Mitchell, the immensely wealthy sister of former governor Harrison Reed (and sister-in-law of former freedman teacher Chloe Merrick Reed) led fundraising for Florida's first hospital in 1872. The motivation was an epidemic that killed Northern visitors, including

Villa Alexandria

The relationship between Martha Reed Mitchell and her husband, Alexander Mitchell, was typical of ambitious couples in the Gilded Age: he made the money (in railroads and finance), and she spent it with tasteful ostentation that raised their class status. They lived at Villa Alexandria only in the winter, but she nonetheless invested heavily in the property.

Writing in 1877, Harriet Beecher Stowe said it had been a "dilapidated plantation" with "worthless" buildings—but within a decade, Mitchell created "a charming villa, built in the Italian Swiss style, with broad verandahs and a picturesque tower." On the grounds she had "date and cocoa palms from Egypt and [the] West Indies, teas from Assam . . . , California nutmegs."

Mahogany cabinets in the dining room, said to have cost fifty thousand dollars, displayed Mitchell's "marvelous collection of teapots from all over the world." Her grandson, David Mitchell, averred that her bathroom was the first south of Charleston to have modern plumbing. His bathroom, built later, had Tiffany windows, a marble tub, and a sink trimmed with ivory and silver as well as a shower and a Turkish bath. He said his grandmother "brought down expert builders and mechanics, so that every item was properly taken care of."

Note: The quotes from Stowe are from Olav Thulesius, *Harriet Beecher Stowe in Florida, 1867 to 1884* (Jefferson, N.C.: McFarland, 2001), 169; those of David Mitchell are From John T. Foster Jr. and Sarah Whitman Foster, *Beechers, Stowes, and Yankee Strangers: The Transformation of Florida* (Gainesville: University Press of Florida, 1999), 99, 69–70.

one who died alone in an outhouse. It eventually became St. Luke's Hospital. Today's Tampa General Hospital began as Emergency Hospital, also under the leadership of women and because of yellow fever.

Hospitals, schools, and similar institutions are what distinguish civilized society from violent anarchy. That women often play a major role in promoting such institutions and are less likely to participate in violence is key to understanding human progress. The "feminine" values of nurturing children, preserving families, and looking to the societal future are fundamental to peace and prosperity. Thinking ahead and making sacrifices for the future is what Madison County's Margaret Vann intended when she said that Civil War Florida was "grander in her daughters."[87]

5 "The World Is Not Suffering for Another Cake Recipe"

Women's Lives Expand, 1881–1900

In both the North and South the Civil War and its aftermath forced women to develop greater independence. Prior to the war, for example, it generally was considered improper for a woman to speak in a meeting or to travel without an escort. Indeed, many hotels would not rent a room to an unaccompanied woman: the assumption was that proper women stayed in the homes of families and friends, not in hotels, and a lone female hotel patron probably was a prostitute. These attitudes changed because the war made travel essential for many women. The taboo on public speaking also faded with the need to raise money and morale for the war.

The most important of late nineteenth-century changes, though, was the development of clubs and organizations for and by women. Men, of course, long had joined organizations for business and politics—and, contrary to stereotypes, men always socialized more than women. Everywhere in the world it was acceptable for men to go to a club or tavern or saloon to socialize with other men, but in both rural and urban areas, women stayed home. Except for church, most women attended no public gatherings. There simply were no clubs for them, let alone to network for business or civic purposes.

George Washington, for instance, was a Mason and attended functions at his local Masonic Hall, but its female auxiliary, the Eastern Star, did not begin until 1875—a full century after Martha Washington might have joined. When they did finally develop, such auxiliaries were subordinate to the male group and were intended to support it with food and accouterments for largely male gathering. America's first organizations composed of women were missionary societies; formed under the aegis of Protestant clergymen, they supplied the clergy's needs. They developed in the North about the 1830s, but even that was controversial, especially in the conservative South.

The first organizations for southern women were mainly memorial associations that arose after the Civil War. Dedicated to maintaining cemeteries for fallen soldiers, they often used "relief" in their names because they also aided disabled veterans, war widows, and children orphaned by the war. Northern women developed such association and also had female abolitionist societies prior to the war. Some towns even had "moral reform" societies that took on issues as serious as prostitution. A tiny minority of northern women had gone further with women's rights societies that evolved into national suffrage associations with the aim of full civil rights for women.

The first such assembly was in 1848 at Seneca Falls, New York, where Elizabeth Cady Stanton lived—but women were so unaccustomed to organizations that James Mott, the husband of Philadelphia's Lucretia Mott, presided. The Motts were Quakers, as were many of the early women's rights leaders, but even though Lucretia Mott had preached in Quaker meetinghouses for two decades, she was unfamiliar with parliamentary procedure, especially in what was then termed a "promiscuous" meeting—a gathering that included men.[1]

Thus it was a huge step for women simply to learn the mechanics of exercising their constitutional right to assemble. Until the late nineteenth century most women never paid dues to an organization, made or seconded a motion, or served as an organizational officer. Without such skills, even the smallest political action is virtually impossible. After that personal growth, however, a critical mass occurred and an explosion of women's organizations was basic to transforming America.

That generally took place between the 1850s and 1870s in the North; in the South, it was the 1880s to 1900s. To a fairly large extent, northern women offered southerners important—if unconscious—role models for this during the 1860s and 1870s. When Yankee women came to towns such as Ocala or Palatka and opened a school, even resentful Florida women could see that women were capable of creating important change. When a Harriet Beecher Stowe or an Esther Hill Hawks held a meeting in her home that proposed societal reforms, other women were inspired to emulate the process, if not necessarily the purpose.[2]

The first national organization of and by women that Florida women were likely to join was the Woman's Christian Temperance Union (WCTU). Like missionary societies, WCTU chapters often developed with clergymen—but the national body was for and by women from its beginning. The WCTU formed in Ohio in 1874 and by the 1880s had spread to Florida. Under the national leadership of Frances Willard, it soon adopted goals beyond temperance, including even "Home Protection," a euphemism for ending prostitution and venereal disease.

Women's nascent yearning to explore ideas and express opinions is clear from the WCTU's rapid growth: when it went worldwide in 1891, the WCTU had thirty-nine issue-oriented "departments" as diverse as world peace, labor law, prison reform, and more. An 1891 "polyglot petition" to governments throughout the world aimed at curtailing not only alcohol and tobacco but also narcotics—most of which were legal at the time—and seven million people, mostly women, signed it.[3]

The WCTU had a broad, if vague, definition of "Christian." Few Catholic women joined the WCTU—or any organizations other than auxiliaries, often auxiliaries of labor unions led by male Catholic immigrants. In contrast, a number of WCTU founders were Jewish. Among them in Tampa were Josie Weissbrod, Grace Zellnicker Gundersheimer, and Mary Sauls, all of whom belonged to the local temple but used "Christian" as if it were synonymous with "good." Both Sauls and Mrs. L. K. Levinson, another charity leader, signed their reports with "Yours in Christian Work," even though they were practicing Jews.

Early WCTU members also were apt to have a fairly broad definition of "temperance," and some did not see it as the total "prohibition" that it became under the Prohibition Party and before women had the vote. It also was socially diverse. The Tampa chapter ranged from wives and daughters of "bankers, merchants, judges, newspaper editors, and lawyers" to women who supported themselves. Among them were storeowners and a boarding-house operator who made a point of not serving alcohol. They alternated their late afternoon weekly meetings between the Baptist and Methodist churches, and they also held "mass meetings every second Sunday night at the Opera House." During their first year these ambitious women raised the money for a "public reading room" to give men a socializing opportunity that did not include smoking and drinking.[4]

They also created a "superintendent for colored work," and Tampa's Emily Charles may have been the first president of an African American WCTU chapter. Born a slave in Georgia in 1824, she married Cyrus Charles, and their marriage was one of the first recorded in 1866, when Florida's blacks finally were allowed to wed legally. They homesteaded five acres of land and prospered, living in a "big two-story house."[5] Cyrus served as a Reconstruction official in 1868, and after his death a decade later, Emily continued to manage their businesses. Her property was assessed at eight thousand dollars in 1889, making her wealthier than most whites. Even in the North, African American chapters of the WCTU were uncommon, and Emily Charles truly was an exceptional woman.

Most WCTU members saw themselves as religious and conservative, not feminists—but no matter how apolitical a woman might be, once she became active for legal reforms, it was hard to remain blind to the need for the vote. Florida's women took their first steps in that direction in the 1880s: indeed, in Tampa, the beginnings of a movement for enfranchisement preceded the WCTU. The WCTU chapter began in 1886, but Kate Binkley had been in touch with nationally known Elizabeth Cady Stanton several years prior to that.

On April 22, 1880, Binkley sent Stanton a petition for an amendment to the U.S. Constitution that would grant women the vote. The fourteen signatures, she said, had been acquired "by hard work," and represented either self-supporting women or the wives of working-class men. They viewed themselves as entitled to vote because they paid taxes. In all probability Stanton responded to the petition and mail was exchanged between the 1880 petition to Stanton and a letter that one signer, Julia Seiver, wrote five years later to Susan B. Anthony:

February 12, 1885

My dear Miss Anthony:

Yours of the 3rd . . . reached me last night. I cannot resist the desire to write you a few lines.

My sympathies are deeply interested in the movement for emancipation of our sex. For 30 years I have been an earnest advocate of Woman Suffrage, and though I have arrived at the age of 52, I am still anxious to labor for our noble cause.

Like yourself, I am a native of Berkshire County, Mass., but the last 24 years of my life have been spent in the South.

The indifference manifested by the women of the South is truly deplorable. . . . We need good public speakers here, women whose sound logic would fall [upon] fossilized ideas. . . .

Owing to impaired health, I am able to appear only occasionally before the public as a lecturer, but my heart is with the good cause, and I shall try to secure a large number of names for the petition for a 16th amendment to the Constitution. Thanks for the Report of the Convention and other papers.

Sincerely yours,
Julia A. B. Seiver[6]

Various national newspapers aimed at feminists went in and out of existence during the nineteenth century, and one of them, *Woman's Tribune*, mentioned that Elizabeth W. Varnum of Florida participated in an 1886 convention of the American Association for Advancement of Women, held at Louisville, Kentucky. This organization evolved into today's American Association of University Women (AAUW). No hometown or other information was listed for Varnum, but she probably was a feminist, at least in terms of seeking women's admission to colleges. *Woman's Tribune* also reported in 1887 that well-known Indiana leader Helen M. Gougar had organized a Florida chapter of the National Woman Suffrage Association, with Mrs. Don Allen of Bartow as president.[7]

Florida's First Feminists

The founders of women's rights organizations in the United States left detailed records in six massive volumes totaling some five thousand pages. The first three volumes were published in 1883; the fourth in 1902; and the last two in 1920, after the vote was achieved nationally. Florida did not have dedicated space in the first three but did in the fourth. The 1900 report was by Mrs. C. S. Burnett-Haney of Stuart:

> The brief history of work in Florida . . . gathers about the name of Ella C. Chamberlain. . . . In January, 1893, she presented the question so forcibly at a social gathering, as a woman taxpayer, that a gentleman suggested forming a society and twenty members were secured, eight of them men. . . .

> In 1894 the president [Chamberlain] addressed the Carpenters' Union twice, and considerable literature was distributed. In December the suffragists of Tampa, aided by those of Melrose [near Gainesville], held a bazar which netted $125.
>
> In January, 1895, a State convention was held in Tampa. . . . During the year Mrs. Chamberlain gave addresses at the De Funiak Springs Assembly, the Adventists' Campmeeting and in various towns. The society paid dues to the National Association until 1897, when the president removed from the State; no one came forward to take the leadership and the movement has since languished.

Instead of the vote, Burnett-Haney focused on the Women's Christian Temperance Union [WCTU]—but she acted in the broad arena of its goals, not mere opposition to alcohol. Her report continued with attention to other feminist issues:

> LEGISLATIVE ACTION AND LAWS: All property of the wife, real or personal, owned by her before marriage or lawfully acquired afterward . . . is her separate estate and is not liable for the debts of the husband without her written consent. . . . It remains, however, under his management . . . , nor can she compel him to account for it. . . .
>
> The wife can not transfer her real or personal property without the husband's joinder. Any married woman who may wish to take charge of her estate . . . must apply to the court for a license. Since 1891 a married woman's earnings acquired by any employment aside from the household are her separate property. . . .
>
> The father has legal control of the persons, education and property of the children, and he alone may appoint a guardian. . . .
>
> OFFICE HOLDING: Women are not eligible to any office, elective or appointive, except that they may serve as notaries public.

Note: Susan B. Anthony and Ida Husted Harper, eds., *The History of Woman Suffrage*, vol. 4 (Indianapolis: Hollenbeck Press, 1902), 240, 577.

Julia Seiver's 1885 letter to Susan B. Anthony may have been influenced by the fact that Florida revised its constitution in 1885, but if so, there was no proposal to enfranchise women. Seiver was right to consider Florida women "deplorable": feminists in other states and territories often took advantage of constitutional conventions to include themselves as full citizens in new governance structures, but the issue seems to have gained no attention in Florida. Instead, the state's 1885 constitution marked the true end of Reconstruction liberalism: it imposed a poll tax that was intended to keep black men from voting. The federal government, including the U.S. Supreme Court, was firmly conservative by 1885, with no more of the protections for African Americans that had been real in 1865. Poll taxes would not be repealed until an amendment to the U.S. Constitution in 1964.

The effect was disenfranchisement for all but white men who could afford the tax. The new constitution also created a plethora of offices that most men viewed as patronage, with eight executive offices in every county (including an elected land surveyor)—but no county mayors to coordinate these separate fiefdoms. State power was distributed in an executive branch with six Cabinet members who were nearly equal to the governor.

Moreover, ballots for all of these offices were cast in separate containers. "The ballot boxes were marked distinctly with the name of the office," a political history explained, and because "most Negroes were illiterate" and election officials "refused to tell them in which box to place the ballots," the votes of black men were "practically eliminated."[8] Indeed, 87 percent of African American men voted in the 1884 election; by 1896, only 5 percent did. The poll tax also dissuaded frugal white men from voting, and their participation declined drastically, from 96 percent in 1884 to 57 percent in 1896.[9]

Florida government did not aim truly to represent the people; instead it was a game limited to white men, most of whom expected to profit personally. Most women saw no reason why they should try to join in such corrupt competition. Instead they created their own voluntary associations and worked without tax money to do the societal good that needed to be done.

* * *

The most vital issue was public health. Yellow fever struck on a regular basis, caused by mosquitoes that flourished because of a lack of sanitation and especially because of a lack of water and sewage systems. As population increased, outbreaks grew worse. An 1887–88 epidemic was the worst: it cut a killer path across the state, with contagion spreading from Cuba to Key West to Tampa to Cedar Key to Jacksonville. In Tampa at least 122 people are known to have died, and local historians believe that as many as 300 were buried in unmarked graves. That was about 10 percent of the town's population—to put it in today's context, in a comparable epidemic more than 30,000 people within the city limits could expect to die.

Many others, of course, were terribly sick and permanently weakened. The epidemic hit Florida's west coast in October, and although it died down during the winter, it flared up again on the East Coast as soon as the weather was warm. As cases were reported in coastal towns, people rushed inland, where they believed—with some accuracy—there would be less chance of getting sick. Most rural women welcomed their city kin and let them stay for months, usually without charge—but some disease-free communities were determined to stay that way. Armed sentinels kept visitors out of Leesburg, and Bartow men guarded their new railroad station and prevented anyone from getting off the train. In contrast, the "ladies of Bartow" sent $30.25 to the Tampa Ladies Relief Society, which quickly formed to deal with the crisis.

The state issued cards to people who had survived yellow fever and thus were immune to it. With an official-looking appearance, they were headlined "Yellow Fever Immunity Card." Personal movement, however, was controlled as late as August 1888, when newlyweds Caroline Taylor and Victor McIlvaine rushed from their Tampa wedding ceremony "to catch a train to escape an impending quarantine." Taylor owned a store but was forced to stay at Cedar Key for months.

Nursing was only barely becoming a recognized profession, and Florida had no nursing schools, but experienced female nurses employed by the state came from Key West. The *Tampa Journal* advertised for nurses in four categories by race and gender, with pay ranges from $3 per day for whites and half that much for blacks. Families who "could afford to pay for the services of such nurses were expected to do so, but the Relief Committee paid for those without means."[10]

WCTU founders Jennie Copeland and Mary Cuscaden gave their lives to fighting the epidemic. "The dread of it never left us," wrote Kittie Martin Lea. Yellow fever "would spread like a forest fire, blaze up . . . taking entire families."[11] Because she was immune, Lea opened her home to the sick, and other women did the same. By far the majority of nursing still was done at home, but Jacksonville had a hospital—and the epidemic prompted Tampa women to create what they called Emergency Hospital. Josie Weissbrod—the same unmarried Jewish woman who was a founder of a WCTU—led others in establishing and furnishing the facility as well as hiring a staff and managing day-to-day operations.[12]

The women did a fine job, but as often happens with successful volunteers, they found their efforts rewarded with a takeover by professionals. After a decade of the women operating Emergency Hospital without taxpayer funds, the Tampa Physicians Protective Association moved to take over the hospital. That there was no medical reason for this was clear in that the hospital had only six deaths among more than two hundred patients treated, but the male county commissioners sided with the male physicians and "demanded that the women relinquish control."[13]

The nine "lady managers angrily refused" to have their status changed to that of an auxiliary. The president of "the Board of Lady Managers" was Meroba Hooker Crane, a member of a pioneer family and the operator of the city's best hotel. But despite her influence and the success of the "lady managers," the change occurred without their consent. An entirely new Women's Auxiliary Board made up of physicians' wives was formed, displacing the founders. Within a few years the physicians were calling on the County Commission for major infusions of tax dollars.

* * *

Immigration to the United States increased dramatically in the 1880s and 1890s, and Florida also had newcomers. It was unique in its attraction for people from the Caribbean, especially Cuba but also other islands. Those who came from places colonized by the Spanish usually were Catholic and spoke Spanish—or occasionally French, as among immigrants from such places as Martinique or Haiti. Others came from British-controlled islands, especially the Bahamas and were Protestant English speakers. Most were dark-skinned, however, and were therefore defined by Americans as "Negroes."

The greatest number of immigrants came from southern and eastern Europe, including Italians and Greeks as well as Jews from Germany, Russia, and the Slavic countries. Despite stereotypes to the contrary, Jews arguably were more welcomed in the South than in the North. Jewish merchants built modern stores and sold better-quality goods than Floridians had previously been able to buy.

Jewish women usually worked in these family stores, and they quickly rose in civic circles. As noted earlier, Jewish women were leaders in the founding of Tampa's WCTU, and Tampa elected the Jewish Herman Glowgowski as mayor four times. Historian Mark Greenberg concluded: "Evidence suggests a high level of acceptance of Jews. . . . Social discrimination, which swept America late in the nineteenth century, touched southern states least of all."[14]

Greeks settled on the west coast, especially at Tarpon Springs, because the waters there contained natural sponges. In a time prior to artificial sponges, the young men of these families specialized in diving for sponges—and the women participated in preparing the sponges for sale. Although Greece did not allow women to emigrate without a male escort until 1920, family-owned businesses typically included women. Some opened restaurants to serve sponge divers who had immigrated without female support, and these families found financial success as Americans discovered Greek food.

Life in Tarpon Springs centered around St. Nicholas Greek Orthodox Church, and even after Greeks spread out from that area, they maintained close ties. Young people were strongly expected to marry within the faith, and marriageable women were carefully supervised. Chaperones were an essential part of courtship, and few women were allowed to leave the community for education. On the other hand, unlike Roman Catholic priests, Greek Orthodox priests could marry, and their wives provided something of a female role model.

For Roman Catholics, that model continued to be nuns—many of whom also were immigrants. Sister Mary Ann, whose birth name was Ellen Hoare, became particularly important to Duval County, where her half-century career established her as "Jacksonville's Angel of Mercy." Just twelve when she fled Ireland's great famine for New York in 1848, she went straight to work; because she never was educated, she could not teach like most Sisters of St. Joseph. She came to Florida during the Civil War, when she began "begging for food for the poor." In 1886, after she took in an orphaned girl, the order was able to open St. Mary's Home, and when Sister Mary Ann died in 1914, the orphanage was home to "more than sixty children."[15]

The Children's Home of Tampa similarly began with an abandoned baby girl in 1896, but its management was secular. Nuns nonetheless brought great change to Tampa in this era, especially in education. Two members of the Holy Name of Jesus, Sister Marie Augustin and Sister Marie Maurice, arrived in August 1881 and began their convent and school in an old livery stable and blacksmith shop downtown. When two more nuns joined them in October, they moved to "a little cottage." Even though relatively few Tampans were Catholic, many were eager for decent education for their children, and by the end of the year, seventy-five students were enrolled in the Academy of Holy Names. It remains extant on Tampa's prestigious Bayshore Boulevard today.

Especially after large numbers of Catholics arrived from Cuba in the following years, Tampa nuns began three more schools: St. Peter Claver for black pupils opened in 1894; a second Convent of the Holy Names served a largely Spanish-speaking population in West Tampa after 1896; and in 1897, St. Ignatius School began in Port Tampa, at the peninsula's end. While nuns operated these co-educational schools, Jesuits ran the school for upper-class boys.

The Cuban influx was the result of the cigar industry, which created uniquely planned development and the subsidized the move of skilled cigar makers, including women. Most had been born in Cuba, and many worked in Key West prior to a strike there. Largely to break the union, Vicente Ybor and other factory owners acquired land around Tampa, and Ybor City was born in 1885. Despite its strike-breaking origin, the new town had many aspects of socialism: workers owned stock in the Ybor City Land and Investment Company, and their homes and jobs were closely linked. By the end of 1886 some three thousand Cubans had arrived—more in this one year than in all the years since Tampa's founding in 1824. The population tripled within five years, and whites became a minority.

Two towns in Sicily, Santo Stefano Quisquina and Alessandria della Rocca, supplied most of the unskilled labor for cigar factories—and many of those families went on to establish dairy and vegetable farms. Their children grew up trilingual, speaking Italian at home and both Spanish and English in public. At the opposite end of the economic ladder, factory owners often spoke relatively little English. They had direct connections to Spain, especially the northeastern provinces of Asturias and Galicia. Because they were wealthier and because Spain is more conservative than its colonies, these women lived more reclusive lives than either native women or most new immigrants. Women directly from Spain seldom joined organizations, whereas Spanish-speaking women with Cuban roots were active in both political and economic life.

Throughout the world, cigar making was one of very few occupations in which women and men were treated nearly equally. The lowest level of worker was a "stripper"—a person who stripped the stems and veins from tobacco leaves. Then came the "bunchers," who measured out the approximate amount of tobacco needed and created a rough "bunch" for rolling. "Rollers" shaped that into a cigar. It was a skill that required appreciable practice, and women were good at it. Because rollers were paid by the quantity of their personal production, skilled women could and did earn as much as men. At the pinnacle were the "packers," who placed cigars in boxes according to fine distinctions of color. Most packers were men—and given what we know now about the higher rates of color-blindness among men, more packers should have been women.

Factory managers nonetheless so valued women's skills that they offered flexible hours, and young mothers freely went home to nurse babies. Because factories had no machines, they were quiet enough for workers to hire "lectors," who read aloud to them. It was routine for cigar makers to know the contents of a half dozen newspapers, many from abroad, and they chose the classical literature that was read. Thus an Ybor City woman who might be illiterate, especially in English, quite probably knew more about the great novelists than did Tampa's society ladies. This was the background for Nilo Cruz's *Anna in the Tropics,* which won the 2003 Pulitzer Prize for Drama; it features cigar makers listening to Tolstoy's *Anna Karenina.*

* * *

All over the nation immigrants clashed with the established elite, and conflict included the issue of alcohol. Whether they were from Europe or Latin America, most immigrants were accustomed to daily beer or wine. Even prudish women from Norway, for example, considered beer to be essential, especially for nursing mothers. In southern and eastern Europe, wine often was more readily available than decent drinking water, and it certainly was less expensive than milk. In places such as Italy, some mothers introduced their children to wine almost as soon as they were weaned. Rosa Cavelleri, for instance, was told by her adoptive mother in Milan at age seven that she was "too old" for milk.[16] Neither Catholics nor Jews had religious bans on alcohol, and most—especially men—resented the Anglo Protestant women of the WCTU who tried to prevent them from drinking.

Obtaining citizenship was not the obstacle to voting that it is now, and illiterate though they might be, most immigrant men voted—while women, no matter what their education or wealth or social status, did not. The first time the Anglo and immigrant cultures clashed in Florida over alcohol was in an 1887 Hillsborough County election. The WCTU persuaded the county commissioners, all of whom were from pioneer Protestant families, to put the question of banning alcohol on the ballot. The *Tampa Journal* enthused:

> WOMEN AND CHILDREN WORK LIKE HEROES
>
> The oldest inhabitants tell us that never in the history of Tampa has there been an election like the one held yesterday. The people were awakened at 5 o'clock in the morning by the ringing of church bells, which was a signal for a congregation of women and children who were to give their work and influence on the side of Prohibition during the day at the polls. By 7 o'clock the women were on the Court-House Square, putting up banners and preparing for the contest. . . .
>
> The women went to work early, pinning "dry" badges upon the coats of the Prohibition voters. . . . It was soon evident that the women and children "had come to stay" and were prepared to brave any amount of indignity [from their opponents]. . . . Under the tents, the ladies served cool drinks and a bountiful dinner free to all.

The WCTU's side lost the election by a mere twenty-five votes. Ballots varied tremendously, depending the number of immigrant men in a precinct. Rural men voted "dry," but urbanites did not, and Hillsborough stayed "wet."

Beyond the wet/dry debate, there were other clashes over Florida's increasing urbanization, and women worked especially on safety and environmental issues. Ranchers had long been accustomed to unfenced land and freely roaming cattle—and springtime fires. To improve grass production, cattlemen set fires to kill underbrush, and not surprisingly, some became wildfires that destroyed property and lives. Mrs. E. E. Pratt sent an assertive letter to the editor objecting to this practice in Polk and Hendry counties. An early environmentalist, she put her point in a broad philosophical context, showing that this class of men ignored the welfare of others when they engaged in such risk:

> Where there is no law . . . [except] promotion of a selfish interest, there is no attractiveness from any point of view. Such a principle, carried out, means isolation. There can be no neighborhood, no town, no city,

no combining of interests for social, religious, or intellectual benefit. All the good that accrues from unity is lost.[17]

"Unity" for the common good was the broad aim of the General Federation of Women's Clubs (GFWC), which formed nationally in 1890. Most GFWC members also were early environmentalists—and one of their first

Formation of women's clubs, 1883–1900

Year	City	Formal Name	Most Prominent Leader
1883	Green Cove Springs	Village Improvement Association	Mrs. A. M. Rutledge
1888	Tampa	Tampa Ladies Improvement Society	Julia Friebele
1889	Crescent City	Village Improvement Association	Bessie Williams
1890	Melrose	Literary and Debating Society	Eliza King
1891	Ormond Beach	Village Improvement Association	not available
1891	Coconut Grove	Housekeeper's Club	Flora McFarlane
1892	Tarpon Springs	Woman's Town Improvement Association	Soledad Safford
1893	Orlando	Orlando Sorosis	Mrs. W. C. Comstock
1894	Jacksonville–Fairfield	Fairfield Improvement Association	Mrs. N. C. Wamboldt
1894	Orange City	Village Improvement Association	Louise Morse
1895	Daytona Beach	Palmetto Club	Celia Doener
1896	Apalachicola	Philaco Woman's Club	Mrs. C. F. Buffam
1897	Palatka	Woman's Fortnightly Club	Mrs. George Gay
1897	Ozona	Village Improvement Association	not available
1897	Jacksonville	Woman's Club of Jacksonville	Mrs. W. W. Kummer
1899	High Springs	New Century Woman's Club	Mrs. Otto Kahlich
1899	Palmetto	Village Improvement Association	not available
1900	Tampa	Tampa Woman's Club	Helen Dick
1900	Miami	Married Ladies' Afternoon Club	not available
1900	Fort Myers	Woman's Club of Fort Myers	Julia Hanson
1900	Titusville	Progressive Club	Mrs. Blake Walker

Source: Compiled by author using information in Jessie Hamm Meyer, *Leading the Way: A Century of Service: The Florida Federation of Women's Clubs, 1895–1995.*

goals affected women in general and Florida in particular. The era's dress standard required a lady to wear a hat, and fashionable women adorned their winter hats with bird feathers. Hunters made significant money by shooting Florida's most colorful birds for their plumes, and during the next decades, GFWC clubs urged women to change that style.

The GFWC had purposes beyond birds and feathers. Its origin had been "study clubs" composed of women who never had the opportunity to go to college. Comparable to modern book clubs, they enabled members to choose a topic that interested them and then read books on it. Sometimes these women hired a (male) professor or (probably female) author to guide them, but often they acted on their own.[18] Conversation almost invariably led to discussion of local needs, and many study clubs thus evolved into service or civic clubs. They took over functions that today are performed by city or county governments—but that in earlier times often were not performed at all, especially in the South.

Florida's first such group that later affiliated with the GFWC was the Green Cove Springs Civic Improvement Association, which despite its gender-neutral name was open only to women and girls. Composed almost entirely of northern women who lived there only from November to May, it made public sanitation its chief priority, and one of the association's first acts was to donate chemicals that residents could use to disinfect their outhouses. Members also lobbied local government to stop cutting down trees and raised money for new landscaping. Ellen and John Borden of the Borden Milk Company donated a cottage that the group used as a clubhouse in 1888.

A similar group began in Tampa in 1888, but it defined itself as exclusively for women. Like the Green Cove Springs group, the Tampa Ladies Improvement Society aimed to improve public property. Sounding much like environmental engineers, they embarked on their first project: landscaping Court House Square. The successfully implemented design included trees, a gazebo for bands, a drinking fountain, curved walks, and benches for pleasant sitting.[19]

Crescent City, which is in Putnam County, consciously modeled its 1889 group on their Clay County neighbors in Green Cove Springs. It had the distinction, however, of building Florida's first library operated by a women's club. Beginning in 1890, the library lasted until 1961, when it was merged into the county system. In the 1890s, though, many viewed such activism a violation of Victorian social codes. Longtime Crescent City member Bessie Williams wrote:

> It was an interesting and disturbing fact that many of our best women did not venture to join this women's organization, fearing to lose the respect of their husbands and families if they became a part of such an audacious group of women, who dared to think they could do for a town what the men had not done.[20]

The club movement benefited tremendously from networking during a year-long World's Fair in Chicago. Also called the Columbian Exhibition, it began on Columbus Day 1892 to commemorate the 400th anniversary of the first voyage to the New World, and it continued until October 1893. Congress appropriated funds for a "Board of Lady Managers" to plan women's activities, which was chaired by part-time Floridian Bertha Honore Palmer.

Each state was entitled to two board members. Florida's were Mrs. E. Nellie Beck, who had just moved from Bartow, where she was editor of the weekly newspaper, to a new job as editorial writer for the *Tampa Times,* and Mary C. Bell, whose residence needs further research. Beck did not submit any recipes to the cookbook published by the board, but both Bell and the alternate "lady manager," Mrs. H. K. Ingram, submitted two. Although a cookbook may seem less than feminist, they were in fact still so new—and publishers still so unaware of the profits to be made—that when Fanny Farmer published her first in 1897, the contract required her to reimburse the company if the cookbook did not sell.

The Board of Lady Managers understood that recipes were something women actually needed in their daily lives—and the cookbook achieved a second purpose in showcasing the nation's varied cuisine. Bell submitted recipes for "Fish Salad" and "Grandmother's Bread Cake," while Ingram's contributions were for watermelon preserves and "Chow-Chow Pickles." Board members also were expected to recruit exhibits from women in their state, and eight female authors from Florida sent books to be displayed. Florida's most unusual exhibit, however, was wall insulation made from palmetto fiber, the creative invention of Julia Daniels Moseley. A talented artist, she pioneered the Limona section of the Hillsborough County town of Brandon.

Moseley's wall art still exists, and it is just one example of the feminist intent of the Chicago event. A female architect designed the Woman's Building; its interior, including statues and paintings by women; the music was composed and performed by women. During the prime week of May 1893, delegates from twenty-seven nations gathered for a World's Congress of

A Most Uncommon Woman: Bertha Honore Palmer

The people who fill newspaper society pages are seldom the same people who live on in the pages of history, but Bertha Honore Palmer was a rare woman who successfully combined the two types of lives. Stunningly beautiful, she was always referred to in her era as "Mrs. Potter Palmer."

Bertha Honore was born in Kentucky in 1849 and married Potter Palmer when she was twenty-one. He was more than two decades older, but she participated in his businesses from the beginning. They took advantage of the 1873 Great Chicago Fire to buy property and eventually owned a large amount of real estate. They also built Chicago's Palmer House, which she personally shaped into one of the world's best hotels. The birth of two sons did not hinder her civic involvement, and when her husband died in 1902, she was worth $8 million—which she would double prior to her own death sixteen years later.

Palmer was a political liberal and a feminist: she supported the Women's Trade Union League and was on the stage with populist Democrat William Jennings Bryan for his high-profile 1896 presidential nomination. She demonstrated great executive skill in chairing the Board of Lady Managers for the Columbian Exposition, creating an unprecedented global event. Palmer shone in managing the often egocentric members of a large board.

Years earlier, Susan B. Anthony had quietly organized prominent Washington women for female inclusion at the exposition, and Anthony defended Palmer against those who complained that she had not been a pioneer in women's rights. Even more impressively, the job that Palmer did was so outstanding that President William McKinley ignored the fact that she had supported his opponent in the 1896 presidential election, and when the World's Fair was held in Paris in 1900, he gave her another major appointment. Again Anthony played a behind-the-scenes role: McKinley had intended to send an all-male delegation to Paris until the aging Susan B. Anthony visited him.

After Potter Palmer died in 1902, his widow spent increasing time away from Chicago, and in 1910, she added a Sarasota home to those she owned in Paris, London, and Chicago. She apparently found great enjoyment in building "The Oaks" in the community of Osprey. She designed and supervised the constructive of a comfortable house with many verandas, extensive gardens, ponds, and guest cottages—as well as her own electrical and water systems. Eventually Bertha Palmer owned some 90,000 acres of frontier land in southwest Florida.

Beyond that, she worked the Palmer Ranch: she studied cattle breeding and disease prevention, and when this research indicated the advisability of fencing some 30,000 acres, she stood up to angry cattlemen accustomed to free range. She raised hogs at another location and also held large tracts of land in and near Tampa, some of which she kept as a hunting preserve: despite stereotypes of frailty, Victorian women did ride horses and shoot rifles.

In an era when mastectomies were still unusual, she had the surgery after discovering breast cancer. The disease nonetheless killed her, and Bertha Honore Palmer died in 1918 at The Oaks. Several modern Sarasota place names recall her prominence.

Representative Women. Although the building could hold 10,000, there were constant lines to get in, and about 150,000 attendees came to 330 workshops on women's issues. Their reports filled six fat volumes.[21]

Bertha Palmer, the stunning executive who led this project, was a multimillionaire, but both she and Tallahassee's very poor "Aunt Memory" Adams were feminists. Born a slave, Adams was aging by 1893, but she was so determined to go to Chicago that she enterprisingly sold photos of herself to fairgoers. Many attendees from the rural North had never seen a black woman, and the photo of a dignified "Aunt Memory" proved popular. It depicted her with an umbrella in her right hand and a short broom in the left; a large leather purse and a food pail hung from her arm.[22] Wearing a traveling cape, she was on her way to the fair.

* * *

Being able to travel is an important part of being free, and a lack of transportation was a huge factor in keeping women confined to their homes. That changed dramatically in turn-of-the-century Florida: in 1881 the state had a mere 550 miles of railroad; just a decade later it had 2,566 miles, and by 1900 it was up to 3,500 miles. The stagecoach trip from Jacksonville to Tampa had taken four days; with the railroad, it was a half day—and from there, connections could be made to the whole world.

This was a real revolution: until then only wealthy women had been able to maintain an expensive horse and carriage; others occasionally rented them from livery stables, but in both cases, they often depended on a man to hitch and drive the horses. With the train, however, even working-class women could buy a ticket and jump aboard. Indeed, a key reason why northern women were able to create organizations sooner than southern women was the simple fact that trains stopped at many small towns in the North, which was not the case in the South.

With Florida's railroads came entirely new cities: Clearwater, St. Petersburg, and Sarasota on the west coast and DeLand, Palm Beach, and Miami on the east. The former military outposts of Fort Myers, Fort Pierce, and Fort Lauderdale became civilian towns and then cities. In the interior, Orlando grew rapidly, as did Sanford, Kissimmee, Lakeland, and Bartow. The latter two towns especially boomed when phosphate, a fertilizer essential, was discovered there in the 1880s, and moving it out to the coasts for shipping also depended on railroads.

To a much greater extent than most people realize, the federal government funded Florida's great railroad barons, Henry Flagler on the eastern Coast and Henry Plant on the west. Plutocrats of both parties controlled Congress, and these men were not embarrassed to give away federal land that benefited both themselves and their financial associates. The congressional charter for the Jacksonville, Tampa, and Key West railroad lines, for example, rewarded investors with 3,840 acres of free land for every mile of railroad built. Henry Plant alone received 1.6 million acres.

Among the place names with which these newcomer landowners gave themselves public recognition were Flagler and Collier counties as well as the towns of Sanford in central Florida and Chipley in the Panhandle; Henry Plant deemed the name of the Hillsborough County town of Ichepuckesassa unpronounceable, and it was renamed Plant City. At the end of construction, railroad magnates owned not only the transportation system but also all the land for miles around it, as Florida continued to be controlled by a minority of very wealthy families.

In this age of "robber barons," many of those families treated their daughters as property to be married off to the highest bidder. Links between prospective husbands and their future fathers-in-law were almost as important as those between bride and groom, and it was not unusual for a man to marry an appreciably younger woman. Henry Morrison Plant followed that pattern: he had visited Florida when his first wife, Ellen Elizabeth Blackstone Plant, was dying of tuberculosis; his second wife was from a family with international business connections.

Like Henry Plant, Henry Flagler came to Florida because his wife was dying of respiratory illness. Mary Flagler had saved him from bankruptcy early in their marriage: when he lost fifty thousand dollars in a Civil War salt mine, they lived on money borrowed from her family. He then became wealthy with Cleveland's Standard Oil Company, and they had moved to New York City by the time she died there in 1881—and in 1883, he married a woman who had nursed her, Ida Alice Shrouds.

Because Ida Alice was just six years older than Flagler's daughter, Jennie Louise, and had been a working woman until they wed, his associates were open about their rejection of the new Mrs. Flagler. The couple went to St. Augustine on their honeymoon, where he conceived the idea of the Ponce de Leon Hotel.[23] It had opened by 1889, and daughter Jennie Louise was on her way there to recuperate from a debilitating childbirth when she died aboard ship. Flagler built St. Augustine's Memorial Church in memory of her and his stillborn grandchild.

Meanwhile, Ida Alice Flagler's mental health was deteriorating. She may have been a psychological casualty of the "Gilded Age," which for wives often meant a "gilded cage." Male historians repeat stories—always from Flagler's perspective—about her obsessive shopping and socializing, her seances and temper tantrums; but it was hard for a working woman—especially a nurse, who had had a purposeful career—to be accepted by the era's upper-class women. Such women sometimes descended into mental illness as a result of their vacuous lives and their frequently absent and unfaithful husbands. All too often physicians worsened the situation by prescribing confinement to bed—the very opposite of what they needed.

State laws also gave husbands great power to send wives to mental institutions, and Henry Flagler had Ida Alice permanently committed to a New York sanitarium in 1897. Without personal resources or family connections, she wasted away there, as Henry "never saw" her again.[24] By 1901 he wanted

Fort Lauderdale Founder Ivy Julia Cromartie Stranahan

Born in White Springs, on north Florida's Suwannee River, Ivy Cromartie moved to primitive southern Florida as a teenager. Her father, North Carolina educator Augustus Whitfield Cromartie, had moved to the north Florida town of Quincy in 1873; he married Sarah Elizabeth Driver, a Hamilton County native, and they eventually had six children. The family moved first to Seffner in Hillsborough County but, after the great freezes in 1894 and 1895, went further south.

Traveling by covered wagon, they settled in 1899 in the new farming community of Lemon City, now a neighborhood of Miami. Young Ivy Cromartie passed the state teachers' examination and taught in the first school in what became Broward County: at the time, there was one school in Dade and one in Palm Beach. She had nine students and taught only briefly: she began in October 1899 but had to give up the job when she married Frank Stranahan in August 1900, as marriage usually disqualified a woman from teaching.

She could, however, teach Seminoles—and Frank Stranahan had established relationships with them. A recent arrival from Ohio, he was eager to live the pioneer life. The young couple moved to the trading post that he had built at Fort Lauderdale, where he also ran a ferry across the New River. They would live there the rest of their lives, while the city grew around them. As in other parts of the nation, the trading post owner was key to contact with natives, who periodically rowed down the river and exchanged their hunted bounty, especially alligator skins, for manufactured goods.

Seminoles came as family groups, with women as well as men engaging in the trading and deal making. As they camped nearby, Ivy Stranahan—who never had children—encouraged the young ones to learn white ways that they would inevitably need to know. Older Seminoles understandably resented the newcomers, and most were reluctant to spend much time with whites. The Stranahans, however, gained their trust, and Ivy taught English to those who were willing to learn. She began by allowing the children to explore her home and play dress-up in her clothing. They eventually called her "Little White Mother."

For centuries as the frontier moved west, many whites who were the first transitional people between natives and newcomers noted that native women usually were more willing than men to adopt the new lifestyle. That was true among Seminoles, too, and it was Ivy Stranahan who brought in the first sewing machines for the colorful garments that are now so strongly associated with Seminole women.

The Stranahans' home served as the Fort Lauderdale post office, community center, and hotel. Expanded and remodeled several times, their residence had two stories of wide verandas by 1913. She was a founder of the Fort Lauderdale Woman's Club in 1911—and the club predated the official founding of the town. Also the founder of "Friends of the Seminoles," she was in charge of that issue for the Florida chapter of the General Federation of Women's Clubs. The GFWC led her into the movement for the vote, and she was president of the Florida Woman Suffrage Association in 1917. She raised money for Liberty Loans during World War I and was active in the Audubon Society, which began working there in 1918. Both Audubon and the GFWC led the movement to discourage women from wearing feathered hats that meant the killing of millions of native birds.

The next decades, however, saw the boom-and-bust cycle of the Roaring Twenties and the Great Depression, and Frank killed himself in 1930. Ivy then leased the first floor of her home as a restaurant and lived on the second. After the economy collapsed, she personally wrote the language that voters added to the Florida Constitution in 1934, which still preserves a taxpayer's homestead rights. When some complained that the homestead exemption would cut revenue for schools, she replied: "No one is a more staunch believer in education than am I . . . , but a family's home comes first. . . . If we lose our homes, we lose everything."

Pioneer life proved healthful, and because she lived to age ninety, her story continues in later chapters of this book. The Stranahan House is now a museum in downtown Fort Lauderdale, and she was admitted to the Florida Women's Hall of Fame in 1996.

Note: August Burghard, *Mrs. Frank Stranahan: Pioneer.* (Fort Lauderdale: Historical Society of Fort Lauderdale, 1968), unpaginated. See also Harry A. Kersey Jr. *The Stranahans of Fort Lauderdale: A Pioneer Family of New River* (Gainesville: University Press of Florida, 2003).

a divorce so that he could wed Mary Lily Kenan of North Carolina, who was about half his age and from a wealthy background. Flagler would spend many millions more on her than on his first wives, including building their palatial Palm Beach home, Whitehall.

Inconveniently, proven adultery was the only grounds for divorce in both New York and Florida—and because Flagler could not plausibly claim that the institutionalized Ida Alice was guilty of adultery, he needed to manipulate the law. He adopted Florida as his legal residence, and the state legislature obliged, amending the divorce code for his convenience. The adjustment was passed in 1901 and repealed in 1905; Flagler "apparently [was] the only person ever to take advantage of the law."[25] Credible historians claim he spent at least twenty thousand dollars lobbying for it.

Unlike railroad men Flagler and Plant, Julia Tuttle did not get any favors from the legislature nor any business subsidies from the federal government—but she was the primary reason why south Florida developed as it did. When the great freezes of the mid-1890s wiped out orange trees in the Jacksonville area, where Flagler was at the time, she sent him citrus blooms to show that Miami had not been hit. It was key to convincing him that it was worthwhile to extend his Florida East Coast Railway to the southern tip of the peninsula—and some three hundred people cheered the first train to arrive in Miami in 1896. For all that Flagler wins praise in economic histories, Julia Tuttle, "the Mother of Miami" demonstrated more business acumen and foresight than he did: his prediction was that Miami never would be more than a "fishing village."[26]

Yet despite her obvious ability, Julia Tuttle could not vote. To meet the minimum number of voters required by the state to become a municipality, Flagler and other men who incorporated the city in 1896 had to reach out to black men. According to Miami historian Marvin Dunn, of the 367 men who met for incorporation, 162 were black, and the first name on the city charter was that of a black man, Silas Austin. A Jewish man, Isadore Cohen, observed that "the best speech" at the meeting was that of another black man, "Alex C. Lightburn or Lighthourn, who was born in England or the Bahamas." The *Miami Metropolis* praised the integrated, international scene: "the color line was obliterated and . . . there was a full determination that the colored fellow should vote just as he wished."[27] But neither the "the Mother of Miami" nor any other woman—black or white, American-born or not—could cast a ballot.

* * *

West Coast Queens: Margaret Plant and Emelia Chapin

Margaret Plant swept into late nineteenth-century Florida and transformed its social scene in so sensational a way that the drama of her simple presence may never be equaled. Born Margaret Josephine Loughman, she was the daughter of a well-connected New York family and grew up in a Fifth Avenue mansion near the Rockefellers. She married Henry Plant in 1873, a dozen years after the death of his first wife, and became the sort of society matron featured in Edith Wharton novels. She had no children of her own but educated her husband and teenage stepson Morton—who accompanied the newlyweds on their honeymoon—in the sophisticated lifestyle of New York and Europe during the Gilded Age.

Henry Plant and Henry Flagler rivaled each other in the grandeur of the hotels they built along their rail lines, especially those at the terminus of each; Flagler built The Breakers in Palm Beach, while Plant created the Belleview Biltmore in Clearwater. These were not designed for Floridians but rather for wealthy people from elsewhere who discovered the joy of winter in Florida. When the Plants were in the area they made their home at the Tampa Bay Hotel, across the Hillsborough River from the city of Tampa. Henry and Margaret had separate first-floor suites in one wing. The hotel was so big that rickshaws took guests from the elevator—the first in Florida—to dining rooms and verandas.

The couple traveled the world collecting millions of dollars' worth of furnishings for its 511 rooms, delivered on eighty train cars. Amusements included a casino and a combination swimming pool–dance floor. Celebrities accepted invitations to entertain at this outpost of civilization, including famous French dramatist Sarah Bernhardt, Australian opera diva Nellie Melba, and Russian ballerina Anna Pavlova. Margaret Plant was queen of it all: although few Floridians were invited to such events, local newspapers used several paragraphs merely to describe her dress.

Those glorious days, however, were brief. No matter how attractive the enclave of Plant's hotels, the fact was that outside its gates, the area was a cultural wasteland. When Henry Plant died just six years after the grandest hotel opened, the Tampa Bay Hotel soon

continued

degenerated into a fading monument to his vanity and competition with Flagler. Margaret and Morton Plant quarreled, and the estate was tied up in legal proceedings for years. Morton became more identified with Pinellas County and its Belleview Biltmore, but neither he nor his stepmother spent much time in Florida. In 1905 the multi-million-dollar hotel was sold to the City of Tampa for a mere $125,000. It deteriorated during the next two decades until finally being taken over by the new private University of Tampa during the Great Depression. The preservation of the Plants' wing is largely due to The Chiselers, a group of women who began by using chisels to chip away defacements on precious marble.

Emelia Chapin was similar in that her West Coast presence was conspicuous but brief. The women differed, though, in that Chapin was the dominant business partner in her marriage. She inherited a fortune from her New York family and married Chester Chapin in New Orleans in 1867: although he also was wealthy, he preferred yachting, while she enjoyed making money. They built a Tampa mansion in 1891 that included its own water system—something the city did not yet provide. Nor was there any electrical system until 1892, when Emelia Chapin became the principal stockholder of the new electric company.

Electricity at the time was not aimed at household use but rather for powering city trolleys—and Emelia Chapin was powerful enough that the company built a separate streetcar line through largely vacant miles to reach her estate on the bay. There she not only boarded her own luxurious car, but the car itself was not bothered by other trolleys: when she "chose to sally forth . . . the rails were cleared for her pleasure."*

Like the hotel's customers, however, she soon found that there was little reason to sally forth. Bored with Florida, she decided to sell less than a decade later. Her decision also may have derived from a failing marriage: her ex-husband soon married a young cousin. Emelia Chapin's legacy, however, lives on in the Tampa Electric Company, now TECO.

Note: * Gary Mormino and Tony Pizzo, *Tampa: The Treasure City* (Tulsa, Okla.: Continental Heritage Press, 1983), 138.

Eleanor McWilliams Chamberlain emerged in the 1890s as Florida's most prominent leader for women's rights. Called Ella, she moved to Tampa from Iowa in 1882, and a decade later, in 1892, attended a women's convention back in her home state. It inspired her, and she used the column she wrote for a Tampa newspaper to broach the subject of the vote for women. "There are those who conscientiously oppose . . . agitation," she said, but "we respectfully ask such to reserve judgment until they have carefully weighed the claims of women to an equality with man." She requested that readers "sincerely ask themselves if manhood has greater gifts, interests, or rights than womanhood." Chamberlain also resisted her male editor's request for more traditional subjects in her column, declaring, "The world is not suffering for another cake recipe."[28]

Within two years she had organized at least one hundred Florida women into the National American Woman Suffrage Association, and in 1895 she and her husband sat with Susan B. Anthony at its national convention, where Anthony told the audience that "for several years" Chamberlain had sent her boxes of oranges. This convention, the first in the South, was held in Atlanta, and that city was eager to show "the New South" to its former Yankee enemies. In the same year more than a dozen members of "the Pensacola Colored Women's Auxiliary Board" also traveled to Atlanta, where they heard Booker T. Washington speak.[29]

When Anthony presided over the 1895 convention, women had full voting rights in Wyoming, Utah, and Colorado. In several other states they could cast ballots in some races, but not others, with school elections being most common. In some places, including Michigan and Oregon, women organized as many as a half-dozen statewide election campaigns before they won rights—but in the South, where rhetoric about the primacy of states was so powerful—women never organized anything like a state-focused strategy. Florida's feminists were highly dependent on Ella Chamberlain, and when she moved away, the association would disappear. When the movement for the vote revived in 1913, she did accept a vice presidency of the suffrage association, but most of its leadership would come from Florida's eastern coast, not from her Tampa.

The formative stage of leadership usually occurs during a person's education, and several of today's colleges and universities had their origins in this era. Florida Memorial College, a private school for blacks, began in Lake City and is now in Miami; Sarah Ann Blocker was one of its founders. The institution that now is Edward Waters College has always been in

Jacksonville. It calls itself "Florida's oldest private college," as it originated in 1866 to educate newly free black men as preachers. Reconstruction financial problems meant that the seminary had to close, and when it reopened in 1883 it included women. It was then known as East Florida Conference High School or East Florida Scientific and Divinity High School. A decade later, the school was permanently named Edward Waters College for the local bishop of the African Methodist Episcopal Church.

The state's first public higher education for blacks was at Florida Agricultural and Mechanical College, which opened in Tallahassee in 1887. By then almost all southern states had "A&M" schools, which were highly vocational compared with the classical education at colleges for whites. Like most historically black colleges, all three of these Florida institutions were open to both women and men. Higher education for whites would remain gender-segregated far into the future, as white women would be limited to Tallahassee's West Florida Seminary, which later became Florida State College for Women.

Wealthy northern families endowed schools that became black colleges, and they also founded Rollins College, where blacks would not be welcome. Begun in Winter Park in 1885, it was typical of the era's new private colleges for white women in its upper-class and Protestant nature. Rollins College was unique in Florida. The first to call itself a college from the beginning, it was neither a female seminary nor a "normal school," the era's term for teacher training institutions that were open to both men and women.

"Prodded by the efforts of Miss Lucy Cross of Daytona," the new institution was named for the largest donor, Alonzo Rollins of Chicago.[30] The charter faculty consisted of three men and two women, Annie Morton and Eva J. Root. Faculty were expected to spend leisure time with students on the lovely lakeside campus, while also providing rigorous education. Mandatory classes included Latin and German, physics and biology, geometry and trigonometry as well as entire courses on ancient writers such as Sophocles and Tacitus. After appreciable debate by the all-male Board of Trustees, gymnastics also became mandatory. At the first graduation ceremony in 1891, Millie G. Hooker read her essay on German astronomer Caroline Herschel, and other speakers were "Misses Hooker, McDuffie, and Fisk."[31] The faculty that year included seven women and seven men, an unusual parity.

Arguably two years older than Rollins, Florida Southern College now advertises itself as the state's first private college. It began in 1883 as Florida Southern Institute, an institution for men in Orlando. With a college

Beginnings for Blacks: Sarah Ann Blocker and Florida Memorial College

Historians do not yet know if Sarah Ann Blocker's family was slave or free or a mixture, but she was born in 1857, four years before the Civil War began. Both her mother and her grandmother had been born in Delaware, the last state to abolish legal slavery. Her father was a slave born in South Carolina, but it was the mother's status that defined freedom.

According to the 1870 census, when Sarah would have been thirteen, they lived in Augusta, Georgia; her mother was listed as the household head and as an illiterate seamstress. The 1880 census repeated that, adding that the younger Sarah, then aged twenty-three, also was a seamstress. The family had at least two sons, and the children may have been educated at a freedman's school. Soon after the 1880 census the younger Sarah A. Blocker went to Atlanta and enrolled at the institution that became Atlanta University. She earned a two-year degree there in 1883 and began to teach back in Augusta.

She may have continued her college education in summer sessions, but it was common for both whites and blacks to teach with much lesser credentials than a two-year degree. It is clear that her siblings also valued education: an 1888 city directory for Augusta listed both her and two brothers as educators. In accordance with the gender bias that was standard, they were school principals and she was a teacher.

Meanwhile, the Florida Baptist Institute for Negroes had begun in 1879 in Live Oak, under the aegis of the American Baptist Home Society. When it moved to Jacksonville and became Florida Baptist College in 1892, Sarah Ann Blocker was recruited to teach there. Its president, Rev. J. T. Brown, soon asked her to be his assistant, and when he retired, she recruited an Atlanta University colleague, Nathan W. Collier, as the new president. Blocker's titles over time varied from teacher to "matron" to vice president, but it seems clear that it was gender that blocked her from the top job.

The school merged with another and moved again in 1918, going to St. Augustine and becoming Florida Normal and Industrial

continued

Institute. "Normal school" was the era's term for teacher-training institutions that granted a teaching certificate, not a college degree; and "industrial institute" showed vocational intent. Classes at industrial schools usually were segregated by gender: female students learned cooking, sewing, and so forth, while male students learned trades such as carpentry and metal work.

The name change shows that the school had lost its earlier theological identity and now was focused on a curriculum that would enable graduates to find better-paying jobs after shorter courses. Sarah Ann Blocker gave the remainder of her life to the school, dying at age eighty-seven in St. Augustine. Her obituary in the *St. Augustine Evening Record* said in part:

> The death of this beloved colored resident will be heard with deep regret throughout St. Augustine, as she had numberless friends among both the white and colored populations. She was known as a leader among Negro educators and had worked for half a century for the progress of her race. When she retired from active participation in the affairs of the Florida Normal a year or two ago, she was accorded many honors.*

The year of her death, 1944, was the hardest year of World War II, which may account for the fact that according to a local historian, her remains lay "in an unmarked, weed-covered grave in St. Augustine, next to the grave of her friend and co-worker, Nathan W. Collier, whose grave [was] marked with a large tombstone." When the school moved to Miami in 1963, "both graves were moved" there. The school was renamed Florida Memorial College and honored her on its new campus with Sarah A. Blocker Hall. She was admitted to the Florida Women's Hall of Fame in 2003, and the following year, Florida Memorial College granted her a posthumous honorary doctorate.

Note: * From a web page associated with www.drbronsontours.com.

curriculum added in 1885, it moved to Leesburg and began admitting women. After additional moves within Pinellas County, it would settle permanently in Lakeland in 1922—but wherever its location, Methodists sponsored the college, and its students were more likely to be middle-class than those at Rollins.

Teaching was well established as a profession for women by the late nineteenth century, and the Florida Education Association (FEA) began in 1886. This was several decades after such organizations of educators had begun in the North, and FEA included white educators only. It was affiliated with the National Education Association (NEA), which was long dominated by administrators, not teachers—and the vast majority of administrators were men. Although women long composed the majority of members, they would not be leaders for most of another century.

Medicine, which would be unwelcoming to women in the twentieth century, was comparatively open in this era. Dr. Mary Safford of Tarpon Springs serves as an example. Born in Vermont in 1831, she grew up in Illinois; she learned French and German and worked as a governess. When the Civil War began, she worked at the giant hospital at Cairo, Illinois, to which wounded Union soldiers were brought on the Mississippi River. Exhausted at the war's end, Safford went to Europe as a governess and then trained at hospitals in Vienna, Austria, and Breslau, Poland. After returning, she graduated from New York Medical College for Women, which had been established by Dr. Clemence Lozier—another pioneer physician who should be better known.

After her 1869 graduation, Dr. Safford practiced in Chicago and in Boston—where she also was one of the first women in the nation elected to a school board. A well-respected physician, she has been credited with operating as the lead surgeon with male physicians as assistants. She was married between 1872 and 1879, but appears to have regretted it, and Gordon Blake may have gone to Georgia to give her grounds for divorce on the basis of desertion. Primary documents do not indicate that she took his name, and she was always called Dr. Safford in Florida, where she began spending winters with her brother, land developer Anson Safford. She and a former student, Dr. Fidelia Jane Merrick Whitcomb, opened a health spa in the Tarpon Springs Hotel about 1882.[32] She spoke on feminist issues, especially urging women to reject fashionable dress with its damagingly tight waists. Dr. Safford died at Tarpon Springs, where the Safford House is open to visitors.

Dr. Ida Bruce and her husband, Dr. Hiram Bruce, came to Tampa from New York City in 1890. She too had been affiliated with Lozier's school and hospital, and she trained female medical missionaries bound for China. Dr. Laura Reading, who also practiced in Tampa in this era, was akin to Dr. Bruce in being well-credentialed and married. The newspapers had great difficulty sorting out the proper honorific for a female physician, especially if she was married to another physician. Because Laura Reading's husband was not in medicine, she always was called "Doctor," but because Dr. Ida Bruce's husband was a physician like her, she often was lumped with him as "Dr. and Mrs. Hiram Bruce."

When Ida Bruce died soon after childbirth, her husband married another physician who also took his name: Dr. Orpha D. Bruce, an Ohio native who graduated from medical school in Boston in 1885. She had practiced in Cleveland, Ohio, and Portland, Oregon, and probably knew the deceased Ida Bruce from mutual medical associations. The confusing—but nonetheless wonderful—result was that Tampa had two female physicians at the turn of the century, both called Dr. Bruce.[33]

Few Floridians knew of Louise Cecilia Fleming, even though she was the niece of Francis Fleming, who was governor between 1889 and 1893. Called Lulu, she was a slave at birth; her mother, Chloe, was a slave who bore her master's child. They lived in the same Jacksonville area as other wealthy mixed-race families, and her father, Lewis Fleming, not only acknowledged his illegitimate child but also gave her a fine education.[34] She was valedictorian of her class at Shaw University, a North Carolina institution for blacks, and then went to Africa, sponsored by the Woman's Baptist Foreign Missionary Society in the West. She returned to the United States in 1891 and, in 1895, graduated from Women's Medical College of Pennsylvania, which had been founded by Quakers before the Civil War. She spent three more years in the Congo before contracting African sleeping sickness; brought back to the United States in a coma, she died in Philadelphia.[35]

Philadelphia, Boston, and New York all featured excellent medical schools for women, and throughout the nation, women progressed much faster as physicians than as attorneys. This was partly because in this era of female modesty, women sought out female doctors; and partly because medicine was less regulated then than now, with the result that people chose doctors without particular regard to credentials and licenses. Having the permission of the state to practice was much more serious for lawyers than for physicians, and consequently it was harder for women to break into law than medicine.

Midwestern states licensed female lawyers, and Nebraska admitted Mary

Baird Bryan to the bar in 1883, even though she was married—to future presidential nominee William Jennings Bryan—and had a three-year-old child.[36] Mae Wood, who also became an attorney in Nebraska, drew newspaper attention upon her 1896 arrival in Tampa, but there is no record that she ever was licensed to practice in Florida. Similarly, we lack records for Alice Johnson of Live Oak, who may have been the second woman admitted to the Florida bar, probably in 1899. The first, however, is certain: Florida's first female attorney was Jacksonville's Louise Rebecca Pinnell, who was admitted in 1898. She was born in Missouri, which had the first law school that allowed women to enroll.

Much more prominent in the media than in law or medicine, women had been journalists since before the United States began, and several Florida women held high places with newspapers. They did not necessarily write on feminine topics, and some had significant political power. As early as the 1880 census, Julia Henderson Magbee was listed as "editor of paper": with her husband, controversial lawyer James T. Magbee, she published the *Tampa Guardian*.

She died in 1885, at just thirty-nine, but she was not singular; former mayor D. B. McKay, of the pioneer McKay family, wrote of other women in key press positions. When the *Tampa Times* was founded, he said, Nellie Beck "was induced to give up her job as editor of a Bartow weekly to become editorial writer" for the new daily. McKay had even more praise for a third woman:

> Brilliant—and beautiful—Lucie Vannever edited the *Tampa Weekly Journal* . . . for several years. She asked no favor on account of her sex and spoke her mind freely on all public questions. In the 1892 [gubernatorial] campaign the Democrats . . . were badly split . . . , and Mrs. Vannever advocated for Laurens Mitchell. . . . The lady editor's advice was followed. The Democrats closed ranks, Judge Mitchell was nominated and elected.

McKay added that once, when "Mrs. Vannevar was engaged in heated debate with an obese and pompous Middle Florida editor," she "descended from her usually dignified attitude" and charged that her opponent was afflicted with "constipation of intelligence and diarrhea of stupidity."[37]

Others emulated the female postmasters of the Reconstruction Era and secured those federal appointments. Victoria Brandon and her husband John built a mansion between Lakeland and Tampa in this era, and she ran

Florida's First Female Attorney

Born on March 31, 1877, Rebecca Louise Pinnell attended the public schools of Crawford County, Missouri, and graduated from nearby Steelville College. When she was in her late teens the Pinnell family moved to the Levy County town of Bronson. Her father was an attorney, and like many male aspiring lawyers, young Rebecca Pinnell learned the legal field through apprenticeship: she worked in her father's office until she was twenty-one and old enough to take the bar exam, which she easily passed.

Even though other states had been licensing female lawyers since 1869, when Iowa was first, Florida's judicial officials in 1898 seemed not to have heard this three-decade-old news. "They just didn't know what to do with me," she said later. The Florida Supreme Court debated the matter from May to October 1898 before admitting Louise Pinnell as the state's first female attorney.

She worked with her father until 1901, when she joined the corporate practice of a Jacksonville attorney and developed a specialty in railroads. It remained a new area of Florida law, and in 1920 Pinnell went to work for the state's biggest transportation magnate, Henry Flagler of the Florida East Coast Railway. Two of her colleagues there were men who became Florida's first and second presidents of the American Bar Association, and she rose to an executive position, assistant corporate secretary.

Pinnell volunteered for the Red Cross in World War I and was a charter member of both the Young Women's Christian Association and the Business and Professional Women in Jacksonville. In the 1930s she was a leader in the National Association of Women Lawyers.

She practiced law for sixty years and was well respected throughout the state. Never marrying, she lived comfortably with two sisters in a waterfront home in Mandarin. Louise Rebecca Pinnell died on May 22, 1966, at age eight-nine. In a 1958 interview, she summarized:

> Women have made wonderful progress in this century. They have proved that they can go into almost any field and be successful if they work at it. Law practice is hard work and demands a lot of study, but it's a fine field for a woman and offers many rewards. If I could pass the bar examination studying in my father's office and reading his books, a woman today shouldn't have any trouble.

Note: Wendy S. Loquasto, ed., *Celebrating Florida's First 150 Women Lawyers* (Charlottesville, Va.: LEXIS, 2000), 14–16.

the post office for the new town of Brandon—which at more than a 100,000 residents is now Florida's largest unincorporated city. She was born as Victoria Seward in 1843. Her name changed to Varn before she married John Brandon; after another widowhood and remarriage, it would change to Sherrill. These name changes and the fact that the city never incorporated make her less well known than later women who followed as land developers.[38]

The little community was then called New Hope, and it changed to Brandon when Victoria—and Julia Moseley in nearby Limona—led its growth.[39] After John Brandon died in 1886, "Victoria Brandon took the initiative to found a town." According to Tampa mayor D. B. McKay, "Victoria had a surveyor . . . lay out about forty acres of land and streets for the town."[40] She named streets for herself and for other female family members. The *Tampa Tribune* declared in 1890, "The site is on a beautiful, level tract of high pine land . . . [and] the beautiful orange grove of Mrs. Victoria Brandon."[41] She built a depot to induce the railroad to stop there and became the town's first postmaster.

As noted, other women served as postmasters too, often combining that with running a store, but Lizzie Carew received a more unconventional federal appointment: the *Tampa Journal* headlined on August 17, 1888, that she would be the local customs inspector. It is true that her husband had held this position until his death the previous Christmas Eve, but it was nonetheless exceptional that she was appointed. Customs inspector positions were prime political patronage, and as a woman, Carew could not even vote. Moreover, because the appointment took place during one of the era's few years when Democrats controlled the White House, there would have been a line of Tampa men—virtually all of whom were Democrats—waiting for the job. Her appointment came from President Grover Cleveland, who was no feminist, and the best explanation for Carew's appointment seems to be merit.

Or the explanation may be that women could have played a larger role in this area of business than historians realize. Business directories for Tampa in the 1890s list Miss Alicia M. Gonzalez as a "custom house broker." Her advertisement explained that she spoke English, Spanish, and French and promised she would "properly attend to all . . . custom house matters."[42] An astute businesswoman, she was Alicia Gonzalez Neve when she became a major philanthropist, especially for Catholic causes, during the dark depression days of the 1930s.

Finally, a huge occupational field opened to women as Florida began to get electrical and especially telephone service in the late 1890s. Although phone companies began in the North with male switchboard operators, managers almost immediately realized that young men would not pay sufficient attention to this tedious yet vital work. Telephone operators soon became almost exclusively women—and in small towns, they often operated switchboards in their homes.

Phone companies could pay women smaller salaries than most men would expect, and women were willing to make themselves available at all hours of the day and night. They were accustomed to such responsibility from child care; they had been schooled all their lives to be diplomatic and patient; and they made ideal telephone operators. For decades into the future, until the installation of self-dialed phones in the 1950s, millions of women around the nation worked as phone operators. In Florida, and as elsewhere, these experienced women almost never rose to executive positions.

The wives of executive and professional men, however, continued to build women's clubs; at least eighteen developed in Florida during the 1890s. Some groups, such as the Melrose Literary and Debating Society, Orlando's Sorosis, and the initial Tampa Woman's Club, were study clubs that explored academic subjects, especially classical literature.[43] Others were civic clubs from the beginning, lobbying for improvements, especially in sanitation and sewage. Those in Ormond Beach, Orange City, and other locales that had "Village Improvement Association" in their name were of this nature—and were made up exclusively of women, even though nothing about their name implied that.

Other groups were even more pointed about their nonfeminist nature: the best examples were in southern Florida, where the Miami women dubbed themselves the Married Ladies Afternoon Club and the Coconut Grove group was the Housekeeper's Club. That was a particularly irony, given that its most prominent leader was Flora McFarlane—an unmarried woman who created the first south Florida school in 1891. But whether feminist in theory or not, their behavior was feminist, and the club movement that they pioneered would expand exponentially in the new century.

* * *

As the curtain closed on the nineteenth century, the United States presaged its global role in the twentieth century by ending the four-hundred-year presence of Spain in the New World. Spain had lost Florida in 1819, and as the century progressed, its Latin American colonies fell like dominoes. When Cuba, the queen of the Spanish Empire for four centuries, joined its sister colonies in rebellion, Spain was determined to hang on to this last jewel deriving from the initiative of Queen Isabella in 1492. Cubans felt differently, and they staged several revolts against Spain between 1868 and 1898.

Florida's interaction with Cuba was so frequent that by the 1890s, upwards of fifty thousand passengers a year traveled on steamships between Tampa and Havana. Political empathy naturally followed, and when Cuba declared its independence in 1895, support groups sprang up in the United States. The WCTU even opened a shelter for war refugees in Cuba: Tampa's Kate P. Stewart "moved to Havana . . . appealing to her sisters at home to supply the clothing, medicine, bedding, and books."[44]

Carolina Rodriguez had worked for Cuban independence for decades and fled from political imprisonment when the 1895 rebellion erupted. Even the *Tampa Morning Tribune,* which usually was antagonistic to Cubans and certainly to rabble-rousers, dubbed Rodriguez "Cuba's Lady Patriot" in 1898, when she was close to seventy.

At the other end of the age spectrum were Cuban-American girls who delivered "spontaneous orations." At one rally, "Miss Louise Sanchez was the feature of the evening . . . , her every sentence filled with patriotic emotion which set the whole house wild with enthusiasm." At another, more than a thousand people came to hear a speech by Martin Herrera—but it was his ten-year-daughter, Pennsylvania Herrera, who charmed the crowd, including a *Tribune* reporter He wrote dramatically:

> Silence reigned. She began her speech and then for 20 minutes she spoke extempore in clear, measured tones, giving emphasis to her well-rounded sentences with graceful gestures which brought round after round of applause. . . . Not a few eyes were dimmed with tears. . . . It was a scene this writer never witnessed before—a little girl pleading with the earnestness of a prince and the eloquence of a sage.

Among the women's revolutionary groups that developed were Cuba Libre (Free Cuba), Estrella Solitaria (Lone Star), 24 de Febrero (February 24, the date of the 1895 outbreak), and Discipulas de Martí (Disciples of José Martí, the Cuban equivalent of George Washington). Some groups were for married women, while others were made up of girls—including Pennsylvania Herrera and her sister, Pocahontas. The main work of these women's

Paulina Pedroso: Protester against Spain

Paulina Pedroso was born and died in Cuba but was very influential during the years that she lived in Key West and Tampa. A descendant of African slaves, she married in her teens but never had children. She and her husband Ruperto moved from their native Pinar del Rio to Havana in the 1860s, where they became skilled cigar makers. Like many other Cubans, they went on to Key West, where they worked until the late 1880s, when they and many other cigar workers moved to new factories in Tampa.

In addition to rolling cigars, they ran a boardinghouse in Ybor City, the Cuban section of Tampa. Cuba's great revolutionary leader José Martí lived there when he was in the United States organizing support for war against Spain. Paulina was a more powerful personality than Ruperto, and it was she who welcomed Martí when he first visited Tampa in 1891. Because Martí was, of course, a revolutionary, and because most cigar factory owners were men from Spain who opposed to Cuba's revolution, she was taking a genuine risk in supporting Martí. In fact, a Tampa conservative once poisoned him, and she nursed him back to health.

Martí and Pedroso also encouraged Floridians to think about racism. He was white, while she was very black—but they walked together in the cities of Tampa and Key West, spreading another subtle message as they led rallies and raised money for the revolution. Her political activism, which Ruperto supported in a subordinate role, showed another kind of independence.

The United States entered the war in April 1898, and within a few months Spain lost both Cuba and Puerto Rico, its last colonies in the Western Hemisphere. In 1900 victorious Cubans met at the Pedroso home and formed La Sociedad Libres Pensadore Martí-Maceo, to honor both José Martí and Antonio Maceo, the black leader of Afro-Cubans.

Paulina Pedroso's goal had been for the general political good, not for personal reward, and she continued to work in Ybor City. Like most of her colleagues in the cigar industry, she also was a strong unionist, and when Tampa cigar workers went on strike in 1910, the couple returned to Cuba. The new government there honored them with free housing for the rest of their lives. Then sixty-five, Paulina Pedroso died at age eighty.

Decades later the Cuban government purchased the land on which her boardinghouse had stood and created a small park dedicated to her, Martí, and Cuban independence from Spain. The nation of Cuba still officially owns it, but after Fidel Castro's 1959 victory against Cuban president Fulgencio Batista, the park became a target for political opponents. Paulina Pedroso was inducted into the Florida Women's Hall of Fame in 1993, one of the first choices of the late Governor Lawton Chiles.

Note: Thanks to Dr. Gary Mormino of the Florida Studies Center in St. Petersburg, who nominated Paulina Pedroso for the Florida Women's Hall of Fame. Other sources are Susan Greenbaum, *More than Black: Afro-Cubans in Tampa* (Gainesville: University Press of Florida, 2002), and Nancy Hewitt, "Paulina Pedroso and *Las Patriotas* of Florida," in *Spanish Pathways in Florida, 1492–1992*, ed. Ann L. Henderson and Gary R. Mormino (Sarasota: Pineapple Press, 1991).

organizations, as ever, was fundraising, primarily to buy guns and ammunition. Many cigar factory workers donated a dollar per week, and America Herrera donated her silver to be melted down for cash. The Sociedad de Beneficencias coordinated shelter for refugees: by early 1898 nearly three thousand Cubans had fled for their lives.

There were other national and international reasons for U.S. entrance into what was termed the Spanish-American War. Congress declared the conflict to be official in April 1898. By then, wrote a Key West historian, "it had become clear that ground zero for this war would be Tampa rather than Key West. . . . Even the most adamant Key West booster had to admit that it was the better choice. After all, Tampa possessed two things that Key West did not: a regular [drinking] water supply and railroad connections."[45] Tampa Bay also had well-organized women, as Anglos joined Cubans in supporting the federal soldiers who set up camps as far away as Lakeland. All had gone to Cuba by June 7, so this memorable time lasted only a few weeks—but its impact was far greater.

Military officers set up headquarters at the Tampa Bay Hotel, where, according to Clara Barton, who had founded the International Red Cross in the 1870s, both Henry and Margaret Plant were in residence. International correspondents descended there to write about the west coast of Florida.

Most noted the incongruity of the fabulous hotel and the town across the river, which *Scribner's* magazine described as "chiefly composed of derelict wooden houses drifting on an ocean of sand."[46] Few Tampans were welcome in the fantastic hotel, and on the opposite coast, in the hotels owned by Henry Flagler, restrictions were even more severe. Florida author Diane Roberts wrote that at Flagler's Royal Poinciana Hotel in Palm Beach, "Regulations said that 'no native of Florida' was allowed inside."[47]

At the Tampa Bay Hotel, the most remembered guest was Colonel Theodore Roosevelt—but Red Cross founder Clara Barton also served in this war and made several trips between Florida and Cuba. She stayed in less expensive lodging and, as she had during the Civil War, discovered a tremendous need for supplies. Fort Brooke closed soon after the Civil War, and although Barton wrote that she met "a bevy of nice people," neither Tampa nor the army was prepared for the twenty-five thousand men who crowded the town.[48]

Women did what they could to pick up the shreds of poor military planning. Seventeen sisters of the Holy Names arose early every morning to cook for soldiers, who were hungry because of sparse and spoiled rations. Enterprising "black women under umbrellas" took the opportunity to sell "fried chicken cooked on Cuban clay stoves."[49] Nuns turned two of their schools into hospitals that soon were needed by malnourished northern men, who also suffered from the Florida heat and mosquitoes. Cuba's climate is similar, and the need for hospitals soon proved great.

Five times more men died from tropical diseases than from wounds in the brief war. Hospital ships bore many back along the East Coast, and especially in the Jacksonville area, women ran convalescent hospitals. Indeed, the Army Nurse Corps, the first military unit in the world to admit women, began in 1901 as a direct consequence of the need for organized nursing in the Spanish-American War.

In addition to famed Clara Barton, two other women were notable at the war's Florida headquarters. Anna Northend Benjamin wrote for the Leslie newspaper chain (run by the very astute Miriam Leslie), while Kathleen Blake Watkins reported for the *Toronto Mail and Express.*[50] Charles E. Hands, a correspondent for the *London Daily Mail,* was impressed with both female reporters. "Mrs. Watkins," he said, "knew everybody worth knowing in about a quarter of a hour. In a little while she was introducing us to general and colonels. She talked to the Cuban women . . . and before the evening was out, she gave us full details of an expedition to send arms and stores to the insurgents—news which we had been trying to get."[51]

"Mrs. Watkins" probably was a young widow, and Hands called her colleague "Miss Benjamin." Unwilling to hang around the headquarters awaiting news, Benjamin moved on to Key West, where she persuaded the captain of a ship hauling coal to Guantanamo Bay to take her along—and arrived in Cuba before the U.S. Navy did. With a similarly daring attitude, Mabel Williams Bean became the "spy on the bicycle." A young assistant at the Port Tampa post office, nine miles down the bay from the city, she later summarized:

> The War Department in Washington had learned that certain Spaniards . . . were sending letters and photographs about Fort Dade and Fort DeSoto on Egmont and Mullet Keys and pictures of military equipment in and around Tampa. I was told to watch these two Spaniards as much as I possibly could and report their actions. I knew them both . . .
>
> I took the mail, everything to and from, these two suspects. . . . I interpreted the letters from Spanish into English and read them to Gen. Shafter. I engaged these two Spaniards in conversation when they came to the post office and when they left I followed them on my bicycle. . . .
>
> The next spring I went to Cuba as a bride and attended the first Memorial Day exercise held in Havana. . . . The American women in Cuba decorated the twisted, rusty wreck that had once been the splendid battleship [USS *Maine*] with flowers and flags. . . . I saw the last of the Spanish soldiers leave Havana.[52]

That was in 1899, the last year of a century that saw more progressive change than any other to that point. This applies especially for women, as the nineteenth century marked the world's first organized movement for their rights. Because of pioneer feminists, the status of women in the United States in 1899 was higher than almost anywhere else in the world—and certainly higher than in Spain, which had been declining since its zenith under Queen Isabella four centuries earlier. The next century would bring even more change for women, including the right to vote.

6 A New Century, 1901–1920

Britain's Queen Victoria—who also reigned over much of Africa, Asia, and the rest of the globe—died at the beginning of the twentieth century. Although she was a monarch in her own right and not politically dependent on her husband, Prince Albert of Germany, she encouraged a cult of domesticity that centered on him and their nine children. Victorianism had great influence in America during her long reign, from 1837 to 1901, and her passing signaled the passing of restrictions on female life implied by "Victorianism."

The queen asked to meet Susan B. Anthony when both women were late in life, but the monarch never officially supported political equality for women in the way that she had taken a firm stand against slavery. That and other crimes against humanity—such as India's burning of widows and Chinese foot-binding that left women unable to walk—declined in colonies under her influence. Yet Victoria never spoke out on the vote for women or even the reform of English law that discriminated against her fellow females.

The first decade of the twentieth century, in fact, saw much feminist regression in the United States, as there were no victories for the vote in any state for fifteen years, between Idaho in 1896 and California in 1911. In Florida the women's movement of the 1890s dissipated, as no Floridian emerged to replace Ella Chamberlain's leadership.

National leaders did not even try: the Reverend Doctor Anna Howard Shaw—who had degrees in both medicine and theology—owned a winter home at Florence Villa, near Lakeland, and Susan B. Anthony visited her there in what turned out to be the last full winter of her life, in 1903–1904, but

States/Territories Where Women Won Full Voting Rights Prior to the Nineteenth Amendment in 1920

Year	*State/Territory*	*Notes*
1869	Wyoming Territory	won on first attempt
1870	Utah Territory	Congress repealed in 1887; re-won in 1890
1883	Washington	lost in 1887 court case; re-won in 1910
1893	Colorado	won on first attempt
1896	Idaho	won on first attempt
1911	California	after losing campaign in 1896
1912	Arizona	won on first attempt
1912	Kansas	after three losses, the first in 1867
1912	Oregon	after six losing campaigns, beginning in 1884
1913	Alaska Territory	won on first attempt
1914	Montana	won on first attempt
1914	Nevada	won on first attempt
1917	New York	after losing in 1915
1918	Michigan	after three losing campaigns, the first in 1871
1918	Oklahoma	third campaign; high barriers
1918	South Dakota	after five losing campaigns, beginning in 1890

For more information on these and other states, see Doris Weatherford, *Women in American Politics* (Washington, D.C.: Congressional Quarterly Press, 2012).

there is no evidence that these international feminists used their opportunity to try to reorganize Florida's feminists. The National American Woman Suffrage Association (NAWSA) held its 1903 convention in New Orleans—just its second one in the South—but although women from other southern states attended, it appears that no Floridian did.

Instead, the society editor of the *Tampa Tribune*, Louise Frances Dodge, went to New Orleans for Mardi Gras and imported that idea. The first Gasparilla parade (and a month of associated parties) was in 1904; now more

Global Expansion of Full Voting Rights

Year	*Nation*
1881	Isle of Man (British territory)
1893	New Zealand
1893	South Australia
1899	Western Australia
1902	all Australia
1906	Finland
1907	Norway
1915	Denmark
1915	Iceland
1917	Union of Soviet Socialist Republics (Russia)
1918	All Canadian provinces except Quebec
1918	Great Britain
1918	Austria
1918	Ireland
1918	Poland
1919	Germany
1919	Luxembourg
1919	Holland
1920	United States

International Meetings

Year	*Location*	*Leaders/Issues*
1878	Paris	Julia Ward Howe; Theodore Stanton
1883	Liverpool	Susan B. Anthony; Elizabeth Cady Stanton
1888	Washington	May Wright Sewall, Indianapolis
1893	Chicago	Bertha Honore Palmer, Sarasota resident*
1899	London	Countess of Aberdeen
1902	Washington	Clara Barton
1904	Berlin	Mary Church Terrell, an African American
1906	Copenhagen	Carrie Chapman Catt
1908	Amsterdam	debate on British militants
1909	London	debate on British militants
1911	Stockholm	Rev. Dr. Anna Howard Shaw
1913	Budapest	Hungarian Rosika Schwimmer
1914	World War I begins, ending international organization	

Note: * See chapter 5.

than a century old, the Tampa parade attracts a half-million people every winter. Instead of improved legal or economic status, women appeared to value the pageantry of beauty queens.

Other nations led the way for feminism. Indeed, one of America's most accomplished women may have been better known abroad than at home: Mary Church Terrell, an African American who lived in Washington, D.C., was the hit at the meeting of the 1904 International Woman Suffrage Alliance in Berlin. She delivered her speech in flawless English, German, and French. International meetings would continue on a regular basis until World War I ended them, but women elsewhere were more successful at winning voting rights than in America.

California finally turned the tide in 1911, when women there won the vote in a very close, very sophisticated campaign. That brought revitalization elsewhere, and Jacksonville women began rebuilding Florida's movement in 1912. Some thirty women met on June 15 at the home of Mrs. Herbert Anderson and formed the Equal Franchise League. The president was Katherine Livingstone Eagan; the vice president was Roselle C. Cooley, and Frances Anderson was secretary. They were sufficiently connected to prosperous men that Heard National Bank gave them space for an office—yet the cause remained so controversial that neither the Chamber of Commerce nor the Jacksonville Woman's Club would rent them space for larger meetings.

The NAWSA sent one of its excellent organizers, Lavinia Engle, to northeast Florida, and in February 1913 women in Lake Helen began the Political Equality Club, with Mrs. S. A. Armstrong as president and Irene Adams as secretary. Two weeks later the Equal Suffrage League of Orlando formed at the home of Mrs. J. C. Patterson. Rev. Mary Augusta Safford, a Unitarian minister who had arrived from Iowa in 1905, was elected president. (She is not to be confused with Dr. Mary Safford of Tarpon Springs, discussed in the previous chapter.)

The Orlando group took immediate political action. According to NAWSA reporter Alice G. Kollock:

> The Mayor issued a notice that all freeholders [property tax payers] must register for the sewerage bond election by the 9th, and a few suffragists saw their opportunity. Very secretly and hurriedly . . . Miss Emma Hainer and Mrs. Helen Starbuck gathered together several women who owned valuable property and they went to the city clerk's office and announced that they had come . . . to register. . . . [They were

> told] that they law did not permit women to register. This they knew, but their action caused a discussion of the question and disclosed a widespread belief that women should have the right to vote.[1]

The national scene changed the next month, when feminists held their first parade in the nation's capital. This also was an imported idea: British feminists had been holding street demonstrations for years—and militants even drew attention to the issue by starting fires in mailboxes and damaging the property of their opponents in Parliament. Some young American women had participated while studying abroad, and Alice Paul in particular brought the ideas home. Presidential inaugurations were in March then, and they scheduled a parade the day prior to President Woodrow Wilson's inauguration.

Such marches had been held in New York and other cities by 1913 but not in the capital. Because Washington police had no experience with female protestors, too many assumed that any woman so brazen as to take to the streets could be treated the same way that police routinely treated prostitutes. The result of this police attitude was that many men jeered and physically assaulted women. In the end the police chief lost his job, while feminists gained admirers for their courage.

Floridians followed up the very next month, when Montana's Jeannette Rankin spoke to the legislature. Just a few years later, in 1916, she would be the first woman elected to Congress, but in 1913 she was employed by the NAWSA. Jacksonville's Roselle Cooley wrote of Rankin's April appearance in the still-extant Old Capitol building in Tallahassee:

> The House of Representatives decided to hear us in a Committee of the Whole, at an evening session. In this case, it meant the whole House, the whole Senate, and the whole town. Seats, aisles, the steps of the Speaker's rostrum were filled, windows had people sitting in them and in the hall, as far as one could see, people were standing on chairs to hear the first call for the rights of women ever uttered in the Capitol of Florida.[2]

The crowd behaved well, and no one heckled. Two other women spoke in addition to Cooley, Safford, and Rankin. The *Tampa Tribune* got Safford's name wrong, calling her "Dr. R. C. Safford of Orlando," and gave no first name for the Montana visitor, saying only "Miss Rankin." The *Jacksonville Times-Union* muffed even that, calling her "Miss Ruskin." Its reporter did take care, though, to detail that she "was dressed in a pannier draped gown of lavender charmouse, leghorn hat and white plume."

Legislators made no response until May 2, when Representative W. A. MacWilliams of St. Johns County used his parliamentary skills to bring a resolution to the floor. It lost 26–39, but as the disappointed women were leaving for their homes, Senator Fred Cone of Lake City urged them to stay. He was the Senate leader, and he told Cooley, "If you will come into the Senate, we will show those men [in the House] how to treat ladies."[3]

The *Tallahassee Democrat* enthused: "The prominent Florida women who are making a brilliant fight . . . for woman suffrage, this morning sprang a decided surprise . . . by challenging . . . [senators] to a joint debate." The paper printed the women's detailed proposal and added its own bit of goading: if the senators refused, it editorialized, it "will not be the first time that a man 'beat it' when so challenged."

The debate occurred the next day, although without the formal conditions the women had proposed. The relevant Senate committee voted to recommend the enfranchisement bill, but finally, after more waiting and more filibustering, on May 28, the question was tabled with a floor tally of 16–15. Senate records indicate that James E. Calkins of Fernandina, who had been a supporter, switched to opposition on the last roll call. Although Senate Leader Cone had put their bill on the special calendar and advised the women on the process, they nonetheless lost, Cooley said, to "the corporation members and the whiskey men."[4]

Several members used less candid and more confused language to explain away their records. Representative W. J. Epperson of Levy County began explicating his negative position by saying that he was actually positive:

> I am in favor of women voting on moral, temperance, and educational questions, also being allowed to become members of School Boards . . . but I am opposed to giving women the full ballot, as it would draw them down from the high pedestal upon which Southern men have placed them. To stand with men at the polls . . . would possibly lower their morals.[5]

Unconcerned about their morality, women continued to organize. At a three-day meeting in early November, they formed the Florida Equal Suffrage Association and elected Rev. Safford as president. The first vice president was Mrs. C. J. Huber of Webster, while Ella Chamberlain, who had returned to Tampa, was second vice president. Caroline Brevard, an unmarried woman from a prominent Tallahassee family, was third vice president, and the corresponding secretary was Miss Elizabeth Askew, a Tampa banker. Other officers included Miss Frances B. Anderson, Jacksonville; Mrs. Anna Andrus, Miami; and Mrs. John Schnarr and Mrs. J. M. Thayer, both of Orlando.

The legislature met only in odd-numbered years, and women devoted 1914 to building membership. Some fourteen hundred people attended a Jacksonville rally, and new chapters began from Miami to Pensacola. Many were in towns that are small now, but were important then: among them were Milton, Pine Castle, Winter Park, and Zellwood. Perhaps the most striking aspect of 1914 activity, though, was the formation of a Men's Equal Suffrage League, with Orlando's Mayor E. F. Sperry as president.

Kate Gordon, a nationally known suffragist from New Orleans, spoke in Jacksonville that year, while the Orlando group had a float in the winter parade and collected petitions for the vote at a fair. In Pensacola women had a booth at a tri-county fair, and Pensacola also hosted the 1914 state convention. Delegates were told to emphasize getting pledges of support from that year's congressional candidates, and "most of the leagues," Alice Kollack added, "formed classes to study history and the duties of citizenship."[6]

* * *

The legislature met again in 1915—and women won a significant if subtle victory that year. The era was prosperous, and many new towns were forming on the lower portion of the east coast. The Indian River County town of Fellsmere had a population eight times larger than that of Palm Beach in 1915, when Fellsmere's founders sent the paperwork for incorporation to that year's legislature. Because women had played a strong formative role, the municipal charter included them as voters: legislators did not notice, and they authorized the charter along with dozens of other local bills that traditionally are not debated. With their vote in municipal elections authorized, the very first Florida woman to cast a ballot was Fellsmere's Mrs. Zena M. Drier.

Other municipalities followed, and the Glades County town of Moore Haven would elect Marian Newhall Horowitz O'Brien as mayor in 1917—just two years after the Fellsmere precedent. Born to a wealthy Philadelphia family, she inherited Glades County land and was a young widow when she moved there to develop it. After marrying John O'Brien, she added credentials as Florida's first female bank president. Mayor O'Brien attracted national publicity for the area, and the town council accepted her 1919 resignation "with extreme regret," praising her "brilliant" work.[7] Moore Haven, which is on the western shore of Lake Okeechobee, was the first municipality in the South to elect a woman as mayor.

By the time that the federal Nineteenth Amendment granted full voting rights to Florida women, they were voting in twenty-three municipalities. The counties in which some towns granted women the vote were, in alphabetical order: Brevard, Broward, Dade, DeSoto, Glades, Indian River, Orange, Palm Beach, Pinellas, Polk, St. Lucie, and Volusia—most in the center part of the state or on its east coast. The known towns included Aurantia, Clearwater, Cocoa, DeLand, Delray, Dunedin, Fellsmere, Florence Villa, Fort Lauderdale, Miami, Moore Haven, Orlando, Orange City, St. Petersburg, Tarpon Springs, and West Palm Beach.

This granting of the vote for city elections happened very much under the radar, with little publicity. Although it included Miami, Orlando, and other municipalities that now are large, it is notable that Florida's oldest and largest towns of the time—from St. Augustine and Jacksonville to Pensacola, Gainesville, Tallahassee, Tampa, and Key West—did not revise their charters to include women.

The state suffrage association held its 1915 convention in Orlando in February, and by then there were sixteen well-organized branches throughout Florida. The women sensibly planned their work by legislative district, and national president Rev. Dr. Anna Howard Shaw traveled with Rev. Safford to several cities, where they interviewed lawmakers. Among those who assisted in arranging this tour were Miss Minnie Kehoe, Pensacola; Miss C. H. Day, Milton; Mrs. Susan B. Dyer, Winter Park; Mrs. Grace Hatchitt, Orlando; Miss Pleasaunce Baker, Zellwood; Mrs. Kate C. Havens, Miami; and Mrs. H. W. Thompson, Coconut Grove.

Although little was achieved in the 1915 legislature, it was hugely significant that the Florida Federation of Women's Clubs (FFWC) endorsed the vote at their annual convention.[8] With six thousand members in 1915, most of them the most prominent women in their towns, the FFWC was politically powerful—even though most women who belonged to it rarely acknowledged that and did not necessarily feel empowered. The FFWC was an affiliate of the General Federation of Women's Clubs, which had begun in New York City in 1890. By the time that the Nineteenth Amendment became an issue, the GFWC had millions of members nationwide, but local clubs made decisions independently, and not all supported women's right to vote. Especially in the South, opposition from GFWC members seriously hurt the movement, including in nearby Georgia.

More than anyone else, the person who can be credited for this positive move of FFWC endorsement was May Mann Jennings, FFWC president from 1914 to 1917 and the wife of former governor William Sherman Jennings. She turned the state's clubwomen from their traditional aims for civic good to securing their own rights, and her leadership would be of inestimable political value. In addition to the FFWC, the Florida branch of the virtually all-male American Federation of Labor endorsed the vote for women in 1915.

With 1916 being another year without a legislative session, Mary Safford went to work in an Iowa campaign, and Mrs. Frank Tracy briefly took over in Florida. Anna Howard Shaw attended that year's state convention, when some 550 delegates met in Miami in March. In the summer some Florida women went on to Chicago, where the Republicans held their presidential nominating convention, and to St. Louis, where the Democrats met. The St. Louis convention featured a "Golden Lane"—women stood with yellow umbrellas along ten blocks between the hotels and the convention center, making it impossible for delegates not to see the outpouring of support for enfranchisement.

President Wilson was reelected in November, and the 1916 elections brought Sidney J. Catts to the Florida governor's office. A populist Democrat, he declared himself "unequivocally and eternally for the enfranchisement of women"—but also vetoed some municipal charters that endowed women with the vote.[9] He did not mention the issue in his speech when the 1917 session began, nor was he among the men who welcomed Mary Baird Bryan to Tallahassee that spring—but other men fell over one another to please her.

Mrs. William Jennings Bryan, as she was identified in the era's media, had a lifetime of political experience. She may have been the world's first young mother to earn a law degree: her daughter Ruth was three when Bryan passed the bar exam in Nebraska in 1888. She helped her famous husband run his campaigns as the three-time Democratic presidential nominee at the turn of the century—and in 1928 she would lay out the strategy for her daughter's successful campaign for Congress. William Jennings Bryan was secretary of state under President Wilson until they disagreed about entering World War I, and he resigned. The Bryans then moved to Miami, where Mrs. William

Jennings Bryan joined her husband's kinswoman, May Mann Jennings, in Florida politics.

Legislators were so eager to hear from Mary Baird Bryan that the 1917 House *Journal* contained seven entries about arrangements for her speech. Senators moved over to the House side for it, and on April 18 she held their attention in the same way that her husband's oratory kept crowds spellbound. She spoke for an hour and a half, and the *Tampa Tribune* called it "the opening of the real campaign that will be waged to . . . grant equal suffrage in Florida."[10]

The "real campaign" began immediately, as other south Florida women went with Bryan to lobby in Tallahassee. They included not only former first lady Annie Broward and Fort Lauderdale founder Ivy Stranahan but also a young Miami newswoman on her way to decades of fame, Marjory Stoneman Douglas.[11] In the face of such feminine power, only two senators mustered up the courage to vote negatively in committee—but Douglas believed the positive committee vote was merely a "gallant gesture," knowing that the House would kill the resolution.

Many men voted positively, knowing that a simple majority was not enough. The resolution, which had been drafted by former governor William Jennings, called for amending the state constitution, and that required a three-fifths majority. After much parliamentary maneuvering, forty House members voted positively and twenty-seven negatively, five votes shy of two-thirds. A motion to reconsider failed by a greater margin, even though legislators spent most of another day speechifying on the status of women.

The 1917 convention of the State Equal Suffrage Association was in Tampa in November, and Ivy Stranahan accepted the presidency for one year. Mary Safford would resume it in 1918, and that year's convention, also in November, was in Daytona.

Governor Catts called a special session to deal with other matters in December 1918, and these feminist leaders astutely decided not to test the limits of their legislative allies by adding to the limited agenda. Into the vacuum, however, rushed young Helen Hunt, a Jacksonville journalist who had been admitted to the bar the previous year. She would be Helen Hunt West after her 1927 marriage, and she led about fifty Floridians who were associated with the National Woman's Party (NWP). Its national leader was Alice Paul, and NWP tactics had become increasingly controversial since the 1913 parade in Washington.

Because Paul and others of these women had been educated in the

Skirts, Spittoons, and Lobbying the Legislature

Allen Morris, longtime historian for the Florida House, interviewed Marjory Stoneman Douglas a few years before her 1998 death at age 107. He wrote this of the 1917 lobbying effort:

> Mrs. [William Jennings] Bryan, Mrs. Frank Stranahan of Fort Lauderdale, and Mrs. Douglas set out [from south Florida] for Tallahassee, where they were joined at the Leon Hotel by the widows of two former Governors, Mrs. William S. Jennings and Mrs. Napoleon B. Broward of Jacksonville. Mrs. Douglas remembered the old Leon as a great barn with wooden porches, brass spittoons in the lobby, and noisy crowds of politicians and political hangers-on, and she felt "as if we were the only women left in the world."
>
> The plan of action agreed upon that evening at the Leon was simple. "We were there to act like ladies: no shouting, no pushing, no picketing. Mrs. Jennings had been promised that the women's suffrage bill would be passed by the Senate so that we would not have to speak before the Senate committee. We understood perfectly the Senate's gallant gesture, since they were sure it would not pass the House."
>
> When they faced the House committee the next day: "A handful of men, reinforced with handy spittoons, sat back against the wall, as we pleaded for votes. . . . I think I have never seen such blank eyes and unlistening faces. I spoke, I know, very badly. Their faces were still hard and unresponsive as they stood while their chairman bowed us out."
>
> Mrs. Bryan spoke that evening to a more responsive audience. . . . Mrs. Douglas was distracted, however, because a legislator seated next to her spat . . . at a spittoon beside her skirt.*

In her 1987 book *Voice of the River*, Douglas further recalled: "Mrs. Jennings was younger than Mrs. Broward and Mrs. Stranahan and I was younger still. All four of us spoke to a joint committee, wearing our best hats. . . . Talking to them was like talking to graven images. They never paid any attention to us at all. They weren't even listening."

Note: Allen Morris, *Women in the Florida Legislature* (Tallahassee: Florida House of Representatives, 1995), 7; *Marjory Stoneman Douglas: Voice of the River*, with John Rothchild (Englewood, Fla.: Pineapple Press, 1987), 107.

British parliamentary system, they never quite grasped that the structure of government differed in the United States, where presidents have no role in amendments to the U.S. Constitution. Despite the fact that a president could neither sign nor veto the constitutional amendment that was needed for women to vote, the NWP targeted President Wilson—and with great political obduracy, NWP members opposed all Democrats because Wilson was a Democrat. In the 1914 congressional elections they went to western states where women could vote and campaigned against Democrats—defeating twenty-two who supported women's right to vote. The NWP began picketing the White House in 1917 and continued even after Wilson offered his public support for the amendment.

May Mann Jennings warned that the NWP, with its open opposition to Democrats, would have a negative influence with the virtually all-Democratic Florida legislature. Representative Edgar W. Waybright, however, probably was unaware of these internal conflicts between women's organizations when he introduced the resolution written by his Jacksonville constituent, Helen Hunt. Even strongly Democratic Governor Catts seemed oblivious to the NWP's national reputation, and he asked the legislature to approve the resolution—which differed importantly from those in the past, in that it was not intended to amend the Florida Constitution but rather the U.S. Constitution. Yet, even though Waybright pointed out that Wilson had recently endorsed the vote for women, that support was not enough for Florida's conservative Democrats. The resolution failed 31–37.

* * *

That was December 1918, and in January, the national association again sent Anna Howard Shaw, who raised several thousand dollars at events in Orlando, Tampa, West Palm Beach, and Miami. With help from experienced organizers Elizabeth Skinner, Maria McMahon, and Mrs. Halsey W. Wilson, petitions were collected in thirty-eight counties urging the enfranchisement of women. National officers Minnie Fisher Cunningham of Arkansas and Marjorie Shuler of New York also spent "several weeks in a quiet campaign to influence U.S. Senator Park Trammell to cast his vote for the Federal Suffrage Amendment—this being considered useless in the case of Senator Duncan U. Fletcher."[12] Trammell never was persuaded, though; neither of Florida's U.S. senators supported women's right to vote.

The mainstream feminists found legislators who introduced two measures in the 1919 legislative session: an amendment to the Florida Constitution as well as a bill to enfranchise women for primary elections only. The latter had been adopted in Arkansas in 1917 and in Texas in 1918, largely because of Minnie Cunningham Fisher, and she came to assist with implementing it in Florida. At the time Arkansas and Texas were akin to Florida in that virtually all registered voters were Democrats—and because there were not yet any presidential primaries, the Democratic primaries for state and local office were the elections that truly mattered. More important, legislators could grant this partial enfranchisement without the two-thirds majority needed for constitutional amendments.

The final act in the Tallahassee drama began in April, with the opening of the 1919 regular session. Senator W. H. Malone of Key West came up with a bright idea to expand on the partial enfranchisement idea—but it also was an idea that would allow his colleagues to dodge another hard vote. He introduced a bill that would have settled "the great conflict of opinions on whether the womanhood of Florida desires the ballot or not" by arranging for the state Democratic Executive Committee to conduct a mock election for women to express their opinion. That he did not want a positive response, however, was hidden in the fine print: "only such women who desire the electorate franchise in Florida be requested to vote . . . and those who do not . . . be ascertained by refraining."[13] In other words, if a woman did not go to the polls and vote, she would be counted as having voted negatively! Mercifully, the bill died in committee.

Feminists finally had reason to believe that they were on their way to victory when their proposed state constitutional amendment received the required two-thirds majority in the Senate on April 18. But their elation was short-lived; the House tally a few days later was 40–33—still four votes short of two-thirds. As it turned out, April 22, 1919, would be the last time that Florida lawmakers debated the issue.

Late on Wednesday June 4, the U.S. Senate passed the Nineteenth Amendment to the U.S. Constitution by the required two-thirds, and it went to the states for ratification.

Back when the federal Constitution was adopted in 1789, the Founding Fathers deliberately made it difficult to change their work: adding an amendment requires not only passage by two-thirds of both houses of Congress but also ratification by both chambers of three-quarters of the nation's state legislatures. By the time that such near-unanimity of opinion is achieved,

Instead of Women's Enfranchisement . . .

While the 1919 Florida House was not dealing with resolutions on enfranchising half of the state's citizens and taxpayers, it did take time to pass dozens of other resolutions. Some of them show the capitol's conditions at the time:

- Resolution Number 8—Drinking Cups—Resolution authorizing sergeant-at-arms to furnish water, ice, and sanitary drinking cups.
- Resolution Number 34—Washington—Resolution to have picture of George Washington in Hall of Representatives covered with glass.
- Resolution Number 58—Birds—Resolution to instruct the Janitor to remove from the hall of the House of Representatives.

Note: *House Journal*, 1919. Researched by author.

any issue is likely to be almost passé—but it was still a hot item in Florida, and Governor Catts was excited. Legislators were scheduled to adjourn on Friday, June 6, and on Thursday morning, he sent them a message:

> While this office has not received verification from Washington, still The Associated Press would not dare publish something of so vast importance as this, if it were not true.
>
> The legislature . . . will adjourn tomorrow and it has an opportunity, while now in regular . . . [session] to be the first state in the sisterhood of states to ratify this great movement.
>
> Therefore, as governor of our great state, I earnestly recommend that you ratify this action . . . and add an imperishable laurel to your state, which can never die; the fact of being the first state of the Union to recognize women as an equal with her brother man.[14]

His language was stirring, but according to the *Tribune*, legislators paid "no attention to the governor's message." That was not surprising. Some were surprised when May Mann Jennings did not rally her thousands of troops, but after years of disappointments, she and other leaders had become wary enough to see that adding this big question to the last day's agenda likely would doom it to defeat.

Their head count showed that they could get a majority vote, but the extraordinary majority needed to take up a bill so late in the session probably would be impossible—and the consequences of losing could be harmful in other states. The *Tampa Daily Times* subhead on the June 7, 1919, summed up the situation: FLORIDA WILL NOT BE FIRST STATE TO RATIFY SUFFRAGE AMENDMENT; Women Leaders Not Willing to Take Chance on Putting Land of Flowers in Line as the First to Turn It Down."

The women dismissed possible personal glory for themselves rather than risk the disaster of having the amendment fail in its first test. Given legislators' propensity for double-dealing, and knowing well how they rushed out of Tallahassee like schoolboys set loose for vacation, Jennings and her colleagues doubtless made the right call in allowing others to take first place. Florida lawmakers adjourned at noon on Friday, and on Tuesday morning, three states—Wisconsin, Illinois, and Michigan—competed to be first to ratify the amendment.

While other states were ratifying during the remainder of 1919, the Florida association held its annual convention October, again in Tampa. The officers elected showed how widely the organization had spread throughout the state: they were president Mrs. John T. Fuller, Orlando; first vice president Mrs. Edgar A. Lewis, Fort Piece; second vice president Elizabeth Skinner, Dunedin; third vice president Dr. Minerva B. Cushman, St. Petersburg; corresponding secretary Mrs. W. R. O'Neal, Orlando; recording secretary Mrs. C. E. Hawkins, Brooksville; treasurer Clara B. Worthington, Tampa; and auditors Mrs. J. W. McCollum and Mrs. J. D. Stringfellow, Gainesville. Mrs. Amos Norris of Tampa was in charge of lobbying, as she chaired the legislative committee.

As events played out, though, Norris never led lobbying: by the time that Florida's next legislative session rolled around in 1921, other states had completed the ratification. Tennessee provided the last crucial approval, and the Nineteenth Amendment was added to the U.S. Constitution on August 26, 1920.

Florida suffragists nonetheless held their 1920 annual meeting in Orlando, prior to voting in the November election. According to Alice Kollack, they were "not quite ready to merge into a League of Women Voters, [but] this was done on April 1, 1921."[15] The charter members of the league then elected Mrs. J. B. O'Hara of Orlando as president.

The National Association Opposed to Woman Suffrage, which was based in New York and had its earliest roots in Massachusetts in 1868, never appeared in Florida—but some opponents hung on even after women voted in the presidential election year of 1920. Maryland's legislature had been the most strongly opposed, with its lawmakers even going to other states to lobby against it. Even after the Nineteenth Amendment was adopted and women voted everywhere, these extreme conservatives argued that the amendment did not apply in states that had not ratified it—a point that had been settled in the aftermath of the Civil War, with the Thirteenth, Fourteenth, and Fifteenth amendments. Some Floridians joined in this legalistic objection, but on February 27, 1922, the U.S. Supreme Court ruled against them. Their regressive opinions became a forgotten footnote in the history of human freedom.

* * *

Virtually all the women who worked for the vote in Tallahassee did not live in that town nor anywhere near it. As other parts of Florida modernized with northern newcomers, the attitudes of Tallahassee women remained more akin to those a few miles to the north in Georgia. Even Georgia, though, had several colleges for women prior to Florida; indeed, Florida's first college graduate went to Georgia for her education.[16]

The Buckman Act of 1905, sponsored by Duval County legislator Henry Holland Buckman, reorganized higher education in Florida. The State Normal School for Colored Students (teacher-training institutions for both races were called normal schools) had been coeducational from its 1887 beginning. Located in Tallahassee, it became Florida Agricultural and Mechanical College with the 1905 act.

The coeducational West Florida Seminary, which also was in Tallahassee and was for whites, became Florida State College for Women (FSCW), while the "eastern seminary" at Gainesville became the University of Florida, limited to white men. Males who had attended the Tallahassee "seminary" were forced to transfer to Gainesville, while women at Gainesville had to move to Tallahassee. The most significant factor in the change, of course, was that white men got university status, while the new institution for white women was merely a college—sans law school or medical school or any other graduate opportunity. The same was true for blacks of both genders.

The 1905 graduating class of what became Florida State College for

Women was the last that included men. There were just ten graduates, almost evenly divided by gender, with six men and four women. One of the women was Ruby Pearl Diamond, and a Tallahassee auditorium was named for her in 1971 to honor the support she had given the college over the decades. Agnes Granberry, an art major who graduated in 1912, designed FSCW's logo. With the new name in a circle, it included the 1905 founding date in Roman numerals (MCMV). The motto was in Latin: "Vires, Artes, Mores," the roots of the English words meaning virtue, art, and morality. Beneath was "Femina Perfecta," which needs no translation.

When FSCW was only a few months old, on December 3, 1905, Nellie Godfrey (whose name changed when she married Charles King) spoke of college life in a letter to her "dear Charlie":

> We had a very pleasant Thanksgiving, had a delightful dinner, then held a little informal tea that night, and the girls all danced. Then Mrs. Bates invited us over to her room and we had a delightful spread . . .
>
> Prof. Buchholz believes in whipping sometimes. . . . He is a fine man, but very, very peculiar. . . . We went to Prof. Murphree about our work, and he is going to teach us algebra and he said he would try to change our English work.
>
> We've just come in from picking violets and they are beautiful. . . . Roses, roses, everywhere and other flowers.
>
> You said you were coming over to see Edna and me before school is out. . . . All the girls said you must come and ask for all the girls you know; then they'll disappear after a while. Don't you see? You know we're not allowed to have a young man call as a special—well, as a beau.[17]

This was not unusual, as most colleges, both single-sex and coeducational, similarly cloistered young women for decades into the future. Nor was FSCW's founding the nation's last launch of a women's college: instead, that was New Jersey College for Women in 1918, as even in the new century, college education for women remained controversial. The timidity of FSCW faculty and students can also be seen in the fact that no one connected with it offered any visible support for the feminists who came to Tallahassee to work for the vote. Nor, of course, did anyone at A&M: they understood that their advocacy would be a negative, not a positive, with the era's lawmakers.

Female attorneys were helpful to the adoption of the Nineteenth Amendment in other states, but Florida was slow on that too. States from Maine

First Women to Pass the Florida Bar Exam

Year	*Name*	*Primary Residence*
1898	Louise Rebecca Pinnell	Jacksonville
1899	Alice Johnson	Live Oak
1908	Mary Stewart Howarth-Hewitt	DeLand
1909	Nell L. Cowan Bostwick	Sanford/Tallahassee
1911	Annie Dorcas Broward Starrett	Jacksonville
	Elsie Young Douglass	Jacksonville
1912	L. Booth Washington	unknown
1913	Minnie E. Kehoe	Pensacola/Miami
1914	Marie Willard Anderson	Miami
1915	Annie Joe Law	Brooksville
	Hedwiga Walicki	Tampa
1917	Cecile Eleanor Vaught Wysong	Miami/Jacksonville
	Rose Gillespy Baldwin	Jacksonville
	Julia A. Harding	Jacksonville
	Helen Hunt (later West)	Jacksonville
1918	L. H. Shoemaker	Jacksonville
	Jane Tillie Wakefield	Bartow
1919	Ella Cramer Kindred	DeLand
	Louise Pencke	Tampa/Miami

to California admitted women to the practice of law during the 1870s, but Florida's first were not until 1898 and 1899.[18] Most of the first decade of the twentieth century passed without additional female lawyers, but in the second decade, at least one woman would be admitted every year except 1916.

Many of them did not truly practice, though, or did so only in a limited way. That was the case for Jacksonville's Rose G. Baldwin, who assisted her husband, and for Marie Willard Anderson, whose husband was a major political and judicial figure in Miami. Ella Cramer Kindred, a graduate of New York's prestigious Vassar College, practiced occasionally with her husband when they were in their winter home in DeLand. L. Booth Washington, who was admitted to the Florida Bar in 1914, also practiced primarily in New York.

Annie Dorcas Broward (called Dorcas) and her orphaned cousin Elsie Young Douglass both attended Stetson University's law school to assist in the career of Governor Napoleon Broward, Annie's father and Elsie's uncle. When he died shortly after being elected to the U.S. Senate, Dorcas Broward married; her surname was Starrett when she died in childbirth in 1923. Douglass never married and instead became a tax attorney; she worked for the IRS until her 1947 retirement.

Some smaller towns may have offered more opportunity than larger ones, as Brooksville's Annie Joe Law and Bartow's Jane Tillie Wakefield appear to have been successful sole practitioners; Wakefield's achievement is especially impressive because her parents were immigrants from Scotland and Germany. The heritage of Tampa's Hedwiga M. Walicki is not known, but she was listed in city directories both as an attorney and as a stenographer, and in different years, she had offices both downtown and in her home. During World War II she would be the clerk for Tampa's draft board.

Jacksonville was by far the most welcoming to women in the legal profession: almost half of the state's female lawyers in this era lived there. A strong factor in this doubtless was the proximity to DeLand, where Stetson University had its law school. Ironically, that was a private institution, and it would be decades before women were admitted to the law school of the so-called public University of Florida.

Cecile Vaught Wysong was one of the Jacksonville women. Only briefly married, she worked as a corporate attorney for a turpentine manufacturer, in an era when that was key to the local economy. Julia A. Harding was with the law firm of Marks, Marks, & Holt, while L. H. Shoemaker practiced independently in downtown Jacksonville. She refused to reveal what "L. H." stood for, but Shoemaker was popular enough to become president of the Florida Federation of Business and Professional Women after that organization began in the next decade.

Nell Cowan Bostwick ran the most unusual legal-related business. A Sanford native, she was educated in Atlanta and New York and then taught school in Orange County and Tampa; she was living in Jacksonville when she was admitted to the bar in 1909. For years afterward she moved to Tallahassee during legislative sessions, where she "operated the 'Nell L. Cowan Bostwick Legislative Bureau.'" From "a booth in the corridor between the Senate and the House in the Old Capitol," she sold subscriptions to her analyses of pending legislation, primarily to lobbyists.[19]

This was a vital and profitable service because at the time, only the sponsor had copies of proposed bills: opponents literally could—and did—kill a bill by stealing it. Bostwick is credited for creating the first copies of bills, a great contribution to a fair legislative process. Based in Jacksonville when she was not in Tallahassee, she worked all her life, despite marriage and two children.

Minnie Kehoe of Pensacola also was quite well known as an attorney, but perhaps the era's best-credentialed woman was Mary Stewart Howarth-Hewitt. After earning her undergraduate degree at the prestigious University of Michigan, Mary Stewart became the first woman to graduate from Stetson's law school in 1908. The precedent was so keenly understood that the Florida Supreme Court conducted her oral examination for admission to the bar. She practiced with her father in DeLand as Stewart & Stewart; "Howarth" was added to her name when she married a Pennsylvanian. The couple moved there, and although she bore three daughters, she was admitted to practice before federal courts in 1915.

When her husband had a heart attack, Mary Stewart Howarth returned her family to DeLand. She again practiced with her father, while also teaching constitutional law at Stetson—and arguing cases before the U.S. Supreme Court. She did not become Howarth-Hewitt until late in life, in 1949, and her second husband did not live long. By then her daughter Catherine Stewart Howarth had joined the family law firm in 1934. With her other daughters, Mary and Sara, she moved briefly to Memphis; while they attended medical school there, she was admitted to the Tennessee Bar in 1936. In 1976, when Mary Stewart Howarth-Hewitt died in DeLand at age ninety-one, she was living with her daughter, Dr. Mary Howarth-Jacobs. Her grandson said that when she was well past the usual retirement age, it was not unusual for her to leave after-dinner card games "to go get someone out of jail."[20]

* * *

One of the most important long-term changes for Floridians, especially African Americans, began in 1904, when Mary McLeod Bethune and her young son moved to Daytona Beach from Palatka, where her husband had toiled at tapping pine trees for turpentine. A native of South Carolina, she was educated at Moody's Bible Institute in Chicago and wanted to be a missionary to Africa—but could not find any church willing to sponsor a black woman.

She was twenty-nine years old and had less than five dollars when she began the Daytona Beach Literary and Industrial School for Training Negro Girls. Her five students lived and learned in an old house, using orange crates for desks and ink made of elderberries; they often did not know how

A Heroine Elsewhere: Attorney Mary Grace Quackenbos

Mary McLeod Bethune's husband was typical of the black men who worked in north Florida's pinewoods, tapping trees for resin that was made into turpentine and other industrial products. That sort of work has been exported to the Third World now, where other dark-skinned workers live in near-slave conditions, just as African Americans did in the Florida of a century ago.

Florida's first female lawyer was a corporate attorney, but numerous northern women worked as labor attorneys. One of the most courageous was Mary Grace Quackenbos. A member of a colonial New York Dutch family, she did not have to work for a living, but she nonetheless traveled the country taking cases on behalf of the exploited.

Appointed as an attorney for the Department of Justice under the administration of President Theodore Roosevelt, Quackenbos investigated cases in the South, including one involving mistreated Italians who had been recruited for work in Mississippi. She also came to the Florida turpentine woods—and despite the unlikelihood of prosecuting powerful white men—won her case. Retired history professor Angus McKenzie Laird explained that his father, a timber company executive, was fired when he became a whistle blower on the situation:

> In early 1906, reports of forced labor, brutality, deprivation, and even murder were filtering out of the turpentine camps. . . . They reached the ears of Mary Grace Quackenbos . . . [who began] a crusade against corrupt New York labor agents and their southern employers . . .
>
> Five officials of the Jackson Lumber Company were convicted of peonage. General Manager W. S. Harlan, described as a "man of very high standing . . . with plenty of money and influence," and four subordinates were sentenced to prison terms. While the convicted men were unsuccessfully employing every legal means of remaining out of jail, Florida civic leaders, politicians, and businessmen began a concerted effort to discredit the federal officials. . . . Mary Grace Quackenbos . . . was one of the most unpopular persons in this part of the country, although a heroine elsewhere.

Note: Angus McKenzie Laird, *Like I Saw It: An Autobiography* (Tallahassee: St. Andrews Press, 1981), 7, citing Jerrell H. Shofner, "Mary Grace Quackenbos, a Visitor Florida Did Not Want," *The Florida Historical Quarterly* 58, no. 3 (January 1980).

their next meal would be obtained. After moving to a junkyard, the girls and Bethune cleaned and resold mountains of trash to earn money—while wearing the big aprons that she insisted upon to disguise disparities in personal possessions.

There was particular need for such a school, not only because the era's all-male school boards routinely refused to educate black children but also because many of the area's African American women were maids and cooks who were expected to move with wealthy families to summer homes in the North. With a strong emphasis on religion and discipline, the boarding school grew rapidly. Bethune trained her girls in singing, and they soon entertained Rockefellers and other winter residents. She was assertive enough to obtain major donations from these men, ultimately resulting in Bethune-Cookman College.[21]

On the Florida west coast Blanche Armwood was a similar black educator, although different from Bethune in that Tampa's Armwood family had been leaders in their community since Reconstruction. She graduated from St. Peter Claver Catholic School in 1902—and at age twelve passed the state teachers' examination. After more education at Atlanta's Spelman Seminary (later a college), she returned to Tampa and began teaching other blacks at age sixteen.

In 1914, when she was twenty-four, Armwood developed a curriculum of "household arts schools for cooks and housewives of the Negro race."[22] She managed to get the cooperation of the school board, and more unconventionally, that of public utilities—which were eager to introduce new electrical appliances for housework. She sold her idea to the U.S. Department of Agriculture and, with federal support, set up household arts schools as far away as New Orleans. Unlike Bethune, Armwood married and changed her name three times, but her influence also would go on into the next decades.

The NAACP began in New York in 1915—and despite an official policy of the national board to avoid recruitment in the apartheid South, Tampa followed only Atlanta as a chapter willing to take the risks. At a founding meeting that same year, 107 black Tampans were brave enough to fill out membership forms, and the chapter's second president—elected just months later—was educator Christina Meacham. She was principal of the town's only school for blacks, Harlem Academy, and in 1916 she organized a "Negro Day" at the state fair, giving Florida's African Americans an opportunity to exhibit their crafts.

Another NAACP founder was Marion E. Rogers, who had been brave enough to threaten to sue the Hillsborough County School Board in 1913; her assertiveness resulted in some improvements for black children. In 1908 Clara Frye had begun caring for sick and injured African Americans in her home; she would build it into a hospital that was the only one available to west coast blacks for decades in the future. "An Englishwoman married to a black barber, Sherman Frye," her mother, Fanny Fordham, had been born in England; Clara's father was Joseph Draughton, and she was born in Alabama in 1872.[23] Although more white than black in appearance, she identified with Tampa's blacks. Her husband, however, was not a factor in her decades of work.

Florida had enough African American nurses that a chapter of the National Association of Colored Graduate Nurses (NACGN) began in Jacksonville in 1915. Its leader was Jerenia Valentine Dial Reid, who had been born to Tillman and Mary Ann Valentine in 1879. She grew up in relative prosperity, and her father was active in the Republican Party in Jacksonville. At age twenty-one—the minimum required by the nursing school associated with Freedmen's Hospital in Washington, D.C.—she went north to train as a nurse. When she returned to Jacksonville after her 1903 graduation, Valentine probably was Florida's first credentialed black nurse. She married twice but lost one husband to illness and the other to World War I. Although she had the financial responsibility for her two children, she nonetheless found time to organize the NACGN. When she attended its 1928 annual convention in New Orleans, she was superintendent of nurses at Pine Ridge Hospital in West Palm Beach.[24]

Mary Cash held a similar status in Tampa. Although Clara Frye was its most prominent health care provider for African Americans, Cash was the area's first black nurse with educational credentials. Sponsored by Frye and Dr. M. R. Winton, Cash graduated from nursing school in North Carolina 1916. She returned to Tampa and spent her life as a nurse and midwife in the black community. The only exception was a five-year period when Cash traveled in Europe as a private nurse for a Sarasota circus-owning family.

Tampa and Jacksonville, of course, were old cities compared with Miami. It was barely a town when widow Florence Gaskins arrived from Jacksonville in 1896. Eventually a successful businesswoman, she ran a laundry associated with Henry Flagler's Royal Palm Hotel, bought real estate, and operated a school for black students. Victoria Ward was another significant black woman: she organized Miami's first burial society for blacks—which was essentially funeral insurance, at a time when insurance companies refused to sell to them.

Many of Miami's black newcomers were not African Americans but immigrants from the Bahamas. The 1900 census showed that besides the Florida born, more black people in Miami were from the Bahamas than anywhere else: 41 percent of black Miamians were native Floridians, 22 percent were Bahamians, while the remainder came from Alabama, Georgia, the Carolinas, and Virginia. Bahamians were native English speakers, and most were better educated than Americans. Some took their British citizenship very seriously: one such descendent recalled that his elderly relatives talked about Queen Victoria as though they viewed themselves as part of the royal family.[25]

Polly Mays, who lived south of Miami, not only operated "the only black medical facility," but also drove a school bus.[26] In an era when most women did not drive at all—let alone a bus—she took children to school in Coconut Grove before there was a school for them in south Dade. The area would have no high school for blacks until 1926—but surprisingly, unlike in most of the South, "pay for white and black teachers at the turn of the century was the same."[27]

Nellie S. Powers ran the south Florida school that was considered the best. Its lengthy name included "normal," a word used throughout the nation to indicate a teaching-training institution. The school soon had some three hundred students, and a 1916 article in the *Miami Herald* said:

> The Miami Colored Normal Industrial Training and Kindergarten School will begin its seventh years' work under the direction of Nellie S. Powers. . . . Mrs. Powers has inaugurated a new idea, in that she has instructed every pupil to provide his or her own individual drinking cup. . . . The course will include Kindergarten, Grammar School, High School, Normal, and Industrial Training.[28]

Other black people lived in Lemon City, which was then north of Miami's city limits. Some of its land had been homesteaded by Ada Merritt, who sold it to Elijah and Rosa Boles about 1915. That couple came to south Florida from Lake City, along with Elijah's sister, Isabel Boles. The Boles family intermarried with the Ford family, who came from the St. Augustine area, and the women of these families went on to be teachers and principals of schools for black children. Among Lemon City's most prominent pioneers was Josephine Dillard Powell, who would lead the area NAACP.

Also outside the city limits was Hardieville. "Miami's first red-light district," it was named for Sheriff Dan Hardie, "who herded all the prostitutes" there. In a 1912 meeting with prominent businessmen, Dr. James Jackson, a white man, candidly proclaimed, "all too many white men contracted venereal diseases from Hardieville prostitutes and then infected their wives." The men pondered the problem and came up with this solution: "removing all immoral women from the streets, and prohibiting 'good women' from going all over town unescorted after 9:00 p.m."

The Dr. Jackson who led this meeting is the namesake of Miami's Jackson Memorial Hospital, while Dr. W. B. Sawyer, who came to Miami in 1903, treated the area's black patients. Decades later his daughter, Gwendolyn Sawyer Cherry, would be the first black woman in the Florida legislature. In 1918, however, when a maid who worked for Mrs. Clarence Bush was refused admittance to Jackson Memorial, Dr. Sawyer led the formation of a facility for blacks. Mrs. Bush, a white woman, donated five thousand dollars and five acres of land. The hospital was not named for her, though: instead its name was Christian Hospital.

* * *

Being a teacher or a nurse was as high as a black woman could aspire; no African American women practiced as lawyers or physicians. Progress for white women in these fields also was slow: indeed, there may have been more female physicians in Florida during the 1880s and 1890s than in the new century.

White male physicians used the legislature to strengthen their hold on the profession with new licensing requirements, and they used quotas to exclude women from medical schools. Because DeLand's Stetson University admitted women to its law school, Florida women had more opportunity in that profession. Even today the disparity shows: the Florida Medical Association has not researched the history of the state's female physicians in the way that the Florida Bar Association sponsored research on pioneer women in law. We thus have no official source for women licensed to practice medicine, but we do know that Florida's female physicians were not natives but instead northern newcomers.

Dr. Orpha Bruce, who earned her medical degree in Boston, continued to practice in Tampa until her 1910 death. That city, which had earlier had more than one female physician, then was left with none. North of Tampa, in

Tarpon Springs, Dr. Mary Safford had been a great community resource until her 1891 death, but again, no one replaced her. Tarpon Springs was larger than Miami when Dr. Eleanor Gault Simmons began her Dade County practice.

South Florida's first female physician, she graduated from Woman's Medical College of Pennsylvania in 1879. After practicing in New York and New Jersey, Dr. Gault married in 1891. Her husband, Albion Simmons, was a lawyer, but they ventured south the next year, where he hoped to get into the business of producing guava jelly. Whether he was successful is unclear, but she continued to practice medicine after marriage, either rowing Biscayne Bay or riding horseback to her patients' homes.

A member of the Miami Housekeepers Club that was affiliated with the Florida Federation of Women's Clubs, Dr. Simmons was in sufficient contact with national feminists that she wrote a letter on the subject to a "Mrs. Blackwell." It probably was not intended for Dr. Elizabeth Blackwell (who, in 1849, was the world's first credentialed female physician) because Elizabeth Blackwell had moved back to her native England in 1869. It may have been addressed to her sister, Dr. Emily Blackwell, who practiced in New York City; but the most likely recipient (if indeed it was addressed to a famous "Mrs. Blackwell") probably would be the Reverend Antoinette Brown Blackwell. Unlike the physicians, she was a married woman and properly addressed as "Mrs." She also was a sister-in-law to Lucy Stone; the featured orator at the first National Women's Rights Convention in 1850, Stone retained her maiden name when she married Henry Blackwell. The letter revealed that Miami's Dr. Simmons was curious about the history of women—but far from leading the movement for the vote like many other female physicians, she remained conservative and ambivalent. Dr. Simmons said in part:

> It is with much interest that I have been looking up the work of women in the field of pure science, and the number counts up well and the quality of the work done is good, considering how short a time women have turned their attention in this direction . . .
>
> Women's suffrage will come by women gradually proving themselves. . . . If it comes at all, [the only way] will be by gaining positions of trust gradually and proving practically that they are capable of sustaining prolonged strain in civil as well as domestic affairs, [and only] if they do nothing to disturb the sentimental relations between the sexes.[29]

Dr. Eleanor Simmons on the Miami River Frontier

When Dr. Eleanor Simmons arrived, Miami was a true frontier complete with saloon brawls and shoot-outs. When two men were killed in such a fight, vigilantes hunted down the perpetrator, Sam Lewis. Both he and posse member Rhett McGregor were shot—and Dr. Simmons bravely insisted on treating both, even though it was clear that Lewis was about to be lynched:

> Someone sent to Julia Tuttle's home on the Miami River to borrow her boat to go to Coconut Grove to get Dr. Eleanor Simmons. By the time Dr. Simmons arrived, it was three in the morning. She dressed McGregor's bullet wounds. . . . Then the doctor spoke to the men in the room: "Men, I'm going to the wounded man to do my duty as a doctor."
>
> Dr. Simmons walked the short distance to the shack and called out, "Mr. Lewis, this is Dr. Simmons. Can I do anything for you?"
>
> "Yes, I am all shot up. Come in quick. If anyone comes with you, I will kill him."
>
> Dr. Simmons, lantern and bag in hand, pushed open the door and went in. She removed two bullets from the right thigh and one from the left leg. The bone of the left leg was broken, and she splinted it. Lewis told her he expected to be lynched and begged her to give him enough chloroform so that he could kill himself. She refused. As morning came, Lewis surrendered.

The shootings occurred in Lemon City, later absorbed by Miami but then an independent municipality. Author Thelma Peters continued:

> The women of Lemon City reacted to the Lewis murders by fighting the saloons. In September 1895 Ada Merritt presented to the county commission a petition signed by fifty-eight women of Lemon City asking that no more liquor licenses be granted in their community. The commission replied that they had no discretion in refusing licenses so long as a majority of electors in a given precinct voted in favor of them. Women had no voting power—and in fact, the very day the petition was presented to the commission, another liquor license was granted.

Note: Thelma Peters, *Lemon City: Pioneering on Biscayne Bay, 1850–1925* (Miami: Banyan Books, 1976), 163, 166.

Apparently unaware that women in western states had held "positions of trust" for decades, Miami's Dr. Simmons was much less assertive than Winter Haven's Dr. Mary Bell Jewett. A leader in the Florida Federation of Women's Clubs and a firm feminist, Dr. Jewett left no doubt where she stood on the issue of the vote. Given all the civic work of women and the fact that they paid taxes like men, she almost sputtered in exasperation at a 1915 meeting in Tampa: "Why, it's humiliating . . . the way women have to beg and flatter men."[30] When the Nineteenth Amendment finally passed Congress in 1919, she said: "The women of Florida . . . owe no thanks to our two reactionaries, Senator Duncan U. Fletcher and Senator Park Trammell."[31]

Born in Ohio in 1858, Dr. Jewett attended Massachusetts' elite Wellesley College when it was a pioneer institution and studied medicine in both Philadelphia and New York. She practiced in New York City from 1897 to 1910, when she joined a widowed sister in the small Polk County community of Florence Villa—where internationally known Rev. Dr. Anna Howard Shaw had a vacation home. In addition to working for the vote and practicing medicine, Dr. Jewett was a co-founder of the Winter Haven library, its Central Park, and—most uncommonly—an affordable housing program. She also demonstrated willingness to defy southern standards when she "insisted that blacks receive an education equal to that of whites and convinced the school board to erect a building for blacks."[32] Dr. Mary Bell Jewett died in 1928; today two schools are named for her.

North Florida also had female physicians. Henrietta Marie VeHeim was born in Paris and spoke with a French accent all her life. Her family immigrated to Chicago in 1874, and she graduated from medical school there. She worked as a physician in the wild frontier of South Dakota's Black Hills, married Charles Wheeler, and bore a daughter named Alix. Charles died, and as a widow with a young child, she daringly moved to DeFuniak Springs and built a practice there. After she married Halfden E. Martens in 1898, the family went south to Lemon City. Dr. Martens—who often was referred to as "Mrs. Martens"—held office hours in Miami's Hatchitt Building in the afternoons and made the rounds of patients' homes in the morning, sometimes riding a tricycle.

Tallahassee's Dr. Ellen Lowell Stevens, an official with the State Board of Health, probably was the era's most distinguished female physician: she was a graduate of the prestigious medical school at Baltimore's Johns Hopkins University. Dr. Stevens traveled the state directing the era's crusade against tuberculosis. The *Pensacola Journal,* the *Ocala Evening Star,* and the *Ocala*

Banner carried stories about her work in those areas in 1908 and 1909, and she worked the northeastern part of the state the next year, with reports in *Daytona Daily News* and the *Nassau County Leader.* The *Tallahassee True Democrat* also ran a 1910 story on her public health work.

Jacksonville's Louise C. Meigs was not a professional woman, but was an FFWC officer, and she hotly defended her state in a 1915 letter to the *New York Times.* It had previously published a calumny saying that women were forbidden to practice medicine in Florida. Meigs countered that this was false and specifically cited not only Dr. Ellen Lowell Stevens but also Dr. Mary Freeman of Perrine, a no longer extant town between Miami and Homestead.

Meigs called Dr. Freeman "a very smart and capable woman."[33] She was unusual in that she was a graduate of a southern medical school, having earned her degree from South Carolina State College in 1912. Not surprisingly, she was the only woman in her class, and she may have been admitted because she was in her forties—and thus posed neither a sexual distraction nor a competitive threat to male classmates. Born in Illinois in 1867, Dr. Freeman practiced in south Florida for two decades prior to being killed by a drunk driver in 1936. Her gravesite in Miami's Woodlawn Park North Cemetery has no marker.

Women were new to law and fairly new to medicine, but they had always run businesses. The hospitality industry was one of the oldest such, and Isabella Peacock—who was a leader in Miami's Housekeepers Club—joined her husband in running the first hotel between Palm Beach and Key West. At the opposite end of Florida, in Apalachicola, sisters Annie and Mary Ella Gibson proved exceptionally successful. They bought a large inn in 1917 that had been built a decade earlier, in 1907, and ran it for the rest of their lives. The Gibson sisters sold it to the U.S. Army in 1942, when the military needed facilities for soldiers in the Panhandle, but it later reverted to its former use. More than a century old, the lovely Gibson Inn still exists near Apalachicola Bay.

Miami had its first Jewish delicatessen in 1915, an enterprise usually conducted by husband-wife teams. Delis were new to America, an innovation brought largely from German cities. Social conditions there had advanced to the point that women no longer were expected to be full-time housewives who cooked everything from scratch—or to be wealthy enough to employ servants for that. Delicatessens provided the first "fast food," with sausages, cheeses, pickles, slaw, potato salad, and other pre-made foods. Ultimately these businesses and their successors would prove important in freeing women from kitchen duties for civic ones.

* * *

The Florida Federation of Women's Clubs had affiliates in at least eighteen towns by the end of the nineteenth century, and three more formed in 1900 alone.[34] The Tampa Woman's Club began in January 1900, with Helen Dick as president. A northerner married to the manager of the palatial Tampa Bay Hotel, she was seen as the leader of proper society on the west coast, and the club was more literary than its predecessor, the Tampa Ladies Improvement Society. Fort Myers and Titusville also began groups that year, with the latter giving itself an ambitious name, "Progressive Club."

Florida clubs adopted the goals of the national General Federation of Women's Clubs, but they also varied according to local needs and interests. Environmentalism, though, was always a key goal, especially an end to thoughtless tree cutting. A related goal was an end to free-ranging cattle; club women argued endlessly that ranchers should fence their cattle to prevent the destruction of gardens and landscaping.

These issues would continue for decades, and the same was true of FFWC efforts to prevent tuberculosis, a disease that brought death to young people. Among the methods of combating the disease was to build fountains in public places, instead of the usual practice—especially in the era's one-room schoolhouses—of drinking from water pails with a common dipper.

FFWC members took a strong interest in schools and worked for the inclusion of music, art, and home economics in the curriculum. They lobbied for better teacher pay and for longer school terms: at the time, the school "year" was not much longer than today's summer vacations—nor was attendance compulsory. At the 1908 convention in Live Oak, FFWC president Clara Raynor of Daytona Beach reported that the state had 217,000 school-age children—but 87,000 never attended school, and only 17,000 had gone beyond the fifth grade.

"Less than half of these are presumably males," said Raynor, "future citizens who will make laws and conduct government."[35] The nation had forty-six states in 1908, and Raynor reported that thirty had mandatory attendance laws. The FFWC endorsed a resolution to require all children to attend school for sixteen weeks of the year, but the legislature—most of them presumably uneducated themselves—did not respond. Electing such women

The Nation's Second Girl Scout Chapter

Famed Girl Scout leader Juliette Gordon Low profoundly understood why girls need self-esteem and assertiveness: when her husband died, she had to sue to recover a fortune that he left to his mistress. She founded the first Girl Scout troop in Savannah in 1912—and the second was in Tampa in 1913. Willie Lowry of the General Federation of Women's Clubs, who was a superb networker, heard about the Georgia group, and she encouraged the Florida founder, the wonderfully named Jessamine Flowers Link. A childless woman, Link quickly took the opportunity to link with Low's group.

Magnolia Troop One began its adventures with motorboat rides and meetings in an airplane hangar—a very modern setting for 1913. The girls adopted a uniform of white blouses, pleated skirts, and green ties. On hikes through the woods Link taught her girls about the natural world. Her husband was a veterinarian, and she also promoted an interest in animals. The girls handed out sandwiches to troops on trains during World War I, and in the extremely serious flu epidemic that followed the war the girls took the risk of delivering soup to sick families.

The healthful lifestyle that Link encouraged was demonstrated in her own life: she lived to 102. Like Low, Link was an excellent organizer, and when she died in 1973, the Suncoast Girl Scouts was a multi-million-dollar body with thousands of members and tens of thousands alumnae.

to school office was the clear answer, but it took Florida a very long time to hear that message.

Women had been elected to school boards in other states as early as the 1870s—often by male voters—and in 1916 Florida women emulated that. Although they could not yet vote for themselves, at least two women ran—and one won. Mrs. William Hocker, who had been FFWC president in 1912, won election to the Ocala School Board. Alice Snow of Tampa might have won her race: during the suspiciously long week that it took to count ballots, her initial lead disappeared; she was declared the loser by a mere 38 of some 4,400 votes.

In northern cities, motivated learners often obtained more education in libraries than in schools, but in Florida neither libraries nor bookstores were easily available. GFWC members throughout the nation built clubhouses and often had libraries in them, but book borrowing usually was limited to members. Public libraries, however, soon became the GFWC's primary achievement, as the national association later could claim with validity that 75 percent of the nation's libraries had their roots in funds raised by their members.

Just months after the Tampa Woman's Club began in 1900, a member named Willie Lowry read about the grants that industrialist Andrew Carnegie was making to build libraries and sought one—but to her surprise, city fathers refused to accept the money, not only because of Carnegie's reputation as a labor exploiter but also and especially because they did not want to incur the future operating expenses nor open the doors to nonwhite users, as Carnegie intended. Records show years of correspondence between the clubwomen and Carnegie's New York–based agent, with Tampa city officials reluctant to commit to a library. West Tampa, however, was then a separate municipality dominated by immigrants, and its men proved more willing to abide by Carnegie guidelines. Its library opened in 1914, and Tampa's in 1917. In both places, the first librarians were women.

The FFWC also adopted a 1907 resolution for "traveling libraries," later called bookmobiles, to serve rural areas. Within a short time women had donated enough books to create four traveling libraries, with two of them funded by the Massachusetts GFWC. By 1910, when Mrs. J. Stanley Frederick of Miami was president, they had ten. The system was methodical: books were shipped in shelved cases that opened on hinges so they could serve as book cases with no need for unpacking. The cases traveled via train to towns that had a railroad but not a library and were usually delivered to the home of an FFWC member, who made it known that books would be available for the next six months.

Not every group that belonged to the national federation specialized in libraries, though. In Tampa, that was the function of the older Tampa Woman's Club, while the all-female Tampa Civic Association, founded in 1911 by Kate Jackson, focused on public sanitation and especially playgrounds. Elizabeth Askew, mentioned earlier as a suffragist, was president of Woman's City Club, which began in 1914.

It soon could cite a string of achievements: a social center that provided wholesome entertainment for young working women, a women's employment bureau and sales exchange, and a "rest room for women and children"—something that especially nursing mothers needed when they came to town from surrounding farms. The Woman's City Club's greatest pride was getting the school board to provide affordable hot lunches—but even today, schools do not operate as the community cornerstones that Askew envisioned: she wanted "the fullest use of the schoolhouse for the public good . . . , including social centers, vocational training, library extension."[36]

Women led such efforts all over the state. The Ormond Beach club "maintained a library and reading room which was never locked. The last person to leave after nine o'clock turned out the light," and misuse was unknown.[37] Tarpon Springs women bought the first streetlights in their town—and paid for the kerosene to light them. The same was true in Orange City, where the women also funded the man who lit the streetlamps. When electricity came to Delray Beach in 1914, club members reported that it was available in the evenings from six to eleven and that once a week, "the electricity was turned on during the day so that those who had electric irons could use them."[38]

Like electricity, trains also were vital to the liberation of women, and Florida trains sometimes delivered passengers exactly where they wanted to get off. Delray Beach pioneer Ethel Sterling, for example, took piano lessons in West Palm Beach as a teenager, and she said, "the train would go north at seven AM and return south at eleven PM. Someone would . . . wave a lantern at the brakeman so he'd know where to leave me off."[39]

Trains were so important to May Mann Jennings's FFWC work that she traveled many more miles that way than by car, even though she knew how to drive. Like highways, city streets were unpaved, and other FFWC clubs hired men to smooth the ruts from the mud during the rainy season. Prior to sidewalks, some clubs paid for boardwalks to be built over deep sand.

Perhaps the most unusual FFWC community effort was by one of the oldest clubs, that in Crescent City. In 1914, "because the town had no movie theatre, they borrowed money from a member's husband and built one. The entire theatre with seats, screen, and machine cost $7,000, and they were able to pay back their loan 'within a short time.'"[40] They were the only women's club in the nation to own a movie theater, and they kept it in operation until the 1930s.

Although FFWC women usually made their community contributions financially, some also put in physical work. When the daughter of a Vero Beach baker died from diphtheria, these generally upper-class women personally cleaned and disinfected the bakery to meet the standards of the State Board of Health. In Winter Haven Dr. Mary Jewitt brought attention to the school outhouses, where "conditions horrified the members."[41]

Botanical Gardens: Mina Edison, Marie Selby, and More

The only way to reach the Fort Myers home of Thomas and Mina Edison was by boat. He was already well known by 1886, when he married twenty-year-old Mina Miller of Chautauqua, New York. A widower, he presented her with three rather difficult teenagers, and they had three children together. Soon after they married, the family began spending winters at their "honeymoon cottage."

The place was not limited to vacationing, however, as Edison also built a laboratory and then a large house that they called Seminole Lodge. There were no passable roads, and for years they depended on a ship that arrived just once a month. Because it stopped only briefly, anyone who wanted a longer visit had to stay for a month.

The Edisons may have had the first family swimming pool in Florida, built in 1900. Thomas Edison did not engage in recreation, however, and instead lived in Florida largely because the climate enabled growing of plants such as bamboo and rubber trees, which he used as experimental materials. Mina Edison was interested in botany too and, especially as her husband aged, took on greater responsibility for their varied botanical garden. Most of their visitors were potential investors, and her hospitality required a great deal of planning. She referred to herself as a "home executive" and, according to biographer John Venable, "also busied herself in aiding the Negroes living in the slums on the outskirts of Fort Myers."

North of Fort Myers, in Sarasota, Marie Selby built a smaller home but a similarly valuable garden. A classical pianist, she married petroleum executive William Selby in Marietta, Ohio, in 1908, and soon after their wedding bought seven acres on Sarasota Bay. Marie was the major developer of the estate's botanical garden. They summered in Montana and sailed the Gulf in winters, and Marie Selby was an accomplished sailor who won regattas. She may have been the first woman to cross most of the country by automobile: as honeymooners, the couple camped their way from Ohio to the Pacific. When she died in 1971, Marie Selby left her impressive botanical garden to the public.

Bok Tower Gardens near Lake Wales also developed about this time. Its creator, Edward Bok, was famous in the early twentieth

continued

century as the editor of *Ladies Home Journal*—and it may be argued that he owed at least some of his success to his wife. An immigrant from Holland, he married Mary Louise Curtis, the daughter of the magazine's founders, Cyrus and Louisa Knapp Curtis. They had published a farm magazine until 1883, when they realized that the "women's supplement" Louisa edited was more popular than Cyrus's farm section. The Philadelphia-based magazine aimed at women was a huge success, and it continued to be so after Louisa Curtis passed the editorship to Bok.

He died in 1930. The museum at Bok Tower Gardens makes little mention of either his mother-in-law or his wife, although it features his Dutch mother. The music offered by Bok Tower's carillon does reflect his wife, whose primary interest was music. Mary Bok endowed Philadelphia's Curtis Institute of Music, which offered free tuition and educated such outstanding musicians such as Leonard Bernstein. She also donated a theater to Rollins College in Winter Park; dedicated in 1932, it was named for her friend Annie Russell, a well-known English actress who had retired there. A 1949 remarriage changed Mary Bok's name to Zimbalist, and she lived on to her ninety-third year, dying in Philadelphia in 1970.

Note: John D. Venable, *Mina Miller Edison: Daughter, Wife and Mother of Inventors: A Brief Biography* (East Orange, N.J.: Charles Edison Fund, 1981), 18.

Nationally the GFWC tried to protect Native Americans, and the Fort Lauderdale chapter took a special interest in Seminoles—but few men in powerful places felt the same. Ivy Stranahan, the original white woman most helpful to the Seminoles, spent 1917 as president of the suffrage association, lobbying in Tallahassee with Lena Shackleford, a past FFWC president. After losing their campaign for the vote, Shackleford especially was struck by how legislators dismissed both women and Natives. "It was disconcerting, to say the least," she wrote, "to have your warm and tender sympathy for the Seminoles crash against the senatorial opinion . . . that Indians are a 'dirty, disease-breeding lot.'"[42]

FFWC leader Mary Barr Munroe of Coconut Grove also befriended the natives: when she died in 1936, a eulogist said, "No one was better informed on the lore and conditions of the Seminole Indians." She led the movement against killing birds, too, and the tribute continued, "The Indians and the birds have lost an especially kind friend."

Commitment to Seminoles and the environment came together in the FFWC's crowning achievement, the beginning of Everglades preservation. The effort was initiated by the Coconut Grove club, especially Edith Gifford and Mary Barr Munroe. May Mann Jennings would later recall:

> It required a great deal of persuasion and manipulation to bring the Legislature of 1915 to the point of presenting 960 acres for a park to a group of women . . . , but the improbable came to pass. Mrs. Henry Flagler met the Legislature's gift with a similar donation of rich land, and the women looked out upon a dooryard of 1,920 acres for their great conservation project. ROYAL PALM STATE PARK was the only possible name for their enterprise, and as such, it was dedicated on November 23, 1916.[43]

Mary Barr Munroe, who pioneered in Dade County before Julia Tuttle did, was an especially strong environmentalist: she "once plucked an egret feather from the hat of a club visitor and refused to apologize." Her colleague Edith Gifford, whose Philadelphia family was in the shipping business, said at the dedication:

> It is the only state park owned by women. . . . We hope to make this Royal Palm Park a model of its kind, and also a tribute to women's enterprise and women's instinct for conservation. . . . This affords an opportunity of which we ought to be so jealous that we should recognize no such word as "fail."[44]

Still another FFWC priority was reforming the reform system, as members objected to the common practice of leasing convicts, usually black men, as laborers for private businessmen, who often treated them worse than slaves. Florida's neglect of its human resources also was reflected in that the only reform school—"for delinquent boys and girls, white and black"—was in the Panhandle town of Marianna. Lucy W. Blackman, who chaired the FFWC's legislative committee, said in 1912 that she had heard rumors of "impoverished and unsanitary conditions" there, and she lobbied lawmakers to investigate. With their appointment arranged long in advance, legislators arrived to find "all spic and span, with a chicken dinner in their honor awaiting them."[45]

But when two of the FFWC committee members, Mrs. Henry Wight and Mrs. W. B. Young, "put on their hats one morning and, uninvited, unannounced, unexpected, and evidently unwanted," they found conditions at Marianna that were entirely different. Their report raised a "sensation," especially as they explained that many of the inmates "were not delinquent but simply were victims of circumstances over which they no control." They lobbied for a separate and more humane facility for girls, and the legislature appropriated funds for that at Ocala. However, when May Mann Jennings later visited the site, she found that no work had been done, and "the girls who were sent to live there [were being] turned back on the streets."[46]

In a number of states GFWC chapters built nursery schools for black children—doubtless with something of a personal interest, as this made absenteeism less likely for their household help. The Florida federation went beyond that to list "race relations" explicitly as a goal, and Mary McLeod Bethune led creation of the Florida Federation of Colored Women's Clubs. In a 1917 letter to her colleagues, she especially emphasized World War I:

> We planned great things at our splendid State meeting in June. . . . Let us not lose a moment's time, dear co-workers. The emergency is here—the need on women's service is greater than ever before. . . . No women in the world, not even the women of Russia, nor of England, nor of France, can bring to their country's need, truer hearts, deeper devotion, more unselfish service than the tried and true women of the Negro race. . . .
>
> Many of the clubs have reported good work already. Many are keeping up their Red Cross and Emergency work, canning, preserving, knitting, . . . doing their bit. . . . Two clubs united into an Emergency Circle have sent $50 for War Relief, prepared fine boxes [for refugees], bought several Liberty Bonds."[47]

These were assertive moves, but GWFC women, both white and black, were viewed as conservative compared with those in the Women's Christian Temperance Union. Its origins had been in Ohio in the 1870s, and chapters began in Florida during next decade.[48] One of the WCTU's primary goals at the turn of the century was raising the "age of consent"—the age at which a man can argue in court that he is not guilty of rape because the "woman" consented. Florida was not the worst in this—that was Delaware, where the age of consent was seven—but Florida was one of many southern states in which it was ten. Women in the Palmetto Club of Daytona adopted a resolution:

> . . . Whereas . . . when men so far forget morality and justice as to place the age when a girl can consent to her own ruin far below the age when she can legally dispose of a few paltry dollars;
>
> When our lawmakers deliberately shield vicious men in the perpetuation of the heinous crime of destroying womanly virtue by making it legal for a girl of ten years to consent to such destruction . . .
>
> Therefore be it resolved, that we do earnestly protest against any legal difference in age between moral and financial responsibility, and that we petition the legislature to raise the age when a girl may legally consent to her legal, social, and moral ruin, to the same age as that at which they are willing to allow their boys to take financial responsibility—twenty-one years.[49]

That legislative session added technicalities to the bill to prevent its passage, but the age of consent was later raised to eighteen. In discussing the issue at their 1906 convention, GFWC members inquired if there was any place in the state devoted to rehabilitating such "fallen" women, the era's phrase for any woman who had borne a child out of wedlock or was viewed as sexually promiscuous. Someone from Tampa, a member of that city's brief-lived Current Events Club, told them about the Door of Hope, an innovative institution that had begun in the last year of the last century. The *Tampa Morning Tribune* ran the organization's 1900 annual report:

> Since the rescue work first began in the hearts of a few WCTU women of Tampa one year ago, twenty girls have . . . been called "ours." The first little one was but thirteen years old. . . . She was enticed by old associates. . . . The age of consent in Florida being at the tender age of ten years, we could not take her by force, but kept, as far as possible, watch and care over her. She was honorably married not long ago. . . .
>
> Eight girls have . . . received honorable employment outside the Home. . . . We are about to take possession of our permanent home. . . . If we can secure one hundred dollars a month, we can maintain our home, pay all bills, and make our regular payment on the new property.[50]

The women's careful budget of approximately $1,200 a year compared favorably with $30,000 that the legislature had approved for the as-yet-unopened Ocala facility for girls—and put to shame the paltry $14.61 that women at the GFWC convention donated to the Door of Hope. But president Jennie Weller, vice president Mary Sauls, and other women persisted. The Door of Hope offered not only a safe place to stay but also a nursery for the children of mothers who wanted to earn a respectable living. The three-story facility employed its residents at sewing—on machines the women had gotten donated from manufacturers—and taught other employment skills. By 1908 its leaders had an arrangement whereby police delivered female vagrants and delinquents to them instead of to jail. They also accepted women who were alcoholics and drug addicts and, in 1914, a woman who was dying of syphilis.

In 1918, however, records for the Door of Hope disappear.[51] The most likely explanation is that it was a casualty of World War I. As women once again put the national interest ahead of their work for each other, the haven may have lacked donors and volunteers. A second probable factor is that Congress passed the Chamberlain-Kahn Act during World War I, aimed at curbing the era's high rate of venereal disease by protecting innocent young soldiers from preying prostitutes. The law mandated, for example, that no unescorted woman could be out after 9:00 p.m.—and even if escorted, she had to carry documentation to prove her respectable connection to her companion. Although Florida was less directly affected by World War I than by the Spanish-American War two decades earlier, Tampa police may have adopted the military attitude and taken troubled women to jail instead of to the Door of Hope.

After World War I, the government would never again try to enforce such moral standards. Everything changed, as the world became smaller—and the effect on Florida women was quick and real. Because French and Belgian women shortened their skirts to drive ambulances from battlefields, more liberated clothing and short hair became socially acceptable in this semi-tropical state, where such fashions logically should be have been implemented earlier. Because of activists in Britain and Scandinavia and Australia, "the new woman" who was educated and who voted came to be seen as acceptable in backwaters such as Florida. Indeed, in the few years between the war's 1914 beginning and the Roaring Twenties, the world saw more dramatic political and social changes than in any other brief span of human history.

7 Up and Then Down, 1921–1940

The Roaring Twenties truly roared in Florida. Streams of northern newcomers brought new attitudes and lifestyles; they lived in new towns with new art deco architecture and decor. Population had boomed 34 percent over the previous decade, and by the end of the 1920s Florida passed the million-residents mark.

The 1920s marked not only a great economic transformation but also the greatest social change of all time for women all around the globe. Following World War I and the example of Europeans, American women shortened their skirts, cut their hair, smoked cigarettes, and drank in speakeasies—during a time when alcohol was prohibited but narcotics were legal. They drove cars, read Freudian psychology, danced sexily to new jazz, and aped fashion and behavior from new movies. The "flapper" of the 1920s was liberated beyond any woman in human history.

Understandably, there was great generational conflict, especially in immigrant families. Mothers and daughters conflicted, and in the midst of all this hurried yet profound change, exercising the vote that older women had worked so hard to obtain in the previous decade seemed almost minor and political feminism almost passé.

Those high-flying days, however, were founded partly on shaky investor pyramid schemes, and Florida plunged into the Great Depression in the mid-twenties, sooner than other states. Back-to-back hurricanes also had devastating effects:

> The storms of 1926 and 1928 wrecked thousands of acres of vegetable and citrus farmland in South and Central Florida and choked off what little remained of the land development and housing markets. Between 1926 and 1930, the assessed value of real estate dropped by approximately one-third, from $623 million to $441 million. . . . In 1926 alone, more than forty banks failed.[1]

As the rest of the nation joined the downward slide after Wall Street fell in 1929, depression worsened in Florida, too. Per capita annual income in the state was $510 in 1929, but by 1933—when Democrat Franklin D. Roosevelt took the White House from Republicans who had held it for twelve years—the annual income of Floridians was down to $289. By the end of that year, 26 percent of Floridians were "receiving public assistance from either state or federal sources."[2]

Even long settled and affluent areas such as Key West were badly hit. The city declared itself bankrupt in 1934, when 80 percent of its residents "were on relief."[3] Things got worse the next year, when a major hurricane destroyed the still-new railroad that linked the keys to the mainland.

But both in that Depression decade and in the Roaring Twenties, women continued to organize for their communities. The years after 1920 when women won the vote nationwide saw an explosion of new groups, including the League of Women Voters, Business and Professional Women's clubs, the Florida Parent Teacher Association, the Florida Junior League and—in this virtually all-Democratic state—the Democratic Women's Clubs. Black women also developed new organizations, and they arguably registered to vote more devotedly than white women.

* * *

The women who ran for office were white. The first was in 1920, when Mrs. C. H. Curtis managed to file as a candidate for the Florida House between the enfranchisement of women in late August and the election in early November. She lived in Zephyrhills, north of Tampa, and the *Tampa Tribune* endorsed her. Rural Zephyrhills, however, was not as liberal as the city newspaper, and Curtis did not come close to winning.

The paper editorialized on the local supervisor of elections and his alleged hardships with women's names. When he insisted that married women register under their husbands' names, the *Tribune* mused: "It is difficult to see how the urbane supervisor will be able to dictate the terms of registration, if a woman would rather register under her own name, rather than that of her husband."[4]

Up in the Panhandle in 1921 Molly Truesdell ran for city commissioner in the Bay County town of Lynn Haven but lost the election. In the 1922 election two women ran for the Florida House. Both were candidates in Democratic primaries, the only state elections that mattered in the Florida of that time. Approximately 90 percent of the state's registered voters were Democrats, as had been the case since the Civil War.

Mytice Vera McCaskill ran in Taylor County, which is on the upper west coast where the Gulf bends into the Panhandle; its biggest town is Perry. She was just twenty-five years old but well qualified. While a student at Florida State College for Women, McCaskill had worked as a House clerk in the 1917 legislature, and she followed that with a Senate clerkship in 1921. During World War I she organized the state for the YWCA, which specialized in refugee needs. With encouragement from those who knew her in the capitol, she ran for a vacant seat—but soon discovered that Tallahassee was more urbane than Taylor County, where she ran. According to House historian Allen Morris:

> McCaskill campaigned from the back of a pickup truck driven by her father or a cousin. Her daughter later related an incident of the campaign: "She walked towards a group of women sitting on the porch of a backwoods shack. They were chewing tobacco. One of the women spat in her direction and called her 'that hussy that's a-running for the Legislature. . . . ' Leave politicking and moonshining to the menfolks. 'That's all they're good for anyway,' she declared and spat again." Reflecting on the campaign later, McCaskill's son noted, "One of the other issues in the campaign, other than Mother being a woman, was that she was roundly criticized for being a college graduate."[5]

At least one other issue affected the campaign: McCaskill supported a state law to treat cattle for wood ticks—something most farmers opposed but that had proven effective in preventing disease. Her opponent, W. T. Hendry, filed just prior to the deadline, and he represented the anti-regulatory view. She lost badly, 835–197—and was especially chagrined when the next legislature passed the mandatory cattle treatment. McCaskill was successful in private business, however, as an agent for New York Life Insurance. She later married attorney James Jordan Tyson, moved to his home in Montgomery, Alabama, and bore three children; she died in 1985.

Katherine Bell Tippett of St. Petersburg was quite a contrast to young McCaskill but also lost her 1922 race. She came closer, however, placing second in a field of four. A Maryland native, Tippett was proficient in five languages, as she had traveled the world with her journalist husband. She also was an author—but hid herself under a pseudonym. The couple retired to St. Petersburg in 1902, and she became active in the Florida Federation of Women's Clubs.[6] Lobbying for its goals showed her how poorly represented most Floridians were. As she said of the 1921 legislature:

> The first great shock to the women new to the methods of the Halls of the Legislature is the fact that . . . the men assembled to thrash out the grave problems of the state act like a bunch of boys unwillingly kept in school. The slightest mention of invitations to picnics or fish fries calls for the motion to adjourn. . . . This practice is causing the Legislature to be kept in almost continuous session, with the Sergeant-at-Arms keeping locked doors to keep the quorum.[7]

An unnamed senator told Tippett "that he wished club women would stop writing him to 'vote for bills so and so. How can I find time to know all their numbers?' Mrs. Tippett quickly informed him, 'If you do not take time, they soon will know your number.'"[8] But an insufficient number of voters paid as much attention to their lawmakers as these clubwomen did, and she lost to M. W. Ulmer, 948–660. Ulmerton Road, an important artery in Pinellas County, reflects him, while except for minor attention in the St. Petersburg History Museum, her legacy has largely been forgotten.

The 1924 and 1926 elections also failed to set milestones, but in 1928, Florida voters established three precedents: for the first time a woman won a statewide race; a woman joined the Florida House; and most impressive, the state's East Coast voters sent the first woman from the South to the U.S. House. The Great Depression was settling in by 1928, and unhappy voters seemed ready to take a chance on a new type of politician.

The statewide winner was Mamie Eaton (later Greene). She was elected to the railroad commission, which was transformed into the Public Service Commission in 1958. This body, now no longer elected, regulates utilities such as electricity and telephones, while its predecessor, the railroad commission, approved franchises and set rates for passengers and freight.

Governor John Martin appointed Mamie Eaton, a resident of Monticello near Tallahassee, to the position in March 1927 to replace her recently deceased husband, R. L. Eaton. She won election in her own right in 1928 and was reelected in 1930 for another two-year term. When she married A. B. Greene of Tallahassee in 1931, the attorney general's office debated whether her ballot identity could or should be changed to Eaton-Greene or other variations that indicated her newly acquired marital status.[9] Voters seemed to have less of a problem with her name than lawyers did, and she won again in the 1932 election.

In 1934, however, she was akin to many other women of the Great Depression who lost their jobs to men. She lost to Jerry W. Carver, who would hold the post for more than two decades. On March 13, 1958, when the status of the Public Service Commission was being debated, the *Sarasota Herald Tribune* ran a column by reporter Allen Morris, later an eminent state historian. Morris reminded voters of how Carver had won the 1934 election: he said he needed the job because had "seven mouths to feed." Carver, said Morris, "ousted the only woman ever to hold statewide elective public office in Florida, the late Mamie Eaton-Greene."[10]

Her 1928 electoral victory made Florida about average in the ranks of states with women in statewide office: North Dakota elected the first in 1892, but a few states did not set this precedent until after 2000. Florida did not rank nearly as well in electing its first female state legislator. Colorado had elected the first in 1894, and Florida's date of 1928 was fourth from the bottom nationally. When Edna Giles Fuller became Florida's first that year, only Louisiana, South Carolina, and the Alaska Territory had yet to elect a female legislator.

She appeared on the ballot as "Mrs. J. T. Fuller" and was a widow whose uncle, James L. Giles, had been mayor of Orlando. An orphan, she grew up in his home, and when she married, he took her husband into the Giles's family business. Fuller inherited appreciable wealth upon her husband's 1912 death, and when she ran for the legislature in 1928, was fifty-five years old.

Active in many Orlando causes, Fuller said she was running on her "record of 20 years of constructive public service," which included organizing Florida's food conservation in World War I. According to her friends, "Miss Edna loves people. . . . She'll encourage you to do right, and if that doesn't work, she'll drive you." In the all-important Democratic primary, she defeated her sole male opponent for the Orange County seat by winning 3,987 to 3,119.

She introduced seven bills in the 1929 session, the most significant of which addressed the era's economic collapse by changing the period of residency for "mother's pensions," the term for financial assistance to women

Initial election of women to state legislatures

Year	State	Number
1894	Colorado	three
1896	Utah	two
1908	Idaho	one
1910	Wyoming	one
1912	Washington	two
1914	Arizona	one
1914	Oregon	one
1916	Montana	two
1918	California	four
	New York	two
	Kansas	one
	Nevada	one
1920	Connecticut	five
	New Hampshire	two
	Indiana	one
	Oklahoma	one
1921	New Jersey	two
	Kentucky	one
1922	Pennsylvania	seven
	Minnesota	four
	Ohio	four
	Arkansas	two
	Georgia	two
	Massachusetts	two
	Missouri	two
	North Dakota	two
	Alabama	one
	Illinois	one
	Maine	one
	Maryland	one
	Rhode Island	one
	South Dakota	one
	Tennessee	one
	Texas	one
	Vermont	one
	West Virginia	one
1923	Virginia	two
1924	Nebraska	three
	Wisconsin	three
	Delaware	one
	Hawaii Territory	one
	Michigan	one
	Mississippi	one
	North Carolina	one
1928	**Florida**	**one**
	Iowa	one
1936	Alaska Territory	one
1940	Louisiana	two
1945	South Carolina	one

Source: Doris Weatherford, *Women in American Politics: History and Milestones.*

Initial election of women to Congress

Rank	State	Year
1	Montana	1916
2	Oklahoma	1920
3	Illinois	1922
4	California	1923
5	New Jersey	1924
6	Massachusetts	1925
7	Kentucky	1927
8	**Florida**	**1928**
8	New York	1928

who had no one to help support dependent children. The House speaker's respect for Fuller is clear in that during her first term he appointed her chair of the House Education Committee's Subcommittee B, and in the next session she would chair Subcommittee A; both subcommittees made major decisions. Jacksonville's Helen Hunt West, who observed the 1929 session, wrote that "the woman member of the house did not appear ill at ease."[11]

Representative Fuller was reelected without opposition in 1930 and rose to chair the House Public Welfare Committee in 1931. During her first term she had also been vice chair of the House Domestic Relations Committee as well as the Committee on Realtors and Agents. In 1932, however, voters throughout the nation ousted incumbents of all parties; that year marked the nadir of the Great Depression. Florida was no different, and a dramatic 78 percent of the House membership lost their elections. Fuller was among them, losing 3,736 to 2,668. She lived on in Orlando for another twenty years, dying in 1952.

The more remarkable thing about the 1928 election was that Florida was the first state in the South to elect a woman to Congress. In contrast to being among the slowest to elect a woman to its legislature, Florida tied with New York as eighth in the nation to put a woman in Congress. She was Ruth Bryan Owen of Miami, the daughter of feminist Mary Baird Bryan and presidential nominee William Jennings Bryan, and her own life history was uncommonly interesting.[12] A widow with four young children, she ran and lost in 1926 but won in 1928.

Florida's population in the 1920s remained so low compared with other states—and power was still so concentrated in Tallahassee and the Panhandle—that her gerrymandered district stretched along the East Coast from the Georgia border to Key West. With her brilliant mother and aunt Mary Baird Bryan and May Mann Jennings plotting strategy and using their multiple contacts, Ruth Bryan Owen made news by driving herself through the vast district. "The Spirit of Florida" was emblazoned on her car, and she usually traveled with another woman or two. While the incumbent, William Sears, spent his time in Washington, she stopped in every village and talked with voters.

But just as Florida women had faced legalistic objections to their right to vote after the Nineteenth Amendment was adopted, Owen had to face down a legalistic loser. The state had accepted her filing fee and put her on the ballot in 1926 and again in 1928, and she clearly prevailed in the second race—but Sears crafted a complex argument to the U.S. House, maintaining that she was not a legitimate candidate and should not be seated. His case depended on an aspect of federal law that applied only to women, not men.

Her second husband had been Reginald Owen, a British army officer, and Sears argued that she lost her American citizenship when she married him. This had been true in the past: native-born women lost their citizenship if they married a foreigner, while men endowed a foreign woman with automatic citizenship when they married. Congress had corrected this inequality with the 1922 Cable Act, but Sears cleverly argued that the routine seven-year waiting period for citizenship had not quite passed when Owen won in 1928. She had to plead for admission to the U.S. House, and a majority of members agreed that Floridians intended her to be their representative. Sears, on the other hand, behaved so badly that the House finally banned him from the floor, a privilege otherwise granted to former members.

Following the aims of the Florida Federation of Women's Clubs, one of Owen's chief priorities was the preservation of the Everglades, and Congress took the first steps for that goal during her tenure. She also creatively proposed a Department of Home and Child, presaging the Department of Health, Education, and Welfare that finally developed in the 1950s. This was too forward-thinking for her era, though, and Congress never took up the proposal.

Her 1932 loss was in the same year that liberal Democrat Franklin Roosevelt ousted incumbent Republican Herbert Hoover by a huge margin—and ironically, Owen was a friend of the Roosevelts. But like Edna Giles Fuller on the state level, Owen could not overcome the anti-incumbent attitude of that year—plus she had a disadvantage because of Prohibition.

A Woman for All Seasons: Ruth Bryan Owen

Ruth Bryan Owen led a complex life, with three marriages and three name changes. She also had three distinctive governmental careers: between the 1920s and the 1950s she was the first congresswoman from the South, the first female diplomat, and an architect of the United Nations.

Born in Illinois to politician William Jennings Bryan and pioneering attorney Mary Baird Bryan, she had role models in both parents. The family, which included a younger brother, soon moved to Nebraska, and from an early age Ruth participated in politics as her father rose to become the only three-time Democratic nominee for president. Fewer people noticed her extraordinary mother, probably the world's first attorney who was also a young mother: Mary Baird Bryan passed the Nebraska bar exam in 1888, when Ruth was three.

By age eleven, Ruth was handling some of her father's correspondence. She entered the University of Nebraska in 1901, when she was just sixteen, but left two years later to marry William Homer Levitt, an artist much older than she. It is possible that she was pregnant; she bore two children, Ruth and John Baird, in quick succession. She and Levitt divorced after a five-year marriage, some of which she and the children spent with her parents.

She was in Germany studying voice when she met Reginald Owen, an English military officer. They wed, and she accompanied him to Jamaica before bearing her third child, Reginald, in England in 1913. When World War I began the next year, she took a course in nursing and went to the British colony of Egypt, where she worked for three years in a Cairo hospital. In 1918, near the end of the war, her husband became critically ill with kidney disease that he had ignored during months of combat at the Dardanelles.

Doctors told him he would not recover and, pregnant with her fourth child, who would be named Helen Rudd, Ruth Bryan Owen led her family around the globe via Asia to the Miami suburb of Coconut Grove. Her parents had retired there after her father, then secretary of state, resigned from Woodrow Wilson's Cabinet because he opposed American involvement in the war.

continued

Despite their abilities, the Bryans had not accumulated wealth, and Ruth Bryan Owen became the chief breadwinner not only for her four children but also for a disabled husband, an aging father, and a mother eventually crippled by arthritis. Owen discovered that she had inherited her family's oratorical skills and joined the national lecture circuit. She also taught speech at the new University of Miami and soon became involved in Florida politics.

In 1926—just six years after Florida women won the vote—she ran for Congress. Her father had died the previous year, with the result that men in the Democratic Party (the only party that mattered in the South) felt free to oppose her. Despite these obstacles, Owen lost by a mere eight hundred votes. Her husband died in 1927, and she prevailed in the 1928 election.

Owen won a precedent-setting seat on the House Foreign Affairs Committee; she worked to preserve the Florida Everglades; and she proposed a Cabinet-level Department of the Home and Child. As noted, after her 1932 loss President Franklin Roosevelt appointed her minister to Denmark, where she served until 1936—when her third marriage again resulted in problems of citizenship that forced her to resign.

She married a Danish noble, Borge Rohde, in 1936; their wedding reception was at the Roosevelts' estate in Hyde Park, New York. But despite these high-ranking connections, no one informed her that marriage could have negative consequences for a female ambassador. She automatically became a Danish citizen, and Secretary of State Cordell Hull used that to push her out of her job. The national media piled on further critique, particularly objecting to the fact that her husband was younger than she.

Forced to resign from her Copenhagen post, she and her new husband lived in the United States and campaigned for Roosevelt's reelection; she again took to the lecture circuit and wrote. She had published *The Elements of Public Speaking* in 1931, while in Congress, and in 1935, while an ambassador, published *Leaves from a Greenland Diary*. The first American diplomat to visit this Danish colony, she continued in this genre with three books in the late 1930s on Scandinavia and its folklore. In 1949 she would add one on the Caribbean, where she had lived early in her second marriage. In between, she wrote the book that most reflected her political views: *Look Forward, Warrior* (1942) was a plea for global harmony.

She was usually called Ruth Bryan Rohde at this point. Roosevelt appointed her to the State Department—from which her nemesis, Secretary of State Cordell Hull, had resigned as World War II wound down. Roosevelt saw her as an excellent choice to work on drafting the charter for the new United Nations, and after the president's death in April 1945, President Harry S. Truman appointed her as an alternate delegate to the first UN General Assembly. She served creditably and, beginning in 1948, chaired a committee for international speakers.

At age sixty-eight she died of a heart attack in Copenhagen, where she had gone to receive the Order of Merit from the Danish king. She was cremated there, and her ashes were buried in Copenhagen's Ordrup Cemetery. She was admitted to the Florida Women's Hall of Fame in 1992 under the name she used in Congress, Ruth Bryan Owen. The Florida Democratic women's PAC, Ruth's List, is named for her, while a school in Miami uses her final surname, Rohde.

Note: Much of this profile is drawn from the author's *Women in American Politics*, published by Congressional Quarterly Press in 2012. See also Sarah Pauline Vickers, *The Life of Ruth Bryan Owen: Florid a's First Congresswoman and America's First Woman Diplomat* (Tallahassee: Sentry Press, 2009).

Roosevelt and Democrats campaigned to repeal the Eighteenth Amendment, the "Noble Experiment" that had banned alcohol throughout the nation during the 1920s. Owen was in a particularly personal predicament on the issue. Having traveled the world, she was accustomed to responsible alcohol use—but her father, famed William Jennings Bryan, had been a strong prohibitionist. To speak against the repeal would have insulted his memory and the many voters who revered him, and she was thus unable to capitalize on the year's wave of anti-prohibition sentiment. President Roosevelt understood her political problems, and soon after his inauguration, he appointed her ambassador to Denmark—the first such appointment ever for a woman.

* * *

Florida women did not give up on running for federal office, however, as Tampa's Hortense K. Wells was a candidate for the U.S. Senate in the next election. The *Tampa Morning Tribune* said on February 8, 1934:

> Mrs. Hortense Wells, Democratic national committeewoman for Florida, yesterday made formal announcement for the United States Senate in the June primary.
>
> [The] first woman to seek this office in Florida, Mrs. Wells informally had announced nearly two months ago that she would go after the job long held by Park Trammell. John Page Jones came out a few weeks ago and Claude Pepper, Tallahassee lawyer, is certain to come in. . . .
>
> [A] native of Georgia, like many other officeholders in this state, Mrs. Wells has made her home in Tampa since early childhood. In 1932, as an early pre-convention backer of [Franklin Delano] Roosevelt, she entered the race for national committeewoman and carried 51 of the 67 counties, with a total vote of 86,000.
>
> "I expect to make a vigorous campaign and my platform will be in harmony with the Roosevelt administration," Mrs. Wells said yesterday."
>
> Mrs. Wells, widely known over the state in civic activities, is state chairman of the Daughters of the American Revolution; served as state publicity chairman of the American Legion Auxiliary; for two years was state president of the Business and Professional Women's club, and now honorary state president of that organization.

The election turned out to be limited to three candidates, Trammell, Pepper, and Wells. Historian Gary Mormino said she "finished a distant third . . . in what was perhaps the most corrupt US Senate election in state history."[13] Trammell won narrowly, and strong evidence showed that it was only because ballot boxes were stuffed for him—in Tampa, where Wells lived. But even in an honest election, she might have been expected to lose: she lacked previous electoral experience, and Roosevelt, who was not on the 1934 ballot, could not be expected to get involved in a Democratic primary, especially against an incumbent. The only woman in the Senate at that point was Hattie Caraway of Arkansas, who had the advantage of being elected to replace her late husband. Not until 1948 would a woman who lacked this sort of advantage win a Senate election—and even then, Maine's Margaret Chase Smith had the advantage of previous election to the U.S. House.

Like Congresswoman Ruth Bryan Owen, the first woman elected as a judge in Florida also lived in Miami. Edith Meserve had moved there from Maine as a child. In 1916, when she was twenty-six, she married attorney Henry F. Atkinson, who had written the city's charter and was elected as a Dade County judge. Although it was unconventional to go to school after marriage, she graduated from Stetson University College of Law in DeLand in 1922. Just two years later, Edith Meserve Atkinson ran for judge of the newly created Juvenile Court. She defeated two male lawyers and is credited with beginning free legal aid to the area's poor.

Mattie W. Tompkins also was an attorney and an elected official. A native of Washington, D.C., Tompkins earned her law degree there and was admitted to the Florida bar in 1925. She settled in Avon Park, where she developed a general practice, and was elected to the city council in 1939. Listed in *Who's Who among Women Lawyers* that year, she helped develop an airport, the city's first garbage control, and assistance for women suffering from the Great Depression. Tompkins would serve until 1947, when she lost her reelection by just five votes.

Hendry County voters elected South Dakota native Mildred M. Taylor to their school board in 1936 "by a large majority."[14] She would go on to elected positions within the Democratic Party and in the 1950s was included in *Who's Who in United States Politics* and in *American Political Almanac.* The mother of four, Taylor lived in LaBelle.

The 1938 election set two precedents. Voters in Lake Wales chose Mada McLendon as a municipal judge—and would reelect her to five two-year terms until 1948. Born Mada Burney Fraser in Putnam County in 1909, she lived most of her life in Lake Wales, where she founded the Business and Professional Women's Club. She earned her law degree at Stetson University in 1932, and her name changed to Babcock with marriage; it was McLendon after she was widowed and remarried. Even after losing her 1948 race, she enjoyed a long and successful practice, including admission to practice before the U.S. Supreme Court in 1981—when she was seventy-two.

The most remarkable of female officeholders in this era, however, remains almost entirely forgotten. In 1938 south Florida's Okeechobee County had a woman as sheriff—something that has yet to happen in most of Florida's sixty-seven counties. Eugenia Simmons, however, was not elected but was the widow of the incumbent: Governor Fred Cone appointed her when her husband was killed. The governor did the same later in the same year at the opposite end of the state, naming Celia Atkinson to replace her deceased husband as sheriff in Walton County. Both women served satisfactorily, but neither ran for election in her own right.[15]

* * *

Although Florida was governed by Republicans during Reconstruction, today's Republican Party of Florida did not form until 1921, and many who registered to vote in that party were African Americans. Since the Civil War it had been regarded in both North and South as the party of Lincoln, and virtually all blacks who dared to vote were Republicans. This would begin to change with the 1932 election of Democrat Franklin Roosevelt, but in the Roaring Twenties, when Florida women first voted, African American women registered as Republicans.

Indeed, Florida Democrats of that era all but banned blacks from Democratic primaries—to the extent that these important elections long were referred to as the "white" primary. These exclusionary party rules, which were approved by the legislature, meant that black citizens effectively were limited to nonpartisan elections and general elections, which Republicans had no chance of winning.

Tampa's Blanche Armwood was a Republican, and she was so influential with black women that the party hired her as a national speaker during the 1920 election. She campaigned successfully for the election of President Warren Harding, but he did not reward her with either a federal job or one for the party. Ironically, it was Tampa's Democratic politicians who next hired her. Armwood men had held office during and after Reconstruction, and whites respected her family. White men named her superintendent of Hillsborough County's schools for black children—a first in the state, as administrators for black schools routinely were white and usually male.

Her name at this time was Beatty; it had been Perkins during a first marriage and would be Washington with a third. She moved to Washington, D.C., with that marriage and graduated with honors from Howard University's law school in 1937. She returned to Tampa and worked with the juvenile court system in 1938, but died of a heart attack during a 1939 visit to Massachusetts. An East Hillsborough County high school is named for her.

While Armwood remained a Republican, Daytona's Mary McLeod Bethune became a strong Democrat during the 1930s—and President Franklin Roosevelt appointed her as the first black person of either gender to hold a major federal position. She was a national figure by that time, but in 1920, after women got the vote, she courageously led registration drives with northeast Florida blacks—despite intimidation. The Ku Klux Klan terrorized her students in a 1920 night appearance at her boarding school, but she continued her organizing with women and also led black men. In a secret strategy session with clergymen and other activists, she said:

> Use your minds, but keep your lips closed. Eat your bread without butter, but pay your poll tax! . . . Do not be afraid of the Klan. Quit running. Hold your head up high. Look every man straight in the eye and make no apology to anyone because of race or color.[16]

Perhaps because Bethune was astute enough to secure support from winter residents such as John D. Rockefeller Jr., the Klan never again threatened her. Indeed, according to two prominent feminist historians, one white and one black:

> Bethune, Beatty [Armwood], and other activists of the period "were perceived as less of a threat than black men by the power structure [and] were allowed to say things that might have gotten a black man lynched or run out of town. [Yet] Bethune did not pull punches in talks like 'The High Cost of Keeping Negroes Inferior,' stressing how much it cost Florida in dollars and sense to keep the Negro in his place."[17]

Lynching was real; many black mothers and wives saw sons and husbands brutally murdered for no reason other than the color of their skin. Perhaps the worst case was in Lake County, where—to get out of trouble with her husband—a seventeen-year-old white woman falsely accused four black boys of raping her, and vigilantes led by notorious Sheriff Willis McCall killed the young men. Several recent authors have addressed the case, known as the "Groveland Boys," and Gilbert King's 2013 book *Devil in the Grove* won a Pulitzer Prize. Less attention has gone to a book by Julie Buckner Armstrong: *Mary Turner and the Memory of Lynching* tells the appalling history of a woman who lived just over the border in Quitman, Georgia. Eight months pregnant, she was hanged upside down; her baby was cut from her belly and stomped to death.

Even white women were not immune from such terrorism: in Jacksonville in 1926 vigilantes stripped two white women naked, tarred and feathered them, and justified their pornographic violence on the grounds that the women were said to be prostitutes. Dora Apel has researched the subject on a national level with *Imagery of Lynching: Black Men, White Women, and the Mob* (2004).

Yet even as they knew the possible consequences of getting "uppity," many black women nonetheless became activists in the 1920s. Mary Jane Lawson not only registered voters in Palatka—she also raised money for a hospital for blacks. Even the town's white newspaper heralded her, saying, "The small amount of one dollar is asked. Can you not spare that?" The *Times-Herald* added: "On Monday night, August 30th, Mrs. E. B. Straughter will preach and close the effort. Come help us. Each who gives a $1 will be given a hospital certificate."[18]

Like Mary McLeod Bethune, Jacksonville's Eartha Mary Magadalene White was born to former slaves who had large, intact families. White was the thirteenth child in her family, yet she managed to be educated in New York City as well as Florida. Author Joyce Ann Hanson, writing of black women's political activism during World War I, said that Floridians "were among the most active and organized of all southern states. Under the direction of black state chair Eartha M. White, each county had appointed a black woman chair and organized committees" to support the Circle of Negro War Relief.[19] When the war ended and the Nineteenth Amendment followed, White turned her attention to voter registration as well as community charity.

She opened the Clara White Mission, named for her mother, during the Great Depression. She would continue to donate property for needs among Jacksonville blacks during the next decades and in 1967 began the Eartha M. M. White Nursing Home, which grew into the area's largest employer of African Americans. She lived almost a century, from 1876 to 1974, and was inducted into the Florida Women's Hall of Fame in 1986.[20]

Another emerging black professional woman of the 1920s was Mary E. Potter, who with her husband, Rev. Marcellus D. Potter, edited and published the *Tampa Bulletin*. They began it in 1915, and a decade later it had a statewide circulation among African Americans. An employee said that although Rev. Potter's kind "spirit pervaded the newsroom," it was "Mrs. Potter who really ran the operation."[21] Almost a hundred years later the paper still is extant as the *Florida Sentinel Bulletin*. It is an invaluable source for historians, as the news it contained was largely ignored by mainstream newspapers.

These women and more networked through the National Association of Colored Women (NACW), which had begun in Washington in 1896. It expanded to the South in the next decades, aiming to fund projects for blacks that local governments refused to provide. The NACW developed nursery schools for working mothers in Florida as well as summer camps and homes for delinquent girls. Such projects usually occurred without any attention from mainstream media, and many whites had no idea how much constructive civic work was being done by black women. More practical than political, the NACW in Florida did not concentrate on voting.

The NACW's founding president, Mary Church Terrell of Washington, D.C., stayed with the Republican Party when many African Americans began switching to the Democratic Party, and that was a factor in Mary McLeod Bethune's decision to form the National Council of Negro Women (NCNW) in 1935. Bethune had been the Florida president of Terrell's NACW from 1924 to 1928, and because she was a Floridian, many organizations of black women in Florida soon affiliated with the new national group. Because it began during the Great Depression, the NCNW's primary goals were more employment opportunity and a more equable distribution of New Deal funds. It also encouraged women to register and vote.[22]

Just as the legal status of black women changed with the vote in 1920, that of Seminoles changed with federal law in 1924. Native Americans were granted U.S. citizenship—but the law also reinforced the reservation system. Especially in Florida, where Seminoles had lived quite freely in the Everglades for decades, this was a negative change. These particular U.S. citizens were forced to move to three reservations in 1924.

The Big Cypress Reservation was established deep in the Everglades, centered in modern Hendry County. The Brighton Reservation was home to the band often called "the Cow Creek Seminoles," and their federal land grant was in modern Glades County on the northwest side of Lake Okeechobee. The Miccosukee Reservation was on the far western side of Broward County. In the crucial year of 1924 their longtime Fort Lauderdale advocate, Ivy Cromartie Stranahan, personally drove four tribal leaders—two women and two men of differing ages—to introduce them to their new forced home. According to a Broward County historian who knew Stranahan:

> She had invited the leaders to inspect the reservation lands. The four . . . were Annie Tommie, an impressive woman, mother of a large family [and] a "medicine woman . . . ," Willie Jumper, a white-haired senior, and two young Indians, Frank Huff and his sister, Pocahontas Huff. . . . [They were] two elders, who knew the past, and two young people who looked to the future.
>
> Not one word was spoken. The Indians stood. Mrs. Stranahan sat behind the wheel of her car. . . . At long last . . . , Annie came alone,

climbed in, and took a seat. Then she was followed . . . by the other three. . . . Mrs. Stranahan drove straight to the reservation. . . . It was a major accomplishment. They had accepted the reservation.[23]

Even on the reservations, most Seminoles continued to live as far as possible in their ancient ways. As late as 1958 a textbook for Florida schoolchildren said that although the Brighton reservation offered "a modern laundry and a shower bathhouse," residents refused to accept the architectural styles of whites and instead built chickees, traditional homes open at the sides and roofed with palm fronds. They had no electricity, but women's feet provided the power for pedal sewing machines that Stranahan had introduced. By the 1920s the Seminoles had developed their now famous style of clothing:

"Hundreds of bright-flowered pieces of cloth [were sewed] into long bands; then the bands sewed together in a beautiful, gay design. . . . The Seminole woman's dress is proper for the climate in which the Indians live and for their way of life. When a Seminole woman walks on wet, swampy ground, as she often must, she can easily lift her long skirt above the water. Her dress is loose and cool. . . .

[A Seminole woman] wears her long, straight hair in a way that shades her eyes. She draws it to the top of her head and ties it. Then she fastens her hair to a piece of cardboard, shaped like a hat brim, and wired around the edge. She draws her hair over this brim-like piece of cardboard. She finishes her hairdress with some colored beads, and puts on a net to keep each hair in place. It makes a most attractive protection for her eyes. . . .

A baby girl is given a string of beads when she is born. She collects them the rest of her life. No woman feels dressed without beads. An Indian woman will work for a long time with beads around her neck that weigh several pounds. She would not think of taking them off in the daytime.[24]

Although Native Americans won the vote with citizenship in 1924, neither Seminole men nor women involved themselves much in American politics. Instead, they continued to be governed by elected tribal councils, and the matrilineal system of property and names continued. In contrast to white women at the time, "the Seminole woman holds a high place in the tribe. She is head of her family. The camp belongs to her. She owns property, which she may sell if she pleases and when she pleases and she may use the money as she wishes."[25]

White women never developed the matrilineal name system that liberated Native American women—and freed their children from any concerns about illegitimacy. Years would pass before Florida women, black or white, had the property rights assured to women by Seminole law.

* * *

Since the formation of women's organizations in the 1880s and 1890s, clubs had been the most effective way of channeling ideas and action for change in Florida communities. The General Federation of Women's Clubs was the chief such body in the first two decades of the twentieth century, and important additions occurred in the third decade—much of this activity motivated by the fact that women now were voters.

The League of Women Voters (LWV) grew directly from the movement for the vote, as the National American Woman Suffrage Association (NAWSA) began transforming itself into the league in 1919. Once again, Florida took longer than some states. According to the report that Alice G. Kolloch sent to the national body, the state's league did not formalize until 1921. Although the Nineteenth Amendment that enfranchised Florida women had been added to the U.S. Constitution in August 1920, Florida suffragists nonetheless held their annual convention in Orlando in October. Kolloch's record said "Mrs. John T. Fuller of Orlando" had succeeded Rev. Mary A. Safford as president in January 1919, and Fuller was reelected at this 1920 meeting ("Mrs. John T. Fuller" was Edna Giles Fuller, who later would be the state's first female legislator). The group met again in April 1921 and formally became the Florida League of Women Voters, with Mrs. J. B. O'Hara of Orlando as its first president.[26]

The league's national president, Maud Wood Park, a thoroughly modern woman, visited Florida in 1922, hosted by the Tampa chapter. Park was a young widow when she became NAWSA's most effective congressional lobbyist; after her 1908 remarriage, she not only retained the name by which she was known but also amicably lived separately from her husband most of the time—few of her colleagues even knew she was married. The league, however, would develop less as a feminist organization than its first president's personal life would seem to indicate, especially in Florida.

Leaguers, for example, did not lobby for the inclusion of women on juries—something that would have dovetailed exactly with its emphasis on civic duty. Instead, Florida women would wait decades for juries of their true peers. The rules of the national LWV also developed, ironically, to discourage true political participation, especially in Florida. League officers were required to be nonpartisan, and in a state where approximately 90 percent of voters were Democrats, this proved a real problem. The Tampa chapter that hosted Park in 1922, for example, later was threatened expulsion from the national league because of what national officers saw as excessive participation in Democratic activities—but that was the only realistic way to be politically active in the South of that time.

There were internal disagreements between chapters within the state, too, and the Great Depression added to the Florida LWV's woes. By 1937 it was in such a poor financial state that the national LWV disaffiliated it—despite the valiant efforts of Marion G. Dickson of Tampa, who had been elected state president in 1936. "Within two years," however, a new Florida Non-Partisan League of Women Voters began with Catherine Poynter as its leader.[27] She was married to Nelson Poynter, the editor who turned the *St. Petersburg Times* into a nationally respected newspaper. Her leadership demonstrated the difference between the two counties on the opposite sides of Tampa Bay: Hillsborough County remained thoroughly Democratic, while Pinellas was attracting more and more Republicans from the North—and in that era, Republicans often were more liberal than Democrats, especially on race-related issues.

Instead of the LWV, many former suffragists turned to the new National Democratic Women's Clubs (DWC). Both parties organized affiliates for women after they won the vote, but most of these groups did not fulfill their promise. Instead of encouraging women to become genuine political leaders, clubs often evolved into little more than cheerleaders for male politicians. Thus the feminism that had been clear in 1920, when the Nineteenth Amendment was adopted, soon dissipated. Neither the LWV nor the DWC carried on with the issues of true equality—such as jury duty and discrimination in education and employment—that had been subjugated during the single-issue campaign for the vote.

The National Women's Party (NWP) offered an alternative, as it introduced the Equal Rights Amendment (ERA) to the U.S. Constitution in 1923. The ERA would have banned state laws and business practices that allowed discrimination on the basis of gender. It met virtually no success in Florida, however, partly because the ideal of true legal equality remained too radical and partly because most NWP leaders were Republicans, which axiomatically made them anathema to most Floridians. Jacksonville attorney Helen Hunt—who became Helen Hunt West after her 1927 marriage—was an exception as a Democrat.[28]

She led approximately fifty women in Florida who belonged to the NWP. They aimed for a straight-line expansion from the Nineteenth Amendment to what they hoped would be the Twentieth Amendment, the ERA. In a 1935 speech to the Florida Federation of Women's Clubs in Lake City, she said:

> Women who are smug in their contentment in comfortable homes with husbands, brothers, and sons of unreproachable character . . . seldom pause to think that their own daughters and granddaughters have to look to an entirely different set of men for justice.
>
> Generation after generation passes. The only measure of security comes through the fundamental law of the land, and that is the reason women need an Equal Rights Amendment to the Constitution of the United States.
>
> By the accident of birth we are women, and we are dissatisfied with our inheritance of injustice and inequality. By the same accident of birth our brothers are men and they have inherited both. All we ask is the right to share that inheritance. . . .
>
> The greatest difficulty in putting over the idea of the Equal Rights Amendment women is that some women do not understand what it means and what it proposes to do. It merely means that the law applies the same to one citizen as it does to another. It makes no attempt to change the laws of nature . . . , but [to] apply the law equally to both men and women.[29]

She was right. Not only were all Florida women banned from juries; a married woman could not sign any sort of contract. In most cases she could not file a suit—or be sued, which discouraged men from transacting business with them. While the national League of Women Voters opposed the ERA because it would nullify protective labor laws for women, Florida had few such laws—and Helen Hunt West probably was correct that most of the laws that ostensibly protected women from harsh labor conditions actually were intended to limit their access to jobs. Night work, for example, often was banned by such laws—but exemptions invariably were made for night work typically done by women, such as that of telephone operators and nurses.

Miami attorney Ethel Ernest Murrell echoed these arguments when she spoke at Florida State College for Women in March 1939. The Associated Press featured a photo of her—wearing a full fur coat—with Sarasota student Leona Howe. Howe was president of the "Twenty-One Club," which was composed of students old enough to vote, and Murrell told the group:

> A single woman in Florida can do almost anything a man can do—but not the married ones, it's the lunatic class for them. By what strange alchemy a woman suddenly changes, when married, from a free-thinking adult citizen to the classification [with declared lunatics] that the statutes place upon her?
>
> A married woman may not make a legal binding contract, and this protects no one except the female swindler. . . . The woman who can afford attorney's fees could have herself declared a free dealer, but . . . one trouble is meeting hubby and explaining it to him. . . . The court will inquire into your competency and, if you are able to remain calm under that insult, he [the judge] will issue to you the same kind of license . . . as he would give to a precocious infant. So then you may go on your way, but if you remarry you have the whole stupid rigamarole to repeat.[30]

Another reason for the Equal Rights Amendment was evident simply in the existence of FSCW: Florida's tax-supported colleges were strictly segregated by gender. By the time that Murrell spoke at FSCW, Stella M. Biddle Fisher had filed an important case on that practice. A DeFuniak Springs native, she served as recording secretary of the Florida Senate in its 1919 session. It probably was marriage that motivated her move to Gainesville, and she sued the University of Florida for refusing to admit women to its law school. The case never wended its way through the courts, however, as Fisher passed the bar exam without attending law school. Although most female attorneys continued to graduate from the private Stetson law school, after 1925 Fisher's friendships with legislators did result in the admission of (white) women to UF's law school—although not its undergraduate school.

Nor was even that limited opportunity truly available. Gloria Floyd (later Gehan) said that "while women were legally allowed to attend the University of Florida College of Law . . . , they were not encouraged to do so." She spoke to the dean about it and he gave her permission to enroll:

On her first day of law school, all the students (male) formed two lines through which she had to traverse in order to enter the law school building. . . ."I was the first young woman. . . . You felt conspicuous, you stuck out like a sore thumb. . . . Some ignored me as a matter of principle."[31]

She graduated with honors in 1933 and went on to a long career in Gainesville. Meanwhile, Jacksonville attorney Helen Hunt West was an active Democrat who nonetheless covered the legislature for Jacksonville and Pensacola newspapers. At the national level, her strongest ally was Molly Dewson, who had led women in electing Franklin Roosevelt in 1932. Dewson saw women as crucial to his 1936 reelection and persuaded Roosevelt to insist on gender equality within the Democratic Party. This had to be done by state law in Florida, and Helen Hunt West led the "50–50" effort in the 1935 legislative session. Molly Dewson sent model legislation, and it appeared ready for passage until:

> Just one day before it was to reach the floor, Chairman S. P. Robineau of Dade County inaugurated a special order calendar requiring unanimous support to introduce a bill. Sensing parliamentary subterfuge, West swung into action. . . . She contacted friends and professional acquaintances . . . and asked them to write letters. . . . She also contacted James Farley [Roosevelt's chief political aide], who immediately pressured Democratic legislative leaders to place the "50–50" bill on the calendar. Finally, she went directly to the chairmen of the powerful committees. . . . When one suggested her best technique might be to "vamp" the chairman of the rules committee, she was understandably irritated.[32]

Her lobbying strategy proved extremely successful, as the bill passed 75–8. The result was that for decades into the future, the Florida Democratic Party functioned under 50–50 rules of governance on its state and county executive committees: if a man chaired, for example, the vice chairmanship automatically had to be filled by a woman.

Molly Dewson, who was more politically experienced and cynical than West, congratulated her but added, "Don't expect too much, for the men will still try to get the most easily manipulated of our sex on to the committees." West, ever the idealist, replied: "By virtue of the bill becoming a law, about 1,400 Florida women take their places in the ranks of the Democratic party in Florida on an equal footing with men. This is the most revolutionary thing in Florida politics since the passage of the Suffrage amendment."[33] Her idealism, however, was not enough to carry West through to victory when she ran for Congress. Her advertising was advanced for its era, as her business card included a photo of the still young-looking woman. It said she was running for Florida's Second Congressional District, and lines beneath that declared: "OPPOSED to any LEGISLATION which does NOT Square with the CONSTITUTION of the U.S. *Please give me your VOTE in the May primaries.*" East Coast voters, however, did not reward her with their congressional seat, and it would not be until 1989 that Florida had its second woman in the U.S. House.

* * *

Less politically active women also felt empowered by their new voting rights, and such mainstream women greatly expanded their lobbying advocacy in the 1920s. The best example may be the Parent Teacher Association (PTA), which had begun in as the National Congress of Mothers in 1897. Florida again ran decades behind the rest of the nation, as its first chapter did not form until 1921. That was the West Riverside PTA in Jacksonville, and within the same year it expanded to other Jacksonville schools. When the national body chartered the Florida PTA in 1923, it was the forty-fifth of the then forty-eight states.

The state association's leadership reflected its East Coast origin. Those who signed the charter were Ruth Nonney, Catherine F. McClellan, and I. E. Phillips of Jacksonville; they were joined by Willie T. Fanger of Hialeah, Amy E. Cook of Miami, Mary Leary of DeLand, and Jennie L. Lemon of Orlando. The only geographical exception was Aldine K. Vinson of Tallahassee.

In the era's rigid segregation, African Americans had a separate organization, but Florida's blacks followed sooner than might be expected, as the Colored Congress of Parents and Teachers organized in Florida in 1927—just four years after the white association. Although women were the leaders in both organizations, the white group chose to give its first honorary life membership to D. P. Davis, the developer of Tampa's Davis Island—who disappeared when his project went bankrupt in the next decade. The second honorary life membership went to Thomas Alva Edison in Fort Myers—who never was as involved in community life as much as his wife, Mina Miller Edison.[34]

The Florida PTA grew quickly and had some legislative success as early as 1924, when members lobbied for an equalization formula in state education spending that would address the disparity across counties. At the time Baker County—a Panhandle county with a large number of blacks—spent an average of 75 cents per child per year, while Pinellas—a largely white community with many newcomers from the North—spent $17.50.

The PTA began a statewide summer leadership program in Gainesville in 1925, and members especially worked to get lunch programs into urban schools. In 1932 the PTA adopted a position of advocating for an eight-month school year—a high ideal during this era of economic crisis. Their positive attitude was reflected in a song composed by Viola Edwards of Tampa, and a songbook would be distributed at the 1941 state convention.

The effect of empowering women with the vote was clear: legislators took them more seriously, and they won results much faster than during the decades when all that they could do was to reason and beg. Moreover, the mothers themselves gained self-confidence to the point that the state had 385 PTA affiliates by 1932, at the depth of the Great Depression. That growth again demonstrated women's ability to network and organize: in the eleven years between 1921 and 1932, they built a strong statewide body under difficult circumstances.

Like the League of Women Voters, the National Federation of Business and Professional Women (BPW) began in 1919. Its roots were in Kentucky, Missouri, and nearby states—but the first Floridians organized prior to official founding of the national body. Z. Ray Ross of Jacksonville, a longtime BPW leader, recalled that "ten brave, wonderful women" met in Jacksonville on June 6, 1919.[35] They pledged themselves to building a state branch, prior to going to St. Louis in July for the first national BPW meeting.

The Florida federation's first president was Lilla White of St. Augustine, and the featured speaker at the 1921 state convention was Edna Giles Fuller of Orlando, who would go on to be the first woman in the legislature. Ruth Rich of Jacksonville was the second president, and when she moved to Washington to edit *Independent Woman*—BPW's excellent national monthly magazine—Hattie Roebuck, also of Jacksonville, replaced her. Elizabeth Barnard, who was postmaster of Tampa, was elected president in 1925, and Mary Randolph of West Palm Beach followed in 1925. Professional women were so eager to network that BPW spread like wildfire: Florida had twenty-seven chapters, some with more than a hundred members, within seven years.

Jacksonville attorney L. H. Shoemaker was president in 1927, and the annual convention featured a skit called "The Flapper Grandmother." Clare L. Wackwitz of St. Petersburg followed as president; she was elected at a convention in Winter Haven, where the Acadia chapter won a prize for civic involvement. The onset of the Great Depression was clear by the time that Dr. Nancy Meek Hain of Miami took office, as BPW's funds included a category for members in need. The decade's last leader was Tampa's Hortense Wells, who also ran for the U.S. Senate.

Another BPW founder, Marie C. Broetzman, led an especially interesting life. She was born in the eastern German town of Colbenz in 1905. Her family immigrated to Jacksonville, and she passed the Florida bar examination in 1932. Broetzman's practice, however, differed from that of most aspiring lawyers: a dedicated Catholic, she visited prisoners condemned to death and charged little or no money on cases for the poor, including racial minorities. Jacksonville judges respected her, and that doubtless was an asset for BPW.

BPW began its first state publication in 1928, and in the next decades, the *Florida Business Woman* would evolve into a slick magazine. The Florida federation also formed an orchestra of musically talented women in 1933, giving businesswomen an opportunity to continue their musical education. More politically active than most women's organizations, the Florida federation of BPW endorsed the Equal Rights Amendment in 1936.

The Junior League had begun in 1901 in New York City, with young women who were wealthy enough that they could volunteer, especially in the era's "settlement houses" that aided immigrants. Its founder was Mary Harriman, a member of a famous family that included many public officials. (Her kinswoman by marriage, Daisy Harriman, went on to be the nation's second female ambassador, following Florida's Ruth Bryan Owen.) One of the first women Mary Harriman recruited for the new group was young Eleanor Roosevelt—and when she was dating future president Franklin Roosevelt, Eleanor purposefully had him pick her up at the settlement house, where he was exposed to poverty.

Thirty branches had developed throughout the nation by 1921, when the organization formalized into the Association of Junior Leagues International. Then and now, local leagues impose obligations on members, with mandatory attendance requirements and measured donations of time and treasure to local projects to benefit the needy. The Tampa chapter began in 1928, and its first project was a home for children with tuberculosis—a prevalent disease that spread through overcrowding in impoverished households.

In addition to these new organizations, those that had begun in the nineteenth century continued, including the Daughters of the American Revolution and the Daughters of the Confederacy. Both became more conservative with time, but in the 1920s the Orlando chapters of these organizations included a female preacher of a liberal faith. Rev. Carolyn Hightower Parsons earned a 1926 doctorate of divinity and was ordained as a minister of Unity Church in Orlando. She remained in that pastorate the rest of her life, and according to a 1950s historian the aptly named Rev. Parsons "was largely responsible for the erection of the Christ Church, Unity, in Orlando in 1942."[36]

* * *

Several women brought national attention to Florida in these decades through their achievement as writers. The foremost of these was Marjorie Kinnan Rawlings of Cross Creek, who won the Pulitzer Prize for *The Yearling* (1938), a short novel set in her rural area near Gainesville. Although Rawlings was a giant of American literature, her neighbors did not necessarily approve of the way they were depicted her in work. Some sued for libel, including Zelma Cason—whose case was brought to the all-male jury by another woman, Palatka attorney Kate Walton.

Much less attention went to Zora Neale Hurston, an African American, but since the 1980s, Hurston has become a feminist icon. Her hometown was the all-black town of Eatonville, northeast of Orlando. Hurston said she was born there in 1901, but modern scholars believe that she actually was born in Alabama a decade earlier. In any case, she lived in Eatonville when she was very young, and her mother, a teacher, soon died. Her father was mayor of Eatonville, but after his remarriage, apparently failed to support her.

After some schooling in Jacksonville, Hurston worked at various jobs as she moved north, eventually entering Howard University in Washington, D.C. Its literary magazine published her first short story, and armed with this success, she won a scholarship to Barnard College. She was the first black student at the elite school, the female affiliate of Columbia University in New York City.

After her 1937 graduation, Columbia anthropologist Franz Boas—a founder of that field—encouraged her to research the folklore of minorities in the American South as well as the Caribbean. In settings that remained exotic to whites, she used the new technology of film to record black life. Among her mentors were best-selling novelist Fannie Hurst, a white woman who employed Hurston as a companion and secretary, as well as famed poet

Langston Hughes, a black man who collaborated with Hurston on a 1931 play, *Mule Bone: A Comedy of Negro Life.*

Moving between New York, Florida, and other places, she wrote *Jonah's Gourd Vine* (1934), which was based on her father; *Mules and Men* (1935), a collection of folklore; and the book considered Hurston's most significant, *Their Eyes Were Watching God* (1937). It ends with the 1928 hurricane that brought down a wall of water on the south shore of Lake Okeechobee; it killed some two thousand Floridians, most of them people of color. A 1938 work, *Tell My Horse,* was based on research in Haiti and religious beliefs there. When Hurston published her autobiographical *Dust Tracks on the Road* (1942), she was at the height of her success.

That she was most productive during the 1930s indicates the new opportunity that arose for blacks during New York City's Harlem Renaissance. She sought and received the patronage of prosperous whites in a time and place when *avant-garde* whites found it fashionable to have black friends—but critics accused her of softening the hard edges of black experience to appease these patrons. Her work has also been criticized, especially by modern African Americans, for using language patterns that can be perceived as stereotypes. Hurston, however, saw herself as honestly recording what her anthropologist's ear heard, using the language that she knew her fictional characters would have used. Moreover, she saw absurd situations for what they were and portrayed them with humor. "I am not tragically colored," she once wrote. "There is no great sorrow damned up in my soul. . . . I have no lurid tales to tell of race discrimination."[37]

But the same 1930s that brought literary success also were the years of the Great Depression; the audience for Hurston's work was limited, and royalties never were sufficient to meet her financial needs. Two marriages also were emotional and economic disappointments. At various times she taught briefly at Rollins College in Winter Park (a white institution) and at Bethune-Cookman in Daytona (a black one), and also did some writing for the Depression-era Federal Writers' Project (FWP). One of the pieces she wrote for the project remains in need of greater attention: it was about the destruction of the African American community in Ocoee, a town west of Orlando, when blacks tried to vote there in 1920.[38]

Finally, through friendship with fellow Floridian Marjorie Kinnan Rawlings, prominent editor Maxwell Perkins added Hurston to his authors' list—but he died before their first project was finished. He funded a trip to Honduras for her because she wanted to travel to an area so unknown that coastal people feared its natives. Before working on that research, however, she finished *Seraph on the Suwanee* (1948), a novel based on poor whites in rural northwest Florida. It was scheduled for publication on October 11, 1947—but on September 13 Hurston was arrested, falsely accused of sexual abuse of her landlady's son. Her life went downhill after that tragic injustice, and when she died in 1960 in St. Lucie County, she was a pauper.

Carita Doggett Corse never was poor, but she understood the desperation of writers during the Great Depression and did everything she could to assist those in Florida. The New Deal programs of Democratic president Franklin Roosevelt reached out to many kinds of people, including white-collar workers embarrassed by their poverty, and among the programs was the Federal Writers' Project. Corse was one of very few female state administrators.

If scholars are right that Zora Neale Hurston was born in 1891, not 1901 as she claimed, then the two women were about the same age, as Carita Doggett was born in Jacksonville in 1892. Although of different races, they also shared educational commonalities: Doggett graduated from Vassar College, which was the first of the women's colleges associated with the male Ivy League. Vassar is just north of New York City, and she went on to earn a master's degree at Columbia University, where women were accepted as graduate students.

Doggett returned to Jacksonville after her 1916 graduation and wrote a 1919 book on Andrew Turnbull, the colonial founder of New Smyrna.[39] Marriage in 1921 changed her name to Carita Doggett Corse; her husband was an engineer. The couple had three children, including a set of twins, but she continued to write. The University of North Carolina published her work *The Key to the Golden Islands* in 1932, earning her an honorary doctorate from Tennessee's University of the South.

The year 1935 was big for Corse. She published two books, a history of Jacksonville sponsored by that city's affiliate of the Florida Federation of Women's Clubs, and *Shrine of the Water Gods,* which was about Silver Springs. The Federal Writers' Project also began in 1935, and despite being the mother of relatively young children, Corse was named its Florida director.

Most states used FWP funding for tourist guides, promoting the resources and history of their states. Corse already had established such a model, having written *Florida: Empire of the Sun* for the state hotel commission in 1930. She supervised the writers of several of these guides as well as a massive compilation published in 1939 and reprinted with additions in 1940. In the introduction to the second addition of *Florida: A Guide to the Southernmost*

State, Corse said "more than 400 experts on special topics served as consultants." Her task in managing this number of individuals was huge, and the six-hundred-page book provides great insight to Florida on the cusp of World War II.

Southern states also used the Federal Writers Project as an opportunity to interview elderly people who had been born in slavery. Corse hired ten African American writers for this and other documentation of black life. Typed up and bound in the 1930s, these slave narratives largely gathered dust for a half century, until black history and women's history came to be acknowledged as an important part of all history.[40] Also unlike other state FWP directors, Corse employed more black women than men. They were Rachel Austin, Rebecca Baker, Violet Muse, Pearl Randolph, and Grace Thompson—along with established author Zora Neale Hurston.

Although Hurston's employment with the agency was relatively brief, she did more than write. She made sound recordings of folklore and African American songs, including at Jacksonville's Clara White Mission. She choreographed a program for young black dancers in Orlando, which earned "the effusive praise of Dr. Corse."[41] Hurston also wrote portions of the *Guide.* In the section with recommended automobile tours, her description of all-black Eatonville soars far beyond the mundane:

> Maitland is Maitland until it gets to Hurst's corner, and then it is Eatonville. Right in front of Willie Sewell's yellow-painted house the hard road quits being the hard road. . . . Take the left side of the road and except for Macedonia Baptist Church, people just live on that side and play croquet in Armetta Jones' backyard behind the huge camphor tree. . . . West of it all, beyond the village and school, everybody knows that the sun makes his nest in some lonesome lake in the woods back there and gets his night's rest.[42]

When the federal project ended in 1942, Carita Doggett Corse became the first Florida director of Planned Parenthood, where she defended women's right to birth control—which was new and highly controversial. She died in 1978, just as the slave narratives were being rediscovered, and was inducted into the Florida Women's Hall of Fame in 1997.

Two Tallahassee historians and writers also began to develop their careers in the 1930s. Dorothy Dodd and Kathryn T. Abbey (later Hanna) were two of the three women present when the Southern Historical Association began in 1934 with a meeting in Atlanta. Some two dozen men were there, but the only other woman was Kathleen Bruce of Virginia's prestigious all-female Hollins College. Other all-female colleges, including Georgia's Agnes Scott College and Virginia's Randolph-Macon, had male representatives.

Kathryn Abbey, listed first because of alphabetical order, was with Florida State College for Women. Born in Chicago in 1895, she earned three degrees at respected Northwestern University, finishing with a doctorate in 1926. She wrote books on Florida both alone and with her husband, Alfred Jackson Hanna. When she was elected president of the Southern Historical Association in 1953, Kathryn Abbey Hanna lived in Winter Park and taught at Rollins College, which, like FSCW, admitted only women. Hanna's most unusual book may be *Confederate Exiles in Venezuela* (1960). Like other works by both Hanna and her husband, it was published out of state—something that indicates Florida's relative backwardness.

Dorothy Dodd was the only Southern Historical Association founder who was listed without an academic affiliation; only "Tallahassee, Florida" followed her name. Dodd was akin to Zora Neale Hurston and Carita Corse in having been educated at New York City's eminent Columbia University. Unlike Corse and Hanna, she never married but devoted her life to Florida history.

Born in Kentucky in 1902, Dodd moved with her family to Florida at age eight. After graduating from Florida College for Women, she earned a master's degree from Columbia in 1925. She supported herself by writing for the *Tampa Daily Times* before earning a doctorate in history at the University of Chicago. Although it was one of the nation's most prestigious schools, Dodd was underemployed until 1941, when she became the state's first archivist: Florida, indeed, was so far behind other states that it had no formal archivist until almost a hundred years after statehood. When she rose to state librarian in 1962, the state's library still was so new that she was just the second person to hold the position.

In addition to writing books such as *Florida Becomes a State* (1945) and *Florida, the Land of Romance* (1957), Dr. Dodd was of incomparable importance in collecting and preserving state records. Dorothy Dodd lived to see her 1986 induction into the Florida Women's Hall of Fame, dying in 1994 at age ninety-two.

Katherine Blood Hoffman likewise graduated from FSCW, in 1936, and earned a master's degree from Columbia University. Called Kitty, she taught chemistry at FSCW from 1940 to the 1980s. She served as a liberating model for women there both before and after the college became FSU. She remembered, though, how difficult it had been to achieve this:

> After my sophomore year began, the Great Depression settled in. My family sadly admitted that they could no longer provide money for my schooling at FSCW. At their suggestion, I contacted the business manager, John Gabriel Kellum, to see if he could suggest a solution.
>
> Mr. Kellum asked me what my father did, and I told him that he grew citrus in Winter Haven [that] was worth little in the current marketplace. Mr. Kellum directed Miss Anna Mae Tracy, head of food services, to purchase sufficient fruit from my father to feed the students and to finance my schooling. . . .
>
> I rode the bus home, helped dad pick three truckloads of oranges, and was able to complete the academic year. There was enough money left over for me to pay for a tonsillectomy at the infirmary, as well as a movie at the Ritz. That cost ten cents and required a chaperone if you went at night.[43]

Hoffman, Dodd, and Hanna probably were present when famed poet Robert Frost visited FSCW in 1940. *Miami Herald* reporter Helen Muir definitely was, and much later, she wrote *Frost in Florida: A Memoir* (1995). Muir also was an artist with words, and she mused, "I want poets to be declared equal I guess, to—what shall I say, scientists? No, big businessmen. I want poets declared equal to big businessmen." No one encouraged FSCW students, however, by telling them that it was Frost's wife, Eleanor, who had been valedictorian of their high school class.

Faculty at nearby Florida A&M in the same era were aware of Augusta Savage, although she never went to school there and few white Floridians ever heard of her. Yet of all the state's artists and writers in this era, she arguably was the most recognized internationally. She was the only black sculptor of either gender whose work was exhibited at the 1939 World's Fair.

Born in Green Cove Springs, near Jacksonville, in 1892, Augusta Christine Fells was akin to Mary McLeod Bethune in coming from a large family: she was the seventh of fourteen children born to Edward and Cornelia Fells. A natural artist as a child, she initially was handicapped by her father, who took literally the biblical injunction against "graven images." "My father licked me four or five times a week," she said later, "and almost whipped all the art out

African American in Paris: Augusta Savage

St. Louis dancer Josephine Baker probably is the best known of the black Americans who went to Paris in the Roaring Twenties. Although in the same time and place, American blacks differed from the "Lost Generation," the disillusioned whites who made Paris their home after World War I. The most famous were Ernest and Hadley Hemingway, Scott and Zelda Fitzgerald, and Gertrude Stein and her partner Alice Toklas. None were racist, but they made little effort to reach out to the Americans who looked different. Indeed, there may have been less contact between black and white Americans abroad than there was in the New York of the Harlem Renaissance.

Parisians were much more likely to befriend blacks, and several African American female artists were glad to live and work there in the 1920s. Florida's Augusta Savage was one for whom Paris was a liberating place. Art historian Theresa Leininger-Miller said:

> She frequently had dinner and played cards with [French] painters and writers, and she produced a witty pair of bronze bookends of men at French urinals. . . . Delighted with the freedom she found in Paris, Savage expressed her exuberance in a small figurine . . . , a racially ambiguous dancing woman with stylish bobbed hair standing on tiptoe. . . .
>
> Savage's *Amazon* is a half-nude figure. . . . The warrior appears to be listening while standing at attention. . . . Savage might have identified herself . . . , an independent woman who was characterized by strength, boldness, perseverance, and nonreliance on men.

Not all of her works repeated that theme, though, as *Mourning Victory* was an antiwar piece. It depicted a woman with "head hung in apparent sorrow as she gazes at the face of a severed head." The woman looked "weary and vulnerable. Her shoulders are slumped, her arms hang limply . . . under the weight of . . . the moment of reckoning."

Note: * Theresa Leininger-Miller, "Heads of Thought and Reflection: Busts of African Warriors by Nancy Elizabeth Prophet and Augusta Savage, African American Sculptors in Paris, 1922–1934," in *Out of Context: American Artists Abroad*, edited by Laura Felleman Fattal and Carol Salus (Westport, Conn.: Praeger, 2004), 99–102.

of me."[44] When she molded a clay statue of the Virgin Mary, however, he changed his mind and stopped beating her.

The family moved to West Palm Beach when she was fifteen, and a school there encouraged her talent—but the era's values were such that she married at sixteen. Like Tampa's Blanche Armwood, she would marry three times—but unlike Armwood, she had two daughters to support as a result of these brief marriages. Her first husband, John Moore, soon died, but despite being a teenage widowed mother, she somehow found the courage to apply for a booth at the Palm Beach County Fair. After fair officials got over their trepidation about renting to a black woman, this proved key to her success. She sold $175 worth of figurines and won a $25 prize.

She had just $4.60 in savings, however, when she arrived in New York City in 1921 and entered Cooper Union, a creative institution that included art. She also briefly remarried and retained the surname of her husband, James Savage, after they divorced. Although she completed the Cooper Union course, she was reduced to working in laundries—a common occupation for black women at the time—to support her family, which included her now disabled father, who also moved to New York.

Her first artistic success in New York was a commission for a bust of controversial civil rights leader W.E.B. DuBois, to be displayed in the Harlem library. Her commission to depict Marcus Garvey, leader of the era's "back to Africa" movement, probably came about because of Garvey's friendship with Robert Lincoln Poston—and Augusta Savage married Posten in 1923. He died the next year, while returning from Liberia, which Garvey promoted as a new nation for American blacks.

With financial assistance that included donations from people at Florida A&M in Tallahassee, Savage was able to go to Paris in 1929, where she studied with well-known sculptors. She stayed two years and, because the French accepted black Americans more than was the case at home, was quite successful. According to art historian Catherine Bernard:

> Augusta Savage concentrated on portraying Black figures. . . . *Gamin*, her portrait of a young boy, won a fellowship. . . . The sculpture demonstrates her ability to convey emotion through facial expression. . . . Throughout her career, she continued to explore the expressive qualities of the human figure.[45]

Although the Great Depression was at its depth when she returned in 1931, Savage nonetheless opened a Harlem studio and continued to build

Documenting the Truth: Female Federal Photographers

While Zora Neale Hurston painted with words and Augusta Savage molded her thoughts into sculpture, two women who were not Floridians were part of the movement that turned photography into an art. Neither Dorothea Lange nor Marion Post Wolcott was yet famous when they came to Florida as employees of the federal Farm Security Administration (FSA) in the late 1930s, with the aim of documenting poverty with pictures.

Florida made for particularly poignant photos, as the opulence of Palm Beach and Miami Beach contrasted with the misery of farm workers just a few miles away in Belle Glade and Homestead. Violet Wood reported to the FSA that working families lived "in shacks, box-cars on railroad spurs, roadside tents, home-made trailers and old Fords." In Glades County, which has some of the richest farmland in the world, she saw "six white children and four adults living in a 12-foot by 12-foot rainbreak with four poles supporting a roof of scrap tin and with walls made of potato sacks and flour bags."

Woods's words were powerful but easily ignored by those who could not visualize. FSA chief Reg Tuxwell wanted members of Congress to understand how difficult things were outside Washington, and he heeded his wife, Grace Tugwell, when she said that "words were simply not enough." Another wife of an FSA administrator, Bernarda Shahn, argued that photos were needed for "the stark presentation of actual conditions, the wordless, statistics-less, visual, inescapable truth."

Tugwell responded by hiring photographers, including Dorothea Lange, who had been doing similar work on her own and who ultimately became the most famous. "This was a revelation," one observer commented, "what this woman was doing." Lange focused on the Panhandle, and especially her photographs in Careyville, a Holmes County lumber town, showed the difficulty of life for both blacks and whites after the local sawmill went bankrupt.

Marion Post (later Wolcott), hired in 1938, was described as "a young photographer of considerable experience who has made a number of very good photographs on social themes."* Formerly employed by the *Philadelphia Evening Bulletin,* she took a series

continued

of photos in Lakeland and Plant City, including white women who picked strawberries while wearing dresses. That contrasted with an Amish woman in Sarasota, covered in black from head to toe, including the sunbonnet that she wore while staring into a drainage ditch.

Wolcott's most poignant shots probably were in Belle Glade, where farm workers have always toiled for very little reward. One of the most interesting was of "Choke 'Em Down Lunch Room," a screened shack that uncommonly advertised "White & Colored Served." Another Belle Glade photo featured "Buddy," a white if dirty toddler, who was perched atop a badly patched bedroll. When unrolled at night, it was the only "bed" available to his six-member family.

Note: * Michael Carlebach and Eugene Provenzo Jr., *Farm Security Administration Photographs of Florida* (Gainesville: University Press of Florida, 1993), 10, 21, 27, 75, 78. See also Dorothea Lange and Paul Taylor's most famous book of photos on homelessness during the Great Depression, *An American Exodus: A Record of Human Erosion* (1939; repr. Paris: J.-M. Place, 1999).

her reputation. In 1934 she became the first African American admitted to the National Association of Women Painters and Sculptors. Savage received some help from the New Deal's Federal Art Project but also attracted large numbers students of all ages and races to her workshops.

Her most important commission was for the 1939 World's Fair in New York, where she depicted the spirit of the song, "Lift Every Voice and Sing," by James Weldon Johnson—also of Jacksonville. Her sculpture was well received but, like other exhibits, was destroyed when the fair ended. Savage did not have the resources for storage of her sixteen-foot piece.

It turned out to be the acme of her career. Increasingly depressed, Savage moved to a farm near Woodstock, New York, in the 1940s and did little more artistic work prior to her 1962 death. Like Zora Neale Hurston, Augusta Savage is achieving recognition long after her death. The Smithsonian in Washington holds some of her work; her home in western New York is on the National Register of Historic Places; a Green Cove Springs art center is named for her; and she was admitted to the Florida Artists Hall of Fame in 1996.

Finally, the era had begun with another woman whose achievement is almost totally forgotten now—but in 1921 Lois K. Mayes was elected by her largely male peers as the first female president of the Florida State Press Association. The owner and publisher of the *Pensacola Morning Journal,* she presumably was a widow: the headline of a syndicated story about her election referred to her as "Mrs." In the same election Miss Ruby Pierce of West Palm Beach was reelected treasurer. Women thus accounted for two of the five-member board—and a Sanford man was secretary.[46]

* * *

The high-flying 1920s were literally so, as aviation became part of American life. Florida was an immediate favorite for pilots with its warm weather, flat land, and ease of take-off over unpopulated land and sea. Many women took up flying along with men, as it seemed natural in an era when both genders also were learning to drive new cars. Indeed, there were predictions that just as almost everyone in the 1920s was learning to drive a car, most people in the future would fly their own plane.

Bessie Coleman was indisputably the era's best African American female pilot. A Texas native, she had earned her credentials in France, as no American aviation school would admit her. In 1921 she became the world's first black person of either gender to earn a pilot's license. With promotion by the *Chicago Defender,* an African American newspaper, her dare-devil aerial acrobatics made Coleman's air shows an immediate sensation. After just five years, though, she died in a crash from the skies over Jacksonville.

It was not pilot error but rather was caused by a wrench left in the plane's gearbox. Some accounts of her Jacksonville funeral on May 2, 1926, say that five thousand people paid their respects, and many more mourned at a second funeral in Orlando three days later. She posthumously received many honors, including having a portion of Tampa International Airport named for her.

Miami was the departure point when Kansan Amelia Earhart began her last, fatal flight in 1937. Her attempt to go around the world and her disappearance in the Pacific continues to fascinate. Back then, people were fascinated by Tampa's Ruth Elder—but she was rather a faux aviator, especially compared to the very competent Earhart.

Elder intended to set a record as the first airplane passenger to cross the Atlantic. A few months after Charles Lindbergh's famous 1927 solo flight, she set out with Lakeland pilot George Haldeman. An oil leak, however, caused them to abandon their plane in the ocean, 250 miles short of the coast of Spain; they deliberately crash-landed near a Dutch ship that rescued them. The public nonetheless was impressed with their daring, and the Elder/Haldeman team was toasted in Paris and welcomed at the White House. Called the "Miss America of Aviation," Elder moved to Hollywood, where she married six times, made movies, and made a lot of money, which she spent freely. She died obscurely in San Francisco in 1977.

Movies, too, were hugely important in the 1920s, especially to women, and Florida initially tried to rival California as the center for making them. Indeed, already in 1917 the world's first famous female film maker, France's Alice Guy Blache, used the Everglades to shoot a movie, and by World War I "Jacksonville hosted thirty production companies, providing work for a thousand local actors and extras."[47] Among the silent film stars who worked there were Theda Bara and Gloria Swanson.

In the next decade Tampa Bay's Rocky Point was the setting for the daringly titled *Hell's Harbor* (1929). That was after Tampa's Colleen Moore was the industry's number box office attraction in 1926 and 1927. Although she is nearly forgotten today, writers such as F. Scott Fitzgerald praised her acting ability. She changed her name from Kathleen Morrison and had prayed for stardom during her days at Tampa's Academy of the Holy Names. Some film historians call her "the first movie flapper."

The era's greatest movie, of course, was *Gone with the Wind* (1939), and it too had a Florida connection. Butterfly McQueen, who played the role of the young slave Prissy, was born as Thelma McQueen in 1911 in Tampa. She attended St. Peter Claver, a Catholic school for blacks, and in adulthood was a life member of the Freedom from Religion Foundation. She also was the star of the television show *Beulah* in the early 1950s. The show was popular with whites, but Beulah was a maid—and although highly paid, McQueen nonetheless crusaded against the limitations on roles available to black actors.

Black Floridians saw movies from theater balconies, entering and exiting from second-story stairs. For women of both races, though, movies were important as trend creators. As Hollywood women cut their hair and shortened their skirts, women all over the nation did the same. The most popular haircut imitated movie star Clara Bow: it was short and straight, and millions of women had their hair styled in the same way. Some enterprising beauticians rented space in the lobbies of theaters, brought in salon equipment, and cut hair right there. Women in fact lined up for the chance to have their hair bobbed while theatergoers watched.

Hollywood, Florida, developed at about the same time as Hollywood, California, as Florida also provided a rich diversity of settings. Directors used the draped Spanish moss on live oak trees to frame stories both romantic and spooky, while the state's swamps provided excellent backgrounds for horror stories. Florida's wide, sandy beaches were sparsely settled and more beautiful than those in California, and palm trees created tropical settings. The state offered a variety of ethnic actors, including African Americans, Greeks, and Hispanics. Opulent places such as Palm Beach and Coconut Grove were easily available as backdrops for many tales, while Sarasota offered both exotic animals and circus workers for another kind of movie. Although the business never reached the hoped-for early potential, hundreds of movies would be shot in Florida. In the darkness of theaters across the country, its image as the Dream State shone brightly.

* * *

Beneath the surface of the Roaring Twenties, however, lay reminders of troubled times and omens of worse times. Racism continued, and among its worst manifestation was in 1923, when the town of Rosewood, in the northwestern part of the peninsula, was completely obliterated by a mob of white men. Almost no white people, though, knew of that or other devastation caused by blind hate. In the words of eighth-generation Floridian Diane Roberts:

> There is a secret history. For the longest time, only black Floridians knew it. They whispered cautionary tales, warned about the terrible things. . . . The lynchings, the riots, the massacres . . .
>
> Even more secret, hidden, or ignored for years, was the Rosewood Massacre. Every detail of it is disputed by somebody, [but] on a hard-frost day in January 1923, a white woman may or may not have been attacked by a black convict who'd run off from the county road gang. He may or may not have hidden somewhere in the cedar-milling village of Rosewood. Model Ts full of white men with Winchesters and shotguns and pistols and kerosene, some Klan, some just Levy County freelancers out for a bit of recreational violence, roared over. . . .

> The vigilantes rolled up in the bright moonlight and shot Sarah Carrier in the head, right in front of her children. . . . Their mother's blood crimsoning on their nightgowns, [they] escaped into the woods.
>
> The white men kept moving, shooting a widow named Lexie Gordon as she crawled out of her burning house. She'd sent her daughters into the swamp when she heard gunfire, but she was . . . too weak to follow. They made an old man dig his own grave, then they shot him, too. They burned the whole place, the churches and the houses and the school.
>
> There are parts of Rosewood victims' bodies, trophies, kept around Levy County—that's the story. . . . A teacher from Chiefland, up the road from Rosewood, told Michael D'Orso, who wrote a book on Rosewood, that he had seen a man's thumb at a gas station. . . .
>
> White people in Levy County still won't talk about this. Or if they do, they claim it never happened. Rosewood itself is gone. White people live in trailers where black people once lived in houses. But like all secrets . . . Rosewood returned. In the early 1980s a reporter from the *St. Petersburg Times* started following up rumors. . . . A black state representative and a Cuban state representative, aided by a lawyer whose daddy had doctored some kin of . . . survivors, filed a bill to compensate the victims. . . . The Rosewood families didn't get much. . . . A handful of survivors received $150,000.[48]

Nor was it only rural rednecks who supported the Klan. Miami had included black men as founders when it was incorporated in 1896, but in 1921 "thousands of people turned out to watch . . . dozens of Klan members march in full regalia." At least some women supported its goals, as on the 4th of July in 1927, the American Legion chapter in northeast Miami presented its first prize for the best float to "the women of the Klan."[49] While their men organized mob violence to terrorize blacks, including the maids who worked in their own homes, the women of the Klan's auxiliary called themselves "kamelias."

Not surprisingly, some blacks responded to the era's "Back to Africa" movement. Led by Marcus Garvey, a Jamaican, it advocated black pride, knowledge of African history, and mass migration to the nation of Liberia. Racists gave no support whatever to the Back to Africa concept: they knew that their economy and lifestyle were based on repressed black labor, and the last thing kamelias wanted was a shortage of docile domestic workers. Miami's Ann Marie Adker, who was raised by a Bahamian grandmother, Mariah Young, recalled:

> The Marcus Garvey people had a great big hall just around the corner from where we lived. . . . Every Sunday that's where we would be. . . . They were all right in there, learning about our history. They would tell folk tales. . . . They told us stories that were told to them at their parents' knees. . . . The people of means—the white folks, you know—came down on the movement and they couldn't meet in that hall any more.
>
> That's when the Garvey people started this church. It was Saint Peter's African Orthodox. They wanted to form this church so that they could have their own place that the whites could not touch. When I was twelve years old my grandmother gave me the privilege of going to any church I chose to. . . . Since I was a Garvey follower, I leaned towards joining St. Peters, and I did.[50]

It would be decades before a black woman could be represented in a court of law by another black woman, but white women continued their rise in the legal profession. The first during the Roaring Twenties, Gertrude Dzaialynski Corbet, was one of the most interesting.[51] Born in 1874 to Jewish parents who moved from Savannah to central Florida, she grew up in Lake Meade, where her father ran a store and her grandmother ran a hotel.

Dzaialynski became a legal secretary and court reporter in Tampa, Gainesville, Tallahassee, and Pensacola—and, with a network of powerful contacts, developed a career in politics. She earned the nickname "Miss Dynamite" while working for winning Democrats, and although Florida women did not yet have the vote, they rewarded her with the federal position of tax collector for the Jacksonville area. She was past forty when she married Scotsman John A. Corbet in 1915, and when she passed the bar in 1921, that was almost an afterthought. An observant Jew who was active in her temple, she practiced law in Jacksonville until her 1931 death and, according to her family, was a member of the Democratic National Committee.

Three times as many women were admitted to the Florida Bar during the Roaring Twenties as had been in the previous decades. During the period between Florida's first female lawyer in 1898 and the beginning of the twenties, just twenty-one women became lawyers, compared with fifty-nine in

Women admitted to the Florida Bar during the 1920s

Year	Name	Notes
1920	Lena Alfman	Pensacola native; practiced in Miami; later moved to Texas
	Jane L. Phillips Armstrong	Largo; admitted at age twenty; diplomatic corps in Cuba, Africa, elsewhere
	Caroline Marie Healy Uebele	moved to Wisconsin and practiced there
	Clarice M. Naumurg	little known; Jacksonville
1921	Gertrude Dzialynski Corbet	active Democrat; federal tax collector for Jacksonville area
1922	Mary Wooster Sutton	brief career in Florida; from New Jersey
	Elizabeth Meserve Atkinson	Miami; first woman elected judge; began free legal aid
	Lelia Russell Byrd	Stetson graduate; practiced in Miami
	Marie Eleanor "Nell" Cooper	Miami; practiced many years
	Helen E. Martin Crabtree	first woman to practice in Palm Beach County
1923	Esther Miriam Finney Sumner	Dade County law librarian; *Who's Who among Women Lawyers*
	Abbie Elizabeth Lapham Gibbons	Brevard County; practiced with husband
1924	Florence M. Hazard Mims	Tampa; criminal law
	Stella M. Biddle Fisher	filed case against UF for its exclusion of women; practiced in Gainesville
	Emily S. Williams Ziegler	Stetson graduate; practiced in DeLand
	Joanna Hamilton Vermilye	Illinois attorney; practiced in Palm Beach
1925	Bernice J. Ayer	George Washington University; Tennessee; partner in Miami firm
	Rubye B. Chalk Godwin	brief career in Florida; practiced in Georgia
	Henriette E. Mednick	little known; Jacksonville
	Allie Richardson Barnes	little known; Lake Wales
	Mary J. Davey	little known; had practiced in Ohio
	Beverly C. Cobb	little known; Clearwater
	Jean Gregory Cole	little known; St. Petersburg
	Dorothy Dorman	little known; Winter Haven

Year	Name	Notes
	Clara C. Cain Gore	George Washington University; Miami, Gore & Gore; admitted to U.S. Supreme Court
	Maurine Sharp	only briefly Florida; Kentucky
	Mattie W. Tompkins	D.C. native; Avon Park; elected to city council; *Who's Who among Women Lawyers*
1926	Lydia Douglass	little known; Miami
	Anne Overman Gibbons	little known; Fort Lauderdale
	Sue K. Hicks	partner in Penny & Hicks, Miami
	Winifred B. Judge	Miami; moved to New York City
	Effie E. Knowles	Miami; won major case for Seminole Tribe in 1955
	Opal Plaisted	no known practice
	Herberta Ann Hathcock Leonardy	Plant City native; practiced in Sanford; taught parliamentary law in Miami
	Gertrude Leonore O'Kell Woods	Miami; listed in *Martindale's American Law Dictionary*
	Rose Shakewitz	little known; Fort Lauderdale
	Pauline G. Wallace	no known practice
	Marian Borros	New Jersey native; Ormond Beach; lived to ninety-seven
	Arax M. Gulizian	little known; Orlando
	Anna Bray Lindsley	St. Petersburg; Florida Attorney General's Office; Washington, D.C.; Coral Gables
	Vivian Selter	St. Petersburg; *Who's Who among Women Lawyers*
1927	Madeline A. Jacobson Cox	New York native; served in World War I; Tallahassee; wedding in Florida Supreme Court
	Dorothy S. McDougall	little known; Georgia
	Anna A. Krivitsky	native of Russia; University of Chicago; Tampa and St. Petersburg; defended women
	Ella Jo Stollberg	Atlanta native; Hollywood and Miami Beach; practiced until 1966
	Zephyr Lillian Thorpe	one of six women who graduated from Stetson College of Law that year
	Susan E. Ervin	St. Petersburg; associate in business law firm
	Laurine Leonore Goffin	Jacksonville; died in 1948
	Mary V. Wakefield Houston	little known; DeLand

continued

Women admitted to the Florida Bar during the 1920s—*Continued*

Year	Name	Notes
	Mary Anne Leddy	New York; Chicago; Miami; *Who's Who in American Women*
	Charlotte Inez Farrington Vogel	longtime feminist leader; Delray Beach
	Mollie M. Parker	no known practice
	Mary L. Esarey	Lake Worth; worked for Equal Rights Amendment
	Victoria Rountree	Tampa; moved to California
	Hilda Meadows Tilton	practiced in Georgia
1928	Lenea I. Stromber Adlehelm	West Palm Beach; founding member of Florida Association for Women Lawyers
	Ireana A. Lawrence	no known practice
	Ruby Fleming Barney	Kentucky native; George Washington University; practiced in Jacksonville
	Susie H. Bell	Green Cove Springs; practiced with husband
	Sidney S. Gober	Maryland native; practiced in Jacksonville
1929	Augusta Beyer Collin	no known practice
	Mabel Claire Altman Hackney	Tampa; specialized in law related to shipping
	Bessie Ethel Sims Williams	Sarasota; practiced with husband as Williams & Williams

Source: Wendy S. Loquasto, ed., *Celebrating Florida's First 150 Women Lawyers*. See the narrative in chapters 5 and 6 for women admitted prior to 1920.

the decade that roared. The highest numbers were in 1926 and 1927, the last years of the great boom. When the national economy crashed in 1929, the number of women who had this opportunity distinctly dropped.

* * *

While Seminoles and Rosewood victims were removed from land that once was theirs, the Florida land boom for whites—most of them newcomers—soared during the early 1920s. Coral Gables in south Florida, Snell Isle in St. Petersburg, and many other places set the new standard of homes built on the Mediterranean model. One can drive through the state today and clearly see the houses that date to that era. Not only did these homes reflect a new style of building in Florida; the new designs also were clearly different from those in the American Northeast and Midwest.

Usually part of a planned community, they were not individual homes built along well-traveled roads—instead, the roads were built for them, and architects laid out the whole town, not just houses. Enclaves set apart from existing communities, they often centered around golf courses and country clubs. It encouraged a lifestyle very different from that newcomers had lived up North, a lifestyle in which they interacted largely with one another, sometimes literally walling off the rest of Florida.

Most of these developers were men, but era's "Queen of Real Estate" was Maud Cody Fowler—although she signed many documents without revealing her gender, calling herself "M. C. Fowler." Born in Memphis, she lived in Kansas City when she married Orin Scott Fowler in 1890. The birth of a son, Cody, did not deter her independence, and as an officer in the Security Underwriters Corporation, she was considered one of the area's most successful businesswomen. She also was a founder of the Kansas City Women's Athletic Club, an indication of feminism.

When she moved to Florida at the beginning of the Roaring Twenties land boom, the *Tampa Tribune* called Maud Fowler "one of the foremost real estate operators in America"—high praise indeed, given that the paper used no qualification by gender. She developed the town of Temple Terrace near Tampa, named for the 350,000 Temple orange trees planted in the area. A golf course was the focal point of the town near the Hillsborough River, and its Club Morocco attracted such entertainers as jazz singer Al Jolson. The nightclub included gambling and alcohol, despite Prohibition, and one early resident said it was not unusual to tip the band fifty dollars to perform a request.

Maud Fowler was elected mayor of Temple Terrace in 1925, the first female elected official on Florida's west coast. The land bubble burst in 1926, however, and the orange trees froze in 1927, and she was among many for whom the Roaring Twenties plunged into the Great Depression. She lost a fortune, had to defend herself in bankruptcy proceedings, and was never again queen of anything. But her son built the major Florida law firm of Fowler and White, and Fowler Avenue, which features the main entrance to the University of South Florida, was named for her.

Julia Tuttle, Bertha Palmer, and others had already demonstrated women's abilities to be successful as real estate developers, but the state had no precedent for Elizabeth Barnard, who headed the postal service in Tampa in

1926. She had come to Tampa as a nineteen-year-old bride in 1900 and within six years was a widow with two children to support. Hired as a secretary at the post office, she took classes to improve her credentials, mapped out a career path, and moved determinedly toward promotions. She was especially astute in insisting on employment with the federal government, which unlike most employers, defined the qualifications for each promotion and pay level—and by 1923 she was postmaster. Barnard headed a system that, during the great growth of the Roaring Twenties, soared from 19 letter carriers in 1923 to 113 just four years later. Sixteen substations were established under her administration. Under these stressful conditions, she proved that a woman could perform well in a chief executive position.

At the top level, though, postmasters remained political appointees who had at least an element of party loyalty. Republican Warren Harding was president when she got the position in 1923, and two Republicans succeeded him. Although Democrat Franklin Roosevelt's 1933 inauguration meant new hope for most during the Great Depression, the effect was the opposite for Bernard. Tampa was a Democratic town; many men wanted the appointment; and although she was not personally partisan, she was forced into retirement at age fifty-two. No corporation had the sense to pick up this proven executive, and she died in Jacksonville at seventy-nine.

The boom-and-bust scene also played out on the opposite coast. "Drunk on Yankee money, borrowed money, and funny money," wrote Diane Roberts:

> Florida in the early 1920s careened about, tripping over its own satin dance slippers. Florida was the endless party, the bottomless cocktail. . . . Finally, inevitably, predictably, the clock struck midnight. The local banks crashed, the land bubble burst, the swindlers skedaddled. . . .
>
> The hurricane of 1926 killed four hundred and left fifty thousand homeless. People called it "the Big One" until the hurricane of 1928, which killed two thousand. There were so many dead around Lake Okeechobee . . . they had to be stacked on funeral pyres. There were so many dead that for years farmers found skeletons in the fields.
>
> In 1928 Florida was $600 million in debt—and the annual state budget was only $29 million. The newspapers up north said Florida was finished, over, gone. . . . By 1928 almost 10 million acres had been seized for nonpayment of taxes, [but still], the state couldn't pay on its bond debt. There were bankruptcies and suicides and general desperation.[52]

Women, who almost always earned less than men, also were on the edge of desperation. There was, however, one federal program in place that assisted them. The Smith-Lever Act, passed in 1914, mostly aimed at providing farmers with expertise from agricultural agents, but it also acknowledged the importance of the farmer's wife with home demonstration agents. Sometimes called "extension agents," in the sense of extending knowledge, they were graduates of the relatively new field of home economics. These women played a very important role in helping Florida's poor, especially its rural poor, through the Great Depression.

With leadership based at Florida College for Women in Tallahassee, home demonstration agents were assigned by county. Most dealt with white women, but probably because of Blanche Armwood, Florida was a leader in this area and had employed black women as home economics experts as early as 1917. Work among African Americans was via Florida A&M College, also in Tallahassee. These women provided education by organizing Home Demonstration Clubs, usually called HD Clubs.

In that social setting and with great sensitivity to the fact that most club members had long experience as homemakers, they provided education in nutrition, health, cooking with modern appliances, and sanitation—at a time when many Floridians had outhouses and pulled their water from wells. They offered expertise in the most productive ways to raise chickens, increase egg and milk production, and market homegrown fruit and vegetables. Perhaps more prized than anything else, agents offered facilities that had electricity, running water, and equipment for sterilization to preserve garden produce safely.

When invited, agents also made home visits. There, too often, they "noted obvious health problems, including malnutrition, pellagra, hookworm, tuberculosis, malaria, and dental problems." Pellagra is a disease caused by a lack of protein and niacin; hookworm reflects improper sanitation and was most commonly found in those who lacked even outhouses; tuberculosis often shows that a victim lives in a home without proper air circulation; and malaria is caused by exposure to infested mosquitoes. All these diseases were preventable, and home demonstration agents were on the front line of trying to abate epidemics. They conducted baby clinics, too, helping to reduce a shameful infant mortality rate. According to historian Lynne Rieff:

> Agents explained in simple terms the relationship between sanitation and good health. They emphasized cleanliness in the kitchen. Screening doors and windows prevented insects from entering the houses but

still permitted breezes to circulate fresh air. In club meetings, members made brooms, mops, and rat and fly traps, and agents taught women how to change straw in mattresses and wash the ticking. For houses infested with bed bugs or lice, agents taught women how to scour a room.[53]

For a woman, of course, the most perilous time of life was when she gave birth. Because they often were undernourished and lived in unsanitary conditions, hundreds of thousands of Florida women faced the reality of death at delivery. Some New Deal programs helped with this—and with the even more frequent infant mortality—and one hero of such government employment was Victoria Joyce Ely, a registered nurse and the first licensed midwife in Florida.

Ely began her career at St. Luke's Hospital in St. Louis, Missouri, but when World War I began she joined the Army Nurse Corps and served in France. She worked with the Red Cross after the war until moving to Florida in 1923, where she was the health officer for workers in the timber industry near Perry. When the legislature passed a Midwifery Practice Act in 1930, the State Board of Health hired Ely to implement it. After earning credentials in this specialty, she became the state's first licensed midwife and, during the next fifteen years, built a program that gave formal training to midwives across the state.

She taught them to record vital statistics, including registering the birth with health departments—which meant greatly increased accessibility for birth certificates that would be so important by the century's end. Ely retired to Ruskin, in southern Hillsborough County, and in 1954, the health department office there was named for her. She died in 1979 and was admitted to the Florida Women's Hall of Fame in 2002.[54]

Nor were sanitation, malnutrition, and other health problems limited to rural areas. Dr. Rosaline Ebersbach (later Murray) testified to the conditions she found in 1938, when she became Tampa's first female psychiatrist. Recently arrived from the North, she was shocked by what she found: "Disease, hunger, and miserable living conditions such as I had never expected to see in the United States."[55] Social workers took her to see one of their most difficult cases, a seemingly mentally ill woman who was incapable of caring for her children. It turned out, Dr. Ebersbach discovered, that the woman simply was severely malnourished. The problems that manifested themselves as mental illness were, in fact, pellagra, and good food healed her.

Such improvement, though, depended on women who had the social skills to interact with other women who needed help without offending them:

> There were agents who encountered suspicious and skeptical people. Some individuals found it difficult to believe that agents would assist them and expect nothing in return; others distrusted extension workers because they worked for the government. Some tenants believed agents were spies for landowners. Overcoming suspicion and gaining trust were goals that were not easily accomplished.[56]

As the Depression worsened, though, more and more women were willing to seek out any assistance they could get. The Federal Emergency Relief Act provided equipment for canning garden produce, including tin cans and glass jars, and Ruby McDavis, agent for northwest Florida, reported that families within her district canned more than 180,000 containers of food during 1933. Club members in Chipley, a Panhandle town, created a distribution system to send live poultry and fresh eggs to Orlando, where affluent customers would pay more than twice as much as they could get in their rural area.

The most common assistance to women under federal programs, however, was sewing. At a time when policymakers assumed that every woman knew how to sew, the Works Progress Administration (WPA) opened "sewing rooms" in virtually every major city. Despite the diminutive nature of that term, many were actual factories, sometimes employing hundreds of women—but at very low wages. A WPA garment factory in Tampa's Ybor City employed mostly Spanish-speaking women, and they were some of the very few anywhere to go on strike against their federal employer.

They earned less than ten dollars a week, and when Congress began cutting WPA funds in 1937, the local administrator—a white man—did what seemed natural to him and cut the women's programs first. To everyone's surprise, the women did not go quietly. About a hundred followed the leadership of Margaret Hagen, who spoke in both English and Spanish. They "sat down" on the job, refusing to leave the factory. That "sit-in" method had worked for Detroit men in the automobile industry the previous year, but after four stormy days, Margaret Hagen and her closest supporters were fired, and their short-lived Workers Alliance died.

The difference between the situations in Michigan and in Florida was in the support from outside: the wives of Detroit strikers brought meals, picketed, and encouraged the sit-down—but no one did that for women. This failure to take seriously the genuine economic needs of working women is particularly ironic because it later was revealed that at the all-male University of Florida, the entire football team and some coaches were living surreptitiously off the WPA payroll.[57]

The government also subsidized some profit-making canneries that offered low-paid, menial work to Florida women, work that would evaporate with the end of the growing season. Women toiled long hours in canneries while the fruit or vegetable crop was fresh, and in 1936, some Tampa women spontaneously went on strike. It happened to be at the same time that the American Civil Liberties Union (ACLU) was meeting there, and because of that, the strike made national headlines. A telegram sent to ACLU headquarters read:

> Steady brutal violation of civil rights. . . . Four hundred and fifty cannery workers, most girls, went out . . . against incredibly low wages and bad working conditions. Police and employer terrorism with arrests and prevention of picketing . . . Tuesday night union formally organized and next day officers of union arrested and clubbed.[58]

Nor was it only working-class women who became poorer with the Great Depression. Middle-class women also suffered, especially teachers. Many school systems were so nearly bankrupt that they cut salaries, shortened school terms, and even simply stopped paying teachers, expecting them to volunteer. Some school boards—almost entirely men—substituted "script" that local stores might or might not accept as equivalent to cash.

The long impoverished Panhandle of Florida especially suffered, but teacher Elsie Jones Hare helped many teenagers during the economic hard times. An accomplished musician and writer, she was educated at Huntington College in Alabama. After two years in Pensacola, she centered her life in the small town of Century, where she taught everything from French to chemistry, shorthand, and typing. Hare held a lifetime teaching certificate from the state, and her students remembered her with such fondness that she was chosen for the Florida Women's Hall of Fame in 1986, the year following her death.

But neither Hare nor most female teachers could expect to rise to administration. Principals, superintendents, and school boards were virtually all male, and their attitudes toward teachers—the majority of whom were women—assumed the right to dictate behavior, even in private life. In

Pinellas County, for instance, Superintendent R. S. Blanton issued an order banning teachers from smoking cigarettes, whether in public or in private. Unlike today, his 1925 mandate was not concerned about the health effects of smoking but because he believed that a female smoker was indicative of immorality. Shocked when he was told "several St. Petersburg women teachers smoked," he issued a written vow that such "will be considered grounds for dismissal." Some board members, however, thought more clearly, and Arthur Norwood zeroed in on the discrimination against women that the cigarette ban implied, as the order did not forbid the use of pipes or cigars. The board failed to uphold the superintendent's mandate, and teachers who could afford cigarettes went on smoking.[59]

There was a good chance that they would not spend money that way a few years later, when the Great Depression meant that teachers sacrificed first. Some who had moved to Florida from the North were shocked by the government's callousness. Among them was Augusta Jox Berg, an educated woman who had moved from Wisconsin to Tampa. She wrote angrily in 1932: "This world is turning into a madhouse! Who ever heard of a time when teachers weren't paid their salaries? . . . Such conditions! No money for anything—only the gangsters and politicians!" She depended for livelihood on two daughters who were teachers. Much later her youngest son, then a child, remembered when this middle-class family had nothing to eat. He said, "Mother prayed that God would provide. And that afternoon a turtle wandered out of a nearby lake. . . . That night we had turtle for supper."[60]

* * *

Spanish-speaking women in Tampa had three Home Demonstration Clubs by 1920, and that decade generally was prosperous for the enterprising women who made cigars. After a 1920 strike in response to inflation caused by World War I, the industry grew, and an Ybor City street dance in 1927 celebrated the best year yet. They rolled more than 500 million cigars in 1929—but that year also marked national financial collapse. Never again would Cuban-American women be as prosperous as they were then.

Their last major strike was in 1931, in response to management's removal of the *lectores*, or readers, who had stretched minds as fingers worked. Taking out the *lectores* was indeed a triumph of capitalist ideology made possible by the depressed economy, as many managers had long resented what they saw as the leftist reading material that workers voted to hear. At least equally important, though, was that the quiet workplace ended because noisy machines replaced human talent. Hand-rolled cigars were expensive, and as the economy plummeted, machines made them more quickly and cheaply.

Florida's Spanish population also was affected by civil war in Spain during the 1930s. Showing the devotion to democracy that they had when Cuba won its independence from Spain in the 1890s, women supported the legitimately elected government in Spain, which was under attack by a coalition of royalists and fascists—with support from Germany's rising Adolph Hitler. On May 6, 1937, more than five thousand Spanish-speaking women marched to Tampa City Hall, where they presented a petition to the mayor requesting American support for the elected government in Spain. They not only boycotted Spanish products—a real sacrifice, especially with olive oil—but also raised money.

Women sold meals to factory workers and used the proceeds for freedom fighters. Many donated 10 percent of their weekly earnings. Despite the poor economy, they managed to buy several ambulances and tons of supplies for their democratic allies on the other side of the Atlantic. Cigarmaker Elisa Moris led much of this activity. A widow in her early forties, she used her maiden name, like many other Spanish-speaking women. She was an ardent orator, but while speaking at the Labor Temple in 1938, she had a heart attack and died. Hundreds of people marched behind her casket to the Centro Austuriano Cemetery, more than two miles away.

Most Anglos, however, did not pay any attention to the message that these pro-democracy people were trying to deliver. Supported by rightwingers in Germany, Italy, and even royalists in faraway Japan, conservatives won the Spanish Civil War. They removed Spain's elected government and restored the monarchy. It was a preview to the next decade and World War II—but few Americans were watching. That would change in 1941, when fascists forced the whole world into war.

Zora Neale Hurston was an anthropologist educated at New York's Columbia University whose work had been published by prestigious houses, but she too was poor by the Great Depression, when she worked for the Federal Writers Project in Florida. A native of the black community of Eatonville, near Orlando, she was the first African American admitted to New York's Barnard College. Her most famous novel is *Their Eyes Were Watching God* (1937), about the horrific 1928 hurricane that killed some two thousand residents of the eastern Everglades, most of them African American farm workers. Courtesy of FWHOF.

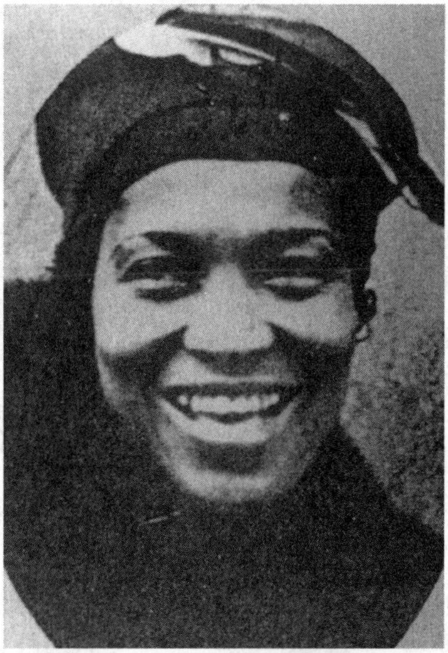

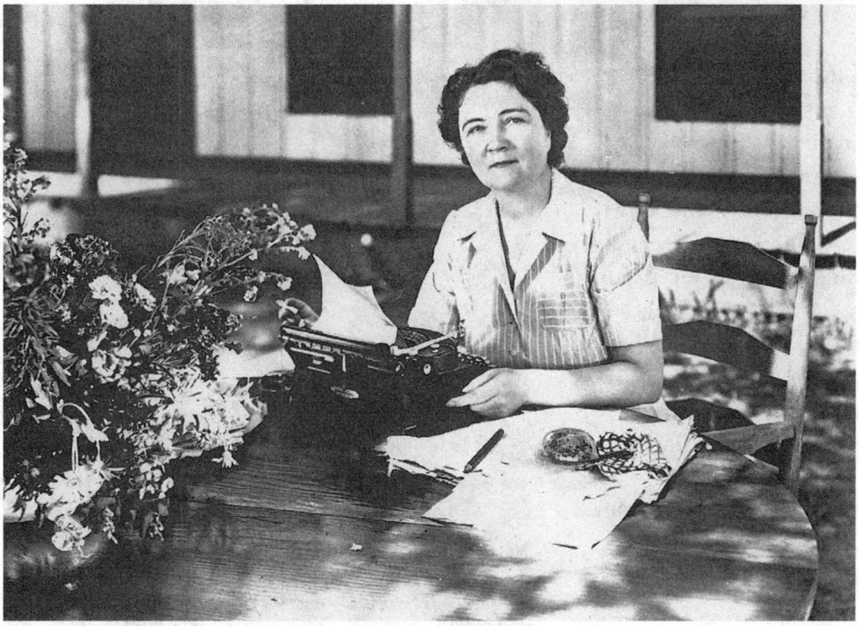

Marjorie Kinnan Rawlings never was so poor that she had to work for the Federal Writers Project, but her rural lifestyle in Cross Creek, near Gainesville, was not much different from that of her neighbors. It was the setting for her classic short novel, *The Yearling*, which won the Pulitzer Prize for 1938. Universally recognized and the recipient of many honors, she was very much a Floridian who enjoyed camping out; she even published an entertaining cookbook based on local food. Courtesy of FWHOF.

Helen Lennehan Muir moved from New York to Miami in 1934 and almost immediately made a name for herself by being the only reporter to hold down the *Miami Herald*'s office during the severe 1935 hurricane. According to a contemporary, she "cranked out stories" while winds that neared 130 miles an hour broke windows in the office tower. A columnist for the Associated Press, she also published books on Florida, as well as articles in national magazines. Courtesy of FWHOF.

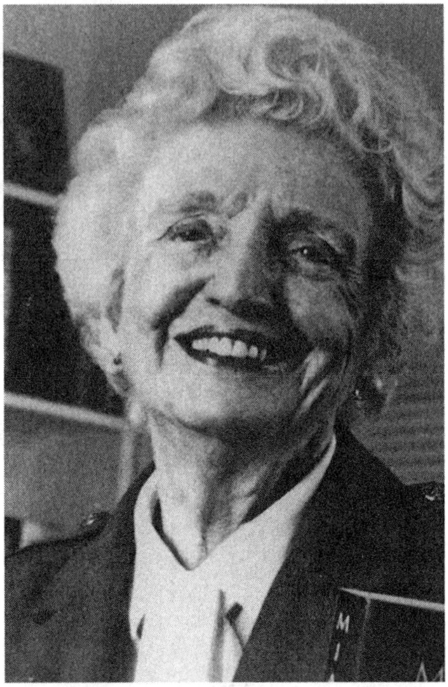

The thirteenth child of a former slave, Eartha Mary Magdalene White was born in Jacksonville in 1876. She attended several schools in Florida and New York, and during the Great Depression of the 1930s established the Clara White Mission in honor of her mother. It served the city's needy for decades, and she later began the Eartha M.M. White Nursing Home, which grew into Jacksonville's largest employer for African Americans. She died at age 97. Courtesy of FWHOF.

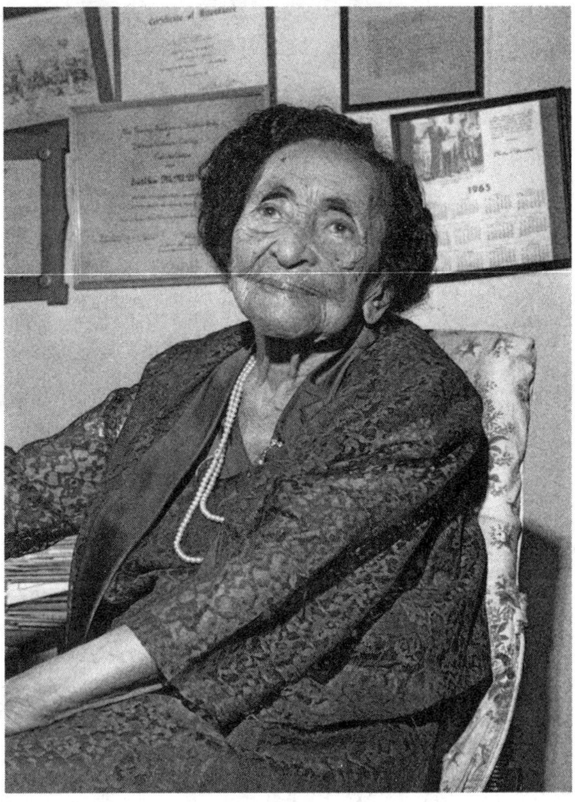

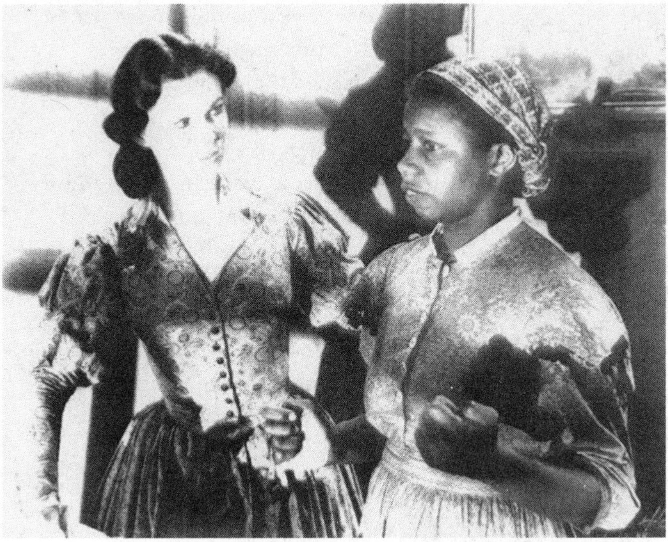

Butterfly McQueen became famous for the 1939 film, *Gone with the Wind*, in which she played the role of Prissy; she is shown here with Vivian Leigh, who portrayed Scarlett O'Hara. Born in Tampa in 1911, her true name was Thelma McQueen. She attended St. Peter Claver School, a Catholic school for blacks, and soon went on to Hollywood. McQueen was successful in other roles but spent her life crusading against the limited opportunities for blacks. State Archives of Florida, *Florida Memory*, http://floridamemory.com/items/show/151580.

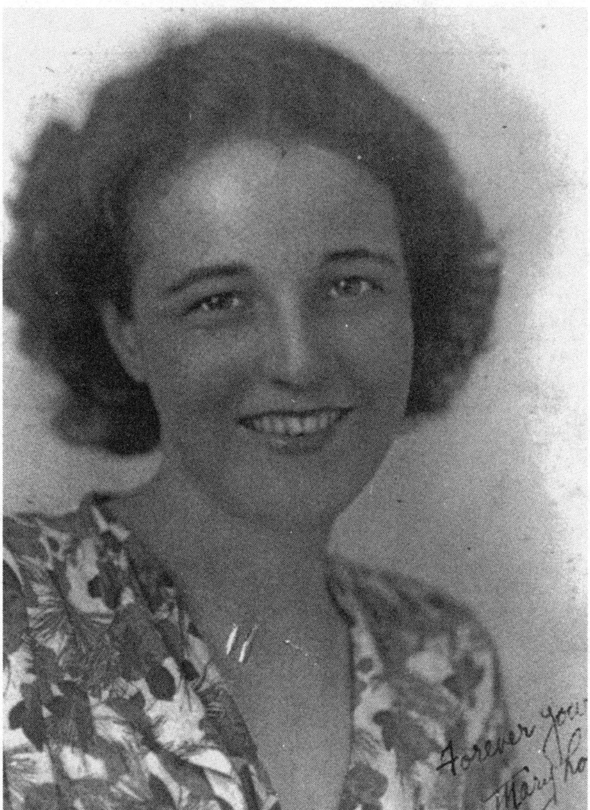

Mary Lou Baker was the second woman elected to the Florida House and perhaps the nation's first woman to be pregnant while serving as a legislator. An attorney from St. Petersburg who kept her maiden name, she won election in 1942 while her husband was in the army. She successfully sponsored bills for women's personal property rights but did not achieve her primary goal—allowing women to serve as jurors. State Archives of Florida, *Florida Memory*, http://floridamemory.com/items/show/20073.

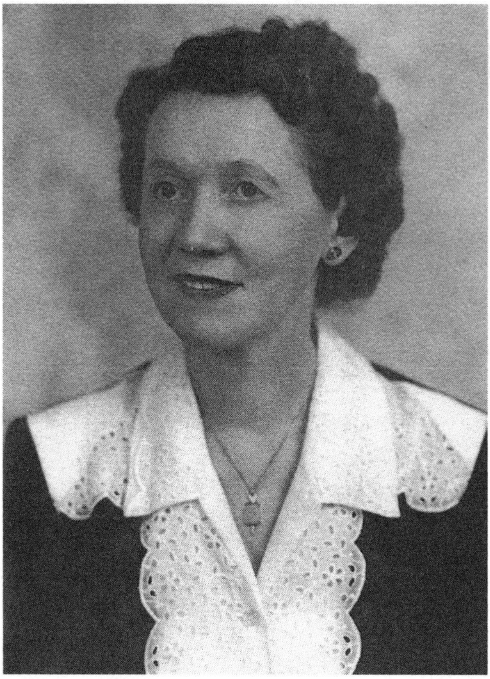

Many new occupations opened to women when the nation needed their labor during World War II. Mary Brennan Karl was one of the first Floridians to recognize that, and she built a Daytona vocational school that trained workers for jobs as welders, riveters, and more. She died soon after the war ended, and Volusia County honored her by naming it the Mary Karl Vocational School; it eventually evolved into Daytona State College. Courtesy of FWHOF.

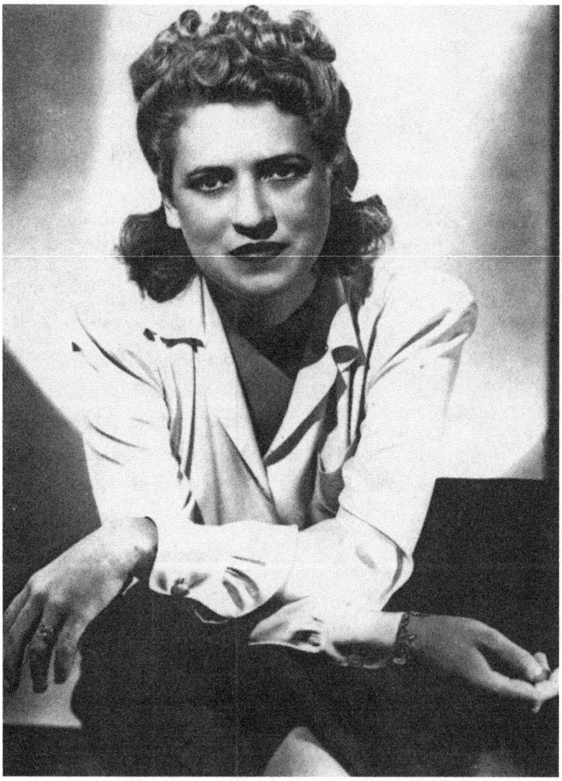

Born in extreme poverty near Pensacola, Jacqueline Cochran nonetheless grew up to be an international celebrity in aviation. She held seventeen international speed records by 1940 and then flew for the British in World War II while America was still neutral. When the United States entered the war, she returned home to head the Women's Air Service Pilots (WASP) and received the Distinguished Service Medal in 1945. After the war, she flew new jets and was the first woman to break the sound barrier. Her autobiography is *The Stars at Noon* (1954). Courtesy of FWHOF.

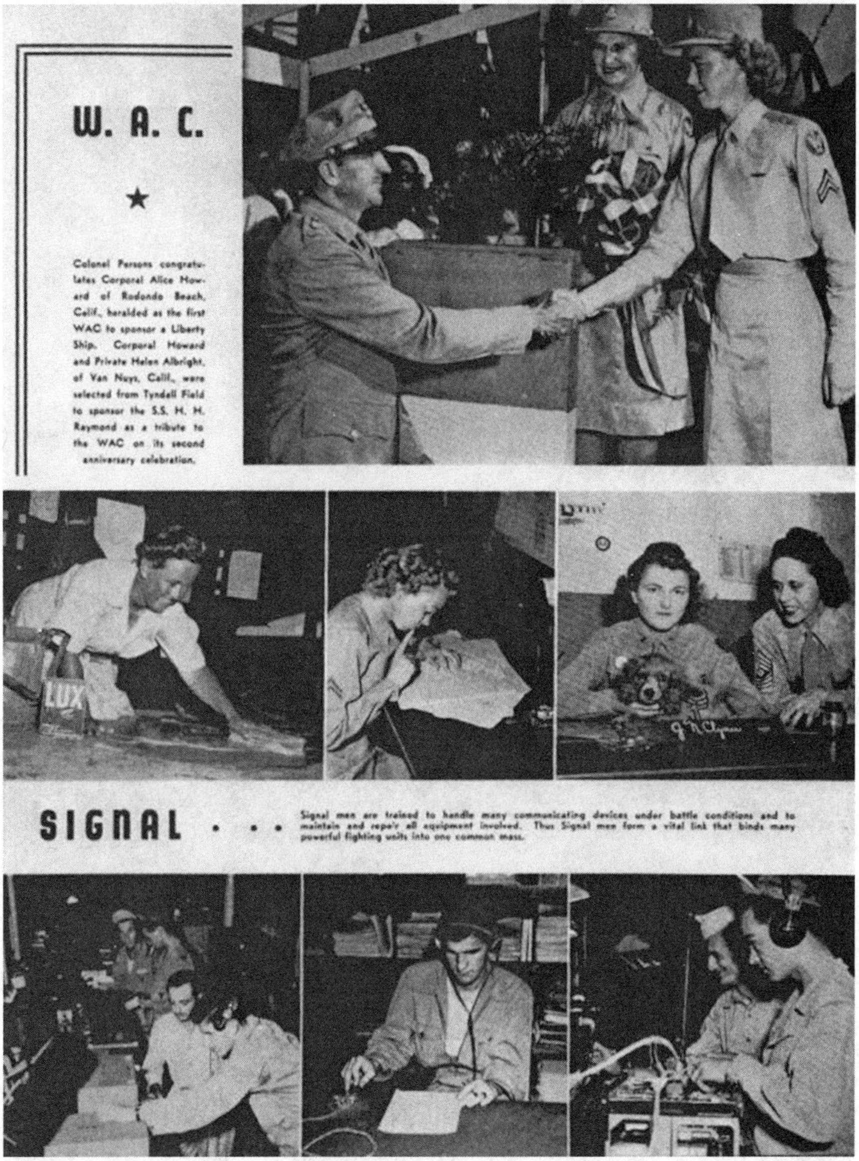

W. A. C.

★

Colonel Persons congratulates Corporal Alice Howard of Rodondo Beach, Calif., heralded as the first WAC to sponsor a Liberty Ship. Corporal Howard and Private Helen Albright, of Van Nuys, Calif., were selected from Tyndall Field to sponsor the S.S. H. H. Raymond as a tribute to the WAC on its second anniversary celebration.

SIGNAL . . .

Signal men are trained to handle many communicating devices under battle conditions and to maintain and repair all equipment involved. Thus Signal men form a vital link that binds many powerful fighting units into one common mass.

This collage shows members of the Women's Army Corps (WAC) working various jobs at Tyndall Field, an air base near Panama City. Some of them probably went through basic training at Daytona Beach, where the WAC had the second of its three boot camps. WACs were required to be better educated than the average army man, and relatively few did the menial labor depicted here. Tyndall Field's specialty was gunnery, and women taught the subject to men, including the firing of large artillery. State Archives of Florida, *Florida Memory*, http://florida memory.com/items/show/152882.

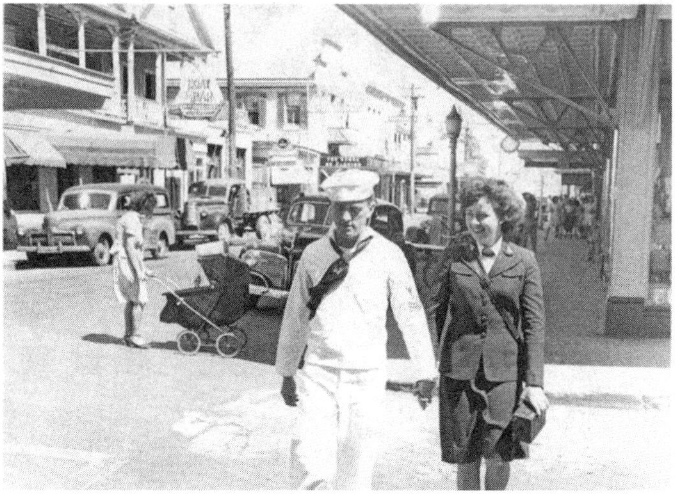

A U.S. Navy couple wears their uniforms as they walk together in Key West. Navy women were called WAVES, while those in the Coast Guard were SPARS. Women Marines were simply Women Marines, or WM. All of those branches, plus the Women's Army Corps and the WASPs of the Air Corps served in Florida. State Archives of Florida, *Florida Memory*, http://floridamemory.com/items/show/35656.

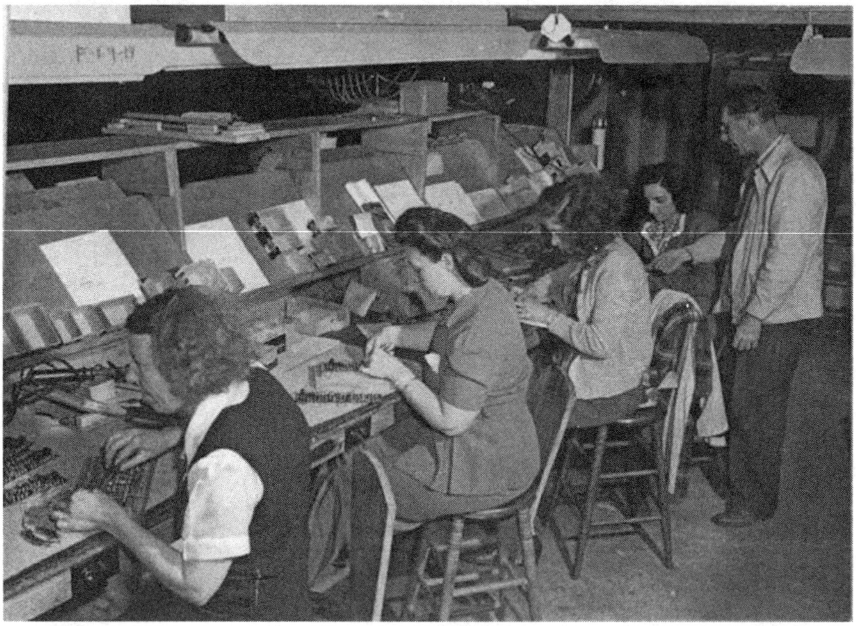

Coral Gables women solder electronic parts for communication systems. Employers preferred women for this delicate and tedious work, and some thus got in on the ground floor of the computer industry. State Archives of Florida, *Florida Memory*, http://floridamemory.com/items/show/65964.

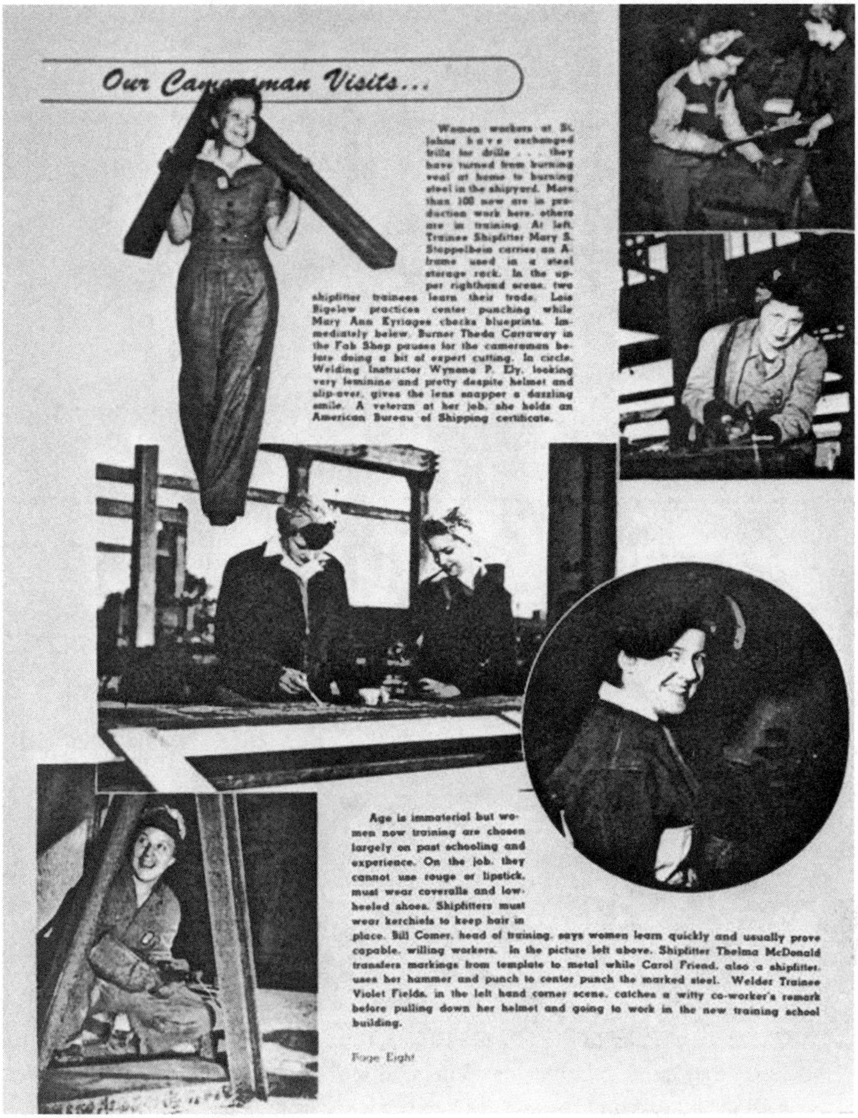

Our Cameraman Visits...

Women workers at St. Johns have exchanged frills for drills . . . they have turned from burning veal at home to burning steel in the shipyard. More than 100 now are in production work here, others are in training. At left, Trainee Shipfitter Mary S. Steppelbein carries an A-frame used in a steel storage rack. In the upper righthand scene, two shipfitter trainees learn their trade. Lois Bigelow practices center punching while Mary Ann Kyriages checks blueprints. Immediately below, Burner Theda Carraway in the Fab Shop pauses for the cameraman before doing a bit of expert cutting. In circle, Welding Instructor Wynona P. Ely, looking very feminine and pretty despite helmet and slip-over, gives the lens snapper a dazzling smile. A veteran at her job, she holds an American Bureau of Shipping certificate.

Age is immaterial but women now training are chosen largely on past schooling and experience. On the job, they cannot use rouge or lipstick, must wear coveralls and low-heeled shoes. Shipfitters must wear kerchiefs to keep hair in place. Bill Comer, head of training, says women learn quickly and usually prove capable, willing workers. In the picture left above, Shipfitter Thelma McDonald transfers markings from template to metal while Carol Friend, also a shipfitter, uses her hammer and punch to center punch the marked steel. Welder Trainee Violet Fields, in the left hand corner scene, catches a witty co-worker's remark before pulling down her helmet and going to work in the new training school building.

Page Eight

Women work at blue-collar tasks at St. Johns River Shipbuilding in Jacksonville. Shipyards in Tampa and Pensacola also provided major employment opportunity for women. Employers were surprised at how good women were at this work, which—except for the noise of riveters—was analogous to sewing. State Archives of Florida, *Florida Memory*, http://floridamemory.com/items/show/141957.

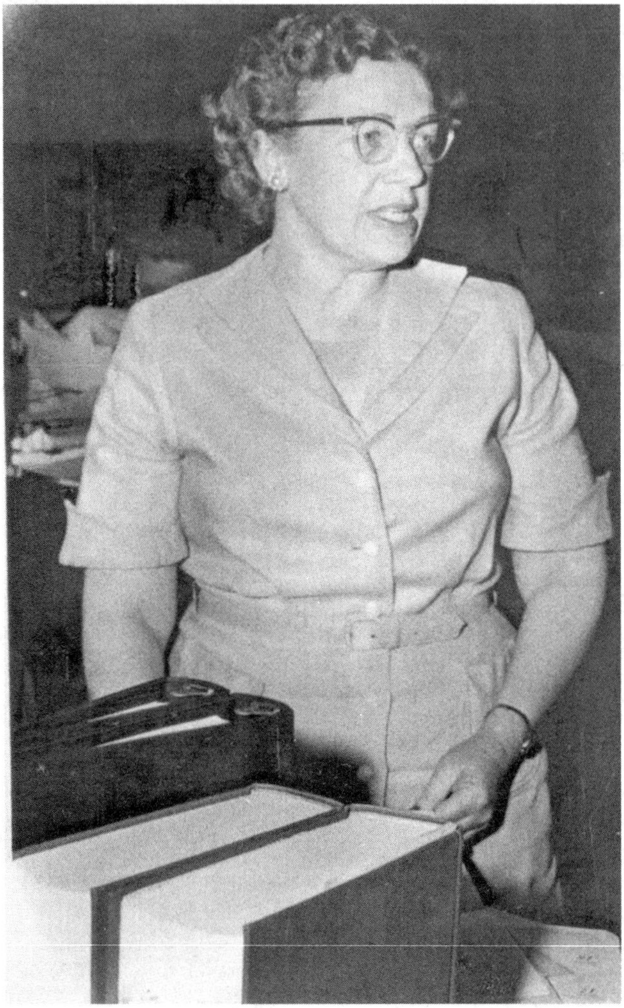

The third woman in the Florida House, Representative Mary Patton of Apalachicola sponsored more than forty bills in the 1955 and 1957 sessions of the legislature; she chaired the Committee on Commerce and Reciprocal Trade. State Archives of Florida, *Florida Memory*, http://floridamemory.com/items/show/42812.

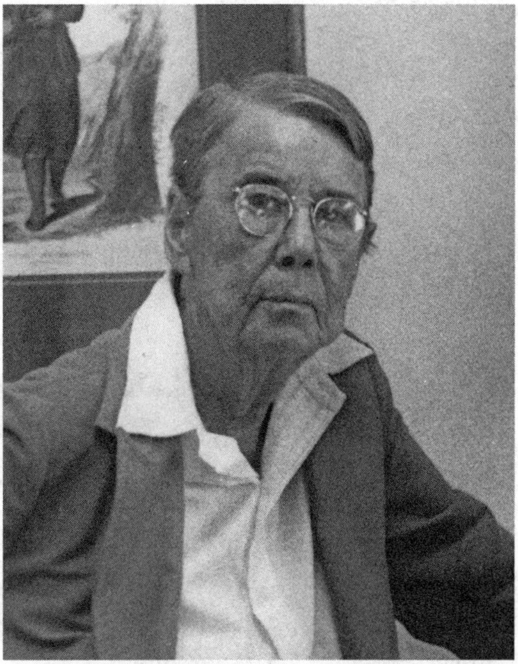

The state's first official archivist, Dorothy Dodd earned degrees from Florida College for Women and from New York's Columbia University. After writing for the *Tampa Times*, she earned a doctorate in history from the University of Chicago and was appointed state archivist in 1941. She rose to state librarian in 1962, the second person to hold that title. Courtesy of FWHOF.

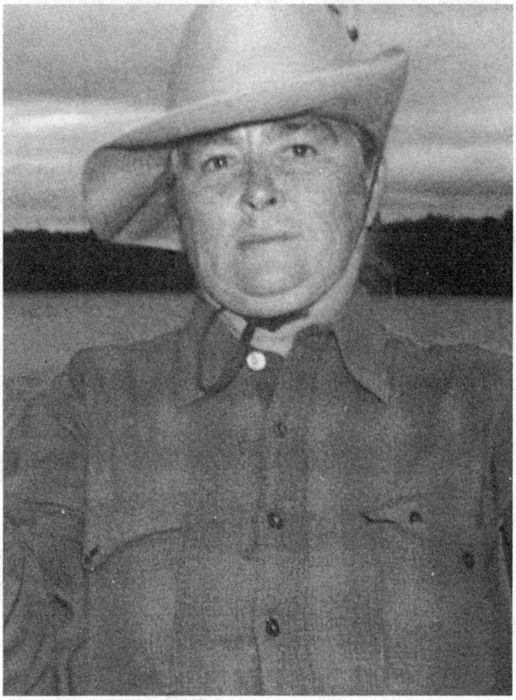

Born in Alachua County in 1906, Dessie Smith Prescott supported herself in nontraditional jobs from age twelve. She served in the Women's Army Corps during World War II but spent most of her life as a hunting and fishing guide in the wilds of north central Florida. Courtesy of FWHOF.

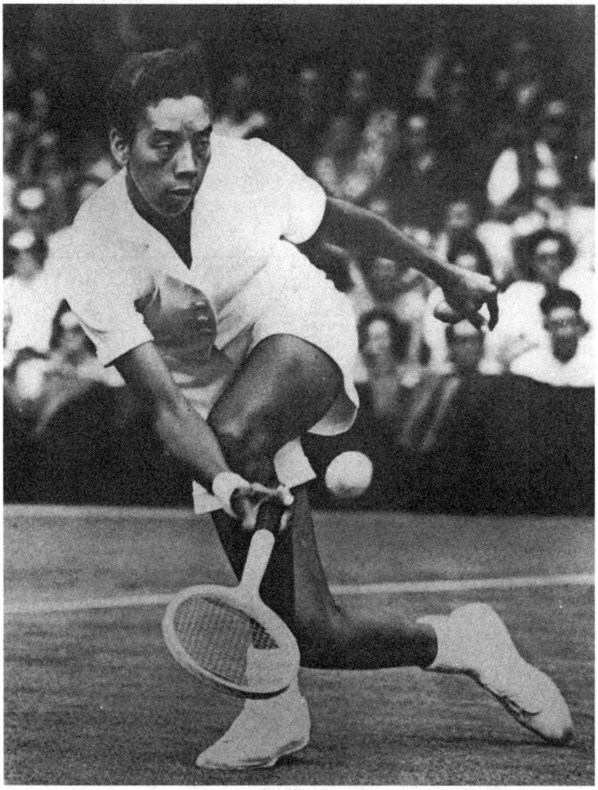

Althea Gibson was the first woman of color to achieve major athletic fame. A 1953 graduate of FAMU, she won England's famous Wimbledon tennis tournament the next year. After achieving the highest awards in tennis, she also became successful in professional golf. Courtesy of FWHOF.

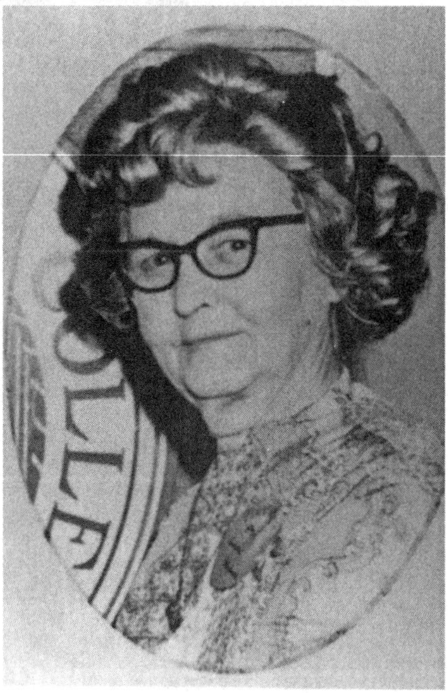

After moving to Orlando in 1957, Lena Smithers Hughes made a major contribution to Florida's economy by developing the Valencia orange, which unlike most citrus, can be harvested in summer. Within a few decades, the majority of the state's orange crop came from roots that Hughes developed. Courtesy of FWHOF.

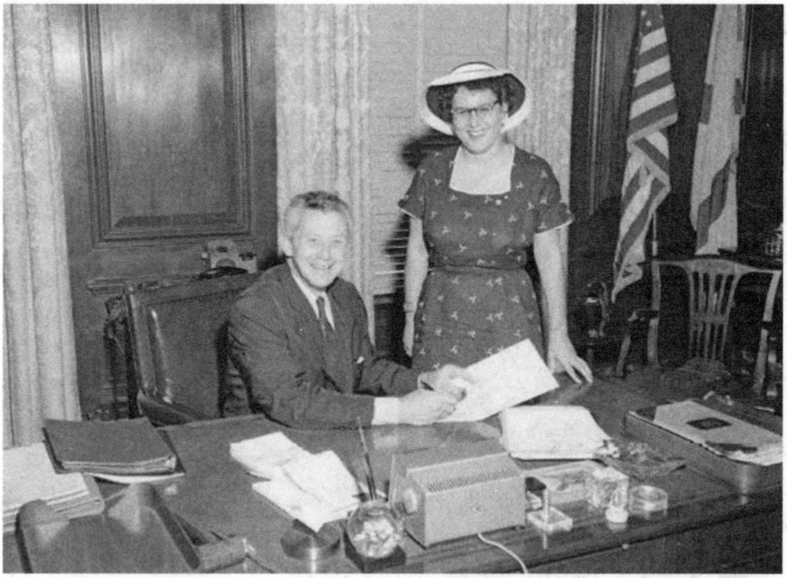

A lobbyist from the Business & Professional Women's Clubs (BPW) talks with Governor LeRoy Collins in 1957. Between the 1920s and 1970s, BPW was the most activist feminist organization in the nation, consistently working for the Equal Rights Amendment and for equality in the workplace. Photo by Red Kerce, State Archives of Florida, *Florida Memory*, http://floridamemory.com/items/show/45500.

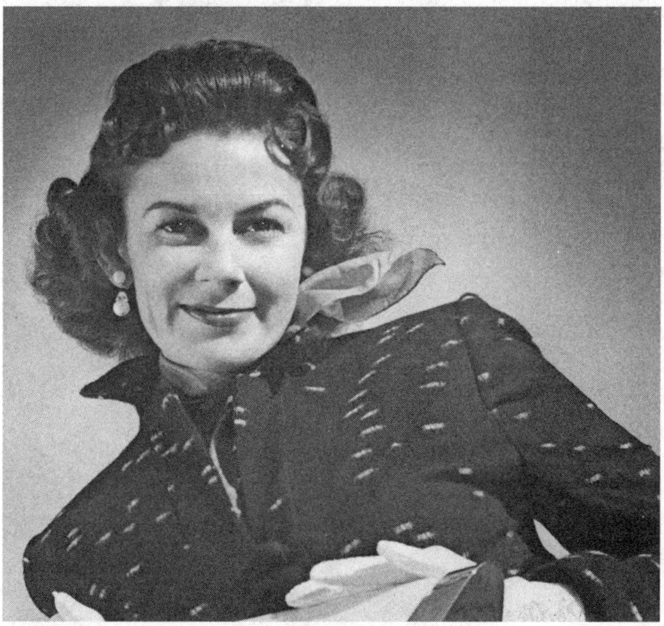

Betty Skelton (later Frankman) set speed records on land and in the air. She won the 1949 world record for altitude in light planes, and after turning to car racing, was the four-time women's winner, with a top speed of over 300 mph. Born in Pensacola, she also lived in Tampa and Winter Haven. Courtesy of FWHOF.

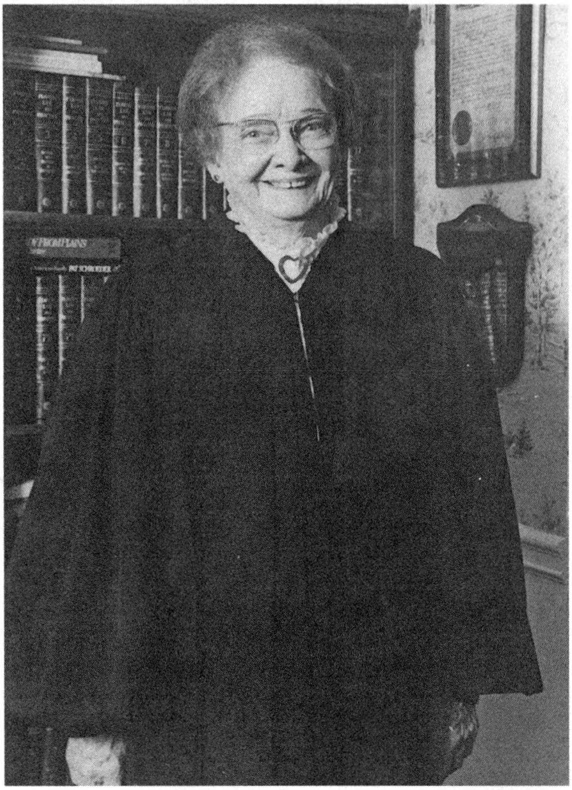

Mattie Belle Davis became Dade County's first female judge in 1959. She pioneered traffic courts that mandated education in safety and, in addition to other honors, was the first Florida woman chosen as a Fellow of the American Bar Association. Courtesy of FWHOF.

Frances Bartlett Kinne worked as a musical entertainer for troops during World War II and after marrying an Army officer taught music in Japan. She earned a 1957 doctorate from Germany's University of Frankfurt and became dean of the College of Fine Arts at Jacksonville University in 1961. She rose to president in 1984, making her the first female president of a Florida university. She also was the first female president of the International Council of Fine Arts. Courtesy of FWHOF.

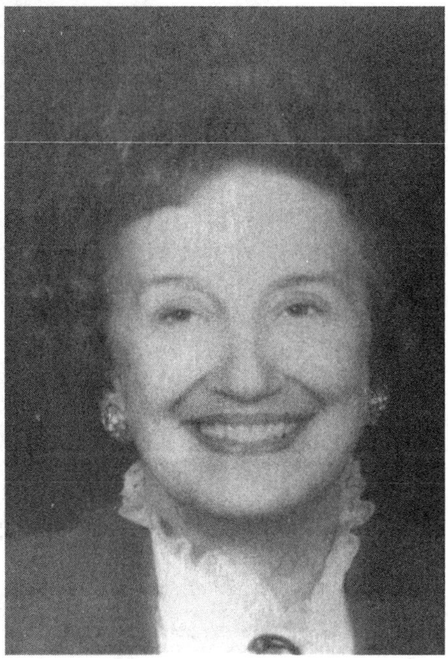

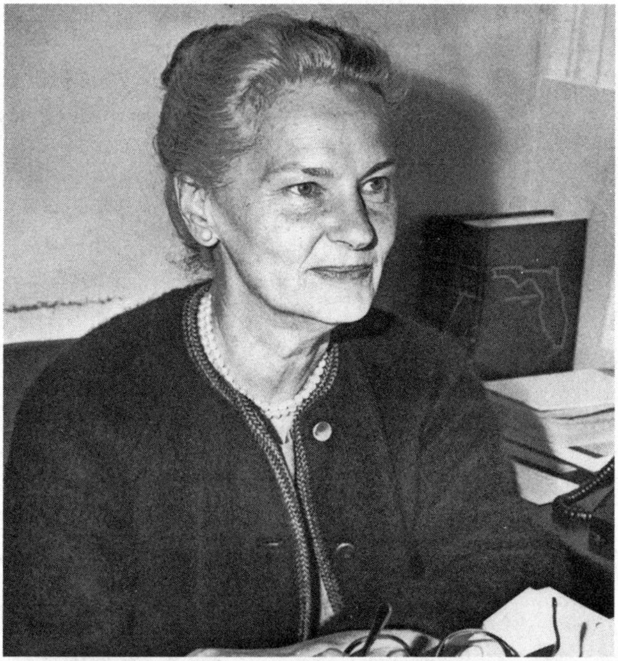

Elizabeth McCullough Johnson, called Beth, was the first woman in the Florida Senate. Elected in 1962 from Orlando, she would be joined by the state's second female senator in 1966; ironically, the second woman, from Cocoa, also was called Beth Johnson. Courtesy of FWHOF.

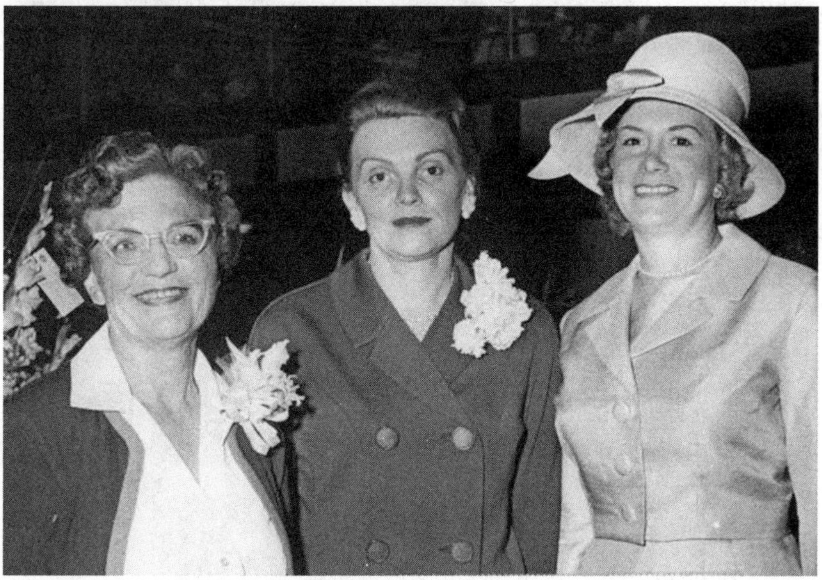

The 1962 election brought three outstanding women to the House. In the middle is Mary Grizzle of Pinellas County, while the others are Maxine Baker and Mary Ann MacKenzie of Dade County. Baker's work on mental health proved of such significance that Floridians now use "Baker Acted" as a verb. Grizzle sponsored the first maternity leave for teachers. State Archives of Florida, *Florida Memory*, http://floridamemory.com/items/show/42907.

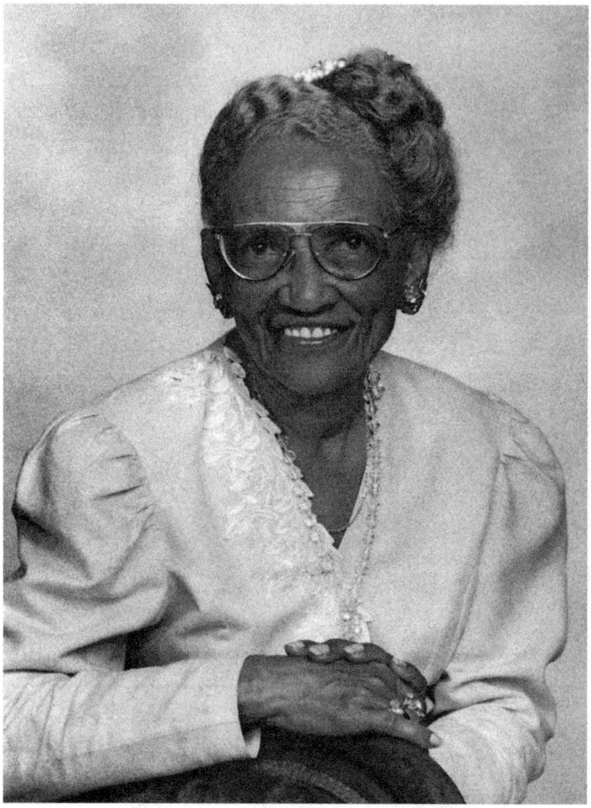

Left: Athalie Range became the first African American woman elected to the Dade County Commission in 1964. Four years later, Governor Reuben Askew appointed her to head the Department of Community Affairs, making Range the first black person to lead a state agency since Reconstruction. Courtesy of FWHOF.

Below: This 1964 photo was taken in the capitol at the first meeting of the Governor's Commission on the Status of Women. Acting chair Lee Leavengood of Tampa is on the left; Senator Beth Johnson of Orlando is on the right; and in the middle is an official from the U.S. Department of Labor. State Archives of Florida, *Florida Memory*, http://floridamemory.com/items/show/43127.

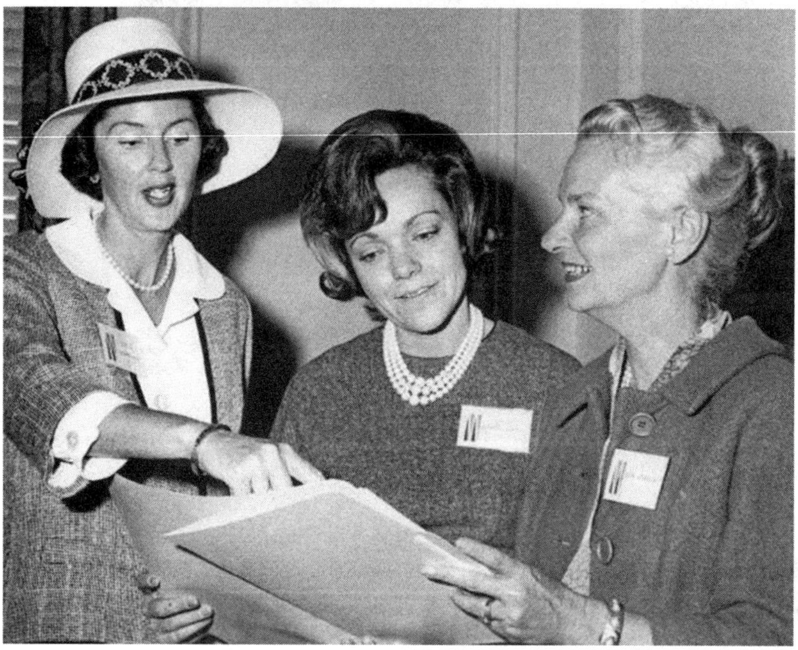

Aleen Kidd (later MacKenzie) of Ocala was the first chair of the Governor's Commission on the Status of Women. She also was a national expert on highway safety and led a campaign for increased funding for higher education. Courtesy of FWHOF.

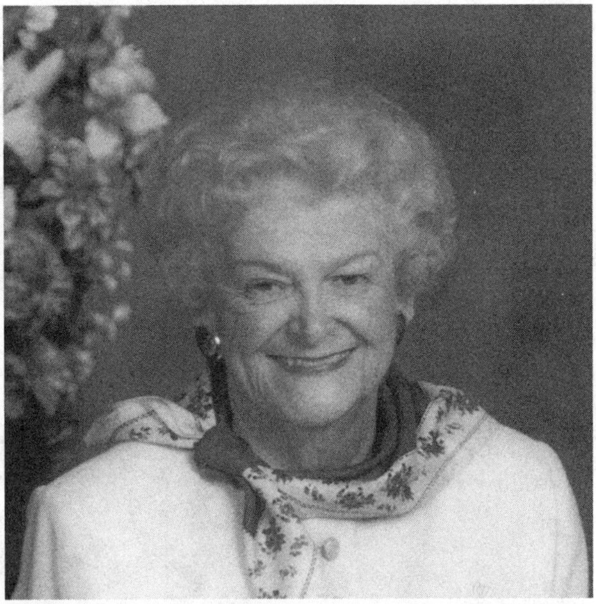

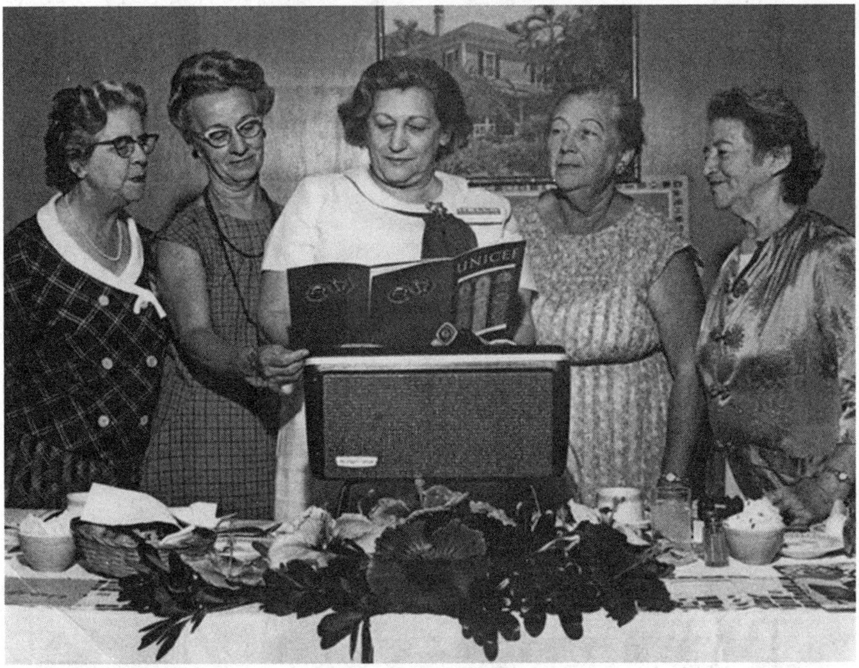

Members of the League of Women Voters in the Fort Myers area look at information about UNICEF on October 24, 1967—the anniversary of the founding of the United Nations. Supporting the UN was a major goal of the League in the 1950s and 1960s. State Archives of Florida, *Florida Memory*, http://floridamemory.com/items/show/257850.

The first woman to head the Seminole tribe, Betty Mae Jumper was elected to that position in 1967. In 1949, she had been the first Seminole woman to earn a high school diploma, at the Cherokee Indian School in North Carolina. She led the tribe in declaring unity with the Choctaw, Cherokee, and Mikasuki, and in 1970 was appointed to the National Congress on Indian Opportunity. Courtesy of FWHOF.

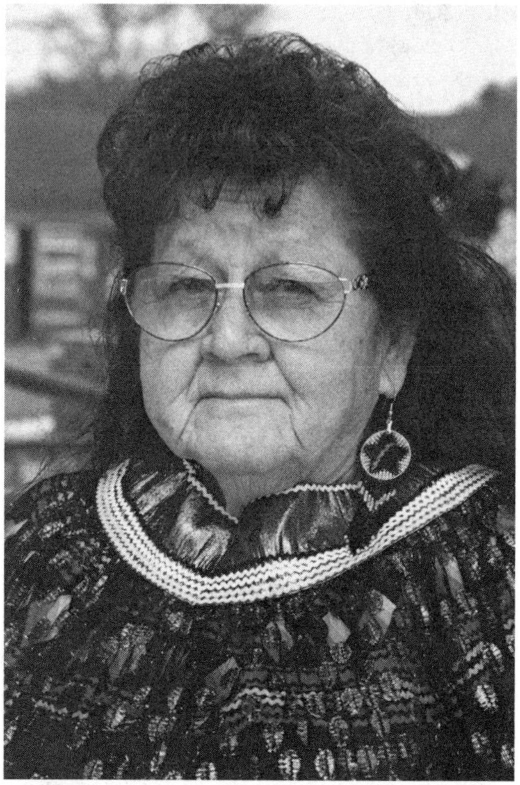

Marjorie Harris Carr founded Florida Defenders of the Environment in 1969, with her major aim being to stop construction of the Cross-Florida Barge Canal. Her court case went on for years, but finally, in 1990, both Congress and the legislature passed acts to end the digging. Courtesy of FWHOF.

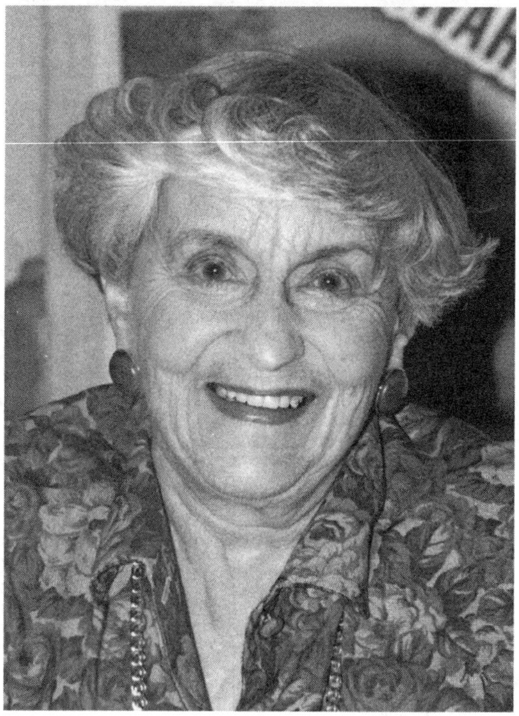

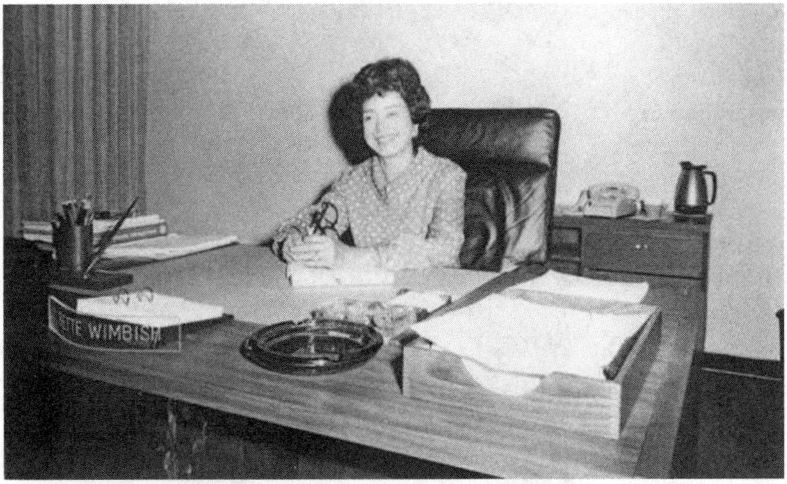

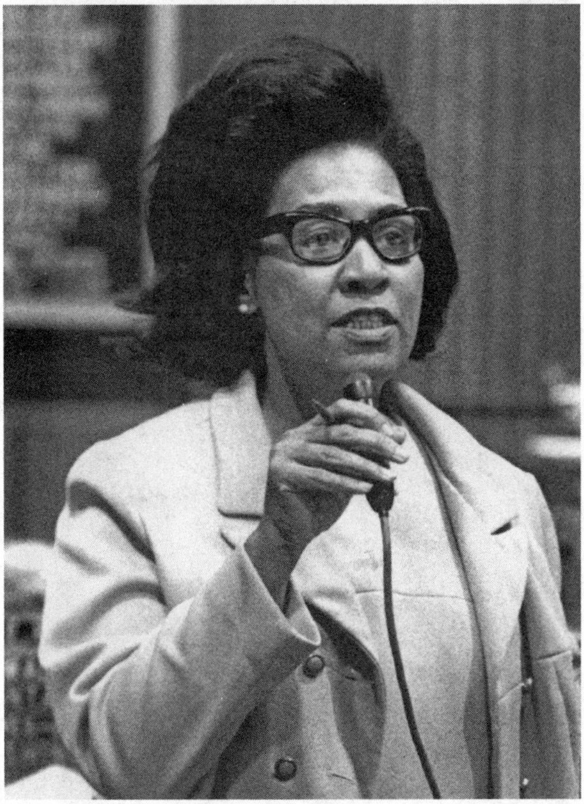

Above: Although she appears to be white in this photo, Bette Wimbush identified herself as black; for many years, her boarding house was the only place available to black members of the New York Yankees during spring training. Elected to St. Petersburg City Council in 1969, she was the first African American of either gender to hold such a position on Florida's west coast since Reconstruction. She is shown here in Tallahassee in 1973, when she was deputy secretary of commerce. State Archives of Florida, *Florida Memory*, http://floridamemory.com/items/show/87264.

Left: Elected in 1970 from Dade County, Gwen Sawyer Cherry was the first African American woman in the Florida House. An attorney and former teacher, she introduced the Equal Rights Amendment in 1972 and chaired Florida's committee for International Women's Year in 1978. She died prematurely in a car accident. Courtesy of FWHOF.

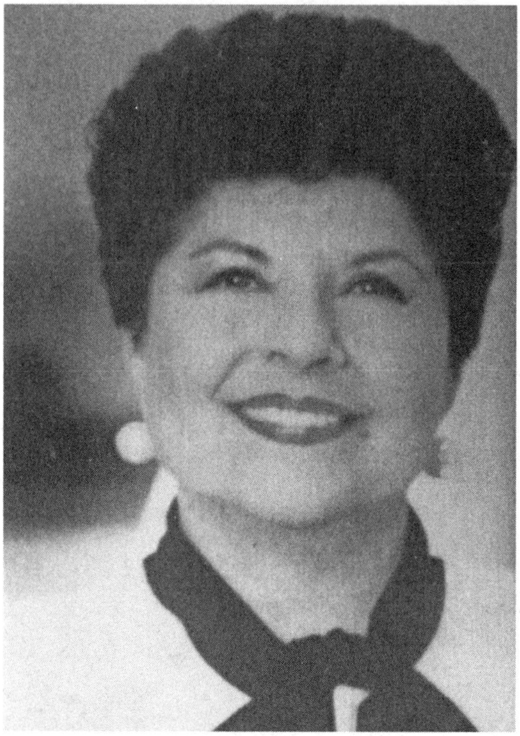

The very first woman chosen for the Florida Women's Hall of Fame when it began in 1982, Elaine Gordon had been elected to the House from Miami in 1972. She pioneered almost every piece of feminist legislation and endured much hostility from those who opposed women's rights. Courtesy of FWHOF.

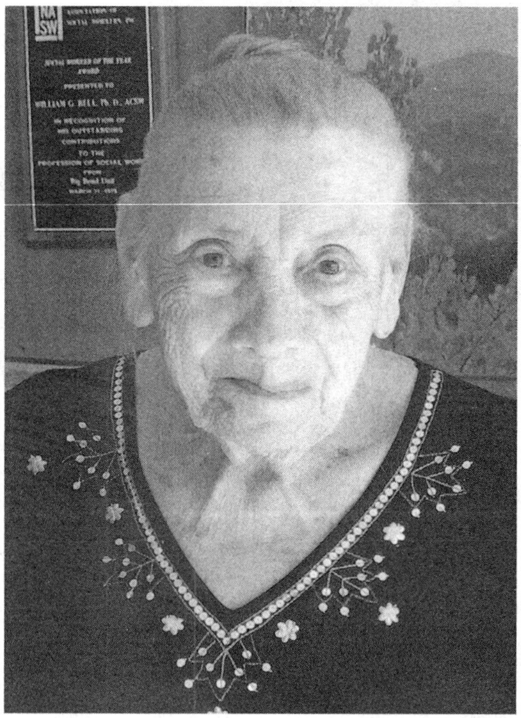

A longtime presence in the capitol lobbying for the needy, social worker Budd Bell formed the Clearinghouse for Human Services in 1974. About a hundred humanitarian organizations joined, and together they made good progress in assisting Florida's underprivileged. She also was one of the first to raise the issue of domestic violence. Courtesy of FWHOF.

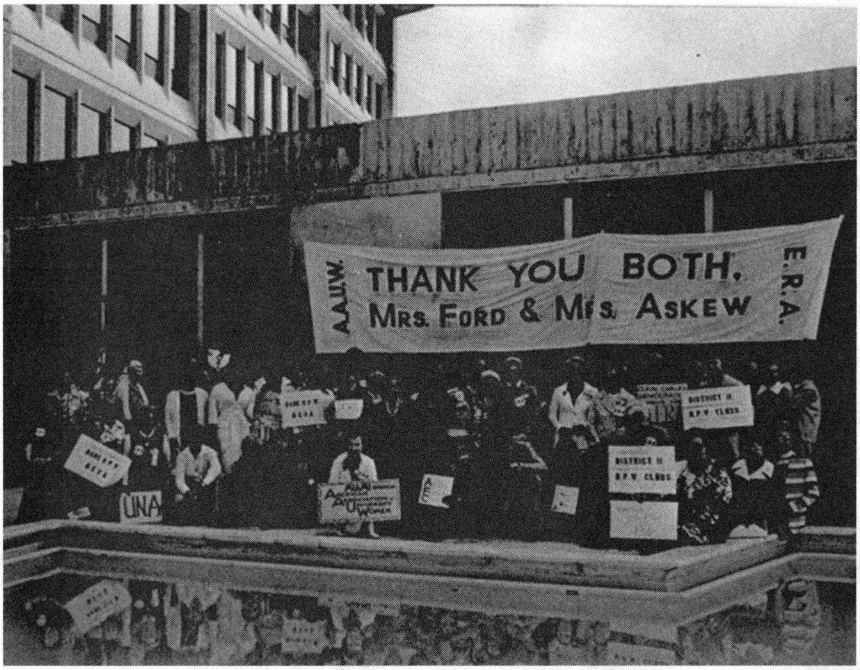

Above: Members of the American Association of University Women lead a rally for the Equal Rights Amendment (ERA) in Miami in 1975. The banner indicates the bipartisan nature of the issue at that time, as both Betty Ford, wife of the Republican president, and Donna Askew, wife of the Democratic governor, supported the ERA. State Archives of Florida, *Florida Memory*, http://floridamemory.com/items/show/139892.

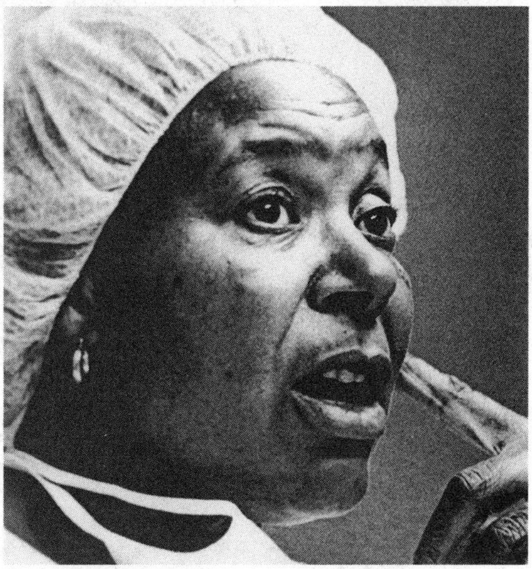

Right: A lifelong resident of the Panhandle's Walton County, Gladys Milton became a nationally known figure in the late 1970s, when she led the opposition to physicians who tried to take away midwives' right to practice. She endured the burning of her home and her clinic, which was the area's first. The Midwives Alliance of North America honored her in 1992. Courtesy of FWHOF.

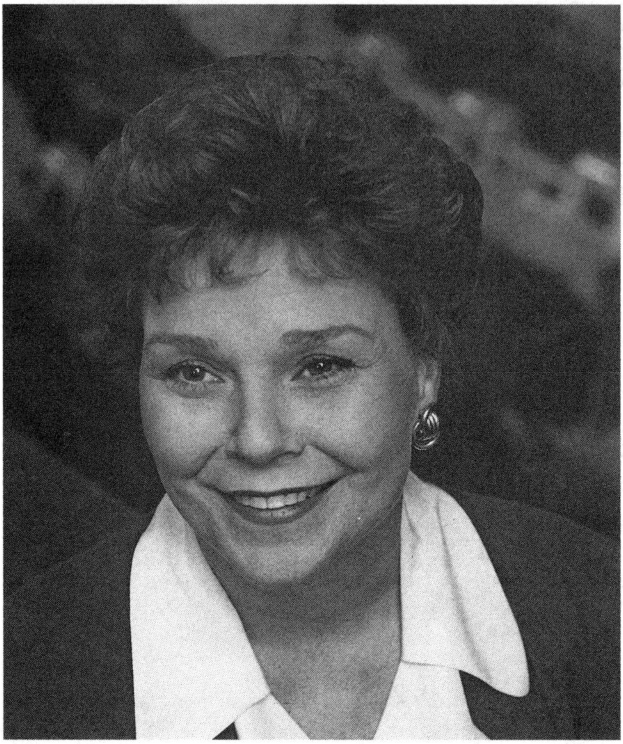

When Congress passed Title IX of the 1972 Education Act, many did not expect that its provision for equity in athletics would be enforced, but as director of women's sports at FSU, Barbara Jo Palmer led that fight nationally and locally. In 1977, her athletes won national championships in five sports. Courtesy of FWHOF.

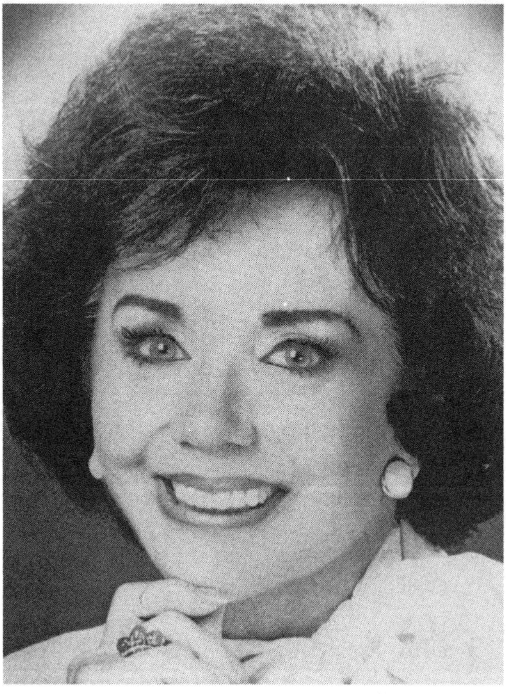

The first woman elected to the legislature from Hillsborough County, Helen Gordon Davis served in its two chambers for eighteen years, from the 1974 to 1992 elections. She fervently championed women's rights, even personally lending the money for Tampa's first center for displaced women and for a statewide study of pay equity. Courtesy of FWHOF.

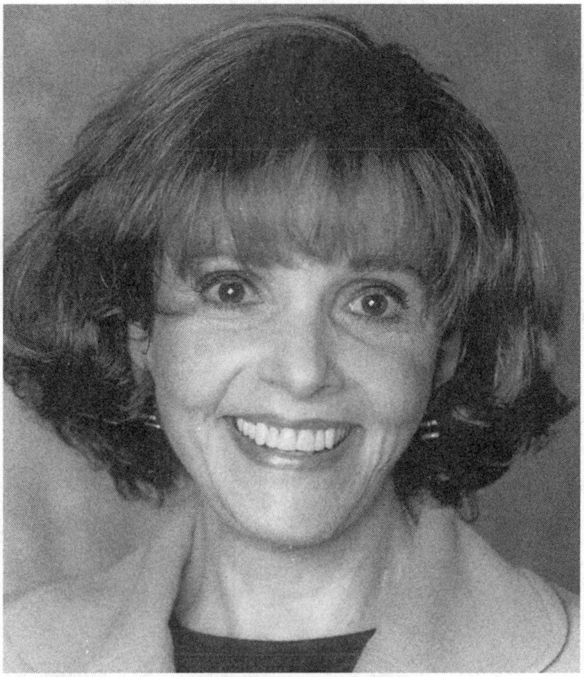

Paula Hawkins of Maitland was the first—and thus far, the only—female U.S. senator from Florida. Voters chose her for the Public Service Commission in 1974, when that body still was elected, and she went on to Washington six years later. Although a half-century had passed since the first woman in the U.S. Senate, Hawkins was the first with no family connections. Courtesy of FWHOF.

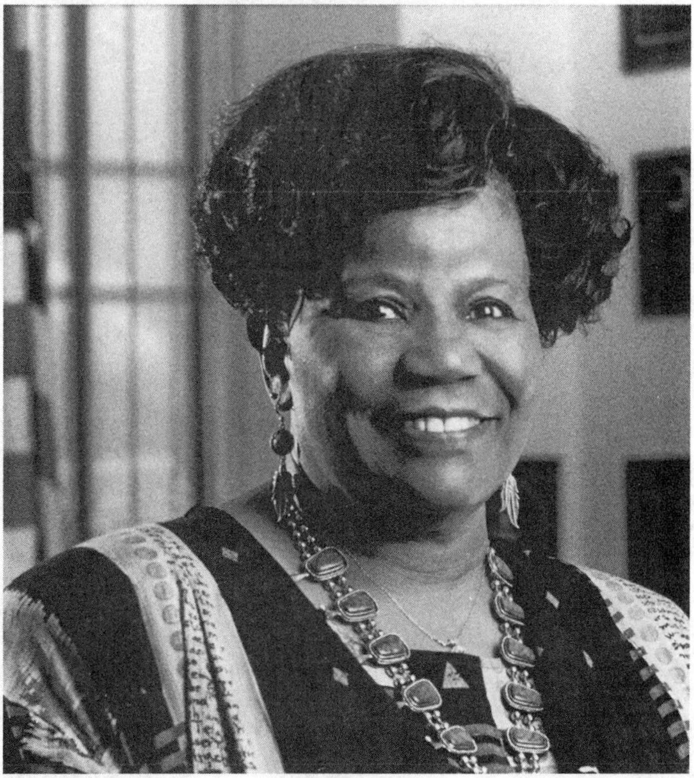

In 1982, Carrie Meek of Miami was elected as the first African American woman in the Florida Senate, and in 1992, she became Florida's first black woman in Congress. A longtime teacher, she was a consistent champion of feminist issues. Courtesy of FWHOF.

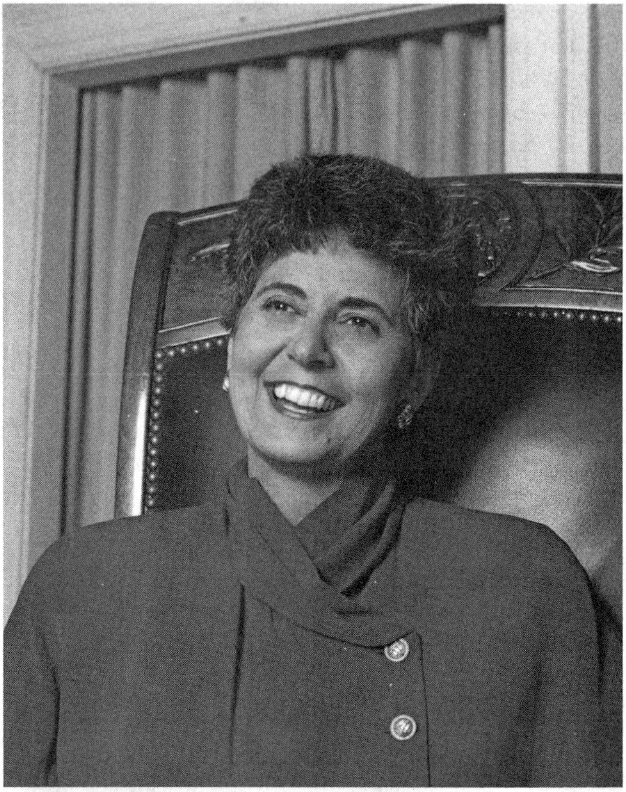

The first woman on the Florida Supreme Court in 1985, Rosemary Barkett had been born in Mexico to Syrian parents. She moved to Miami as a child, speaking no English, and entered a convent at age 17. After eight years as a nun, she went on to law school at the University of Florida, where she was voted the outstanding senior in 1970. In 1993, President Bill Clinton appointed Barkett as a federal judge. Courtesy of FWHOF.

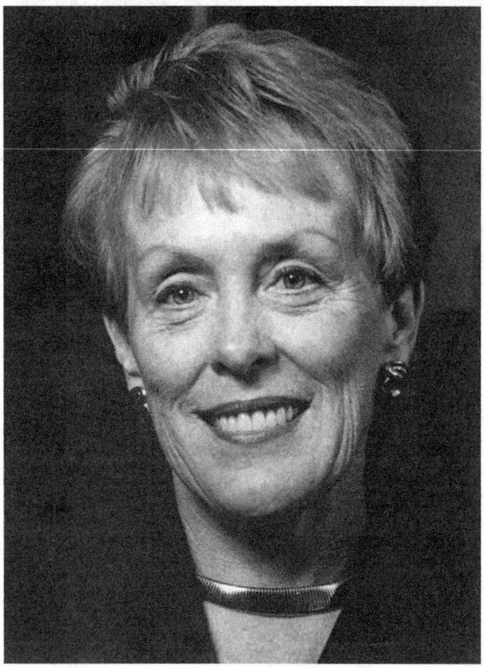

Betty Castor of Tampa was the first woman on Florida's exceptionally powerful cabinet, winning her election for education commissioner in 1986. Prior to that, in 1972 she had been the first woman on the Hillsborough County Commission and was Hillsborough's first woman in the Florida Senate. She went on to be president of the University of South Florida. Courtesy of FWHOF.

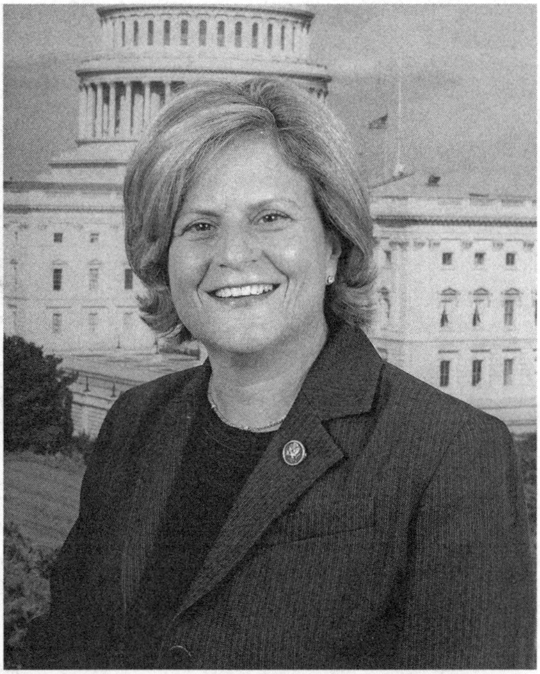

The first Cuban-American woman in Congress, Ileana Ros-Lehtinen won a special election in Miami in 1989. Also the first Republican congresswoman from a former Confederate state, she had been the first Hispanic woman in the Florida legislature when she was elected as Ileana Ros in 1982. As of 2014, she remains in the U.S. House. Courtesy of FWHOF.

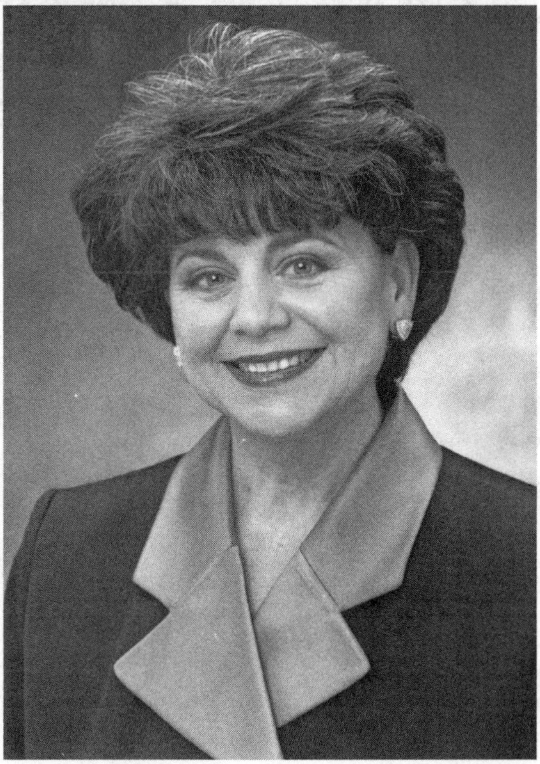

A fifth-generation Floridian, Lynda Keever became publisher of *Florida Trend* in 1991. With her business magazine, she has led policymaking for the state during the last quarter-century. Courtesy of FWHOF.

Miami native Janet Reno was the nation's first female attorney general, appointed by President Bill Clinton in 1993. She served the entire eight years of his term and previously had set precedents as the prosecuting attorney for Dade County. Courtesy of FWHOF.

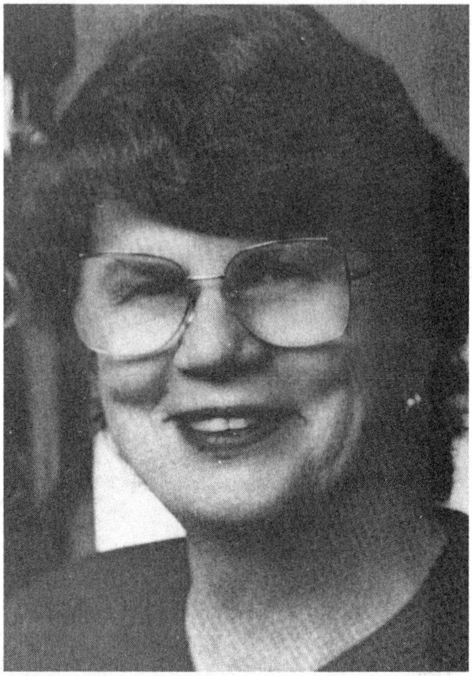

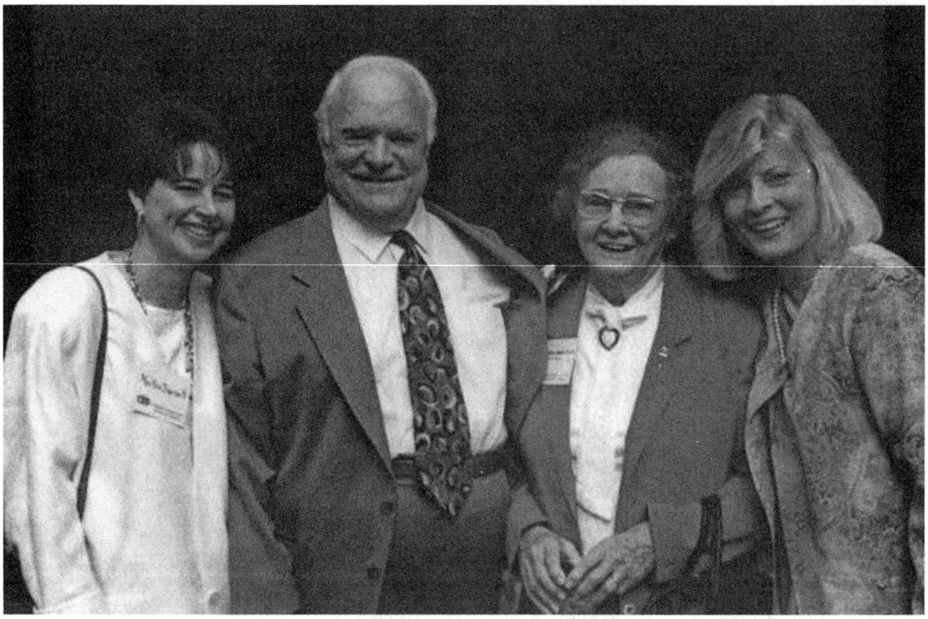

Martha Barnett, on the left in this 1993 photo, is a Pasco County native who in 2000 became the second female president of the American Bar Association. Barnett is shown here with Chesterfield Smith, a previous ABA president, pioneer Miami Judge Mattie Belle Davis, and attorney Lynn Parks. State Archives of Florida, *Florida Memory*, http://floridamemory.com/items/show/47251.

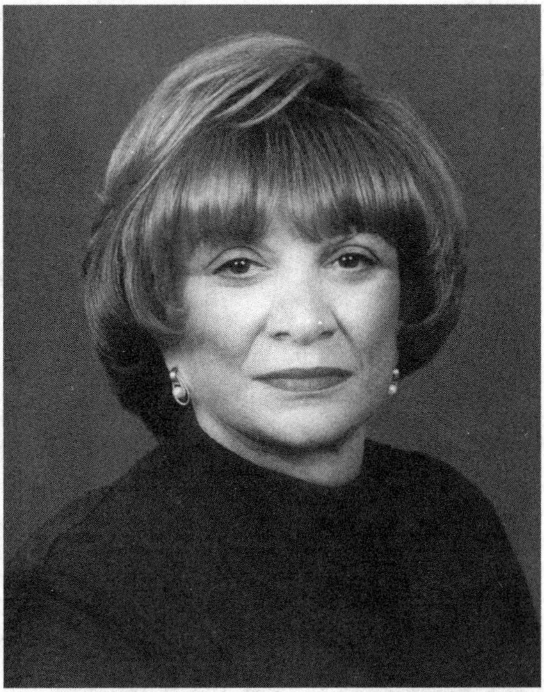

Gwen Margolis of Miami was chosen by her peers as the first female president of the Florida Senate. That was in 1993, and she was just the fourth female senate president in the nation. Margolis is unusual in having returned to the legislature with the 2002 election; most former senate presidents retire or become lobbyists. Courtesy of FWHOF.

In 1997, Republican Toni Jennings followed the precedent set by Democrat Gwen Margolis as president of the Florida Senate. Jennings set a new precedent by serving two terms in that position, something no Florida man has achieved. Courtesy of FWHOF.

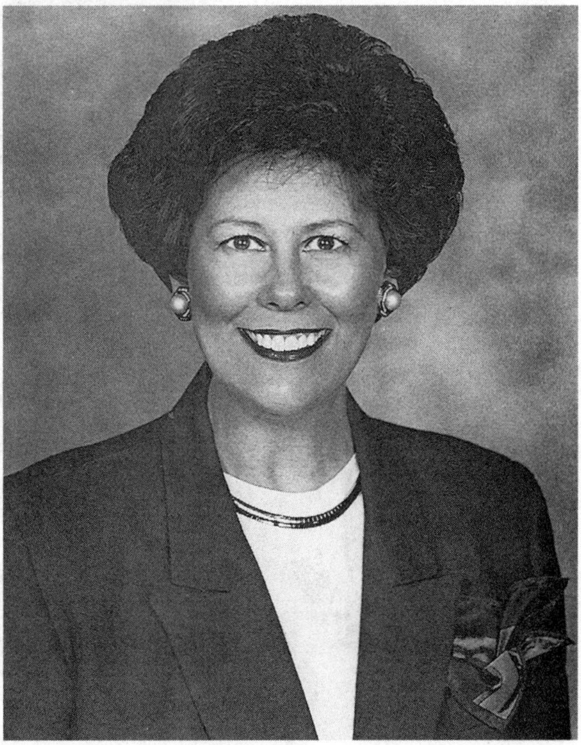

Right: Born in India in 1950, physician Pallavi Patel began her medical career in Zambia. Since association with the University of South Florida, she and her husband have built a prosperous health care company and donated millions to causes, including women's health. Courtesy of FWHOF.

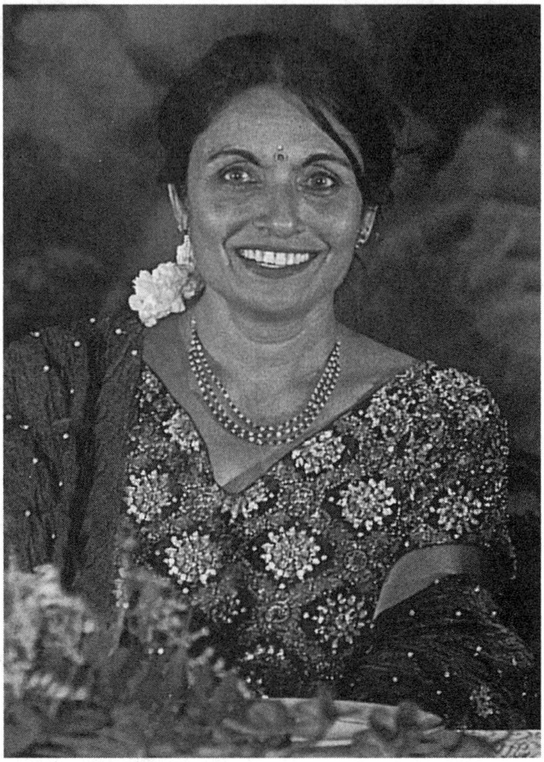

Below: Florida's Chief Financial Officer (CFO) Alex Sink of Tampa speaks at a news conference shortly after winning her 2008 election. Sink narrowly lost a 2012 race for governor, and Florida has yet to join the majority of states that have elected at least one woman to top office. Photo by Bill Cotterell, State Archives of Florida, *Florida Memory*, http://floridamemory.com/items/show/23819.

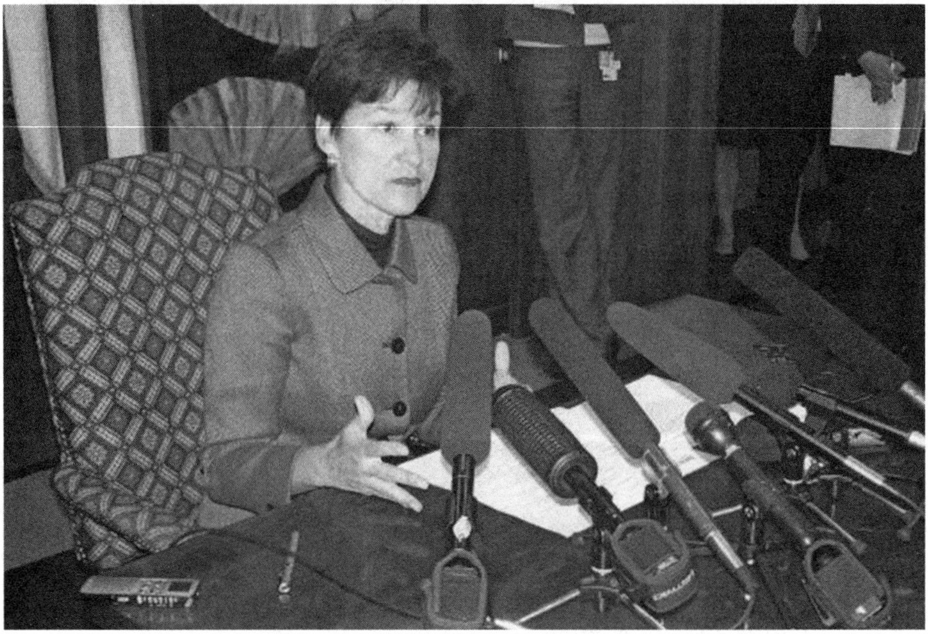

8 World War II and Its Aftermath, 1941–1960

Nothing changed Florida as much as World War II. Literally millions of people moved here during its four years, and after the war's end, many became permanent Floridians. The 1940 census showed Florida to rank twenty-sixth in state population; by 1960 it had soared to be the tenth most populous of the fifty states.

Because of predictable weather and flat land for flight training, hundreds of thousands of pilots for both the army and the navy learned to fly in Florida. The Air Force was not yet a separate entity, but many women who were recruited into the Women's Army Corps (WAC) called themselves "Air WACs." They were not allowed to fly, but all across the state, they taught men the basics of flight in classrooms and simulation labs; they ran air traffic control towers and were mechanics for planes. WACs served around the globe, with the first assigned near battlefields in North Africa in the war's first full year, 1942.[1]

Navy women generally had to meet higher qualifications, yet were not allowed to go overseas until very late in the war. They were called WAVES, an acronym for the seldom-used formal name of Women Accepted for Volunteer Emergency Service. Like WACs, WAVES worked as mechanics, controlled air traffic for navy planes, forecasted weather for both planes and ships, and from far away, plotted trajectories for targets to be hit by great guns on the navy's ships. Jacksonville, Key West, and Pensacola were strategic ports, and civilian women built ships for the navy, especially in Tampa.

The U.S. Marine Corps and the Coast Guard, also under the Department of the Navy, likewise enlisted women for stateside duty. "Women Marines" were called simply that, while the Coast Guard's female unit was the SPARS.[2] These entities were new in World War II, with the Army's women's service being created first, in the summer of 1942; the Marine Corps was last, the following summer.

The Army Nurse Corps, however, had existed since 1901; the Navy Nurse Corps followed in 1908. Both would expand greatly to meet wartime needs, and some nurses served in Florida. Often they worked in temporary facilities, as tourism ended with the war and many hotels became hospitals. The favorite places for men to recover from wounds were converted hotels on the beach, including the luxurious Don Cesar in St. Petersburg and The Breakers in Palm Beach.

Florida had 172 military installations, many more than most states. Some, such as the Sopchoppy Bombing Range, were small, but others were huge. Camp Blanding, in north-central Florida near Starke, was so big that it would have been the state's fourth largest city had it been counted as a municipality. Long gone now, it was viewed as temporary, and most other military installations also were converted to new uses after victory. Tampa, for example, had three big air bases, but only MacDill Air Force Base remains: Drew Field became Tampa International Airport, while what was Henderson Field is now the University of South Florida.

Per square mile, more military personnel trained in Florida than in any other state. For America's military women, though, the most important Florida site was Daytona Beach, home to the second basic training camp of the Women's Army Corps.

* * *

Leftists, especially Miami's Jews and Tampa's Latin community, had been warning for years about the dangers of rightwing governments in Germany, Italy, and Spain, but most Americans were shocked when, without warning, Imperial Japan attacked the naval fleet at Hawaii's Pearl Harbor. It was on Sunday December 7, 1941, and Mrs. Brooke E. Allen was visiting her parents at MacDill Field, saying goodbye before she joined her husband at Honolulu's Hickam Field. She was on the phone with him, planning her arrival, just five minutes before the first bombs fell. She would endure great anxiety before she knew if he was among the 2,300 dead.

"The Day that Shall Live in Infamy"

Almost all Americans could remember where they were on December 7, 1941, when they got the news that without warning or declaration of war, Japanese planes had attacked the American naval fleet docked at Honolulu. Thousands of sailors still asleep on a Sunday morning were killed. When he asked Congress to declare war the next day, President Franklin D. Roosevelt called it "the day that shall live in infamy," and virtually everyone agreed.

Tampa's Maria Leto Pasetti, then eighteen years old, recalled: "Sunday was the most exciting day of the week for us. . . . We would spend all morning getting ready for the Tea Dance at the Centro Espanol," she said, but "that afternoon . . . Don Francisco stopped the music and told us the Japanese had bombed Pearl Harbor."

Pasetti's family had emigrated from Sicily not long before, but Mildred Cox was a ninth-generation Floridian. She was engaged to an army man, and their wedding was scheduled for December 7:

> It was cold, gloomy, rainy. So miserable. I was Catholic and Jim was Protestant, so we got married at the rectory of Sacred Heart. . . . We went back to our home . . . and I was packing a bag, and my aunt came upstairs and said, "Hurry up! Get in the car and go!" . . . Jim's brother had heard about Pearl Harbor. . . . The guests said, "Get in the car!"
>
> Jim seemed so different. One of my dreams was to go down Franklin Street with tin cans behind the car . . . but Jim got out and cut the cans. He gets back in and he's still not talking.
>
> We're heading towards Indian Rocks Beach [in Pinellas County]. So I turn on the radio and he flipped it off. I started crying. My mom told me this would happen—men were different after the wedding! . . .
>
> We got to the causeway and the . . . toll taker asked, looking at Jim's uniform, "Soldier, where are you stationed?"
>
> Jim said, Camp Blanding. . . . The attendant then looked at the "Just Married" sign on the window and said, "Soldier, take your coat and cap off and git! I never saw you!"
>
> The next morning a telegram was slipped under our door. "Report to Camp Blanding." I went with him on the bus. Jim walked across the street and waved at me. Soldiers were everywhere."

Note: Gary Mormino, *Hillsborough County Goes to War: The Home Front, 1940–1950* (Tampa: Tampa Bay History Center, 2001), 69.

Germany, under Nazi Adolf Hitler, and Italy, under fascist Benito Mussolini, joined Japan's emperor in declaring war on the United States before Congress declared war on them on Monday, December 8. Partly because much of the Pacific naval fleet was destroyed at Pearl Harbor, and partly because by then Britain stood alone as Europe's only outpost of democracy, the war in Europe was prioritized. This strategy made especially good sense in Florida, where Nazi submarines were discovered off the East Coast just weeks after Pearl Harbor. Miami reporter Helen Muir wrote:

> The German U-boats that had been waging a devastating war in the North Atlantic moved into the shipping lanes off the Florida coast on the night of February 19, when the tanker *Pan Massachusetts,* loaded with one hundred thousand barrels of gasoline, oil, and kerosene, became a flaming torch after being struck twenty miles south of Cape Canaveral. It lit up the ocean for a full mile. The eighteen survivors of the thirty-eight man crew were picked up by a British passenger vessel that also loaded aboard many of the dead and headed for Jacksonville.
>
> Within the next week, the Nazi wolf pack struck again and again up and down the coast. . . . Citizens with every kind of old fishing scow, motorboat, and sailboat, millionaires with elaborate yachts, all answered the screams of the injured and dying. . . .
>
> The landing of saboteurs at Ponte Verde [in northeast Florida] was not a false alarm, and these men were later caught and executed. It was no rumor either that the FBI picked up twenty-nine German, Italian, and Japanese aliens before February was out. They were all neatly ensconced close by the Naval Air Station at Opa-Locka, [caught with] with guns, cameras, binoculars, and spyglasses.[3]

Compared with some other states, Florida had few "enemy aliens," the term applied to those who had a recent history of immigration from an enemy nation. Nonetheless, many Italian Americans, especially in Tampa, were interrogated by the FBI, which also confiscated their cameras, maps, guns, and ammunition. Very few Japanese lived in the state, but those who did drew immediate attention. Aiko Sone, a native of Japan who ran a gift shop in St. Petersburg, was arrested the day after Pearl Harbor. Her property was boarded up, but—unlike most Japanese-Americans in western states—she soon was allowed to reopen her business. Law enforcement, however, kept a close eye on her and her compatriots. They were not allowed to leave the city and their bank accounts were frozen.[4]

Potential saboteurs threatened not only from under the sea but also from the sky, as Floridians had reason to fear that their coast would be bombed just as England's had been. Women joined men in the Civil Air Patrol, a quasi-military organization that watched the skies for enemy planes. Called "spotters," they worked from isolated towers on beaches. When they spotted a plane, they used a specially installed telephone extension to a central location and reported the longitude and latitude of the plane as well as its type.

Relatively few Floridians lived on the beaches then compared with now, but after the submarine attacks, those who did were not allowed to go out at night. Indian Rocks resident Marjorie M. Cochran said that because of tight security and limited gasoline, she "never left the island" between the Gulf and the Pinellas County mainland "for three months." Civil Defense wardens, some of them women, also enforced blackout rules. All windows had to be covered with heavy black fabric so that no light could be seen by enemy planes.

In preparation for the possibility of an air raid, Jean Fyfe and Margaret Lee Moody flew over Tampa Bay during a mock drill conducted by the Civil Air Patrol in September 1942. They dropped paper as potential bombs, and residents were supposed to learn where to evacuate. Many people criticized this, however, seeing it as the sport of elitists fortunate enough to own planes as well as a lamentable waste of fuel when troops in North Africa were desperately short of it.

It was such activities by eager but misguided civilians that prompted Congress to use women's enthusiasm and skills when it created the military's first corps that accepted women who were not nurses. The first post for the Women's Army Corps was at Iowa's Fort Des Moines, an army cavalry facility that was not needed in modern warfare. The third basic training post was at Fort Oglethorpe, Georgia—and in between, the corps experimented with a nonmilitary locale, Daytona Beach.

Because the entire idea of military training for women was new in the United States (although not for its allies, especially Britain), it was reasonable to test the viability of a nonstandard site. Beyond that, military installations all over the country were overcrowded with new soldiers, and it was difficult for WAC officials to find commanders of extant facilities willing to accept these untested female volunteers. Daytona Beach therefore was a logical choice. Because tires and gasoline were rationed, tourism essentially ended; hotels and other businesses stood virtually empty, and their owners were desperate for dollars.

That was true in other tourist locales throughout the nation, however, and the largely unspoken reason that Daytona Beach won out was because the city's Mary McLeod Bethune, the African American founder of Bethune-Cookman College, was on the WAC advisory board.[5] WAC Director Oveta Culp Hobby, a white Texan, made the corps more welcoming to black women than any other women's military unit. She initially tried to secure Clearwater's Fort Harrison but was unable to get approval from male superiors, who argued that it was needed for men. With assurances from Bethune—and because Fort Des Moines women already had overflowed into hotels—Hobby allowed the second WAC facility to be a civilian setting. It was authorized in October 1942; leases with private owners were quickly signed; and the "army camp" opened on December 1.

New recruits lived in a tent city and studied in "classrooms" all over town. *Collier's* magazine reported on the transformation: "You can find the Fifth Avenue Gown Shop, but you won't find any gowns inside. Instead, you'll find a . . . WAAC teacher and a couple of hundred WAACs students."[6] A *Reader's Digest* story said recruits in Daytona were so dedicated that "an order had to be issued prohibiting WAACs from drilling by flashlight."[7]

After four weeks of life in the tent cantonment, women were considered trustworthy enough to be billeted in hotels and apartment houses. In these settings, officials did their best to replicate life in a regular army camp. Superiors regularly checked that beds were made properly, shoes shined, uniforms ironed, and everything stowed in as military a style as possible. If one woman took a Florida-vacation attitude and failed to follow regulations, the entire "barrack," which ranged in size from thirty-seven to six hundred, might lose weekend passes.

Most recruits agreed that life was better in Daytona than Des Moines, partly because of the weather and partly because—although some ten thousand women could be stationed in Daytona at any given time—even larger concentrations of young men were nearby. Local citizens arranged dances and other weekend entertainment, and soldiers flocked there from Jacksonville's naval bases and from the area's army posts, especially Camp Blanding. Despite early fears of riotous behavior, a *Collier's* reporter said on May 29, 1943, that these Saturday nights were simply "thousands of young men and women who quite naturally enjoy one another's company."

Some people, of course, objected to women in the military at all, while others bemoaned their presence as a loss of personal peacetime privilege. Fred Huntress, a winter resident of Daytona, complained in a 1943 letter to

Senator Claude Pepper that WACs were having "a grand vacation at government expense . . . [and] the Army group monopolizes our few sizeable restaurants to the detriment of civilians." As elsewhere, rumors flew about sexual misconduct, but an army investigation showed that most were false, perpetrated by "well-to-do property owners . . . the elderly conservative type."[8] Military police detained an average of eleven Daytona WACs per week, many fewer than rates for men—and most offenses were minor, such as failure to wear a hat.

At the end of basic training, women returned to the tent city where they had arrived for out-processing. They went on to dozens of other locations for training in some four hundred military occupational specialties, and new recruits replaced them in Daytona Beach. The process continued until March 1944, when Iowa's Fort Des Moines and Georgia's Fort Oglethorpe became the army's only basic-training posts for women.

By then the military had already absorbed those who were most eager to volunteer, and officials had to step up their enlistment promotions aimed at women. A male recruiter who was disappointed in Florida was gracious enough not to name the city of which he complained:

> When our team hit one Florida city, we closed the place—actually got the mayor to close schools and stores so everyone would come to our parade and rally. We got important speakers, generals, war heroes. Better than 50 planes flew overhead forming the letters WAC. That night we had a big dance for prospects, with good-looking pilots as dates. Results? We didn't get one Wac in that town. Some of the local girls put in application to please their escorts, but withdrew them the next day.[9]

Earlier in the war, though, Florida contributed its share of eager volunteers. The first WACs had truly excellent credentials, and Miami attorney Mary Cinthya Vann Racey was among them. A graduate of North Carolina's eminent Duke University, she earned her law degree at the University of Miami in 1931, just a year after the university granted its first degree to a woman.[10] Racey was practicing law in Miami when the war began, and she joined the army as soon as the opportunity arose. She was discharged as a captain, a significantly higher rank than most women achieved.

The military did not allow women to be chaplains, but Ruth Braddock was a chaplain's assistant who counseled men and performed other services. Years after settling in Miami, where she ran a swim school, Braddock became the founding president of Herstory of Florida, which attempted to archive and publicize the history of the state's women.

Hortense K. Wells rose from private to corporal while serving in Wales, a climate very different from her Tampa home. Politically ambitious, Wells had risen to the powerful Democratic National Committee prior to the war, when she also ran unsuccessfully for the U.S. Senate. After her military service, she ran for Congress in 1950 and again lost.[11] Wells was a leader in the Business and Professional Women's Clubs, which had lobbied Congress for the creation of the military units for women. Wartime BPW also developed a nationwide system, called a "talent bank," that created a database of credentialed civilian women by their skills. The aim was to make male leaders aware of such women and to include them in war agencies.

Nellye Friedman, also of Tampa, was chosen as one of the army's pioneer women, when credentials were extremely high. As a Jew, she felt a particular urgency about Hitler and had worked as a plane spotter before the WAC began. "I was among the first that went," she said, and "I got all kinds of publicity." Although most such publicity was positive, some right-wingers fed the belief that these women were little better than prostitutes. Friedman was not the only one who encountered such attitudes. "I went for my country," she explained, "and the sort of stuff I'd hear was why is 'a nice Jewish girl like you from the South joining the Army?'"[12]

Dessie Smith Prescott, who also was a WAC, probably would have slugged anyone who gave her such a "compliment." Born in 1906 in Alachua County, she was orphaned at age twelve. At nineteen, she built her own log cabin and supported herself with nontraditional jobs such as selling cars. Before and after her wartime service, Prescott worked as a professional guide to hunters and fishers—probably the first such woman in the state. Marjorie Kinnan Rawlings wrote of boat trips on the St. Johns with Prescott, who knew Florida's backwoods like the back of her hand. She died in 2002, after her 1999 admission to the Florida Women's Hall of Fame. She came to the capital for the recognition, an important acknowledgment of an unconventional woman who dressed and lived like a man.

* * *

Critics of women in the army doubtless snickered at Prescott's seeming lesbianism, and WACs indeed were more likely to be the target of negative rumors than were women in the navy. Because the navy's branches for women crafted a more elitist image, they were more apt to meet their recruitment quotas—but the naval units also were smaller. They were much less likely than the army to accept black women, and most naval women trained in civilian facilities, not military camps. Colleges were their most common sites, but the Coast Guard's SPARS were quartered on the Atlantic in Palm Beach. For more than seven thousand SPARS, boot camp was the magnificent Biltmore Hotel, temporarily serving as barracks. A former SPAR recalled:

> By May 1943, the news was flashed around the country that on June 14, the first class of Spars would be indoctrinated at a fabulous new training station of their own: the Palm Beach Biltmore Hotel. Disgruntled civilians with reservations for the winter season read the headlines and wept: HUGE PINK PALACE IS SPARS' NEW FLORIDA TRAINING SCHOOL. . . . We hupped over the sunkissed soil of one of America's favorite playgrounds.[13]

The hotel was divided navy style, using the terminology of a ship. Now called the quarterdeck, its basement held offices, the clothing store, sick bay, and more. The first "deck" had the mess hall, library, and the captain's quarters, while the mezzanine featured a recreational hall. The third and fourth "decks" contained classrooms, including those for two specialty schools: Storekeeper plus Cooks and Bakers. On three levels above were the "boots and new booties," meaning recruits and advanced recruits; the "ship's company," or sleeping quarters for these yeomen; and officers' quarters at the top.

Air WACs at MacDill Field lived in barracks, and it was not a training site: instead the women assigned there were graduates of boot camp and specialty schools. They performed many functions that supported the young male air cadets who trained there—where so many accidentally plunged into the coastal waters that the slogan was "A Plane a Day in Tampa Bay." Some WACs were reporters and photographers for the *Thunderbird,* a quarterly magazine that provided information and promoted *esprit de corps.*

Such military occupations offered young women valuable skills that they could use for peacetime employment. In particular demand were those who trained in new technologies that would transform the economy in the century's second half. Some Air WACs, for example, were sent to Orlando at army expense for a six-week course in keypunching, the term used for early database creation.

Other women, however, were unable to develop their new skills when their jobs reverted to men at the war's end, most notably the WAVES stationed in Pensacola, whose ship-related tasks were not easily transferable. Women trained at a gunnery school there and, after graduation, taught gunnery to men. Marie Kimball said of her experience in Pensacola:

> We took the same course the boys took who went out as aerial gunners. Our drill sergeant was a Marine who did not believe that women should be in the service. The rougher he was on us, the more determined we were to show him how good we were. . . .
>
> There was always someone who just couldn't believe that a girl could not only teach the men how to operate the guns, but actually fire them.[14]

The women who worked at Embry-Riddle School of Aviation were civilians, but they functioned in a quasi-military atmosphere. The school on Miami's Biscayne Bay began in 1939, when the war began in Europe, and expanded after Pearl Harbor. In April 1942 Henrietta Klein was the first woman to enroll in a sheet metal class there, and soon other women paid tuition for courses that they could use as credentials for getting into the military or to obtain better-paid jobs in defense plants—jobs that had been reserved for men until the war emergency. Women at Embry-Riddle studied drafting and designing, parachute packing, instrument building, plane repair, and radio communications. One told a reporter: "Never before would I admit in public that a carburetor was more fascinating to me than a fresh manicure. . . . But now that it's patriotic for women to be mechanically minded, I can tinker around with motors . . . without fear of masculine scorn."[15]

By January 1943 Embry-Riddle employed forty women as instructors, including a mother-daughter team and two women who were sisters. Like most managers who had no experience working around women, some were skeptical about male response to a woman at the head of the class. One army commander "who doubted that women could be effective" soon acknowledged that "the boys don't seem to notice whether their teachers are men or women."[16]

"The boys" did see a difference, though—and many said that they preferred women. Female instructors, they said, "had more patience" and "seemed to take more interest." Jean Blood Criddlebaugh taught plane inspection—or, as she said, "what to look for that would ground a plane." She taught eight or nine hours a day, but put in "ten or twelve studying and reading after my classes."[17] She was like other female instructors at Embry-Riddle who were experienced pilots but who had to teach because they were not allowed to fly. Except for the Civil Air Patrol, private planes were not permitted to use fuel, and opportunities for female pilots were extremely limited.

Some expressed gratitude to Embry-Riddle's founder for giving them a chance to contribute to the war effort. Many years later Nancy Graham said: "To work for Mr. John Paul Riddle was a stroke of fortune for anyone but particularly for women. Mr. Riddle treated women pilots as equals to male pilots." When one of his female employees, Mary Brooks, was killed while flying with a student on his solo test, Riddle announced: "She gave her life for her country, just as surely as if she had been fighting over enemy lines."[18]

While young men were trained to fly at government expense, women who already had these skills could not use them except in the quasi-military WASP (Women Airforce Service Pilots) and its predecessor, the WAFS (Women's Auxiliary Ferrying Squadron). Both groups were small and elite, requiring women to be highly credentialed—and those credentials had to be earned at their own expense and prior to fuel restrictions. Headquartered in Texas, they flew all over.

WASPs performed many functions, including serving as targets for gunnery students who fired live ammunition. Even though WASPs were not allowed to go overseas, the work was dangerous enough that thirty-eight died on duty—with no compensation for their lives or their burial costs. Their chief job, and that of the earlier WAFS, was "ferrying"—flying planes from the plant where they were built to military posts. This was relatively dangerous because new planes might have undetected mechanical problems, and many men doubted women's ability, especially with newly designed and heavy planes. *Flying* magazine quoted a male pilot who was in Orlando, where he expected a powerful plane to be delivered:

> The overcast was so deep that Orlando had practically knocked off flying. . . . My Thunderbolt was due. . . . The apron sort of filled up with guys who wouldn't admit they were worried, of course, but they did want to see what was coming in through this stuff. Sure enough, a Thunderbolt broke out at about 500 feet, making a smooth turn to the end of the runway and rolled to as pretty a stop . . . as I ever saw. . . .
>
> I ran up to the wing and out stepped the teeny-weeniest little girl. . . .
>
> "Your plane, captain?" she asked me, and I nodded. . . .
>
> Just then the tower man ran up. "Look here, you, why didn't you tell me you were a girl?"[19]

The "girls" of the WASP were commanded by superstar aviator Jacqueline Cochran. A native of the Florida Panhandle, she grew up so poor that no one would have anticipated this adult success: it was through sheer genius and force of will that she gained international fame. The winner of many air races, she volunteered for the British air forces prior to American involvement in the war, and after the war she set records for supersonic speed. Cochran's autobiography is *The Stars at Noon* (1954). Governor Lawton Chiles remembered her from when he was young, and in 1992 he made certain that she was one of his administration's first inductees into the Florida Women's Hall of Fame.

* * *

The military strongly resisted women who chose to be "camp followers," living near a husband's training post while he remained in the United States. Many young women nonetheless followed their man as long as they could, moving from place to place for a year or more before he finally went overseas. Despite advice from experts, especially clergymen and physicians, they started families in such numbers that MacDill Field, for example, had added a maternity unit to its hospital by 1944. Because women with children were not allowed to serve in the military, this maternity ward was for the use of "dependents," as soldiers' wives were called.

Like the army, the navy eventually came to see that sailors' morale would be improved if at least some men were allowed to be near their wives when they returned from overseas duty. *Business Week* announced in February 1944 that navy "brass relented" and leased "two swank hotels" in Miami Beach for the use of women who wanted to stay near their husbands while the men trained on new planes.[20] For young couples in love, this was a poignant chance to be together before the husband returned to the real possibility of death.

Sometimes a woman could not follow because she did not know where her husband was stationed. Margaret Wilder, a sophisticated New York City resident who was not prone to hysteria, believed that hers was in Miami. She could not confirm it, though, and the telephone system was frustratingly inadequate. She pored out her thoughts on paper, explaining to the husband for whom she had no address: "The long distance telephone operator tried to get me a line for three hours this evening, and when she finally did reach the hotel all they could say was that you hadn't left any forwarding address, that they were under the impression that you were moving on orders. . . . That this had to come so suddenly, without one last Christmas together . . . is the worst part."[21]

She was older, with teenage children, and so did not try to move with her husband, but the many younger women who did often found themselves treated as pariahs. They had the lowest transportation priority, and it was not unheard of for a woman and her babies to be bumped from overcrowded trains and buses so that her space could be taken by a soldier or by a businessman with defense contracts. Motels of the modern sort did not yet exist, and few young women could afford the era's hotels—or find a vacancy in military towns, even if they could afford a room.

Ladies Home Journal ran a story about a Florida woman whose experience was late in 1941, while car travel still was possible, before gasoline rationing was implemented. She and her fiancé had planned their wedding for December 19, 1941, when he was scheduled to come home on leave. Instead he got orders sending him to the Pacific, and she determinedly drove to him in Salt Lake City. They got a marriage license and were planning a different sort of wedding when he had thirty minutes notice to leave for California. She followed, going through a snowstorm and a car breakdown. After several hassles with two judges over a waiting period that was partly fulfilled with their Utah license and partly with a California one, they finally had their wedding—with air-raid sirens drowning out the music.[22]

Later in the war, after rationing made private transportation almost impossible and public transportation became overcrowded, *Collier's* wrote of "a very young mother with a three-week old baby in her arms who got off to change trains in Jacksonville, Florida, and toppled in a faint." She was headed for Mississippi, where her husband was stationed, but instead was hospitalized in Jacksonville for two weeks. Then, "with no money and faint prospect of a roof over her head if she did get to Mississippi . . . , she meekly accepted a ticket back home."[23] Doubtless it was Jacksonville women who cared for her baby and raised the money for this ticket, as hundreds of Florida women volunteered for Travelers Aid, which helped with situations of this kind.

Once such a woman reached her destination, finding "a roof over her head" was a severe problem. Port cities such as Jacksonville, Tampa, Miami, and Pensacola were crowded not only with other wives but also with the thousands of people who moved there to work in shipbuilding. In the interior, small towns such as Camp Blanding's Starke quickly ran out of housing when swarms of newcomers arrived. Building materials had to go for construction directly related to defense, and civilians could not expect a share.

The government and other agencies ran advertisements urging families to "share your space," and as a result many Florida women became landladies. Scarce supplies sometimes could be obtained for small renovations: outside of some older houses today, for example, exterior staircases provide evidence of second-story apartments that were created during the war. Most camp-following women could not get an entire apartment, however, and instead rented rooms—sometimes with kitchen privileges and sometimes without.

Some landladies welcomed them and made part them feel part of the family—but some charged exorbitant rent, parsimoniously counted out the sheets of toilet paper, and required that no electricity be used after 10:00 p.m. Comparatively few civic groups paid any attention to these lonely young women, and knowing that they would be temporary, employers seldom offered them jobs. Most lived in isolation, motivated only by the hope of seeing their man for a few hours on weekends.

Instead, local organizations concentrated on soldiers and sailors—and on their own young women, who were expected to entertain young men at United Service Organization (USO) clubs and other recreational facilities. Tens of thousands of Florida women who were teenagers during World War II have bittersweet memories that center on dancing with strangers. Most recall new swing styles, gaiety and fun, but doubtless there was a hidden cost in these unnatural relationships. Girls quickly had to learn to steel their hearts, to say no firmly, to reject hurried marriage proposals from boys who wanted to leave part of themselves behind by putting a ring on a feminine finger. At too early an age for such cynicism, they had to accept the fact that next week's USO dance would bring a new set of passing strangers.

Clergymen and other advice givers strongly warned young women not to accept marriage proposals from men they had known only briefly. Millions of couples nonetheless wed before the husband was shipped overseas, and the unsurprising result was a soaring divorce rate a few years later. Simple divorce by mutual agreement was virtually unavailable, as most states insisted on specific legal grounds for breaking the marital contract—indeed, South Carolina had no provision at all for divorce. Those seeking to end marriages often had to go to Nevada or a handful of other states with more lenient law.

A 1942 case is illustrative: that was the war's first year, and a couple who married too hastily found that they had to go all the way to the Florida Supreme Court to divorce. The case originated in Miami, where a Georgia man married a Minnesota woman, and the marriage broke down over cultural differences that centered on cooking. "He liked hot biscuits and corn bread at every meal," said the Tallahassee judge, "and [her] light bread and crackers were not on the Georgian's menu." The ruling upheld the Miami court, where the judge had said that even though the case lacked the usual serious grounds, "the couple never should have been married, as they were ill-suited . . . for each other."[24] Under the urgency of war, though, many ill-suited couples met in artificial settings such as USO dances, where men who were old enough to die for their country concluded, reasonably enough, that they also were entitled to marry.

Most who came to USO dances truly were boys, wholesome lads lonesome for the companionship of girls. Those more directly interested in sex searched for prostitutes, as soldiers and sailors ever have done. To cope with an explosion of venereal disease in World War I, Congress had passed the Chamberlain-Kahn Act, which put the burden of male behavior on women by imposing curfews for women in towns near military bases. The result had been police harassment of respectable women, and the approach during the Second World War was more realistic. Federal authorities recognized how Florida would be affected by large numbers of men without women, as the Associated Press reported from Jacksonville on November 7, 1942:

> Work is expected to get underway shortly on three Florida camps for diseased prostitutes now that federal funds have been made available. . . . President Roosevelt authorized expenditure of $687,000 for eight such camps in three states earlier this week. . . .
>
> The camps, to be known as Florida State Board of Health hospitals, will be located in abandoned CCC [Civilian Conservation Corps] camps in the Ocala National Forest, at Wakulla [near Tallahassee] and in the Myakka River State Park near Sarasota.
>
> Dr. Henry Hanson, state health officer, said they would have a combined capacity of 600 women and that their opening would greatly relieve overcrowded conditions in jails. . . .
>
> The camps will be available only for detention and treatment of diseased women. Those not infected will not be admitted. Every effort will be made to teach the women useful occupations to rehabilitate themselves.

The story was not widely publicized, though, and most women remained unaware of such camps—and even of prostitution in general. Instead, all across the state, older women arranged dances and other social activities to introduce young women to soldiers and sailors. They also reached out to young men in other ways. They used their clubs and churches as networks to invite strangers for Sunday dinner. Women's organizations that owned clubhouses often transformed them into recreational facilities to be used by off-duty military personnel. At Camp Blanding alone, the Florida Federation of Women's Clubs contributed a hundred thousand books that soldiers could read. "Over at Miami Beach," wrote journalist Helen Muir:

> The women turned the Million-Dollar Pier, where Minsky's burlesque shows had lightened prewar days, into the Servicemen's Pier. They ran it on businesslike lines, working in shifts. Volunteers from Coconut Grove, Coral Gables, Miami Shores, and other sections sliced sandwiches and waxed floors, handed out stationery [to write letters home] and arranged dances. They did a remarkable job. Eighteen thousand volunteers headed by Katherine Pancoast . . . entertained more than four million servicemen over a four-and-a-half year period.[25]

Women also organized recruitment rallies; they recycled paper and even bacon grease, which was used in making explosives. Girl Scouts and other organizations ran salvage drives, collecting items, especially metal, that could be melted down and reused for war materiel. On Florida's west coast, the Girl Reserves specialized in getting women to donate their old pots and pans as well as metal coat hangers. Women washed their emptied tin cans, flattened them, and gave them to a youngster who pulled a wagon door to door. St. Petersburg's Charlotte Harris did so much newspaper recycling that the sixteen-year-old girl was crowned "Salvage Queen" by the U.S. Victory Waste Paper campaign.

* * *

As they had in World War I, women's organizations sold war bonds, which essentially are loans to the government. Again the Florida Federation of Women's Clubs came through, raising almost $4 million dollars in its "Buy a Bomber" campaign. Hendry County's Belle Glade long has been impoverished, but that town's Business and Professional Women's Club managed to sell $160,000 worth of war bonds. Tiny Wachula, in Hardee County, bought more bonds than any similar-sized town in the nation.

Black women's organizations participated in war bond sales, too. Fannye Mae Ponder was president of the State Federation of Colored Women's Clubs during the war years, and she was credited with selling $85,000 worth of bonds just in her hometown of St. Petersburg. Like their white counterparts, black women entertained soldiers with dances and other social events. Celebrities such as Billie Holiday, Bessie Smith, and Josephine Baker performed in Florida, while Ella Fitzgerald introduced her hit "A Tisket, A Tasket" in Miami. Such talented entertainers attracted many white soldiers, and Bernice Sawyer, a member of a prominent black family, said they often "had more whites than colored" at their hotel's nightclub.[26]

Those women were from out of state, however. Florida's biggest homegrown success story in World War II entertainment probably was a white woman, Frances Langford, a native of Mulberry in Polk County. Although largely forgotten today, she became one of the most popular of USO celebrities for soldiers overseas. Her career began in the 1930s, when Hollywood superstar Rudy Vallee was in Florida and heard her on the radio. He invited her to sing on his radio show, and she soon appeared with several of the era's most prominent big bands.

Langford also made movies: the biggest hit of her wartime ones was *Yankee Doodle Dandy* (1942), co-starring James Cagney. She also wrote a column for Hearst newspapers called "Purple Heart Diary," in which she told of the military hospitals she visited all around the world. Like other women overseas, she shared the hardships of sleeping in barracks and eating unpalatable mess hall food. Her name changed to Stuart with a postwar marriage, and she retired back in Florida at Jensen Beach. She was honored by veterans after the war, and such men also successfully pushed for her admittance into the Florida Women's Hall of Fame in 2002.

Although they were not as glamorous as the USO women, the Red Cross also sent many women overseas, to support soldiers' morale and especially to assist refugees. Australia was crowded with both, as in addition to soldiers, civilians from Japanese-held territory escaped there. Mary Irene McKay did not tell her parents that she intended to go overseas when she left for the Washington headquarters of the Red Cross, but she soon was running a facility in Australia for soldiers on leave. As a Floridian in a time before air conditioning and pest control, she was accustomed to insects, and that was the main topic of her letter that ran in the *Tampa Morning Tribune* on June 17, 1943:

> It's been so long since I've had a hot bath that I've lost all previous ideas of cleanliness and sanitation. I just try to keep the edges clean and my fingers crossed.
>
> The house is twenty minutes from [work] by the oldest form of transportation, i.e., the feet. Cockroaches fly around, as big as my hand, and the spiders resemble dinner plates. I've seen snakes . . . built like balloon tires, but fortunately not in the house. . . .
>
> The boys are thrilled to find someone just over from the States, as an American girl is still a rarity. There are plenty of Australian girls who are completely enamored of our boys. Much to the chagrin of the Australian men, and who can blame them?[27]

Her Red Cross canteen probably served food to these soldiers that was in new forms. To lower shipping costs and still deliver vitamin-rich foods, the government subsidized experiments that created many new dehydrated and frozen products during the war. Frozen orange juice concentrate may have been the most popular, and this, too, had a transforming effect in Florida.

Fanny-Fern Smith Davis contributed to this change in the food economy with her work in plant hormones. From the federal government's experimental farms in Beltsville, Maryland, and other sites, she used her doctorate in botany to specialize in grasses. Ultimately her work helped unlock the secrets of plant growth and led to better pasturage for dairy and beef cattle. She later retired to the Florida Panhandle, where Dr. Davis founded the biology department at Okaloosa-Walton Community College.

Food, unfortunately, is a weapon of war, and millions of starving allies whose crops were destroyed by war also had to be fed. American women responded to the food shortage by growing victory gardens, and some—especially college students off for the summer—joined the Women's Land Army (WLA), a nonmilitary organization that supplied farmers with labor during peak seasons. In Florida, where different crops can be grown at every time of year, female participation in agriculture soared. Already by July 1942, less than a year after the United States entered the war, the *Saturday Evening Post* reported that 24 percent of Florida's farm workers were female, the highest ratio in the nation.[28] Most did not join the WLA but instead were simply women who took on agricultural work in addition to their usual tasks.

Floridians were exceptionally fortunate to have access to year-round food because it and other scarce materials were rationed. Books of ration coupons were distributed nationally by household so that each family could get its fair share of coffee, sugar, meat, dairy products, canned vegetables, and more—without the soaring prices that scarcity brings. Although the official decision makers on rationing boards often were men, women were likely to be the volunteers who ran rationing offices and inspected retail stores for compliance under aegis the Office of Price Control. Even fabric and shoes were rationed, and Floridians again had an advantage in not needing winter coats and boots.

Women rarely served on the Selective Service boards that drafted men for military duty, but a few credentialed women worked in that area, too. While retaining her position as an elected judge in Lake Wales, for example, Mada McLendon responded positively to a request from the Polk County Selective Service Board to assist with its duties.[29]

Another wartime lawyer was Charlotte Van Cortlandt Washburne. Admitted to the Florida Bar in 1941, she had come to DeLand's Stetson University from New York, where the Van Cortlandts had pioneered the Dutch colony in the early 1600s. Soon after her law school graduation, she moved to Washington, D.C., and there married fellow Stetson graduate James Faircloth. As an attorney with the Department of Justice, she spent the war years helping prosecute Nazi saboteurs on the East Coast. The couple later settled in Quincy.

Faircloth was a civilian, but two of her legal colleagues joined the naval branches. Anne E'del Deacon of Lantana was admitted to the Florida Bar, married, and enlisted in the navy's WAVES—all in 1942. Her husband was an air corps pilot, and the WAVES allowed married women to enlist if their husbands were not in the navy. Holding the rank of lieutenant junior grade, she was a counter-intelligence officer in Miami. After several years away from Florida and a divorce, Deacon would return and, at age fifty-two, establish a solo practice in Lantana. In 1956 she was appointed as the first female municipal judge in Palm Beach County.

Caroline Adams graduated in 1942 from the law school of Nashville's Vanderbilt University. She took the Florida bar exam in Tallahassee a few months later—and was the only one of thirty-three test takers who passed. When the Marine Corps began accepting women in 1943, Adams served at its base at Cherry Point, North Carolina, and after the war ended was assigned to New York City as a demobilization officer.

In contrast, Ann Marcus had been a lawyer in her native Austria but was unable to practice in the United States—or in Vienna, after Jews were barred from professions. She got out before Jews were confined to Vienna's ghetto and twice escaped death on her trip: because of a reservation mistake, she was not on a ship that was torpedoed, and she lived through an iceberg crash in Canadian waters. Marcus settled in Orlando in 1942 and worked feverishly to defeat the Nazis.

While such individual women made significant contributions to the war effort, the most vital group was arguably the tens of thousands who worked in defense industries. That was most likely to be in Tampa or Jacksonville, both cities with industrial histories and expertise in shipbuilding. Tampa had three major shipyards with some thirty thousand employees, many of whom were women. Although Florida did not have nearly the number of aircraft manufacturers as some other states, especially California, even in the tourist town of Miami, about four thousand women and men worked at Vultee, a major manufacturer of plane parts.

By using the power of their defense contracts, the federal government prodded aircraft plants, shipyards, and other industries to use all available labor—and as a result, black women and men also began to get jobs previously unavailable to them. Tens of thousands left their jobs as maids or fruit pickers for better work. This was often up North, as Florida continued to be segregated, but even in Florida some racial walls began to crack.

Doris McClure, a white woman who was a "labor leaderman" at Tampa's McCloskey Shipyard said "30 [white] men, 32 white women, and 66 colored women worked under me." Among them may have been Mary Glenn Horton of Bealsville, a black community begun after the Civil War. She left her badly paid job as a teacher and instead welded ships on the midnight shift. "For the first time," said her son Sam, "we had things we never had before—like two pairs of shoes!"[30]

The war in fact created the beginnings of the modern civil rights movement, as black soldiers from the North objected to segregation. Miami historian Marvin Dunn wrote:

> Local whites had feared that black military personnel in Miami might have to be allowed to use the whites-only beaches, which were being used to teach white sailors to swim. In order to avoid this, the Dade County Commission on March 14, 1944, gave the Navy permission to establish a temporary beach for Negro trainees on Virginia Key. . . .
>
> Miami blacks began agitating for a permanent bathing beach in

> Dade County. . . . To press home the point, a group of blacks . . . tested their right to use county-owned beaches by swimming by whites-only Baker's Haulover Beach on May 9, 1945. With this event, the civil rights movement in Dade County began, more than a decade before it did in other cities in the South.[31]

Women participated in these beach occupations, while other black women went to court to sue for pay equal to that of white women. Hilda Turner, who was born in 1903, grew up first in Tampa and then in Tallahassee—where she went because Tallahassee had the only high school for blacks on Florida's west coast. After further education in Atlanta, she taught in Hillsborough County schools for blacks. As an unmarried woman without financial support, she needed particular courage to file the equal pay lawsuit. She won at least a limited victory but nonetheless left Tampa for Chicago and did not return until retirement. When interviewed in the early 1990s at Valencia, a longtime downtown restaurant, she would not say that she had feared for her safety, but she did note that it was the first time she had eaten inside the restaurant. In her time, blacks had to get their food at the kitchen window.

Turner's use of the federal courts to establish the principle of equality—and the school board's acceptance of her right to do that—demonstrated that a more serious attitude toward the law was beginning to evolve. In the 1920s a black teacher who sued the board, even a female teacher, risked lynching. At the same time the power elite, including elected officials, continued to make decisions that they saw as suitable for the situation, regardless of what the law said about procedure. The most illustrative example is that a woman was part of Hillsborough's school board when Turner filed her case—even though Hillsborough voters would not elect their first woman to the board until 1967.

The wartime female presence happened because when board member Alfonso Chiaramonte went to war in 1942, no election was held for the vacancy: instead, his male colleagues simply allowed his sister, Frances Chiaramonte (later Fielding) to "fill in." She got her brother's name on the ballot in the 1944 election and campaigned hard for the absent candidate. Winning by thirty-two votes, she surrendered the seat when he returned.

Although few women ran for office—even in the surrogate way that Chiaramonte did—female voters did dominate the 1944 election. An Associated Press article by Jane Eads that circulated in Florida made note of June

4, the twenty-fifth anniversary of Senate passage of the Nineteenth Amendment in 1920 that had given all women the right to vote. Eads recounted that struggle and also pointed out:

> With millions of men away at war, both political parties believe that the women's vote will be the decisive factor in next November's elections. Not only do both parties want the women's vote, they want the women to help with the spade work in their precincts and at headquarters, getting people to register, getting them to the polls on election day.

The League of Women Voters worked to get ballots to soldiers for the 1944 election, and at home it probably was women who formed the majority that gave President Franklin Roosevelt his last term in office. Reelected in November, he would die the following April, just weeks before the war in Europe ended with victory against fascism. Some Florida women had experienced fascism on a personal level.

Future Miamian Ana Raab had a close encounter. Born Jewish in the Carpathian Mountains of Transylvania, she had gone to medical school in Paris. She presented her thesis, "Nietzsche and Psychiatry," just a week before the Nazis invaded France. Hitler was strongly opposed to psychiatry and all intellectualism, especially among Jews, and so with her future husband, Federico Marrero, she fled to the Mediterranean and then on to his home in Cuba. In 1960 they would flee again as Castro took over Cuba. Dr. Marrero retook her medical exam in English and practiced psychiatry until retirement in 1983.

Future Hillsborough County School Board member Yvonne McKitrick was a child in the 1930s when Mussolini's dictatorship began limiting Italian freedom. Her name then was Tomei, and she lived in Italy with her mother while her father, a dishwasher in New Jersey, hurriedly saved enough money to get them to America. She said of her childhood: "I had to wear a Fascist uniform because only Fascists could go to school. I remember the Fascists signs everywhere and having to raise my hand to salute Mussolini."

* * *

The war in Europe ended in May 1945, and the fighting stopped in Asia in September. Among those who came home to Pinellas County was a marine, Colonel Bob Goddard, who brought with him a newspaper clipping about Wanda Wilson, St. Petersburg's Azalea Queen of 1942. Goddard and

Wilson had never met, but he had carried her picture since August 1943, after finding it on the body of a dead Japanese soldier on the South Pacific island of Bougainville. Although neither Wilson nor Goddard knew a local soldier who fought there, they surmised that some American man had seen the newspaper and clipped the story because he found Wilson attractive; perhaps he pretended with other men that she was his girlfriend. Presumably the Japanese man took it from the dead American for similar reasons, and then Goddard took it from him.

The story indicates the great longing these young men had for the girl back home, but some had to wait as much as a year before a ship was available to transport them back. Soldiers who had not served enough time to be eligible for discharge stayed to occupy former fascist nations—but some of those might have the chance to meet American women, as the military began lifting its restrictions on women overseas. The State Department and other governmental agencies also began recruiting civilian women who contracted for overseas work. Jane Steele (later Brannon) was one of those.

Described as "a 90-pound bit of feminine dynamite," she had passed the Florida law exam in 1931 and, after the war, worked in Yugoslavia as legal counsel to the War Crimes Commission. She helped prosecute fascists who had failed to follow the rules of war that had been established by the League of Nations. Eastern European states saw some of the greatest terrorism of the war, and her life amid bombed rubble there was not entirely comfortable. At the same time, though, she enjoyed this rare opportunity to work in international law.

> When I tell you I lived in the Corini Villa, headquarters for the Allied Military Government, the only woman with 57 men—it might sound a bit unconventional to some of my Tampa friends. But all I can say is that they were wonderful—and good bridge players!
>
> Soldiers came to me for everything—love affairs, allotment papers, insurance problems—anything for an excuse, I decided, to just talk to an American woman.[32]

Soldiers' wives back home often had genuine legal problems as well, particularly in Florida, where women's property rights still reflected nineteenth-century attitudes. Changing that was the greatest goal of St. Petersburg's Mary Lou Baker, the second woman in the Florida legislature. She was an attorney married to an army officer, which made her especially aware of the benighted legal status of the state's married women. A Democrat and remarkable feminist, she kept her maiden name. She defended that in the *St. Petersburg Times* of February 12, 1944, saying:

> The purpose of a name is to distinguish an individual, and to distinguish that individual from others. I received my law degree and my certificate to practice as Mary Lou Baker. Mary Lou Baker is my name, and I am entitled to every particle of good will attached to the use of my name as a result of my own efforts, but nothing more. It might even be considered unsportsmanlike for me to use the name of my husband on the ballot.

She had won her first election in 1942, defeating one-term incumbent Stanley C. Minshall and a third candidate, Henry D. Goff, in the Democratic primary. Goff's platform was largely limited to a proposal to exclude non-native Americans from the legislature—and it was not coincidental that both of his opponents were Canadians at birth. That platform was not popular with Pinellas voters, most of whom had been born elsewhere, and Goff was last in the first primary, winning just 1,884 votes compared with 4,783 for Minshall and 5,034 for Baker. In the runoff, she defeated the incumbent by 5,988 to 3,978, carrying 69 of the county's 77 precincts. Even in Pinellas, a stronghold of midwestern newcomers who usually voted Republican, that party still was so weak that Baker had no general election opponent.[33]

In the 1943 session she successfully sponsored two bills that were important to women's civil rights. One permitted married women to manage their separate property independently and to make contracts without a husband's signature. The other allowed powers of attorney to be executed by either husband or wife. This was particularly vital when husbands who were ignorant of state law went overseas without granting a power of attorney to their wives. Many married women, for example, did not have their name on the family savings account or safe deposit box, and therefore could not get access to it. Some were not allowed to take their own jewelry from a safe deposit box.

In its July 1943 issue the *Florida Law Journal* called Baker's new legislation "the most historic change which has occurred in the basic law of the State of Florida in the past generation." Yet it barely passed, with the margin in the House being a mere 46–38. The *Journal* editorialized that it was only "through her tenacity and courage [that] it was finally enacted into law in the closing days of the session."[34]

Florida's Second Woman in the Legislature: Mary Lou Baker

Like Florida's first female lawmaker, Edna Giles Fuller of Orlando, Mary Lou Baker grew up in a political household—but she was younger and more ardently feminist than Fuller—and Mary Lou Baker was among the first American women to be pregnant while in office.

She was born in British Columbia in 1915. Her family moved first to Provo, Utah, and then to Pinellas County in 1925. Determined from her youth to be a lawyer like her father, Judge Lee L. Baker, she also followed in the footsteps of her mother, Mary Vesgar Baker, who was president of the Florida Democratic Women's Clubs and twice a delegate to national Democratic conventions.

After graduation from Clearwater High School, Mary Lou Baker studied at Florida Southern College in Lakeland and then, like most female attorneys in Florida, went on to Stetson College of Law in DeLand. During college she also worked in the 1935 and 1937 sessions of the legislature. Baker earned her law degree in 1938 and married Searle Harris Matthews a few months later. She nonetheless worked during both the 1939 and 1941 sessions, the first as a lobbyist for social services and the second as head of indexing for the official journals of both chambers.

Her husband joined the army and had risen to the rank of captain by 1942, when she was elected to the legislature. He served in the Pacific theater of operations while her brother, Robert Warren Baker, flew combat missions over Europe. At her 1944 reelection, both endorsed her from afar.

She won by a commanding 12,335 votes to 7,643.

Her newborn son, conceived when her husband was home on leave, was not a determent to her ability to represent Pinellas in the next legislative session. In addition to her jury bill, Baker also introduced bills ranging from improved transportation to enriching bread with vitamins and regulating eyeglass sales. By the 1946 election, however, the *St. Petersburg Times* backed off from its previous support. The ostensible reason was that she had failed to fulfill a campaign promise to create a local commission to regulate electricity rates. Baker responded that Florida Power had voluntarily lowered rates and

continued

that there was no political consensus on whether such commissions should exist at a county or city level.

It is entirely possible, though, that the editors succumbed to the era's general belief that with the war over, women should return to their "proper place" and leave public affairs to men. On May 1, 1946, the paper reneged on its original pride in her and instead said in endorsing a young man: "It has been no advantage to the best interests of Pinellas for Miss Baker to have been the only female member of the legislature. . . . Rather, it would probably constitute a legislative liability."*

Voters agreed, choosing her opponent, Democrat Charles J. Schuh Jr., by 8,820 to 4,552. The legislature returned to being all male. Baker and her son sailed for Okinawa, where her husband was part of the occupation forces. She maintained a public presence, though, through weekly columns in the *Tampa Tribune* on postwar Asia. When the family returned in 1948, she continued to practice law. She worked for Planned Parenthood, then a new organization in Florida, and died in 1965. She was just fifty years old.

Note: * Thanks are due to Lois Riccardi of USF's St. Petersburg's campus for her 2010 paper on Mary Lou Baker. See also Ellen J. Babb, "Women and War: St. Petersburg Women during World War II," *The Florida Historical Quarterly* 73, no. 1 (1994): 43–61, and especially Allen Morris, *Women in the Florida Legislature* (Tallahassee: Florida House of Representatives, 1995), 12–14.

The conservatism of the state's lawmakers was even more evident with her bill to make it lawful for women to serve on juries. The Nineteenth Amendment to the U.S. Constitution had granted only the vote, and the proposed Equal Rights Amendment that would ensure other civil liberties made little progress.[35] Every state enacted different laws on whether women could be jurors, and southern states were slow to include them. Male attorneys, especially prosecutors, argued that women were too emotional to hear testimony on murder and other serious crimes, and many men were reluctant to allow women to make decisions in rape cases.

Representative Warren Sanchez of Live Oak was typical when he proclaimed his certainty that his colleagues did not want their wives and sisters exposed to the embarrassment of hearing evidence in such cases—and he also fretted about the cost of providing women's restrooms in courthouses.

These arguments prevailed, as Baker's bill to allow women to serve on juries was defeated in both the 1943 and 1945 legislative sessions.

Although the status of Florida women remained low, the national Democratic Party elected Dorothy Vredenburgh Bush, who eventually retired to Naples, as its secretary in 1944. She was a feature of every nominating convention through 1988, calling the roll of states in the accent of her native Alabama. Efficient and calm during sessions that sometimes were tumultuous, she earned the respect of both politicians and the media. She would die in 1991 at age seventy-five and was entombed at Naples Memorial Gardens.

In the same election year of 1944, Edith S. Stearns had her name on the general ballot in Florida's fourth congressional district, which centered in Miami. The founder and president of the Pan American League, Stearns ran to support such global views. As a Republican, however, she stood no chance in overwhelmingly Democratic Florida. She died in Miami in 1958.

Irene Ann Byram of Jacksonville set another sort of record when she became Florida's first licensed female bartender in 1944. Although female innkeepers freely poured alcohol in colonial days, the nation became more puritanical in the nineteenth century, and male bartenders promoted fears that having women behind the counter would encourage prostitution. Florida was not the only state that enacted laws prohibiting women from this occupation, but during the war, when able-bodied men were supposed to be in the military and women were expected to fill their jobs at home, legislators began repealing such laws. After a Michigan woman won her court case on the subject, other women followed, and in Florida, Governor Spessard Holland publicized the innovation by personally swearing in Irene Byram.

Her personal history did not fit the public image of bartenders. Her parents, Adolph and Mary Makowski, had emigrated from Poland, and she was born in Detroit in 1912. She married and had two children, and the family moved first to Wauchula and then to Jacksonville in the 1930s. When she was licensed, Byram was a thirty-two-year-old mother with young children, and her marriage would last forty-nine years, until her husband's death. According to her obituary in the *Tampa Tribune*, she had twelve great-grandchildren when she died just short of her hundredth birthday.

Most women, of course, did not want to become bartenders—and few fought to retain the jobs they had held during the war or ran for political office. Judy Cooper of the *St. Petersburg Times* inadvertently summed up women's limited status more than a decade later when she wrote that "1945 was a big year for women. Miss [Mary Lou] Baker was appointed chairman of a newly-created women's rights committee, Mrs. Lamar Bledsoe became Clerk, and a woman was Secretary of the Senate. That was Miss Hazel Seymour, who served during the military absence of Secretary Robert W. Davis."[36] What the author failed to point out, however, was that the latter two women were legislative employees, not elected officials, and that most states had women in these clerical positions much earlier.

On the other hand, in addition to chairing the new Women's Rights Committee mentioned in the *Times*, Mary Lou Baker also was vice chair of the House Education Committee in the 1945 session—a position coveted by many men. Her bills on both property rights and jury duty were influenced greatly by Miami attorney Ethel Ernest Murrell. She had a prestigious education that culminated in Paris at the Sorbonne and was wealthy enough to travel in Europe and Asia, where she lectured on women's rights. Settling in Miami, she married widower John Murrell and became one of the first female graduates of the law school at University of Miami. Having already been an active feminist on the international stage, Murrell took on her adopted state:

> She promoted a three-point program to achieve women's equality . . . in the new state constitution. She started a ten-year campaign in 1933 to get the state legislature to pass an act endowing married women with the same property rights as men. During her campaign for women's rights, she wrote a column, "Law for the Ladies," which was carried in eight Florida newspapers, and she conducted a legal forum over radio station WKAT. As chair of a Florida State Bar Association committee, she drafted . . . and worked for the passage of the Florida Married Women's Act in 1943, as well as for legislation permitting women to serve on grand and petit juries in Florida. Ms. Murrell tried to get the Equal Rights Amendment made a part of the Florida Constitution in 1946. She was elected chairperson of the National Woman's Party . . . in 1951.[37]

But Murrell's 1946 attempt to revise the state constitution was unsuccessful, and Mary Lou Baker lost her bid for reelection to the legislature that year. Baker had attended coeducational institutions and supported the concept of coeducation, but her electoral defeat meant that it was entirely male legislators who made the decision to change the nature of the state's two universities for whites.

The War and the Equal Rights Amendment

On March 3, 1943, a little more than a year after U.S. entry into World War II, the *St. Petersburg Times* ran an article on the Equal Rights Amendment (ERA). Written by the National Woman's Party, which grew out of the movement for the vote, it was filed in 1923 as an amendment to the U.S. Constitution. Until World War II, Democratic Senator Hattie Caraway of Arkansas was the only female member of Congress to support it.

Members of the Business and Professional Women's Clubs (BPW) worked hard for it, but other liberals shied away because of concerns that a constitutional mandate for equality would nullify protective labor laws for women. It rarely occurred to anyone that the obvious solution to this "problem" was to extend such labor protections to men, but the entrance of women into wartime blue-collar jobs—in which women were invariably paid less for doing the same task as men—brought the ERA to public attention again. With eight women in Congress, only one of whom was in the Senate, the *Times* said:

> Half of the women members of Congress have now announced their support of the proposed "equal rights" amendment to the Constitution—for the first time since the amendment was introduced in the national legislature 20 years ago. Four of the eight women legislators have definitely come out for the amendment since the opening of the present Congress, and a fifth has made a statement which seems to indicate that it will have her support if and when it reaches a vote in the House.
>
> Mary Norton [D-NJ], chairman of the House Labor Committee, opposes the amendment; Frances P. Bolton [R] of Ohio and Jessie Sumner [R] of Illinois have not committed themselves. [The] latest of the women legislators to come out for the amendment is Clare Boothe Luce [R], author of "The Women" [a play and movie], now serving her first term as representative from Connecticut. Margaret Chase Smith [R] of Maine and Winifred Stanley [R] of New York announced their support a few days earlier.

continued

Edith Nourse Rogers [R] of Massachusetts, dean of the women members of Congress, said in a speech on the birthday of Susan B. Anthony, Feb. 15: "With women in every phase of war work, from the WAACs and WAVES to welders, it is only justice that they should have equal rights with men."

Opposition to the amendment lines up about as it did in 1923. . . . Women's trade union organizations oppose it on the ground that women in industry need special protection, and the League of Women Voters says the business of remedying discriminatory laws should be left to the states. . . .

Florida is pointed out by the Woman's Party as the state whose laws best illustrate the discrimination against women. . . . Florida, says the Woman's Party, classifies married women as "financially and legally irresponsible. . . ."

California and Nevada also require wives to obtain court orders . . . to engage in business separately from their husbands. Certain limitations on the making of contracts by wives in Louisiana, Michigan, and Nebraska are also complained of. . . . In Idaho, Virginia, and Texas, the support of illegitimate children rests solely with mothers. Earnings of minor children belong to the father in Massachusetts, Michigan, and New York, and in Alabama and Georgia, the father is preferred as a guardian. . . . A Kentucky law makes drunkenness a ground for divorce of wives, but wives may not divorce husbands for drunkenness. . . .

Despite wartime change, the ERA never made it to the floor of either chamber of Congress—and thirty years later, when it did pass out of Congress by the required two-thirds majority, an insufficient number of state legislatures failed to ratify it.

Notes: See chapter 7 for more about the 1923 filing in Congress. For biographies of these women and more information on the amendment, see Doris Weatherford, *Women in American Politics: History and Milestones* (Washington, D.C.: Congressional Quarterly Press, 2012).

In the 1947 legislative session Tallahassee's Florida State College for Women (FSCW) became Florida State University (FSU), while the University of Florida (UF) at Gainesville opened to women. Prior to this, women could enroll in only three graduate departments at UF: architecture, pharmacy, and law. As late as 1941 there were just thirty female students among more than three thousand men at the Gainesville campus. Each semester these women had to sign an affidavit swearing that they were over age twenty-one and could not obtain the courses they needed anywhere else in Florida. Lois Thacker Graessle, the only woman in her 1941 law school class, recalled she "had to learn not to blush during the daily verbal assaults from the university's male population. . . . Fellow students would shuffle their feet as she entered the classroom."[38]

The reason that the legislature made the two institutions coeducational was not sudden enlightenment on the issue of equality. Instead, it was the flood of veterans who returned home eager to catch up on their lives—and to take advantage of the G.I. Bill of Rights, which paid the cost at any college where the veteran could gain admission. Universities were so overwhelmed with applicants that some states flatly banned admission of female students. There was no Equal Rights Amendment to prevent this, and women nationwide acquiesced: they quietly paid the higher tuition at private, single-sex colleges rather than insisting on a right to enroll at their tax-supported public institutions.

In Florida far too many veterans were eligible for admission to the all-male university in Gainesville than could be accommodated. The legislature resolved the problem by making Tallahassee's Florida State College for Women coeducational, renaming it Florida State University. Both institutions remained all white, and men became the strong majority in both.

Some FSCW students regretted the change, but no one asked the opinions of young women. Appearing to be opposed to veterans was taboo, and the result was that this haven for developing female leadership was transformed into a football-oriented school much like UF. Male students soon led the school's organizations, and young women who once had been club presidents became secretaries—or held no offices at all. On the other hand, women could finally go to the state's premier university. For decades into the future, though, they were discouraged from enrolling in male-dominated schools such as medicine and law, where informal quotas limited their numbers. Top administrators at both universities were male; female faculty were few and almost always paid less.

Mary Lou Baker's jury bill finally passed in the 1949 session because of Florida's third female representative, Edna Pearce. A descendent of pioneer ranching families in Highlands County, she was educated at Florida Southern College in Lakeland and at Florida College for Women in Tallahassee. She was "a prosperous, attractive 37-year-old cattlewoman from Fort Basinger" when she won the 1948 election—without ever facing an opponent on the ballot.[39] Pearce was so widely respected that when the incumbent announced that he would not seek reelection, she visited all potential candidates and let them know of her intention to run. No one chose to file against her.

She downplayed the jury issue in her campaign, instead emphasizing her chief goal—paving the only road from Fort Basinger to Sebring. Representative Pearce had friends in Tallahassee from her days at FSCW and her activism on behalf of the State Cattlemen's Association as well as the Florida Farm Bureau. The result was that she won appointment to both the powerful Appropriations Committee and the Committee on Public Roads. Not surprisingly, her constituents soon were able to drive on something other than rutted sand and mud.

Handily reelected in 1950, Pearce also sponsored bills that were in line with the agenda of the Florida Federation of Women's Clubs: among them were bills establishing a hospital for alcoholics, the labeling of containers with poisons, and accurate labeling of Florida beef. She chaired the Women's Rights Committee that had been created in the 1945 session, and was sufficiently respected by the House leadership that she chaired the Committee on Public Health and Safety in the 1953 session. Neither chamber, however, was willing to take up her bill to "abolish discriminatory wages based on sex."[40]

After the 1953 session Pearce vacationed on the *Queen Mary*, where she met an Englishman. They married and, giving up her political career, she moved to London. Much later, after returning to Florida, she was honored by the 1983 legislature for her "significant contributions to her community and to the State of Florida." Even in the revived feminism of the 1980s, though, no one was sufficiently aware of women's history to point out her successful sponsorship of the jury bill.

Women's history indeed is so ephemeral, and their lack of civil rights is considered so much an embarrassing aside, that even feminists did not know about the jury issue—but worse, the story was not yet complete. Pearce's act was limited by the political reality of her time: it merely allowed women to serve on juries, and they still were treated differently from men in that women would not be routinely called for duty. Only members of the League of Women Voters and a few other conscientious women were willing to follow its provisions, which required a woman to go to her courthouse and actively volunteer to be called. Thus female attorneys, defendants, and witnesses still usually faced a juror box with only men—and white men at that.

* * *

Black people had almost no chance of being judged by their peers, as they were rarely chosen for juries. Discrimination continued in education, too, as black students, both male and female, had to seek professional education elsewhere. Florida remained so adamantly segregated that no racial minorities were admitted to the state's graduate schools. Those who earned bachelor's degrees from the public Florida Agricultural and Mechanical College or from private institutions could not further their education within Florida. Instead, the state was so dedicated to all-white status at its Gainesville and Tallahassee universities that it paid tuition for Florida blacks at out-of-state institutions rather than integrate.

This prejudice had an ironic effect, though, as some African Americans obtained excellent credentials at superior universities. Evelyn Stocking Crosslin was one. A Daytona Beach native, she graduated from Bethune-Cookman and went on to Meharry Medical College, a historic institution for blacks in Nashville. She returned to Volusia County, where she provided medical services, especially to the poor, for almost a half century. Dr. Crosslin maintained her career even after she married and bore three children. An activist in civic and professional causes, she mentored the careers of many during her forty-seven years on the staff of Halifax Medical Center. She died in 1991 and was posthumously inducted into the Florida Women's Hall of Fame in 1995.

But the state paid only tuition for black graduate students who were forced out of state; it did not pay living expenses or travel costs. African Americans had to figure out how to leave their homes for long periods of time and sustain themselves in a place that was not home. The biggest positive change for Florida blacks, however, came in 1946, after the U.S. Supreme Court ruled in a Texas case that voters could not be blocked from party primaries on the basis of race. The Florida Democratic Executive Committee quietly changed its rules to eliminate its longtime "white primary" but did not advertise that fact to potential black voters.[41]

The postwar legislature decided that rather than pay out-of-state tuition for black law students, segregation would be more cost efficient if a law school were created at Florida A&M. Its first alumna was Bernice Gaines (later Dorn), who graduated in 1958 in a class that included a dozen men. After brief practice in her hometown of Jacksonville, Gaines returned to Tallahassee and taught contract law. She then married, moved north, and finally retired in Satellite Beach. Her 1958 admission to the Florida Bar came sixty years after the admission of the first white woman, in 1898.

But even in A&M's coeducational undergraduate setting, gender bias was axiomatic. Although the college had existed for decades, Gaines's roommate, Norma Solomon (later White), "was the first woman to march" with the band that made the school famous at football games.[42] Decades later the band remains largely male—with a history of egregious hazing that brought a 2011 fatality.

The legislature elevated A&M's status from a college to a university in 1953—the same year as the graduation of its most prominent student of the era, Althea Gibson. She went on to be the first African American woman to achieve major athletic fame. Born in South Carolina in 1927, she grew up in New York, where at age fifteen she won the 1942 state tennis championship for black women. She would go on to claim the National Negro Women's Tennis championship from 1948 to 1958.

Gibson nonetheless struggled financially before enrolling at Florida A&M in 1949. It gave a firm foundation to her career, however, and she won national tournaments during her four years as a student. Just three years after graduation, in 1956, the U.S. State Department sponsored her on a tour of Southeast Asia, with the aim of demonstrating that Americans were beginning to overcome the racial prejudice from which Gibson had suffered earlier.

The next year she became the first woman of color to compete in England's famous Wimbledon—which she also won. Associated Press named her the 1957 Woman Athlete of the Year, another first for black women. Welcomed home with a parade in New York City, she published her autobiography, *I Always Wanted to Be Somebody,* in 1958. After claiming the World Professional Tennis Championship in 1960, she played professional golf for another decade. In 1973, when she was forty-five, she surprised the sports world by announcing her intention to return to professional tennis. Soon afterward she became one of the relatively few women inducted into the Black Sports Hall of Fame, and she was inducted into the Florida Women's Hall of Fame in 1999. Althea Gibson died in New Jersey in 2003.

Much less attention has gone to another black athlete, Theresa Manuel. A lifelong resident of Tampa, she was Florida's first female Olympian of any race. She specialized in track and field and was good enough to be chosen for the 1948 Olympics in London—the first time that black women had a significant Olympic presence. As a teenager, she led the girls' basketball team at Tampa's segregated Middleton High School and then went on to graduate from Alabama's Tuskegee Institute, a historic school for blacks. It was at Tuskegee that she switched from basketball to track, and in the Olympics she competed both in the eighty-meter dash and in javelin throwing. Manuel then returned to Middleton as a coach and, in 1976, was chosen Florida Basketball Coach of the Year. In 2014 she was still living in West Tampa.

Like Theresa Manuel, Carrie Patterson and Wilhemina Jakes should be better known, in their case for their role as civil rights leaders. When the two young women paid their fare and boarded a Tallahassee city bus on May 27, 1956, all the seats were full except in the "white" section. The driver ordered them to stand in the back of the bus, the "colored" area. Tired and not wanting to stand, they asked for a refund of their fares. Instead, the driver called the police and the two were arrested. Racists later terrorized them by burning a cross in front of their residence.

Like Rosa Parks in Birmingham a few months earlier in December 1955, they found that their action prompted a bus boycott. Tallahassee blacks formed car pools to take one another to and from work, and because of the drastic decline in revenue, the bus company closed for a month. "We would rather walk in dignity than ride in humiliation" became the motto, and many African Americans held out for two years. The boycott succeeded in May 1958, when the company capitulated and agreed to all demands, including the hiring of black (male) drivers. A monument on the FAMU campus has been erected to honor the young women, but they remain less recognized than the men who followed up on their action.

Another woman who merits more attention is Patricia Stephens Due. She was a student at Florida A&M in February 1960, when she and others were arrested for "sitting in" at a whites-only lunch counter. According to Morgan Watkins, who wrote her obituary in the *Gainesville Sun* (February 8, 2012), "Due and several others refused to pay their fines, spending 49 days in jail. It was considered the civil rights movement's first jail-in, which became a powerful tactic in the following years." Her husband, John Due, was a civil rights attorney, and the two spent their lives working for the cause—even though Patricia was so light-skinned that she could have passed for white. As a result of injury by a tear gas bomb that "a police officer threw in her face," she wore sunglasses for the rest of her life.

Dr. Danzelle Dean Simpson was a Miami pediatrician who, in 1955, became the first African American of either gender appointed to the Florida Board of Medical Examiners. Her mother, Kate Stirrup Dean, had begun a forty-year career as a Dade County educator in 1922; despite being widowed in 1924, she brought up her daughter to great success. The valedictorian of George Carver High School, Danzelle Dean graduated magna cum laude from Fisk University and was at the top of her class at Meharry Medical College, both historic institutions in Nashville, Tennessee. She married in 1949 and spent the rest of her life in Miami, where she was the first woman and the first black on the admissions committee of the University of Miami Medical School. Her white peers also elected her as a Fellow of the American Academy of Pediatrics—but when she traveled, she could not rent a room at most Florida hotels.

Some whites, especially Jews, stood up for black civil rights. Indeed, John O. Brown of the Congress of Racial Equality (CORE) said two-thirds of the sit-in participants who integrated public facilities were white. He added that "had it not been for white people, there never would have been a CORE chapter in Miami. Jack Gordon of Miami Beach, who later became a powerful state senator, and his wife, Barbara, were among our most visible supporters."[43] CORE was a more radical organization than the NAACP, and Miami Beach librarian Ruth Perry, a white woman, served as CORE's secretary for many years.

Mabel Norris Reese probably made the greatest sacrifice for black rights of any white woman in Florida. In 1947, two years after World War II ended, she and her husband bought the *Mount Dora Topic*, a weekly newspaper in Lake County's historic town of Mount Dora. They came from Ohio, where "this delicate young woman and mother was a hard-nosed journalist with . . . the *Akron Beacon-Journal*."[44] When they settled in Lake County, she did not realize that because she was a liberal woman from the North, powerful Sheriff Willis McCall would see her as a challenge.

Despite her determination to make a financial success of the paper (which suggested not rocking the local boat), Reese's journalistic training told her to interview both sides on issues—and the sheriff strongly objected to any

Giving Her Life for Liberty: Harriette Moore

Harriette Vyda Simms met Harry Moore when both taught in Cocoa, at the town's only school for black children. They wed on Christmas Day, 1926, and Harriette continued teaching after the births of their two daughters. Her parents gave them land to build a house in the Brevard County village of Mims.

The area's segregated school system allotted $27.04 per black student, compared with $69.05 for whites. Such disparities motivated the Moores to establish a chapter of the NAACP in 1934. Several lynchings of black men impelled them to greater activism, and by 1944 a resentful school board fired the couple. Times were changing, though, as African American expectations rose because of their experience during World War II. The Progressive Voters League that Harry organized soon registered massive numbers of black voters across Florida. Racists took note and began to threaten the Moores.

In 1948 Harriette finally got another job at Lake Park Elementary School in Palm Beach County. The Moores rented rooms there but used their Mims home during school holidays. On Christmas Day in 1951 they quietly celebrated their silver wedding anniversary and went to sleep. At 10:20 a bomb exploded under their bed, powerful enough that people in Titusville, four miles away, heard the explosion.

The nearest hospital that would accept blacks was in Sanford, thirty-five miles away. Titusville had an ambulance service, but it was for whites only—and in any case no one in Mims had a telephone to call an ambulance. George Simms, Harriet's brother, used his car to drive the badly wounded Moores to Sanford, but Harry died at midnight. Harriette lived long enough to talk to FBI agents, but knowing that many local officials were Klan members, she refused to allow them into her hospital room. Harriette Moore died the day after Harry Moore's funeral.

Note: Ben Green, *Before His Time: The Untold Story of Harry T. Moore, America's First Civil Rights Martyr* (New York: Free Press, 1999). See also Robert W. Saunders, *Bridging the Gap: Continuing the Florida NAACP Legacy of Harry T. Moore* (Tampa: University of Tampa Press, 2000).

version of a news story other than his own. Their first clashes were over issues concerning white men, but she stepped up her criticism of him when local blacks told her that he had murdered two young black men after falsely accusing them of rape. She editorialized against him again when the sheriff led opposition to the admission of the children of a family named Platt to Lake County schools. They were descendants of North Carolina's Lumbee tribe, and the sheriff objected to educating them—saying of a girl, "I don't like the shape of that one's nose."[45]

Things came to a head in 1954, when Reese advocated obeying the Supreme Court's decision on school integration and criticized McCall for his activism in the National Association for the Advancement of White People. His Ku Klux Klan henchmen burned a cross on her property, poisoned her dog, and left their KKK signature on her office windows. Her advertisers withdrew their business, subscriptions plummeted, and she was forced to flee to Volusia County. The *Daytona Beach Journal* hired her—but, of course, at a lower status. Its publishers were a couple named Davidson, German Jews who understood the dangers of racism.

While Mabel Norris Reese escaped with her life, Harry and Harriette Moore died because of their political activism. Racists bombed their home in the Brevard County town of Mims on Christmas night, 1951—on their twenty-fifth wedding anniversary.

* * *

With World War II won, women's organizations returned to their original aims. The Business and Professional Women continued to lead on feminist politics, as it used the massive increase of women in the wartime labor force to point out how routinely women were paid less than men for the same work. BPW found congressional sponsors—especially Miami Democrat Claude Pepper—for the proposed Women's Pay Act of 1945. If such wage discrimination had not been banned during the war, however, it was hardly likely to happen after the emergency was over; it would not pass until 1963, when John F. Kennedy was president.

At its conventions immediately following the war, the Florida Federation of Women's Clubs "set goals for a peacetime society" that included expansion of women's clubs abroad. The 1948 FFWC convention, held in St. Petersburg, was called "Pan American," as women attended from Canada, Cuba, Brazil, Ecuador, and the Dominican Republic. In the next decade some members would follow through by visiting Cuba and even the Philippines. The FFWC also promoted:

> Efforts on behalf of the United Nations, the European Recovery Program, assistance to those in need abroad . . . , scholarships for foreign students, and an international good will program to promote friendly contacts among women of the world. . . . Isolationism as a political ideology was no longer a factor in the thinking of most citizens. Optimism prevailed.[46]

Women's participation in civic affairs rose throughout the nation, as many felt they had earned that right during the war. The FFWC was not unusual in seeing its membership soar: during the first two years after the war's end, it rose by more than five thousand, with thirty-six new clubs in the state. Its horizons broadened enough that although the organization remained all white, the highest priority on its state legislative agenda was an "industrial school for Negro girls, staffed by trained and capable Negroes."[47]

The clubs lobbied the Railroad Commission, which regulated transportation, to mandate that bus and train stations be kept clean. Other points of its legislative agenda included expanded education in music and art, a juvenile court system, and laws on adoption—saying that it was a known fact that babies were being sold in Florida. The 1949 national convention of the General Federation of Women's Clubs was in Hollywood, and former first lady Eleanor Roosevelt spoke on human rights. In 1950 the FFWC finally won its long campaign for mandatory fences to keep cattle off highways, and it began another long effort to ban billboard advertising.

The federation's most important decision of the decade, though, was to donate to the federal government the Everglades land that members had bought during the past two decades. Known as Royal Palm Park, it demonstrated the women's willingness to put money where their mouths were: during the boom years of the 1920s, when many developers wanted to drain the swamp, FFWC women throughout the state contributed to buy the land for preservation.

They built a three-story lodge that was used primarily by visiting scientists but otherwise left their portion of the Glades undisturbed. In 1947 they granted their lodge and land to the National Park Service. With additional federal land, President Harry Truman dedicated Everglades National Park on December 6, 1947. Seminoles sat on the dais with him, as did FFWC officials, including pioneer Ivy Stranahan and former congresswoman Ruth

Bryan Owen.[48] The state road department soon hired "Indian women to plant grass along the shoulders of the highways."[49]

The state president of BPW in 1952–53 was Wilhelmina Harvey of Key West, who was so busy as a civic activist there that people referred to her as the mayor—although it was her husband who actually held that office. She graduated from Florida State College for Women in 1937 and was an educator and businesswoman all her life. In 1982 she was chosen as one of four living women admitted to the inaugural Florida Women's Hall of Fame.

The postwar period brought another new organization of women. Although Florida had its first female lawyer in 1898, no state organization existed until 1951, when the Florida Association for Women Lawyers (FAWL) began. Among its founders was Emma Roesing, a Chicago native who was educated at New York's Columbia University. She had moved to Miami in 1925, when she was hired as the office manager of the legal department at Florida Power and Light. Admitted to the bar in 1933, she worked in private practice with future Judge Mattie Belle Davis.[50] Roesing was active in the National Association of Women Lawyers (NAWL) and co-chaired two NAWL conventions when they were held in Miami Beach. Another FAWL founder was Frances M. Lovelace of St. Petersburg, a member of the Democratic National Committee and an unsuccessful candidate for the Florida House in 1952. Had she won, it would have been the same seat formerly held by Mary Lou Baker.

FAWL's first president was Anna Brenner Mankes Meyers, who had been born in Poland in 1896. Also educated at Columbia University, she moved to Miami and was admitted to the Florida Bar in 1936. Her name changed from Mankes to Meyers when she was widowed and remarried, and in 1941 she was admitted to practice before the U.S. Supreme Court. After appointment to the Dade County School Board in 1953, Meyers would be reelected to that post for almost two decades. She also held office in the International Federation of Women Lawyers.

Rebecca Bowles Marks followed Meyers as FAWL president, but she was illustrative of the limited roles for female attorneys. She spent her life in Tallahassee, where she was a research assistant to Supreme Court Justice B. K. Roberts. The status of women as judges also rose only slowly. Florida had had its first female judge soon after the First World War, as Edith Meserve Atkinson won election to the Juvenile Court of Dade County in 1922.[51] A decade later Mary Kennerly Buckles was appointed to the Putnam County court, but she served only briefly. Voters in Lake Wales consistently reelected

Judge Mada McLendon after 1938—but despite the presumed shortage of men during the war, the state had no new women as judges in the 1940s.

Countless male lawyers and judges were exempted from the military draft—often by draft boards on which they and their colleagues sat—and the judicial system remained overwhelmingly male. Ida Rountree Pridgen of Gainesville, however, was an exception as a law professor. A librarian and administrator at the University of Florida College of Law since 1929, she passed the bar in 1943—and because of the war "was called upon to serve as a faculty member."[52] Her husband had been disabled in World War I, and she supported their two children by supplementing her meager pay from the university by running a boarding house. It catered exclusively to (male) law students, and many of her "boys" said she influenced their years in Gainesville more than anyone else.

Jeanette Gifford Mullens Smith did not find any professional advantage during the war, but when the University of Miami was crowded with veterans after the war, she was hired as an assistant professor. She was an alumna of that school, having graduated magna cum laude in 1937. She went on to be the first librarian of the Dade County Law Library—which turned out to be essentially a teaching position, as she discovered that many male lawyers "had only rudimentary ideas of looking up law." She had preschool children when the University of Miami hired her in 1949—a time when female professors with children were unconventional in any field. Colleague Daniel Murray later recalled:

> The UM Law School would take someone with a brain regardless of their sex. . . . [She] was unassuming and modest, with an incredible ability to argue on any subject, and win! She was not soft, but she was simpatico with her students . . . [who discovered] a woman professor with a mind as sharp as a razor![53]

Smith still had young children when she co-authored the first edition of *Florida Constitutional Law* in 1958. Promoted to full professor in 1969, she was the only woman among twenty-two men at the University of Miami who held that rank. She also served on many commissions, including one to create a program in poverty law. Two other women, Minnette Massey and Sonia Mentschikoff, would join her on the UM law school faculty, and when Mentschikoff retired in 1976, she was its dean.

Monroe County voters elected Eva Warner Gibson as a judge of the juvenile court in 1950. Gibson had taught math and worked as a deputy tax collector, as well as other government jobs, and no one opposed her when she ran for reelection in 1956. In that same year Anne Deacon was appointed as a judge in Palm Beach County.

The most surprising thing for women in the legal profession was in 1944, when "after a whirlwind campaign on a bicycle," Mary Schulman won election as prosecuting attorney in Leon County, home of the state capital. Reelected in 1948, Schulman later worked for the attorney general. According to *Florida Women of Distinction*, published by Eloise N. Cozens in 1957, Schulman was overseeing the legal aspects of more than twenty-five state boards, ranging from accountancy to water research.

Academia, however, is not as liberal as many people believe, and at the University of Florida, Ida Pridgen was not invited to continue teaching law after World War II ended. She turned to selling real estate, an occupation in which women remained rare but in which incomes soared during the postwar years. Although the mortgage was rarely in a woman's name, many women had saved their good paychecks from wartime jobs and were able to finance family homes. In addition to its educational benefits, the G.I. Bill could be used to buy a home or business, and with building materials again available after the war, Florida real estate roared as it had in the 1920s. Because the postwar federal government ensured mortgages, however, the 1950s boom would not sour as it had in the 1920s.

Florida's new homes and rising population could be seen even in towns so small that they are still rural today. Palmetto, which is between Sarasota and Tampa, had a woman as postmaster during this era, and growth can be seen in her career. Edith Mathis Cox was an experienced bookkeeper when she assumed the job in 1947, after her husband's death. Records showed that the post office had done $7,112 worth of business in 1935; that almost doubled in 1940, with $12,209; in 1945, when the war ended, it was $23,361; and by 1950 it had grown to $33,129. A 1954 newspaper article featuring Cox said that just three years later, revenue had jumped to $52,221. In less than twenty years, it had increased more than fivefold, even in this isolated town.

Yet the headline for this story did not recount Cox's executive abilities but instead was titled "Palmettoans Dispute Bradenton Claim to Prettiest Postmaster."[54] The *St. Petersburg Times* was unembarrassed to say that a week earlier, it had published a story declaring Bradenton's female postmaster to be the prettiest in the state. She may well have been, given that Palmetto's Cox was old enough to have two married daughters—but in a reasonable journalistic world, beauty never should have been a consideration for judging postal management. Much attitudinal change remained to be done.

* * *

The 1950s marked the fourth decade that Florida women had the vote, and in 1951 Fort Myers had a female mayor. Florence Fritz was a popular local writer, whose work included *Bamboo and Sailing Ships: The Story of Thomas A. Edison and Fort Myers.* The *Miami News* published her 1950 story, "Old Indian Route Becomes a Modern Highway," about the opening of the completed road between Fort Myers and Immokalee. She served just one year as mayor and merits further research.

The Florida House finally had its fourth female member in 1954. Mary Patton was born in the Indian Territory, before that became the state of Oklahoma, and was educated there and in Texas. She worked as an aide to her husband, a representative from Apalachicola, a coastal town in the Panhandle's Franklin County, and when Bryant Patton died in 1954, she easily won the special election to replace him. Myth has it that women rise in politics because of their husbands, but Patton was the only such case among early women in the Florida legislature.

Reelected in 1956, Mary Patton sponsored or co-sponsored more than forty bills in the 1955 and 1957 sessions. Leadership was aware of her abilities because of her service when her husband held the office and promoted her to vice chair of the House Public Health Committee in the 1955 session. In 1957 she rose to chair the Committee on Commerce and Reciprocal Trade. More than other pioneer women in the legislature, though, Mary Patton remains in need of research from feminist scholars.

In a special election in 1957 Orlando voters sent their second woman to the House—but Beth Johnson followed Edna Giles Fuller by thirty years. She and Mary Patton were the first women to serve simultaneously. After the 1957 session, however, Johnson would be alone until the 1960s, when feminism began to revive.[55]

Marjory Stoneman Douglas had worked in the feminist movement that brought the right to vote and was fifty-seven years old when she launched an international career as an environmentalist with her 1947 book, *The Everglades: River of Grass.*[56] Born in Massachusetts in 1890, she lived most of her 108 years on the edge of the Glades, in Miami. Writing and speaking in

Significant female political activists in Florida, 1920 to 1960

Name	Residence	Party	Era	Achievement
Alderman, Carlotta Townsend	Jacksonville	D	1940s	delegate to three national conventions
Alford, Maysel	Jacksonville	D	1940s	member, Democratic National Committee
Ausherman, Katharine E.	Fort Lauderdale	R	1920s	presidential elector in 1928
Barfield, Edith Herlong	Miami	D	1930s	delegate to two national conventions
Bird, Lena	rural Tallahassee area	D	1920–40s	delegate to three national conventions
Carroll, Mrs. Frank X.	Pensacola	D	1950s	delegate to two national conventions
Coe, Evalyn S.	Pensacola	D	1930–40s	delegate to two national conventions
Fuller, Eula	Flagler County	D	1940s	delegate to two national conventions
Lieb, Helen Bowman	Tampa	R	1950s	member, Republican National Committee
Mayes, Lois K.	Pensacola	D	1920s	member, Democratic National Committee
McChesney, Ruby	Madison County	D	1940–50s	delegate to two national conventions
McGregor, Louise W.	DeLand	D	1930–40s	delegate to three national conventions
Morse, Mrs. F. W.	Tampa	R	1920s	member, Republican National Committee
Nooney, Mrs. Fred T.	Jacksonville	D	1920–50s	delegate to four national conventions
Pearce, Pearl	Sebring	D	1930s	delegate to two national conventions
Pickle, Louise	Washington County	D	1940s	delegate to two national conventions
Ramsey, Mrs. J. Reid	Tampa	D	1940–50s	delegate to two national conventions
Stritzinger, Gloria R.	Pensacola	D	1950s	delegate to two national conventions
Tally, Lucile Cottrell	Tavares	D	1940–50s	delegate to two national conventions
Wedgworth, Ruth S.	Belle Glade	D	1940s	delegate to two national conventions
Wells, Hortense	Tampa	D	1930–40s	member, DNC and Credentials Committee

Source: Created from alphabetical analysis of The Political Graveyard (http://www. http://political graveyard.com/).

elegant prose, Douglas spent seven decades trying to stop the destruction of Florida's life-giving water system, from the boom days of the 1920s to her death in 1998.

Not nearly as famous now as she was then, Lois Lenski also was a popular Florida writer. She won the Newbery Medal, still the most prestigious prize in children's literature, for *Strawberry Girl* (1949). Set in Polk County a few decades earlier, this story of a fictional ten-year-old girl introduced hundreds of thousands of young readers to a place where crops grow in winter. An Ohio native, Lenski had developed a reputation in New York and London as an illustrator before she began to write. She kept her maiden name when she married in 1920 and published her first book in 1927. By the postwar period, she may have been the nation's most distinguished author for young readers: she won numerous prizes, published some forty books, and illustrated many more. After wintering in Florida in 1942, Lenski spent at least part of the year there for the next three decades, first in Lakeland and then in Tarpon Springs.

Lenski was sufficiently candid about life in rural Florida that "some teachers and librarians objected to Lenski's plots as 'too grimly realistic.'"[57] But Floridians knew the facts of their lives, disagreed with critics, and welcomed her. It was true that around Lakeland and Plant City, youngsters worked on farms during strawberry season. For decades, "strawberry schools" ran on a different schedule, as students worked the fields during the spring semester and went to school only when summer rains began. Lenski broke more rules when she featured children who did not go to school at all: *Judy's Journey* (1946) was about migrant families around Lake Okeechobee. In an introduction aimed at adults, she spoke of a shame still too prevalent:

> I have seen and talked to migrant children and heard them tell of their experiences. One girl of eleven picked twenty-two hampers of beans in a day; a seven-year-old girl picked five hampers. They go to the field at six in the morning and return at dark. They have never had books or playthings. Some of them are no longer childlike, but are already old before they are ten. They do not know how to play, [but] they are good fighters. Everything in their life is against them.[58]

After her husband's death, Lenski sold her Connecticut home in 1964 and lived full-time in Tarpon Springs. She avoided writing about its Greek community, but she often read her works to students at the area school for black children. *Journey into Childhood: Autobiography of Lois Lenski* came out in

1972; *Florida, My Florida* in 1975; and she died in Tarpon Springs the next year.

Farther south, in Key West, lived another writer who also was better known then than now. Elizabeth Bishop won the 1956 Pulitzer Prize for poetry. Vassar-educated and independently wealthy, Bishop lived most of her life in Massachusetts, but she purchased a house at 624 White Street in Key West in the mid-1930s and spent winters there. She became friends with Pauline Pfeiffer Hemingway, who lived there with her famous husband, Ernest.

Bishop was poet laureate of the United States from 1949 to 1950 and, shortly before her death in 1979, won the National Book Award. She also wrote plays, prose, and children's literature and translated Brazilian works from Portuguese. Collections of her letters were published after her death, as was her literary autobiography, *The Voice of the Poet: Elizabeth Bishop* (2000).

Like Hemingway and other writers, Bishop struggled with alcoholism, and so did journalist and author Susan B. Anthony II, who also lived in Key West. She was born in 1916, a decade after her famous aunt died, and was gifted with the same keen intelligence. Her most important book probably was *Out of the Kitchen and Into the War* (1943), which not only urged women to take on nontraditional jobs but also offered visionary ideas on wartime housing shortages, model child care facilities, and more.

Employed by the *Key West Citizen,* Anthony eventually overcame her addiction enough to be certified as an alcoholism counselor. Much later, in 1975, she co-founded the Wayside House, a Delray Beach center for female alcoholics. In a brochure for the shelter, she commented on the irony: "Here I was—an alcoholic—and did you know Aunt Susan's first public speech was a temperance lecture?" Susan B. Anthony II died in Boca Raton just short of her seventy-fifth birthday.

Jeanne Bellamy was a much more successful journalist of the era. Born in 1911, she was an award-winning journalist at the *Miami Herald* from 1937 through the 1960s. Her investigative reporting resulted in prison reform, attention to the city's diminishing water supply, and action on other Miami issues that were just beginning to gain public support. In 1958 Bellamy became the first woman on the *Herald*'s editorial board, and four years later she was elected president of the Florida Society of Editors.

In 1958, when Bellamy rose to the editorial board, biochemist Florence Seibert began her "retirement" in St. Petersburg. Born in 1898, she exhibited courage and strength as a child, when polio left her with crippled legs. Seibert attributed her intellectual success to that physical disability: because she

"Florida Women of Distinction"

Eloise N. Cozens, a writer and radio broadcaster who lived in New Smyrna Beach, thought of herself as progressive—but she was akin to others of her era in deeming a woman of "distinction" to be inherently white, preferably past middle age, and usually the wife or widow of a prominent man. In 1955 she published a ninety-page volume featuring such women, usually with at least two entries per page.

The book began with endorsements by the wives of U.S. Senator George Smathers and U.S. Representative Syd Herlong—printed on their husbands' official congressional stationery. Many of the women included professed no profession other than wife and mother, but all were busy with volunteerism. Among the most significant achievers were:

- Several musicians, including Martha Martin Bigelow of St. Petersburg, an organist who performed on radio; Lenore Johanson of Miami, a classical composer; Faustine Lasseter, a master pianist who also was the music critic for the *Fort Lauderdale News*; Grace Willett Synder of St. Petersburg, a composer of popular songs who "once was billed as the Champion Lady Coronet Soloist of the World"; and Bertha Foster, who retired to Coral Gables after entertaining troops in Europe during World War I and heading the music department at Florida College for Women from 1921 to 1943.
- Several authors, including Sara Albertson of Eustis, who published works on subjects from predatory animals to the history of the Florida Dental Society; Olive Bown Goin of Gainesville, who wrote on zoology for both scientific journals and popular audiences; Mattie R. Logan of Tampa, who wrote and lectured on Latin America; and Marie Tello Phillips of Miami Beach, whose books on a number of subjects earned international honors.
- Media members Eve Bacon, co-founder and editor of the *Winter Park Sun;* Ruby Edna Pierce, a Palm Beach journalist called "the Dean of Newspaper Women in Florida"; and Ruth Smith of the *Orlando Sentinel-Star*, who also appeared on Orlando radio and had worked for the *Jacksonville Times-Union*.
- Sports figures Lucille Paul Heintz of Sarasota, who held "numerous medals and trophies in the difficult art of fencing," and Dorothy B. Palmer of Fort Pierce, a citrus farmer who also held championships in fishing, swimming, and tennis.

continued

- Civic figures Louise Hettinger, a member of the Osceola County school board; Elizabeth Skinner Jackson, a city commissioner in Dunedin; and Sara W. Wood, who served on the Marion school board.
- Entertainers Dorothy P. Horsfall, who conducted a Jacksonville radio show under the pseudonym "Ann Daly," and Evelyn Barton Rittenhouse, who had acted on the same stage as Lionel Barrymore before moving to St. Petersburg, where she appeared on radio.
- Eve Lyn Weeks of Fort Lauderdale, who was born blind but learned to teach the blind and to enjoy a full life of other activities; and Julia Marie Perkins, who lost her sight as an adult but continued as a Miami realtor.
- Esther Sawyer Bates, a Daytona Beach bookstore owner listed in national directories of influential women.
- Dr. Betty Blumer, a Melbourne chiropractor.
- Lennie Lanier Humphries, one of the few women in the nation employed as an expert on highway safety.
- Edith Mae Kester, an artist who studied at the Louvre in Paris and who "exhibited and lectured in almost all of the larger cities" before retiring to Daytona Beach.
- Isabel McKay of Miami Beach, "director of Aeronautical Training Society, a large Miami company."
- Alyce D. McPherson of Ocala, formerly superintendent of both the Florida Industrial School for Girls (white) and the Forest Hill Female Correctional Institution for Negro Girls.
- Mary Agnes Blankenship Miller of Live Oak, a nurse who believed that women "should take more interest in politics"; among the first to vote in 1921, she was a member of the Democratic National Committee.
- Grace L. Snyder, who held the unusual position of chairman of the Department of Religion at Florida Southern College in Lakeland.

Approximately two hundred women were included in the volume, and most indicated their religion, often in the context of listing charities. Of those who did so, just one was Catholic: Alix Gress Sellers Marshall of Jacksonville. The three Jewish women were Ruth Hope Leon of Jacksonville, Betty Bloom Rubin of Pensacola, and Ann Marcus of Orlando, who had been a lawyer in her native Vienna.

There were just two examples of ethnic diversity, both from Tampa: Anita Quintana, a social worker who also taught Romance languages, and Molly Ferrara, a popular businesswoman who was honorary mayor of the Ybor City section of Tampa.

could not go out to play, she read and thought—and was admitted to medical school at Yale University. With a picture of Nobel Prize winner Marie Curie on her desk to help her cope with hostility from male students, she earned a doctorate. Even before that, she developed a method of eliminating contaminants from distilled water—something that was key to intravenous therapy.

The University of Chicago rewarded Seibert with a position and she began her research on tuberculosis there. After nine years she moved to the University of Pennsylvania, where she taught mostly male students and continued to work on TB. Dr. Seibert ultimately made one of the most important contributions to public health of the twentieth century, as tuberculosis was a leading cause of death. A 1937 fellowship allowed her to work with a colleague in Sweden, and it was this joint effort that led to the development of a skin test for what is usually a lung-based disease. With the assistance of her sister, Mabel Seibert, she had the test ready by 1941, but the medical establishment was reluctant to accept it, and World War II meant more delays.

Finally, in 1952, Dr. Seibert testified before a condescending committee of the World Health Organization: "They thought," she said, "that if they didn't have a big man there arguing the test, they could push out this method."[59] Her scientific evidence was persuasive, however, and the test became standard—thereby identifying the contagious disease before it could kill. With her sister, she retired to St. Petersburg in 1958 but used her skills to research cancer at Bay Pines Veterans Hospital for another two decades. She lived to see her induction into the Florida Women's Hall of Fame in 1986 and died in 1991, the year after she was admitted to the National Women's Hall of Fame.

Like Siebert, Lena Smithers Hughes was not a native Floridian, but she had a major impact on her adopted state through research on the Valencia orange. Most citrus ripens in winter, but the Valencia can be harvested in summer and thus extends the season. Born in Tennessee, Siebert earned degrees there and at Michigan's Wayne State University. She taught in several northern states prior to moving to Orlando in 1957, after the 1944 death of her husband, Charles Hughes. He had been an employee of the U.S. Department of Agriculture specializing in citrus, and she independently continued their quest for a sweeter Valencia orange. When she was admitted to the Florida Agricultural Hall of Fame in 1986, 60 percent of the state's orange crop came from Hughes's roots. In addition to her important research, she endowed scholarships at the University of Florida and at Florida Southern

College in Lakeland. Inducted into the Florida Women's Hall of Fame in 1984, Lena Smithers Hughes died in 1987 at age seventy-seven.

Unlike those women, Betty Skelton was a native Floridian. She drew national attention in the postwar period in the most daring of areas: she was a racecar driver and aviator who established more records in those combined fields than any other person. Born in Pensacola in 1926, she grew up in Tampa and would retire to Winter Haven and then to The Villages. She made her first solo flight—illegally—at age twelve but was not old enough to join any of the women's military services in World War II.

Taking to the skies again when fuel was available after the war, she flew in the same 1946 air show in Jacksonville that debuted the navy's now famous Blue Angels. Just twenty-three when she won the World Light Plane Altitude Record in 1949, she soared even higher to be the champion again in 1951—defeating male aviators both times. *Look,* a popular mass magazine, featured her in 1960, when she underwent NASA's experiments for putting humans in space—but despite her credentials, neither she nor any other woman, including Pensacola's superstar aviator Jackie Cochran, was allowed to become an astronaut at that time.

Skelton turned to land racing and won its women's record four times, with a 1965 speed of 315.72 mph. She was the first woman admitted to the International Automotive Hall of Fame operated by NASCAR, the most prominent car racing organization. The internationally famous Smithsonian Air and Space Museum displays her airplane. Marriage changed her name, and she was known as Betty Skelton Frankman when she was inducted into the Florida Women's Hall of Fame in 1993. How much feminism changed the nation during her lifetime is clear in the fact that when she died in 2011, female astronauts were accepted as routine.

More than fast cars and planes, though, what changed the nation in the 1950s, especially for women, were household appliances—and in Florida, the air conditioner in particular. People who had been winter residents became full-time residents, selling businesses up north and building new ones in Florida. Literally millions of people who would not have moved there without air conditioning now did so. The population soared: in 1940 the state had 1.9 million residents, and the 1960 census showed nearly 5 million.

Homebuilders changed their styles, constructing dozens of similar houses, usually with the new method of concrete block and without prepayment from a specific buyer. The effective motto was "if you build it, they will come"—and millions of northerners did. In the affluence of the postwar

"Florida Women of Distinction," Part Two

Eloise Couzins apparently learned how difficult it is to choose among one's contemporaries for a biographical dictionary, as she soon issued a second volume. Her introduction acknowledged "some errors," and concluded with, "We really tried." Among the most notable women included in the second volume were:

- Sybil Smith Cooper of Gulfport in Pinellas County, who was featured in *House Beautiful* and other national publications for her mail-order gourmet food. A retired home economics teacher, Cooper sold fruitcakes, frosted nuts, "liquored grapefruit peel," and other creative products.
- Rachel Stearns Corbett, a Miami artist whose paintings were published in *Life* magazine, and Teresa Holloway, a Jacksonville writer published in the *Saturday Evening Post*; these were the era's biggest magazines.
- Miamian Thelma Stewart Cureton, who rose to an executive position in life insurance during World War II; in 1955 she was elected as the first female president of the Miami Association of Life Underwriters.
- Snead Young Davis of Ponte Vedra, who "has the distinction of being one of the few women owners and breeders of Florida's fine purebred cattle."
- Jacksonville musician Jessie Jay deVore, the 1932 founder of the state's first elementary school orchestra.
- Dr. Viola Graham of Tallahassee, who earned her doctorate in biochemistry from Cornell University and taught at FSU; she also was included in the era's biographical dictionary, *Men of Science*.
- Marjorie Bartlett Silver, a Fort Pierce writer who also pioneered educational television in Florida.
- Betty Vance, whose writing for the *Tampa Tribune* had won twenty-two Florida newspaper awards.
- Two Winter Park artists: E. Fairfax Davenport, the first American woman admitted to the Ecole des Beaux Arts in Paris, was unmarried and a cousin of famed James Whistler; her work was exhibited internationally, and the king of Belgium honored her for a World War I poster that she created. Wilhelmina Freeman Greene was younger; she specialized in flower paintings and created a slide show of "Gardens around the World."

world, middle-class people could afford to buy these new houses, and with new appliances, women could comfortably keep house without help from a domestic servant. Many maids and cooks who took wartime jobs never returned to working in the household of another woman.

Saving for a "dream kitchen" motivated many women during the war. Manufacturers that made tanks and guns during the war ran ads in women's magazines promising that as soon as the fighting ended, they would be making machines to ease home life. The 1950s indeed transformed housekeeping with automatic washing machines, clothes dryers, and dishwashers. Women no longer had to scrub clothes on a washboard or transfer them between tubs of wash water and rinse water, nor did they have to consider the weather for hanging clothes to dry outside. Refrigerators meant no more waits for the iceman to refresh the icebox, and freezers meant women could shop less frequently.

The biggest factor in cultural transformation, though, was television. It offered new opportunities to many female entertainers, as much early programming was by local performers. Moreover, new television stations not only hired singers and dancers but also created shows aimed at a female audience, usually broadcast live in the daytime. In the evenings, instead of people going out to movie theaters, television brought families together at home. A June 1953 newspaper article said:

> The Tampa Bay area's first television [station] opened here only a month ago, but its impact is being felt already. . . . Evidence of this change in St. Petersburg's way of life is forthcoming from Mrs. Doris Isler, switchboard operator at WSUN-TV, who says she receives more calls about the station's late movie program, called Your Home Theater, than any other single program. . . .
>
> A very large number [of callers] request the station to move the show up to an earlier hour. It doesn't go on the air until 10:35 and "that's way past our bedtime," they tell Mrs. Isler. . . .
>
> She gets many calls from persons whose sets are not operating properly, asking if the "picture will get any better," or if the station is on the air at all. "I've actually helped dozens of persons tune their sets," Mrs. Isler said. "I believe some of them don't touch the sets after their installation and think the picture will automatically appear."[60]

As with computers a few decades later, televisions improved to the point that such technical problems disappeared, and the medium soon fulfilled its larger purposes in broadening the minds of millions. Many young Americans had been exposed to other cultures during the war, and after television entered the living room of almost every household, older people also began to see that not everyone lived and thought as they did. It was a major factor in the profound cultural transformation of the next two decades, as the women's liberation movement arose in the 1960s and 1970s.

9 Agents of Change, 1961–1980

Rock concerts, marijuana, long hair on men, and miniskirts (as well as granny dresses), were the most visible signs of cultural change in the 1960s and 1970s—but more important, the era also brought the crest of the civil rights movement for African Americans and the women's liberation movement. No decade was as important for Florida women as the 1970s. For women who were then politically active, those years defined their lives and Florida's future.

Increased opportunity began with increased educational access, which is the basis for all progress. The University of South Florida (USF) graduated its first class in 1960. Until that Tampa institution opened, all public higher education had been in the small towns of Gainesville and Tallahassee, limiting the university experience to those affluent enough to go to north Florida.

Private institutions that admitted women did exist at Rollins College in Winter Park, Stetson in DeLand, and the universities of Jacksonville, Tampa, and Miami. But even in urban settings, those colleges were nonetheless considered a four-year, live-on-campus commitment: commuters and older students were almost unknown at the time. Florida's private colleges also were small and selective, and their tuition was too high for most.

Jacksonville University, however, set a precedent with a female president in the last year of this era. Except for the nuns who ran Miami's Barry College, Frances Bartlett Kinne was the state's first white woman to be president of an institution of higher education. Two black women—Mary McLeod Bethune of Bethune-Cookman and Sarah Ann Blocker of Florida Memorial

College—preceded her at private institutions, but Kinne was the state's first white female university president.

Born in Iowa, she earned degrees in music education in 1940 and 1944. She married an army officer and lived in China, Japan, and Germany, earning her doctorate from Germany's University of Frankfurt in 1957. Dr. Kinne became dean of the College of Fine Arts at Jacksonville University in 1961, rose to the presidency in 1979, and was named chancellor in 1989. She retired in 1994, after being admitted to the Florida Women's Hall of Fame in 1986. The recipient of many awards, she also was the first woman elected president of the International Council of Fine Arts.

Community colleges burgeoned in the 1960s, too, and Paula Mae Milton was a leader in the creative arts at Miami-Dade Community College. Born in Kentucky in 1939, she moved to Florida in 1954, graduated from Stetson University in 1961, and earned a master's degree from the University of Miami in 1963. Her doctorate was from Florida State University in 1967, two decades after graduate degrees became available there with coeducation in 1947.

Miami-Dade Community College still was new, and young Dr. Milton would inspire thousands of students there. She also founded a Miami theater company, co-chaired a television drama series that was produced in conjunction with the British Broadcasting Company, and co-authored a textbook on drama. Her 1982 entry into the Florida Women's Hall of Fame was posthumous, as her promising life was cut short at age forty-one.

Grace Rushing Maxwell never was nominated for the Hall of Fame, although she was involved in the founding of several community colleges. According to her obituary in the *Tallahassee Democrat* on August 8, 2012, she was born in Polk County in 1920. She graduated from Florida State College for Women in 1942, married and had four children, and then went on to earn a master's degree from the University of Florida in 1955 and a PhD from FSU in 1964. She served as charter faculty and/or administrator at four new community colleges: Florida Keys in Key West, Indian River in Fort Pierce, St. Johns in Palatka, and North Florida in Madison. Dr. Maxwell finished her career back in Tallahassee, at FAMU, from which she would retire in 1992.

But back when legislators used the word "south" in their 1956 charter for the University of South Florida, they signaled their intention to build no universities farther south than Tampa—a west coast city only midway down the peninsula. They were not afraid of political retaliation because, like many legislatures in former Confederate states, Florida's legislative districts were drawn to give great power to rural areas, ignoring urban population increases. Especially unfair to newer cities in Dade, Broward, and Palm Beach counties, this was undemocratic even for older populous counties, such as Hillsborough.

"Multi-member" districts also meant that several legislators represented the same geographical area, living close together in affluent neighborhoods, while leaving poor and minority communities without any true representation. The U.S. Supreme Court ruled against this, and although Floridians did not immediately acquiesce, after the 1970 census the "one man, one vote" principle established by the Court finally began to change the state. As more representatives from the cities of south Florida took their seats in Tallahassee, the "pork chop gang" of rural north Florida began to lose power in the 1970s, and the state became more progressive. Women, too, benefited from single-member districts, as a smaller number of constituents made it easier to run low-cost, grassroots campaigns.

* * *

Even before the one man, one vote decision and the creation of single-member legislative districts, more Florida women began to win elections than in previous decades. This was not necessarily the case everywhere: in some states, women were more likely to win elections in the 1920s and 1930s than in the 1940s and 1950s. By 1962, however, forty of the fifty states had women in their state senates, when Florida finally had its first female senator.

Orlando voters sent Elizabeth McCullough Johnson, known as Beth, to the Florida Senate. That was sixty-six years after the nation's first female state senator, Dr. Martha Hughes Cannon, in Utah in 1896. Orlando merits credit, too, for having elected the first woman to the Florida House, Edna Giles Fuller in 1928. Although both precedent-setting women were from the same area, more than three decades passed between election of the first female House member and the first senator.

Beth Johnson moved to the Senate from the House, where she had won a special election to fill a vacancy in 1957. She was born in Pennsylvania, graduated from New York's prestigious Vassar College, and moved to Orlando in 1934. A Democrat, she was active in the League of Women Voters and other civic groups, where she worked to introduce the concept of planning and zoning to a largely unregulated Florida.

Male colleagues in the House respected her enough that Representative Johnson was vice chair of a committee on governmental reorganization in

Women in the Florida House to 1980

Year	Name	Residence	Party
1928	Edna Giles Fuller	Orlando	D
1942	Mary Lou Baker	St. Petersburg	D
1948	Edna Pearce	Highlands County	D
1954	Mary Patton	Apalachicola	D
1957*	Beth Johnson	Orlando	D
1962	Maxine Baker	Miami	D
1962	Mary Grizzle	Pinellas County	R
1962	Mary Ann MacKenzie	Miami	D
1970	Gwen Cherry	Miami	D
1970	Jane W. Robinson	Cocoa	R
1972	Betty Easley	St. Petersburg	R
1972	Elaine Gordon	Miami	D
1972	Mary Singleton	Jacksonville	D
1974	Elaine Bloom	Miami Beach	D
1974	Karen Coolman	Fort Lauderdale	D
1974	Helen Gordon Davis	Tampa	D
1974	Nancy O. Harrington	Coral Gables	D
1974	Mary Ellen Hawkins	Naples	R
1974	Gwen Margolis	North Miami Beach	D
1976	Beverly Burnsed	Lakeland	D
1976	Fran Carlton	Orlando	D
1976	Linda C. Cox	Fort Lauderdale	D
1976	Marilyn Bailey Evans	Melbourne	R
1976	Roberta Fox	Coral Gables	D
1976	Pat Collier Frank	Tampa	D
1976	Toni Jennings	Orlando	R
1976	Dorothy Eaton Sample	St. Petersburg	R
1978	Virginia Rosen	North Miami Beach	D
1978	Eleanor Weinstock	West Palm Beach	D
1979*	Carrie Meek	Miami	D

Notes: Names are listed only once, by year of first election; within year, names are listed alphabetically by surname.
* Special election to fill a vacancy.

Women in the Florida Senate to 1980

Year	Name	Residence	Party
1962	Beth Johnson	Orlando	D
1966	Beth Johnson	Cocoa	R
1970	Lori Wilson	Merritt Island	I
1976	Betty Castor	Tampa	D
1978	Pat Frank	Tampa	D
1978	Mary Grizzle	Pinellas County	R

Note: Names are listed only once, by year of first election; within year, names are listed alphabetically by surname.

the 1959 session, and she rose to vice chair of the powerful House Finance and Taxation Committee in 1961. Her chief goal, however, was the establishment of the University of Central Florida, which eventually offered a low-cost public choice for local students who could not afford Rollins College. When Beth Johnson died in 1973, former Governor LeRoy Collins eulogized her as "one of the very best public officials." She was inducted into the Florida Women's Hall of Fame in 1986, and an Orlando park is named for her.

The 1966 election created a political science curiosity: the second woman in the Florida Senate was also named Beth Johnson. Cocoa voters chose her, in a district adjacent to that of Orlando's Beth Johnson. To avoid confusion with the senior senator, the junior woman referred to herself in Tallahassee as Elizabeth Johnson. She set a precedent as the first Republican woman elected to the legislature; when she served in the 1960s, the body remained overwhelmingly Democratic. That did not mean, however, that these white men were liberals: most came from a "Dixiecrat" heritage of racial segregation and conservatism.

Although of differing parties, both Beth Johnsons were progressives who made significant contributions to the state. The Orlando senator worked closely with the Disney brothers to build Disney World, while the Cocoa senator held office at the same time that NASA was building its rocket launch site in her district. Both were reelected and played strong roles in the extraordinary change of the 1960s, as Disney and NASA became huge factors in the state's economy. The women also showed the foresight to push the legislature to spend the revenue necessary to provide a transportation system adequate for the many millions of visitors who would come. One result was the building of Interstate 4, which proved crucial to central Florida.

From 1962 to 1973 Florida had at least one senator named Beth Johnson. The Orlando woman died in April 1973, and the Cocoa woman did not run for reelection in 1972. Her husband had died, and she later told an interviewer, "As a widow, I could not raise my family on $12,000 a year."[1] That thought would have occurred to few male lawmakers: if widowed, they might have left a senate seat to spend time with their children, but few would leave because they could not afford to stay. Legislators are paid as part-timers, and a legislator with NASA in his district would probably have found a consultancy if he needed money. Women held themselves to a higher standard, though, and Senator Johnson was akin to most women in seeing her job as true representation, not as a way to supplement her income.

When NASA began construction, Brevard County's JoAnn Hardin was a teenager with a strong interest in science. She began working at Cape Canaveral on the day after her graduation from Titusville High School. While studying at the University of Florida and at Jacksonville State University in Alabama (where she had been born in 1940), she continued with the space program during summers. National publications pictured her with the Apollo moon launch team, the only female face among hundreds of men.

After earning a degree in mathematics, she married and became JoAnn Morgan, and went on to obtain a master's degree in engineering from California's Stanford University. All the while she maintained her contacts at NASA, where ultimately she became the first female senior executive. During a career spanning five decades, Morgan won medals and other honors as an engineering manager. She worked on the pioneer launches not only of Apollo missions but also of Apollo-Soyuz and Skylab, rising to director of payload projects management. When she became director for safety and mission assurance, Morgan was one of the last two people who verified that a shuttle was ready to blast off. President Bill Clinton honored her in 1995, the same year that she was admitted to the Florida Women's Hall of Fame.

Judith Kersey was just a few years younger than Morgan and followed a similar path to become NASA's first female guidance systems engineer. She played a major role in the creation of the Space Station and held national offices with the Society of Women Engineers. Kersey also developed a workshop, "Introducing Girls to Engineering," that attracted some eighteen hundred girls during its first four years. She would join the Florida Women's Hall of Fame in 2004.

* * *

The Cape Canaveral site where these and other women worked was renamed the Kennedy Space Center after President John F. Kennedy was assassinated. In the first year of his presidency, 1961, he created the President's Commission on the Status of Women, an early indication of growing feminist revival. Former first lady Eleanor Roosevelt chaired it, and the president called upon governors to follow up with similar commissions on the state level—where, much more than on the federal level, thousands of unthinking legalisms had created a complex mass of inequalities for women.

Florida governor Farris Bryant, a Democrat like Kennedy and his successor Lyndon Johnson, complied with the request and appointed the Governor's Commission on the Status of Women. Bryant was encouraged to do so by a delegation of Business and Professional Women who visited him early in 1964. Although Bryant would leave office with the November election, the commission continued under Governor Haydon Burns.

The commission's first meeting was on November 9, 1964, in the Cabinet room of what now is the Old Capitol building, with "ten women from six metropolitan areas" who had been appointed by Governor Bryant. The members adjourned to FSU for a program sponsored by the university's Committee on Continuing Education, where two out-of-state women spoke to more than a hundred attendees. The afternoon speaker was from New York's Sarah Lawrence College, a school that was a leader in "the unfinished business of women's education."[2] At dinner they heard from Dr. Mary Dublin Keyserling, director of the Women's Bureau of the U.S. Department of Labor, an agency begun by President Woodrow Wilson during World War I.

Commissioners elected Aleen Pridgen Kidd (later MacKenzie) of Ocala as their chair. Usually referred to in the press as Mrs. William Kidd, she had "spearheaded the drive for a constitutional amendment that permitted selling bonds for higher education" and "headed up the women's committee in Florida for the [1964] Democratic ticket."[3] She also was a national leader in highway safety.

That issue was major, as cars could go as fast as they do now but did not have seatbelts and certainly not airbags. Most roads were two lanes wide, often without shoulders or guardrails, and thus invited head-on collisions. Moreover, the prerogative to drink and drive was virtually unchallenged until women took up the cause. Kidd's work on this issue preceded that of Mothers Against Drunk Driving (MADD) by two decades, and both the state insurance commissioner and Governor Burns appointed her to positions dealing with highways. The National Association of Women Highway Safety Leaders was among those who nominated Aleen Kidd MacKenzie for the Florida Women's Hall of Fame, and she was inducted in 2013.

The vice chair of the Governor's Commission on the Status of Women was Lee Bird Leavengood of Tampa, and the commission's attention to lifelong learning reflected her goals. After rearing three children, Leavengood created a highly successful program in this area for USF. She truly practices what she preaches: after a long career at USF, in 2012, the tireless Leavengood was an executive with the Tampa Bay History Center. She and Kidd attended national meetings on behalf of women, and Leavengood's scrapbook contains a picture of her with First Lady Jackie Kennedy.

The *Tampa Daily Times* Editorializes on the Governor's Commission on the Status of Women

Male editors at Tampa's afternoon newspaper began their 1964 piece on the new commission by congratulating Governor Farris Bryant and his three Tampa appointees. They were the *Times*'s own journalist Polly Henry, attorney Josephine Howard Stafford, and Lee Leavengood, who would soon be elected as the commission's vice chair but was listed in the editorial merely as "Mrs. Victor Leavengood."

The writers no doubt thought that their words would evoke chuckles, as the editorial continued:

> Actually, we had assumed that the status of women was exceptionally good. . . . Take politics, for instance. . . . Grandmother would never have thought of casting a ballot without prior consultation with Grandfather. . . . Grandmother didn't even know how to write a check until the necessity arose in widowhood. It's only fair to note, however, that she caught on to the trick quite easily. . . .
>
> As far as civil rights are concerned, the ladies we see generally manage to get a seat in the front of the bus—sometimes one just vacated by a man. And most can take their pick of restaurants. The law also reacts quickly in their favor. Take a look, for instance, at the statutes on divorce.
>
> In fact, we are rather surprised that the status of women is even an issue. But Governor, have you given any consideration to improving the status of us hard-working, neglected men?

In contrast, an article in the *Tampa Morning Tribune* took a serious approach:

> The governor's commission on the status of women, created by Gov. Farris Bryant last July, held its first meeting yesterday, although many have been working in smaller projects for months. They decided that their present job is mostly research—trying to pinpoint any glaring inequality affecting women. . . .

continued

Since they were created by an executive order, with no legislative sanction, the commission exists at the will of the governor and several of the women wondered whether incoming Gov. Haydon Burns was sympathetic. . . .

Katherine Warren, dean of women at Florida State University [said] "too few women have become effective human beings as a result of advanced education." Mrs. Helen Parades of Perrine, head of the committee on employment . . . said an estimated 795,000 women work in Florida. She said there is no state labor law for women and several bills seeking to guarantee women equal pay with men for equal work have failed in the legislature.

It may not be coincidental that the sneering, dismissive *Tampa Times* went out of business in the next decade, while its competitor continues today.

Note: Undated *Daily Times* editorial in the scrapbook of Commissioner Lee Leavengood; *Tribune* article syndicated from Tallahassee by United Press International, November 13, 1964.

Esther Peterson, who traveled from Washington for a January 1966 commission meeting in Tallahassee, was a household name in her time. She had been a close aide to Eleanor Roosevelt when Roosevelt chaired the President's Commission on the Status of Women. Also an advisor to President Lyndon Johnson, Peterson pointed out that women were living longer than ever, "yet they use only about 15 years of their lives in raising a family." She specialized in consumer issues and told commissioners that "government and private business are making great strides towards standardization of package sizes, clothing sizes, and a requirement that clothing contain a label outlining how it should be cared for."[4]

The commission released a fifty-three-page annual report, "Women in Florida," in 1966. By then the volunteer body—with no paid staff—had expanded to twenty-eight members, who demonstrated great diligence in collecting data for Governor Burns. The first twenty-five pages of the report covered women's status in education, including higher education, as reflected by responses to a detailed questionnaire.

Katherine Warren, dean of women at FSU, chaired the committee on education, while Tampa's Lee Leavengood chaired the committee on "Home and Community." That survey included responses to questions on child care, care for the aged, consumer issues, and family service associations. Although all commissioners were white, Leavengood's concern for others was reflected in the report's indication that among "major concerns [was] the general unavailability of quality day care for children of low income families, particularly Negroes and migrants."

Louise Hewlett, Alma Lee Loy, Phyllis Rabiner, and Jo Stafford chaired other report sections on employment and on the legal status of women. The latter was lengthy and legalistic, pointing out specific state statutes that discriminated against women and especially recommending legal changes on divorce, child custody, property rights, and other issues. Virginia Smith of the League of Women Voters did not serve on those committees, but she emphasized to the press the most serious legal inequality: "jury service in Florida is mandatory for men, but voluntary for women"—a real handicap for any woman who found herself in court, whether as a plaintiff, defendant, witness, or lawyer.[5]

Recommendations to Governor Burns were drafted by Orlando Senator Beth Johnson and three of the state's rare female judges.[6] They included a state equal pay law and a state minimum wage law—but no recognition of the federal Equal Rights Amendment. On the other hand, the report's last paragraph was quite radical: a list of subjects for further study included "legal abortions, sterilization laws, and required birth control for unwed mothers."

Equal pay soon became a high priority for the commission, even though that fight should arguably have been considered won. Shortly before his 1963 death, President Kennedy prodded Congress into passing the Equal Pay Act, which had been ignored since World War II. Florida congressman Claude Pepper played a major role in that, but traditional southern focus on states' rights vs. federal law meant that many Floridians believed the national law did not apply to them. The federal act, in fact, was based on the interstate commerce clause of the U.S. Constitution, and many businesses claimed they did no out-of-state commerce and thus were free to ignore the law, including pay scales based on gender. Passing a Florida law on equal pay thus became a major goal.

With the Business and Professional Women's Clubs, the commission held a 1968 session on equal pay at the Miami Airways Hotel. They had secured co-sponsors in the legislature, a Republican and a Democrat, both men from south Florida. At the conference feminists pointed out that this was an "act to abolish discriminatory wages sex based on sex . . .

The bill "provides for the abolishment of artificial differentials in pay between women and men."

It "requires that employees who perform comparable work, requiring comparable qualifications of skill, effort, and responsibility, shall be paid at the same rate. . . .

The bill "does not disturb pay differentials based on established seniority or merit increase systems as long as they do not discriminate on the basis of sex."[7]

Governor Haydon Burns lost a contentious 1966 Democratic primary, and as a result Claude Kirk became the first Republican governor of the twentieth century. He would increase the number of commissioners to twenty-six. Reubin Askew, a progressive Democrat, displaced Kirk in 1970, and he would provide the commission's first executive director in 1974. Until then, commission members shared the office's clerical duties as volunteers. No commission with a mostly male membership, of course, functioned without state-supported clerical workers.

Attorney Jo Stafford of Tampa chaired the commission's legislative committee in 1969, and nonmember Adele Weaver, a lawyer in the office of Congressman Claude Pepper, lent her expertise to the equal pay bill. To help with passage, though, they added a clause saying that enforcement would be "up to the employee to put to civil action." In other words, instead of using state resources to enforce state law, a victim of discrimination had to find a lawyer willing to take her case and go to court. The law merely promised to provide her with grounds to sue—but even in this limited form, it did not come close to passage.

That was particularly embarrassing because the similar women's commission in Georgia had succeeded in passing an equal pay bill. Its body "was composed of 115 women, and while the Legislature was in session," the Georgians reported, the "members of the Commission never left. Seeing the unrelenting women in the galleries, Georgia's legislators finally passed the bill six minutes before adjournment." Georgia commission chair Mamie K. Taylor also "offered the following astute advice: 'be sure the bill you draw up has teeth in it to get it implemented.'"

At their November 1968 gathering in Miami Springs, Florida commissioners identified nine areas of concern on which they intended to make

Members of the Governor's Commission on the Status of Women, late 1960s/early 1970s

Name	Area Represented	Notes
Anderson, Anne	Bradenton	"Mrs. George"
Anderson, Marie	Miami	*Miami Herald*; author
Akerman, Mildred	Fort Lauderdale	judge in Small Claims Court
Alexander, Lucile S.	Jacksonville	state president of Altrusa, a women's charity
Armistead, Betty	Rockledge	WWII veteran; NOW leader
Arnold, Mamie	Sebring	American Legion Auxiliary
Baker, Annette	Clearwater	Democratic National Committee
Barthlemy, Frances	Jacksonville	American Association of University Women
Bettner, Elizabeth	Miami	realtor
Bird, Audrey	Jacksonville	served on Property Rights Committee
Bishop, Virginia	Lake City	Insurance Women of Florida
Blackwell, Dr. Louise (Mary)	Tallahassee	FAMU English professor
Blee, Charlotte	Boca Raton	PTA national board
Brady, Dr. Marna V.	Gainesville	dean of women at UF
Brewer, Sam	Tallahassee	first male appointee
Butler, Mildred	North Miami	"Mrs. Edward"
Canariis, Billie	Tampa	Red Cross
Carleton, Edythe	St. Petersburg	Florida Federation of Women's Clubs
Chapman, Dorothy	Orlando	*Orlando Sentinel*
Dick, Jackie	Ft. Pierce	State Board of Cosmetology
Dover, Jilene	Fort Lauderdale	
Elmendorf, Mary	Sarasota	Internationalist; New College administrator
Emmel, Lois	Gainesville	Florida Federation of Women's Clubs
Foley, Ruth	Bradenton	"Mrs. Charles"
Ford, Dr. Clinita	Tallahassee	FAMU home economics
Freede, Beatrice	Dunedin	Business and Professional Women's Clubs
Gibson, Dr. Juanita	Tallahassee	FSU director of institutional research and service
Grizzle, Mary	Pinellas County	legislator and commission chair in 1968
Harold, Margaret	Ft. Lauderdale	"Mrs. Gilbert"

continued

Members of the Governor's Commission —*Continued*

Name	Area Represented	Notes
Hawkins, Paula	Maitland	future U.S. senator
Henry, Polly	Tampa	Florida Women's Press Club
Hewlett, Louise	Miami	Florida Federation of Garden Clubs
Holley, Gladys S.	Quincy	Pilot International, a women's charity
Johnson, Senator Beth	Orlando	Florida's first female state senator
Kidd, Aleen	Ocala	commission's first chair
Kovachevick, Elizabeth	St. Petersburg	future federal judge
Leavengood, Lee	Tampa	Tampa Art Institute
Leslie, Helen K.	St. Petersburg	BPW; commission chair in 1968
Light, George	Miami Beach	second man
Loy, Alma Lee	Vero Beach	future county commissioner
Moore, Thelma	West Palm Beach	Hotel and Restaurant Commission
Myers, Martha	Miami	National Council of Jewish Women
Perry, Betty	Tallahassee	vice chair in 1969
Parades, Helen	Perrine	advocated equality of women on juries
Rabiner, Phyllis F.	Daytona Beach	bank executive
Rudy, Jane	St. Petersburg	Republican Women's Clubs
Semler, Jane	Fort Lauderdale	Insurance Women of Florida
Sobieski, Anne Dion	Key West	juvenile court judge
Smith, Virginia	Coral Gables	League of Women Voters
Squires, Dr. Gretchen	Pensacola	physician
Stafford, Jo	Tampa	Tampa municipal judge
Stritzinger, Gloria	Pensacola	Democratic Women's Clubs
Tait, Edna	Jacksonville	past president, Florida Education Association
Wander, Irene	Melbourne	
Warner, Anne Kenan	Tampa	
Warren, Katherine (Kay)	Tallahassee	dean of women at FSU
Woodford, Mae	Hernando	Civil Air Patrol
Yeaman, Dr. Dorie	Palm Beach County	

Note: Because of turnover, not all these women served simultaneously.

recommendations to the new governor. The topics, and the woman in charge of studying legislative needs on them, were:

Education	Marie Anderson[8]
Nurses Resources	Marna Brady
Labor Law	Thelma Moore
Employment Prejudice	Elizabeth Kovachevick
[federal] Economic Opportunity Act	Clinita Ford
State Civil Service System	Jane Rudy
Women's Property Rights; juvenile law	Anne Sobieski
Migrant Labor	Mary Elmendorf
General Legislation	Martha Myers

In a discussion on "Employed Women," four panelists addressed "the dual role of women today, being homemaker and careerist." The speakers were Dr. Lynn R. Barlett of the University of Miami; Roberta Jackson, who was about to graduate in library science from Miami-Dade Junior College; Rebecca Carney of the Council on Continuing Education of Women; and Terry Maureau, a recent nursing school graduate of Miami's Catholic Barry College.

Marie Anderson, who led the education committee, was not an educator but rather a journalist for the *Miami Herald*. In 1980 she would publish *Julia's Daughters: Women in Dade's History*, a scholarly work of some 150 pages; it included women both before and after the "Mother of Miami," Julia Tuttle. Anderson was very active on the commission, especially with linking it to the Florida Women's Press Club to help publicize its feminist work. In this she had particular support from two *Herald* colleagues: by 1959, Juanita Greene held a policy-setting role at the newspaper, while Jeanne Bellamy was a member of the editorial board.[9]

Another of Anderson's projects was developing "a roster of women in Florida who could be recommended to the Governor for possible appointment by him."[10] This reflected a longtime BPW goal: since the Great Depression and World War II, BPW members had collected resumes for a national "Talent Bank" to encourage appointments of women to the many governmental agencies created during those eras. BPW aimed to counter the argument that no women had the credentials to serve—and indeed the Roosevelt and Truman administrations appointed more women to federal positions than had any previous president. In Florida, however, BPW's Talent Bank would have almost no effect for another decade.

Dr. Marna Brady, who was in charge of resources for nurses, extended her mandate far beyond that—indeed, other categories of employment got much more attention than nursing in the comprehensive agenda that she proposed. It included not only more vocational education for girls but also programs in which an older woman could "train or refresh her training for employment." The aims included "child care centers and retirement and/or nursing homes for the aged" to enable middle-aged women to develop careers. In a clause that now seems outdated but that was then a real concern, the commission's report called for the elimination of "all restrictions on the employment of married women in public high schools."

Mary Grizzle, a legislator from Pinellas County, chaired the commission under Governor Claude Kirk, but already in 1965, when Haydon Burns was governor, she had led a meeting in St. Petersburg. "It's up to the woman," Grizzle said, "to show she is willing to know the economics of daily life, to be aware of what is going on." The meeting featured Mrs. Wilda Cook, registrar of voting in Pinellas County." In introducing Cook, Grizzle said: "Sometimes women are their own worst enemies. Often they aren't sure exactly what they want—and if they are, they don't make the effort to do something about it." Mrs. Cornelius Vanderpoel, president of the local Republican women's club, added:

> Women are the majority group that has less than minority rights. . . . Four hundred thousand more women than men are registered to vote. They are in a position to sway the results of any issue. Women in the past have used the traditional methods of persuasion and charm to achieve their ends—now they also can use power.[11]

Florida women in the teaching profession led the way with a powerful example of insisting on fairness. Fed up with uncertain revenue, they forced the state to recognize that the era's expectation of Space Age education was a farce without funding. Their only fiscal certainty was that salaries were low: a 1967 report showed that Florida teachers were paid $7,200 less annually than the national average—and even less than their colleagues in Alabama and Georgia. When school began in the fall of 1968, they took the radical step of going on strike. It was the first statewide teachers' strike in the nation's history.

Although men were the majority of the leaders, women made up the majority of the strikers. Some, such as Pasco County's Mary and Merton Gates, were married couples with children, and walking out meant no income for either parent. At the national level Janet Dean, president of the Council of Urban Education Associations, particularly encouraged the strike. Louise Alford, president-elect of the Florida Education Association, stepped down from that position to become an organizer for the American Federation of Teachers.

After tens of thousands of teachers demonstrated their solidarity by filling the Orange Bowl for a statewide rally, the legislature responded. Republican Claude Kirk lost his 1970 reelection bid partly because of the issue, as teachers endorsed his Democratic opponent. Over the next years collective bargaining mechanisms would be established in both K-12 systems and the universities, and Florida became a leader, not a follower, in unionized faculty with rights protected by mutual contract.

One (seldom noted) result was that whimsical actions by school board members—almost all of them male—were less likely because unit-wide contracts and pay scales made it much more difficult to single out a particular teacher for privilege or punishment. Especially for women in small counties where isolation meant a lack of power, this was very helpful in preventing male administrators or school board members from sexually harassing female teachers.

* * *

Miami voters in 1961 elected their first woman to the city council, Alice Cutts Wainwright. (According to Miami historian Marie Anderson, Anna M. Perry had been appointed to a vacancy in 1930 but never was elected.) Wainwright's youth had been difficult; she was pregnant and widowed just five months after her 1934 wedding. Among other things she worked as an aircraft mechanic during World War II and, after earning a 1950 law degree at the University of Miami, lost her first election. She persevered to become a very effective leader, however, especially in the development of the city's convention center. Governor Reuben Askew appointed Wainwright to his innovative land management commission, and in 1974, "the last natural hammock on the bayfront" was named for Alice Wainwright.[12]

When Wainwright joined the city council, Jane Stevens Roberts was already on Miami's school board, and in 1961 she rose to chair it. She joined Anna Brenner Meyers, who had been appointed in 1953 and was elected thereafter. By 1969 three of the four winners of school board elections would be women.

In comparison, Hillsborough County had just one woman on its board by the end of the 1960s. She was Cecile Waterman Essrig, a member of a Jewish family long active in Tampa's civic and economic life. Pat Collier Frank, a future state senator, lost three school board elections but persevered, winning in 1971. Both women were important to finally ending segregation in the area's schools—but both encountered prejudice. At her funeral in July 2012, Essrig's daughters—both successful professionals—recalled how a neighbor had congratulated their mother on running, and even donated money, but said he would not vote for her because he didn't vote for women. Later, when it was her turn to chair the board, two male colleagues came to her home to tell her that they would not vote for a female chair. They did the next time, though, and voters reelected Cecile Essrig for two decades.

With the legislature reapportioned after the 1960 census, three women joined the Florida House in 1962, the most ever. All three were stellar legislators, and one made such a significant contribution to the state that her name is now used as a verb. When Floridians say—as they often do—that someone has been "Baker acted," they mean that the person has been taken into custody for treatment of mental health problems. Maxine Baker—not to be confused with Mary Lou Baker, a legislator during the 1940s—was its author.

Maxine Baker was sixty-five years old when she entered the Florida House, and she had never before held public office. A native of Maryland, she graduated from Radcliffe College, the female affiliate of Harvard University, and moved to Miami with her husband in 1924. After rearing two children, she volunteered in the 1950s on the area board of the State Welfare Board, campaigned for Dade County's new charter, and won appointment to the 1958 Governor's Advisory Committee on Constitutional Revision. The *Miami News* named Baker as one of "Six Outstanding Women" in 1963.

She initially did not intend to specialize in mental health, and assignment to that House committee was considered lowly. Intelligent and studious woman as she was, though, she soon became an expert. "Nobody wanted to talk about it and nobody wanted to spend any money on it," she said in a 1988 interview with *Tampa Tribune* reporter Mark Davis. "I found," she said, after visiting almost every institution in the state, "people who were in mental hospitals—old aunts, mothers, and fathers—who just shouldn't have been. They were sent there just to get them out of the way. I didn't like seeing people being held against their will."

Florida's chief facility for the mentally ill was an old military arsenal and prison at Chattahoochie in the Panhandle. It was widely known for cruelty and mistreatment of patients, which officials ignored. Representative Baker visited facilities in England and learned that such state-sponsored abuse did not have to be accepted. By 1971 she had researched and written a reform bill—and she was sufficiently astute politically that, amazingly enough, the House approved it by a 100–6 vote. Because the Senate was led by progressive Democrats Richard Pettigrew of Miami and Louis de la Parte of Tampa, no senator voted against it. The law worked so well that it has never been repealed, and it proved a model for emulation elsewhere.

According to House historian Allen Morris, the Baker Act "strengthened the civil and due process rights of mentally ill persons, established specific criteria for involuntary treatment, and required the development of community-based treatment programs as alternatives to institutionalization."[13] The act required that a diagnosis of mental illness be made within three days of incarceration, and if that time was extended, two psychiatric professionals had to sign an affidavit as to the need for confinement.

This reform benefited women more than men, as they were more likely to be incarcerated against their will. It was an old problem for feminists: more than a century earlier, Susan B. Anthony had defied both the law and male "progressives" to hide a perfectly sane woman from the woman's philandering husband, a Massachusetts state senator who repeatedly institutionalized his wife while abusing their daughter. Mental institutions were full of women who found themselves adjudicated insane if they challenged husbands. Maxine Baker was a hero both to those who were mentally ill and to those who were not.

Miami voters also elected Mary Ann MacKenzie, another progressive Democrat, to the House in 1962. She was an attorney, and her bill for safety in water skiing—a new sport—gained attention. Reelected in 1964, she was vice chair of the House Mental Health Committee in the 1965 session; Maxine Baker chaired it in the following session. This marked measurable progress since the 1963 session, when no woman was either chair or vice chair of any legislative committee.

The third woman who won in the 1962 election was the first from Florida's west coast since Mary Lou Baker, who set this precedent in 1942. Mary Grizzle of Indian Rocks Beach was a progressive Republican and represented her constituents well. She rose to vice chair of the Committee on Hotels and Restaurants and, in the 1970s, would render significant Senate service to feminists.

The 1964 election brought no change in the legislature, but in Miami Athalie Range became the first African American woman elected to the Dade County Commission. Born in Key West, she attended the New England Institute of Anatomy and Embalming, and this background as a funeral director proved crucial when she became a widow with four young children to support. Her children also led to her activism in the PTA, where she fought for improved education for minorities. Those credentials enabled Range to win her commission race, and she showed additional courage in introducing a number of innovative ordinances, including restrictions on handguns. In 1970 Governor Reuben Askew appointed Range as secretary of community affairs, making her the first African American of either gender to head a state agency. Athalie Range was inducted into the Florida Women's Hall of Fame in 1997. Born in 1916, she was still living in 2012.

Jacksonville voters made serious change on their city council in 1967, with eight of nine incumbents losing their seats. Even more significant, African Americans Mary Singleton and Sallye Mathis were elected at large, with support from many whites. Mathis was a Bethune-Cookman graduate who was active with both the NAACP and the League of Women Voters. After retiring from her job as an educator in 1962, she integrated the Jacksonville YWCA and became sufficiently respected that she won her 1967 election handily. Singleton would go on to the legislature in 1972.[14]

In the same year that they were the first African American women on the Jacksonville City Council, Betty Mae Jumper became the first female chief of the Florida Seminoles. Born in Indiantown in 1923, she attended the Cherokee Indian School in North Carolina and, in 1949, was the first Florida Seminole to earn a high school diploma. That was three years after she married Moses Jumper in 1946. Elected to head the Seminole Tribe of Florida in 1967, Betty Mae Jumper was a founder of the United South and Eastern Tribes, which lobbied for Native Americans in Washington.

President Richard Nixon appointed Jumper to the National Congress on Indian Opportunity in 1970; she was one of just two female appointees. She wrote two books, *And with the Wagon, Came God's Words* and *Legends of the Seminoles.* Florida State University awarded her an honorary doctorate in 1994, the same year she entered the Florida Women's Hall of Fame. Other Seminole women wearing traditional dress came with her to a garden party at the Governor's Mansion, where Governor Lawton Chiles would welcome her.

At the same time that Jumper was working for Seminoles, Alicia Baro advocated for Puerto Ricans. Born in San Lorenzo, Puerto Rico in 1918 as Alicia Santos, she grew up in New York City and graduated from its prestigious Hunter College in 1940. After marrying and relocating to Miami, she began speaking out on behalf of migrant workers, which led to the formation of the Puerto Rican Democrats Organization. She said of the Florida where she arrived in the 1950s, "Three or four Puerto Ricans could not stand on a corner without fear of police breaking them up."[15]

Baro helped establish a health clinic for low-income Hispanics and went on to be a founding member of the National Conference of Puerto Rican Women, the Coalition of Hispanic American Women, and the Women's Chamber of Commerce of South Florida. She also worked with Mollie Brilliant, a leader in the Jewish community, on a highly successful 1976 Miami convocation. Following a conference of the Organization of American States' Inter-American Commission of Women, some six hundred women from countries throughout the Western Hemisphere attended a three-day meeting that emphasized feminist issues. Inducted into the Florida Women's Hall of Fame in 1997, Alicia Baro died on January 2, 2012, at age ninety-three.

Much farther north, in a culture that was very different from Miami's, Bay County voters greeted Gladys Chapman as supervisor of elections when Governor Ferris Bryant appointed her to a vacancy in 1961. The move took some courage on the governor's part, as no woman had yet held public office in this Panama City area. Moreover, Chapman was something of a radical, in terms of having led the formation of the local Classroom Teachers Association in the 1940s. She and other CTA leaders—most of them women—were threatened with firing but ultimately were able to convince the all-male school board of their right to organize. Even as a teenager, when she was Gladys Alford, she showed her devotion to education: she moved temporarily to Alabama because Bay County had no high school.

Governor Bryant knew this history, respected her, and appointed Chapman to the elections office. She went on to win eight reelections, and her thirty-six-year tenure was the longest of any county elected official. She retired with the 1996 election and died on October 31, 1999. According to her obituary in the *Panama City News Herald*, Governors Bryant and Askew both attended her funeral. She attracted fans from both sides of the political spectrum: Charlie Whitehead, former state chair of the Democratic Party, said, "she was probably as strong a Democrat as I've ever known"—while a self-described conservative said she was the only Democrat for whom he had ever voted. In his anonymous 2009 blog "Around the Capertree," this man recalled that Gladys Chapman "always spoke in clear, concise, grammatically correct sentences, and as a reporter, I appreciated that."

* * *

The event that transformed Florida more than anything else in the 1960s actually occurred elsewhere: revolution in Cuba brought waves of immigrants to Miami. Unlike many earlier newcomers to the United States, most of these new arrivals had been affluent until they fled into exile when Fulgencio Batista fell to Fidel Castro's rebels in 1959. The new government confiscated their property, and most arrived without assets. By the end of the 1960s, about such 400,000 immigrants had arrived in south Florida, especially Miami. They were Spanish speakers with a distinctive culture and life experience, and over the next decades they would change Miami into a city akin to Havana. Helen Muir, well-known reporter for the *Miami Herald*, spoke to the particular impact for Miami's black women:

> You heard their protests first in your own kitchen. They began, "Them Cubans . . ." What they [black women] were saying was "they work longer hours for less money and are taking our jobs away from us. They are moving in on all the service jobs and we are losing out. The United States is giving them allowances and food stamps and low cost housing, but what about *us*?"
>
> Dr. Jean Jones Perdue, whose longtime work among the elderly won . . . national honors, remembers paying a first visit to the Claude Pepper Towers. "It was built for the black elderly, who were displaced when I-95 cut through their community. . . . It was filled with Cubans. . . . The director spoke only Spanish. . . . There were less than a dozen blacks in the whole place. . . .
>
> [Dr. Perdue said] when the Cubans came in and signed up for their allowances and food stamps, they were immediately put on the list for low-income housing. People who had lived and worked for generations in Miami were not.[16]

Everyone, poor or rich, Cuban or not, was affected by the Cuban missile crisis of 1962. Reconnaissance planes revealed that Russian missiles in Cuba were aimed at the United States. The island nation is just ninety miles from

Key West, and all across the United States people stayed glued to their televisions, fearful of a third world war that could be nuclear. Muir continued:

> Miamians learned about the missile crisis first hand by waking up to the sight of convoys of military trucks and extra trains filled with soldiers. . . .
>
> Some people packed up and fled. . . . Others battened down and discussed the possibility of bomb shelters. On the whole, Miamians responded as they always had to hurricanes—by laying in extra supplies of food and drinking water.
>
> At Doctor's Hospital [for blacks] blocks of beds were being set aside in case of emergency. One influential lady was most insistent about installing her elderly mother for safekeeping. She was turned away.[17]

President Kennedy won the political war: Russia removed the missiles; Castro agreed to allow regular "Freedom Flights" that carried departing Cubans to Miami for more than a decade; and the United States kept its southern Cuba naval base, Guantanamo. But the president did not encourage another invasion—something that had been a disaster the previous year, when exiles aided by the CIA failed in their attack on Cuba's Bay of Pigs. That unwillingness to depose Castro, in Helen Muir's words, "would earn President Kennedy lasting hatred" in Miami's Cuban community. They "became staunch Republicans and opened up an entirely new way of playing politics in South Florida, with passions unleashed and no holds barred. Miami became a hotbed of plotting and terrorist activity by extremist Cubans."[18] And just days after visiting Miami (and Tampa) in November 1963, the president was killed in Dallas.

While those who transformed Miami politics were mostly male, Cuban women arguably were accustomed to greater business leadership than American women of the time. Ofelia Tabares de Fernandez was perhaps the most impressive: she had been director of commerce in Cuba under the Batista government. Based in Miami, she developed ties with the United Nations to assist with the transition of immigrants. Another early refugee was Mignon Perez de Medrano, who had been "in charge of technical personnel training for the Esso corporation's oil refinery operations."[19] She set up an office in Coral Gables and began finding new jobs for her former employees in the new country.

Yvonne Zita Santa Maria is still another example of these enterprising women. Born to an upper-class family in Havana in 1928, she was bilingual and did public relations work for Barcardi Rum. She and her mother were arrested as counter-revolutionaries in 1961 and, after their release from prison, came to Miami with one suitcase and fifty dollars each, provided by the Red Cross. In less than twenty years, Santa Maria went from homelessness to being the first female Hispanic president of a savings and loan association. Appointed to the Governor's Commission on the Status of Women in 1977, she was its delegate to the United Nations International Women's Year convocation in Mexico City.

Most, but not all, Cuban exiles went to Miami. One important exception was Gladys Pumariger Soler, who had been born in the Cuban town of Pedro Betancourt in 1930; after earning her medical degree in 1955 at Havana University, she did her internship in Jacksonville. She practiced in Mantanzas, Cuba, until the revolution motivated her to return to Jacksonville, where she devoted herself to the care of indigent children. As director of pediatrics at Jacksonville University's Medical Center from 1964 to her retirement in 1992, Dr. Soler became widely known in children's medicine. She served on numerous medical and civic boards and in 1984 was inducted into the Florida Women's Hall of Fame. Dr. Soler died in 1993.[20]

Adela and Cesar Gonzmart lived permanently in Tampa after the revolution. They had gone back and forth between there and Havana earlier in their lives, as Adela Hernandez was the granddaughter of the founder of the Columbia Restaurant, which began in the Ybor City section of Tampa in 1905. Both Adela and Cesar were classical musicians; she a pianist and he a violinist. She had trained at New York's famed Juilliard School of Music, and they performed internationally. Adela Hernandez Gonzmart also is considered the founder of Florida's Ballet Folklorico.

Cuban immigration would continue to be controversial, as would another issue of the 1960s, the construction of the Cross-Florida Barge Canal. This had been an engineering dream since the first maps of Florida revealed how easily the chain of lakes connected to the St. Johns River could cross the peninsula to the Gulf of Mexico. Many people supported this transportation shortcut, which would save ships hundreds of miles. However, especially after Ohio's Lake Erie literally caught fire because of oil-based pollution, objections arose.

Women were a strong part of the environmental movement. In Jacksonville they fought shipping interests to clean up the St. Johns River, and they created an oceanside park named for early activist and historian Kathryn Abbey Hanna. Area women also were deeply involved in ending the stench of paper mills that hung over the air—something that businessmen argued was too expensive until women became active as environmentalist voters. Governor Bob Graham supported these efforts and others, especially with his precedent-setting appointment of Vicky Tschinkel as secretary of the Department of Environmental Regulation.

Marjory Stoneman Douglas, of course, was Florida's iconic environmentalist, known for decades as an opponent of draining the Everglades. Farther north, Marjorie Carr followed as the chief opponent of the Cross-Florida Barge Canal. In both cases, reworking natural waterways was destroying the habitat for native plants and animals, and women continued the leadership that they had already demonstrated in this cause since the turn of the twentieth century.[21]

Marjorie Harris Carr was born in Boston in 1915 but moved to Florida at age three. After earning a bachelor's degree in zoology from Florida State College for Women in 1936, she became the first female wildlife technician in the United States. She married naturalist Archie Carr in 1937 and bore five children while earning a 1942 master's degree from the University of Florida. From her Gainesville base she founded the Florida Defenders of the Environment in 1969.

Opposition to the canal did not seem likely to succeed. Parts of the project had been completed during the Great Depression and World War II, and President Lyndon Johnson set the explosives that resumed work in 1964. Carr and her organization filed suit in 1969, arguing that destruction of natural waterways would deplete the Florida Aquifer, and she withstood criticism as the case wound its way through the courts. A preliminary injunction was issued in January 1971, and just four days later, President Richard Nixon surprised many by following up with an executive order suspending construction.

By then $74 million had been spent and the canal was one-third complete. Nixon resigned in disgrace the following year, and the Army Corps of Engineers and its supporters aimed to continue digging. Carr and her forces failed to lobby through Congress a 1979 de-authorization bill, but she nonetheless continued her fight. Finally, in 1990, both Congress and the state legislature passed acts that ended the canal. Marjorie Carr died in 1997, a year after her admission to the Florida Women's Hall of Fame and a year prior to the naming of the land along the waterways as the Marjorie Harris Carr Florida Greenway.

* * *

No female judges served on the courts that handled Carr's case, and discrimination against women in the legal profession remained routine, even after the 1964 Civil Rights Act. Jeanne Crenshaw, who graduated from law school at the University of Florida in 1967, recalled in 2000 that law firms coming to campus to recruit new hires "tacked announcements of interview times on the bulletin board that included the loud-and-clear message: 'No women.'"[22]

Yet some older women did continue their slow ascent. Perhaps the most esteemed was Mattie Belle Davis. Born in Georgia in 1910 as Mattie Belle Edwards, she moved with her family to Miami in 1926. Unable to afford higher education, she worked as a legal secretary and studied on her own for the bar exam. Her effort made the front page of the *Miami Herald,* which announced on November 29, 1936, that she was the only area resident and the only woman in the state to pass that year's exam.

She married Troy C. Davis in 1937, and they practiced together for eleven years until he died. Left to support his teenage daughters from an earlier marriage, she carried on a solo practice at a time when that was difficult for women. Davis was active in both the Florida Association for Women Lawyers and the National Association of Women Lawyers, and she was an officer in the Business and Professional Women's Clubs. All this paid off in 1959, when she won appointment as the first female judge of the Metropolitan Court of Dade County. Judge Davis sometimes handled as many as two hundred traffic cases a day, and that expertise led President Lyndon Johnson to appoint her to the National Highway Safety Advisory Committee in 1967. Governors Reuben Askew and Bob Graham named her to similar state bodies in the next decade. Most significant, she pioneered defensive driving classes that have since been taken by millions of people, often under court order.

When municipal courts merged with county courts in 1973—partly because of efforts by the League of Women Voters—Davis would consistently win reelection as a county judge until mandatory retirement. In 1970 she became Florida's first woman elected as a Fellow of the American Bar Association, a very high honor. She presided over the founding meeting of the National Association of Women Judges and continued her activism during a long retirement. Judge Davis received many honors prior to her 2004 death, including her 1998 admission to the Florida Women's Hall of Fame.

In 1965 Governor Haydon Burns named Dixie Herlong Chastain to the Dade County Juvenile and Domestic Relations Court. A graduate of Stetson University in DeLand, she also studied sociology and government at

North Carolina's Duke University, and in 1930 Dixie Herlong had been the first woman to complete law school at the University of Miami.

After marrying businessman R. B. Chastain in 1935, she continued to practice law while also rearing three children. She ran two losing races for county court in the 1950s—but Governor Burns knew of her abilities and appointed her to a newly created judgeship. She won future elections, rising to the circuit court in 1973. Dade County commissioners named a new building for her prior to her 1979 retirement.

Like Judge Chastain, Edith E. House was admitted to the Florida Bar in 1930. She had been co-valedictorian of the law school at the University of Georgia in 1925, a credential so stellar that she had offers from two St. Petersburg firms in 1930, despite the Great Depression. After four years there, she moved to Jacksonville and joined the staff of the federal district attorney. Never marrying, House spent the rest of her career there. When the district was divided in 1963, she was named acting U.S. attorney for the Southern District of Florida, headquartered in Miami. Gender barriers were such, though, that she was not promoted from acting status, and after eight months in the interim job, she retired when a man took over. Edith House died in 1987, and her native Georgia has honored her memory more than has Florida.

The first black woman admitted to the Florida Bar was Bernice Gaines Dorn, in 1958, and almost a decade passed before there was a second. She was Gwendolyn Sawyer Cherry, who also would be the first African American woman in the state legislature. The Sawyer family long played a leading role in Miami's business community, as Gwen's father was Dade County's first black physician and her mother operated a hotel. They sent their daughter to New York for better educational opportunity, and she graduated from Florida Agricultural and Mechanical College in 1946 with a degree in chemistry and biology.

Returning north again, she earned a master's degree from New York University in 1950 and then taught at Miami's Northwestern Senior High School. She was the first African American of either gender to attend law school at the University of Miami, but graduated—at the top of her 1965 class—from Florida A&M. Her husband was James L. Cherry, and she was the first black woman to practice law in Miami.[23]

Ruby Burrows McZier, also an African American, did not have an affluent family, but she also was admitted to the Florida Bar in 1965. Born in the impoverished town of Belle Glade, she graduated from a historic black college in Talladega, Alabama. After teaching in Lake Wales she moved to Washington, D.C., where she graduated from Howard University's law school. Begun just after the Civil War, Howard was the nation's first university for blacks. The reality of gender bias, however, can be seen in that a century after Howard's founding, she was the only woman in her law class.

She married Arthur McZier, bore a daughter, and spent most of her career in Washington. Her first job there reflected her background in Belle Glade, as she advised Senator Edward Kennedy on farm worker issues. McZier moved on to the Equal Employment Opportunity Commission (EEOC), which enforced new federal laws that curbed discrimination. After 1971 McZier practiced privately, specializing in taxes, and served on the Metropolitan Washington Airports Authority. She did not forget her Florida roots, though, and was a trustee of Bethune-Cookman College and a founder of DeLand's Museum for African-American Art.

C. Bette Wisbish was admitted to the Florida Bar in 1968, passing the bar exam just days after her husband died. Always called Bette, which was pronounced "bet," she did not use her formal first name, Carrie. After graduating from Florida A&M in 1944, she had married Ralph Wimbush, and the couple led civil rights activism for the rest of their lives—although Bette was so light-skinned that she could have passed for white. He became a physician, while she changed her aspirations from medicine to law. She bore three children and would be forty-three years old when she finally earned her 1967 law degree at FAMU. Elected to St. Petersburg City Council in 1969, she was the first African American of either gender elected to such a position on Florida's west coast since Reconstruction; she rose to vice mayor in 1971. For many years, the Wimbushes ran a boardinghouse that was the only available housing for black members of the New York Yankees during baseball's spring training.

The fifth black woman admitted to the Florida Bar was the only one who risked her legal career with arrest. Arthenia Joyner, a state senator after the millennium, was arrested twice, once in her youth in the 1960s civil rights movement, and again in 1985, when she joined a Washington demonstration against apartheid in South Africa. Born in Lakeland in 1943, Joyner grew up in Tampa's downtown black community, where her father was a businessman. When she went to Tallahassee's FAMU in the early 1960s, Florida's civil rights movement was burgeoning, and Joyner was arrested when she joined demonstrators.

After graduating in 1964, she taught at Tampa's Booker T. Washington Junior High School and then returned to FAMU to earn her 1968 law degree. Admitted to the bar the following year, she has been in private practice longer than any other black woman in Florida. Joyner, who retained her maiden name during her marriage to civil rights attorney Delano Stewart, led Floridians in support of African American presidential candidates. She worked for New York congresswoman Shirley Chisholm in 1972, and in 1982 and 1984 led those supporting Jesse Jackson's nomination. A longtime member of the Florida legislature, Joyner has received many honors, including the 1984 presidency of the National Bar Association, the black equivalent of the American Bar Association. *Ebony* magazine chose Joyner as one of its 100 Most Influential Black Americans in 1985, and she was a delegate to two United Nations convocations on women's issues, in Africa and China.[24]

* * *

All of the African American women who became lawyers in the 1960s supported the civil rights movement, as did other women, both black and white. Important precedents had been set by black women in the 1940s and 1950s—especially by Hilda Turner, Harriette Moore, and young women at FAMU—but the movement would explode in the 1960s.[25]

Yet very little attention went to a 1962 case in Miami, when Connie Hoffman, a white woman, and her lover, seaman Dewey McLaughlin, were arrested for miscegenation—even though he was Honduran, not African American. They were sentenced to a month of hard labor, but Hoffman managed to carry the case to the U.S. Supreme Court. Two years later, it struck down Florida's law banning interracial sex.

More than the racial identity of sex partners, most minorities focused on segregation in daily life. In his book on Jacksonville politics, James B. Crooks compared life for black and white women as the 1960s got underway:

> The typical wife was white, American-born, and a high school graduate. She did not work outside the home. Locally only one-fifth of married women worked outside the home, and then usually only until becoming pregnant. . . . She visited the newer shopping centers on occasion but made major purchases of furniture and appliances at downtown stores. . . . Splurges for dinner, a movie, or dancing generally took place at a downtown restaurant, theater, or hotel. . . .

African-Americans constituted 42 percent of the population. . . . Most of them were not middle class; they lived in substandard housing . . . and were barred from the segregated downtown restaurants, theaters, or hotels. Still, they had begun to dream of a better world. . . . For Janet and Earl Johnson, who moved to Jacksonville in 1959 following Earl's completion of law school at Howard University, the time had come for action. It began during the holiday shopping season between Thanksgiving and Christmas in 1959. Black youths began picketing downtown stores. . . . [The next month], Jacksonville blacks entered . . . stores downtown requesting service at lunch counters.[26]

At Cohen Brothers, a major downtown store, about 500 of Jacksonville's 894 black teachers held charge accounts—but they were not allowed to eat there. By the end of the year, however, the *Pittsburgh Courier*, the longtime national standard of black journalism, reported significant change. "All over town," a December 1960 report said, "the 'White' and 'Colored' signs . . . were torn down and tossed into garbage cans.[27]

Such victories were piecemeal, with steps forward and steps backward. Although integration occurred at Jacksonville stores, public school integration was such that, in 1962—eight years after the Supreme Court ruling—only thirteen black children were enrolled in previously all-white schools. In response to that tiny bit of progress, the Ku Klux Klan bombed the home of a student who lived with his grandparents, Mr. and Mrs. George R. Gilliam, and an all-white jury acquitted the five men charged with the crime. More violence broke out in March 1964, and Johnnie Mae Chappell, an African American mother of ten, was fatally shot by a white man as she searched for the wallet she lost in the melee. Two hundred people, mostly young black men, were arrested, but no one was charged with Chappell's killing.

Tampa had the second NAACP chapter in the South, back in 1915, but some regard the city's civil rights movement as having begun on February 29, 1960, when—after a delay caused by a bomb threat—Rev. Martin Luther King spoke at Fort Homer Hesterly Armory. More than 4,200 people attended. Teacher Florene Jones "worked the hardest to get King to come," and in a 2011 interview, she said:

People dressed up in their Sunday best. Well, it was just very motivating and it gave you the sense that you really wanted to go out and do something, that you wanted to demonstrate. You didn't worry about whether you might lose your job—you just wanted to go for the equal rights and what it meant to us as African Americans. Our eyes did not begin to come open until Dr. King came to town and he started telling us about the injustices that, as a race of people, we faced everyday.[28]

Nine days later, some young blacks "did something," and among them was future Hillsborough County Commissioner Sylvia Rodriguez Kimbell. They attempted to eat at Woolworth's, which like many stores of that era had a lunch counter stretching along one wall from front to back. "Rather than being presented with menus, they were presented with a sign: Closed."[29] But after more such attempts—all non-violent, in line with King's philosophy—the Tampa Bi-Racial Commission formed, and lunch counters were desegregated.

After NAACP activists Harry and Harriette Moore were killed by racists who bombed their Brevard County home, Bob and Helen Saunders of Tampa took over the NAACP state leadership role.[30] This took courage, especially because Helen had been born in Mims, the town where the Moores were attacked. When Helen Saunders died in 2011, longtime NAACP leader Leon Russell of Pinellas County said in his eulogy, "Helen was a civil rights warrior long before she met Bob, but they were a perfect civil rights union."

As Helen Strickland, she was the 1940 valedictorian of Titusville Negro High School and attended Bethune-Cookman College; she married Bob Saunders in 1954. The Saunders's six-year-old son was Hillsborough County's first black student to attempt integration, and "carloads of people followed an NAACP Youth Council group to the Saunders home . . . and threw garbage and racial epithets. 'Danger was something you just had to accept in those days,'"[31] Bob later wrote in his memoirs. Bob Saunders Jr. was finally accepted in a West Tampa elementary school where the children were largely from Cuban families.

Ironically, the successful 1960s integration of dime-store lunch counters was the action of private enterprise, while in so-called public schools, segregation continued. Almost two decades after the 1954 U.S. Supreme Court decision on this, Hillsborough schools finally integrated fully in 1971. Among the leaders of this integration were Gwen Miller, an African American educator and future member of Tampa City Council, and future mayor Pam Iorio, who was then student president of her middle school.

By that time Fort Lauderdale schools had been integrated, largely because of a suit filed by Eula Gandy Johnson, a middle-aged African American. She also led the area fight for integrated beaches, and her "swim-in" made the pages of nationally syndicated news, including the mass magazine *Look*. On July 4, 1961, Johnson encouraged teenage blacks, mostly male, to "wade-in" to the Atlantic. The City of Fort Lauderdale sued her, but a court ruled in her favor. As president of the local NAACP, Eula Johnson suffered several threats on her life and businesses. She was a widow with three children but nevertheless achieved ownership of a grocery store and two gas stations. A decade after her death in 2001, some of that property is being turned into a museum.

Others challenged segregation on beaches in other coastal cities, and blacks finally had access to cool waters. Prior to this, the only decent beach accessible to them was privately run American Beach, on the Atlantic in far northeast Florida, where the influence of Mary McLeod Bethune had long been a beneficial factor. Farther south in Johnson's area, blacks were limited to a Port Everglades beach that people reached via a ferry—and once there, they found no fresh water, toilets, tables, or other facilities.

On the national level the Young Women's Christian Association had a longtime commitment to both wholesome recreation and racial equality, and even though this was difficult to implement in Florida, there was evidence of success by 1964. In its USF edition the *Tampa Tribune* published a photograph of an integrated committee meeting. Three of the young women were white, and three were black. The caption read: "Y-Teen leaders plan work and fun activities for a regional conference held at USF last week."

Among other white women who supported the black civil rights movement was Dr. Helen Taylor Dexter, who moved from Cincinnati to Pinellas County in 1954. She had grown up privileged, attending boarding school in France, going to college at Pennsylvania's exclusive Bryn Mawr, and adventuring with archaeology in Alaska and Russia. One of four women in her medical school class at New York's Columbia University, she married her biology professor and specialized in dermatology. But Clearwater in the 1950s contrasted with her previous life, and some patients were so poor that Dr. Dexter accepted garden produce or chickens as payment. When Dexter died in 2011, at age 101, her daughter said: "At that time, black people came in through the back door of the office, but she insisted that people of color would be going through the front door."[32]

In addition to attention to civil rights, President Lyndon Johnson and his Democratic Congress created several programs in the mid-1960s that attempted to end poverty in America. These were aimed at poor and uneducated people of all skin colors, but some Floridians objected to such efforts even though they included whites. The Job Corps, intended to equip high-school dropouts with work skills, was one such, and it developed a curriculum for women, teaching skills such as hairdressing. St. Petersburg was chosen as the first site, but local people rejected it.

Sargent Shriver, brother-in-law of the late President Kennedy and head of the Job Corps, announced on May 14, 1966, "the nation's first Job Corps Center for Women will be moved from St. Petersburg, Fla., because of the 'hostile environment' there." That Associated Press story ran throughout the nation, and the *New York Times* reinforced the city's negative attitude by saying, "This is the first time that a center has been forced to move, although other centers have been embroiled in local controversies." The *Washington Post*'s lead sentence was "The nation's first Job Corps Center for Women was run out of St. Petersburg, Fla. Today." The local paper ran these comments and concluded that the unwelcoming image "won't help the tourist trade." Nothing was said about the loss of career opportunity for young women.

* * *

Future historians will probably judge that for half of the population, nothing else was as important during the second half of the twentieth century as the women's liberation movement and its chief incarnation, National Organization for Women.

NOW began as a direct result of President Kennedy's Commission on the Status of Women. After a meeting of that body in Washington, some members expressed their frustration about working within governmental constraints, and they formed NOW on October 29, 1966.

Few Floridians realized it, but the movement's pioneers in cities such as New York and Chicago were much influenced by female theorists in Gainesville. According to historian Carol Giardina:

> In 1967, the first women's liberation group . . . in Chicago . . . floundered [until] a paper arrived from Gainesville, a small town in North Florida . . . , [which] transformed our thinking. After that paper, there would be no turning back for us or for the rest of the movement. . . .
>
> "Toward a Female Liberation Movement," known as "The Florida Paper," [was] self-published in June 1968 by Beverly Jones and Judith Brown. The paper provided the crystallizing idea needed by the emerging movement. Women must fight their own battles, said Jones and Brown. Women must stop fighting other people's battles. . . .

In Search of Equity: NOW

Unlike during the earlier campaign for the vote, southern states formed chapters of the National Organization for Women about as quickly as did northern states. The Gainesville Women's Liberation Movement began in 1967, just months after NOW began nationally, and Jacksonville, Miami, and other Florida cities followed within the next few years. Under the leadership of Von Kerik and her sister, Lee DeCesare, for example, the Tampa chapter began in May 1972.

Women from south Florida attended a national meeting of NOW in Washington on February 13, 1973, and national leaders appointed Broward County's Karen Coolman as coordinator for Florida. After follow-up meetings in Orlando and Tampa, a committee meeting in Gainesville in August nominated Coolman as the elected leader (initially called "coordinator"; later changed to "president"). Coolman was elected at the first statewide meeting, in Orlando in September 1973, and served until the following September, when she resigned to concentrate on her successful race for the legislature.

By then the national office had issued charters to eleven local NOW chapters. In alphabetical order they were Broward, Dade, Gainesville, Jacksonville, Orlando, Pensacola, Polk, South Dade, South Palm Beach County, Tallahassee, and Tampa. Fifteen others soon were added, ranging from Key West in the south to Pensacola in the far northwest.

Turnout for NOW's first state convention was impressive. The speakers at an evening banquet were Jackie Frost, the regional director from Atlanta, and Wilma Scott Heide, who had replaced Betty Friedan as national president. Almost two dozen workshops met in the afternoon. Hundreds of women attended these workshops, and they went home to energize thousands. Their efforts permanently changed the future.

Note: All information taken from Florida NOW: Brief History, www.flnow.org/history.

"The Florida Paper" spread like wildfire across the United States. ... In January 1969, Carol Hanisch left New York for Gainesville, joined Gainesville Women's Liberation, and opened ... Freedom for Women, with funding for a staff organizer. That March, Carol Hanisch wrote ... "The Personal is the Political," the article that coined the phrase and provided the earliest formulation of this key concept.[33]

Betty Friedan, best-selling author of *The Feminine Mystique* (1963), was the first president of NOW, and by the time she stepped down in 1970, after only a little more than three years, 750 delegates from 118 chapters attended that year's national convention. Delegates promoted a one-day national strike by women on August 26, 1970, which was the fiftieth anniversary of the Nineteenth Amendment that granted all women the vote. Women's history was so little known that almost no one was aware of the anniversary, but feminist writers managed to garner a great deal of press attention, including in Florida. Not all the attention was positive, of course, as conservatives objected to the strike—but the overall effect for NOW was excellent, and membership soared.[34]

Vicki Wengrove formed the Jacksonville Women's Movement (JWM) in 1970. According to historian James Crooks, the JWM "began with consciousness raising, moved on to lobbying Mayor Tanzler to appoint more women to public boards, secured the formation of the Mayor's Advisory Committee on the Status of Women," and after the 1973 Supreme Court ruling in *Roe vs. Wade*, "established self-help clinics to offer abortion counseling."[35]

The women's movement tackled a widening range of issues. One of its most significant early victories was pressuring newspapers to end employment ads that routinely segregated jobs by gender. At the time, classified ad sections of newspapers read "Help Wanted—Men" and "Help Wanted—Women," instead of today's "sales," "professional," and so on. Under the leadership of English professor Lee DeCesare, the *Tampa Tribune* was one example of success in this area. DeCesare also sued the local CBS Television station for its failure to have any female reporters on the air, successfully transforming that important arena. The Miami area already had set a major precedent in 1967, when WTVJ employed Jane Chastain as the nation's first female sports broadcaster. Molly Turner likewise pioneered in Miami television, beginning as a singer in 1951 and retiring in 1989 as an Emmy-winning investigative reporter.

Burgeoning NOW chapters also worked on education reform. Along with the older American Association for University Women, NOW can claim major credit for ending school practices that routinely routed girls into home economics and secretarial classes, while boys were assigned to agriculture or business. Publishers were pressured into eliminating similar stereotypes in textbooks, and feminists spent years lobbying school boards to provide equity for girls in athletics.

Conservatives in Congress had found the notion of equality for blacks to be so far-fetched that when President Lyndon Johnson forced debate of the 1964 Civil Rights Act, they added women—believing this was so obviously absurd that it would cause the bill to fail. They were wrong: progressives had enough votes that the law passed with women specifically included, and pioneer feminists used its provisions to file many court cases against discrimination. With the era's other burning issues, including opposition to the Vietnam War, many conservatives lost their elections, and by 1972 voters had elected enough progressives that another congressional act extended educational equity. Title IX of the 1972 act became famous, as it provided the legal framework for increased participation of girls in athletics; because of heavy focus on football, schools spent much more money on male students than on females. Fortuitously, Barbara Jo Palmer began her career at Florida State University at the same time.

A Pennsylvania native born in 1948, she earned bachelor's and master's degrees at FSU; in 1977 she became director of women's athletic programs. Her teams would win five national championships, but her true legacy was her lobbying for Title IX. She helped write the legislation and devoted decades to its enforcement, both before and after her 1982 induction into the Florida Women's Hall of Fame. Because of her, many discriminatory practices ended: prior to Title IX, girls in public schools had to buy their uniforms, while boys did not; boys got free meals on out-of-town trips, while girls went hungry or paid for their own; boys got access to gyms at reasonable hours, while girls had to practice early in the morning or late at night.

NOW chapters in several Florida cities filed lawsuits to allow women to become firefighters and police officers. Until then women were hired only as "meter maids" who collected money from parking meters, and most sheriffs and police chiefs argued that women were physically incapable of law enforcement work. Some women who worked for this change truly were fearful of false arrests by resentful police. Miami State Representative Elaine Gordon joined Lee DeCesare in arguing the point with Tampa Mayor Dick Greco. Today's female police officers and firefighters owe a great deal to such women, who had no interest in obtaining these jobs for themselves but took real risks to open doors for others.

NOW members led the building of women's centers and shelters for victims of domestic violence. State Representative Helen Gordon Davis personally guaranteed the mortgage on an old mansion that became the Centre for Women in Tampa, an institution aimed at "displaced homemakers"—women who found themselves divorced or widowed and without income-producing skills. Along with Betty Castor in the Florida Senate, Davis successfully sponsored legislation that raised the cost of marriage licenses to fund such programs. Feminists also lobbied to reform laws on rape and insisted that it be treated like other crimes: at the time in Florida, for example, victims had to pay for expensive medical kits that provided the material evidence to prosecute the rapist.

NOW also took on the issue of reforming maternity practices, along with Lamaze, a French-based group that promoted natural childbirth, and La Leche, which advocated breast-feeding. Physicians, most of them male, had a vested interest in doing things they way they had long been done, using general anesthetics in labor and delivery as well as keeping new mothers isolated from husbands and supportive family. Since the beginning of the postwar baby boom, an entire industry had developed to supplant breast-feeding with bottle-feeding, and most physicians insisted that the artificial method was more "scientific." Led by feminists who argued that their grandmothers' ways were superior, thousands of Florida women joined Lamaze and La Leche and overturned systems that removed them from controlling their bodies and babies.

Without intending to become controversial, Gladys Nichols Milton soon was a symbol of this "back to the future" thinking. An African American born in rural Walton County in 1924, she learned to deliver babies in an era when no area hospital admitted black women. Herself the mother of seven, she had no opportunity to obtain educational credentials, but she safely delivered more than two thousand babies. She welcomed women of all races to her Milton Memorial Birthing Clinic in Laurel Hill, the first such institution in the Panhandle. Local (male) physicians responded by calling on their friends in the legislature to outlaw midwives.

Racists set fire to both Milton's home and her clinic, and she was featured in several national magazines. Feminists, especially Miami's Nikki Beare, who lobbied for nurses in Tallahassee, took up her cause, and legislation on midwives absorbed feminists for several sessions in the 1970s and 1980s. As

Stop Rape

Women Against Rape was a national nonprofit organization with the goal of educating the public about the legal, medical, and psychological aftermath of rape. In 1973 an organization member, Sharron Long, who was originally from New Zealand, came to Tampa via California, where she had been instrumental in opening a Rape Crisis Center.

Her work in California inspired two local women, Terry Casto and Virginia Daire, to spearhead such a movement in Tampa. It began with a panel discussion, "After the Rape," at the Ashley Street Library Auditorium on Tuesday, November 20, 1973.

Panelists included Ms. Long; Major Frank Bowen of the Tampa Police Force; Betsy Colson, formerly of the Hillsborough County Sheriff's Department and an investigator for the University Police Department; Delores Turner of Miami, who at the time was the director of Miami's Women in Distress, Inc.; the Honorable Harry Lee Coe, a circuit court judge; Barbara Godfrey, who revealed that she was a rape survivor; Major Walter Heinrich, a police officer later elected sheriff; Dr. Julian Rice, the director of Hospitals for Hillsborough County; Faith Weatherington of the University of South Florida; Baya Harrison III, an assistant attorney general to then attorney general Robert Shevin; and Richard Levinson, a local assistant public defender.

The auditorium was full to overflowing. As it turned out, a number of the attendees were survivors of rape who, for the first time in their lives, felt they could speak out against the emotionally brutal treatment that they had received, not only at the hands of their rapists but also from people in law enforcement and in the medical and legal communities after reporting the rape.

This led to the founding the Rape Crisis Center. In 1974 Virginia (Reber) received an award from the Florida West Coast Professional Chapter of Women in Communications, Inc. The organization said:

> Rape is not a pretty topic and perhaps, for that very reason, it has never had much done about it, until recently. Women haven't always reported it, courts haven't always prosecuted it, neither the public nor the police were sympathetic about it, and not very

many people wanted to talk about it. Our next winner is one of the people who had the stick-to-it-iveness to see this project to fruition. Calmly, through intelligent action and soft-spoken dignity, she has helped to bring rape, the country's fastest growing violent crime, to the public eye.

Note: Casto is now known as Terry Wollin and is a city council member in Pinellas County's Indian Rocks Beach. Daire, then known as Ginger Reber, became a Tallahassee attorney and directed the Florida Supreme Court's Gender Bias Study. She wrote this sidebar.

women's participation in their own health care became more acceptable, Gladys Milton would be admitted to the Florida Women's Hall of Fame in 1994, five years prior to her death. She had already earned the Sage Femme (wise woman) award, the highest honor of the Midwives Alliance of North America, in 1992 and had written her autobiography, *Why Not Me?* (1993).

NOW did an immense amount of lobbying under the guidance of young lobbyists Alyce McAdam and future legislator Anne Gannon—but it was not an entirely political organization. Many members felt a stronger attraction to "consciousness raising," which was essentially a form of group therapy. Personal discussions in informal groups without official leaders focused on the way gender bias permeates all aspects of life and how women could deal with the hurt it caused. Some members boycotted products that used advertising denigrating women, and others emphasized dress reform: indeed, the national press fixated on alleged "bra burnings" in New Jersey.

Without breaking from NOW and its wide agenda, many women whose interests were more political than social formed the National Women's Political Caucus (NWPC) in 1971. Florida quickly followed that too, as NWPC branches developed with chapters from Fort Myers to Jacksonville. Like the older League of Women Voters, the caucus was bipartisan, and both groups worked for the Equal Rights Amendment. The league, however, took stands on issues but not on candidates, while the chief goal of the caucus was to elect feminist women to office. Among the top leaders were Democrats Katherine C. Kelly of Palm Beach, Marjorie Head of Broward County, Edna Saffy and Sharon Laird of Jacksonville, and Barbara Dunn and Roxanne Dow of Tallahassee. Leading Republicans included Tomah Smith of Sarasota and Kate Gooderham of Fort Myers.

"We Believed We Could Change the World": Hospice Pioneer Mary Labyak

Another of the era's significant changes was acknowledgment of the need for specialized care for the terminally ill. The word "hospice" did not enter the language until 1967, when the first such institution opened in London. Almost a decade later, in 1975, there were just two hospices in the United States. But under the Carter Administration, Congress began to provide funding to these facilities, where everyone knew that the patient would not recover but should be entitled to end life with dignity.

In 1979 Pinellas County social worker Mary Labyak joined with "like-minded volunteers seeking to improve care for the dying." By 1983 she headed Suncoast Hospice, and given the large number of elderly people who retire to Pinellas, it soon became one of the nation's largest. Labyak provided a pioneering model for today's 2,500 hospices.

In addition to caring for the dying elderly, Labyak created programs for children, AIDS patients, and survivors of trauma and suicide. In a 2011 speech she said, "We always believed that our hospice didn't exist to be simply a provider of Medicare. . . . We believed we could change the world."

When Mary Labyak died in 2012, board member Marsha Lederman said of Suncoast: "When they started, it was very small, mainly volunteer based. It was Mary who created what we have today, and 99 percent of it was her inspiration. She was a brilliant person."

Nikki Beare, who defended feminist interests in the drafting of midwifery law, was a founding member of NWPC on all levels, from the national to Dade County. She hosted the first radio talk show for women in Florida, "Women's Powerline," and published a statewide newspaper, *Women's Almanac.* She also represented Florida at United Nations international gatherings on women's rights in Kenya (1985) and Beijing (1995). Born in 1928, she lives in retirement in Havana, a north Florida town where she moved with her daughter, Sandy Beare, after Hurricane Andrew destroyed their Miami home. Nikki Beare was admitted to the Florida Women's Hall of Fame in

1994; in 1991 Sandy Beare became the first executive director of the reestablished Florida Commission on the Status of Women.

Roxcy Bolton also was affected by the disastrous 1991 hurricane and, like Nikki Beare, had been a founder of both NOW and the Women's Political Caucus. While retaining the accent and manners of her 1926 birthplace in Mississippi, Bolton became active in Dade County Democratic politics while in her thirties. The charter president of the local NOW chapter, she was elected as a national vice president in 1969, when the national body was less than three years old. She established the first women's rescue shelter in modern Florida, in 1972, an action very soon emulated in other cities. In 1974 Bolton founded the first rape treatment center at Jackson Memorial Hospital; it was named for her in 1993.

Women's Park in Miami also is her brainchild, and the *Miami Herald* honored her with its Spirit of Excellence award in 1988. Roxcy O'Neal Bolton was inducted into the Florida Women's Hall of Fame in 1984.

* * *

The legislature moved from biannual to annual sessions after voters approved a major revision of the state constitution in 1968, and that was a factor in making the 1970s "the Golden Age" of Florida lawmaking. The League of Women Voters led a successful effort to unify the court system and to encourage better-qualified judges. Voters also adopted laws that required candidates to disclose their sources of income, which cut down on conflict of interest and bribery. The third major change was adoption of "Sunshine" laws that were the best in the nation: they insisted on open governmental meetings and access to public records.

The league was the key organization in developing and passing these innovations, which fundamentally changed the nature of government. Many men accustomed to the old style of doing business dropped out of elective office rather than obey the new laws, which banned personal meetings among local elected officials and mandated disclosure of financial interests. The nature of the women in the legislature also changed, as female lawmakers became much more assertive.

One aspect of 1970s feminism can be seen simply in name usage. In the 1960s the media routinely referred to married women by their husbands' names, and those who were unmarried saw that status spelled out with "Miss." When the legislature included the two Beth Johnsons, for example, newspapers called the Orlando senator "Mrs. George W. Johnson" and the Cocoa senator "Mrs. Peter Johnson."

Lori Wilson, the third woman elected to the Florida Senate, might also have been referred to as "Mrs.," but like Mary Lou Baker in the 1940s, Wilson used her own name and not that of her husband, Gannett newspaper executive Al Neuharth. Underscoring her independence, Senator Wilson was elected in 1970 as an independent, declining to identify with either party. Independently wealthy, she spent almost $55,000—a fortune at the time—to win the right to represent Merritt Island, east of Orlando. Florida's first three female senators thus were from that region.

Much more feminist than the first two female senators, Lori Wilson led the fight for the Equal Rights Amendment. The outspoken senator was not handicapped by the fact that she was a beautiful blonde, and everyone of that era remembers her trademark white pantsuits—which she wore when they were considered radical apparel, especially in a legislative body where pants appeared to challenge a longtime male prerogative. She left the Senate at the end of 1978, after rising to vice chair of the Judiciary-Civil Committee in her last term. A Space Coast park on the beach has been named for Senator Lori Wilson.

Two women entered the Florida House in the 1970 election: Gwen Sawyer Cherry, an African American Democrat profiled earlier in this chapter in her role as an attorney, and Jane W. Robinson, who followed in the tradition of Senator Elizabeth Johnson as a liberal Republican from Cocoa.

Born in Oklahoma, Robinson had married, borne three children, and lived in many places before settling in Florida in 1965—just five years prior to her election. A photographer and former journalist in Washington, D.C., she also was an aviator and ran a Brevard County public relations agency. Robinson later mused of the 1971 session, which had four women in the House and one in the Senate:

> While five women certainly didn't constitute a majority, subtle changes began to take place. Lobbying efforts that had taken the form of "stag parties" suddenly became "family parties." While many wives had always accompanied their husbands to Tallahassee for the session, it became more common . . .
>
> Why is it that female politicians are always introduced by the number of children they have, but the fact rarely is noted in regard to men?
>
> I recall one of the lobbyists plopping down next to me during a committee recess and candidly asking, "We always send a case of beer to

> each of the legislators, but we don't know what to send to you women. Perfume? Candy?
>
> I remember asking him, "Why not a case of beer?" He was taken aback, but I believe, came to grips with the fact that women wanted the same treatment as men. . . .
>
> My first committee meeting was a social fiasco. . . . I had sat up late to read and underline all the bills on the agenda. I arrived first and took a seat at the long committee table. As the Members arrived, they took up positions at the table—in every chair but the ones at my right and left. I was quarantined as Typhoid Mary. . . .
>
> Staff members began to feed me some of their research, especially when they . . . hadn't been allowed to offer negative information in the staff report. They frequently made me look a lot smarter than I deserved![36]

Armed with insider knowledge from staff, she found that her colleagues came to respect the new female representative and saw the advantages of lifting their "quarantine." After three terms, Robinson left the House in 1976 to become chief of the Division of Consumer Services in the Department of Agriculture. It was a new bureau, and the rising awareness of consumer issues was still another indication of increased female participation in politics.

Gwen Sawyer Cherry marked an even more visible change in the 1971 session, as she was the first black woman in the legislature. She was a vital part of all the major reforms during that decade, but her life was cut short when she died in a Tallahassee car accident during the 1979 legislative session. In his eulogy, Governor Bob Graham called her "a champion for the rights of all people, and a voice of reason and concern." She was posthumously inducted into the Florida Women's Hall of Fame under his administration, in 1986. Because she had worked for child care, in 1991, Education Commissioner Betty Castor would name the child care center that opened in the Department of Education's new building for Representative Cherry.

Gwen Cherry was the first to introduce the Equal Rights Amendment to the House, in 1972, and that autumn's election brought more change. Four women, the most ever, won House seats. All were strong feminists, and Mary Littlejohn Singleton of Jacksonville joined Cherry as the second black female representative.

Singleton's political career began on Jacksonville City Council, where she was elected vice president in 1967—appreciably earlier for either white or black women than in most cities. She served nearly four years in the House before resigning to become head of the Division of Elections under Secretary of State Bruce Smathers, another Jacksonville Democrat. Secretary of state was an elective office at that time, and Smathers's appointment of a black woman to head a major bureau was preceded only by Governor Reubin Askew's 1970 appointment of Athalie Range.

Two white women also won in 1972. Betty Easley was a Republican who represented St. Petersburg and, like other Republicans of her era, supported the Equal Rights Amendment. She also strongly supported noise control and successfully sponsored legislation—rarely enforced—to limit the volume of car audio systems. Born in 1929 as Betty Chapman in Victoria, Texas, the self-described "Army brat" was educated all over the world. She was sufficient talented artistically to work as a medical illustrator at famed Walter Reed Army Hospital in Washington, D.C., before marrying Kenneth Easley and moving to Florida in 1957. She bore five children while also working in various jobs and was active in a number of organizations, including Business and Professional Women.

Easley would serve in the legislature from 1972 to 1986, and colleague Peter Dunbar said "we used to call her the 'House Mother' because she was a conscience helper for all of us."[37] Representative Marilyn Jones-Evans, who served with Easley in the 1980s, remembered:

> I loved to see her get that gleam in her eye, pull out that microphone and begin debating. Most of the women Members, at that time, really didn't have the knowledge, the courage or the ability to debate all the issues, but Betty was there ready, willing, and able. The only times that I would have liked Betty to sit down was when she was debating against one of my bills. She reminded me of a tea bag in hot water. She just got stronger and stronger.[38]

Easley and the other newcomers from the 1972 election actively supported the ERA, but the most important victory for feminists was that of Miami's Elaine Gordon. She would serve more than two decades, until her retirement at the 1994 election; in 1992 she became dean of the Florida House, having been reelected to that body longer than anyone else. She established this record despite strong opinions that included sponsoring or co-sponsoring every bit of legislation that liberated women's lives during this important era. Elaine Gordon's significance can be seen in that she was the very first inductee into the Florida Women's Hall of Fame at its 1982 beginning.

Born in New York, she moved to Miami in 1964 and won election to the House just eight years later, after working as an aide to Representative George Firestone. Like him, she was a strong Democrat. Progressive Democrats controlled the House in this era, and Gordon rose to significant roles, especially in appropriations for health and children. Her career was not without struggles large and small, however, as Gordon recalled of her first arrival:

> I peeked into the Chamber, thrilled, of course, about being elected and longing to see my seat. Lo and behold, the tag designating my name on the front of my desk said, "Mrs. Gordon." I quickly contacted the Sergeant and said, "That is not correct. I'm not 'Mrs. Gordon,' I'm 'Ms. Gordon.'" He said that he would fix it up, so that afternoon I looked and it said, "Mr. Gordon." I called him again and he said, "Oh, it was a terrible mistake . . ." Well, by now, it was 10:00 Tuesday and time to go in for the swearing in. When I walked in, the tag said, "Miss Gordon."[39]

Perhaps because she was young, divorced, and the first Jewish woman in the legislature, her male colleagues directed a disproportionate amount of venom at Representative Gordon. One example was early in her career, when the Old Capitol was still in use. Rooms were small and poorly ventilated, and most men smoked either cigars or cigarettes. She was allergic to tobacco and asked the smokers to group themselves in one area of the committee table. Although also a Miami Democrat and a physician, Wally Sackett instead blew smoke in her face. Even more egregious, Representative Ray Maddox had the temerity to change the parliamentary phrase "lay the bill on the table" to "lay Ms. Gordon on the table."[40]

In addition to the election of these women, the other distinctive thing about 1972 was the beginning of the Women's Studies program at the University of South Florida. It has a legitimate claim to being considered the nation's second oldest, as it appears to have followed only San Diego State University, where such a program began in 1970. USF's founder was Dr. Juanita Williams, a psychologist born in 1928. She wrote a popular textbook, *Psychology of Women,* the first edition of which was published by prestigious W. W. Norton in 1977.

Historian Judith Ochshorn was slightly older, having been born in 1922, and she also pioneered Women's Studies in 1972; she would go on to publish *The Female Experience and the Nature of the Divine* (1981). With political scientist Janice Snook, who taught Woman and Law, Williams participated in the founding convention of the National Women's Studies Association, held in San Francisco in 1977. Yet despite the credentials of these and other founders, the program would not win departmental status until 1992, two decades after its founding and—not coincidentally—when the first female president, Betty Castor, headed USF.[41] After Castor left, it again declined from departmental to program status, as the university has failed to acknowledge its rightful pioneer status in this academic field.

Many Florida cities conduct municipal elections in odd-numbered years, and the 1973 cycle brought a female mayor to Fort Lauderdale. Virginia Shuman Young, born in 1917, had grown up in the then small town; her father signed the city's incorporation papers in 1911. After marriage and a family, she won election to the Broward County school board in 1953 and served there for twelve years, until her 1965 defeat. Successful in a 1971 race for the Fort Lauderdale City Commission, she went on to be mayor in 1973. The city's system was a one-year term that was awarded by her peers on council, not a direct election by the people. Young was mayor again in 1981 and was continually reelected to the city council until 1985, when she declined to seek an eighth term. Boca Raton had a similar system, and Dorothy Wilken, a Pennsylvania native, was mayor in 1976–77.

* * *

The 1974 election brought more feminists to the Florida House, notably the first woman from Hillsborough County. Helen Gordon Davis was no kin to Elaine Gordon, but both were Jews originally from New York City. Helen Gordon Davis—who always used her maiden name as part of her unhyphenated full name—came to Tampa after World War II with her husband, Gene Davis. He built a successful business as a liquor distributor, while she bore three children and was active in numerous organizations. The first white member of the area NAACP, she was motivated to join by segregation on the city's buses: her black nanny was forced to sit at the back, while Davis had to sit in the front and manage the children without assistance from her employee.

As president of the Hillsborough County League of Women Voters, Helen Gordon Davis played a major role in rewriting state laws that reformed the judiciary in the 1970s. Although the county still had multi-member districts in 1974, she easily won her first election and was popular enough to have no opponent in 1976. Her 1978 Democratic primary was close, but Davis prevailed. She established herself as perhaps the state's chief champion of those in need, including prisoners and migrant laborers and, in the next decade, would move on to the Senate.[42] In a 1995 interview, she said:

> The election of women to the State Legislature in the early seventies was both an outgrowth of the feminist movement . . . and a reaction to the abuse and misuse of power. . . . And so the public turned to women as the panacea to all their ills.
>
> Those women who were elected at that time were older, mostly in their forties [and] more issue-oriented—coming from their studies with the League of Women Voters and the PTAs. . . .
>
> However, they were naive about power politics and unprepared for the condescension and derision that greeted every issue related to women. From alimony based on years of marriage . . . to displaced homemaker training, from mandatory Pap tests to sex education, the issues were so distorted and denigrated by male colleagues that it was difficult to be gracious and to persevere to another year.
>
> Yet, with a few great men, women were the conscience of the Legislature. . . . [They] opened new avenues . . . for farm workers, child abuse, mental health, day care . . . all the social issues of the day.[43]

The west coast elected a second woman to the House in 1974, and Mary Ellen Hawkins was the first from the southwestern portion of the state. A Republican, she represented the wealthy community of Naples but understood historic discrimination against women of every class. A divorcee with three children, she said of attitudes in her Alabama youth:

> Women weren't expected to have planned careers. A woman was expected to work at a job only while waiting for a prince. . . . Someone like me [who] wanted to spend the money for a medical education and, even worse, take up a slot at a medical school, was vigorously discouraged. . . . I never got over my resentment of the Old South's double standard, and I resolved to do what I could to make things better for women who wanted to pursue untraditional jobs and participate in public affairs.[44]

After attending the University of Alabama, Hawkins moved to Washington and worked for her local congressman. She discovered that he was extremely lax in carrying out his duties and that she and other women in his office were expected to cover for him. "It was great training," she recalled wryly, adding that women, no matter how highly placed they were, were not allowed to join the male-only Congressional Secretaries Club and were paid about half as much as men. Marriage took her to Americus, Georgia, where she may have been the first local woman on a grand jury—in a courthouse that had no restroom for her. After divorcing, Hawkins came to Florida in 1972, worked as a political reporter for the *Naples Daily News,* and just two years later was elected to the legislature. She would go on to be dean of Republican women in the House, serving through 1994. She recalled at that time:

> When I arrived in Tallahassee for my first session, I noted that what is now the "Spouses Lounge" was then the "Wives Lounge," even though there were married women Members of the House. I also noted that amendment forms said "Mr. ________ moves the amendment." Invitations from lobbyists urged me to bring my wife.[45]

Hawkins was the only Republican of either gender elected in 1974, and it would be Gene Davis, husband of Democrat Helen Gordon Davis, who was most responsible for the gender integration of the "wives" lounge. He brought coffee and other refreshments, and when the wives saw that he made himself comfortable there, they suggested the change to "Spouses Lounge."

In addition to Hawkins and Davis, four women from south Florida, all Democrats, won House races in 1974. Nancy O. Harrington of Coral Gables served just one term and had the least influence. Fort Lauderdale's Karen Coolman also served one term but achieved more. The first woman elected from Broward County, she had graduated magna cum laude from the University of Michigan, with a degree in art history. Coolman, who was married to Charles Douglas when she served in the legislature, was the first female legislator whose retention of a maiden name was not widely publicized.

Few knew that she was the young mother of two when Coolman became a founder of Florida NOW, and NOW members worked hard to promote her electoral victory at age twenty-seven. She was a leader for women's rights in the legislature, but after assuring that her aide Linda Cox would replace her, she left for law school. As Karen Coolman Amlong, she achieved a successful career in employment discrimination. In 1992 she won a significant sexual harassment judgment, *Stockett vs. Tolin.*

In retrospect, the most striking thing about the 1974 election may be that three of the six female winners were Jewish. Elaine Gordon, who was elected in 1972, had been the first, and like her, 1974 winners Elaine Bloom and Gwen

Margolis were from Miami. Helen Gordon Davis of Tampa was the fourth Jewish woman in the House in 1974, but she was not widely perceived as being Jewish. The result, she told the author, was that some so-called Christians said "very anti-Semitic things" in her presence.

Like Davis and Gordon, Elaine Bloom and Gwen Margolis went on to long political success and did much for women. Margolis learned her feminism the hard way: brought up, she said, to "get married, have children, and live happily ever after," she instead found herself a divorcee with four children. She had attended Temple University in Philadelphia, where she was born in 1934, but after moving to Florida in 1960 returned to school and became an appraiser in commercial property.

Her 1974 election victory was especially significant because it centered on the Equal Rights Amendment, and she defeated an incumbent who opposed the ERA. That, however, did not win the respect of those in Tallahassee who assigned offices and other perks. Margolis said of herself and other women in the House:

> Our status in those days wasn't impressive. My first office in the Old Capitol was upstairs from the Speaker's office in a room with his staff. No one could find me. . . . You literally had to go through the Speaker's office and climb an old spiral staircase to get there. Every morning when I came in I had to clear the termite dust off my desk.[46]

Elaine Bloom had a similar background. Born in New York in 1937, she was educated at prestigious Barnard College. She and her husband moved to Florida in 1962, and he eventually became a judge while she reared their two children. Her life changed when she accepted the founding chairmanship of the Dade County Commission on the Status of Women in 1971. That and other civic experience motivated her to run for office in 1974. Bloom had just finished a term as president of the 2,500-member Dade County chapter of the National Council of Jewish Women, and support from them and others enabled her to win the Democratic primary with 61 percent of the vote. She noted, however, "the standard contributor who gave 100 dollars to a man normally sent only 25 dollars to a woman."[47]

The year also brought the first female president to the Florida Education Association (FEA). The organization was nearly a century old in 1974, having been founded in 1888, and women long were the majority of its members. It was affiliated with the National Education Association, which had chosen a female president back in 1909, but Dr. Ella Flagg Young was superintendent of schools in Chicago and not a true classroom teacher. As teachers and administrators separated nationally, Florida joined other states in electing teachers as organizational presidents.

FEA's first female president was Catherine Luther of Duval County. She served in 1974–75, and nearly a decade passed before election of the second woman, Ruth Holmes of Bay County in the Panhandle; her term was 1983–85. Pinellas County's Kathy Bell would follow in 1987–90, and the most recent was Maureen Dinnen, of Broward Community College, who was FEA president in 2000–2003. Miami's Yvonne Burkholtz was a well-respected lobbyist for FEA during the years of organizational transformation; indeed, she walked the Capitol halls on behalf of teachers to the point that her foot was permanently damaged.

* * *

The 1966 report of the Governor's Commission on the Status of Women had estimated that there were only seventy-five child-care facilities in the huge state—and most of those were aimed at upper-income families who could afford nursery school to give their child an academic edge. Although the German concept of kindergarten had been introduced in the United States prior to the Civil War, more than a century later most Florida counties did not offer kindergarten.

A decade after the report, in 1976, Pat Collier Frank joined Helen Gordon Davis as Tampa's second woman elected in the House. Frank had been the second woman on the Hillsborough County School Board, and she would champion early childhood education in the legislature, including public school kindergarten. She worked closely with Congressman Sam Gibbons of Tampa—who was a leading reason why the nation has enjoyed the highly successful Head Start program. Tampa social worker Delia Sanchez also was key to the implementation of such facilities, which hugely changed the lives of working women. Pat Frank would rise to the Florida Senate in the next decade, but like Gwen Margolis, her initial House assignment was to a tiny attic office.[48]

Pat Frank was among the eight women who won their Florida House races in 1976—the most ever. They were more diverse by geography and ideology than in the past. Three, including Frank, can be said to be from the Tampa Bay area: Beverly Burnsed was from Lakeland, while Dorothy Sample represented St. Petersburg.

Although a Democrat, Burnsed was not as feminist as previous women in the House and did not support the ERA; Sample was a Republican and not nearly as liberal as her Republican Pinellas predecessor, Mary Grizzle. A Florida native who was respected by her male colleagues, Burnsed served for twelve years and chaired committees that had previously gone to men. In 1988, under Republican Governor Bob Martinez, she became assistant secretary of state. Dorothy Sample served a similar period of time, but although her St. Petersburg constituents reelected her, she achieved less in Tallahassee.

Eastern central Florida sent three women to the House in 1976. Fran Carlton was a Democrat from Orlando, while Toni Jennings began her long career as a Republican also representing Orlando. The third Republican woman was Marilyn Bailey Evans of Melbourne.

Fran Carlton had the same tenure as Beverly Burnsed and Dorothy Sample, from the 1976 to the 1988 elections. A married woman, she was a striking blonde who exercised by running the steps of the eighteen-floor capitol. Carlton's primary achievement was raising the legal age for alcohol beyond eighteen years. It took her a decade, and she had to overcome strong opposition from the liquor industry and the generally young and male House leadership. The third woman, Melbourne's Marilyn Bailey Evans, was elected under that name, but was Marilyn B. Evans-Jones by the time she left the House in 1986. In contrast, Toni Jennings remained unmarried her entire life; her long career is covered in the following chapters.

South Florida added two more liberal Democratic women to its delegation in 1976, with Roberta Fox of Coral Gables and Linda Cox of Fort Lauderdale; Cox replaced her former boss, Karen Coolman. An active feminist, she married and became a mother while serving in the legislature, and in the 1982 election would successfully support her aide, Ann MacKenzie, as her replacement. Fox, who was married to Myron Gold, had the longer tenure, serving in both the House and Senate. Her colleague Elaine Gordon said Roberta Fox "was a rising star—very valuable to both houses in which she served. Dynamic, impressive, and a formidable debater, she had a quick mind and was extremely persuasive and forceful."[49]

The nation celebrated its two-hundredth birthday in 1976, and New York publisher W. W. Norton made a strong effort to issue individual histories of each state. Most authors were men, but Gloria Jahoda of Tallahassee wrote *Florida: Bicentennial History* (1976). She had issued *Trail of Tears* the previous year, as well as *The Other Florida* (1967), published by prestigious Scribner's.

Her fiction was with Houghton Mifflin, while other nonfiction books on Florida also attracted national publication. A Chicago native with degrees in English and anthropology, Jahoda had come to Tallahassee in 1963 when her husband took a library job at FSU. The Florida Senate honored her in 1973, prior to her unexpected death in 1980 at age fifty-three. Governor Bob Graham issued a proclamation saying Gloria Jahoda "has given the generations of today and the future the opportunity to understand and appreciate the beauty of our environment."[50]

The bicentennial year of 1976 also brought a close national election in the fall, as Democrat Jimmy Carter narrowly ousted incumbent Republican Gerald Ford. The only president who was never elected, Ford became an appointed vice president when Republican Spiro Agnew left in 1973 because of corruption scandals; in 1974, Richard Nixon resigned in disgrace. Both of the 1976 presidential nominees supported the Equal Rights Amendment, and Florida feminists circulated a flyer with ERA endorsements from Betty Ford and Rosalyn Carter. Along with information about the constitutional amendment, it included the Republican first lady's recipe for Angel Food Cake and the Democrat's Plains Cheese Ring, which featured pecans and strawberries from her Georgia hometown.

Annie Ackerman was part of the reason that Carter prevailed in 1976. Condominiums, or condos, were still new, and after moving to Miami Beach in 1969, Ackerman became known as the "Condo Queen" because of her political influence with residents. Like many of these newcomers, she was Jewish; the daughter of immigrants from Russia, she learned urban politics in Chicago. Over the next two decades, thousands of Democrats who lived in the condos of southeast Florida would vote according to her recommendations. Jimmy Carter was just one of many high-level candidates who sought her endorsement, and she was a mentor to such luminaries as Governor Bob Graham and U.S. Attorney General Janet Reno. Born in 1914, Annie Ackerman died in 1989, three years after she was inducted into the Florida Women's Hall of Fame. "I really believe she revolutionized condominium living," Dade County Mayor Steve Clark said at her funeral.[51]

Rita Reutter was a similarly charismatic woman adored by those who knew her. She had worked in a Connecticut airplane factory during World War II, raised a family, and followed her daughters to Florida in 1976, where she enrolled in graduate school at Florida Technological University. The very next year, the student body there elected the fifty-eight-year-old woman as homecoming queen. The unconventional act meant national publicity for the nine-year-old school, and Reutter was a hit on Johnny Carson's late night TV show.

Many women supported JoAnn Saunders of Gainesville in her attempts to win a seat in the U.S. House in both 1974 and 1976. They were not successful; no Florida woman had won a congressional race since Ruth Bryan Owen's second term in 1930. The 1976 election, however, did bring a new woman to the Florida Senate. The fourth female senator, Betty Castor of Tampa, followed only Lori Wilson and the two Beth Johnsons. She would be far more influential than the average elected official, however, as Castor would go on to a long and respected career.

She left the Senate briefly in 1978, when Florida set a milestone with two women—one of them black—running for lieutenant governor. Betty Castor was on the ballot with Jim Williams, a credible candidate in the style of former Governor Reuben Askew. Representative Mary Singleton of Jacksonville ran with former governor Claude Kirk, who switched parties from Republican to Democrat. Both tickets, however, lost in the first Democratic primary, which was won by Attorney General Bob Shevin and State Senator Bob Graham. Both Shevin and Graham were strong ERA advocates who built early campaigns, and by the time that Williams chose Castor, most feminists had committed to either Shevin or Graham. The Kirk-Singleton slate had no realistic chance: especially after he switched parties, Kirk could not be expected to retake the governor's office. Governor Graham, however, appointed Mary Singleton as director of the Department of Banking and Finance, and she held this position when she died in 1980.

In the 1978 legislative races, two women joined each of the two chambers. Pat Frank and Mary Grizzle rose from the House to the Senate, while south Florida voters elected two more liberal Democratic representatives, both Jewish. Virginia Rosen of North Miami Beach would serve three terms, from the 1978 to the 1982 elections, while Eleanor Weinstock of West Palm Beach won reelections to the House until 1986, when she moved up to the Senate.

Weinstock's long career did not start out with easy victories. She had been active in the PTA and was president of the Florida League of Women Voters when the Equal Rights Amendment was the league's top priority. It was after a 1977 ERA loss in the legislature, she said, that "I realized I was a strong, committed feminist." Her husband asked, "Why don't you quit lobbying and beat one of those guys who voted against the ERA?" She defeated a male

Republican in a race so close that, she said, "my family and I went to sleep thinking that I had lost. Early the next morning, I was awakened by a phone call from a friend . . . I had won!"[52]

President Carter appointed an unprecedented number of women to office during his four-year administration, especially to the diplomatic corps. He revolutionized the State Department by choosing ambassadors for their credentials, not their partisanship or campaign donations, and as a result, many more women headed embassies abroad. Among them was Florida native Frances Cook, a career diplomat who would represent the United States in Burundi, Cameroon, and Oman.

The career of Clearwater native Nancy V. Rawls began slightly earlier, as she had become ambassador to Togo in 1974. She served there and as ambassador to Africa's Ivory Coast until 1983. Like most female foreign service officers of her era, Rawls never married; she died in Connecticut in 1985.

Eileen R. Donovan had an even more pioneering career in foreign service. A member of the Women's Army Corps in World War II, she had been the first female ambassador in the western hemisphere when President Lyndon Johnson appointed her to Barbados in 1969. She eventually retired to Spring Hill, north of Tampa, where she would die in 1996.

The decade's last year, 1979, brought Carrie Meek to the House. After Miami's Gwen Cherry died in a Tallahassee car accident, Meek won the special election for Cherry's seat. Born in Tallahassee in 1926, Carrie Pittman Meek grew up "with her parents and 11 brothers and sisters not far from the capitol building in a ghetto area called Black Bottom. Her father was a farmer, and her mother washed clothes for others."[53] She nonetheless managed to graduate from Florida A&M, and in an era when Florida preferred to pay out-of-state graduate tuition for blacks rather than integrate its universities, she earned a master's degree at the prestigious University of Michigan in 1948.[54]

Internationally known Mary McLeod Bethune became Meek's role model when she taught at Bethune-Cookman College, and in 1961 Meek joined the staff of the new Miami-Dade Community College. Her 1979 victory over thirteen other Democratic candidates was an appropriate conclusion to the exciting 1970s, as Carrie Meek would go on to do tremendous good for women in the years ahead.

10 Through the Twentieth Century, 1981–2000

The 1980 election, called the "Reagan Revolution," signaled a reverse for feminism throughout the nation. In Florida perhaps the most striking way to measure the conservative impact of 1980 is that it marked the first election since 1968 when no new women entered the legislature.

With no female newcomers in the House of Representatives, the thirteen women in the 120-member body—a little more than 10 percent—all were incumbents. Four women were in the 40-member Senate—exactly 10 percent. They included just two new members, Republican Toni Jennings of Orlando and Democrat Gwen Margolis of Miami—both of whom moved up from the House. These statistics indicated a profound pause in progress, but few noted it at the time.

A similar lack of attention was true of the changes in the federal judiciary wrought by President Jimmy Carter. During his four years in office, between the 1976 and 1980 elections, he appointed thirty-six women as federal judges. That is four times the nine women chosen by the previous seven presidents, since the first under Franklin Roosevelt in 1934. Carter's appointments were very much based on a woman's qualifications, not on partisanship, but his revolution in beginning to equalize the federal judiciary went largely unheralded.

In Florida the first woman appointed to the federal judiciary was Susan Harrell Black, whom Carter named to the Middle District of Florida, based in Tampa, in 1979. Born in Valdosta, Georgia, she graduated from Florida State University in Tallahassee and earned her law degree at the University of

Female members of the Florida House, 1980–1982

Name:	Listed in Clerk's Manual as:	Residence:	Party	First elected
Beverly B. Burnsed	"Mrs."	Lakeland	D	1976
Fran Carlton	Mrs. Ernest E.	Orlando	D	1976
Linda Cox	Mrs. William H.	Fort Lauderdale	D	1976
Helen Gordon Davis	Mrs. Gene	Tampa	D	1974
Betty Easley	Mrs. Kenneth E.	Largo (Pinellas)	R	1972
Marilyn Evans-Jones*	"Ms." (Mrs. Edward E. Jones, Jr.)	Melbourne	R	1976
Roberta Fox	Mrs. Myron Gold	Miami	D	1976
Elaine Gordon	"Ms."	North Miami	D	1972
Mary Ellen Hawkins	"Ms."	Naples	R	1974
Carrie P. Meek**	"Ms."	Miami	D	1979**
Virginia Rosen	Mrs. Maurice	North Miami Beach	D	1978
Dorothy Eaton Sample	Mrs. Richard L.	St. Petersburg	R	1976
Eleanor Weinstock	Mrs. Sander	West Palm Beach	D	1978

Notes: * Until this session, her name was Marilyn Bailey Evans; ** special election to fill the vacancy left by Gwen Cherry's death.

Female members of the Florida Senate, 1980–1982

Name	Listed as	Residence	Party	First Elected to: Senate	First Elected to: House
Pat Collier Frank	Mrs. Richard Harlan	Tampa	D	1978	1976
Mary R. Grizzle	Mrs. Charles H. Pearson*	Belleair (Pinellas)	R	1978	1962
Toni Jennings	"Miss"	Orlando	R	1980	1976
Gwen Margolis	"Ms."	North Miami	D	1980	1974

Notes: *Remarriage after widowhood; she was Mrs. Ben F. Grizzle when first elected in 1962.

Florida in Gainesville in 1967. The difficulties that female lawyers faced at the time can be seen in the fact that she taught high school in Jacksonville before finding a job in the legal profession. The public showed significant willingness to vote for women as judges, however, and in 1973 Black won election as a Duval County judge; at the next election voters elevated her to the Circuit Court. After her 1979 federal appointment, she would join the U.S. Court of Appeals based in Atlanta in 1992.

President Carter also assisted Miami's Gisela Cardonne Ely's legal career by inviting her to a 1978 White House conference, and in 1980 she became the first Hispanic woman in the Dade County court system. Ely would go on to the circuit court in 1988 and, in 1997, became the first Hispanic woman to chair the Florida Circuit Court Judges.

At the polls in 1980 voters made a very significant—but little noted—addition to the Florida Constitution. Floridians had revised it during the previous decade with Sunshine amendments to ensure that elected officials held open meetings and disclosed their financial interests. Although she favored these reforms, Patricia Dore worried that their language could be used to justify making personal information about nonelected citizens available to the press and public. A brilliant attorney who was the first woman on the law school faculty at Florida State University, Dore drafted a constitutional amendment that read:

> Right of privacy—Every natural person has the right to be let alone and free from government intrusion into the person's private life except as otherwise provided herein. This section shall not be construed to limit the public's access to public records and meetings as provided by law.

Added as Section 23 of the Florida Constitution, this "privacy amendment" has been used especially to protect the personal records of women who seek reproductive choice. Dore intended that interpretation, and she made it unambiguous by including "the right to be let alone and free from government intrusion." She was still young when she led this important action, and her 1992 death, at age forty-seven, saddened many. Dore died alone in her home, from complications of diabetes. According to legal scholar Victor Tipton, she was "the first person who was not a Supreme Court justice to have memorial services held in the Supreme Court Building."[1]

The biggest headline of 1980 undoubtedly was Florida's first election of a woman to the U.S. Senate. Paula Hawkins of Maitland was the nation's first female senator who had no family connections to Congress, and she also was a Republican in an era when Republicans were only beginning to win elections in the South. Playing down both her party affiliation and her Mormonism, she won with support from women, including many Democrats, who simply were eager to see a woman representing Floridians in the U.S. Senate. As she had done when she was elected to the Public Service Commission (PSC) in 1974, Hawkins won her race with an image of fighting for consumers.

Because of scandals about excessive influence by campaign donors from regulated utilities, voters amended the Florida Constitution in 1978 to make the PSC appointed, not elected. One of Governor Bob Graham's first appointees to it was Susan Leisner of Tampa, who already had made feminist history in New York. With a prestigious MBA and some experience, she wanted to enter the management ranks at the phone company where she worked but discovered that no woman started higher than the company's "Level Seven," whereas men—even men who lacked her credentials—were hired at "Level Ten."

A handful of women joined her in a class-action suit, *Leisner et al. versus New York Telephone Company.* Judge Constance Baker Motley—the first black woman in the federal judiciary, appointed by President Lyndon Johnson in 1966—ruled in favor of the women. As a result of Leisner's courage, tens of thousands of women employed in such companies could see genuine careers, not merely jobs, in their futures. Leisner moved to Tampa with her attorney husband in 1972, and she joined the PSC in 1981.

That was Paula Hawkins's first year as a U.S. senator, and although Hawkins did not support the Equal Rights Amendment (ERA), most women in the state legislature continued to work for it. The task, however, became much more challenging. The Republican Party, which had endorsed the ERA since World War II, withdrew that support at its 1980 convention. Although the Florida legislature remained overwhelmingly Democratic, many of its men were conservative Democrats, and in 1982 it would be the Florida Senate that dealt the final blow to the amendment that would have added legal equality for women to the U.S. Constitution.

Florida's first ladies and their husbands had supported the ERA in the previous decade. Dozens of members of the American Association of University Women and the Business and Professional Women, for example, were pictured with a huge banner thanking first ladies Betty Ford, a Republican, and Donna Askew, wife of Democratic Governor Reuben Askew, for their ERA efforts. Askew's 1978 Democratic successor, Bob Graham, also supported the federal amendment—but not enough to prevent his former colleagues in the Florida Senate from killing it.

To recap what has been detailed in earlier chapters, the ERA was introduced in Congress in 1923. Its authors were members of the National Woman's Party who had worked for the Nineteenth Amendment that granted women the vote in 1920. That amendment addressed only the vote, however, and other discrimination against women remained legal. State legislatures could (and did) treat women differently from men in areas such as jury service, college admissions, and so forth. Businesses could (and did) discriminate against women in insurance, credit, and many more cases.

The ERA was intended to address such legal bias, but organized opposition arose from business interests and from fundamentalist churches. Mormons were particularly active, and Sonia Johnson, a Utah English professor and the mother of four, visited Florida to tell the story of her ex-communication from the church because of her ERA support. It was published as *From Housewife to Heretic* (1982).

In south Florida one of the strongest opponents was Shirley Spellerberg, a realtor who ignored the long history of her industry's discrimination against women in granting mortgages. Until the feminist revolution, most unmarried women found it impossible to buy a house in their own name, while the income of married women routinely was excluded from repayment plans because the industry believed that a married woman might get pregnant and thus lose her income.

In Tampa, Jean Putney (who referred to herself as Mrs. Louis Putney) led the opposition because the ERA would subject young women, as well as young men, to the military draft. The fact that the draft ended soon after the Vietnam War did not lessen the theoretical truth of this argument. Attorney Ann Kerr also led Tampa opposition, arguing that widows would lose obscure dower rights under the Florida Constitution. Again, that such rights could easily and justifiably be extended to widowers did not lessen the appeal of the argument to legalistic minds content with the status quo.

The ERA opponent with the longest career in Tallahassee may have been Carole Griffin. Although Governor Bob Graham appointed her to his Commission on the Status of Women, she went on to oppose almost all of the legislation that the commission championed. She worked for other conservative causes, too, and ran unsuccessfully for Congress in 1994. When she died in 2012, at age seventy-three, the *Tallahassee Democrat* said: "Griffin spent two decades in the Capitol opposing abortion and pornography. She also worked against tax increases and ratification of the Equal Rights Amendment."

Florida's fight over the ERA was a decade long, from its 1972 introduction to its 1982 death in the Senate. By then Representative Gwen Cherry was dead, too, but it was she—an African American Democrat from Miami—who first introduced the ERA. The 1972 House vote was an overwhelmingly 91–4 in favor, but senators did not act. By the next session:

> Opponents . . . brought busloads of anti-ERA women to Tallahassee, and deluged members with mail. . . . The amendment failed in the House 54 to 64. . . . In the years that followed, ERA proponents

brought a host of celebrities to the state—Gloria Steinem, First Lady Betty Ford, and sensitive guy Alan Alda. But in four subsequent votes and informal consideration other years, the amendment never mustered a majority of both houses. By the early 1980s, the Senate, under Dempsey Barron's leadership, had taken on a markedly more conservative cast. So in 1982, as extended authorization expired, Florida could claim the dubious honor of being a key state in the ERA's defeat.[2]

Congressional authorization for ratification expired on June 30, 1982, and the Florida Senate was the nation's last legislative body to vote. The tally, on June 22, 1982, was 19 in favor and 21 opposed—with one of the negative votes cast by Tampa's Guy Spicola, who had campaigned as a supporter and accepted campaign contributions from the National Organization for Women and other ERA proponents. When he won his Senate seat, his Democratic primary rival had been had been Representative Elvin Martinez, and the Hillsborough County League of Women Voters withdrew an award it had given to Martinez because he would not promise to vote for the ERA. After Spicola reneged on his campaign commitment, Governor Graham nonetheless appointed him as a judge.

A few weeks before they killed the ERA, conservative senators also tried to eliminate the Governor's Commission on the Status of Women. When the Senate Committee on Governmental Operations debated abolishing it on May 8, 1980, Senator Pat Frank appeared before them:

> An amused committeeman suggested [that] if there must be a committee on the status of women, there should be one on the status of men.
>
> "Gentlemen," said Senator Frank, "there is a committee on the status of men," pausing for emphasis. "It's called the Florida Senate."
>
> The abashed committee voted to continue the Commission.
>
> An interstate banking lobbyist ended a conversation with Senator Frank by saying, "We'll talk about this later, honey."
>
> The Senator called the lobbyist's attention to a button that said, "Don't call me 'honey' or 'baby' or 'lady.' Just call me Senator."[3]

* * *

Senator Frank also was a leader in the Florida Network of Executive Women (NEW), which began in 1980 as an outgrowth of the Florida Women's Network.[4] More informal than older national organizations such as the BPW and the AAUW, Florida branches of NEW often took names that did not express affiliation to NEW, but from the Miami's Women's Forum to the Pensacola Women's Alliance, they not only provided an opportunity for business networking but also supported feminist legislation. That was most easily tracked through the Governor's Commission on the Status of Women.

Having survived the May 1982 challenge to its existence, the commission began the Florida Women's Hall of Fame later that year. Its first honoree was Representative Elaine Gordon of Miami.[5] Other 1982 inductees were internationally known Mary McLeod Bethune of Daytona, "Mayor" Wilhelmina Harvey of Key West, Paula Mae Milton of Miami-Dade Community College, and Barbara Jo Palmer of Tallahassee, all discussed in earlier chapters.

Helene S. Coleman also was inducted in 1982. Born in New York City in 1925, she graduated from that city's famous Hunter College in 1945, and after marrying and moving to Jacksonville, became a full-time volunteer, especially for children. She helped pioneer guardian *ad litem* programs that became a national model, assuring that minors and others incapable of advocating for themselves in court would have an objective representative with judges who make decisions on their welfare. Coleman chaired boards in foster care, mental health, juvenile justice, and other endeavors, and she reached the height of her activism as president of the National Council of Jewish Women.

Raquel Cohen never was nominated for the Hall of Fame but arguably should have been. Prior to her move to Miami in 1980 she had earned a master's in public health and then a medical degree from Harvard University. Born in Peru, Dr. Cohen specialized in cross-cultural mental health issues. Her psychiatric expertise proved especially helpful during the Mariel Boatlift of Cuban exiles, and she developed an international reputation for dealing with victims of trauma and terrorism.

The 1982 election brought new districts based on the 1980 census, and as a result, an unprecedented number of women entered the legislature. Eighteen won seats in the House and nine in the Senate, and some went on to long success. A decade later two of the newcomers, Miami Republican Ileana Ros and Jacksonville Democrat Corrine Brown, would win election to Congress. Democrat Anne MacKenzie of Fort Lauderdale rose to be majority leader of the House, while Republican Toni Jennings of Orlando became the minority leader pro tempore of the Florida Senate. Yet this 1982 pinnacle soon plateaued, and three decades later, no woman yet has made the leap from majority leader to speaker of the House.

Female newcomers to the Florida legislature in the 1980s

Name	District	Party	Notes
1982 election, House:			
Patricia Bailey	Pinellas	D	served just one two-year term
Virginia Bass	Pensacola	D	three terms; state agency head
Corrine Brown	Jacksonville	D	went on to Congress
Mary Figg	Tampa	D	served ten years; Healthy Kids
Carol Hanson	Boca Raton	R	twelve-year tenure; Boca Raton mayor, 1995–2001
Anne MacKenzie	Fort Lauderdale	D	first female majority leader
Elizabeth Metcalf	Coral Gables	D	six years; psychologist and children's advocate
Ileana Ros	Miami	R	went on to Congress
Deborah Sanderson	Fort Lauderdale	R	appointed to major committees by Democrats
Peggy Simone	Bradenton	R	ten years
1982 election, Senate:			
Roberta Fox	Miami	D	moved up from House
Jeanne Malchon	St. Petersburg	D	ten years; League of Women Voters
Carrie Meek	Miami	D	moved up from House; went on to Congress
Karen Thurman	Dunnellon	D	went on to Congress
March 1984, special election, House:			
Irma Rochlin	Brevard County	D	less than four years
Dixie Sansom	Brevard County	R	almost eight years
1984 election, House:			
Arnhilda Gonzalez-Quevedo	Coral Gables	R*	four years
Frances "Chance" Irvine	Orange Park	R	eight years
1984 election, Senate:			
no newcomers among the nine women in the forty-member Senate			
1986 election, House:			
Lois Frankel	West Palm Beach	D	later West Palm Beach mayor; Congress
Susie Guber	Miami	D	six years; Commission on Status of Women
Marian Lewis	North Palm Beach	R	six years; wife of U.S. Rep. Tom Lewis
Sandra Mortham	Pinellas County	R	went on to secretary of state

Name	District	Party	Notes
1986 election, Senate:			
Ileana Ros-Lehtinen	Miami	R	moved up from House; went on to Congress
Eleanor Weinstock	Palm Beach	D	moved up from House
Marlene Woodson (later Howard)	Bradenton	R	four years
May 1988, special election, House:			
Betty Holzendorf	Jacksonville	D	went on to Senate in 1992
1988 election, House:			
no newcomers among the sixteen women in the 120-member House			
1988 election, Senate			
Helen Gordon Davis	Tampa	D	moved up from House
Sherry Walker	Jefferson County	D	one four-year term

Notes: See previous table for women elected before the beginning of the decade.
* Changed to Democrat in 1988.

The 1982 female freshmen included six Democrats and four Republicans, but women of both parties continued to work for shared goals. Democrat Mary Figg represented part of Tampa, and one of her chief goals was cleaning up Tampa Bay. She achieved that through Southwest Water Improvement Management (SWIM). At the other end of bay Peggy Simone, the first Republican woman elected from Manatee County, mused in 1995 about the conflicts between state and local governments over water and other related issues:

> I asked these questions of myself: Can local government do it and will they do it? Protection of the environment, my special area of interest, is a good example. We knew local city councils and county commissions could protect the environment, but they weren't doing it, or at least not well enough. So, we have enacted some tough environmental protection laws. The most unpopular with some local governments and special interest groups was the Growth Management Act of 1985. . . . We're not saving Florida fast enough and are now spending millions of dollars to correct environmental damage of the past.[6]

Another quality-of-life measurement is music, and a Florida woman gained international attention in 1983: Ellen T. Zwilch became the first woman anywhere to win the Pulitzer Prize in music. A Miami native, she was a child prodigy who was born as Ellen Taaffe in 1939. She begged for piano lessons at age five and by age ten was composing her own works. After graduating from Florida State University she went on to become the first woman to earn a doctorate in composition from New York's famed Juilliard School of Music. That was in 1970, and she benefited from the feminist revolution, becoming one of very few women to earn a living as a classical composer. The nation's most prestigious orchestras played her music, and Zwilch performed one of her works for the opening of the National Museum for Women in the Arts in Washington, D.C. Cartoonist Charles Schultz often referenced her in his "Peanuts" comic strip, and Zwilch has won many significant awards.

Lenore Carrero Nesbitt became a federal judge in 1983. Born in 1932, she had been valedictorian of her 1957 law school class at the University of Miami—a time when very few women went to law school, let alone graduated at the top of the class. The presidential appointment made her the first woman on the federal bench for the Southern District of Florida. Statewide, she followed only Susan Black, who had been appointed to the Middle District four years earlier. Judge Nesbitt also served on numerous committees and boards, including that of the Miami Children's Hospital. She died of cancer in 2001, the same year as her admission to the Florida Women's Hall of Fame.

In Tallahassee the 1983 municipal election began a trend that remains relatively unnoticed: the nation's disproportionate number of female mayors in capital cities. Although few political scientists have yet commented on this phenomenon, it appears that capital cities—where awareness of government is highest—are more likely than other municipalities to choose women as leaders. Indeed Florida may hold the record, with Tallahassee having elected five female mayors—more than any other capital city in the nation.

The first was Carol Bellamy, elected in 1983, and Betty Harley followed in 1987. Dorothy Inman-Johnson, an African American, served twice, with one-year terms that began in 1988 and 1993. In between was Debbie Lightsey, elected in 1994, and Penny Herman followed her in 1994. After Inman-Johnson's second term, however, the city changed its charter to increase the mayor's powers, and no woman has held the office since.

* * *

A similar situation developed within academia. A woman reached the pinnacle of power in the state university system in 1981: to the surprise and joy of feminists, the Board of Regents (appointed by Governor Bob Graham) hired Barbara Newell as chancellor. A graduate of New York's elite Vassar College, she held a doctorate in economics from the University of Wisconsin. Dr. Newell had wide experience, including having represented the United States in Paris with the United Nations body UNESCO and having held the presidency of Massachusetts' historic Wellesley College. Her tenure in Tallahassee, however, was rocky. The patrician intellectual—whose husband had a different surname—did not fit into the capital culture, and in 1985 she was eased out of her job. The method was particularly insulting: when the chairman of the Board of Regents released her resignation letter to the press, it was news to Newell.[7] No woman has since headed the state university system.

Unlike the Board of Regents, which set policy for all of the public universities, local boards of trustees governed community colleges. They also are appointed by governors, and Governor Graham's trustees at Polk County Community College created a milestone in 1982, when they made Maryly VanLeer Peck the first female president of a Florida community college. A 1951 graduate of prestigious Vanderbilt University, she earned her doctorate from the University of Florida—in the unconventional field of chemical engineering and in the unconventional year of 1963. Perhaps because she was a Gator and because she was not so close to Tallahassee, President Peck did not experience the problems of Chancellor Newell. She served Polk Community College successfully until her 1997 retirement, dying in West Palm Beach in 2011.

The pattern repeated in 1984, when trustees at two rural community colleges chose women presidents. Lake City Community College hired Muriel Kay Heimer that year; she was just the second president of the still-new college. Heimer served for the next thirteen years, retiring in 1997. In Avon Park, where South Florida Community College, is based, Catherine Cornelius became president in 1984. Dr. Cornelius had been a top administrator at Daytona Beach Community College in Volusia County. She served with distinction until her 2002 retirement and was especially supportive of other women.

Barbara Newell was still chancellor of the state university system in 1983, when Helen Popovich became the state's first female president of a public university, Broward County's Florida Atlantic University (FAU). It was not

Making It Big: Pulitzer Prize Winners

Although few noted it then or now, Florida's emergence as an increasingly sophisticated state could be measured during the 1980s by national recognition of its newspapers. After decades of no paper that won Pulitzer Prizes—the first of which were awarded in 1917—Florida had repeated winners during the 1980s. Even more remarkably, most were women.

The first was Bette Orsini of the *St. Petersburg Times*, who shared the 1980 prize for national reporting with colleague Charles Stafford. The award was for their investigation of the Church of Scientology, which was building its international headquarters in Clearwater. Angry Scientologists focused on Orsini much more than on Stafford, however, and according to her obituary on March 29, 2011, "the Guardians of Scientology called their plan 'to restrain' Orsini 'Operation Bunny Bust.'"

In the next year, 1981, two *Miami Herald* women earned Pulitzers. Madeleine Blais won in the category of feature writing for her story on a local pacifist who had been dishonorably discharged from the army in World War I. The other winner was Shirley Christian in international reporting. She took on the danger of the era's revolutions in Central America and won for her reports on Nicaragua.

Unlike Blais and Christian, who moved away, Lucy Morgan of the *St. Petersburg Times* covered Florida politics for decades. Her 1985 award was for her investigation of corruption in the Pasco County sheriff's office. Back in 1973 she had demonstrated her devotion to investigative reporting by going to jail rather than reveal the name of a source. Morgan was inducted is into the Florida Women's Hall of Fame in 2006.

The competition between her St. Petersburg paper and the Miami one continued when the same prize that Morgan won in 1985 went to Edna Buchanan of the *Miami Herald* in 1986. A crime reporter since the 1960s, Buchanan developed a specialty in rape, uncovering many cases that law enforcement had ignored. More active in the community than most journalists, her empathetic coverage of victims resulted in the nation's first rape treatment center. After winning numerous awards from fellow journalists, she turned to writing mysteries and won international awards in that arena, too.

In addition to Buchanan, the *Herald*'s Carol Guzy was a 1981 co-winner in spot news photography for her pictures showing the devastation of a volcano in Colombia. Guzy had grown up in Pennsylvania and was halfway through nursing school when a new camera changed her life. She has won four Pulitzers and numerous other awards, and as of this writing, worked primarily for the *Washington Post.*

The *Orlando Sentinel* joined the prestigious group in 1988, when Jane Healey won the Pulitzer for editorial writing. She had begun working for the paper as a political reporter in 1974 and joined the editorial board in 1981. Healey's 1988 Pulitzer was for a series of editorials on Orange County's failure to plan and manage its growth. She went on to be editor of the *Sentinel*'s editorial page and is routinely listed as one of the area's most powerful people.

Janet Chusmer did not win a Pulitzer for her own writing, but was executive editor of the *Miami Herald* when the newspaper won two prizes, plus several other awards from the Society of Professional Journalists. Her peers chose Chusmer as Newspaper Editor of the Year in 1990, and when she died later in the year, the National Press Foundation said that she was "transforming the *Herald* to serve the unique multicultural population of Greater Miami."

Note: Please see chapter 11 for a continuation of Pulitzer winners.

yet a true university, as the state's educational system had expanded so rapidly that the Board of Regents attempted to keep down costs by offering classes only at the junior and senior level: students were expected to transfer from community colleges or other institutions. Dr. Popovich changed that at FAU, adding freshmen and sophomore classes to give students a full university experience. Originally on the faculty of the University of South Florida, she made a strong effort to reach out to minorities and women.

In an article on April 8, 1985, the *Boca Raton News* said that Dr. Popovich attracted a more than capacity crowd when she spoke on women and the arts; thirty people who wanted luncheon reservations were turned away. "She cited a study," the paper said, "in which the same set of papers were judged by two sets of judges; the only difference being that the names of women authors were changed to men in one set. Each time the highest scores went to papers with the names of men as authors, demonstrating how much the perception of the piece was affected by the sex of the author." Graduate programs and research grants also rose during Popovich's administration, but she left FAU after five years to become president of Michigan's Ferris State University.

Farther north in Brevard County, political dominos fell when two male legislators resigned just prior to the 1984 session. In a special election, voters chose women of opposite parties, Republican Dixie Sansom and Democrat Irma Rochlin. Sansom had been an aide to legislator Clark Maxwell, who resigned to head Florida's Community College Board, and she won the House seat of the man who replaced Maxwell in the Senate. A reporter for the *Melbourne News,* Sansom decided to run, she said, because "nothing is accomplished through silence."[8] Meanwhile, Hazel Tally Evans of St. Petersburg ranked high enough on the Democratic National Committee that she was co-chair of arrangements for the 1984 national convention.

An additional milestone in 1984 was that Miami Democrat Elaine Gordon won election by her peers as speaker pro tempore of the Florida House. She was the first woman to hold this position, which is second in House leadership—and only one more woman has followed in the nearly three decades since. As of 2014 no woman had won the top spot, speaker of the Florida House. A majority of states have set this precedent, with North Dakota being first in 1933.

The 1984 Florida Women's Hall of Fame ceremony had eight honorees. The three from Miami—NOW founder Roxcy Bolton, writer Helen Muir, and land developer Julia Tuttle—are profiled in earlier chapters. Also profiled earlier are Jacksonville physician Gladys Soler; Orlando author Zora Neale Hurston; and Orlando horticulturist Lena Smithers Hughes, who improved breeding strains of the Valencia orange.

The other two women honored in 1984 were Tallahassee residents. Barbara Landstreet Frye reported from there for United Press International (UPI). She had been born in Lancaster, Pennsylvania, in 1922 and graduated from the University of Georgia in 1943. That was during World War II, and because the war opened new opportunities to women, she began working for UPI in Tallahassee in 1944. During her thirty-eight-year career, Frye covered eleven governors. Her standards of accuracy and fairness were somewhat new to the mostly male Florida press corps, and when she was UPI bureau chief, younger reporters adopted her as a model for a more objective style of journalism. Married and the mother of two, she died in 1982. Barbara Frye is credited with reforming state politics through her carefully researched writing; she turned down promotions because of her love for Florida.

Sybil Collins Mobley had a similarly long career in Tallahassee as the founder of FAMU's School of Business and Industry. An African American born in 1925 in Shreveport, Louisiana, she earned an excellent education at a time when that was only beginning to be possible for black women. She graduated from Philadelphia's Wharton School of Business—perhaps the best such in the nation—and the University of Illinois granted her doctorate in 1963.

Dr. Mobley joined FAMU that year, and she founded an innovative program that allowed students to earn a master of business administration degree in five years. While mothering three children she also served on the boards of such prominent corporations as Hershey Foods, Anheuser-Busch, and Sears, and she was a consultant to the U.S. Agency for International Development for a number of African countries. Dean Mobley was at FAMU for forty years. When she retired in 2003, she said that what made her program different from others was its international aim, which included internships abroad. She explained:

> We don't let them [students] go without the language, the economy, the culture, the history. We say the globe is the unit of analysis for anything. . . . The world moves on, and that's why we . . . have an approach that changes with time, both the methodology and the content.[9]

At the same time that Mobley worked for young people at FAMU, Representative Fran Carlton, Democrat from Orlando, worked to save their lives by raising the legal age to buy alcohol. In 1980 she succeeded in raising the minimum from eighteen to nineteen. Liquor lobbyists could not credibly argue for law that allowed high school seniors to drink, but they strongly opposed any further increase. Carlton's bills to raise the age to twenty-one were defeated until 1985, when she jubilantly—yet somewhat cynically—finished her journal entries on the issue:

> The petition drive is going well. Some of the legislative players have changed, and public support is beginning to have an impact. Mothers Against Drunk Driving [MADD] is a new, emerging voice. Raising the drinking age was a popular campaign issue in the 1984 elections.
>
> Help from Washington! The Congress passes a bill: raise the drinking age or lose transportation funds. That should have settled the issue—making it easy to pass. *Not* in the *Florida* legislature. The opposition

attempted to kill it by placing [a controversial] discrimination issue on the bill. . . .

All appeared lost until the Speaker and the [Senate] President agreed to appoint a conference committee. . . . I was elated! The final vote on the bill in 1985 was unanimous—of course![10]

In the 1985 municipal elections Rosario Kennedy became the first Hispanic woman on the Miami City Commission. Born in Cuba to a prominent family, she challenged other expatriates by having all her campaign materials printed in English. Some Cuban conservatives were angry, but she won the election and went on to be vice mayor in 1988.

* * *

Florida feminists were elated about the 1985 appointment of the first woman on the Florida Supreme Court, Rosemary Barkett. She was born in 1939 in Ciudad Victoria, Mexico, to Assad and Mariam Barakat, who were immigrants from Syria. Rosemary had six siblings and did not speak English when the family arrived in Miami in 1946. At age seventeen she entered the Sisters of Saint Joseph, which she served for eight years, working as a nun in elementary schools in Jacksonville, St. Augustine, and Tampa. After leaving the order she graduated from Spring Hill College in Alabama, one of several Catholic institutions with that name, in 1967.

From this cloistered background Barkett made the transition to the previously all-male University of Florida—and in 1970 was the first woman honored as the outstanding senior in the College of Law. Governor Bob Graham was aware of her brilliance and integrity, and after she practiced law in Miami for almost a decade, he appointed her as the first woman on the state's highest court.

The men there, she said in a 2011 interview with the author, "were extremely welcoming." Because all justices worked in the same Tallahassee building and saw each other daily, "it became really rather intimate, like a little family." Ethical restrictions limit the socializing that judges can do with the public, and so, she said, they often spent holidays and other occasions in one another's homes. With the men's wives and children joining in, it became "very comfortable, like an extended family. In retrospect," she added, "they were just very sweet."[11]

Feminists celebrated Barkett's appointment at a Tallahassee party organized by Tampa State Senator Betty Castor, and the next year Castor won

First Woman on the Florida Cabinet: Betty Castor

With her twin sister Janet, Elizabeth Bowe was born in Glassboro, New Jersey, in 1941. Her father became mayor, and Betty grew up determined to make the world a better place through the influence of government. While a student at Glassboro State College, she organized aid for schools in Uganda and was so successful that in 1962 President John F. Kennedy named her to a delegation celebrating that new nation's independence.

After enrolling in a prestigious graduate school, Teachers College of Columbia University, she returned to Uganda to teach. One of her proudest achievements—which also demonstrated her innate feminism—is that she led an expedition of African girls in climbing Tanzania's hazardous Mount Kilimanjaro. No men accompanied them, and the feat was widely hailed in a culture where such female independence was rare.

She met Don Castor in Damascus, Syria, and after returning to the United States and marrying, moved with him to his native Florida. They settled in 1965 in Miami, where she completed her master's degree in education while bearing the first of their three children—Kathy Castor, who now is a member of Congress. They moved to Tampa in 1968, and Don practiced law while Betty bore daughter Karen and son Frank—and also became president of the League of Women Voters in 1970.

In 1972 she audaciously ran for the Hillsborough County Commission, and politicos were stunned when she defeated ten Democrats and a Republican for the countywide seat. Castor was the first woman on the commission, and because the incumbents were under investigation for profiting personally from voting machine sales, this was a clear victory of reformers over traditionalists.

Fran Davin, a newcomer from Massachusetts and California, managed Castor's campaign, and in 1974 she joined Castor on the commission. In that same year Helen Gordon Davis became Hillsborough's first female legislator. Women in government were so new, however, that in separate incidents, both Representative Davis and Commissioner Castor were asked to leave governmental meetings at downtown private clubs from which women were banned

continued

in the daytime. Castor drew attention to her exclusion by calling TV cameras to film her eating a hot dog at her desk. The resulting bad publicity reached as far as the *New Yorker*, and male elected officials finally realized that they could no longer conduct public business in private clubs.

She moved on to the Florida Senate in 1976, defeating Julian Lane, an incumbent who had been mayor of Tampa. In that race and others, she never campaigned against an individual as much as she ran for a position, with positive platforms that emphasized education and the environment. She and Fran Davin also earned their environmental credentials in a long contest with the three other county commissioners over zoning issues, and the men eventually went to prison for taking bribes from developers. Again the case made national news, including television's *Sixty Minutes*.

Castor and Jacksonville legislator Mary Singleton became Florida's first female candidates for lieutenant governor in 1978, and after she lost, Governor Bob Graham appointed Castor to head the Division of Elections, another first for women. She and Don Castor—who had been elected as a judge in 1976, the same year that she won her Senate race—divorced in 1978. The couple remained a model of amicability in rearing their teenage children, and the divorce did not hurt her in 1980, when she again defeated an incumbent, Republican David McLain, to return to the Senate. Castor's peers had so much respect for her that they elected her president pro tempore in 1985—still another precedent for women.

In 1986 she was the first woman in the Florida Cabinet. She married former legislator Sam Bell in 1989 and was easily reelected as education commissioner in 1990. In 1994 she became the first female president of the University of South Florida, which saw tremendous expansion under her administration. She developed programs in China and Africa; the endowment rose from $65 million to $200 million; and USF was designated as a Research I university. In 1999 Castor left USF to take the presidency of the National Board for Professional Teaching Standards. Its mission is to encourage teachers to pursue rigorous goals, and during her tenure, the number of board-certified teachers increased tenfold.

From 1972 onward Castor had never lost an election, but 2004 was a bad year for progressive Democrats. She ran for the U.S. Senate seat that Bob Graham vacated and narrowly lost to Republican Mel Martinez—who resigned before his term ended. Ever indefatigable, Castor continued to work for good causes, especially for women, as head of the Patel Institute for Global Solutions and through other organizations.

Her children are married to spouses with their own successful careers, and she has six grandchildren. Congresswoman Kathy Castor has two teenage daughters; Dr. Karen Dentel is a school teacher in Orlando, the mother of a son and daughter, and in 2012 won a seat in the Florida House; and Frank Castor is a Palm Beach judge and the father of two girls. Betty Castor was inducted into the Florida Women's Hall of Fame in 1996.

Note: See chapter 9 on the race for lieutenant governor.

election as the first woman on the Florida Cabinet. Floridians elected their commissioner of education then, and the position was one of seven on Florida's uncommonly powerful Cabinet, which sometimes could overrule the governor. Teachers—most of them women—were the biggest factor in her victory. Castor, who had taught in Miami and in Ghana, especially reached out to educators by personally teaching at least one class in every one of the state's sixty-seven counties.

The race began as a contest between two candidates named Betty, both from the Tampa Bay area. Republican Betty Easley of St. Petersburg was a respected legislator, but she showed less frugality than Betty Castor. Expenditure reports showed that Easley spent campaign nights at Hyatts and hired a janitorial service for her office, while Castor slept at the homes of supporters, and her staff did their own cleaning. When the time came to qualify for the ballot, Easley's bank account did not predict victory, and she dropped out. The Republican primary was between men, and the party's voters nominated the less competitive, who had the same name as actor Ron Howard. In the Democratic primary Castor defeated both a female school board member and a male legislator who had been confined to a wheelchair since the Vietnam War.

Commissioner of education was abolished as an elected office under Governor Jeb Bush in the 2000s, but before that, the office—as well as that of the elected secretary of state—was an excellent steppingstone for women in government. Feminists knew that importance from elsewhere: when North Dakota set the precedent of electing women to statewide office in 1892, the position was state superintendent of schools. In 1922 New Mexico was the first to elect a female secretary of state (who also was Hispanic). Florida lagged far behind most states in having no woman win statewide election until 1986. Even Alabama and Mississippi had chosen several women for statewide offices, including treasurer, many decades earlier.

But Florida women were making progress, and the 1986 Hall of Fame ceremony was the largest ever, with thirteen honorees, including new Supreme Court Justice Rosemary Barkett. Six other women also were from Miami: Annie Ackerman, Gwen Cherry, and Marjory Stoneman Douglas have been profiled earlier, while Miami's Arva Moore Parks and Marilyn K. Smith also were inducted in 1986. Parks, born in 1939, graduated from the University of Florida in 1960 and earned a master's degree from the University of Miami in 1971. A film producer and the author of a half dozen books on south Florida, she chaired the Florida Endowment for the Humanities in 1982. Smith, a philanthropist who died prematurely the year prior to her induction, was a Chicago native and national leader in Jewish causes.

Jacksonville had two 1986 inductees, African American nursing home founder Eartha Mary Magadalene White and Jacksonville University President Frances Bartlett Kinne. Both are included in earlier chapters, as are the remaining winners: Tallahassee archivist Dorothy Dodd; Pensacola area educator Elsie Jones Hare; Pulitzer Prize–winning novelist Marjorie Kinnan Rawlings of Cross Creek, near Gainesville; Dr. Florence Seibert of St. Petersburg, who invented the skin test for tuberculosis; and Beth Johnson of Orlando, Florida's first female state senator.

Tampa's Stella Ferguson Thayer, an accomplished horsewoman, got the attention of businessmen and sportsmen in 1986, when she outbid well-known New Yorker George Steinbrenner for ownership of Tampa Bay Downs. She had earned her law degree from prestigious Columbia University in 1965, an era when few women went to law school. As managing partner of Macfarlane Ferguson and McMullen, Thayer has also served on the boards of many businesses and nonprofits. Horseracing thrived under her leadership at Tampa Bay Downs, and in 2012 she was president of the National Museum of Racing.

Representative Marilyn Evans-Jones of Melbourne set a precedent for Republican women in the 1986 gubernatorial race, when Congressman

Louis Frey chose her as his running mate. However, like the 1978 Democratic candidates for lieutenant governor, Betty Castor and Mary Singleton, this mixed-gender ticket did not survive the party primary.

U.S. Senator Paula Hawkins lost her 1986 reelection to Washington—and as of 2012, no Florida woman has followed her—but in Tallahassee, the year arguably was the acme for women in state government. Not only did Betty Castor become the first woman on the Cabinet, but women also held precedent-setting positions in legislative leadership. When she was elected as education commissioner, Castor, a Democrat, held the title of Senate president pro tempore, while Republican Toni Jennings of Orlando was the minority leader pro tempore. In the House, Democrat Elaine Gordon of Miami was finishing up her term as speaker pro tempore, while Republican Betty Easley of St. Petersburg was minority leader pro tempore. Although these are second-in-command positions, it was—and still is—unusual for women to hold all of them, in Florida or in other states. Moreover, the women made it clear in public statements that their power was real, not ceremonial.

They were models for Lois Frankel, who won a secret ballot for the most promising freshman in the class that was elected in 1986. During the next decade she would lead a task force on AIDS—a huge new issue in the era—as well as the "Save the Children" campaign. The June 6, 1989, issue of the *Miami Herald* proclaimed:

> Lois Frankel has a bag of buttons . . . that say in crayon script, "Kids Are Special People . . ." She's wearing a lawyersque black suit as she circulates through the Florida House of Representatives, toting a printed list of lawmakers' names on . . . the latest bill she's shepherding. . . . She's . . . [the] majority whip, lining up the votes one by one, ignoring no one, not even the most recalcitrant rural Republican. Her hands are dual word processors. . . . Another box checked off. She moves on.

In this atmosphere of female power, it would have been hard for anyone at the 1986 Women's Hall of Fame ceremony to foresee that it would be the last time things felt this way for the next six years. Nor, apparently, did anyone realize that of the twenty-seven inductees between 1982 and 1986, there were none from Tampa, even though it is older than most Florida cities. Moreover, the city arguably led the state's women in this era: not only did Tampa's Betty Castor become the first woman on the Florida Cabinet in 1986 but also, in 1987, Tampa was the state's first major city to elect a woman as mayor.

Sandra Warshaw Freedman, called Sandy, was a Tampa native and a tennis star in her youth. She bore three children after marrying attorney Michael Freedman and won election to the city council in 1974. She joined Jan Platt, who also won that year, and the city's first councilwoman, Catherine Barja, elected in 1971. But Freedman never intended to stop at that level, as she said in a 2004 interview with the author:

> I wanted to be the mayor from the time that I was in the sixth grade. My teacher required us to bring in current events every day and then we'd talk about them—world affairs, politics, city and state government. I continued my interest in government from that time forward, got my degree in government with an emphasis on state and local government [at the University of Miami in 1965], and then began to build my life back in Tampa.

Her peers elected her as city council chair, which meant that she automatically became mayor when the incumbent, Bob Martinez, resigned to run for governor. Although women had made appreciable progress in the last decade, some men nonetheless remained convinced that the only place for them was in the home. Freedman spoke of a Republican activist when she continued:

> Knowing that I would run for mayor in 1987, I began making contacts with influential members of the business community in hopes that I could secure their support. The most memorable visit was to a very prominent developer. . . . I had known him for several years and made an appointment . . . to talk about my candidacy. He was very cordial as we sat facing each other in his spacious office. . . .
>
> After a few minutes of normal chitchat, he leaned forward in his chair and said, "How many children do you have?" I was taken aback, but answered "three." Then he said, "How old are they?" I told him their ages, something like 13, 16, and 19. Then he said, "How do you think you can be mayor and raise those children the right way?" I quickly told him that they knew more about government and were better citizens than he ever would be, gathered my briefcase and stormed out of his office. Needless to say, he did not support me—but he did the second time I won the mayor's office.[12]

Freedman won huge majorities in elections for both of her four-year terms. Downtown was transformed during her administration, especially with the innovative Florida Aquarium. She also emphasized rehabilitation of old housing, and after she campaigned for President Clinton in 1992, he intended to appoint her as chief of Housing and Urban Development, a Cabinet-level position. That was disrupted by a "scandal" involving her husband's position as an attorney for a bank. No charges were filed, but press coverage of the non-case was enough to deter the appointment. Sandy Freedman, however, is one of few Floridians who has slept in the Lincoln bedroom of the White House.

In contrast to Tampa's smooth city government under Freedman, Jacksonville government attracted extremely negative press in 1989, when African American city council members were arrested. Two of the three were women, Dietra Meeks and Denise Lee. With Warren Jones, they had tried for months to secure funding for drainage and sanitation improvements in black neighborhoods, where floods had caused two deaths. On September 26, when the final vote on the annual budget came up with no money for the problem, the three walked out, leaving the council without a quorum to adopt the budget. According to Jacksonville historian James Crooks:

> Council president Tillie Fowler recessed the meeting, ordered a lockdown of city hall to prevent the council members' departure, and issued warrants to force their return to the meeting. They were returned with council member [Dietra] Meeks in handcuffs. . . .
>
> The arrests triggered outrage in the African American community. At a news conference the next day . . . state representatives Betty Holzendorf and Corrine Brown, NAACP president Willye Dennis, and numerous black clergy attacked the council president for her disrespect of the black council members. . . . [13]

After more than a thousand north-side residents marched on city hall, the needy district got its sewage improvements in a budget passed on October 10. Black women clearly led this success, and the female NAACP president later would be elected to the legislature. Council president Fowler also mended her reputation sufficiently that she would go on to Congress in the next decade.

Farther south, the last year of the 1980s brought the first Florida congresswoman since Ruth Bryan Owen's initial victory in 1928. During the sixty-one years in between, Florida changed immensely—especially Miami, which was home to both women. The winner of the special election, caused by the death of legendary Democrat Claude Pepper, was Ileana Ros-Lehtinen. She was the nation's first Cuban American congresswoman as well as the first Republican congresswoman from a former Confederate state. Both precedents indicate the era's tremendous transition.

Born in Havana in 1952 as Ileana Ros y Adato, she was among the earliest exiles from Castro's Cuban government, coming to Miami in 1959. Her family valued education, and after earning degrees from Miami-Dade Community College and Florida International University, she founded a private elementary school; she would go on to obtain a doctorate in education from the University of Miami in 2004, after she was in Congress.

When first elected to the Florida House in 1982, Ileana Ros was the first female Hispanic legislator. Her name changed in 1985, when she married fellow legislator Dexter Lehtinen. He had been a rising politician, but his career became mired in charges of sexual harassment before they wed. Her career, in contrast, would take off on a national level. She moved on to the Florida Senate in 1986, also bearing two daughters.

The vacant Miami congressional seat for which Ros-Lehtinen ran in 1989 had been dependably Democratic since its 1962 creation, but its base of retirees from the urban North faded over the years as Cubans displaced them. With targeted turnout in a special election, she won 52 percent of the vote and has been handily reelected ever since. She is the strongest congressional voice against the Cuban government. Her district also covered the Keys, and Ros-Lehtinen brought in millions in federal funding for revitalization projects both there and in Miami.

Jeanie Austin of Orlando was a powerful factor in the victories of Ros-Lehtinen and other Republicans in this era. She won a tight 1984 race to become the first woman to head the Florida Republican Party, despite opposition from Paula Hawkins, a fellow Republican who in 1986 would become Florida's first female U.S. senator. Although Austin lost her reelection bid for the state chairmanship, she went on to co-chair the Republican National Committee with nationally known strategist Lee Atwater. She helped elect the first President Bush in 1988, and upon her 2005 death from bone cancer, Governor Jeb Bush declared, "she was fiercely loyal to my Dad and my family." Florida Republicans can perhaps thank Jeanie Austin more than any other person for making their party a viable force.

* * *

Jeanie Austin's Republican victories also included the 1986 election of Bob Martinez as governor. He had been a Democrat—indeed, a radical, as he was a leader in the 1968 teachers strike. He headed the Hillsborough County Classroom Teachers Association, then owned a popular restaurant, and ultimately became mayor of Tampa. His 1986 election made Martinez the first Hispanic and the second Republican governor since Reconstruction. (Claude Kirk, who later switched to Democratic, had been elected as a Republican in 1966.)

While Martinez took the governor's office, Bob Graham moved from there to the U.S. Senate when he defeated incumbent Paula Hawkins. With Graham's departure from Tallahassee, the Governor's Commission on the Status of Women disappeared. Martinez did not appoint a new commission, and its associated Hall of Fame went out of existence. Indeed, women's history proved so ephemeral that when the Hall of Fame resumed operation in 1992, basic information on some members could not be found. The plaques that had hung in the governor's office were missing; when discovered several years later, they were at the back of a high shelf in a broom closet.

Thus for many feminists, the 1990 gubernatorial election focused on a decline in the status of women. Martinez reinforced their motivation by calling a special legislative session to take advantage of a U.S. Supreme Court decision, *Webster vs. Missouri Reproductive Health Systems* (1989). The ruling was not as dramatic as the public was led to believe, as the Court merely confirmed the right of states to regulate abortions in the interest of public health, which had been the case all along. Some politicians, however, saw it as an opportunity to repeal the 1973 *Roe vs. Wade* decision, and Martinez was among the Republican governors who called special sessions of legislatures to enact more restrictive law. Democrats still controlled the Florida legislature, however, and the session proved a waste of money.

Feminists, including many Republican women, remembered that the next year, when Martinez was up for reelection. After twelve years as an advocate for women in the legislature, Pat Frank had competed unsuccessfully in the 1988 race for the U.S. Senate seat that Lawton Chiles vacated. In 1990 she quietly led a sophisticated campaign to help Chiles defeat Governor Martinez—whom she had known since her days on the school board, when Martinez led the teachers' union.

Although the effort was definitely under the radar, a surprising number of largely anonymous Floridians donated money to the cause, including a ninety-one-year-old man who memorialized his youthful girlfriend's death from an unsafe abortion by sending three one-dollar bills. Frank used these donations for a professional phone bank, which joined with volunteers in calling "infrequent voters"—women who were registered to vote and did so in presidential years but usually not in gubernatorial years. Republican and independent women were specifically targeted, and the effort doubtless was a factor in Martinez's loss to former U.S. senator Lawton Chiles.

Chiles pledged that he would send a bill to the legislature to enact the Commission on the Status of Women into law, so that no future governor could abolish it merely by ignoring it. With lead sponsors Elaine Gordon in the House and Carrie Meek in the Senate, the 1991 legislature passed two relevant acts.

Whereas previous governors had appointed commissioners without any particular guidelines, the new law not only spelled out the number of commissioners (twenty-one) but also allotted some appointments to other Cabinet members as well as House and Senate leaders. The commission was housed in the Office of Attorney General, where Bob Butterworth gave it enthusiastic support. The result was a stronger commission with a more diverse membership and influence with more elected officials.

The second 1991 legislative act created standards for the Florida Women's Hall of Fame. It provided that the commission would forward ten annual nominations to the governor, from which no more than three could be chosen each year. Deadlines were imposed so that a governor's failure to act would be a violation of the law. Thus, for the first time since 1986, Hall of Fame induction ceremonies returned in 1992. Governor Chiles's three choices were Jacqueline Cochran, head of the Women's Air Force Service Pilots in World War II; Ruth Bryan Owen, Florida's first congresswoman in 1928; and Carrie Meek, the first black woman in the Florida Senate.[14]

The Florida Senate that passed the legislation was particularly noteworthy, as Gwen Margolis, a Democrat from Miami, presided over it.[15] Her mostly male colleagues elected her as their first female president, giving Margolis tremendous power over legislation. Although few people, even feminists, noticed it at the time, she was only the fourth female senate president in the nation. Vermont's had been first, in 1955; New Hampshire followed in 1983; and then came Alaska in 1987. Florida's 1991 precedent with Gwen Margolis was truly a national milestone, especially for the South. That the state's senators would elect a woman, especially a Jewish woman, would have been nearly inconceivable a few years earlier, prior to the feminist movement.

Gwen Margolis specialized in economics, but she also supported bills on traditional women's issues, and other female senators were thrilled with her

Female newcomers to the legislature, 1990s

Name	District	Party	Notes
1990 election, House:			
Mary Brennan	St. Petersburg	D	eight years; champion for children
Cynthia Chestnut	Gainesville	D	African American; rose from mayor of Gainesville
Kathy Chinoy	Jacksonville	D	served just one term
Patricia Muscarella	Clearwater	R	served just one term
1990 election, Senate:			
Patsy Ann Kurth	Palm Bay	D	served to 2000; died in 2011
1992 election, House:			
Lois Benson	Pensacola	R	served just one term; daughter later elected
Shirley Brown	Sarasota	D	eight years; went on to school board
Larcenia Bullard	Miami	D	African American; went on to State Senate
Mandy Dawson	Fort Lauderdale	D	African American; went on to state Senate
Willye Dennis	Jacksonville	D	African American; forced to resign in 1999 scandal
Lori Edwards	Lakeland	D	went to on Polk County supervisor of elections
Addie Greene	West Palm Beach	D	African American; went on to county commission
Suzanne Jacobs	Delray Beach	D	served eight years; active feminist
Mimi McAndrews	Royal Palm Beach	D	first Korean American; one term
Julie McClure	Bradenton	D	served just one term
Sharon Merchant	Palm Beach Gardens	R	eight years; lost 2000 Republican primary for state Senate
Beryl Roberts-Burke	Miami	D	African American; eight years
Debbie Wasserman Schultz	Broward County	D	went on to state Senate and Congress
Kimberly Shepard	Winter Park	D	defeated longtime incumbent, but lost next election
1992 election, Senate:			
Ginny Brown-Waite	Hernando County	R	went on to Congress
Patricia Grogan	Merritt Island	D	served just one term
Betty Holzendorf	Jacksonville	D	moved up from House
Karen Johnson	Leesburg	D	served just one term
1994 election, House:			
Annie Betancourt	Miami	D	active feminist; long tenure

continued

Female newcomers to the legislature, 1990s—*Continued*

Name	District	Party	Notes
Lisa Carlton	Sarasota	R	eighth-generation Floridian; went on to state Senate in 1998
Faye Culp	Tampa	R	president of National Federation of Women Legislators
Sally Heyman	North Miami Beach	D	strong feminist; elected to Dade County Commission in 2002
Debbie Horan (later Ritchie)	Key West	D	married Pensacola legislator and moved
Evelyn Lynn	Ormond Beach	R	sixteen years in House and Senate
Deb Prewitt	New Port Richey	D	two terms; rose from mayor
Helen Spivey	Pasco County	D	one term; environmentalist; Crystal River City Council
Marjorie Turnbull	Tallahassee	D	eight years; old Florida family
1994 election, Senate:			
Katherine Harris	Sarasota	R	went on to secretary of state and Congress
1996 election, House:			
Nancy Argenziano	Dunnellon	R	moved to Tallahassee; switched to Democrat in 2011
Janegale Boyd	Monticello	D	nurse; two terms
Paula Dockery	Lakeland	R	long tenure; quite independent of her party
Margo Fischer	St. Petersburg	D	lost in 1998; wife of mayor; died in 2005
Suzanne Kosmas	Volusia	D	went on to Congress
Sandy Murman	Tampa	D	elected as a Democrat; soon switched to Republican
Stacy Ritter	Coral Springs	D	moved on to Broward County Commission
1996 election, Senate:			
Betty Holzendorf	Jacksonville	D	moved up from House
1997 Special Election, House:			
Deborah Tamargo	Tampa	R	lost the next election in this Democratic Hispanic district
1998 election, House:			
Nancy Detert	Sarasota	R	long career in both chambers
Heather Florentino	New Port Richey	R	went on to Pasco County school superintendent
Carole Green	Fort Myers	R	went on to Department of Elder Affairs

Name	District	Party	Notes
Bev Kilmer	Quincy	R	ran unsuccessfully for Congress in 2004
DeeDee Ritchie	Pensacola	D	1990 Florida Teacher of the Year
Eleanor Sobel	Hollywood	D	long career; chaired Women's Caucus
Leslie Waters	Pinellas County	R	after term limits, elected to Seminole City Council
Frederica Wilson	Miami	D	went on to Congress
1998 election, Senate:			
Anna P. Cowin	Leesburg	R	went on to Lake County school superintendent
Debbie Wasserman Schultz	Broward County	D	went on to powerful position in Congress

election. Writing about Palm Beach senator Eleanor Weinstock and presiding officer Margolis, House historian Allen Morris said:

> For Senator Weinstock, the personal highlight of the 1991 Session came in the final moments. Just seconds before the banging of the gavel [and adjournment], a bill revising domestic violence laws sponsored by Senator Weinstock was taken up on special order, after a real battle to have the bill heard. President Margolis requested that the bill be read, stating that "the women of the Senate want this bill, and we're going to pass it right now!"

Margolis used the style that male presiding officers adopted when they deeply wanted a bill enacted into law. Without pausing for breath between sentences, let alone for any debate that might try to justify violence against women, President Gwen Margolis hurriedly continued:

> Senator Weinstock moves the bill. All Members vote. All Members voting. Let the record show that the bill passes unanimously.[16]

Because the Senate membership was nearly tied by party, Margolis shared power with Republican Toni Jennings, who became the first woman to chair the powerful Senate Rules Committee. When she was elected to the House in 1976, Jennings, at age twenty-seven, set a record for the youngest woman in the Florida legislature. This record would be broken later by Democrat

Debbie Wasserman Schultz, who won a Broward County seat filled with senior citizens when she was twenty-six. Both Democratic women are mothers, but Jennings has remained single. Her mother consciously gave her a name that could be interpreted as masculine, which Toni Jennings has used as the longtime CEO of the family construction company, Jack Jennings & Sons. House historian Allen Morris wrote:

> Senator Jennings' father was a traditionalist who got converted. He named his business with the thought that his daughter would grow up to take . . . traditional "women's roles. . . ." A lot of the credit must go to Mrs. Jennings, who named her daughter "Toni." Over the years, both in business and in politics, Toni Jennings has gotten a lot of mileage out of her name. It gets very interesting when a customer or constituent calls and wants to speak to Mr. Toni Jennings. Even in the 1990s, people assume that someone in the construction business and the State Senate will be a man.[17]

Jennings was a friend of Glenda Hood, who made history in the spring of 1992 by becoming the first female mayor of Orlando. She followed only Tampa's Sandy Freedman as the mayor of a major Florida city. Born as Glenda Evans, she was a fourth-generation Floridian and attended Rollins College. She won election to city council in 1982 and a decade later was elected mayor. A popular Republican, Hood would be easily reelected in 1996 and 2000. The Orlando area indeed was a center for female power, as Linda Chapin, a Democrat, served as mayor of Orange County at the same time.

Born Linda Welch in Connecticut, she graduated from Michigan State University and met her husband at the 1964 World's Fair in New York—at the "It's a Small World" expo that predated Orlando's Disney World. They married and moved to Orlando, where she served as president of the League of Women Voters and bore two children. Once they were in school, she went into banking and soon led the Chamber of Commerce in revising Orange County governance to elect a countywide mayor. Chapin was the first person in that position. She served from 1990 to 1998, and won her second term with an overwhelming percentage of the vote, but would lose a congressional attempt in 2000. The Linda Chapin Theatre in the Orange County Convention Center is named for her.

* * *

The 1992 presidential election was the most surprising in years, as Democrat Bill Clinton ousted incumbent Republican George H. W. Bush. Clinton's feminist coattails proved effective in Florida: fourteen new women won election to the Florida House, all but two of them Democrats. This was by far the highest number of female freshmen legislators in the state's history—yet even with incumbents added, they were just 23 of the 120 representatives. Several incumbents lost or chose not to run, making the total just three more women than in the previous election cycle.

In the Florida Senate, Miami Democrat Elaine Bloom became president pro tempore in 1992; she was the first woman to hold that position since Betty Castor in 1986. Initially elected to the House in 1974, Bloom lost a race for the Senate in 1978 and then returned to the House in a special election in 1986. Her time away from Tallahassee gave her an unusual opportunity to see how much priorities had changed—and how women had built an agenda that called for greater attention to all Floridians. She said:

> Because of the progress of individual women, we've . . . truly benefited those concerns with which women have always been identified. Child care, preventative health care, child and spouse abuse, and other vital social services were rarely top agenda items for male legislators. Every female elected, however, regardless of other areas of interest . . . became involved with some aspects of these issues, thereby making them more visibly acceptable and important.[18]

But the most significant recognition that women should be part of representative bodies was in the 1992 congressional races, when four Florida women won seats in the US House. In all of the twentieth century, Florida had had only two congresswomen—Ruth Bryan Owen in 1928 and Ileana Ros-Lehtinen in 1989—and yet this one election resulted in four. It was indeed "The Year of the Woman," as national pundits dubbed 1992, and it marked the acme of work that feminists had done in the previous two decades.

Because Florida gained congressional seats after the 1990 census, at least seven women ran for Congress in 1992, including Democrats Cheryl Knapp and Dr. Karen Moffitt in the growing towns around Tampa Bay as well as future mayor Lois Frankel in West Palm Beach. The four winners were from north Florida, south Florida, and west Florida: Tillie Fowler, the only Republican among the four, won in suburban Jacksonville; Corrine Brown, an African American, won its downtown and areas to the south; Carrie Meek, also an African American, won a Miami seat; and Karen Thurman waged a tough campaign to carry a rural district north of Tampa.

Tillie Kidd was born in Atlanta in 1942; her father was a Georgia legislator for more than four decades. She earned undergraduate and law degrees at Atlanta's Emory University and moved to Washington, where she worked as a congressional aide and as legal counsel in the White House Office of Consumer Affairs under the Nixon Administration. After marrying Buck Fowler in 1968, she came to Jacksonville in 1971. While rearing two daughters she was president of the Jacksonville Junior League and chaired the Florida Humanities Council. In 1985 she was the first Republican elected to the Jacksonville City Council, and she rose to be its first female chair.

Fowler won a vacant seat in Congress with 56 percent of the vote, defeating a Democratic man who had been a prominent legislator. In Congress she specialized in military issues that affected Jacksonville's naval facilities. Her Republican Party was more moderate then than now, and Fowler suffered no repercussions when she voted for federal funding if a medically needy rape victim chose to have an abortion. She also expressed feminist views when she said of her female colleagues in Congress:

> I think as mothers, home-workers, people who usually had to juggle a lot of different priorities, we get pretty good. . . . I think we bring a different view to issues such as child care. But I don't think there is any one set of issues that is just women's issues because I think women's perspective is needed in defense; that's one of the reasons I wanted to be on the Armed Services Committee. I think women are concerned with defense issues and our perspective is needed.[19]

In this, Fowler followed in the footsteps of Colorado Congresswoman Patricia Schroeder, who in 1973 had been the first woman on the House Armed Services Committee. After retiring from Congress and moving to Orlando, Schroeder told Florida women about being the first on that macho committee: forced to accept her and the committee's first black man, the chairman made them share one overstuffed chair at the committee's table. With her strong sense of humor, Schroeder has laughed many times recalling how she and California Democrat Ron Dellums sat "cheek-by-cheek."

By the 1990s when Fowler served, things had gotten much easier for women in Congress, and Fowler eventually rose to the vice-chairmanship of the Republican Conference, making her the fifth-ranking member of her party in the House. Like other Republicans of the era, however, she had campaigned on the slogan of "eight is enough," and Fowler was one of relatively few who kept their promise for term limits. She retired at the 2000 election, stayed in Washington, practiced law, and in 2004 served on a panel investigating abuse of Iraqi prisoners of war. She was visiting Jacksonville early in 2005 when she suffered a brain hemorrhage and died. Tillie Fowler was inducted into the Florida Women's Hall of Fame later that year.

The other Jacksonville-based district was drawn to include black voters from inner-city precincts, and it extended far south to incorporate East Coast areas that long had been home to black Floridians. Corrine Brown, its winner, was born in Jacksonville in 1946. She overcame the trials of being a single mother to graduate from Florida A&M in 1969, and she followed that with graduate work both there and at the University of Florida. She taught at Jacksonville's Edward Waters College, a private institution for blacks, before moving to Florida Community College, where she would work from 1977 to 1992. Also a leader in the American Federation of Teachers, she was a delegate to the Democratic National Convention in 1980. In 1982 Brown won election to the Florida House and was reelected until running for the newly created U.S. House seat in 1992. In this "Year of the Woman," she won by eighteen points and never again faced a serious competitor.

Brown has long tenure on the House Transportation and Infrastructure Committee, and in 1998 succeeded in raising revenue for Florida projects by nearly 60 percent. She has been an advocate for rail as well as for the welfare reforms implemented by the Clinton Administration. Brown used her seat on Veterans Affairs to be "particularly attentive to the needs of women veterans and health issues" and, after Florida's problems in the 2000 election, was a leading sponsor of the 2002 Help America Vote Act.[20]

Although Carrie Meek was appreciably older, she was akin to Corrine Brown in moving from the Florida legislature to Congress. Both had been inspired by friendship with Gwen Cherry, the first black woman in the legislature, and like Brown, Meek had a long career in education.[21] Despite the humble demeanor of a retired schoolteacher, Meek was an astute politician, and she managed to secure a seat on the powerful Appropriations Committee—a rare achievement for a freshman.

In addition to obtaining funds for Miami—especially in the wake of Hurricane Katrina—Meek also looked out for Haitian refugees. She successfully sponsored legislation to extend Social Security to domestic servants, and she consistently advocated for the least advantaged. In a 1997 debate, for example, she said:

> The spending cuts that the House approved today fall mainly on the sick and on the elderly. Tomorrow we will be voting on tax cuts that mainly favor the wealthy. . . . Today, the House voted to rob from the poor so that tomorrow the majority can help the rich.[22]

The third Democratic woman elected to Congress in 1992, Karen Thurman, was the first congresswoman from Florida's west coast, a precedent that had been set on the East Coast in 1928. Thurman also had begun her career as a teacher. Born Karen Loveland in Rapid City, South Dakota, in 1951, she moved to Florida and graduated from Santa Fe Community College in 1970, when it was quite new. After earning her bachelor's degree at the University of Florida, she taught middle school math. In 1973 she married John Patrick Thurman, and they had two girls. It was her students who convinced her that she should run for city council in Dunnellon, a town between Tampa and Ocala. She won her 1974 race and moved up to mayor in 1979. Her emphasis was on the environment, especially clean water, and she continued that after being elected to the Florida Senate in 1982. She drew attention to the issue of pollution with a cleverly named bill: LUST stood for Leaking Underground Storage Tanks.

Her colleagues respected Thurman enough that she was the first woman to chair the Senate Agriculture Committee, and after the 1990 census she chaired the reapportionment committee that drew Florida's new congressional maps. Even with this advantage, however, her 1992 congressional campaign was not easy: she won the three-candidate race with 49 percent of the vote. Republicans targeted her in the next election—the 1994 rightwing revolution led by Newt Gingrich in which many congresswomen lost—but Thurman stunned pundits by winning 57 percent, soundly defeating car racer opponent "Big Daddy" Don Garlits.

Her biggest constituent bloc was blue-collar retirees, and she worked to protect Social Security and to reduce the cost of health care, especially prescription drugs. Veterans also were a great concern, and Thurman pushed for clinics in areas where there were no VA hospitals. After cruising through the 1996 election, she won a coveted seat on the House Ways and Means Committee, which deals with taxes. When the committee chairman lobbied her for a tax increase to cut the deficit, she replied: "This is not about you. This is not about the President. This is about the 600,000 people I represent."[23]

Among the fourteen new women who won seats in the Florida House in 1992 was Mimi McAndrews of Royal Palm Beach, the legislature's first

Korean American of either gender. She had grown up in Missouri, graduated from Florida Atlantic University, and finished her Georgetown law degree just two months prior to running for an open seat. Surprised at her own victory, she said, "I did not run as a minority candidate, nor [were there] a large number of minorities in my district." Despite her image of herself as an average American, she said: "I was overwhelmed with attention. . . . The Korean Broadcasting Station, the largest television station in the world, sent a three-man crew to follow me around. . . . I immediately became a role model for Asian children."[24]

The biggest milestone of 1992 in the Florida House, however, may have been the election of Debbie Wasserman Schultz, who at twenty-six was the youngest woman ever elected to the legislature. She looked even younger than the married woman that she was, and she said that a typical reaction from the Broward County senior citizens whose votes she sought was: "You're the candidate? You look like you're sixteen years old!" Yet "without any money, and very little of the right kind of support," she knocked on enough doors to win the Democratic primary without a run-off. Continuing to go door-to-door eight hours a day and seven days a week, she won the general election with 64 percent of the vote.

Nor did she slow down in the legislature, where her 1993 priority was a bill mandating gender equity on the dozens of state boards that control many areas of life—everything from the Board of Regents governing universities to boards that license chiropractors and cosmeticians. The goal was to have approximately even numbers of women and men on these boards, most of which are appointed by the governor. Although a freshman, Wasserman Schultz took on its sponsorship:

> The bill had been introduced by several different Members in the past . . . but never passed both Houses in the same session. . . . No one expected this year to be any different: especially when Governor Chiles expressed serious reservations and called it a "Noah's Ark" proposal. The supporters of the bill bent over backward to address the concerns of the Members and the Governor. The debate was heated almost every step of the way. . . .
>
> As the questions and debate dragged on, I turned around . . . and realized that, one by one, every woman in the House had come . . . to stand behind me. . . .
>
> I was asked to "TP" it [temporarily pass, which effectively means to

drop] because . . . debate was taking too long and it might not pass. I turned around to the women behind me and mentioned this to Representative Mary Brennan, a normally mild-mannered legislator from Pinellas County. Her adamant response was, "Don't you TP that bill!" Buoyed by her comments and the women surrounding me, I turned around, the debate ended, and the bill passed 73 to 39."[25]

* * *

As the Reagan and Bush administrations continued in the 1980s, the nation saw—but did not clearly acknowledge—a great increase in illegal immigrants. In Florida most arrivals were extremely poor people from the Caribbean, especially Haiti and Jamaica, and from Mexico. They could not meet the standards of immigration law—but were willing to work in citrus groves, strawberries fields, and cultivating Florida's other winter crops. Countless farmers turned a blind eye to the law, and as ever, women and girls toiled along with men and boys.

Their numbers increased as the general population increased. The 1970 census showed that about a half million Floridians were foreign-born; in the 1980 census they topped a million; and in 1990 there were almost 1.7 million. Cubans were by far the largest group, accounting for about a third of all immigrants—but the law accommodated exiles from that communist country to make them legal. The situation was:[26]

Country of Origin	*1990 Census for Florida*
Cuba	497,619
Haiti	83,249
Canada	77,559
Jamaica	74,863
Nicaragua	72,060
Colombia	66,614
United Kingdom	61,069
Germany	55,321
Mexico	55,316
Italy	28,693
Poland	26,313
Dominican Republic	23,373
Philippines	22,353
Peru	22,087

Honduras	20,825
China	15,237
Spain	14,648
Bahamas	14,416
Venezuela	13,998
Argentina	13,135
Vietnam	12,843
India	12,221
Ecuador	11,084

Haitians risked their lives to reach Florida's east coast by sea, and often were deported back home or held in detention centers. Most immigrants lacked educational opportunity in their homelands, and they worked in badly paid jobs, usually agriculture or service industries. Women who were not in the fields toiled as cleaners in hotels and offices or in the kitchens of restaurants, places where their inability to speak English was less important. Like immigrants in the past, they struggled to learn the new ways and to send their children to school, and they made countless sacrifices to give their families a better life.

Asians were more likely to have some financial stability, especially the Vietnamese and Filipino women who married American soldiers—or, as was often the case for Filipinos, who were mail-order brides. They often were entrepreneurial and built small businesses, opening restaurants and nail salons. The latter transformed a feminine portion of Florida's economy, as millions of women who had seldom enjoyed manicures and pedicures in the past could indulge themselves at low-cost salons run by Asian women.

Other Asians, including some from the Middle East, were more visible because they had enjoyed the benefit of affluence and education back home. China, Japan, and India were most often the places of origin of such women. Among them in Tampa, for example, was Renu Khator, who rose to the second-highest position at USF before moving on to Texas, where she became president of the University of Houston. She dressed in western clothing and spoke with no accent—but her marriage to another Indian had been arranged in their youth by their parents. He was a USF scientist, and both Drs. Khator were perfectly happy with that: in their cultural view, young people should concentrate on education and trust their parents to find a suitable mate, which allowed the young to avoid the distractions and disappointments of dating.

A New Kind of Immigrant: Mona Jain

Mohinder Jain—whom almost everyone calls "Mona"—was born to Indian parents in Karachi, Pakistan. When the British Empire broke up after World War II, Pakistan became a Muslim theocracy, while India would be a secular state. Religious tolerance was not an empty phrase for eleven-year-old Mohinder: on August 15, 1947, "We moved to India wearing what clothes we had. . . . We had to run; otherwise our family will be killed."

Her family was educated, though, and that enabled their financial recovery in New Delhi. Profoundly understanding that education is the only investment that cannot be taken away, she earned two degrees at Delhi University. She was one of nine children—all of whom have earned college degrees—and was voted "best all-round student" in 1952.

She also met Kalish Jain at university, and unlike many Indian couples whose property-related marriages were arranged, they married because of love. Their families did not object, even though she was of the Sikh faith, while he practices Jainism. Their home in Manatee County has shrines to both—and they also celebrate Christmas.

Their daughter, Anila, was five years old when Mohinder won a slot as a Fulbright exchange teacher. Kalish encouraged her to accept the opportunity, and she taught biology at Riverview High School in Sarasota. Newspaper stories from the time show that the community welcomed her—and with her beautiful silk saris, traditional jewelry on five body parts, and cosmetic "marriage mark" on her forehead, she was indeed an exotic presence.

She arrived in 1964, when America's quota law allowed just one hundred immigrants from India per year. A major rewrite of the law in 1965, under Democrat Lyndon Johnson, changed the system from being based on nationality to individualism that encouraged immigrants with assets, including educational and business assets. Mohinder had liked what she saw in Florida, and Kalish and Anila soon were able to follow her. They were the only Indian family south of Tampa.

Kalish built businesses, while Mona not only continued to teach biology but also became a lifelong student. With a National Science Foundation grant she earned a 1971 master's degree from FSU; in the next decade, she added a PhD from USF in educational leadership as well as an MD degree, for which she traveled to the Caribbean. Instead of practicing medicine and making money, though, she used all this background to provide health services to disadvantaged children, primarily as director of Manatee County Head Start.

Dr. Jain kept a busy calendar as an activist in numerous organizations, some of them international. She has earned dozens of honors, including USF's Distinguished Alumnus Award, as well as recognitions from the American Medical Women's Association and the American Association of University Women. Among the celebrities she has met are Queen Elizabeth, presidents from Eisenhower to Clinton, Indian leaders including Indira Gandhi, and perhaps most distinguished on the long list, the Dalai Lama and Mother Teresa; with the latter she had a private meeting.

Governor Lawton Chiles appointed Dr. Jain to the new Florida Commission on the Status of Women in 1991, and with reappointments by other officials, she has served longer than any other member. It was largely her leadership that made the Sarasota-Manatee observance of women's right to vote into an event that attracts as many as five hundred people every August. Dr. Anila Jain, a pediatrician, is following in her mother's traditions.

All this was not exactly what she envisioned when young Mohinder first came to America. In a 1965 interview with the *Sarasota Herald Tribune*, she explained that she was doing her own housework for the first time—and coming to understand women's busy lives. Saying that its women were what she particularly admired about America, she added: "In India, we always thought American women did nothing but ride around in big cars all day. Now I know these women work hard at jobs and take care of the home as well."

The children of Egyptians Sami and Nahla Al-Arian, in contrast, chose their own mates. They were born in the United States—and as women from places such as Italy and Spain had discovered earlier in the century—the second generation allowed greater personal freedom. Earlier second-generation women, however, seldom had a college education, while Laila and Leena Al-Alrian have credentials from prestigious universities and pursue promising careers even after marriage. The children of another USF couple, Kwasi and Mary Wiredu, also follow this pattern. Natives of Ghana, they were educated in English schools, but even though they had been gone from Africa for decades, Mary felt pressure from family there to arrange a marriage for her eldest daughter. The daughter ultimately did marry an African—but not before earning her medical degree. Dr. Amanda Wiredu, who practices in Lakeland, had a traditional American church wedding as well as a Ghanaian ceremony in her parents' home.

Many Middle Easterners encountered deep prejudice from Americans, especially after Iran took American hostages in the late 1970s. To escape political arguments, some learned to disguise their origins. Brandon's Sahebzaman family escaped from the Shah of Iran but obscured their identity by telling people that they were from Persia. That was true; it is the ancient name for Iran, and with most Americans geographically clueless, Mahee Sahebzaman has enjoyed long success with a large beauty salon. Her customers judge her by her business ability, unaware of the nuances of nationalism.

* * *

Although 1992 was designated "The Year of the Woman," it was not a winning proposition for Pinellas County Senator Mary Grizzle. She had supported women as far back as the 1960s, when she championed the right of female teachers to take maternity leave; now she lost her Republican primary to a more conservative man. The new districts for the Florida Senate, drawn after the 1990 census, arguably discriminated against women. Of the forty incumbent senators, only two were forced to run against each other—and they were women.

Both were progressive Democrats and former leaders in the League of Women Voters. Senator Jeanne Malcohn represented southern Pinellas County, while Senator Helen Gordon Davis represented southern Hillsborough. Instead of district lines that would keep one seat in Pinellas County and one in Hillsborough—as had long been the case—the new district crossed the bay to take in Malcohn's home in St. Petersburg as well as Davis's in south Tampa. Davis defeated her friend Malcohn in the Democratic Party but then lost the general election to St. Petersburg newcomer Charlie Crist. With Republican Mary Grizzle's loss in northern Pinellas, Florida women lost three of their best longtime advocates.

Davis paid the bills to take the case all the way to the U.S. Supreme Court, but although election districts routinely are drawn to favor African Americans, no case law protects women against such discrimination. Nor did the court, which had only one female member at the time, indicate any interest in setting a precedent on behalf of women.

Rosemary Barkett, the only woman on the Florida Supreme Court, also was the target of a vicious 1992 campaign to remove her from the bench. Her opponents could cite no evidence that she voted differently from her male colleagues in any major cases: instead, their action indicated increased sexism as well as a rightwing attempt to make the judiciary less independent and more political. Her colleagues had great respect for her, and they elected her chief justice earlier that year. In the summer and fall, though, she had to walk the tightrope of asking voters to cast a positive ballot on her retention, while also respecting judicial canons that severely limit campaigning.

With help from many women and most judicial figures, Justice Barkett retained her seat with 61 percent of the vote, and President Bill Clinton elevated her to the federal court in Atlanta the following year. Two decades later, Rosemary Barkett remains a federal judge. The Founding Fathers ensured an independent federal judiciary by providing in the Constitution that those appointments are for life.

President Clinton also made history by appointing Janet Reno as the nation's first female attorney general. A Miami native born in 1938, she grew up near the Everglades in a still-extant house built by her mother, Janet Wood Reno. Her father, a Danish immigrant, was a reporter for the *Miami Herald,* while her mother wrote for the *Miami News.* Young Janet made a great transition when she went from tropical Miami to upstate New York, where she graduated from prestigious Cornell University in 1960 with a degree in chemistry.

That was an unconventional field for women, and the same was true when she switched fields and won acceptance at Harvard Law School, in an era when law schools kept strict quotas on the number of women admitted. The legal profession was just beginning to welcome women when Reno returned to Florida, and despite her Harvard degree, she worked at small firms until

1971, when she became staff director of the House Judiciary Committee in Tallahassee.

She served there during an exciting time in state government, as Florida transformed from "good old boy" dominance to "government in the sunshine." Reno was part of the movement that wrote new law requiring open meetings, financial disclosure, and campaign donation limits. She also was lead counsel to the Senate Judiciary Committee, where she handled a major revision of the state's criminal code. Crime would be the focus of her reforms when she returned to Miami and worked as a prosecutor. When the incumbent resigned in 1978, Governor Reuben Askew appointed her as state attorney—a position no Florida woman had ever held.

Reno won reelection five times, and she reduced crime among Miami's heterogeneous population with innovative drug courts and juvenile courts that became models for the nation. With the strong recommendation of fellow Miamian Bob Graham, President Clinton appointed her attorney general, and the U.S. Senate confirmed the nomination on March 12, 1993.

In that same year Patricia Seitz, called Pat, became the first female president of the Florida Bar Association. Born in Washington, D.C., Seitz earned her law degree at prestigious Georgetown University in 1973. When she was campaigning to be the bar's first female president, Seitz said some men had fretted to her husband, attorney Alan Greer, that a woman might not be strong enough to discipline miscreant members. After Seitz issued her first reprimands, however, a male board member told her husband, "She scared me more than my third-grade teacher!"[27] Greer reminded him that Seitz's father was a three-star general, and she had learned from youth how to issue orders.

Very few women held the top position as prosecutors in the nation's major cities, but Governor Lawton Chiles appointed Katherine Fernandez Rundle as Reno's replacement in Miami. Like Reno, she has since been reelected without any serious opposition and retained the office at the time of writing. A Miami native, she graduated from the University of Miami and earned her 1976 law degree in England, at the University of Cambridge. She created Florida's first unit for prosecuting domestic violence. Elected president of the Cuban American Bar Association in 1991, she also was the first Hispanic woman appointed to Florida's Constitutional Revision Commission.

Busy in Washington, Janet Reno was unable to attend the ceremony for the Florida Women's Hall of Fame for her 1993 induction. The other two winners that year were Tampa's Paulina Pedroso, a leader in the fight for

Cuba's independence from Spain in the 1890s, and Betty Skelton Frankman, who set speed records both on land and in the air. Both are profiled in earlier chapters.[28]

President Clinton appointed another Miami native, Carol Browner, as head of the Environmental Protection Agency. Appreciably younger than Reno, Browner also began her career as a staff attorney in Tallahassee, for committees that dealt with the environment. She moved on to Washington in 1983, where she worked for environmental organizations, married, and bore a son. After Lawton Chiles was elected governor in 1990 he named Browner to head the Florida Department of Environmental Regulation, and she held that position until her federal appointment in 1993. Reno and Browner stayed with the Clinton Administration for its entire eight years, unlike many male appointees. Both had to deal with frequent controversy, but both ended their tenure with praise from previous critics.

The head of the Florida Democratic Party in the 1990s—during the state administration of Lawton Chiles and the national administration of Bill Clinton—was Terrie Brady of Jacksonville. She has spent decades with the United Teachers of Duval County, much of the time in Tallahassee, where she also was an official with the Florida Education Association. It was an easy move to go to a new office a few blocks away, as the Democratic Party had its headquarters in the Towle House—an 1846 mansion that Brady's male successor sold.

Pinellas County Commissioner Carol Sheen Todd, a moderate Republican, was a candidate for lieutenant governor in 1994. She had demonstrated unusual creativity in the 1989 case of three Ohio women who were drowned in Tampa Bay. She insisted that police publicize the clues they had, and just one day after a sample of the suspect's handwriting went up on billboards, someone called to identify him. After twenty-two years as a county commissioner, Todd retired in 1994 and became the gubernatorial running mate of longtime Tallahassee politician Jim Smith, formerly a Democrat. Republican women did not turn out in great numbers to vote for another woman, however, and the team lost the primary to Jeb Bush and Frank Brogan—who in turn lost the general election to incumbent Democrats Lawton Chiles and Buddy MacKay.

On the national level the 1994 election was a loss for Democrats, as Georgia's Newt Gingrich led a successful Republican campaign to take over the U.S. House. The Gingrich revolution was not reflected in the Florida House, however, where six Democratic and three Republican women won their first elections. The Republicans—Lisa Carlton of Sarasota, Faye Culp of Tampa, and Evelyn Lynn of Volusia County—were moderates with long careers. Culp, who was pro-choice, used her tenure to rise to the presidency of the Washington-based National Federation of Women Legislators.

The 1994 Democratic winners in the Florida House were Annie Betancourt of Miami, Sally Heyman of Miami Beach, Debbie Horan of Key West, Marjorie Turnbull of Tallahassee, and Deb Prewitt and Helen Spivey, both of Pasco County. Spivey was unusual in that she was past retirement age at election, and Prewitt led her female colleagues in (vainly) opposing an extremely conservative House leader. Turnbull had long been a force in Tallahassee, including service with FSU and FAMU. Heyman was an especially strong feminist; she served on the Commission on the Status of Women and held other offices in Dade County. Betancourt would go on to activism in the League of Women Voters, leading leaguers on tours of Cuba during the next decade. She had been born there, and her 1994 election marked the first legislative victory for a female Cuban American Democrat.

Annie Betancourt is not kin to Kathy Betancourt, who for decades was one of the most popular and effective lobbyists in Tallahassee. She represented the Hillsborough County Classroom Teachers during the 1970s, and when its president, Bob Martinez, became mayor of Tampa, Betancourt lobbied for the City of Tampa. She stayed with his successor, Mayor Sandy Freedman, but moved back to her alma mater, the University of South Florida, when Betty Castor became president there. Prior to her 2011 retirement, Kathy Betancourt brought hundreds of millions of dollars to USF and the city of Tampa.

All three of the 1994 Women's Hall of Fame winners have been discussed earlier. Miami's Nikki Beare, a founder of NOW and a longtime lobbyist for women, especially nurses, had supported Gladys Milton, another 1994 inductee, in Milton's fight to practice as a midwife. The third winner was Betty Mae Jumper, chief of the Seminole tribe.

The year saw a milestone in the Florida Cabinet, as Republican Sandra Mortham of Pinellas County became the first female secretary of state. Her 1994 victory was the first for women at the Cabinet level since Democrat Betty Castor broke the barrier as education commissioner in 1986.

Born as Sandra Barringer in Erie, Pennsylvania, in 1951, she graduated from St. Petersburg Junior College in 1971. In 1989 she would complete her bachelor's degree at St. Petersburg's private college, Eckerd. Meanwhile she married educator Allen Mortham and bore two sons. Elected as a city

The Right to State the Truth: Silvia Safille Ibanez

The legal struggle that Silvia Safille Ibanez endured to use the credentials she earned seems almost incredible—but the reality is that in many professions, even fairly recently, older men protected their interests by using the law to deny newcomers the opportunity to advertise. Except for staid listings in phone books, lawyers could not advertise until young trial attorneys forced that change.

Silvia Ibanez was both a lawyer and a certified public accountant (CPA). She had earned bachelor's and master's degrees in accounting at the University of Miami and won a 1974 award as the Outstanding Graduate Student in Accounting. After nearly a decade of work with international firms she moved to San Juan and completed law school at the University of Puerto Rico. Admitted to the Florida Bar in 1983, she practiced in St. Petersburg before moving with her twin daughters to Polk County and then to the Orlando area.

Her business cards stated the facts about her status as an attorney and a CPA, and it was the accounting governing board, under the state's authority as the Florida Department of Business and Professional Regulation, that told her she could not advertise her earned credential.

She took the case all the way to the U.S. Supreme Court in Washington—and made it more powerful by arguing it herself. It was a stunning move, as she had not yet argued any case in any court, but she won a unanimous victory that overthrew the decision of the lower court—where a male attorney had presented her case. The Supreme Court spelled out in its final ruling:

> Petitioner Ibanez is a member of the Florida Bar; she is also a Certified Public Accountant. . . . She referred to these credentials in her advertising and other communication with the public. . . . Notwithstanding the apparent truthfulness of the communication . . . the Board [Florida Board of Accountancy] reprimanded her. . . . The District Court of Appeals . . . affirmed.

The U.S. Supreme Court overturned the district court decision unanimously, with Ruth Bader Ginsberg writing the opinion.

continued

President Bill Clinton had appointed Ginsburg to the Supreme Court in August 1993, and she issued the Court's decision the following June. All her colleagues signed off on the opinion, which read:

> Held: The Board's decision censuring Ibanez is incompatible with First Amendment restraints on official action. . . . The State may ban such speech only if it is false, deceptive, or misleading. . . . The State's burden is not slight: It must demonstrate that the harms . . . are real. . . . Measured against these standards, the order reprimanding Ibanez cannot stand. . . . As long as she holds a currently active CPA license from the board, it is difficult to see how consumers could be misled by her truthful representation to that effect.*

The real truth was that a mostly male judiciary had supported a mostly male state board in trying to limit the career of a young Hispanic woman. At appreciable personal expense, Ibanez courageously took her case to the highest level and thereby created more opportunity for newcomers, both male and female. An increase in providers naturally lowers costs, and Silvia Ibanez thus helped make business and legal services available to more people—and thereby strengthened democracy.

Note: Ibanez v. Florida Dept. of Business and Professional Regulation, Board of Accountancy—512 US 136 (1994), *Justia US Supreme Court* (https://supreme.justia.com/cases/federal/us/512/136/).

commissioner in the Pinellas County town of Largo, Mortham won a seat in the Florida House in 1986. She quickly rose in Republican leadership, establishing a reputation as strongly anti-tax, and that stance helped her win election as secretary of state in 1994. The Florida Federation of Business and Professional Women honored her with their Glass Ceiling Award.

The next year, 1995, a Miami woman, Ann Moliver Ruben, made national headlines for her promotion of girls' aspirations. Ruben was licensed to use the "Margaret" figure from the "Dennis the Menace" cartoon, and she created a t-shirt declaring, "Someday a Woman Will Be President." She had a contract with Wal-Mart, but when—amazingly enough—some Wal-Mart customers objected to this gentle feminism, the retail giant pulled the shirts. After complaints from people nationwide, Wal-Mart restocked the shirts.

* * *

The three women inducted into the Florida Women's Hall of Fame in 1995 were African American physician Evelyn Crosslin of Daytona Beach; engineer JoAnn Morgan of Titusville, who was the first female executive at NASA; and Sarah Brooks Pryor, pioneer postmaster in Fort Walton Beach. The 1996 inductees were Gainesville environmentalist Marjorie Carr; Tampa's Betty Castor, the first woman on the Florida Cabinet; and Ivy Stranahan, Fort Lauderdale founder and president of the Florida Suffrage Association in 1917. All are profiled in earlier chapters.

Except for Democrat Jimmy Carter, who appointed an amazing thirty-six women to the federal courts during his four years in office, President Bill Clinton put more women into the judiciary than any previous president. In 1993 during his first year in office, Clinton named Susan Bucklew as the first female federal judge in Tampa. A Tampa native, she had been Hillsborough County's first female judge of any sort when appointed by Democratic Governor Bob Graham in 1984. Bucklew had not always been in the legal profession, however: like many women of her era, she began her career in education and taught high school English for a decade prior to going to law school.

President Clinton appointed Joan Lenard as a federal judge for the Miami district in 1995. She arrived there from Ohio in 1976 and rose in the ranks of prosecutors until 1982, when she became a lower-level judge. Lenard has presided over trials of terrorists and Cuban spies and, in 2012, issued a strong decision against the state of Florida, directing that it must spend Medicaid money to assist financially needy children who have autism. According to the *Tampa Bay Times* of April 9, 2012, she said the investment in treating these children "ultimately will save public funds."

Judge Joan Lenard should not be confused with Marilyn Lenard, who was a member of the Electoral College that reelected President Clinton in 1996. Marilyn Lenard became the first female president of the Florida AFL-CIO in 1993. Her union roots were with Communication Workers of America, and she was president of the Space Coast Labor Council when she won the top state post. Vicki Vaughn of the *Orlando Sentinel* wrote on October 11, 1993:

> Years past her Kentucky childhood and move to Florida, a divorce, single parenthood, and a second marriage, Lenard has undergone a transformation. And so has the Florida AFL-CIO. Last month, in a stunning upset, Lenard, 43, ousted Dan Miller as president of the

133,000-member Florida labor coalition, a post he had held for 16 years. She is the only woman heading a state AFL-CIO.

The article went on to quote a male labor leader who said, "The work force is changing, and Marilyn represents that change." Moreover, two of the three top AFL-CIO officers during this period were women, as Susan Wilson of Ocala served as secretary/treasurer. A leader in the obsoletely named International Brotherhood of Electrical Workers, Wilson also served on the Florida Commission on the Status of Women.

In the 1996 election three women were among the four candidates for the Democratic nomination for Tampa's seat in the U.S. House. Longtime representative Sam Gibbons—who had supported women in Congress and was a founder of Head Start—retired, and the race to replace him was hotly contested. The women were former Mayor Sandy Freedman, County Commissioner Phyllis Busansky, and Pat Frank, a former legislator who held various offices after she was the second woman on the Hillsborough County School Board in 1972.[29] All were excellent choices, and the ultimate winner was a man, Jim Davis. He too was a progressive Democrat, and he would hold the seat until giving it up to run for governor in 2006.

The 1996 legislative elections gave Republicans a majority in the Florida Senate, and they followed the precedent set by Democrats earlier in the decade, when Gwen Margolis became the first female president of that body. The Republican majority elected Toni Jennings, and she set another precedent by serving four consecutive years—something that no Florida man ever has achieved. A moderate who worked with Democrats, Jennings proved so popular that she presided until 2000, when term limits required her to retire from her Orlando seat.

One of President Clinton's initiatives after his 1992 election was controversial within his own Democratic Party, but Democratic Governor Lawton Chiles joined in Clinton's "Welfare to Work." The Commission on the Status of Women took an active role in this effort to give young mothers the tools—especially job training and child care—that they needed to become economically independent. With money won by suing tobacco companies for promoting deadly diseases, Chiles and Attorney General Bob Butterworth also implemented health care for needy children, which axiomatically meant support for women. When Chiles died suddenly in 1998, the *St. Petersburg Times* summarized this achievement. "Look around" at the change, the editorial began. "You can see it everywhere.

It's in the face of every poor child who has health care, as Chiles' chief of staff Linda Shelley put it eloquently yesterday [at his funeral]. Before Chiles started the Healthy Start program in 1992, Florida's record on infant mortality was worse than that of some African countries, as Chiles himself used to say. Six years later, infant mortality is down 26 percent—the biggest drop in the nation. Chiles' initiative has, quite literally, made life possible for hundreds of Florida children.

So has his other "healthy" passion: Healthy Kids, which provided health insurance to some 60,000 . . . children. . . . Last May . . . a quarter of a million more children [became] eligible for coverage. . . .

As Florida's welfare-to-work efforts took hold, Chiles also fought hard so that participants in the Work and Gain Economic Self-Sufficiency program, or WAGES . . . would have child care for their children. Chiles knew that without subsidized child care, work is an empty promise for many families.[30]

Promises had been made on legal reforms too, and partly at the instigation of Justice Rosemary Barkett, the Florida Supreme Court did a 1990 study of gender bias. That was updated in 1996, with attorney Winifred J. Sharp as its chair and Betty Morris as staff director. The commission had six subcommittees: family law, education, domestic violence, criminal justice, the courts and judges, and the legal profession. In too many cases the members found that the recommendations made six years earlier had not been implemented.

Three men and three women served on the family law subcommittee, for example, and they wrote candidly: "The original Commission recommended that the laws dealing with spousal support require judges to set amounts . . . consistent with the supported spouse's marital standard of living. This has not been done . . . The problem of collecting child support still remains a major one."[31] The education subcommittee reported similarly:

The original Commission Report recommended that the judiciary and legal profession need to be educated about the nature of sexual battery and the root causes of prostitution. Little has been done about this recommendation. The Legislature has passed amendments to the Rape Shield law to try to protect victims of sexual battery from attacks on them in court . . . but [they] are still vulnerable in many regards.[32]

Judge Jennifer Bailey chaired the subcommittee on domestic violence, and among its nine members was Robin Hassler, a Governor's Office specialist on this issue. The subcommittee pointed to some successes—including amending law to make it easier for judges to deny bail for abusers—but needs remained. One was the fifteen-day life of an injunction against a potential abuser, which was too short to change habits. The experts proposed extending this to thirty days, but "due to a lack of funds, the Commission was not able to pursue this inquiry."[33]

The most important issue for the subcommittee on courts, chaired by Judge Karen Cole, may have been a mechanism for women in divorce cases who had no financial resources to appeal decisions. Members also "considered a proposal to revise [statutes] to provide that spouse abuse should be a valid basis to make an award of attorney fees." The earlier commission also had recommended that a pamphlet on divorce be given to couples when they applied for marriage licenses. The committee especially intended to warn new brides about pre-nuptial agreements—but, the writers said, "this has not been worked on."[34]

The subcommittee on criminal justice, chaired by attorney Jerri Blair, began its report by saying that "prisons and detention facilities in Florida for women and girls are much inferior to those for men and boys." Members visited several sites and "noted that girls are not being provided with adequate basic hygiene items, such as shampoo . . . underwear, combs. . . . Some of the girls reported that they were not receiving needed prenatal care." Members added that, again because of a lack of funding, "the Commission . . . could not survey . . . whether female employees in the DOC [Department of Corrections] are being given equal opportunity for pay and advancement."[35]

Attorney Ellen Freidin, who championed many causes, chaired the subcommittee on women's status in the legal profession. It "noted with approval the Florida Bar's . . . workplace model policies on sexual harassment, family leave, and alternative work levels."[36] A decade earlier, few female attorneys had dared to raise such issues, but because of feminist efforts, workplace policies attuned to women's needs were offered as models for other professions. The commission appended more than sixty pages to its general observations and recommendations, including dozens of proposed additions and deletions to state statues.

At least as significant, Governor Chiles appointed the second and third women to the Florida Supreme Court. The first had been Rosemary Barkett, appointed by Governor Bob Graham in 1985, and after she left for the federal court in 1993, Florida reverted to having no woman on its highest bench for four years, until Chiles appointed Barbara Pariente in 1997.

Pariente was born in New York City in 1948. She graduated with highest honors from Boston University and was fifth in her law school class at George Washington University. After arriving in Fort Lauderdale in 1973 she clerked for a federal judge and then practiced privately in West Palm Beach for eighteen years. Her colleagues repeatedly honored her, especially for her legal work in protecting children. Pariente had retained her maiden name when she married Frederick Hazouri, who also became a judge. They had three children and by 2012 eight grandchildren. Barbara Pariente frequently speaks and writes about the court's work, and she is particularly cognizant of women's issues.

The very next year, in 1998, Chiles named another female justice, and Peggy Quince was the court's first African American woman. Like Pariente, Quince was born in 1948, and when she married attorney Fred Buckine, she too retained her maiden name. A native of Norfolk, Virginia, Quince graduated in 1970 from Howard University, the historic institution for blacks in Washington, D.C., and earned her law degree at Catholic University, also in Washington. She joined the Florida Attorney General's Office soon after moving to Bradenton in 1978 and rose to chief of the division based in Tampa, while also rearing two daughters. In 1994 Governor Chiles appointed Peggy Quince to the area's circuit court, where she also was the first black woman, and four years later he named her to the state's highest court.

Both women have consistently been praised by those in the legal profession. At the federal level President Bill Clinton appointed Pat Seitz, who had been the first female president of the Florida Bar Association, to the top court in Miami in 1998. That year marked a slowdown, however, as no women have been added to the Florida Supreme Court since the 1997 and 1998 appointments of Pariente and Quince. Democratic governor Bob Graham had appointed Rosemary Barkett in 1985, but no woman joined her during the four years of Republican governor Bob Martinez's tenure. Nor were any chosen during the millennial years of Republican governors Jeb Bush, Charlie Crist, and Rick Scott.

The three women who have served at this highest state level, moreover, are arguably "two-fers" in that they are seen as representing both women and ethnic groups. Although Catholic, Rosemary Barkett is an Arab American born in Mexico; Barbara Pariente has a Hispanic heritage; and Peggy Quince is black. As of this writing no white woman has joined the hundreds of white men who have served in this powerful position.

* * *

The 1997 Women's Hall of Fame inductees were Miami's Athalie Range, the first African American to head a state agency; Carita Doggett Corse, who headed the Federal Writers Project in Florida during the Great Depression; and Alicia Baro, longtime advocate for Puerto Ricans. They are profiled in earlier chapters, as are 1998 winners Senator Helen Gordon Davis of Tampa and Judge Mattie Belle Davis of Miami. The third winner in 1998 was Christine Fulwylie-Bankston of Pensacola.

A native of Paducah, Kentucky, born in 1916, she began teaching in a one-room Kentucky school in 1937. She was instrumental in merging black and white YWCA facilities there in 1959 and then moved to Pittsburgh, where she directed the city's Negro Education Emergency Drive. After earning a 1974 doctorate in education at the University of Pittsburgh, she came to Pensacola in 1980. There she established a free tutoring program and served numerous Escambia County causes. Christine Fulwylie-Bankston died just prior to her 1998 induction, but dozens of her supporters memorialized her by wearing red when they came to Tallahassee.

For feminists, the most notable thing about the 1998 election was that it was the first for a Cabinet position in which all the major candidates were women. State Senator Katherine Harris of Sarasota ousted incumbent Sandra Mortham in the Republican primary for secretary of state and went on to defeat the Democratic nominee, attorney Karen Gievers of Miami, in the general election. Gievers, whose husband had been killed by a drunk driver, would go on to become a top trial lawyer. She gave generously of her time with lawsuits on behalf of children, even suing the state for inadequately supporting children. In 2010 Gievers would be elected as a circuit court judge in Tallahassee.

In 1998, however, the rivalry between Republicans Sandra Mortham and Katherine Harris may have been the most vicious in any campaign between Florida women. Harris won, but scandals would eventually kill her elective career. Mortham suffered even after she lost her renomination for secretary of state. Republican gubernatorial nominee Jeb Bush then chose her as his running mate, but that did not work out either. The December 1997 issue of the *Tampa Business Journal*, for example, said Secretary of State Mortham had "a lengthy list of transgressions, including spending thousands of taxpayer dollars to promote herself . . . with an amazing range of knicknacks."

The magazine also charged her with spending tax dollars "to pay for her husband to accompany her on trips to Russia, Africa, Asia and South America." Fort Lauderdale's *Sun Sentinel* of January 7, 1998, defended Mortham,

Building the Basics of Governance: Women on Constitutional Revision Commissions

The Florida Constitution, the state's fundamental governing document, underwent a major rewrite in 1968—at the same time that the national women's movement was just beginning to organize. The new constitution mandated that ten years later a new commission would analyze the results of reform and then, every twenty years, a Constitutional Revision Commissions (CRC) would meet. More than in most states, the Florida Constitution is a living document intended to keep up with change.

Without aiming to, these mandates also offered a way to measure of the status of Florida women. In 1968 only one woman worked on the major revision: Senator Beth Johnson of Orlando, profiled in chapter 9. The growing impact of feminism was clear a decade later, as five women won the coveted 1978 CRC appointments:

- Yvonne Burkholz of Miami, who lobbied for teachers through the Florida Education Association
- Dr. Freddie Grooms, the highest-ranking African American administrator at Florida State University
- Lois Harrison, later of Polk County and state president of the League of Women Voters at the time
- Jan Platt, a member of Tampa City Council and a future Hillsborough County commissioner
- Stella Thayer, an attorney who earned her 1965 law degree at prestigious Columbia University

In an article on July 10, 1977, announcing appointments, Associated Press reporter John Van Greson featured only Burkholz, who was well known in Tallahassee. He wrote of the others: "two might be described as housewives, but one is a city councilwoman and the other is the wife of a newspaper publisher." His dismissive comment belies the individual credentials of these women. The unnamed councilwoman was Jan Platt, and the writer failed to note that she had joined Governor Rubin Askew in creating the first "Sunshine" laws on financial disclosure and open meetings. The "wife of a newspaper publisher" presumably was League of Women Voters president Lois Harrison. Exactly which women he had in mind as

continued

"housewives" remains mysterious; only someone wearing sexist blinders could dub either Dr. Grooms or attorney/businesswoman Thayer as such.

Although Van Greson did not mention it, both the commission's alternate slots also went to women. These were political scientist Charlotte F. Hubbard and Sybil Mobley, an African American who was dean of the School of Business and Industry at FAMU.

By 1998, when the CRC met again, attitudes had improved, and women's credentials were seen as valid: none was termed a housewife. Ten women—double the number in 1978—won appointments in 1998:

- Martha Barnett, a Tallahassee attorney who was then president-elect of the American Bar Association
- Pat Barton of Naples, a retired realtor, Republican activist, and anti-drug educator
- Valerie W. Evans, a leader in the home-school movement
- Marilyn Evans-Jones, a former member of the Florida House from Melbourne
- Katherine Fernandez-Rundle, who had replaced U.S. Attorney General Janet Reno as Dade County prosecutor
- Barbara Williams Ford-Coates, tax collector of Sarasota County
- Ellen Freidin, a Miami attorney and president of the Florida Association for Women Lawyers
- Toni Jennings of Orlando, who, as president of the Florida Senate, was able to appoint herself
- Jacinta Mathis, an African American attorney from Orlando
- Judith Byrne Riley of Valparaiso, national chair of the Private Industry Council and member of the Commission on the Status of Women

Five of the ten women were appointed by Democratic governor Lawton Chiles: Barnett, Ford-Coates, Freidin, Riley, and Fernandez-Rundle. He also named Lyra Blizzard Logan of Miami as an alternate; a graduate of Harvard Law School, she was thirty-four and the youngest.

Senate president Toni Jennings had nine appointments, but used only three for women: herself, as well as Republicans Pat Barton of

Naples and Marilyn Evans-Jones, who had retired to Amelia Island; both are very wealthy communities.

House Speaker Daniel Webster, a Republican like Jennings, also had nine appointments, and the two women he chose arguably were the least qualified on the commission. The *Landland Ledger* of June 4, 1997, described Valerie Evans as "an Orlando homemaker who holds a law degree from Florida State University"; her age was listed as forty-seven and there was no indication that she ever practiced law. His second female appointee, Jacinta Mathis, was also from Orlando and an attorney, but her credentials were slim compared with those of others.

The judiciary was entitled to four appointees but chose no women, although candidates certainly were available, including such qualified attorneys as Pat Seitz, the first female president of the Florida Bar, and the many female judges elected in the past two decades.

Although a definite improvement over the solitary female commissioner in 1968, the ten women among the thirty-seven members in 1998 still made up only 27 percent of the whole. The CRC meets again in 2018, offering another opportunity to measure the inclusion of half of the population.

pointing out that "museums in Florida have flourished during her tenure"—but the paper nonetheless concluded that she was an "albatross on the Republican ticket." Bush replaced her with a man after the most damaging revelation, that Mortham had not paid rent for her son's wedding reception in the Old Capitol.

Of much more long-term importance, however, was that voters in the 1998 election approved an amendment to the Florida Constitution that granted women equality with men. Its author and chief advocate was Miami attorney Ellen Freidin, who wrote in the final report of the Constitutional Revision Commission:

> If you read the Constitution of the state of Florida, you see that there is no express mention of the rights of women. . . . The only rights of women expressly stated in our state are those mentioned in statues.

> It is past time for the state of Florida to explicitly recognize in its Constitution the equal rights of women. . . .
>
> [The majority] of the Constitutional Revision Commission has agreed, and will give citizens of Florida the chance on Nov. 3 to ensure that females and males alike are equal before the law. If Revision 5 on the November ballot is approved, Article I, Section 2 of the Constitution will read: "All natural persons, female and male alike, are equal before the law and have inalienable rights. . . ."
>
> Florida then will join 17 other states in putting equal rights amendments in their Constitution. . . .
>
> There are, of course, a couple of common arguments against such an amendment. Commissioner Dick Langley [Republican state senator from Clermont, appointed by House Speaker Daniel Webster] has said that equality for women is covered in the Constitution by the words "all natural persons." Also Commissioner Ken Connor [Florida Right to Life, also appointed by Webster] has argued that the amendment could pave the way for the legalization of same-sex marriages.
>
> My response to the former argument is that the additional language in the constitution—"female and male alike"—is a matter of emphasis, and a matter of explicit recognition of equality.
>
> Traditionally, if we did not have the historical basis for male supremacy in our society, we probably wouldn't be dealing with this today. If women always had been allowed to vote, always had been allowed to make decisions for themselves, and always had equal opportunity, this additional clause would not be necessary. . . .

Voters understood the point and approved the amendment. Thus, although the federal Equal Rights Amendment never was ratified, Florida women are assured of legal equality under their state constitution. In addition, the 1980 privacy amendment to the state constitution, authored by attorney Patricia Dore, grants unusual legal standing for individualism in reproductive matters. Florida women who want to make their own decisions owe great debts to Dore and Freidin.

Governor Chiles had made the last of his appointments to the Florida Women's Hall of Fame prior to his death in December 1998, and those women were admitted to the Hall of Fame in a March 1999 ceremony at the Capitol. They included international athlete Althea Gibson and Alachua woodswoman Dessie Smith Prescott, both featured in chapter 8. The third choice was Sister Jeanne O'Laughlin of Miami.

Born in 1929, she grew up in Detroit cared for by her widowed father and, at age sixteen, joined the Dominican Sisters. They educated her at Siena Heights College in Adrian, Michigan, and she went on to earn a master's degree at the University of Arizona. After working as an educational administrator in St. Louis, Sister Jeanne came to Barry College, then a small Miami Catholic school for women. Named for its founder, Ireland-born Mother Gerald Barry, it had begun in 1940, and she served as president until 1961. Three other nuns then followed her, including Sister Trinita Flood, who oversaw the admission of male students during the 1970s. No Barry College president, however, had the impact of Sister Jeanne O'Laughlin. During her twenty-three-year tenure she increased enrollment to more than nine thousand, raised an endowment of more than $24 million, and built a law school in Orlando. It became Barry University in 1981, and O'Laughlin's colleagues elected her to several offices, including the chairmanship of the Independent Colleges and Universities of Florida.

Sister Jeanne also was known for aiding immigrants, including Haitians who fled their impoverished country in the 1980s. In 1992 she "intervened on behalf of three Chinese women who spent more than a year in a room at the Miami International Airport, waiting to be granted asylum."[37] She also was deeply involved in the case of young Elian Gonzalez, whose mother drowned attempting to leave Cuba. In recommending that the boy stay with extended family in Miami, she differed from Attorney General Janet Reno, also from Miami, who ultimately returned him to his father in Cuba. No matter what side of this and other controversies one took, it was indisputable that women had reached positions powerful enough to make such decisions.

In the last election of the century, 1998, just nine new women joined the House of Representatives, compared with fourteen in 1992. Twelve of the fourteen in 1992 had been Democrats, but in 1998, six of the nine newcomers were Republicans. Partisanship would sharply increase after 2000, and women in Tallahassee no longer were the cohesive whole that they had been in the 1970s. Term limits also began to have their predictably conservative effect, as instead of mounting campaigns as challengers, more and more candidates simply waited until incumbents had served the eight allowable years.

Such caution was reflected in the bills that women sponsored, as greater conservatism would be the hallmark of the first years of the new millennium.

Goals such as gender equity on state boards would no longer receive the attention that they had in the 1970s and 1980s. As of 2013 the Florida Senate had not repeated its 1991 precedent of electing a woman as president; the House never has chosen a female speaker; and voters who elected the state's first female U.S. senator in 1986 have not done that again. Progress is not inevitable and, as Thomas Jefferson said long ago, eternal vigilance is the price of liberty.

11 After the New Millennium

Those who take on the challenge of writing a history of their own times face a daunting task, and most historians wisely avoid doing that. However, because it is important for young people to know the record of their short lifetimes, and especially because most women's political history has occurred relatively recently, the conveyance of current information seems to outweigh the perils of possible criticism.

One indisputable fact is that the 2000 election was the nation's most controversial presidential race since 1876. In that post–Civil War contest, the man with the most popular votes, Democrat Samuel Tilden, failed to achieve the presidency. A similar thing happened in 2000, when Democrat Al Gore won the votes of a half million more people than voted for Republican George W. Bush. The tally of the Electoral College vote, which is mandated by the Constitution, was difficult to determine, and everything focused on Florida with its twenty-seven electoral votes.

Leftist Ralph Nader took some 90,000 votes, leaving the margin between Gore and Bush at fewer than 600 of some 6 million votes cast—too close to call. There were no precedents for recounting so many ballots in a state so large, and to complicate things further, Jeb Bush, brother of candidate George W. Bush, was governor. Several women played key roles, too.

Republican Katherine Harris was secretary of state and therefore in charge of the election—but she also co-chaired Bush's campaign committee, and many of the national reporters who descended on Tallahassee did not see her as objective. Theresa LaPorte, a Democrat, was supervisor of elections in Palm Beach County, where most attention focused. She designed what she thought was a space-saving "butterfly"-shaped ballot, but the effect was that many ballots were disqualified because confused voters chose two presidential candidates. Most were elderly Jewish Democrats who inadvertently canceled out their intended vote for Gore.

The woman who earned the most respect was Pam Iorio, Hillsborough County's supervisor of elections and president of the state association of the sixty-seven county supervisors. Iorio had no problems in her county, but there were issues in several others beyond Palm Beach. Iorio did some four hundred interviews with national media, urging calm and a careful, detailed recount. That was begun, but the U.S. Supreme Court intervened, ending the recount in *Bush vs. Gore* on December 12, 2000, and Bush became president in January.

Meanwhile, it was easy to overlook the fact that women, especially Democratic women, won a big victory in the Florida House in 2000. Sixteen women were newcomers to the House that year, the greatest number ever—and unfortunately, more than would be the case in later election years. In alphabetical order, the ten Democrats were Lorranne Ausley of Tallahassee, Dorothy Bendross-Mindingall of Miami, Susan Bucher of Palm Beach County, Joyce Cusack of DeLand (one of the legislature's historically few nurses), Anne Gannon of Delray Beach (a former NOW lobbyist), civil rights pioneer Arthenia Joyner of Tampa, Cindy Lerner of Miami, Nan Rich of Broward County, Sara Romeo of Tampa, and Shelly Vana of Palm Beach County. Ausley, Joyner, and Rich would go on to long careers.

The six Republican House winners in 2000 were Holly Benson of Pensacola, Kim Berfield of Clearwater, Marty Bowen of Winter Haven, Jennifer Carroll of Jacksonville, Donna Clarke of Sarasota, and Gayle Harrell of St. Lucie County. Benson would go on to an agency appointment under Governor Charlie Crist, while the only African American Republican, Jennifer Carroll, later became lieutenant governor.

The Senate added only two women in 2000, and neither was a newcomer. They were Republican Lisa Carlton of Sarasota, a member of the longtime land-owning Carlton family, and Mandy Dawson, a young African American Democrat from Fort Lauderdale. Both moved up from the House, and thus all nine women in the forty-member body could be considered incumbents. After sixteen years of legislative service, Dawson, unfortunately, would plead guilty to tax evasion in 2012.

Female newcomers to the legislature, 2000s

Name	District	Party	Notes
2000 Election, House:			
Lorranne Ausley	Tallahassee	D	Democratic nominee for state chief financial officer in 2010
Dorothy Bendross-Mindingall	Miami	D	after term limits, went on to Dade school board
Holly Benson	Pensacola	R	appointed to state agency in 2006
Kim Berfield	Clearwater	R	lost 2006 Senate race to a Democrat
Marty Bowen	Winter Haven	R	speaker pro tempore in last term
Susan Bucher	Palm Beach	D	went on to be Palm Beach supervisor of elections
Jennifer Carroll	Jacksonville	R	African American; lieutenant governor, 2010-2013
Donna Clarke	Sarasota	R	environmental engineer; lost in 2006
Joyce Cusack	DeLand	D	nurse; minority leader pro tempore in 2006
Anne Gannon	Delray Beach	D	former NOW lobbyist; subsequently reelected
Gayle Harrell	St. Lucie	R	term limited in 2008, but returned in 2010
Arthenia Joyner	Tampa	D	African American; went on to Senate in 2006
Cindy Lerner	Miami	D	attorney; longtime guardian ad litem advocate
Nan Rich	Broward	D	long career in both chambers
Sara Romeo	Tampa	D	lost in 2002 but built program for female veterans
Shelly Vana	Palm Beach	D	teacher; went on to county commission in 2008
2000 Election, Senate:			
Lisa Carlton	Sarasota	R	moved up from House
Mandy Dawson	Fort Lauderdale	D	African American; moved up from House
2002 Election, House:			
Sandy Adams	Oviedo	R	went on to Congress in 2010
Ellyn Bogdanoff	Fort Lauderdale	R	attorney; rose in leadership
Mary Brandenburg	Palm Beach	D	after term limited, ran for mayor of West Palm Beach
Audrey Gibson	Jacksonville	D	African American; went on to Senate in 2011

continued

Female newcomers to the legislature, 2000s—*Continued*

Name	District	Party	Notes
Sheri McInvale	Orlando	D	after switching to Republican, lost to a Democrat
Yolly Roberson	Miami	D	Haitian attorney; after term limits, ran for Congress
2002 Election, Senate:			
Debbie Wasserman Schultz	Broward County	D	moved up from House; went on to Congress
Gwen Margolis	Miami	D	returned after earlier career; see chapter 10
2004 Election, House:			
Anitere Flores	Miami	R	attorney; moved on to Senate in 2010
Susan Goldstein	Broward	R	first Jewish Republican; lost next election
Denise Grimsley	Sebring	R	nurse; citrus grower; rose to chair Budget Committee
Dorothy Hukill	Daytona Beach	R	educator; attorney; lost congressional race in 2010
Priscilla Taylor	West Palm Beach	D	African American; went on to county commission
2004 Election, Senate:			
Nancy Argenziano	Crystal River	R	moved up from House
Larcenia Bullard	Miami	D	moved up from House; African American
Paula Dockery	Lakeland	R	moved up from House
Evelyn Lynn	Ormond Beach	R	moved up from House
Nan Rich	Broward County	D	moved up from House; candidate for governor in 2014
Frederica Wilson	Miami	D	moved up from House; went on to Congress; African American
Trudi K. Williams	Fort Myers	R	environmental engineer
2006 Election, House:			
Debbie Boyd	upper West Coast	D	realtor; rural area south of Tallahassee
Marti Coley	Panama City	R	teacher; widow of legislator
Janet Long	St. Petersburg	D	won seat previously held by Republican Leslie Waters
Betty Reed	Tampa	D	educator; African American
Maria Sachs	Broward	D	Broward Women Lawyers Association
Elaine Schwartz	Hollywood	D	attorney; sponsored legislation for pay equity

Name	District	Party	Notes
Kelly Skidmore	Boca Raton	D	Arthritis Foundation; former legislative aide; lost in 2010
Geraldine Thompson	Orlando	D	college administrator; museum founder
2006 Election, Senate:			
Arthenia Joyner	Tampa	D	African American; moved up from House
Ronda Storms	Tampa	R	former Hillsborough County commissioner
2008 Election, House:			
Janet Adkins	Fernandina Beach	R	charter schools advocate
Rachel Burgin	Brandon	R	lost Republican primary in 2012
Gwyn Clarke-Reed	Broward	D	retired educator; African American
Debbie Mayfield	Vero Beach	R	Indian River school board; succeeded deceased husband
Mia L. Jones	Jacksonville	D	African American; MBA; Jacksonville City Council
Marlene H. O'Toole	The Villages	R	retired IBM executive
Michelle Vaslinda Rehwinkel	Tallahassee	D	attorney and college professor
Hazel Rogers	Broward	D	African American; banker
Kelli Stargel	Lakeland	R	property manager
2008 Election, Senate:			
Nancy Detert	Sarasota	R	moved up from House
Eleanor Sobel	Hollywood	D	moved up from House
2010 SpecialElection, January, House:			
Janet Cruz	Tampa	D	Hispanic district; feminist
2010 Election, House:			
Lori Berman	Broward	D	attorney; feminist
Daphne Campbell	Miami	D	African American; nurse
Ana Rivas Logan	Miami	R	defeated Miami Beach mayor Millie Herrara, a Democrat
Jeanette Nunez	Miami	R	health care administrator
Kathleen Passidomo	Naples	R	attorney; Status of Women Commission
Elizabeth Porter	Lake City	R	health care administrator
Cynthia Stafford	Miami	D	attorney; African American
Dana Young	Tampa	R	attorney; defeated Democratic female attorney Stacy Frank

continued

Female newcomers to the legislature, 2000s—*Continued*

Name	District	Party	Notes
2010 Election, Senate:			
Lizbeth Benacquisto	Palm Beach	R	Realtor; marketing; lost Republican nomination in a 2014 special election for Congress
Ellyn Bogdanoff	Fort Lauderdale	R	moved up from House; rose in Republican leadership
Anitere Flores	Miami	R	moved up from House
Maria Sachs	Broward	D	moved up from House
2011 Special Election, March, House:			
Barbara Watson	Miami	D	African American; public school advocate
2011 Special Election, September, Senate:			
Audrey Gibson	Jacksonville	D	moved up from House
2012 Election, Senate:			
Kelli Stargel	Lakeland	R	moved up from House
Geraldine Thompson	Orlando	D	moved up from House
2012 Election, House:			
Karen Castor Dentel	Orlando	D	teacher; mother of school age children
Katie Edwards	Broward	D	degrees in agriculture and law
Heather Dawes Fitzenhagen	Fort Myers	R	Attorney
Marylynn Magar	Hobe Sound	R	Republican activist
Kathleen M. Peters	St. Peterburg	R	Chamber of Commerce
Sharon Pritchett	Miami	D	law enforcement
Holly Merrill Raschein	Key Largo	R	former legislative aide
Linda Stewart	Orlando	D	Orange County Commission

The highest-ranking Republican woman in 2000 was Paula Dockery of Lakeland, who was the Senate majority whip—but by the end of the decade, she often would differ with her party. In the House, Republican speaker Johnny Byrd of Plant City failed to offer leadership positions to women of his party, even though some had experience that exceeded his. The 2000 election, in fact, would mark the acme of women's electoral victories for the decade: future elections would bring fewer women, and the legislature was increasingly dominated by white male Republicans.

Nor did Florida women advance in Congress, as longtime Miami legislator Elaine Bloom lost her 2000 attempt to go to Washington. But the first year of the new millennium was a positive in that it brought the first Florida woman as president of the American Bar Association. Martha Barnett, a Dade City native who practiced with Holland and Knight in Tallahassee, was only the second woman to preside over the association in its century-plus history.[1] Barnett used her tenure to speak to many groups about issues related to women.

At the same time that Barnett served nationally, Edith Osman became the second female president of the Florida Bar. Seven years had passed since the first, when Pat Seitz was elected in 1993, and Osman acknowledged that, saying, "A strong motivating factor for running, aside from personal gratification, was that I thought we needed to have another woman president of the Florida Bar. . . . Women needed to be considered capable of running, winning, and doing a good job."[2]

The year 2000 was a trifecta for Florida's female attorneys, as Evett Simmons became president-elect of the National Bar Association, the longtime organization for black lawyers. Her mother had died when she was ten, and she was reared by an aunt, Eartha Holzendorf, in Fernandina Beach. With scholarships and part-time work, Simmons graduated from law school at Mercer University in Macon, Georgia, in 1982; she remained unmarried and rose to partner in a St. Lucie firm. One of her mentors was Tampa's Arthenia Joyner, who had preceded her as National Bar Association president.[3]

Miami's Marilyn Milian had almost two decades of judicial experience when she became the first woman to preside on the reality television show *The People's Court* in 2001. A summa cum laude graduate of the University of Miami, she earned her law degree at prestigious Georgetown. She worked for Janet Reno as an assistant state attorney until Governor Lawton Chiles appointed Milian as a judge. She said of her television experience:

> I have the honor of being the first female . . . in the show's twenty year history, and the first Hispanic (male or female) to preside over a nationally syndicated court show. This opportunity has provided me with a platform to showcase the Hispanic culture, and my Miami roots in particular.
>
> I often share Spanish witticisms my mother or grandmother used to say, life lessons that I promptly translate. I receive hundreds of emails a week asking me to repeat those sayings, most from our country's heartland, from people who have never even met a Hispanic.[4]

* * *

Helen Popovich of Florida Atlantic University in Broward County had been the first female president at a Florida public university in 1984.[5] At the millennium, the most noted new woman came at the end of the Clinton administration, when Secretary of Health and Human Services Donna Shalala left Washington to accept the presidency of the University of Miami. Dr. Shalala had been chancellor of the University of Wisconsin prior to joining the Cabinet; she was the second woman in the nation to head a major public research university. After doing a great deal to elevate the image of that private institution, she announced that she would retire in 2015.

The University of South Florida was the first—and has thus far been the only—public university in the state to have a woman succeed a woman in the top job. When Betty Castor left the Tampa-based school in 1999, New York's Judy Genshaft replaced her.[6] Genshaft is a career academic, and her husband, Steven Greenbaum, takes the primary role with their two adopted children. She remains in office at the time of writing.

In contrast to the service of Genshaft and Shalala, Anne H. Hopkins's presidency of the University of North Florida was brief. She was an administrator at such prestigious places as the University of Minnesota and was chosen for the presidency of the Jacksonville school in 1998 but resigned in 2002 because of heart disease. Her academic specialty is political science, and she returned to teaching and writing in that field. Former Jacksonville mayor John Delaney succeeded her at UNF.

Boards of trustees hire college and university presidents, and those trustees are appointed by governors. The legislature created many more such appointive opportunities for Governor Jeb Bush by abolishing the statewide Board of Regents and creating individual boards of trustees at the state universities (something that had always been the case for community colleges). Despite hundreds of additional appointments, the result was not especially significant for women, as the gender equity bill that had been passed in the 1990s was ignored.[7]

Trustees at Florida A&M hired Castell Vaughn Bryant—an African American—in 2005, but she was merely an interim president, and her contract specified that she could not apply for the permanent job. Her successor, James Ammon, resigned in 2012 after a scandal about fatal hazing in the school's marching band. In 2014, FAMU made history by hiring its first female president, Elmira Mangum, an African American who came to Tallahassee from New York's prestigious Cornell University.

Trustees at the University of West Florida named Judy Bense as its fifth president and first female president in 2008, during the administration of Governor Charlie Crist. Although she is the older sister of Allan Bense, who was House speaker in 2004–2006, Dr. Bense had spent thirty years with the Pensacola school, and she has notable academic credentials in anthropology and archaeology.

It was the Tampa area, though, that arguably led the way for women in higher education, including community colleges. Betty Castor was still president of USF in 1997, when Gwen Stephenson became the first African American woman to head a Florida community college. She served at Hillsborough Community College for more than a decade, retiring in 2009 after cleaning up the school's longtime reputation for cronyism and corruption. Dr. Stephenson died of cancer in 2013.

At the same time that Stephenson was reforming Tampa's community college, Sarah Pappas rose to the presidency of Manatee Community College, based in Bradenton. Born in Puerto Rico, she had a Greek heritage and lived in Cuba and Mexico before beginning her career at USF. In addition, Laurey Stryker, who had been Castor's chief assistant at the State Department of Education, was president of USF's Sarasota campus until Dr. Stryker's 2007 retirement.

Other women who were community college presidents at the turn of the twenty-first century included Beverly Grissom at North Florida Community College, which is based in the Panhandle town of Madison, and Ann McGee, who became president at Seminole Community College, based in Sanford. Another woman was added at the university level in 2010, as Mary Jane Saunders became president of Florida Atlantic University, based in Broward County. Saunders, too, had previous experience at Tampa's USF.

All these women had spotless reputations—something that has not always been the case for male educational administrators—yet their total numbers remained much lower than desirable. Of Florida's eleven public universities in 2012, only four—FAU, UNF, USF, and UWF—have had women in the top post. The state has twenty-eight lower-level public colleges, just eight of which have ever been headed by a woman.

The first were during the 1980s: Maryly Peck of Polk Community College in Lakeland and Catherine Cornelius of South Florida Community College in Avon Park.[8] The 1990s added four: Beverly Grissom at North Florida, Ann McGee in Seminole County, Sarah Pappas at Manatee, and Gwen Stephenson at Hillsborough.

The new century, however, brought no new wave. Reorganization turned several two-year community colleges into four-year colleges, but that made little difference in the status of women as presidents, as their number actually decreased early in the 2000s. Although Ann McGee continued at Seminole, men were hired to replace retirees Grissom, Stephenson, and Pappas. Moreover, all the women who served as presidents had doctorates, while, as of this writing, three of the male presidents at the twenty-eight colleges do not.

The female newcomers at this lower level during the 2000s were Carol Eaton at Daytona State College; Katherine Johnson at Pasco-Hernando; and early in 2013, Carol Probstfeld at Sarasota-based State College of Florida. Those three are the only women who won the top position during the fourteen years of trustees appointed by Governors Jeb Bush, Charlie Crist, and Rick Scott.

Florida's history of private higher education is older than that of its public schools, and as detailed in earlier chapters, some women have carved out places there. Rita Bornstein was president of Rollins College in Winter Park between 1990 and 2004: although that school was founded in 1885 for female students, she was the first woman among its thirteen presidents. In 2004, the same year that Bornstein left Rollins, Anne B. Kerr became president of Florida Southern College in Lakeland. She has done a commendable job, especially supporting historical archives and restoring that institution's buildings by famed architect Frank Lloyd Wright. Dr. Kerr, too, was the first female president in the history of the school, which was begun by Methodists in 1883.

Sarasota's New College prided itself on its counter-culture flavor when it began as a private college in the 1960s, but although it now is tax-supported, it has never had a female president. Other private colleges, such as the University of Tampa and Eckerd College, also have failed to put a woman at the helm. The same was true at Florida College for Women in Tallahassee before it became Florida State University, and as of 2015 neither FSU nor Gainesville's University of Florida has even seriously considered a woman as president.

To summarize, Florida has thirty-nine publicly funded colleges and universities as well as a dozen long-established private colleges (not counting vocational, religious, and for-profit institutions that are called colleges). Yet among many decades of operation at approximately fifty institutions of higher education, the number of female presidents can be counted on one's digits.

* * *

A similar neglect continues in the fine arts, as the years 1999 and 2000 marked the only time that women were chosen successively for the Florida Artists Hall of Fame. Painter and sculptor Doris Leeper died in 2000, a year after her admission; she was nationally known as the founder of the Atlantic Center for the Arts in New Smyrna Beach. Elaine Konigsburg, inducted in 2000, is a Jacksonville author and illustrator of children's books. Born in 1930, Konigsburg is one of just five members of her profession who have twice won the highest award in that field, the Newbery Medal.

But they were the last female artists to be honored. As of 2013 only seven women were among that hall's forty-eight honorees—who include musicians and writers as well as visual artists. In addition to Konigsburg and Leeper, the others are writers Marjory Stoneman Douglas, Zora Neale Hurston, and Marjorie Kinnan Rawlings, sculptor Augusta Savage, and composer Ellen Zwilch, all discussed in earlier chapters.[9]

Authorized by the legislature in 1986—earlier than the Women's Hall of Fame—the Artists Hall continues to function under the secretary of state. That officeholder, however, was then elected but is now appointed by the governor. Voters chose two women as secretary of state when it was an elective office, but no woman has held a permanent appointment under the three male Republican governors who have served since. This recent lack of women as secretary of state may be a factor in the noninclusion of any woman in the Artists Hall of Fame for more than a decade.

The three inductees into the Florida Women's Hall of Fame in 2000 were from diverse parts of the state. Florida native Chris Evert was internationally known as a tennis star from the time she was a teenager training in Fort Lauderdale. Ranked number one in the world for seven years, she was the first player of either gender to win a thousand single matches and eighteen Grand Slam titles. Born in 1954, Evert retired from professional sports in 1989. She has three sons and actively promotes charities with her foundation.

U.S. Senator Paula Hawkins of central Florida, discussed in the previous chapter, was inducted into the Hall of Fame in 2000; she would die in 2009. From the northern part of Florida, Major General Marianne Mathewson-Chapman was also inducted in 2000. The Kansas native was chosen for this honor because she earned her 1995 doctorate in nursing at the University of Florida and because she was assigned to duty in Florida locales, including Jacksonville and Miami. A strong advocate for public health, she was the first woman promoted to four-star general. She retired in 2000.

The 2001 Hall of Fame honored Judge Lenore Carrero Nesbitt, featured in chapter 10, and also reached back a century to include Jessie Ball duPont of Jacksonville. The wife of Alfred duPont, a scion of the Delaware family that became rich from gunpowder sales during the War of 1812, Jessie Ball duPont inherited his vast Florida business enterprises, especially timber and paper mills. Her brother, Ed Ball, was a powerful factor in Florida politics for decades, and long after her 1970 death, the Jessie Ball duPont Fund continued to support many state charities.

DuPont was only a part-time Floridian, but Lynda Keever, also inducted in 2001, is a fifth-generation native. Born in 1947, she became publisher of *Florida Trend* in 1991. In a September 2008 editorial for that magazine's fiftieth anniversary, Keever said of the business-oriented magazine, "What I hear people say most about us is that *Florida Trend* helps set the agenda for the state." In addition to publishing the monthly magazine, Keever served on the boards of major state think tanks, including Leadership Florida and the Collins Center for Public Policy.

Because she stayed in Florida, Lynda Keever is better known than Clearwater native Sara Blakely, who headquartered her new business in Atlanta. The prestigious national magazine *Forbes* featured Blakely in 2012, when—at age forty-one—she was the youngest billionaire on *Forbes*'s list of the super rich. She invented something particular to women, the underwear known as Spanx. Using five thousand dollars in savings for a patent, she got a North Carolina textile company to start production—and a decade later she was a billionaire.

* * *

Having completed her role in the complex 2000 election, Pam Iorio entered the contest for mayor of Tampa-and just weeks later, in the spring of 2001, defeated several well-qualified male candidates who had been running much longer. Voters overwhelmingly reelected her four years later, approving her action in cleaning up the city's messy financial situation. Iorio took special pride in Tampa's Riverwalk, calling the two miles of parks a "string of pearls." A children's museum, a history museum, and a newly renovated art museum opened under her administration—despite the national economic collapse. In 2012 individual statues began to be added, and among the first six were two women—African American nurse Clara Frye and women's rights advocate Eleanor Chamberlain.[10]

At the Florida AFL-CIO, Cindy Hall replaced Marilyn Lenard as president in 2001.[11] The labor coalition had long been dominated by men, and it was still so unusual for women to win the top post that Florida may have been the nation's first state to have a woman follow a woman as AFL-CIO president. Hall had begun her career as Cindy Yrabedra, lobbying for the United Teachers of Dade.

The 2002 election brought new districts to comply with the 2000 census. In Florida's congressional delegation, the net result was a gain of one woman: Republican Katherine Harris left the secretary of state's office and succeeded Republican Dan Miller in Sarasota. An heir of citrus magnates, she downplayed her rather elite education: she attended schools in Spain and Switzerland. A careerist who did not have children, she was thirty-nine when she married Ander Ebbeson in 1996. Because of her controversial role in the 2000 election, Harris's 2002 congressional race again brought national attention to Florida. She defeated another woman, Harvard-educated attorney Jan Schneider, with 54 percent of the vote in the heavily Republican district.

A second 2002 congressional race also was between two women and made national news. Republican Ginny Brown-Waite defeated Democrat Karen Thurman, who had held the rural district north of Tampa for a decade. Brown-Waite's legislative colleagues drew the area's new congressional district to be virtually contiguous with her district as a state senator. Because Karen Thurman thus had many new constituents during a year dominated by Republicans, she narrowly lost. Thurman went on to chair the Florida Democratic Party through 2010, and Brown-Waite would serve the next eight years in Congress.

Although few noted it, the redrawn districts brought a shocking drop in the number of female representatives in Tallahassee. In contrast to sixteen newcomers in 2000, only one new woman entered the House in 2002. In the Senate, every female newcomer had previously served in the lower chamber. Nothing had been done to prevent gender discrimination in the decade since 1992—when districts were drawn so that the only senators who had to run against each other were Helen Gordon Davis and Jeanne Malcolm, both Tampa Bay Democrats—and the 2002 districts again seemed to protect the status quo of mostly male incumbents. It would be harder for women to win elections in the 2000s than it had been a generation earlier, in the 1970s.

The only House newcomer in 2002 was Ellyn Setnor Bogdandorf of Fort Lauderdale, a Republican in a county that traditionally had been Democratic.

An attorney, she rose in the leadership until term limited in 2010. In the Senate, six women—three Democrats and three Republicans—moved up from the House. The Republicans represented suburban communities of the I-4 Corridor: they were Evelyn Lynn of Volusia County, Paula Dockery of Lakeland, and Nancy Argenziano of the rural area northwest of Tampa; Argenziano later changed parties. The Democrats all were ethnic minorities from the Miami area: Larcenia Bullard and Frederica Wilson were African American, while Gwen Margolis was Jewish. Wilson would go on to Congress, and when Bullard died of heart disease in 2013, Senate President Don Gaetz, a Republican, called her "the biggest heart in the Senate."[12]

But in 2002 the most striking news may have been Gwen Margolis's return to the Florida Senate, where she had been president in the previous decade. This is unusual: most presiding officers reach that pinnacle and then leave for better-paid jobs, usually as lobbyists or judges. Businesswoman Margolis, however, had made a fortune independently of government, and she—and her Miami constituents—believed that her experience was valuable in a legislature that lacked institutional memory because of tenure limits.

While the status of women in the legislature regressed, some made progress in local government. Barbara Carey-Shuler, who was appointed to the Dade County Commission by Governor Bob Graham in 1979, became the first African American woman to chair that body in 2002. Lois Frankel had been a reformer in the Florida legislature since her 1986 election, and in 2003, she became mayor of West Palm Beach: she defeated the incumbent man 56 percent to 38 percent. Like Tampa mayor Pam Iorio, Frankel would be overwhelmingly reelected and served until term limited in 2011. In 2012 she would go on to Congress.

The year that Frankel won the mayorship of West Palm Beach, 2003, also saw Carole Jean Jordan of Indian River County become chair of the Republican Party of Florida. She rose quickly in national leadership and was appointed "chairman of the chairmen" of state parties in 2005. Jordan would be replaced by a man, though, after Republican Charlie Crist won the governorship in 2006—and in 2013 that man, Jim Greer, would go to prison on corruption charges.

Florida had its first female lieutenant governor in 2003, but Senator Toni Jennings—who entered the Women's Hall of Fame the previous year—was not elected to the post. Instead, she was appointed by Governor Jeb Bush in February—just months after he successfully ran for reelection in November 2002. His running mate, Frank Brogan, resigned to become president of

Florida Atlantic University, and Jennings served as lieutenant governor until the end of Bush's term.

In addition to Toni Jennings, the Florida Women's Hall of Fame inductees for 2002 were public health nurse Victoria Joyce Ely and Frances Langford Stuart, who was an internationally popular singer during World War II; all three women are discussed in earlier chapters, as are educator Sarah Ann Blocker and Senator Mary Grizzle, who entered the hall in 2003. The third winner that year was Gloria Estefan, whose name was known to every young person of the era, as she became the most successful crossover performer in Latin music history. She was born as Gloria Milagrosa Fajardo in Havana in 1957. Her father was a bodyguard to Fulgencio Batista, Cuba's dictator since 1934. When Batista fell from power in 1959 the Fajardo family fled to Miami. Gloria graduated summa cum laude from the University of Miami in 1978, with a degree in psychology, and married Emilo Estefan of the Miami Sound Machine. Despite having a son in 1980 (and a daughter fourteen years later, in 1994), she became a huge star, winning five Grammy Awards.

Shirley Coletti, a St. Petersburg advocate for substance-abusing women and their families, joined the Florida Women's Hall of Fame in 2004. Other inductees that year were Marion P. Hammer of Tallahassee, who had become the first female president of the National Rifle Association in 1996, and Judith Kersey, NASA's first female guidance systems engineer. All were still living as of 2012, while two of the three inductees for 2005 have since died. They were Caridad Asensio of Miami, who founded south Florida's first free health clinic for migrant workers, and former congresswoman Tillie Fowler of Jacksonville.[13] The third, Lucy Morgan, longtime Tallahassee bureau chief for the *St. Petersburg Times,* still occasionally does investigative reporting; the press gallery of the Florida Senate was named for her in 2005.[14]

In 2004, when George W. Bush won a second presidential term, the only Democratic woman to enter the Florida House was an African American, insurance agent Priscilla Taylor of Riviera Beach. The five Republican newcomers included Denise Grimsley of Sebring, Dorothy Hukill of Daytona, Trudi Williams of Fort Myers, Anitere Flores of Miami and Susan Goldstein of Broward County; Goldstein was the first Jewish Republican woman in the legislature. Leslie Waters of Pinellas County rose to speaker pro tempore as a result of the 2004 elections, but this precedent had been set in 1982. As of 2013 no woman has reached the pinnacle, speaker of the house; nor is any scheduled to do so until at least 2017.

The most important result of the 2004 congressional elections doubtless was the rise of Broward County's Debbie Wasserman Schultz to the U.S. House. Born in New York, she earned both her 1988 bachelor's and her 1990 master's degrees at the University of Florida. Just two years later she won election to the legislature: at twenty-six, she was the youngest woman ever elected to it.[15] She bore three children, including twins, and they were still young when she carried an astonishing 70 percent of the vote in her 2004 congressional race. In 2009 she reluctantly revealed that she had endured seven surgeries for breast cancer—but she remained so energetic that President Barack Obama chose her to head the Democratic Party. She successfully led the party through the 2012 presidential election.

In Gainesville in 2004 Margaret "Pegeen" Hanrahan won election as mayor. A Democrat and a professional engineer, she was described in a national magazine as a "vegetarian, bike-riding environmentalist."[16] Hanrahan won the nonpartisan election with 57 percent of the vote and would be reelected in 2008 with 73 percent. Married to Tony Malone, she was twice pregnant while in office, with children born in 2005 and 2007.

On the other end of the age scale, internationally known Shirley Chisholm retired to Palm Coast and died in Ormond Beach in 2005. In 1968 she had been the first African American woman in Congress, and in 1972 she was the first black woman to mount a serious campaign for the presidency. Continuously reelected to represent a portion of New York City, Chisholm had retired from Congress but accepted a 1993 appointment from President Bill Clinton as ambassador to Jamaica. Born in 1924 as Shirley Anita St. Hill to immigrants from Barbados, she led a life that exemplified the century's changes.[17]

In the nonpresidential elections of 2006, Democratic women won a surprising number of seats in the Florida House. The sole Republican who won that year was Marti Coley, a Panama City teacher; she soon rose to vice chair of the House K-12 Education Committee. Democrat Debbie Boyd won a rural district in the Big Bend area south of Tallahassee, while the other Democratic winners represented urban areas: Janet Long of St. Petersburg; Betty Reed, an African American from Tampa; Geraldine Thompson of Orlando, also a black woman; and Maria Sachs, Elaine Schwartz, and Kelly Skidmore, all of southeast Florida. In the Senate, Sarasota's Lisa Carlton rose to president pro tempore as she served out the last of her eight years, but there were no new female senators in the 2006 election.

On the congressional level former Hillsborough County commissioner Phyllis Busansky, a Democrat, lost a race for the seat based in northern

Hillsborough and Pinellas. Democrat Anita de Palma of Clearwater would follow Busansky with unsuccessful races for that seat in 2008 and 2010. De Palma was a graduate of New York's famed Juilliard School of Music and after a career in entertainment was state director of the League of United Latin American Citizens. Both have died: Busansky in 2009 and De Palma in 2013.

Katherine Harris was in the national news again in 2006, when she attempted to rise to the U.S. Senate. That left her Sarasota-based House district vacant, and Christine Jennings won the Democratic nomination for it, defeating Jan Schneider, who had lost general elections to Harris in 2002 and 2004. An Ohio native and formerly a Republican, Jennings—who is not kin to Orlando's Toni Jennings—began working as a bank teller at age seventeen. Without graduating from college, Christine Jennings was able to found her own business, Sarasota Bank, in 1992. She sold it for $40.5 million in 2003 and ran for Congress in 2006.

Because she long had been active in community life, Democrat Jennings did very well in this usually Republican district—in fact, she may have won. Election officials declared her Republican opponent, car dealer Vern Buchanan, to be the winner by 369 of 238,249 votes. Jennings did not concede, especially because more than 18,000 ballots failed to reflect any vote in this major race. She won by 52.8 percent in Sarasota County, where there was a one-in-six presumable error rate. Floridians were tired of ballot disputes, though, and her appeals to examine the results were in vain. Since then two political scientists who have studied the race in detail determined "at a 99.9% confidence level" that Jennings should have won, with a "margin of victory of 639 votes."[18]

Katherine Harris's race for the U.S. Senate ended less dramatically, as she carried only 39 percent of the vote against incumbent Democrat Bill Nelson. Even detractors agreed that her party treated her badly. Governor Jeb Bush did not invite her on his post-primary unity tour with other Republican nominees, and George W. Bush—to whom she had virtually awarded the presidency in 2000—snubbed her in front of television cameras. All the state's twenty-two major daily newspapers endorsed her opponent, and Harris's colorful career ended.

In the same year, however, Florida had its first female chief financial officer (CFO) in Democrat Alex Sink. Never using her birth name of Alexandra, she grew up in North Carolina and began doing bookkeeping for the family farm as a child. After graduating from Wake Forest College with a degree in math, she joined the Peace Corps and taught math in Africa. She then rose

Women in top state elective executive positions

Year	Name	Position*	Party	Notes
1986	Betty Castor	Commissioner of education	D	first woman in Cabinet
1994	Sandra Mortham	Secretary of state	R	first in this position, which is no longer elected
1998	Katherine Harris	Secretary of state	R	defeated Mortham
2003	Toni Jennings	Lieutenant governor	R	appointed, not elected
2006	Alex Sink	Chief financial officer	D	elective position consolidating two old ones
2010	Jennifer Carroll	Lieutenant governor	R	Elected with governor; resigned 2013
2010	Pam Bondi	Attorney general	R	always elected; Cabinet member

Notes: *See index for Mamie Eaton Greene and Paula Hawkins, who won statewide races that were not Cabinet positions.

in the executive ranks of North Carolina National Bank, moved to Miami, and, after a merger with Bank of America, became president of its Florida branches. She encouraged other young women to major in math, saying in a 2010 interview, "without a math degree, I might never have succeeded in banking, and without that banking background, it probably would have been difficult to be elected CFO."[19]

She was the only woman in the Cabinet, which had been reduced from seven to four in 2003. The change left just the governor, CFO, attorney general, and agricultural commissioner. The offices of insurance commissioner and comptroller were combined into the new CFO post, and the change also eliminated two previously elected offices, education commissioner and secretary of state. Although voters had elected three women to these two positions, no women have been appointed since—except for the brief tenure of Sue Cobb, a Coral Gables attorney, appointed by Governor Bush in 2006. Cobb also was named ambassador to Jamaica under George W. Bush and had been Jeb Bush's first lottery secretary in 1999.

Beyond Sink's victory as CFO, the 2006 election set another precedent, as Kathy Castor became the first congresswoman from Tampa Bay. Democrat Jim Davis, who had defeated three women in 1996, gave up his congressional seat to run for governor that year. Castor defeated four men in the Democratic primary, winning 54 percent of the vote, and easily won the general election. The daughter of political pioneer Betty Castor and Judge Don Castor, she earned degrees in political science and law. Her colleagues elected her president of the Florida Association for Women Lawyers; voters put her on the Hillsborough County Commission in 2002; and during this busy time, she also married attorney Bill Lewis and bore two daughters. California Congresswoman Nancy Pelosi campaigned for Castor, and when Democrats won a majority in 2006, Pelosi became the first female speaker of the U.S. House. She assigned Castor to the powerful Rules Committee, which essentially sets the House agenda—an extraordinary achievement for a freshman.

* * *

The 2006 induction ceremony for the Florida Women's Hall of Fame was the first since its 1982 beginning with just two inductees. Instead of the usual three, Governor Jeb Bush chose only Supreme Court Justice Peggy Quince, an African American who is included in chapter 10, and Maryly VanLeer Peck, the first female community college president in Florida.[20] The following year, 2007, saw the induction of Supreme Court Justice Barbara Pariente, who had been the second woman on the court in 1996. Like Pariente and Quince, a second 2007 Hall of Fame inductee, U.S. Representative Ileana Ros-Lehtinen, remains in office. All are discussed in the previous chapter.

The third 2007 inductee was Tampa physician and philanthropist Dr. Pallavi Patel. Born in India in 1950, she began her medical career in Zambia. She and her husband built a successful health care business based around the University of South Florida's medical school, and they have since donated millions to various international causes, including women's health.

The 2008 Hall of Fame honored Miami Senator Gwen Margolis, who in 1991 had been the first female president of the Florida Senate. A second 2008 honoree, Louise Cortelis, also was from Miami. The widow of Republican fundraiser Alec Cortelis, she was an accomplished horsewoman and especially supported veterinary medicine in her roles with the University of Florida, including a trusteeship. Betty Sembler of Pinellas County was similar: her husband, Mel Sembler, was a Republican fundraiser and ambassador, and she worked for anti-drug programs.

In the off-year elections of 2007 Mattie Herrara Bower became the first female and the first Hispanic mayor of Miami Beach. Her activism had begun with the PTA, when she worked to save an elementary school from closing, and for the next three decades, she was at the heart of revitalization of Miami Beach. Her leadership is bringing the town back to its glory days of the 1950s, when national television shows broadcast from there. Since 2009 Mayor Bower has led an annual conference on the status of women. Held in the convention center, it features a lunch in the nearby botanical garden with female chefs and restaurant owners.

Also in 2007, Orlando Mayor Buddy Dyer appointed Val Demings as the first female police chief of Orlando. An African American, native of Jacksonville, and the youngest of seven children, she held degrees in criminology and public administration. Demings rose through the ranks of the Orlando police force, and violent crime fell 40 percent during her tenure as chief, partly because she waged campaigns to get guns off the street. Married to fellow police officer Jerry Demings, she has three sons. Demmings lost a close 2012 race for Congress to incumbent Republican Daniel Webster.

Tampa Mayor Pam Iorio, a Democrat like Dyer and Demmings, appointed Jane Castor (no relation to Betty or Kathy Castor) as police chief. A basketball star while a student at the University of Tampa, she rose through the ranks as a police officer. Both Jane Castor and Val Demings were recognized by their peers as exceptional leaders early in their careers, when each was elected president of her police academy class. Although Castor was popular with her peers and the public, it arguably took courage for Mayor Iorio to appoint Jane Castor because she is a lesbian—and also is the mother of two boys.

Crime fell dramatically under Chief Castor. Mayor Bob Buckhorn retained her when he replaced Iorio in 2011, and Castor led policing during the 2012 Republican National Convention in Tampa. It was the state's first national political convention that was not in Miami, where both parties held their 1972 conventions. Women were not a viable part of police forces in the 1970s, and both conventions saw street violence. In 2012, under female administration, Tampa police did an excellent job of crowd control.

In the smaller city of Fort Myers, Donna Hansen had been the police chief for five years in the late 1980s and early 1990s. She reduced crime by focusing on juveniles, and Attorney General Bob Butterworth appointed her to the Florida Commission on the Status of Women. All these women did measurably good jobs—but it is notable that they were appointed as police chiefs in cities, not elected as county sheriffs. Although a few women served as sheriffs in rural counties early in the twentieth century, they replaced husbands and were not elected in their own right.[21]

Susan Benton changed that in 2004, when voters in Highlands County elected her as sheriff. A fifth-generation Floridian, she grew up in Miami and her first job was teaching physical education. After moving to Highlands County, she bore two children while also rising through governmental ranks. Benton held positions both in and out of the sheriff's office, including as an investigator for the State Department of Children and Families; she had returned to the sheriff's office when she was elected to its top position. A Democrat, Benton won reelection in 2008, and in 2012 her peers elected her head of the Florida Sheriffs Association.

* * *

The 2008 presidential election was the change of a lifetime for most voters, as the nation chose its first black president, Democrat Barack Obama. In state government, however, the election made little difference, as no Cabinet seats are up in presidential years, nor was there any significant increase in the number of female legislators. Eight new women joined the House in 2008, five Republicans and three Democrats, but because of term-limited retirements, the total remained approximately the same. Only one of the four new senators was a newcomer to lawmaking: Palm Beach voters elected Republican Lizbeth Benacquisto, but the other three female senators moved up from the House.

Aside from Florida's vote for the nation's first African American president, pundits in 2008 were most surprised by the victory of Democrat Suzanne Kosmas for Congress. She defeated Republican Tom Feeney in the U.S. House district east of Orlando, which stretches along the Space Coast to Daytona. Kosmas had served in the state legislature, and the national Democratic Party recruited her to take on the challenge of upsetting a well-funded incumbent. Feeney's ethical problems were well publicized, but even Kosmas's supporters were surprised by her margin of victory: she won with 57 percent to his 41 percent—the largest margin of loss for a Republican incumbent anywhere in the nation that year.

The 2008 election also marked the first election of a female prosecutor in the Jacksonville area. Angela B. Corey won the race for state attorney in the area that includes Duval, Nassau, and Clay counties. A Jacksonville native of Syrian heritage, she was educated at Florida State and the University of Florida, and her mentors were legendary prosecutors Ed Austin and Harry Shorstein, both Democrats. She became a Republican, though, and defeated

Florida women in Congress

First Elected	Name	Area Represented	Party	Notes
U.S. House:				
1928	Ruth Bryan Owen	East Coast (Miami)	D	defeated after four years
1989*	Ileana Ros-Lehtinen	Miami	R	still in Congress as of 2014
1992	Corrine Brown	Jacksonville	D	still in Congress as of 2014
1992	Tillie Fowler	Jacksonville	R	retired after eight years
1992	Carrie Meek	Miami	D	retired after ten years
1992	Karen Thurman	north of Tampa	D	defeated in 2002
2002	Ginny Brown-Waite	north of Tampa	R	retired after eight years
2002	Katherine Harris	Sarasota	R	one term
2004	Debbie Wasserman Schultz	Broward County	D	still in Congress as of 2014
2006	Kathy Castor	Tampa	D	still in Congress as of 2014
2008	Suzanne Kosmas	east of Orlando	D	defeated in 2010
2010	Sandy Adams	east of Orlando	R	lost 2012 Republican primary
2010	Frederica Wilson	Miami	D	still in Congress as of 2014
2012	Lois Frankel	Palm Beach	D	still in Congress as of 2014
U.S. Senate:				
1980	Paula Hawkins	Orlando	R	defeated after one term

Note: * Special election.

Shorstein's chosen successor, a man, with 64 percent of the vote. Since then, however, Corey has become controversial. Feminists have protested her prosecution of Marissa Alexander, a black woman sentenced to twenty years in prison for firing a pistol in the direction of her abusive husband—an incident in which no one was injured.

Corey took office in January 2009, and the 2009 Women's Hall of Fame ceremony changed from its traditional November date, when legislators are sworn in, to March, which is National Women's History Month. The most unusual inductee may have been swimmer Dara Grace Torres, who has inspired many athletes to continue in their sport beyond their youth. Born in Miami in 1967, she competed in her first Olympics in 1984 and has won twelve medals in five Olympics. Torres continued to swim for international titles long past the usual age and in 2012 became the oldest swimmer ever to qualify for a place on the U.S. Olympic team. In 2007, when she was forty—and just fifteen months after bearing her first child—she won the national gold, and then went on to beat the record that she had set at age fifteen.

Bonnie Blair is not a native Floridian and is not yet a member of the Hall of Fame, but she moved to Plant City after becoming the most decorated woman in U.S. Olympic history at the 1994 games: she won five gold medals for speed ice-skating. Most Floridians have forgotten that a black woman, Tampa's Theresa Manuel, was the state's first female Olympian. She competed in track and field in London in 1948.[22]

The second 2009 Hall of Fame inductee from Miami was Claudine Ryce. After her son was kidnapped and murdered in 1995, she worked for passage of the Jimmy Ryce Act, which required that violent sex offenders be incarcerated for treatment. The act passed unanimously in 1998, and Governor Lawton Chiles signed it into law. She also founded Team Hope, which assists families through the trauma of trying to determine what has happened to a missing relative. Claudine Ryce died soon after her induction.

The third 2009 inductee, Eugenie Clark, called Genie, is the founder of Sarasota's famed Mote Marine Laboratory. Known as "the shark lady," Dr. Clark came to Sarasota from the University of Maryland. The center expanded its research to numerous marine mammals, and its founder continues to dive into the oceans. At the time of her induction she had spent her eighty-seventh birthday piloting a research submarine.

The first Women's Hall of Fame that honored just two women, instead of the three that its enabling legislation allows, was under Governor Jeb Bush in 2006, and Governor Charlie Crist repeated that in 2010. The two winners were Mary Brennan Karl of Tampa and Anna Rodriguez of Bonita Springs. Karl was nominated by her son, former Supreme Court justice Fred Karl of Tampa, who grew up in Daytona Beach.

Prior to her 1948 death, Mary Karl promoted vocational education. Working with Daytona's famed Mary McLeod Bethune and others of the Roosevelt Administration, she administered a large campus that trained defense workers for World War II. Its programs ran twenty-four hours a day, and at the war's end the federal government conveyed the substantial property to Volusia County, which honored her by naming it the Mary Karl Vocational School. It went on to become Daytona Beach Community College and then, recently, Daytona State College. Mary Karl is considered the college's founder.

Anna Rodriguez is much younger, born in 1957 in Puerto Rico after Mary Karl was dead. Rodriguez has lived in Florida since 1974 and is considered an international expert on human trafficking. She has conducted workshops on the subject throughout Latin America and was honored by the government of Argentina. The head of the Florida Coalition against Human Trafficking, she calls its victims "the invisible slaves" of the twenty-first century.

* * *

Despite Florida's vote for Obama in 2008, the political pendulum swung back toward conservatism in 2010, as two Democratic women lost statewide races. Lorrane Ausley, who had been a Tallahassee senator since 2000, lost her bid for CFO to Republican Jeff Atwater. A graduate of a historic women's college, Virginia's Randolph-Macon, Ausley earned her law degree at prestigious Washington and Lee University, also in Virginia. She kept her maiden name after marrying Bill Holliman and was pregnant while in the Senate. Thousands of Floridians joined in the prayer chain that she requested when her son was born prematurely. As of this writing Lorrane Ausley chaired the board of the Healthy Kids Corporation.

Alex Sink recruited Ausley to run for CFO, while Sink made a strong bid to become Florida's first female governor in 2010. In a year when Democrats did poorly everywhere, largely because of the new Tea Party, Sink came very close. It was widely assumed that the Republican nominee would be Bill McCullom, the current attorney general and a longtime member of Congress, but he lost to newcomer Rick Scott. Although Scott spent $70 million dollars of his personal money, she lost by only some 65,000 votes—a better record than might have been expected in the face of such unprecedented spending.

Jennifer Carroll, an African American legislator from Jacksonville, was Scott's running mate. When she became lieutenant governor with the 2010 election, Florida was the thirty-seventh state to have elected a woman to this post—which eight states do not have. The first was Vermont in 1954, but no other followed until 1974. Even then, progress was slow; just five states elected women as lieutenant governors in the 1970s and six in the 1980s. The explanation probably is that lieutenant governor is the ultimate insider office, and many male candidates perceive successful women as too independent to be running mates.

Carroll did not have enough of a statewide image for that to handicap her, and the fact that she is African American may have brought enough votes in the black community that her presence on the ticket could have made the difference in Scott's narrow victory. In March 2013, however, Carroll suddenly resigned the office after it was revealed that she had played a role in an internet gambling company that promised to give a generous share of its profits to veterans but did not do so.

The lieutenant governor does not sit on the Cabinet, but even after Alex Sink left the Cabinet, it had one woman among its four members. Voters chose Pam Bondi, a Tampa Republican, as attorney general. Pennsylvania also elected a female attorney general in 2010, and Florida tied with that state as the nation's eighteenth to choose a woman for this powerful post. The first was Rhode Island, where former nun Arlene Violet won in 1984.

Bondi enjoyed appreciable recognition on television, as she had expanded her role as an assistant prosecutor into frequent commentary on judicial cases, especially for Fox News. She had grown up in politics: her father was mayor of the Hillsborough County town of Temple Terrace. After graduating from the University of Florida in 1987 and from Stetson University College of Law, she was admitted to the bar in 1991. The race for attorney general was her first, but she defeated Lieutenant Governor Jeff Kottkamp in the 2010 Republican primary as well as State Senator Dan Gelber in the general election. Republican vice-presidential nominee Sarah Palin campaigned for her, and one of Bondi's first acts as attorney general was to lead Florida into the court case that unsuccessfully attempted to overthrow the Affordable Care Act.

Lori Edwards, who had been a legislator from Polk County and was its supervisor of elections in 2010, won the Democratic nomination for the area's congressional seat, but in a year dominated by Republicans, she lost the general election to a Republican man, Dennis Ross. The trend also held in the district east of Orlando, where two women ran against each other in the general election. With lower Democratic turnout in 2010, one-term incumbent Suzanne Kosmas lost her congressional seat to Republican Sandy Adams, likewise a former state legislator. An Air Force veteran, Adams also had support from Alaska's former governor Sarah Palin. Like Kosmas, however, Adams would hold the seat for only one term.

Miami's black community continued to vote Democratic, and they elected Frederica Wilson, also a former legislator, to Congress in 2010. Born in Miami in 1942 as Frederica Smith, she earned science degrees. An educator, she began her elective career on the Dade County School Board. Wilson is more literally visible than most congresswomen because of her habit of wearing hats. She has served on the House Science and Space Committee as well as the prestigious Foreign Affairs Committee.

Perhaps the most important result for the long term, though, was that voters in 2010 amended the Florida Constitution to mandate fair districts. Gerrymandering to elect members of the dominant party had become increasingly common after single-member districts were adopted in the 1970s, and by the beginning of the 2000s most voters were confused about who really represented them. The small Hillsborough County community of Temple Terrace, for example, was split between three members of Congress.

In an effort for more compact community representation and greater accountability to voters, Miami attorney Ellen Friedan led "Fair Districts."[23] Because the legislature refused to put the question on the ballot, she organized the necessary collection of hundreds of thousands of petitions. Able at last to vote for a more sensible system of representation, voters adopted the two constitutional amendments calling for fair reapportionment of districts for Congress and the legislature.

Some new districts remained under court challenge, but most Florida congresswomen had no strong opposition in 2012. Four Democratic women won reelection: Kathy Castor of Tampa, Corrine Brown of Jacksonville, Broward's Debbie Wasserman Schultz, and Miami's Frederica Wilson. That also was the case for longtime Republican Ileana Ros-Lehtinen of Miami. Sandy Adams of the Space Coast, however, was redistricted so that she had to run in a Republican primary against incumbent Congressman John Mica; she lost.

In Dade County, Gloria Romero Roses, whose family roots were in Colombia, sought the Democratic nomination against Joe Garcia, intending to oppose incumbent Republican David Rivera in the general election; she lost to Garcia, who went on to defeat Rivera. In Pinellas County, young attorney Jessica Erhlich took on Republican Bill Young, who had been in Congress for forty-two years, since 1970. She lost the general election, as did Democrat Val Demmings, who ran against Republican incumbent Daniel Webster in Orlando.

But Palm Beach Democrats chose Lois Frankel over County Commissioner Kristen Jacobs in their primary, and Frankel, former mayor of West

Palm Beach, handily won the general election. Thus as 2013 began, women accounted for six of Florida's twenty-seven seats in the U.S. House. Mathematical analysis makes it clear, though, that there is a strikingly large difference between the parties. Republicans held seventeen seats and included just one woman, Ileana Ros-Lehtinen. Florida's delegation to Washington had ten Democrats, half of them women.

New districts did not make much difference in Tallahassee, as the only female newcomers to the Florida Senate were women who moved up from the House. Two were Democrats, Maria Sachs of Miami and Geraldine Thompson of Orlando; the third was Republican Kelli Stargel of Lakeland. With female incumbents, the forty-member Senate had twelve women, equally divided with six Democrats and six Republicans.

New districts did bring greater turnover in the House, with forty-six newcomers. Female freshmen were evenly divided by party, with four Democrats and four Republicans. Orlando featured the most striking races, with two Democratic women defeating Republican men in districts that usually vote Republican. Karen Castor Dentel, daughter of former Cabinet member Betty Castor and sister of Congresswoman Kathy Castor, centered her campaign on educational issues. It was her first run for office, but Linda Stewart, a grandmother, had twice been elected to the Orange County Commission, and she too successfully ran against the Tallahassee establishment. The third Democrat, Katie Edwards, won in usually Democratic Broward County. She has an unusually diverse background: active in both the conservative Farm Bureau and liberal Jewish organizations, she attended a Catholic high school. The fourth female Democratic newcomer was Sharon Pritchett of Miami Gardens; she earned multiple degrees in criminology and at the time of her election was a retired chief investigator.

The four female Republican winners in 2012 were moderates from affluent areas. Kathleen Peters won the district based in the southern beaches of Pinellas County; she had been mayor of the small town of South Pasadena. Marylynn Magar—called "ML"—represents the opposite coast, with a district based in the beach communities of Martin County. Heather Dawes Fitzenhagen is an attorney in Fort Myers; she graduated from Hollins College, a historic institution for women in Virginia. Holly Merrill Raschein lives in Key Largo, and her race probably generated the most attention; she ran as a Republican after resigning her position with longtime Democratic leader Ron Saunders.

In the House as a whole, female representation continued at about the same proportion, with women holding 26 of its 120 seats, or 22 percent. While the number of male Democrats increased because of redistricting, the relative number of Republican women fell. The House nonetheless remained solidly Republican (76–44), but of the twenty-six women, the fourteen Democrats outnumbered the twelve Republicans. Nor were any of these women highly visible in a leadership team that, headed by Pasco County's thirty-something Will Weatherford, was uncommonly white, male, and young. No statistical analysis can make the case that the current leadership is equal in gender equity to that of a generation ago.

* * *

Women in the Florida judiciary also slowed in their progress during new century: no woman has been named to the Florida Supreme Court since 1998—and the two who serve had to endure expensive merit retention races in 2012. Both Barbara Pariente and Peggy Quince survived attacks by right-wingers but only because more responsible members of the profession came to their defense. To date just three women have served on the court, and all three have been openly targeted for removal.[24]

The next level below the Supreme Court is the district courts of appeal (DCAs), which hear cases that are appealed from circuit and county courts. These were created in 1957, when the League of Women Voters led judicial reform. Florida now has five DCAs, where judges are appointed by governors and retained (or rejected) by voters every six years.

In 2012 women held just 20 percent of all DCA seats, with 80 percent held by men. The First District, which covers the Panhandle and is based in Tallahassee, has the highest percentage of female judges at 33 percent. Even though it abuts the First District, the Fifth District of northeast Florida, centered in Jacksonville, has the lowest, a mere 10 percent. Two courts at this level have women as chief judges, Linda Ann Wells of the Third District, based in Miami, and Melanie G. May of the Fourth District, which runs along the East Coast north to Brevard County.

At the next level down, in the circuit courts, judges are elected, not appointed. Populous Dade County has the highest percentage of women at this level, with an equitable 52 percent—but next door in Monroe County the number of women is zero. Florida has twenty circuit courts, but just two have female chief judges, Leandra G. Johnson in Lake City and Martha Ann Lott in Gainesville. Overall, women made up 30 percent of circuit court judges in 2012, as voters continue to be more likely to elect women than governors are to appoint them.

Every county has a county court, and those judges also are elected. Overall, women at this lesser level do only slightly better than at the more prestigious circuit level, with 34 percent of county judges being female in 2012. The highest percentages of women are in the mid-size counties of Lake, Osceola, and Sarasota.[25] In thirty-eight of the sixty-seven counties, however, no woman was a county court judge.

The legal profession itself voted at a similar ratio, with three women chosen by their peers as president of the Florida Bar Association during the first twelve years of the new century. Tallahassee's Pat Seitz had been the first in 1993, and Miami's Edith Osman was second, elected in 1999 to serve in 2000.[26]

The third woman, elected in 2004, was Kelly Overstreet Johnson of Tallahassee. Educated at Florida State, she has won cases in disability rights and civil rights as well as in more traditional areas of law. Mayanne Downs of Orlando followed as Bar president six years later, in 2010; she previously had been legal counsel to Orlando Mayor Buddy Dyer. Downs is an Orlando native and earned both undergraduate and law degrees at the University of Florida. Less time passed before the powerful association elected another female leader, as Tampa's Gwynne Young was president for 2012–13. Her degrees are from Duke University and the University of Florida, and she has practiced complex litigation with the firm of Carlton Fields for decades. Like others of these women, Young has been honored for pro bono work and is listed in *The Best Lawyers in America*.

The Florida Women's Hall of Fame inducted three women for 2011–12: Dr. Ruth H. Alexander, Elizabeth "Budd" Bell, and Vicki Bryant Burke. Born in 1938, Dr. Alexander pioneered women's sports at the University of Florida. She was quick to take advantage of Title IX of the 1972 Education Act, which assured female equity in school sports, and Richard Nixon appointed her to the President's Council on Physical Fitness, where she was the first woman. Reappointed by Presidents Ford, Carter, and Reagan, she was inducted into the Hall of Fame for the National Association of Sport and Physical Education in 1987. She also developed an exchange program in sports management with England's University of Longborough and is the author of eight books, including *Lady Gators—Simply the Best* (1991).

Everyone who frequented the halls of the capitol from the 1970s onward recognized Budd Bell as a presence on behalf of those who needed help. A

Inductees into the Florida Women's Hall of Fame

Name	Residential Area	Birth Year	Notes
1982—Governor Bob Graham			
Mary McLeod Bethune	Daytona Beach	1875	internationally known African American leader
Helene S. Coleman	Jacksonville	1925	president, National Council of Jewish women
Elaine Gordon	Miami	1931	feminist state representative
Wilhelmina Harvey	Key West	1912	leader known as "Mayor"
Paula Mae Milton	Miami	1939	dramatist; Miami-Dade Community College
Barbara Jo Palmer	Tallahassee	1948	nationally recognized for sports equity
1984—Governor Bob Graham			
Roxcy Bolton	Miami	1926	NOW founder
Barbara Frye	Tallahassee	1922	United Press International
Lena Smithers Hughes	Orlando	1910	Valencia orange horticulturist
Zora Neale Hurston	Orlando	1901	nationally recognized novelist on African Americans
Sybil Mobley	Tallahassee	1925	dean of FAMU business school
Helen Muir	Miami	1911	*Miami Herald* reporter
Gladys Soler	Jacksonville	1930	Cuban immigrant; pediatrician
Julia Tuttle	Miami	1848	developer of Miami
1986—Governor Bob Graham			
Annie Ackerman	Miami	1914	condominium activist
Rosemary Barkett	Miami	1939	first woman on Florida Supreme Court
Gwen Cherry	Miami	1923	first black woman in the legislature
Dorothy Dodd	Tallahassee	1902	state librarian; author
Marjory Stoneman Douglas	Miami	1890	nationally known author; Everglades preservationist
Elsie Jones Hare	Pensacola	1903	teacher; postmistress in rural Panhandle
Elizabeth McCullough Johnson	Orlando	1909	first woman in Florida Senate
Frances Bartlett Kinne	Jacksonville	1917	president of Jacksonville University
Arva Moore Parks	Miami	1939	author; film maker

Name	Residential Area	Birth Year	Notes
Marjorie Kinnan Rawlings	Gainesville	1896	Pulitzer Prize–winning novelist
Florence Seibert	St. Petersburg	1898	invented the test for tuberculosis
Marilyn K. Smith	Miami	1936	Jewish activist
Eartha Mary Magadalene White	Jacksonville	1876	founder of institutions for African Americans
1987–1991—Governor Bob Martinez			
No inductees			
1992—Governor Lawton Chiles			
Jacqueline Cochran	Pensacola	1906	headed Women's Air Force Service Pilots in World War II
Carrie Meek	Miami	1926	first black woman in Florida Senate; congresswoman
Ruth Bryan Owen	Miami	1885	first woman elected to the U.S. House from the South
1993—Governor Lawton Chiles			
Betty Skelton Frankman	Lakeland	1926	held national racing records for both air and land
Paulina Pedroso	Tampa	1845	led Cuban Americans in the Spanish-American War
Janet Reno	Miami	1938	first female attorney general of the United States
1994—Governor Lawton Chiles			
Nikki Beare	Miami	1928	NOW founder; feminist lobbyist
Betty Mae Jumper	Indiantown	1923	chief of the Seminole Tribe of Florida
Gladys Milton	Walton County	1924	fought for the right to practice as a midwife
1995—Governor Lawton Chiles			
Evelyn Stocking Crosslin	Daytona Beach	1919	Daytona Beach physician; African American
JoAnn Hardin Morgan	Titusville	1940	first female executive at Kennedy Space Center
Sarah Brooks Pryor	Fort Walton Beach	1877	appointed postmaster of Fort Walton Beach in 1917
1996—Governor Lawton Chiles			
Marjorie Harris Carr	Gainesville	1915	nationally recognized environmentalist; stopped barge canal

continued

Inductees into the Florida Women's Hall of Fame—*Continued*

Name	Residential Area	Birth Year	Notes
Betty Castor	Tampa	1941	first woman elected to the Florida Cabinet
Ivy Stranahan	Fort Lauderdale	1881	Fort Lauderdale founder; suffrage association president in 1917
1997—Governor Lawton Chiles			
Alicia Baro	Miami	1918	advocate for Puerto Ricans
Carita Doggett Corse	Jacksonville	1891	headed the Florida Writers Project in the Great Depression
Athalie Range	Miami	1916	first black woman to head a state agency
1998—Governor Lawton Chiles			
Helen Gordon Davis	Tampa	1926	legislator; personally funded feminist projects
Mattie Belle Davis	Miami	1910	pioneer judge; first Florida woman elected as an ABA Fellow
Christine Fulwylie-Bankston	Pensacola	1916	educator; *Who's Who among Black Americans*
1999—Governor Lawton Chiles			
(Appointments made prior to his death in December 1998)			
Althea Gibson	Tallahassee	1927	international tennis champion; African American
Sister Jeanne O'Laughlin	Miami	1929	nun; president of Barry College
Dessie Smith Prescott	Gainesville	1906	pioneer woodswoman; professional hunting and fishing guide
2000—Governor Jeb Bush			
Chris Evert	Fort Lauderdale	1954	international tennis champion
Paula Hawkins	Orlando	1927	first Florida woman in the U.S. Senate
Marianne Mathewson-Chapman	Eglin Air Force Base	1948	first woman in U.S. Army to reach the rank of Major General
2001—Governor Jeb Bush			
Jessie Ball DuPont	Jacksonville	1884	philanthropist; businesswoman of the duPont Corporation
Lenore Nesbitt	Miami	1932	first female federal judge for south Florida
Lynda Keever	St. Petersburg	1947	*Florida Trend* publisher

Name	Residential Area	Birth Year	Notes
2002—Governor Jeb Bush			
Victoria Ely	Perry/Ruskin	1889	Red Cross nurse; pioneer health officer
Toni Jennings	Orlando	1949	Senate president; appointed lieutenant governor
Frances Langford Stuart	Lakeland/Jensen Beach	1913	international singer during World War II
2003—Governor Jeb Bush			
Mary Grizzle	Pinellas County	1921	first Republican woman in the legislature
Gloria Estefan	Miami	1957	internationally known Latina singer
Sarah Ann Blocker	Jacksonville	1857	founder of Florida Memorial College for blacks
2004—Governor Jeb Bush			
Shirley Coletti	St. Petersburg	1935	expert on substance abuse
Marion Hammer	Tallahassee	1939	president, National Rifle Association
Judith Kersey	Cape Canaveral	1943	first female guidance systems engineer at NASA
2005—Governor Jeb Bush			
Caridad Asensio	Miami	1931	founder, Migrant Association of South Florida
Tillie Kidd Fowler	Jacksonville	1942	one of the four Florida women elected to Congress in 1992
Lucy Morgan	Tallahassee/St. Petersburg	1940	Pulitzer Prize winner for *St. Petersburg Times*
2006—Governor Jeb Bush			
Peggy Quince	Bradenton	1948	Florida Supreme Court justice; African American
Maryly VanLeer Peck	Winter Haven	1930	first community college president
2007—Governor Charlie Crist			
Barbara Pariente	Palm Beach	1948	second woman on Florida Supreme Court
Pallavi Patel	Tampa	1950	physician and philanthropist; born in India
Ileana Ros-Lehtinen	Miami	1952	first Cuban American woman in Congress; born in Havana

continued

Inductees into the Florida Women's Hall of Fame—*Continued*

Name	Residential Area	Birth Year	Notes
2008—Governor Charlie Crist			
Louise Cortelis	Miami/ Micanopy	1930	philanthropist; horse business; Republican activist
Gwen Margolis	Miami	1934	first female president of Florida Senate
Betty Sembler	Pinellas	1931	Republican activist; anti-drug programs
2009—Governor Charlie Crist			
Eugenie Clark	Sarasota	1922	internationally known oceanographer; Mote Marine Institute
Claudine Ryce	Miami	1943	activist for missing children
Dara Grace Torres	Miami	1967	Olympic speed swimmer who set age records
2010—Governor Charlie Crist			
Mary Brennan Karl	Daytona Beach	1890	founded World War II vocational school that became college
Anna Rodriguez	Bonita Springs	1957	activist against sex trafficking
2011—Governor Rick Scott			
Ruth H. Alexander	Gainesville		pioneer in women's sports
Budd Bell	Tallahassee		social worker and lobbyist for children, elderly, women
Victoria Burke	Jacksonville		founder of PACE centers for girls in juvenile justice system
2012—Governor Rick Scott			
Clara Frye	Tampa	1872	founded hospital for blacks in 1908
Aleen Kidd MacKenzie	Ocala	1911	chaired first Status of Women Commission in the 1960s
Lillian Pierce Voss	Palm Beach	1876	pioneer in southeast Florida

Note: Names listed by year, alphabetically within year. See index for details.

Tallahassee resident, she was past middle age when she founded Kids Incorporated of the Big Bend in 1972, and in 1974 Bell went on to found the Clearinghouse for Human Services, a network that ultimately included a hundred humanitarian organizations. In the legislature she led the successful effort for kindergarten and then moved on to champion other groups. She worked with Senator Maxine Baker to create the Baker Act for treatment of the mentally ill. Bell developed programs for the elderly; "Dial A Ride" was her innovation on transportation needs. A strong feminist, she also lobbied for victims of domestic violence. Born in 1915, Budd Bell died in 2009.

Like Bell, Vicki Bryant Burke of Jacksonville was a social worker. After graduating from the University of South Carolina, she came to Jacksonville in 1978. The juvenile justice system focused heavily on boys, and in 1985 she founded the PACE Center for Girls. It provided guidance to girls released from juvenile detention and, by 2011, was so successful that judges had encouraged expansion to seventeen such centers throughout the state. Burke, who was born in 1953, has moved on to working for adult females in the penal system.

The 2012–13 entries into the Women's Hall of Fame truly honored history, consisting of a woman past ninety and two who were deceased. The living woman was Aleen Kidd MacKenzie of Ocala and Tallahassee, who was the first to chair the first Commission on the Status of Women, back in the 1960s.[27] The other two honorees were Clara Frye, discussed in chapter 6 as the founder of Tampa's only hospital for blacks, and Lillian Pierce Voss of Delray Beach.

Born in 1876, Lillian Pierce was the first white child in southeast Florida. Her brother had been born before the family moved to Lake Worth, in what now is Palm Beach County, and his memoirs tell of how his mother nearly died after Lillian's birth. She had convulsions, and the closest woman who could help was seventeen miles away. They sent for this woman, Mrs. David Brown, and she used homemade medicines that slowly healed the new mother.[28] Daughter Lillian was healthy and grew up to work in the family marina. On both sailboats and rowboats, they transported cargo and passengers on the Atlantic and on inland waterways—and both Lillian and her mother were boat pilots. Lillian also played the organ for Palm Beach's pioneer church (with services held in their home). She married Fredrick C. Voss, a steamship engineer originally from Maine. The couple lived at Hypoluxo for more than fifty years, and Lillian Pierce Voss established much of what made Palm Beach County what it is today.

For most of her life, however, she could not vote; she never was eligible to serve on a jury. The struggle for full equality still continues. As of this writing, no woman has been governor or speaker of the House, and Florida has far to go before women hold an equitable half of public offices. The private world is even less inclusive, as studies show that the percentage of female directors on corporate boards hovers at about 15 percent—and has done so for years.

Yet from the time when Ponce de León arrived with two women aboard to the time when women flew rockets to the moon, the female half of the population has made giant, but too often unacknowledged, contributions to Florida history. Countless women have overcome great obstacles and yet are ignored. An alien from another planet could read our history books and conclude that men created modern civilization on their own—but the simple fact is that without women, history ends in a generation. Without women, there is no history—nor any future.

Notes

Chapter 1. A Time Before

1. Keith Morelli, "Excavation Ends at Spring," *Tampa Tribune*, February 3, 2013.
2. McCarthy, *Native Americans in Florida*, 23.
3. William M. Goza, in Brinton, *A Guide-Book of Florida*, lvii.
4. Hann, *History of the Timucua*, 121.
5. Ibid., 82.
6. McCarthy, *Native Americans in Florida*, 50.
7. Milanich, *The Timucua*, 28.
8. Dickinson, *God's Protecting Providence*, 54–55.
9. Purdy, *Indian Art of Ancient Florida*, figure 89.
10. Milanich, *The Timucua*, 25.
11. Jerald T. Milanich, "Original Inhabitants," in Gannon, *New History of Florida*, 4.
12. Hann, *History of the Timucua*, 114.
13. McCarthy, *Native Americans in Florida*, 90.
14. Milanich, *Florida Indians*, 44.
15. Purdy, *Indian Art of Ancient Florida*, 6.

Chapter 2. Newcomers: The First European Women, 1513–1819

1. Morison, *Christopher Columbus, Mariner*, 13.
2. Ibid., 21.
3. Cited in Fuson, *Juan Ponce de Leon*, 35–36.
4. Wagenheim and Jimenez de Wageheim, *The Puerto Ricans*, 16.
5. Ibid., 18–19.
6. Gannon, *New History of Florida*, 17.
7. Ibid., 19.
8. Barcia, *Barcia's Chronological History*, 2. This 1740s work appeared in English translation in 1951 as a book of 426 exceptionally large pages and dedicated to Emily Lloyd Wilson of the St. Augustine Historical Society. Without explanation of who she was, the translator dedicated his lengthy foreword to Marjorie Burke.
9. Gannon, *New History of Florida*, 21.
10. Barcia, *Barcia's Chronological History*, 6.
11. Ibid., 10.

12. Schneider, *Brutal Journey,* 113.
13. Ibid., 177.
14. Ibid., 14.
15. Milanich, *The Timucua,* 198.
16. Jose Rabasa, "Violence in the Soto Narratives," in Galloway, *Hernando de Soto Expedition,* 385.
17. Chang-Rodríguez, *Beyond Books and Borders,* 15.
18. León, *San Cristóbal de la Habana.* Translated from Spanish by Delia Sanchez of Tampa; a more extended quotation on the de Soto expedition is available in Weatherford, *Real Women.*
19. León, *San Cristóbal de la Habana,* 35.
20. Ibid.
21. Ignacio Avellaneda, "Hernando de Soto and His Florida Fantasy," in Galloway, *Hernando de Soto Expedition,* 211.
22. Ewen and Hann, *Hernando de Soto among the Apalachee, 164.*
23. Ibid.
24. Chang-Rodríguez, *Beyond Books and Borders,* 141.
25. Ibid., 30.
26. Barcia, *Barcia's Chronological History.*
27. Ibid., 27.
28. Ibid.
29. Gannon, *Cross in the Sand,* 12.
30. Ibid.
31. Barcia, *Barcia's Chronological History,* 30.
32. Ibid., 35.
33. Ibid., 36.
34. Ibid., 43.
35. Ibid., 45.
36. Stone, *Pedro Menendez de Aviles,* 44.
37. Tebeau, *A History of Florida,* 29.
38. Ibid., 31.
39. Ibid., 35.
40. Barcia, *Barcia's Chronological History,* 74.
41. Ibid., 70.
42. Stone, *Pedro Menendez de Aviles,* 24.
43. Ibid.
44. Ibid.
45. See Connor, *Pedro Menéndez de Avilés: Memorial,* 9–11. More than three centuries passed between the 1567 chronicle and its full publication in Spanish in 1893; more than another half century passed prior to Connor's English translation.
46. Barcia, *Barcia's Chronological History,* 163.
47. Gannon, *Cross in the Sand,* 24.
48. Ibid., 26. Gannon is especially known for advocacy of Florida as the site of the first Thanksgiving.
49. T. Frederick Davis, *History of Jacksonville,* 23.

50. Eugene Lyon, "The Captives of Florida," in Lyon, *Pedro Menendez de Aviles*, 181–82.
51. Davis, *History of Jacksonville*, 18.
52. Manucy, *Florida's Menendez*; in a foreword by Father Michael V. Gannon, 4–5.
53. Barcia, *Barcia's Chronological History*, 103.
54. Ibid., 103. A number of secondary sources feature Doña Antonia, and Albert Manucy's work, *Florida's Menendez: Captain General of the Ocean Sea*, devotes an entire chapter to her.
55. Barcia, *Barcia's Chronological History*, 106.
56. Ibid., 121.
57. Ibid., 122.
58. Ibid., 139.
59. John H. Hann, "Father Juan de Paiva: Spanish Friar of Colonial Florida," in Henderson and Mormino, *Spanish Pathways*, 160.
60. Barcia, *Barcia's Chronological History*, 163.
61. Milanich, *The Timucua*, 95. For more on Juanillo's Revolt, see Francis and Kole, *Murder and Martyrdom*.
62. Hann, *History of the Timucua*, 158–59.
63. Bushnell, *Situado and Sabana*, 112.
64. Milanich, *The Timucua*, 117.
65. Milanich, *The Timucua*, 190.
66. Hann, "1630 Memorial," 99.
67. Amy Turner Bushnell, "A Requiem for Lesser Conquerors," in Chang-Rodríguez, *Beyond Books and Borders*, 72.
68. Ibid., 73.
69. Hann and McEwan, *The Apalachee Indians*, 34.
70. Ibid., 36.
71. Ibid., 56.
72. Ibid., 149.
73. Ibid., 155.
74. Weatherford, *Milestones*, 16.
75. Deagan and MacMahon, *Fort Mose*, 23.
76. Barcia, *Barcia's Chronological History*, 163.
77. Milanich, *The Timucua*, 202.
78. Hann and McEwan, *The Apalachee Indians*, 167.
79. Ibid., 174.
80. Mormino and Pizzo, *Tampa*, 18.
81. Deagan and MacMahon, *Fort Mose*, 19.
82. Ibid.
83. Dodd, *Florida, the Land of Romance*, 92. Although Dodd is deservedly lauded as Florida's first state archivist, she apparently was so fearful of being seen as a feminist that she drew almost no attention to other women. The 98-page book names only one woman, Rachel (Mrs. Andrew) Jackson—who lived in Florida less than four months.
84. Deagan and MacMahon, *Fort Mose*, 37.

85. Robin F. A. Fabel, "British Florida, 1763–1784," in George, *A Guide to the History of Florida*, 37.
86. Dodd, *Florida, the Land of Romance*, 25.
87. Griffin, *Mullet on the Beach*, 6.
88. Dodd, *Florida, the Land of Romance*, 26.
89. Wright, *Florida in the American Revolution*, 7.
90. Ibid., 84.
91. Ibid., 99.
92. Ibid., 142.
93. Ibid., 142.
94. Brevard, *History of Florida*, 6–7.
95. Ogle, *Key West*, 35.
96. Landers, "Francisco Xavier Sanchez, Floridano Planter," 180.
97. Ibid.
98. Blackman, *Miami and Dade County*, 11.
99. William S. Coker, "The Moreno Family of the Gulf Coast," in Henderson and Mormino, *Spanish Pathways*, 230.
100. Giddings, *Florida Exiles*, 35.
101. Ibid., 35–36.
102. Ibid., 43.
103. Brevard, *History of Florida*, 1:45.
104. Ibid., 1:46.
105. Ibid., 1:50.
106. Ibid., 1:53, 55.

Chapter 3. From Spanish Colony to Statehood and Secession, 1820–1859

1. Brevard, *History of Florida*, 1:63, quoting a letter from Rachel Jackson to Eliza Kingsley, July 23, 1821.
2. Ibid., 1:65.
3. Ibid., 1:64, quoting James Parton, *The Life of Andrew Jackson* (Boston: Houghton Mifflin, 1887), 1:607.
4. Tebeau, *A History of Florida*, 119.
5. Johnson, *Red, White and Bluebloods*, 5–6.
6. Some sources spell this "DuVal."
7. Johnson, *Red, White and Bluebloods*, 32.
8. Ibid, 33.
9. Ibid., 101.
10. Long, *Florida Breezes*, 143.
11. Ibid., 143, 172.
12. Ibid., 100.
13. This word is variously spelled, including "Mikisuki."
14. Florida State Library, *Florida Becomes a State*, 45.
15. Johnson, *Red, White and Bluebloods*, 50.
16. A. J. Hanna, *A Prince in Their Midst*, 122.

17. Ibid.
18. According to historian T. Frederick Davis, "there is no authentic record" that Andrew Jackson "ever visited this part of Florida" (*History of Jacksonville*, 56).
19. Davis, *History of Jacksonville*, 65.
20. Ibid., 46.
21. Tebeau, *A History of Florida*, 146.
22. See Weatherford, *Real Women*, for more on the first babies at Fort Brooke, and Weatherford, *History of the American Suffragist Movement*, for more on the early women's rights movement.
23. See Penney and Livingston, *A Very Dangerous* Woman, and Bacon, *Valiant Friend*, for more on the Coffin sisters.
24. Her maiden name was Mary Elizabeth Cleland Randolph; she seems not to have used Mary.
25. Johnson, *Red, White and Bluebloods*, 11.
26. Ibid., 12.
27. Ibid., 20–21.
28. Brevard, *History of Florida*, 1:108.
29. Johnson, *Red, White and Bluebloods*, 108, quoting Margaret Eaton, *The Autobiography of Peggy Eaton* (New York: Scribner's, 1932). For more information on Margaret O'Neale Timberlake Eaton, see Weatherford, *American Women's History*.
30. Fairbanks, *History of Florida*, 286.
31. Mormino and Pizzo, *Tampa*, 37.
32. Pleck and Rothman, *The Legacies Book*, 97.
33. Fairbanks, *History of Florida*, 288. Repeated with additional information in Brevard, *History of Florida*, 1:166–67.
34. Fairbanks, *History of Florida*, 315–16.
35. Ibid., 295, 300–1.
36. Davis, *History of Jacksonville*, 81.
37. Ibid., 324.
38. Blackman, *Miami and Dade County*, 12–13.
39. Brevard, *History of Florida*, 1:280.
40. Ibid., 1:340.
41. Rivers, *Slavery in Florida*, 13.
42. Sprague, *Origin, Progress*, 69.
43. Weatherford, *Real Women*, 20.
44. Johnson, *Red, White and Bluebloods*, 24.
45. Davis, *History of Jacksonville*, 68.
46. Tebeau, *A History of Florida*, 187.
47. Federal Writers Project, Works Progress Administration, *Slave Narratives*, vol. 17.
48. Rivers, *Slavery in Florida*, 159.
49. Denham, "Cracker Women and Their Families in Nineteenth Century Florida," in Greenberg et al., *Florida's Heritage of Diversity*, 26.
50. Rivers, *Slavery in Florida*, 159.
51. Denham, "Cracker Women," 26.
52. Rivers, *Slavery in Florida*, 86.

53. Ogle, *Key West,* 46–47.
54. Daniel L. Schafer, "U.S. Territory and State," in Gannon, *New History of Florida,* 225.
55. Davis, *History of Jacksonville,* 96.
56. Denham, "Cracker Women and Their Families," 16.
57. Ibid., 17–19.
58. Brown, *Women on the Tampa Bay Frontier,* 8–9.
59. Brevard, *History of Florida,* 1:181.
60. Brown, *Women on the Tampa Bay Frontier,* 9.
61. Tebeau, *A History of Florida,* 196.
62. Weatherford, *Real Women,* 34.
63. Ephesians 6:5 and Colossians 3:22.
64. Rivers, *Slavery in Florida,* 123.
65. Ibid., 89.
66. John K. Mahon and Brent R. Weisman, "Florida's Seminole and Miccosukee Peoples," in Gannon, *New History of Florida,* 199.

Chapter 4. "We Live On Cornbread and Hope," 1860–1880

1. Proctor, *Napoleon Bonaparte Broward,* 14.
2. Van Landingham, *Pioneer Families of the Kissimmee,* 10.
3. Daniel L. Schafer, "U.S. Territory and State," in Gannon, *New History of Florida,* 228. Some sources say that "Princess" Catherine Murat, discussed in chapter 3, fired the first gun.
4. Canter Brown Jr. "The Civil War, 1861–1865," in Gannon, *New History of Florida,* 232. See also Brevard, *History of Florida.*
5. Johns, *Florida during the Civil War,* 20.
6. Schmidt, *The Civil War,* 1:31, citing *St. Johns Mirror,* July 17, 1861.
7. Griffin, *Mullet on the Beach,* 35.
8. Johns, *Florida during the Civil War,* 63.
9. Ibid., 68, quoting *The War of Rebellion: A Compilation of the Official Records of the Union and Confederate Armies,* as well as the diary of Jesse Bernard, October 1861.
10. Schmidt, *The Civil War in Florida,* 1:121–22, citing letter from George W. Richardson, June 22, 1862; diary of Henry Haskell; and Official Records of . . . the Armies, 14:356.
11. Schmidt, *The Civil War in Florida,* 95, citing diary of Elias A. Bryant, 4th New Hampshire Regiment.
12. Ibid., 36; citing *Philadelphia Inquirer,* August 24, 1861.
13. Revels, *Grander in Her Daughters,* 75.
14. Long, *Florida Breezes,* 312.
15. Pearce, *Pensacola during the Civil War,* 54.
16. Ibid., xi.
17. Revels, *Grander in Her Daughters,* 114.
18. Ibid., 188.
19. Eppes, *Through Some Eventful Years,* 135.
20. Brown, *Women on the Tampa Bay Frontier,* 236, quoting "Suffering of Southern Women," in the Florida State Archives.

21. Johns, *Florida during the Civil War,* 175, quoting Eppes, *Through Some Eventful Years,* 210.

22. Cox and Dovell, *Florida from Secession to Space Age,* 19, quoting Catherine Cooper Hopley, *Life in the South, from the Commencement of the War* (London, 1863), 289–90.

23. Cox and Dovell, *Florida from Secession to Space Age,* quoting William Lamar Gammon II, "Governor John Milton of Florida" (master's thesis, University of Florida, Gainesville, 1948), 91.

24. Long, *Florida Breezes,* 330.

25. Johns, *Florida during the Civil War,* citing the *Florida Sentinel,* November 17, 1863.

26. Long, *Florida Breezes,* 324.

27. Ibid., 369. See also Fries, *Mary Martha Reid.*

28. Pearce, *Pensacola during the Civil War,* 92.

29. Ibid.

30. Ibid.

31. Revels, *Grander in Her Daughters,* 114.

32. Johns, *Florida during the Civil War,* 110.

33. Brown, *Florida's Peace River Frontier,* 35.

34. Brown, *Tampa in Civil War,* 237, citing "The Heroines of the Southern Confederacy," in the Florida State Archives.

35. Ibid., citing "The Burdens Women Bore," by Mrs. John M. Taylor, Mrs. R. L. Harper, and Miss B. Kelly, in the Florida State Archives.

36. Ibid., 177–78.

37. Long, *Florida Breezes,* 339.

38. Schmidt, *The Civil War in Florida,* 1:122.

39. Ibid., 1:190.

40. Davis, *History of Jacksonville,* 135.

41. Foster and Foster, *Beechers, Stowes,* 9.

42. Ibid., 14.

43. Ibid., 12, quoting *Syracuse Journal,* September 4 and 6, 1863.

44. Schwartz, *A Woman Doctor's Civil War,* 63. Some of the soldiers of whom Dr. Hawk wrote belonged to Massachusetts' 54th Regiment, the nation's first unit of African American soldiers. Commanded by an idealistic white man, Robert Gould Shaw, the regiment was featured in the 1990 film *Glory!*

45. Ibid., 69–70.

46. Long, *Florida Breezes,* 355–56.

47. Johns, *Florida during the Civil War,* 160.

48. Cox and Dovell, *Florida: From Secession to Space Age,* 17, quoting Catherine Cooper Hopley, *Life in the South, from the Commencement of the War* (London, 1863).

49. Blakely et al., *Rose Cottage Chronicles,* 341–43.

50. Ibid., 355–56.

51. Schwartz, *A Woman Doctor's Civil War,* 117.

52. See chapter 2 for more on the Mallorys.

53. Pearce, *Pensacola during the Civil War,* 179.

54. Ibid.

55. Long, *Florida Breezes*, 385–86.
56. Peek, *Lawlessness*, 10.
57. Shofner, *Nor Is It Over Yet*, 95.
58. Peek, *Lawlessness*, 104.
59. Ibid., 60, quoting *Semi-Weekly Floridian* and the *Gainesville New Era*.
60. Ibid., 63, quoting a Freedman's Bureau report by D. M. Hammond in Fernandina.
61. Ibid., 96, quoting a Freedman's Bureau report by J. A. Remley in Ocala.
62. Ibid., 137–38, quoting U.S. House Report 22, 1872, 1:80.
63. Shofner, *Nor Is It Over Yet*, 230.
64. Ibid., 140, quoting *West Florida Commercial*, October 2, 1869.
65. Ibid., 199, quoting U.S. House Report 22, 1872, 1:66, and *Florida Sentinel*, July 1, 1871.
66. Ibid., 194, quoting U.S. House Report 22, 1872, 1:268.
67. Schmidt, *The Civil War in Florida*, 1:235.
68. Ibid.
69. Milanich, *Frolicking Bears*, 67–71, quoting Amos Jay Cummings.
70. Brown, *Women on the Tampa Bay Frontier*, 59.
71. The quotes from Anna M. Kidder were taken from her original letters, which are archived in Schlesinger Library at Radcliffe College, an affiliate of Harvard University.
72. Foster and Foster, *Beechers, Stowes*, 16.
73. Anna M. Kidder letters, Schlesinger Library, Radcliffe College.
74. Peek, *Lawlessness*, 64–65, quoting Freedmen's Bureau papers, September 29, 1867. The official's name was illegible, but he was a lieutenant attached to the U.S. 7th Infantry.
75. From records in the Tampa Bay History Center.
76. Laurel Grove had previously belonged to Anna Madgigine Jai Kingsley, who was born in Africa and enslaved in Florida but married her master and became a slave owner herself; for an account of her life, see Schafer, *Anna Madgigine Jai Kingsley*.
77. Thulesius, *Harriet Beecher Stowe in Florida*, 49–50, citing A. Brooks ("Sylvia Sunshine"), *Petals Picked from a Sunny Clime* (Nashville: Southern Methodist Publishing House, 1880), 38–40.
78. Lanier, *Florida: Scenery, Climate, and History*, 122.
79. Stowe, *Palmetto Leaves*, 295–319.
80. Brown, *Genealogical Records*, 67–69.
81. Federal Writers Project, Works Progress Administration, *Slave Narratives*, vol. 17, 169.
82. Shofner, *Nor Is It Over Yet*, 146.
83. Edward F. Keuchal, "Sister Mary Ann: Jacksonville's Angel of Mercy," in Greenberg et al., *Florida's Heritage of Diversity*, 100.
84. Foster and Foster, *Beechers, Stowes*, 80, quoting New York's *Christian Advocate*, March 2, 1876.
85. Ibid., 78.
86. Brown, *Florida's Peace River Frontier*, 69.
87. Revels, *Grander in Her Daughters*, 146, quoting Margaret (Mrs. Enoch) Vann, *Fragments of the Confederacy*, Jacksonville Historical Records Survey, 1937.

Chapter 5. "The World Is Not Suffering for Another Cake Recipe," 1881–1900

1. See Weatherford, *History of the American Suffragist Movement*, for further information.
2. See chapter 4 on Stowe and Hawk.
3. For further information on the WCTU and prohibition, see cross-referenced entries in Weatherford, *American Women's History*.
4. Weatherford, *Real Women*, 109, citing Nancy A. Hewitt, "Varieties of Voluntarism: Class, Ethnicity, and Women's Activities in Tampa," 1986, a paper that Hewitt has since expanded into the book *Southern Discomfort*.
5. Weatherford, *Real Women*, 104.
6. Ibid., 123–29. Thanks to authors Canter Brown and Gary Mormino, as well as the late Leland Hawes, men who continually keep an eye open for women's history as they do their research in Florida archives.
7. Thanks to the late Leland Hawes of the *Tampa Tribune*, who published this research by Lucy Patrick, a graduate student at Florida State University. *Woman's Tribune* was the name of an Indianapolis paper begun by Amanda Hill and Sarah Underhill in 1859, but it is doubtful if that was the same periodical still being published in the 1880s. Except for *Woman's Journal*, which lasted from 1870 to 1917, most feminist newspapers had short lives.
8. Cox and Dovell, *Florida: From Secession to Space Age*, 103.
9. Neil Bradley, "Old Discrimination Doesn't Die; It Doesn't Even Fade Away," a paper issued by the Atlanta branch of the American Civil Liberties Union, 2000.
10. Weatherford, *Real Women*, 95, citing Milly St. Julien, "The Role of Women in Tampa's Benevolent Organizations, 1895–1915," a paper for the University of South Florida History Department, 1986.
11. Ibid.
12. Ibid., 92–97, citing a 1984 paper by Eirlys Mair Barker, then a student at the University of South Florida. Titled "Seasons of Pestilence: Tampa and Yellow Fever, 1824 to 1905," it is now available in electronic form from the University of South Florida Library.
13. Ibid., 97, citing Nancy A. Hewitt, "Varieties of Voluntarism" (see note 4 to this chapter).
14. Mark Greenberg, "Tampa Mayor Herman Glogowski," in Greenberg et al., *Florida's Heritage of Diversity*, 67.
15. Edward F. Keuchal, "Sister Mary Ann: Jacksonville's Angel of Mercy," in Greenberg et al., *Florida's Heritage of Diversity*, 100.
16. See Weatherford, *Foreign and Female*, especially the chapters on maternal health and on food.
17. Brown, *Women on the Tampa Bay Frontier*, 60.
18. Several books have been written on this subject. See especially Martin, *The Sound of Our Own Voices*.
19. Eirlys M. Barker, "Daughters of the Pioneers: Women in Tampa, 1880–1890," a paper written for Dr. Nancy Hewitt and the History Department of the University of South Florida, ca. 1983.
20. Meyer, *Leading the Way*, 12.
21. An exhaustive history of the event is Weimann, *The Fair Women*. See also Moseley

and Crislip, eds., *Come to My Sunland: Letters of Julia Daniels Moseley from the Florida Frontier, 1882–1886.*

22. Shofner, *Florida Portrait,* 127.
23. For more on Florida's Gilded Age hotels, see Braden, *Architecture of Leisure.*
24. Cox and Dovell, *Florida: From Secession to Space Age,* 126. See also Standiford, *Last Train to Paradise,* 52.
25. Shofner, *Florida Portrait,* 120.
26. Cox and Dovell, *Florida: From Secession to Space Age,* 59.
27. Marvin Dunn, *Black Miami,* 58–59.
28. Thanks to the late Leland Hawes of the *Tampa Tribune,* who provided primary documents on Chamberlain.
29. Cox and Dovell, *Florida: From Secession to Space Age,* 59. For more on Susan B. Anthony and Ella Chamberlain, see Weatherford, *History of the American Suffragist Movement.* Chamberlain was commemorated with a statue on Tampa's Riverwalk in 2012.
30. Lane, *Rollins College,* 6.
31. Ibid., 31. Family names among the founders probably reflect the Florida influence of Harriet Beecher Stowe. The first chairman of the Board of Trustees (all were men, as were the presidents) was Frederick Lyman, and the Beecher and Lyman families were connected through marriage. The college's first president was Dr. Edward Hooker, who may have been related to Stowe's half-sister, Isabella Beecher Hooker.
32. A married woman, Dr. Whitcomb appears to have returned to New York State.
33. Weatherford, *Real Women,* 117–18, with thanks to Leland Hawes, longtime history columnist for the *Tampa Tribune.*
34. See chapter 3 for other mixed-race polygamous families. Ironically, Governor Fleming is remembered for removing a Key West judge from office because the judge allegedly performed a wedding ceremony for a black woman and white man—even though the man took an oath swearing that he was a mulatto. See Allman, *Finding Florida,* 304.
35. Weatherford, *Real Women,* 301–2. See also Lulu Fleming's entry in Hine, *Black Women in America.*
36. The next chapter has more on Mary Baird Bryan and her daughter, Ruth Bryan Owen.
37. Weatherford, *Real Women,* citing McKay's column, *Tampa Sunday Tribune,* June 10, 1951.
38. See the next chapter.
39. For more on Moseley, see Moseley and Crislip, *Come to My Sunland.*
40. James Michael Denham, "Victoria Seward Brandon Sherrill, 1843–1926: Community Builder," in Rivers and Brown, *Varieties of Women's Experiences,* 54.
41. Ibid.
42. Weatherford, *Real Women,* with additional thanks to Leland Hawes.
43. The very first organization of professional women was called Sorosis. Rooted in the Greek word for "sorority" or sisterhood, it began in New York City in 1868 after female journalists were excluded from a function for popular British author Charles Dickens.

44. Hewitt, "Varieties of Volunteerism" (see note 4 to this chapter).
45. Ogle, *Key West*, 106.
46. Charles H. Brown, *Correspondent's War*, 69.
47. Roberts, *Dream State*, 163.
48. Hampton Dunn, *Tampa: A Pictorial History*, 39. Clara Barton left dozens of unpublished diaries of her daily activities, some of which were researched by the author for this era. The American Red Cross maintains archives on her in Washington, and her home in Glen Echo, Maryland, is open to visitors.
49. Mormino and Pizzo, *Tampa*, 128.
50. See Leslie's profile in Weatherford, *American Women's History*.
51. Charles H. Brown, *Correspondent's War*, 69–71.
52. Mabel C. Bean (nee Williams), "My Service in the Spanish-American War," Historical Records Survey, State Archives Survey, 1937, unpaginated.

Chapter 6. A New Century, 1901–1920

1. Harper, *History of Woman Suffrage*, 6:114. For a full history of the vote, see Weatherford, *History of the American Suffragist Movement*. For detailed histories of campaigns in every state, see her four-volume *History of Women in the United States*.
2. Harper, *History of Woman Suffrage*, 6:118. For more on Florida see Kenneth Ray Johnson, *The Woman Suffrage Movement in Florida*, a doctoral thesis submitted at Florida State University in 1966.
3. Harper, *History of Woman Suffrage*, 6:118.
4. Ibid., 6:119.
5. Florida House *Journal*, May 2, 1913, 571.
6. Harper, *History of Woman Suffrage*, 6:115.
7. Morris, *Women in the Florida Legislature*, 121.
8. Harper, *History of Woman Suffrage*, 6:116.
9. Weatherford, "Last Instead of First," 20.
10. *Tampa Morning Tribune*, April 26, 1913.
11. See chapter 5 sidebar for more about Ivy Stranahan.
12. Harper, *History of Woman Suffrage*, 6:117.
13. Florida Senate *Journal*, April 18, 1919, 342.
14. *Tampa Daily Times*, June 7, 1919.
15. Harper, *History of Woman Suffrage*, 6:121.
16. Emma Miller of Tampa attended Georgia's Wesleyan Female College during the Civil War; see chapter 4 sidebar Confidence amidst Crisis.
17. Stern, *FSU Voices*, 33.
18. See chapter 5.
19. Phillip Tomberlin Jr., in Loquasto, *First 150 Women Lawyers*, 5.
20. Jane Loewinger, Saundra G. Swift, in Loquasto, *First 150 Women Lawyers*, 5.
21. See later chapters for more on Bethune.
22. This phrase is used in Armwood's promotional material, in archives at the University of South Florida's Special Collections.
23. Weatherford, *Real Women of Tampa*, 219.

24. Esther Spencer, "Jerenia Valentine Dial Reid, 1879–1962—Woman's Work by a Pioneer of African American Nursing," in Rivers and Brown, *Varieties of Women's Experience*, 287–310.
25. Saunders, *Bridging the Gap*, 28.
26. Marvin Dunn, *Black Miami*, 102.
27. Ibid., 103.
28. Ibid., 70.
29. Karen Davis, *Public Faces—Private Lives*, 121. Davis does not offer a citation for the letter, nor its date. For more on the Blackwell family, including Lucy Stone, see Weatherford, *American Women's History.*
30. Weatherford, *Real Women*, 171.
31. Harper, *History of Woman Suffrage*, 6:119.
32. Beverly Mercer Scott, "Quiet Hero," *Her Voice*, published by the *Winter Haven News Chief*, November–December 2005.
33. Meyer, *Leading the Way*, 64.
34. See chapter 5 for the beginnings of the General Federation of Women's Clubs and its state affiliate, the Florida Federation of Women's Clubs, during the 1890s.
35. Meyer, *Leading the Way*, 67.
36. Ibid., 67, 74.
37. Karen Davis, *Public Faces—Private Lives*, 78.
38. Ibid.
39. Meyer, *Leading the Way*, 11.
40. Ibid.
41. Ibid., 91.
42. Ibid., 82–83.
43. Ibid., 95.
44. Ibid., 69.
45. Ibid.
46. Ibid.
47. Townsend, *Age of Barbarity.*
48. See chapter 5.
49. Meyer, *Leading the Way*, 42–43.
50. *Tampa Morning Tribune*, January 5, 1900.
51. Credit is due to David L. Chapman, "The Door of Hope: Women's Christian Temperance Union and the Purity Crusade in Tampa, 1899–1918." A highly original piece of historical research, this was a paper Chapman wrote for Dr. Gary Mormino of the University of South Florida History Department in the spring semester of 1987.

Chapter 7. Up and Then Down, 1921–1940

1. Carlebach and Provenzo, *Farm Security Administration Photographs*, 2.
2. Ibid., 4.
3. Knowles, *Category 5*, 30.
4. *Tampa Tribune*, September 20, 1920.
5. Morris, *Women in the Florida Legislature*, 9.

6. See chapter 6.
7. Morris, *Women in the Florida Legislature*, 11.
8. Ibid.
9. The problem is further compounded in that some sources spell her new name as Green, but a majority of records indicate that it should be Greene.
10. Morris, *Women in the Florida Legislature*, 12.
11. James R. McGovern, "Helen Hunt West," *Forum* (Florida Humanities Council), Winter 1995–96, 38.
12. See chapter 6.
13. Gary R. Mormino, "Praise for Not-So-Famous Women," *Tampa Tribune*, October 26, 2008.
14. Eloise Cozens, *Florida Women of Distinction*, vol. 1.
15. See chapter 6. For more information on the women who were sheriffs, see Rogers and Denham, *Florida Sheriffs*.
16. Townsend, *Age of Barbarity*, 18. See both the previous chapter and the next chapter for more on Bethune.
17. Hewitt, "Varieties of Women's Suffrage," 25, quoting African American historian Maxine D. Jones.
18. Hanson, *Mary McLeod Bethune*, 97.
19. Ibid. Many books have been written on McLeod; among those that have the immediacy of her era are Catherine Owens Peare, *Mary McLeod Bethune* (New York: Vanguard Press, 1951), and Rackham Holt, *Mary McLeod Bethune: A Biography* (New York: Doubleday, 1964).
20. See Carolyn Williams, "Eartha Mary Magdalene White," in Rivers and Brown, *Varieties of Women's Experience*; Jones and McCarthy, *African Americans in Florida*, also includes White.
21. Saunders, *Bridging the Gap*, 36.
22. Chapter 8 includes more on the NCNW.
23. Burghard, *Mrs. Frank Stranahan*, 24. See also Kersey, *The Stranahans of Fort Lauderdale*.
24. Rainwater and Hanna, *Our Journey through Florida*, 211–13.
25. Ibid., 219.
26. Harper, *History of Woman Suffrage*, 6: 113–120. See also chapter 5.
27. "The Long Hard Climb," *Forum* (Florida Humanities Council), Winter 1995–96, 43.
28. See chapter 6.
29. McGovern, "Helen Hunt West," 36.
30. Associated Press, "Sarasota Girl Meets Law Reformer," *St. Petersburg Times*, May 4, 1939, 24.
31. Betty Taylor, in Loquasto, *Florida's First 150 Women Lawyers*, 58. For more on Gehan, see chapter 9.
32. Ibid.
33. Ibid.
34. See chapter 6 sidebar on Edison.

35. DVD created for the 75th anniversary of Business and Professional Women in Florida, 1994; in the author's files, with thanks to Suzanne Dalton.
36. Cozens, *Florida Women of Distinction*, 1:39.
37. Hemenway, *Zora Neale Hurston*, 69, 124; see chapter 4 for more on Eatonville.
38. The typescript of this 1939 article is in the P. K. Yonge Library at the University of Florida. See also Jones and McCarthy, *African Americans in Florida*, 82.
39. See chapter 2.
40. Federal Writers Project, Works Progress Administration, *Slave Narratives*, vol. 17.
41. Hurston, *Go Gator*, 37.
42. Federal Writers Project, *Florida: A Guide*, 362.
43. Stern, *FSU Voices*, 69.
44. Perry, *Free Within Ourselves*, 155.
45. Bernard, *Afro-American Artists in Paris*, 9. Both Augusta Savage and Zora Neale Hurston are included in *Harlem Renaissance Art of Black America*, which was published in New York by the Studio Museum of Harlem in 1987.
46. Associated Press, "Mrs. Lois K. Mayes, Pensacola, First Woman to be Elected Head of Florida Press Body," *St. Petersburg Times*, April 3, 1921. Thanks to Gary Mormino for locating this article.
47. Fernández and Ingalls, *Sunshine in the Dark*, 3.
48. Roberts, *Dream State*, *276*. See also D'Orso, *Like Judgment Day*.
49. Dunn, *Black Miami*, 117.
50. Ibid., 125–27.
51. Some sources spell this married surname Corbett, but Canter Brown, who did the original research, assures us that it was Corbet, with one *t*. For more information, see Canter Brown Jr., "Gertrude Dzaialynski Corbet, 1874–1931—'Miss Dynamite,' A Jewish Woman in the Progressive Era South," in Rivers and Brown, *Varieties of Women's Experiences*, 215–36.
52. Roberts, *Dream State*, 274–77.
53. Lynne A. Rieff, "Improving Rural Life in Florida," in Davis and Frederickson, *Making Waves*, 111.
54. Kim Curry, PhD, ARNP, "Pioneer in Public Health Nursing: The Work of Victoria Joyce Ely, RN," *Florida Public Health Review* 2 (2005): 17–22.
55. Weatherford, *Real Women*, 244.
56. Rieff, "Improving Rural Life in Florida," 112.
57. Laird, *Like I Saw It*, 78, 97. Laird was a political science professor at the University of Florida.
58. Weatherford, *Real Women*, 236.
59. *St. Petersburg Times*, April 2, 1925.
60. Weatherford, *Real Women*, 228.

Chapter 8. World War II and Its Aftermath, 1941–1960

1. The initial name was Women's Army Auxiliary Corps, or WAACs. After complicated legal problems, Congress changed the authorizing legislation to eliminate "auxiliary."

2. For much more information, see Weatherford, *American Women and World War II*, which is a narrative book. *American Women during World War II: An A-Z*, also by Weatherford, uses an encyclopedic approach, with approximately four hundred entries on individuals and topics.
3. Muir, *Miami, U.S.A.*, 204–6.
4. Ellen J. Babb, "Women and War: St. Petersburg Women during World War II," *Florida Historical Quarterly* 71, no. 1 (July 1994): 43–62.
5. See also chapters 6 and 7.
6. Octavus Roy Cohen, "Municipal Love Affair: Daytona Beach Takes the WAACs to Its Heart," *Collier's*, May 29, 1943.
7. Blake Clark, "Ladies of the Army," *Reader's Digest*, May 1943.
8. Treadwell, *Women's Army Corps*, 208–9.
9. Kathleen Williams Boom, "Women in the AAF," in Craven and Cate, *The Army Air Forces in World War II*.
10. See chapters 6 and 7 for more on early female attorneys.
11. See chapter 7 for more about Hortense Wells.
12. Mormino, *Hillsborough County Goes to War*, 75.
13. Lyne and Arthur, *Three Years behind the Mast*, 26.
14. From WAVES archives at the University of Central Arkansas.
15. Craft, *Embry-Riddle at War*, 108.
16. Ibid.
17. Ibid., 110.
18. Ibid., 143, 145.
19. John Stuart, "The WASP," *Flying*, December 1943, 73. For more on WASP commander Jacqueline Cochran, see Doris Weatherford, *American Women During World War II: An Encyclopedia*.
20. "Services Relent," *Business Week*, February 5, 1944.
21. Wilder, *Since You Went Away*, 69.
22. "Bombardier's Bride," *Ladies Home Journal*, September 1943.
23. Helen Huntington Smith, "G.I. Babies," *Collier's*, December 4, 1943.
24. "He Likes Biscuits, She Likes Bread, So They're Divorced," Associated Press, datelined Tallahassee, December 2, 1942.
25. Muir, *Miami, U.S.A.*, 210.
26. Marvin Dunn, *Black Miami*, 146.
27. Mormino, *Hillsborough County Goes to War*, 104–5.
28. "Our Land Army Is Different," *Saturday Evening Post*, July 25, 1942.
29. See chapter 7 for more on McLendon.
30. Mormino, *Hillsborough County Goes to War*, 59.
31. Marvin Dunn, *Black Miami*, 160.
32. Weatherford, *Real Women*, 280.
33. Numbers are from Morris, *Women in the Florida Legislature*, 13.
34. Morris, *Women in the Florida Legislature*, 13.
35. See chapter 7.
36. Judy Cooper, "Women Have a Part to Play, Too, As Florida's Laws Are Made," *St. Petersburg Times*, April 4, 1959.

37. Ruth Ezell, in Loquasto, *Florida's First 150 Women Lawyers*, 47. For more on Murrell, see chapter 7.
38. Loquasto, *Florida's First 150 Women Lawyers*, 93.
39. Morris, *Women in the Florida Legislature*, 15.
40. Ibid.
41. For more on the "white primary," see Pam Iorio, "Colorless Primaries: Tampa's White Municipal Party." *The Florida Historical Quarterly* 79, no. 3 (Winter 2001): 297–318. Iorio is the former mayor of Tampa and former Hillsborough County supervisor of elections.
42. Loquasto, *Florida's First 150 Women Lawyers*, 106.
43. Marvin Dunn, *Black Miami*, 218.
44. Green, *Before His Time*, 78.
45. Ibid., 196. Thanks also to Lee Jay (Jack) Price of Gainesville, formerly of New York and the National Council of Christians and Jews, for his personal memories of the Reese case.
46. Meyer, *Leading the Way*, 156–57.
47. Ibid., 155.
48. See chapters 6 and 7 for more on Stranahan and Owen, respectively.
49. Rainwater and Hanna, *Our Journey through Florida*, 222.
50. See chapter 9.
51. See chapter 7.
52. Loquasto, *Florida's First 150 Women Lawyers*, 103.
53. Ibid., 79.
54. Bob Hanscom, "Palmettoans Dispute Bradenton Claim to Prettiest Postmaster," *St. Petersburg Times*, August 7, 1954.
55. See chapter 7 for more on Fuller and chapter 9 for more on Johnson.
56. See chapter 6 for Douglas's voting rights activism.
57. Kathleen Hardee Arsenault, "Strawberry Fields and Bean Rows," in Davis and Frederickson, *Making Waves*, 132.
58. Ibid., 136.
59. Weatherford, *History of Women in the United States*, 1:295–96.
60. Clyde Shaffer, "Even St. Petersburg Oldsters Change Way of Life during First Month of Television," *Tampa Morning Tribune*, June 27, 1953.

Chapter 9. Agents of Change, 1961–1980

1. Mary Carolyn Ellis and Joanne V. Hawks, "Creating a Different Pattern: Florida's Women Legislators, 1928–1986," *Florida Historical Quarterly* 66, no. 1 (July 1987): 75.
2. Ann Waldron, "Community Leaders Meet to Discuss 'Status,'" *Miami Herald*, November 9, 1964.
3. Ibid.
4. Associated Press, "Back-to-Work Women: 'Stable Employees,'" *Tampa Tribune*, January 13, 1966.
5. "Education Aims at Status Improvement," United Press International, datelined Tallahassee, November 13, 1965. See also a *Tampa Tribune* story at the same time by

Alexandra Frye, "Members of Governor's Commission on Status of Women Define Goals."

6. For more about judges in this era see discussion later in this chapter.
7. Minutes of the Florida Commission on the Status of Women, November 16, 1968, archives of the FSCW, donated by Commissioner Mary Elmendorf of Sarasota.
8. For more information about these women, see table 9.1.
9. Anderson, *Julia's Daughters*, 119.
10. Item in the scrapbook of Lee Leavengood, a commissioner from Tampa.
11. Janet Hunter, "Status of Women: It's Up to Them," *St. Petersburg Times*, November 17, 1965.
12. Anderson, *Julia's Daughters*, 85.
13. Morris, *Women in the Florida Legislature*, 17
14. See later text for more on Singleton. Both women are discussed in Crooks, *Jacksonville*.
15. Elinor J. Brecher, "Alicia Baro, Puerto Rican-American Activist," *Miami Herald*, January 23, 2012.
16. Muir, *Miami, U.S.A.*, 263–64.
17. Ibid., 247.
18. Ibid., 249.
19. Anderson, *Julia's Daughters*, 126.
20. See also Bettinger-Lopez, *Cuban-Jewish Journeys*.
21. See chapters 6 through 8 for environmentalists.
22. Jan Pudlow, "Women in the Florida Bar," *Florida Bar Journal*, April 2000.
23. See later text for Cherry's political career.
24. For more on Joyner, see chapter 11.
25. See chapter 8 on Turner and Moore.
26. Crooks, *Jacksonville*, 17–18.
27. Ibid., 18.
28. Rodney Kite-Powell, "Freedom for All," *Tampa Tribune*, November 27, 2011.
29. Ibid.
30. See chapter 8.
31. Saunders, *Bridging the Gap*, 169.
32. Andrew Meacham, "Ex-Bellair Commissioner Was Medical Trailblazer," *St. Petersburg Times*, September 24, 2011.
33. Carol Giardina, "Origins and Impact of Gainesville Women's Liberation, the First Women's Liberation Organization in the South," in Davis and Frederickson, *Making Waves*, 312–14.
34. Ibid.
35. See chapters 5 and 6 for examples of earlier such institutions. In the 1970s Skippy King led Tampa's first women's center. Although the mother of many children, she also provided the area's first legal abortions. See Weatherford, *Real Women*.
36. Morris, *Women in the Florida Legislature*, 26.
37. Ibid., 3.
38. Ibid., 4. See also chapter 10.
39. Morris, *Women in the Florida Legislature*, 56–57.

40. Morris, *Women in the Florida Legislature,* 58.
41. Based on a timeline created by Marilyn Myerson, who came to the University of South Florida in 1973. Judith Ochshorn is not to be confused with Kathleen Ochshorn, who later taught Women's Studies at the University of Tampa; Kathleen married Judy's ex-husband, Myron Ochshorn.
42. See also chapter 10.
43. Morris, *Women in the Florida Legislature,* 97.
44. Ibid., 69.
45. Ibid., 70.
46. Ibid., 108.
47. Ibid., 29. See also chapter 10.
48. See chapter 10 for more on Pat Frank.
49. Morris, *Women in the Florida Legislature,* 60.
50. Bob Holladay, "Searching for Glorida Jahoda: One Man's Quest to Discover the 'Outsider' Writer Who Captured the Spirit of North Florida," *Tallahassee Magazine,* May–June 2008.
51. Monica Rohr, "300 Attend Service for Anne Ackerman," *Sun-Sentinel,* May 4, 1989.
52. Morris, *Women in the Florida Legislature,* 118.
53. Jones and McCarthy, *African Americans in Florida,* 128.
54. See chapter 8.

Chapter 10. Through the Twentieth Century, 1981–2000

1. Eulogies by Victor Tipton, Stephen Maher, and others can be found in a resolution passed by the legislature, 19 Fla. St. U. L. Rev, 951 (1991–1992).
2. "How the ERA Faltered," *Forum* (Florida Humanities Council), Winter 1995–96, 46.
3. Morris, *Women in the Florida Legislature,* 126.
4. Other leaders of the network were Nikki Beare in Miami, Nancy Ford in Tampa, and Cecilia Bryant of Jacksonville, the daughter of former governor Farris Bryant.
5. See chapter 9.
6. Morris, *Women in the Florida Legislature,* 93.
7. *Ocala Star Banner,* March 28, 1985.
8. Morris, *Women in the Florida Legislature,* 91.
9. Ben Hammer, "Legendary Florida A&M Business Dean Set to Retire," *Black Issues in Higher Education,* June 19, 2003.
10. Morris, *Women in the Florida Legislature,* 22 (paragraphing added).
11. Weatherford, *Women in American Politics,* 377.
12. Interview with Doris Weatherford, in Weatherford, *Real Women,* 350–51.
13. Crooks, *Jacksonville,* 168–69.
14. Please see the index for more information on these women.
15. See also chapter 9.
16. Morris, *Women in the Florida Legislature,* 119.
17. Ibid., 102.
18. Ibid., 28. See chapter 9 for more on Bloom.
19. U.S. House of Representatives, *Women in Congress,* 709.

20. Ibid., 795.
21. See chapter 9 for biographical details about Meek.
22. U.S. House of Representatives, *Women in Congress,* 722.
23. Ibid., 738.
24. Morris, *Women in the Florida Legislature,* 80.
25. Morris, *Women in the Florida Legislature,* 94–95. See also Schultz, *For the Next Generation.*
26. 1990 U.S. census, as reported by Bouvier et al., *Shaping Florida,* 9–10. See also Immigration Policy Center, *New Americans in Florida,* and Camarota, *Immigrants in the United States.*
27. Jan Pudlow, "Women in the Florida Bar," *Florida Bar Journal,* April 2000.
28. See chapter 5 for Pedroso and chapter 8 for Skelton (later Frankman).
29. See chapter 9 for more on Frank and Freedman; Busansky died suddenly in 2009, soon after becoming Hillsborough County supervisor of elections.
30. "Continue Chiles' Work for Children," *St. Petersburg Times,* December 17, 1998.
31. Florida Supreme Court, *Gender Bias—Then and Now: Continuing Challenges in the Legal System,* December 1996, 2. The women on this subcommittee were attorneys Sandra Allen and Nancy Palmer as well as State Representative Debbie Wasserman Schultz.
32. Ibid., 5. More men than women served on this subcommittee. The most notable woman was Judge Jeri Cohen.
33. Ibid., 6. Among other women, Judge Joan Lenard served on this subcommittee.
34. Ibid., 6. Among other women, Judge Joan Lenard served on this subcommittee as well.
35. Ibid., 9. Three female attorneys and two female judges served on this subcommittee with three men.
36. Ibid., 12. Tallahassee attorney Virginia Daire was a member of this group; she had been a founder of Tampa NOW in the 1970s.
37. Undated Barry University press release.

Chapter 11. After the New Millennium

1. See chapter 7 regarding the 1923 Rosewood Massacre; Barnett's legal expertise and lobbying abilities played a strong role in obtaining compensation for victims. Her father, a physician, had treated survivors. See Michael D'Orso, *Like Judgment Day.*
2. Jan Pudlow, "Women in the Florida Bar," *Florida Bar Journal,* April 2000.
3. Sandy Strickland, "Evett Simmons, Star of the National Bar," *Jacksonville Times-Union,* September 20, 2000. See also chapter 9 for more on Joyner.
4. "Marilyn Milian," in *Beyond Julia's Daughters,* unpaginated.
5. See chapter 10.
6. See chapter 10 for more on Betty Castor.
7. See chapter 10 for the Gender Equity Act as well as information on Grace Rushing Maxwell, who played a founding role with several community colleges but never was rewarded with a presidency.
8. See chapter 10.

9. Please use the index for these names.
10. See chapter 6 on Frye and Chamberlain.
11. See chapter 10 on Lenard.
12. *Palm Beach Post*, March 15, 2013.
13. See chapter 10 for more on Fowler.
14. See other references to Morgan in the chapter 10 sidebar on Pulitzer Prize winners.
15. See chapter 10.
16. "Progressive City Leaders," *Nation*, June 18, 2005.
17. See more on Chisholm in Weatherford, *Women in American Politics*. Chisholm's autobiography is *Unbought and Unbossed*.
18. Arlene Ash and John Lamperti, "Florida 2006: Can Statistics Tell Us Who Won Congressional District 13?" American Statistical Organization, *Chance* 21, no. 2 (Spring 2008): 18–27.
19. Weatherford, *Women in American Politics*, 1:67.
20. See chapter 10.
21. See Rogers and Denham, *Florida Sheriffs*.
22. See chapter 8.
23. See chapter 10 for more on Friedan.
24. See chapter 10 for the attempt to recall Rosemary Barkett.
25. Thanks to Veronica Vasquez of the Florida Commission on the Status of Women for much of this information.
26. See chapter 10.
27. See chapter 9.
28. Pierce, *Pioneer Life*, 73–75.

Bibliography

Adovasio, J. M., Olga Soffer, and Jake Page. *The Invisible Sex: Uncovering the True Roles of Women in Prehistory*. New York: HarperCollins, 2007.

Allman, T. D. *Finding Florida: The True History of the Sunshine State.* New York: Atlantic Monthly Press, 2013.

Anderson, Marie. *Julia's Daughters: Women in Dade's History.* Miami: Herstory of Florida, 1980.

Anthony, Susan B., and Ida Husted Harper, eds. *The History of Woman Suffrage*, vol. 4. Indianapolis: Hollenbeck Press, 1902.

Apel, Dora. *Imagery of Lynching: Black Men, White Women, and the Mob.* New Brunswick, N.J.: Rutgers University Press, 2004.

Arnade, Charles W. *The Architecture of Spanish St. Augustine.* Washington, D.C.: Academy of American Franciscan History, 1961.

———. *The Siege of St. Augustine in 1702.* Gainesville: University of Florida Press, 1959.

Armstrong, Julie Buckner. *Mary Turner and the Memory of Lynching.* Athens: University of Georgia Press, 2011.

Arsenault, Kathleen Hardee. "Strawberry Fields and Bean Rows: Lois Lenski's Florida Children." In *Making Waves: Female Activists in Twentieth-Century Florida*, ed. Jack E. Davis and Kari Frederickson. Gainesville: University Press of Florida, 2003.

Arsenault, Raymond. *St. Petersburg and the Florida Dream, 1888–1950.* Gainesville: University Press of Florida, 1996.

Avellaneda, Ignacio. "Hernando de Soto and His Florida Fantasy." In *The Hernando de Soto Expedition: History, Historiography, and "Discovery" in the Southeast*, ed. Patricia Galloway. Lincoln: University of Nebraska Press, 1997.

Babb, Ellen J. "Women and War: St. Petersburg Women during World War II." *The Florida Historical Quarterly* 73, no. 1 (1994): 43–61.

Bacon, Margaret Hope. *Valiant Friend: The Life of Lucretia Mott.* Philadelphia: Friends General Conference, 1999.

Bakeless, John. *America as Seen by Its First Explorers: The Eyes of Discovery*. Mineola, N.Y.: Dover Publications, 1989.

Barcia, Andres de. *Barcia's Chronological History of the Continent of Florida.* Trans. Anthony Kerrigan. Gainesville: University of Florida Press, 1951.

Bernard, Catherine. *Afro-American Artists in Paris: 1919–1939.* New York: Hunter College of the City University of New York, 1989.

Bettinger-López, Caroline. *Cuban-Jewish Journeys: Searching for Identity, Home, and History in Miami.* Knoxville: University of Tennessee Press, 2000.

Betz, Myrtle Scharrer. *Yesteryear I Lived in Paradise: The Story of Caladesi Island*. Revised edition by Terry Fortner. Tampa: University of Tampa Press, 2007.

Beyond Julia's Daughters. Miami: Women's History Coalition of Miami-Dade County, 2006.

Billinger, Robert D., Jr. *Hitler's Soldiers in the Sunshine State: German POWs in Florida*. Gainesville: University Press of Florida, 2000.

Blackman, E. V. *Miami and Dade County: Its Settlement, Progress, and Achievement*. 1921; repr. Chuluota, Fla.: Mickler House, 1977.

Blakey, Arch Fredric, Ann Smith Lainhart, and Winston Bryant Stephens Jr., eds. *Rose Cottage Chronicles: Civil War Letters of the Bryant-Stephens Families of North Florida*. Gainesville: University Press of Florida, 1998.

Bloodworth, Bertha E., and Alton C. Morris. *Places in the Sun: The History and Romance of Florida Place-Names*. Gainesville: University Presses of Florida, 1978.

Bouvier, Leon F., William Leonard, and John L. Martin. *Shaping Florida: The Effects of Immigration, 1970–2020*. Washington, D.C.: Center for Immigration Studies, 1995.

Braden, Susan R. *The Architecture of Leisure: The Florida Resort Hotels of Henry Flagler and Henry Plant*. Gainesville: University Press of Florida, 2002.

Brevard, Caroline Mays. *A History of Florida from the Treaty of 1763 to Our Own Times*. DeLand: Florida Historical Society, 1924.

Brinton, Daniel Garrison. *A Guide-Book of Florida and the South*. 1869; repr. Gainesville: University Presses of Florida, 1978.

Brown, Canter, Jr. *Florida's Peace River Frontier*. Gainesville: University Presses of Florida, 1991.

———. *Genealogical Records of the African American Pioneers of Tampa and Hillsborough County*. Tampa: Tampa Bay History Center, 2000.

———. *Tampa in Civil War and Reconstruction*. Tampa: University of Tampa Press, 2000.

———. *Women on the Tampa Bay Frontier*. Tampa: Tampa Bay History Center, 1997.

Brown, Charles H. *The Correspondents' War: Journalists in the Spanish-American War*. New York: Scribner, 1967.

Burghard, August. *Mrs. Frank Stranahan, Pioneer*. Fort Lauderdale: Historical Society of Fort Lauderdale, 1968.

Bushnell, Amy Turner. *Situado and Sabana: Spain's Support System for the Presidio and Mission Provinces of Florida*. American Museum of Natural History, Anthropological Papers, vol. 74. Athens: University of Georgia Press, 1994.

Camarota, Steven A. *Immigrants in the United States, 2007: A Profile of America's Foreign-Born Population*. Washington, D.C.: Center for Immigration Studies, 2007. http://cis.org/immigrants_profile_2007.

Carlebach, Michael, and Eugene F. Provenzo Jr. *Farm Security Administration Photographs of Florida*. Gainesville: University Press of Florida, 1993.

Cash, William Thomas. *The Story of Florida*. New York: American Historical Society, 1938.

Chang-Rodríguez, Raquel, ed. *Beyond Books and Borders: Garcilaso de la Vega and La Florida del Inca*. Lewisburg, Pa.: Bucknell University Press, 2006.

Cochran, Jacqueline. *The Stars at Noon*. Boston: Little, Brown, 1954.

Coker, William S., and Jerrell H. Shofner. *Florida: From the Beginning to 1992: A Columbus Jubilee Commemorative.* Houston, Tex.: Pioneer Publications, 1991.

Connor, Jeannette Thurber, trans. and ed. *Pedro Menendez de Aviles: Memorial by Gonzalo Solis de Meras.* Gainesville: University of Florida Press, 1964.

Covington, James W. *The Seminoles of Florida.* Gainesville: University Press of Florida, 1993.

———, ed. *Pirates, Indians and Spaniards: Father Escobedo's "La Florida."* Translated by A. F. Falcones, with a foreword by Charles Arnade. St. Petersburg: Great Outdoors Publishing, 1963.

Cox, Merlin G., and J. E. Dovell. *Florida: From Secession to Space Age.* St. Petersburg: Great Outdoors Publishing, 1974.

Cozens, Eloise. *Florida Women of Distinction.* 2 vols. Daytona Beach: College Publishing Company, 1955, 1956.

Craft, Stephen G. *Embry-Riddle at War: Aviation Training during World War II.* Gainesville: University Press of Florida, 2009.

Craven, Wesley F., and James L. Cate, eds. *The Army Air Forces in World War II,* vol. 7. Chicago: University of Chicago Press, 1958.

Crooks, James B. *Jacksonville: The Consolidation Story, from Civil Rights to the Jaguars.* Gainesville: University Press of Florida, 2004.

Davis, Jack E., and Kari Frederickson, eds. *Making Waves: Female Activists in Twentieth-Century Florida.* Gainesville: University Press of Florida, 2003.

Davis, Karen. *Public Faces—Private Lives: Women in South Florida—1870s–1910s.* Miami: Pickering Press, 1990.

Davis, Mattie Belle. *History of the Florida Association for Women Lawyers, 1951–2002.* Miami: Florida Association for Women Lawyers, 2002.

Davis, T. Frederick. *History of Jacksonville, Florida and Vicinity, 1513 to 1924.* St. Augustine: Florida Historical Society, 1925.

Deagan, Kathleen, and Darcie MacMahon. *Fort Mose: Colonial America's Black Fortress of Freedom.* Gainesville: University Press of Florida, 1995.

DeLand, Margaret Campbell. *Florida Days.* Boston: Little, Brown, 1889.

Denham, James M. *A Rogue's Paradise: Crime and Punishment in Antebellum Florida, 1821–1861.* Tuscaloosa: University of Alabama Press, 1997.

———. "Cracker Women and Their Families in Nineteenth Century Florida." In *Florida's Heritage of Diversity: Essays in Honor of Samuel Proctor,* ed. Mark I. Greenberg, William Warren Rogers Jr., and Canter Brown Jr., 15–28. Tallahassee: Sentry Press, 1997.

Denham, James M., and Canter Brown Jr., eds. *Cracker Times and Pioneer Lives: The Florida Reminiscences of George Gillett Keen and Sarah Pamela Williams.* Columbia: University of South Carolina Press, 2000.

Derr, Mark. *Some Kind of Paradise: A Chronicle of Man and the Land in Florida.* New York: William Morrow, 1989.

De Quesada, Alejandro M., Jr. *A History of Florida Forts: Florida's Lonely Outposts.* Charleston, S.C.: History Press, 2006.

Dickinson, Jonathan. *God's Protecting Providence; Being the Narrative of a Journey . . .*

1699; repr., ed. Evangeline Walker Andrews and Charles McLean Andrews, New Haven: Yale University Press, 1945.
Dodd, Dorothy. *Florida, the Land of Romance*. Tallahassee: Peninsular Publishing, 1957.
D'Orso, Michael. *Like Judgment Day: The Ruin and Redemption of a Town Called Rosewood*. New York: G. P. Putnam's Sons, 1996.
Douglas, Marjory Stoneman, with John Rothchild. *Marjory Stoneman Douglas: Voice of the River, an Autobiography*. Englewood, Fla.: Pineapple Press, 1987.
Dunn, Hampton. *Tampa: A Pictorial History*. Norfolk, Va.: Donning Company, 1985.
Dunn, Marvin. *Black Miami in the Twentieth Century*. Gainesville: University Press of Florida, 1997.
Eppes, Susan Bradford. *Through Some Eventful Years*. 1926; repr. Gainesville: University of Florida Press, 1968.
Ewen, Charles R., and John H. Hann. *Hernando de Soto among the Apalachee: The Archaeology of the First Winter Encampment*. Gainesville: University Press of Florida, 1998.
Fairbanks, George R. *History of Florida: From Its Discovery by Ponce de Leon in 1512, to the Close of the Florida War, in 1842*. Philadelphia: J. B. Lippincott, 1871.
Federal Writers' Project of the Works Progress Administration for the State of Florida. *Florida: A Guide to the Southernmost State*. New York: Oxford University Press, 1940.
Federal Writers' Project, Works Progress Administration. *Slave Narratives: A Folk History of Slavery in the United States, from Interviews with Former Slaves*, vol. 17: *Florida*. Washington, D.C.: Library of Congress, 1936–38; Scholarly Press, St. Clair Shores, Mich: 1976.
Fernández, Susan J., and Robert P. Ingalls. *Sunshine in the Dark: Florida in the Movies*. Gainesville: University Press of Florida, 2006.
Florida State Library. *Florida Becomes a State*. Tallahassee: Florida Centennial Commission, 1945.
Foster, John T., Jr., and Sarah Whitmer Foster. *Beechers, Stowes, and Yankee Strangers: The Transformation of Florida*. Gainesville: University Press of Florida, 1999.
Francis, J. Michael, and Kathleen Kole. *Murder and Martyrdom in Spanish Florida: Don Juan and the Guale Uprising of 1597*. New York: American Museum of Natural History, 2011.
Freitus, Joseph, and Anne Freitus. *Florida: The War Years, 1938–1945*. Niceville, Fla.: Wind Canyon Publishing, 1998.
Fries, Elaine Lewis. *Mary Martha Reid: A Florida Woman of the Nineteenth Century*. Master's thesis, University of South Florida History Department, Tampa, 1994.
Fuson, Robert H. *Juan Ponce de León and the Spanish Discovery of Puerto Rico and Florida*. Blacksburg, Va.: McDonald and Woodward, 2000.
Galloway, Patricia, ed. *The Hernando de Soto Expedition: History, Historiography, and "Discovery" in the Southeast*. Lincoln: University of Nebraska Press, 1997.
Gannon, Michael V. *The Cross in the Sand: The Early Catholic Church in Florida, 1513–1870*. Gainesville: University of Florida Press, 1983.
———, ed., *The New History of Florida*. Gainesville: University Press of Florida, 1996.
George, Paul S., ed. *A Guide to the History of Florida*. New York: Greenwood Press, 1989.

Giddings, Joshua Reed. *The Florida Exiles and the War for Slavery*. New York: Follett, Foster and Company, 1863.

Green, Ben. *Before His Time: The Untold Story of Harry T. Moore, America's First Civil Rights Martyr.* New York: Free Press, 1999.

Greenbaum, Susan D. *More than Black: Afro-Cubans in Tampa.* Gainesville: University Press of Florida, 2002.

Greenberg, Mark I., William Warren Rogers, and Canter Brown Jr., eds. *Florida's Heritage of Diversity: Essays in Honor of Samuel Proctor.* Tallahassee: Sentry Press, 1997.

Griffin, Patricia C. *Mullet on the Beach: The Minorcans of Florida, 1768–1788.* Jacksonville: University of North Florida Press, 1991.

———, ed. *Fifty Years of Southeastern Archaeology: Selected Works of John W. Griffin.* Gainesville: University Press of Florida, 1996.

Hann, John H. *A History of the Timucua Indians and Missions.* Gainesville: University Press of Florida, 1996.

———. *Indians of Central and South Florida, 1513–1763.* Gainesville: University Press of Florida, 2003.

Hann, John H., and Bonnie G. McEwan. *The Apalachee Indians and Mission San Luis.* Gainesville: University Press of Florida, 1998.

Hann, John H., ed. and trans. "1630 Memorial of Fray Francisco Alonso de Jesus on Spanish Florida's Missions and Natives." *The Americas* 50 (1993): 85–105.

Hanna, Alfred Jackson. *A Prince in Their Midst: The Adventurous Life of Achille Murat on the American Frontier*. Norman: University of Oklahoma Press, 1946.

Hanna, Kathryn Abbey. *Florida, Land of Change.* Chapel Hill: University of North Carolina Press, 1941.

Hanson, Joyce Ann. *Mary McLeod Bethune and Black Women's Political Activism.* Columbia: University of Missouri Press, 2003.

Harper, Ida Husted, ed. *History of Woman Suffrage.* Vol. 6. New York: J. J. Little and Ives, 1922.

Hawkins, Paula. *Children at Risk, My Fight against Child Abuse: A Personal Story and a Public Plea.* Bethesda, Md.: Adler and Adler, 1986.

Hemenway, Robert E. *Zora Neale Hurston: A Literary Biography.* Urbana: University of Illinois Press, 1977.

Henderson, Ann L., and Gary R. Mormino. *Spanish Pathways in Florida, 1492–1992.* Sarasota: Pineapple Press, 1991.

Hewitt, Nancy A. "Paulina Pedroso and *Las Patriotas* of Florida." In *Spanish Pathways,* ed. Ann L. Henderson and Gary R. Mormino. Sarasota: Pineapple Press, 1991.

———. *Southern Discomfort: Women's Activism in Tampa, Florida, 1880s–1920s.* Urbana: University of Illinois Press, 2001.

———. "Varieties of Women's Suffrage." *Forum* (Florida Humanities Council) 18, no. 3 (Winter 1995/1996): 22–27.

Hine, Darlene Clark, ed. *Black Women in America: An Historical Encyclopedia.* Brooklyn, N.Y.: Carlson Publishing, 1993.

Holt, Rackham. *Mary McLeod Bethune: A Biography.* Garden City, N.Y.: Doubleday, 1964.

Hurston, Zora Neale. *Go Gator and Muddy the Water: Writings by Zora Neale Hurston from the Federal Writers' Project,* ed. Pamela Bordelon. New York: Norton, 1999.

Immigration Policy Center. *New Americans in Florida.* Washington, D.C.: American Immigration Council, 2012. http://www.immigrationpolicy.org/just-facts/new-americans-florida.

Ingalls, Robert P. *Urban Vigilantes in the New South: Tampa, 1882–1936.* Knoxville: University of Tennessee Press, 1988.

Iorio, Pam. "Colorless Primaries: Tampa's White Municipal Party." *The Florida Historical Quarterly* 79, no. 3 (Winter 2001): 297–318.

Jabour, Anya. *Marriage in the Early Republic: Elizabeth and William Wirt and the Companionate Ideal.* Baltimore: Johns Hopkins University Press, 1998.

Jahoda, Gloria. *Florida: A Bicentennial History.* New York: Norton, 1976.

———. *The Other Florida.* Port Salerno, Fla.: Florida Classics Library, 1984.

Johns, John E. *Florida during the Civil War.* Gainesville: University of Florida Press, 1963.

Johnson, Malcolm B. *Red, White and Bluebloods in Frontier Florida.* Tallahassee: Rotary Clubs of Tallahassee, 1976.

Johnson, Sandra, and Virginia Parks. *Pensacola, the Old and the New: A Guide to Pensacola and Surrounding Areas.* Pensacola: Pensacola Historical Society, 1988.

Jones, Maxine D., and Kevin M. McCarthy. *African Americans in Florida.* Sarasota: Pineapple Press, 1993.

Kennedy, Stetson. *Palmetto Country.* Tallahassee: Florida A&M University Press, 1989.

Kersey, Harry A., Jr. *The Stranahans of Fort Lauderdale: A Pioneer Family of New River.* Gainesville: University Press of Florida, 2003.

King, Gilbert. *Devil in the Grove: Thurgood Marshall, the Groveland Boys, and the Dawn of a New America.* New York: Harper, 2012.

Knowles, Thomas Neil. *Category 5: The 1935 Labor Day Hurricane.* Gainesville: University Press of Florida, 2009.

Laird, Angus McKenzie. *Like I Saw It: An Autobiography.* Tallahassee: St. Andrews Press, 1981.

Landers, Jane G., ed. *Colonial Plantations and Economy in Florida.* Gainesville: University Press of Florida, 2000.

———. *Fort Mose, Gracia Real de Santa Teresa de Mose: A Free Black Town in Spanish Colonial Florida.* St. Augustine: St. Augustine Historical Society, 1992.

———. "Francisco Xavier Sanchez, Floridano Planter." In *Spanish Pathways,* ed. Ann L. Henderson and Gary R. Mormino. Sarasota: Pineapple Press, 1991.

Lane, Jack C., ed. *Rollins College: A Pictorial History.* Winter Park: Rollins College, 1980.

Lange, Dorothea, and Paul Taylor. *An American Exodus: A Record of Human Erosion.* 1939; repr. Paris: J.-M. Place, 1999.

Lanier, Sidney. *Florida: Its Scenery, Climate, and History.* 1875; repr. Gainesville: University of Florida Press, 1973.

Leininger-Miller, Theresa. "Heads of Thought and Reflection: Busts of African Warriors by Nancy Elizabeth Prophet and Augusta Savage, African American Sculptors in Paris, 1922–1934." In *Out of Context: American Artists Abroad,* ed. Laura Felleman Fattal and Carol Salus. Westport, Conn.: Praeger, 2004.

León, René. *San Cristóbal de la Habana: Desde su fundación hasta 1599*. Miami: San Lázaro Graphics, 1990.
Loquasto, Wendy S., ed. *Celebrating Florida's First 150 Women Lawyers*. Charlottesville, Va.: LEXIS, 2000.
Long, Ellen Call. *Florida Breezes; or, Florida New and Old*. 1883; repr. with introduction by Margaret Louise Chapman, Gainesville: University of Florida Press, 1962.
Lyne, Mary C., and Kay Arthur. *Three Years behind the Mast: The Story of the United States Coast Guard SPARS*. Washington, D.C.: n.p., 1946.
Lyon, Eugene. *Pedro Menéndez de Avilés*. New York: Garland Publishing, 1995.
MacKay, Buddy, with Rick Edmonds. *How Florida Happened: The Political Education of Buddy MacKay*. Gainesville: University Press of Florida, 2010.
Mahon, John K., and Brent R. Weisman. "Florida's Seminole and Miccosukee Peoples." In *The New History of Florida*, ed. Michael Gannon. Gainesville: University Press of Florida, 1996.
Manucy, Albert. *Florida's Menéndez: Captain General of the Ocean Sea*. St. Augustine: St. Augustine Historical Society, 1965.
Martin, Theodora Penny. *The Sound of Our Own Voices: Women's Study Clubs 1860–1910*. Boston: Beacon Press, 1987.
Maxwell, Bill. *Maximum Insight: Selected Columns by Bill Maxwell*. Gainesville: University Press of Florida, 2001.
McCarthy, Kevin M. *Native Americans in Florida*. Sarasota: Pineapple Press, 1999.
McGovern, James. "Helen Hunt West." *Forum* (Florida Humanities Council) 18, no. 3 (Winter 1995/1996): 34–39.
McGuire, Nina. *An Uncommon Guide to Florida: A Glove Compartment Companion for Residents, Newcomers, and Tourists*. Lake Buena Vista, Fla.: Tailored Tours Publications, 1992.
Meyer, Jessie Hamm. *Leading the Way: A Century of Service: The Florida Federation of Women's Clubs, 1895–1995*. Lakeland, Fla.: General Federation of Women's Clubs, 1994.
Milanich, Jerald T. *Florida Indians and the Invasion from Europe*. Gainesville: University Press of Florida, 1995.
———. *Frolicking Bears, Wet Vultures, and Other Oddities: A New York City Journalist in Nineteenth-Century Florida*. Gainesville: University Press of Florida, 2005.
———. *The Timucua*. Cambridge, Mass. Blackwell, 1996.
Morison, Samuel Eliot. *Christopher Columbus, Mariner*. Boston: Little, Brown, 1955.
Mormino, Gary R. *Hillsborough County Goes to War: The Home Front, 1940–1950*. Tampa: Tampa Bay History Center, 2001.
———. *Land of Sunshine, State of Dreams: A Social History of Modern Florida*. Gainesville: University Press of Florida, 2005.
Mormino, Gary R., and Anthony P. Pizzo. *Tampa: The Treasure City*. Tampa: Continental Heritage Press, 1983.
Mormino, Gary R., and George Pozzetta. *The Immigrant World of Ybor City: Italians and Their Latin Neighbors in Tampa, 1885–1985*. Urbana: University of Illinois, 1987.
Morris, Allen. *Women in the Florida Legislature*. Tallahassee: Florida House of Representatives, 1995.

Moseley, Julia Winifred, and Betty Powers Crislip, eds. *Come to My Sunland: Letters of Julia Daniels Moseley from the Florida Frontier, 1882–1886*. Gainesville: University Press of Florida, 1998.

Muir, Helen. *Miami, U.S.A.* 1953; expanded edition, Gainesville: University Press of Florida, 2000.

Ogle, Maureen. *Key West: History of an Island of Dreams*. Gainesville: University Press of Florida, 2003.

Parker, Idella, with Mary Keating. *Idella: Marjorie Rawlings' "Perfect Maid."* Gainesville: University Press of Florida, 1992.

Pearce, George F. *Pensacola during the Civil War: A Thorn in the Side of the Confederacy*. Gainesville: University Press of Florida, 2000.

Peare, Catherine Owens. *Mary McLeod Bethune*. New York: Vanguard Press, 1951.

Peek, Ralph Leon. *Lawlessness and the Restoration of Order in Florida, 1868–1871*. Master's thesis. Gainesville: University of Florida, 1964.

Penney, Sherry H., and James D. Livingston. *A Very Dangerous Woman: Martha Wright and Women's Rights*. Amherst: University of Massachusetts Press, 2004.

Pérez, Louis, Jr. *Cuba: Between Reform and Revolution*. New York: Oxford University Press, 1995.

Perry, Regina A. *Free Within Ourselves: African-American Artists in the Collection of the National Museum of American Art*. Washington, D.C.: National Museum of American Art, 1992.

Peters, Thelma. *Lemon City: Pioneering on Biscayne Bay, 1850–1925*. Miami: Banyan Books, 1976.

Pierce, Charles W. *Pioneer Life in Southeast Florida*. Ed. Donald Walter Curl. Coral Gables: University of Miami Press, 1970.

Pleck, Elizabeth H., and Ellen K. Rothman. *The Legacies Book: A Companion Volume to the Audiocourse Legacies—A History of Women and the Family in America, 1607–1870*. Washington, D.C.: Annenberg/CPB Project, 1987.

Proctor, Samuel. *Napoleon Bonaparte Broward: Florida's Fighting Democrat*. Gainesville: University of Florida Press, 1950.

Purdy, Barbara A. *Indian Art of Ancient Florida*. Gainesville: University Press of Florida, 1996.

Rainwater, Cleo, and Kathryn Abbey Hanna. *Our Journey through Florida*. New York: American Book Company, 1958.

Rawlings, Marjorie Kinnan. *Cross Creek Cookery*. New York: Charles Scribner's Sons, 1942.

Reid, Thomas. *America's Fortress: A History of Fort Jefferson, Dry Tortugas, Florida*. Gainesville: University Press of Florida, 2006.

Revels, Tracy J. *Grander in Her Daughters: Florida's Women during the Civil War*. Columbia: University of South Carolina Press, 2004.

Ricciardi, Lois. "Mary Lou Baker." *Tampa Bay History* 24 (2010): 1–12.

Rivers, Larry Eugene. *Slavery in Florida: Territorial Days to Emancipation*. Gainesville: University Press of Florida, 2000.

Rivers, Larry Eugene, and Canter Brown Jr., eds. *The Varieties of Women's Experiences:*

Portraits of Southern Women in the Post-Civil War Century. Gainesville: University Press of Florida, 2009.

Roberts, Diane. *Dream State: Eight Generations of Swamp Lawyers, Conquistadors, Confederate Daughters, Banana Republicans, and Other Florida Wildlife.* Gainesville: University Press of Florida, 2004.

Rogers, William Warren, and James M. Denham, *Florida Sheriffs: A History, 1821–1945.* Tallahassee: Sentry Press, 2001.

Saunders, Robert W. *Bridging the Gap: Continuing the Florida NAACP Legacy of Harry T. Moore.* Tampa: University of Tampa Press, 2000.

Schafer, Daniel L. *Anna Madgigine Jai Kingsley: African Princess, Florida Slave, Plantation Slaveowner.* Gainesville: University Press of Florida, 2003.

———. "U.S. Territory and State." In *The New History of Florida,* ed. Michael Gannon. Gainesville: University Press of Florida, 1996.

Schmidt, Lewis G. *The Civil War in Florida: A Military History.* 4 vols. Allentown, Pa.: Self published, 1991.

Schneider, Paul. *Brutal Journey: The Epic Story of the First Crossing of North America.* New York: Henry Holt and Company, 2006.

Schultz, Debbie Wasserman. *For the Next Generation: A Wake-Up Call to Solving Our Nation's Problems.* New York: St. Martin's Press, 2013.

Schwartz, Gerald, ed. *A Woman Doctor's Civil War: Esther Hill Hawks' Diary.* Columbia: University of South Carolina Press, 1984.

Shofner, Jerrell H. *Florida Portrait: A Pictorial History of Florida.* Sarasota: Pineapple Press, 1990.

———. *Nor Is It Over Yet: Florida in the Era of Reconstruction, 1863–1877.* Gainesville: University Presses of Florida, 1974.

———. "Mary Grace Quackenbos, a Visitor Florida Did Not Want." *The Florida Historical Quarterly* 58, no. 3 (January 1980): 273–290.

Smith, Patrick D. *A Land Remembered.* Sarasota: Pineapple Press, 1996.

Sprague, John T. *The Origin, Progress, and Conclusion of the Florida War.* New York: D. Appleton and Company, 1848.

Standiford, Les. *Last Train to Paradise: Henry Flagler and the Spectacular Rise and Fall of the Railroad that Crossed an Ocean.* New York: Crown Publishers, 2002.

Stern, Maxine, ed. *FSU Voices: An Informal History of 150 Years.* Tallahassee: Florida State University, 2002.

Stone, Elaine Murray. *Pedro Menéndez de Avilés and the Founding of St. Augustine.* New York: P. J. Kennedy, 1969.

Stowe, Harriet Beecher. *Palmetto Leaves.* 1873; repr. with introductions by Mary B. Graff and Edith Cowles, Gainesville: University of Florida Press, 1968.

Tebeau, Charlton W. *A History of Florida.* 3 vols. Coral Gables: University of Miami Press, 1971.

Thomas, Hugh. *Rivers of Gold: The Rise of the Spanish Empire, from Columbus to Magellan.* New York: Random House, 2003.

Thulesius, Olav. *Harriet Beecher Stowe in Florida, 1867 to 1884.* Jefferson, N.C.: McFarland, 2001.

Townsend, Billy. *The Age of Barbarity: The Forgotten Fight for the Soul of Florida.* Self-published, 2012.
Treadwell, Mattie. *The Women's Army Corps.* Washington, D.C.: Office of the Chief of Military History, Dept. of the Army, 1954.
U.S. House of Representatives. *Women in Congress, 1917–2006.* Washington, D.C.: U.S. Government Printing Office, 2007.
Van Landingham, Kyle S. *Pioneer Families of the Kissimmee River Valley.* Privately published, 1976.
Venable, John D. *Mina Miller Edison: Daughter, Wife and Mother of Inventors: A Brief Biography.* East Orange, N.J.: Charles Edison Fund, 1981.
Verrill, A. Hyatt. *Romantic and Historic Florida.* New York: Dodd, Mead and Company, 1935.
Vickers, Sarah Pauline. *The Life of Ruth Bryan Owen: Florida's First Congresswoman and America's First Woman Diplomat.* Tallahassee: Sentry Press, 2009.
Wagenheim, Kal, and Olga Jiménez de Wagenheim, eds. *The Puerto Ricans: A Documentary History.* Princeton, N.J.: Markus Wiener Publishers, 1998.
Weatherford, Doris. *American Women and World War II.* New York: Facts on File, 1990.
———. *American Women during World War II: An Encyclopedia.* New York: Routledge, 2009.
———. *American Women's History: An A-Z of People, Organizations, Issues and Events.* New York: Prentice Hall, 1994.
———. *Foreign and Female: Immigrant Women in America, 1840–1930.* New York: Facts on File, 1995.
———. *A History of the American Suffragist Movement.* Santa Barbara, Calif.: ABC-CLIO, 1998. Introduction by Geraldine Ferraro.
———. *A History of Women in the United States: State-by-State Reference.* 4 vols. New York: Scholastic Library–Grolier, 2003.
———. "Last Instead of First." *Forum: Magazine of the Florida Humanities Council* (Winter 1995): 20.
———. *Milestones: A Chronology of American Women.* New York: Facts on File, 1997.
———. *Real Women of Tampa and Hillsborough County from Prehistory to the Millennium.* Tampa: University of Tampa Press, 2004.
———. *Women in American Politics: History and Milestones.* Washington, D.C.: Congressional Quarterly Press, 2012.
Weimann, Jeanne Madeline. *The Fair Women.* Chicago: Academy Press, 1981.
Weisman, Brent Richards. *Excavations on the Franciscan Frontier: Archaeology at the Fig Springs Mission.* Gainesville: University Press of Florida, 1992.
Wright, J. Leitch, Jr. *Florida in the American Revolution.* Sponsored by the American Revolution Bicentennial Commission of Florida. Gainesville: University Presses of Florida, 1975.
Wilder, Margaret Buell. *Since You Went Away: Letters to A Soldier from His Wife.* Garden City, N.Y.: Sundial Press, 1944.
Williams, John Lee. *A View of West Florida.* Philadelphia, 1827; repr. Gainesville: University Presses of Florida, 1976.
Williams, Joy. *The Florida Keys: A History & Guide.* New York: Random House, 1991.

Index

Boxes, figures, and tables are indicated by *b*, *f*, and *t* respectively.

Doris Weatherford is a leading women's historian and has been publishing books on women's history since 1986. She has served on the board of the Center for Florida History at Florida Southern College, as an adjunct professor at the University of South Florida, and is extensively recognized for her contributions to the field of women's studies. She served as executive editor for *Women's Almanac* (2000 and 2002) and wrote the four-volume *A History of Women in the United States: State-by-State Reference*. Her most recent work, the two-volume *Women in American Politics*, won an award from the American Library Association.

*   *   *

The Florida Commission on the Status of Women is dedicated to empowering women in achieving their fullest potential, to eliminating barriers to that achievement, and to recognizing women's accomplishments. Through programs such as the Florida Women's Hall of Fame, the commission has touched the lives of thousands of women throughout Florida. Both the commission and the Hall of Fame were established by law in 1991.

*   *   *

The University Press of Florida is the scholarly publishing agency for the State University System of Florida, comprising Florida A&M University, Florida Atlantic University, Florida Gulf Coast University, Florida International University, Florida State University, New College of Florida, University of Central Florida, University of Florida, University of North Florida, University of South Florida, and University of West Florida.